D1577095

# ENVIRONMENTAL SCIENCES AND APPLICATIONS

*Series Editors:* MARGARET R. BISWAS
             ASIT K. BISWAS

---

Volume 12

# DESERTIFICATION

# ENVIRONMENTAL SCIENCES AND APPLICATIONS

*Other titles in the series*

## NOTICE TO READERS

Dear Reader

If your library is not already a standing order customer or subscriber to this series, may we recommend that you place a standing or subscription order to receive immediately upon publication all volumes published in this valuable series. Should you find that these volumes no longer serve your needs your order can be cancelled at any time without notice.

The Editors and the Publisher will be glad to receive suggestions or outlines of suitable titles, reviews or symposia for consideration for rapid publication in this series.

ROBERT MAXWELL
Publisher at Pergamon Press

# DESERTIFICATION

Associated Case Studies prepared for the United Nations
Conference on Desertification

*Edited by*

MARGARET R. BISWAS
*Balliol College, University of Oxford, UK*

and

ASIT K. BIWAS
*Biswas and Associates, Ottawa, Canada*

PERGAMON PRESS
OXFORD · NEW YORK · TORONTO · SYDNEY · PARIS · FRANKFURT

U.K. Pergamon Press Ltd., Headington Hill Hall, Oxford OX3 0BW, England

U.S.A. Pergamon Press Inc., Maxwell House, Fairview Park, Elmsford, New York 10523, U.S.A.

CANADA Pergamon of Canada, Suite 104, 150 Consumers Road, Willowdale, Ontario M2J 1P9, Canada

AUSTRALIA Pergamon Press (Aust.) Pty. Ltd., P.O. Box 544, Potts Point, N.S.W. 2011, Australia

FRANCE Pergamon Press SARL, 24 rue des Ecoles, 75240 Paris, Cedex 05, France

FEDERAL REPUBLIC OF GERMANY Pergamon Press GmbH, 6242 Kronberg-Taunus, Pferdstrasse 1, Federal Republic of Germany

First edition 1980

**British Library Cataloguing in Publication Data**

United Nations Conference on Desertification,
*1st, Nairobi, 1977*
Desertification, - (Environmental sciences and applications ; vol.12).
1. Desertification - Control - Congresses
I. Title II. Biswas, Margaret R
III. Biswas, Asit K IV. Series
910'.02'154  GB611  80-40024
ISBN 0-08-023581-6

*Printed in Great Britain by A. Wheaton & Co. Ltd, Exeter*

# Contents

# *Preface*

The drought in the Sahel, which extended from 1968 to 1973, focused governmental and public attention on the problem of desertification as a whole. In response, the United Nations' General Assembly resolved to initiate concerted international action to combat the spread of desert conditions, and called for a world conference to give impetus to international action. The United Nations Conference on Desertification (UNCOD) was accordingly convened in Nairobi, Kenya, from 29 August to 9 September 1977, and was attended by representatives of 95 governments, almost all the United Nations organs and specialized agencies, liberation movements , and 65 non-governmental organizations. Dr. Mostafa Kamal Tolba, Executive Director of the United Nations Environment Programme, was the Secretary-General of the Conference. The case studies discussed in this book were prepared for this Conference by the following countries: Australia, Iran, Israel, Peoples Republic of China, USSR and the United States.

Desertification is the diminution or destruction of the biological potential of land and can lead ultimately to desert-like conditions: grazing lands cease to produce pasture, dryland agriculture fails, and irrigated fields are abandoned owing to salinization, waterlogging, or some other form of soil deterioration. Desertification is a self-accelerating process, "feeding on itself", and, as it advances, rehabilitation costs rise exponentially.

The U.N. Conference on Desertification did not deal with the natural occurrence of deserts, but concerned itself with human activities which degrade land that would otherwise be productive. Of the identified causes of desertification, most can be traced to human mismanagement of soil, water, energy, flora, or fauna—the five basic factors of a land-use system. Excessive pressures of land-use—such as over-grazing, farming marginal lands, and improper irrigation—cause damage beyond the resilience of the ecosystem. When drought appears, the degradation is accelerated and dramatized. Man's activities have desertized an area about the size of China.

Desertification hazards, including deserts, though directly affecting only about one-third of the land surface and one-sixth of the world's population, have their indirect influence on the whole world through:

—reduction of food-producing capacities of the world and causing imbalances in world food markets and reserves;

—causing unplanned mass-immigration with socio-economic and socio-political repercussions on adjoining countries;

—causing dust-storms that bring, to the global circulation of air-masses, added
loads of particulate matter whose impact on global climate has not yet been
assessed; and

—loss of genetic resources of plants and animals.

In his opening statement, Dr. Tolba outlined the principal points of the problem.
First, desertification is a serious threat to the welfare of mankind. Degradation
of land has accelerated in recent decades, precisely at a time when population
growth and rising expectations began to demand enormous increases in food production.
Yet it is estimated that between 50,000 and 70,000 square kilometres of useful land
are going out of production every year, largely due to desertification.

Second, the problem is urgent. As land suffers degradation, the costs of reclaiming
it, modest at first, rise steeply until a threshold is passed beyond which reclamation becomes economically impractical.

Third, the causes of desertification are known, and, in particular, the reasons for
its recent acceleration. A change to a more arid climate could be a cause, but no
firm evidence is available that climate is so changing: rather it is Man himself
who must be viewed as the agent of desertification. It is Man's action that
degrades the land by misuse or overuse as he seeks to wrest a living from fragile
ecosystems under unpredictable and often harsh climatic conditions, and under a
variety of social and economic pressures. Too frequently Man acts in this way
because no better alternatives are apparent to him.

Fourth, Man has now in his possession both the wealth of knowledge and adequate
technical means to bring desertification to a halt. The key to combative measures
is to be found in proper land-use.

Finally, desertification must be seen as a human problem, rather than as one
concerned solely with the deterioration of ecosystems. If Man is its agent, he is
also its victim. The degradation of land is invariably accompanied by the degradation of human well-being and social prospects. All efforts to combat desertification must therefore centre on the welfare of Man.

The views of the scientific advisers, based on the case-studies carried out as part
of the Conference preparations, provide grounds for optimism—desertification can be
halted. It is interesting to note that there are now few developmental activities
in which countries—even the poorest—are not already well equipped with knowledge
of how to avoid desertification. Countries can describe their scientific and
technological needs and deficiencies in precise detail. The Plan of Action to
Combat Desertification places a strong emphasis on public participation. In the
educational and community efforts through which popular participation is stimulated,
technological capacities are extended to the grass-roots.

Desertification can be halted by the year A.D. 2000, and the Plan of Action was
formulated with this goal in mind. Action against desertification cannot, however,
yield results unless governments perceive it as an integral part of their established plans for social and economic development, and as part of their collective
effort to meet the requirements of a 'New International Economic Order'. A
powerful current of contemporary thought views a firm and self-reliant agricultural
base as an essential prerequisite to national development. From this perspective,
productive lands and waters are the key national resources. Dr. Tolba concluded
that enough is known to combat desertification right now: governments have already
begun to act, and are ready to work together to overcome a problem that affects at
least two-thirds of the countries of the world.

The solution to this situation could lie in the development and application of proper land-use practices and management of water resources, which would involve both a technological and a human aspect.  One should consist of measures designed to sustain land productivity or to rehabilitate degraded lands, while the other should be concerned with the commitment of the people who live on vulnerable lands and who will determine the success or failure of efforts to combat desertification.

Perhaps the Conference differed most from previous U.N. conferences in the stature of its Secretary-General.  Dr. Tolba had served the governments well as the Executive Director of the United Nations Environment Programme, and had demonstrated his outstanding capability for practical action already in the United Nations.  In addition, governments recognized his command of the subject, and were prepared to trust his recommendations as being the correct road to implement demonstrated resolve.  Under his direction, the Conference convened in a spirit of unusual harmony and cooperation, and enjoyed an unusual degree of consensus on both causes and solutions.  At no time did politics disrupt the proceedings, and political interventions were few and minor.

It may be concluded quite confidently that, globally, we now have the basic technology, human resources, and finance, to solve desertification problems.  The outstanding problem is a lack of awareness and political will both nationally and internationally.  A world conference is one of the few options available for creating awareness and political will at the global level.  Nothing has done more, for example, to raise the world's consciousness regarding the lack of basic needs of an impoverished thousand million people, than has this major event.  The United Nations Conference on Desertification has had and will have a profound impact on thinking and practice during the coming decades, when we can, as Dr. Tolba frequently stated, bring desertification to a halt.

Finally, we gratefully acknowledge the cooperation of the countries concerned, who prepared these case studies for the Conference, in updating the information, and providing us the necessary permission to publish them.

MARGARET R. BISWAS
Balliol College, Oxford University
Oxford, England
ASIT K. BISWAS, Director
Biswas & Associates
Ottawa, Canada, and Oxford, England

# Australia

# The Gascoyne Basin*

## O. B. Williams,** H. Suijdendorp,† and D. G. Wilcox‡

## INTRODUCTION

Heavy rains on the Gascoyne Basin in January and February 1961 caused severe flooding of the small Western Australian town of Carnarvon (25° S, 114° E, 3300 inhabitants) and of the vegetable and plantation crops along the lower reaches of the Gascoyne River. The flooding and erosion were extensive enough to suggest that run-off from the Basin was excessive. Sheep have been grazed on the Basin for almost 100 years. The location of Carnarvon, the boundaries of the arid Gascoyne Basin (area 64,000 km², mean annual rainfall 200mm) and isohyets for the two cyclonic depressions which crossed the Basin in early 1961 are displayed in Figs. 1 and 2. In terms of Meig's maps of the world distribution of arid and semi-arid homoclimes as set out in McGinnies $et$ $al.$ (1968), the Basin is Aa 24 with a tendency to Ac 23-24 at the western end and Ab 24 on the northern margin. Similar homoclimes are found in parts of the northern and western circum-Saharain regions, the Karoo-Kalahari areas of southern Africa, regions bordering the Red Sea and Persian Gulf, and the northern Thar desert.

An aerial reconnaissance was made by two officers of the Western Australian Department of Agriculture in September 1961 and a summary of their observations was included in the report of the Gascoyne River Erosion Committee (Lightfoot, 1961). The report noted that excess run-off was due to degradation of the basin area and suggested that steps should be taken to prevent further denudation and erosion.

A Second Catchment Erosion Committee in June 1969 recommended that a joint survey team consisting of officers of the Departments of Agriculture and of Lands and Surveys be set up to investigate conditions on the Basin. A report of the joint team's work in the field in 1969 and 1970 described the Basin in terms of its rangeland types and their susceptibility to erosion (Wilcox and McKinnon, 1972).

---

* Based on "A Report on the Condition of the Gascoyne Catchment" by D. G. Wilcox, Department of Agriculture, Western Australia, and E. A. McKinnon, Department of Lands and Surveys, Western Australia (1972). Additional material from officers of the Rangeland Management Branch, Department of Agriculture, Western Australia.
** CSIRO, Division of Land Resources Management, Canberra, A.C.T.
† Department of Agriculture, Rangeland Management Branch, Carnarvon, Western Australia.
‡‡ Department of Agriculture, Rangeland Management Branch, South Perth, Western Australia.

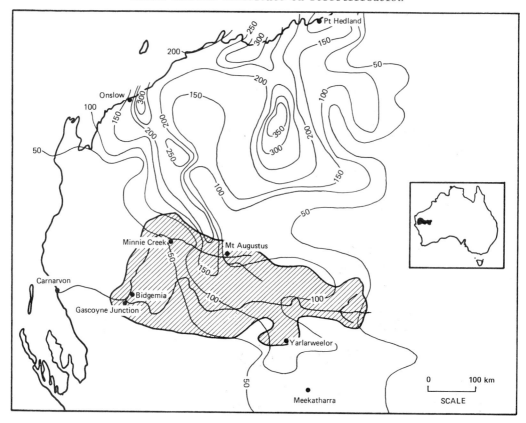

Fig. 1.   The isohyets for the cyclonic depression which
crossed the Basin in January 1961.

The land system or "rangeland type" approach adopted by Wilcox and McKinnon allowed
a logical and sequential examination of all parts of each property or "station" as
they are known.  The occurrence of erosion and degradation in each rangeland type
was thereby determined for each station.  It was from an examination of the total
records for each rangeland and for each station that the whole situation on the
Basin was determined.

Recommendations on stocking rates and remedial treatments were included for each of
the fifty-one rangeland types identified in the survey.

The influence of climate on erosion and on recovery was discussed and the rangeland
types were also described in relation to their respective geomorphological types.
The pastures were described and recommendations for the grazing management of these
pastures were given.

Wilcox and McKinnon reported that 9412 km$^2$ (14.9 per cent) of the Gascoyne Basin
were badly eroded and could become irreversibly degraded unless removed from the
available grazing area; 33,160 km$^2$ (52.4 per cent) were degraded and had some
erosion; they needed careful use if they were not to degrade further.  The remaining
20,575 km$^2$ (32.6 per cent) were in an acceptable condition.  However, this category
was mostly hill or short grass country of poor natural productivity.

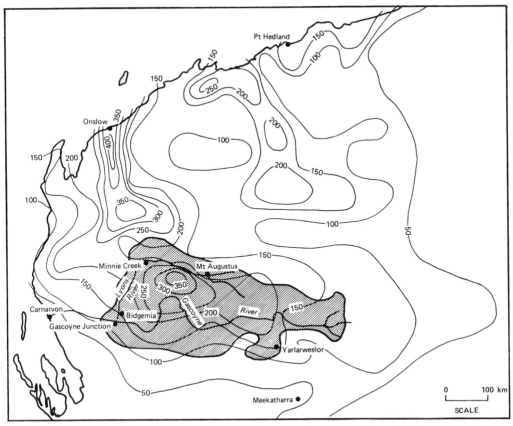

Fig. 2. The isohyets for the cyclonic depression which crossed the Basin in February 1961.

The eroded areas were those which had soils susceptible to erosion and were capable of supporting palatable and durable pastures. They received frequent run-on water from areas upslope, were readily accessible to sheep and maintained high levels of animal production. Their preferential use, when combined with systems of heavy continuous grazing, has produced the devastated areas.

Wilcox and McKinnon suggested that a system of sheep unit capacities (SUC) based on current quantitative data should be adopted to control the use of supervised rangelands and that rangeland productivity under a range of conditions should be established for many rangeland types. Continuous use of many rangelands should be avoided, particularly after severe droughts and in degraded and incipiently eroding pastures. This will require some supervision. The authors recommended a reduction of stock numbers from 416,833 to 237,290 sheep units in order to prevent further erosion and to assist in rangeland rehabilitation.

In effect, the Government of Western Australia was presented with a report which recommended a severe reduction in the number of sheep grazed in the Basin so as to curtail serious erosion and production losses inside and outside the Basin. A decision was made to proceed with the recommendations and, in due course, maps were sent to each station delineating the types of rangeland, their condition, the areas to be removed from grazing and the numbers of livestock to be grazed in each property.

In hindsight the ensuing storm could have been expected in view of the extremely limited prior contact between those in whom the State had vested administration of Crown lands and the pastoralists who, as users of these lands, had paid annual rentals to the Government as well as paying a previous vendor for the lease and improvements on the basis of livestock numbers substantially in excess of the Stock Unit Capacity figures presented in the Report. In practice, if not in law, the lessees (as the State termed them) considered themselves to be owners.

The population is small relative to the vast area of the Gascoyne Basin and is likely to stay small so long as there is a uniform wage, and free capital and population movement within the Australian continent. In the case study there is particular emphasis on the socio-demographic and economic aspects needed for national and international understanding of desertification in the study area, viz. two commercial, community and administrative centres distant from 100 to 400 km and one miniscule local administrative centre with one shire clerk, one school teacher and one policeman for an area of more than 5 million ha in which 320 people live on thirty-one sheep and cattle stations in an arid environment whose products, wool and meat, valued in excess of $2,000,000 pass in their entirety to the export market.

The Upper Gascoyne Shire is the local government authority (Fig. 3). It contains twenty-four stations but seven of these are wholly outside the Basin. The Gascoyne Survey of Wilcox and McKinnon (1972) covers thirty-one stations (Fig. 4), twenty-two of which are in the Upper Gascoyne Shire and nine of which occupy a small part of Meekatharra Shire which lies to the east. It is unlikely that the inclusion of the seven stations which lie outside the Basin and the exclusion of the nine stations which are in the Basin but in Meekatharra Shire will substantially change the picture given by statistics based on the Upper Gascoyne Shire area. Throughout this case study we differentiate between the Gascoyne *Basin* and the Upper Gascoyne *Shire*.

The facilities and services in the larger towns of Carnarvon and Meekatharra will be outlined later.

The Gascoyne Catchment Survey and its Report are fruits of the Carnarvon flood. Now that the pattern of investigation into the condition of arid rangelands has been established, other pastoral regions of Western Australia are either being examined or are to be examined without the necessity for further catastrophes. For example, the survey of West Kimberley has been completed and the first inspection has started; the large proportion of absentee lessees who are interstate and overseas companies differs markedly from the Gascoyne and another set of political problems may eventuate. The survey of the eastern Nullarbor has started, but old aerial photographs and extensive recent fires in the featureless landscape have led to a temporary postponement until the new aerial photography is available. A reconnaissance survey of the Ashburton Catchment is in progress; it is a prelude to the main survey which will start in 1977.

Even with this ongoing survey programme of the type sought by the Pastoral Appraisement Board and pioneered by Wilcox and McKinnon, the estimated time to complete the pastoral regions of Western Australia will exceed 20 years; the monitoring programme planned to follow each survey will, on a state-wide basis, eventually require a large professional staff.

Although we have come to emphasize the influence of catastrophes, we deplore their apparent necessity in Australia and elsewhere as a precursor to the wise management of land resources. It is fortunate that the Carnarvon catastrophe was small, that indigenous ecological expertise was utilized and that prompt and firm political support was given when the socio-economic deficiencies were recognized.

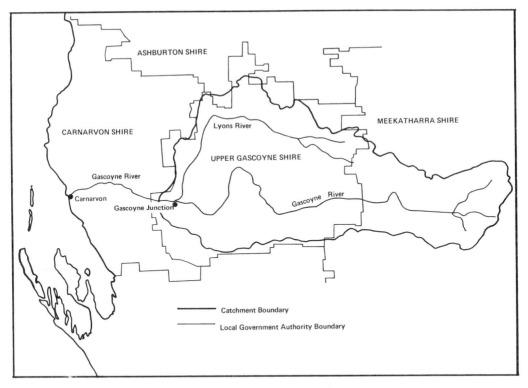

Fig. 3.  The relationship of the catchment boundary to the
local Government Authority Boundary.

The Gascoyne Basin has been chosen for the UNEP Case Study on Desertification
because it is the only Australian pastoral area to the present in which:

(a) a survey of the composition and condition of the vegetation and the erosional
    status of the associated soils on a property and paddock basis has been
    published;
(b) individual agreements have been negotiated with each pastoralist, covering
    the reduction in livestock numbers to take place over a 10-year period, as
    well as excluding livestock partly or entirely from particular portions of
    the property;
(c) a series of monitoring sites has been set up on properties in order to
    determine the trend under livestock-free conditions and future inspections
    have been planned;
(d) a series of long-established exclosures has been monitored for possible
    vegetation changes; and
(e) extension workers have conducted field days at which pastoralists have
    participated in rangeland assessment exercises.

This case study will describe the types of past and present desertification, the
factors which caused and are causing it, and the rangeland appraisal methods
devised by Wilcox and McKinnon (1972) to define the levels of desertification.  We
will describe the adjustments made by pastoralists in the technological, social
and economic spheres.

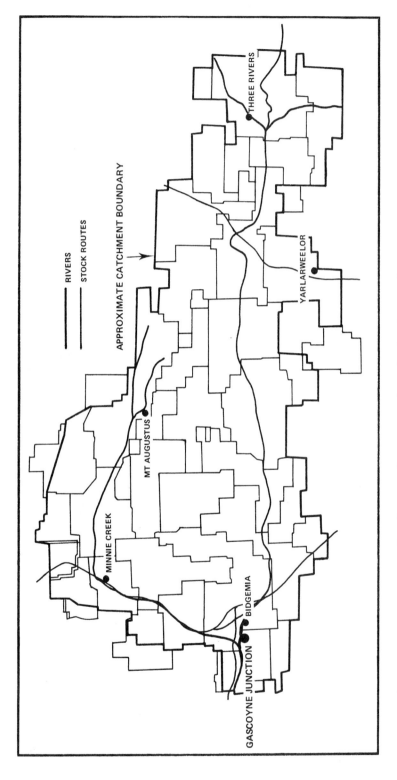

Fig. 4.  Station boundaries within the catchment area.

The research and extension approach inherent in the report by Wilcox and McKinnon, the follow-up to the surveys and in this case study has a long history in the agricultural and livestock industries of mesic Australia, but a short history in Australian regions prone to desertification.

We draw attention to desertification studies in progress elsewhere in Australia (Anon, 1974) where the ecological framework differs substantially from that of the Gascoyne Basin.

However, these differences do not submerge the similarities in

(a) the mode of pastoral usage,
(b) the reduction or removal of long-lived plants upon which the maintenance of flocks and herds depends during long rainless periods,
(c) the inability to maintain the high levels of animal reproduction attained in the early settlement period,
(d) the dominant and continuing water erosion which follows intense summer rains on surface soils devoid of protective vegetation cover in arid environments,
(e) the long-term nature of natural restorative measures in a region of erratic rainfall,
(f) the unrelenting pressure exerted by domestic herbivores on the vegetation and the apparent inability of the pastoral industry to reduce this pressure.


GENERAL DESCRIPTION

*Demographic, Sociological and Cultural Characteristics of the Present Population*

The European settlement of the Gascoyne commenced with C. S. Brockman in 1876 and Carnarvon township was gazetted in 1886. The railway to Mullewa, 400 km south of Gascoyne Junction, was completed in 1894 to service the Murchison goldfields. Travelling stock-routes with government wells and bores ran from Mullewa through Gascoyne stations such as Dairy Creek and Bidgemia and up to the Ashburton River.

Because the costs of transport over land to developing pastoral areas was prohibitive compared with transport by sea, harbours were established at the mouths of the west-flowing rivers. These dry sandy rivers and the plains each side of them became the transport routes from the ports to the stations, water being found at waterholes or wells in the sand.

There has never been a substantial population either aboriginal or European in the Gascoyne Basin, though the environmental constraints were different for these two peoples. Water was a direct and indirect limit in the hunter-food gatherer economy. Permanent water sources away from the river were uncommon and open water was limited to isolated sections of the river; extended drought periods made hunting more difficult at a time when vegetable foods were scarce.

In recent decades, demographic changes have been marked, but these are difficult to quantify because the aborginal population in its entirety was not counted until the 1966 census. By 1966 many aborigines had moved from the Upper Gascoyne Shire to Carnarvon and this possibly explains the anomalous growth in population between 1961 and 1966 from 354 to 462 and the decline between 1966 and 1971 from 462 to 320. There are few aborigines now resident in the Shire and they are employed by the Shire Council or are dingo hunters and kangaroo shooters. Approximately 1800 of the 7000 residents in Carnarvon Shire are part or wholly aboriginal.

The complementary relationship between the aboriginal and European settlers which succeeded the initial settlement and disturbance of aboriginal land ownership no longer exists.

In 1971, when the population in the Upper Gascoyne Shire was 320, 202 were males and 118 were females, a masculinity ratio of 1.71:1.0 which is characteristic of isolated pastoral regions and mining towns in arid Australia. The population aged 19 or less is 53 males and 44 females, but between 20 and 64 years is 141 males and 70 females. There are few old people. Of the 320 people in the Shire, 185 were employed (152 males and 33 females) and only 1 unemployed. Infant mortality over the 7 years 1967 to 1973 totalled 3, births totalled 34 and deaths totalled 17.

In the Shire in 1971 there were 74 dwellings of which 69 were occupied by 278 people. In the 5,573,000 ha of the Shire the stations with their small communities of from three to ten people are separated by road distances of from 35 to 70 km.

The religious allegiance of the society is of the Western Christian tradition. The nearest churches are in Carnarvon. Both the Australian Inland Mission and Salvation Army visit stations by means of light aircraft. Social activities include the picnic races (horse races, gymkhana, foot races) at Landor and at Gascoyne Junction; polocrosse is played and tennis courts are venues for tennis evenings and barbecues. Sporting events throughout Australia are covered by radio. Football and horse racing are popular. There is no television reception in the area.

Sociological changes have followed the reductions in real income and reliance on non-aboriginal labour. The old division between "the Establishment" of long-established pastoralists and newcomers has gone and the society is in a continual state of flux. Pastoralists and employees mix socially if they wish to do so; there are not enough people in the area for a class system to develop, even if it were to be desired. The majority of lessees reside on their stations. All people including staff can take holidays and paid holidays are included in the pastoral award. Those working on stations generally have their own personal transport.

Voting in the triennial elections for the State and Federal legislatures is compulsory for all residents aged 18 years and upwards. In the latest round of elections the population of Upper Gascoyne preferred Liberal (conservative) candidates for all legislatures.

Local government (shire) elections have not involved State or national political parties and are generally fought on local issues. The Shire is divided into "wards" and several councillors are elected from each ward. The main function of the Upper Gascoyne Shire is road works and maintenance; this accounts for 70 per cent or $213 per head of population of the Shire revenue and 100 per cent or $70 per head of loan fund receipts. The budget is funded from rates levied on the properties, from local government grants made by the State government and from charges paid by pastoralists for contract road work done on their stations.

Because there is no urban centre, the Shire is not involved in the larger range of activities which fall to most local government authorities; these include electricity and water reticulation, sewerage and drainage, health and sanitary services, land planning and building supervision. The provision of these services on stations in the Upper Gascoyne Shire is the responsibility of the individual pastoralists.

The shire, through the Council and its administrative officer the shire clerk, is the formal administrative and financial link between the electors and the Local Government Department of the State Government, but this link is less political than other organizational and informal links. The most important of these organizations is the Pastoralists and Graziers Association (P and G) with a local committee based on Gascoyne Junction, communicating directly with the Association Headquarters in Perth. The "P and G" is influential at the political level and its contact with members of the State Legislature is closer than that it has with the Shire Council and the Local Government Department even though the membership of council and the local P and G committee are similar.

There appears to be little conflict within the Basin; differences of opinion arise on individual local issues, but the protagonists change. The population at Gascoyne Junction consisting of shire clerk, school teacher, hotel licensee and policeman, is too small to engender antagonism of the anti-urban type that is normal in the Australian countryside. Factions, as perceived, are both external and institutional. One hears of *the* unions, *the* government, *the* people in *the* cities, *the* department. This, in part, may explain some of the reaction to the Wilcox and McKinnon report.

Such feelings are in no way diminished by the fact that the pastoralist and his family may be of urban origin themselves.

The infra-structure, though slight, is efficient. The shire has modern road-making plant, and the policeman and school teacher are routinely replaced from outside the region. The shire clerk is within the local government system and promotional opportunities involve moving to a shire with larger annual revenue.

The flying doctor service operates out of Carnarvon and Meekatharra where there are large hospitals; maternity cases go to Carnarvon or Meekatharra (it is the practice for Australian women to be admitted to hospital and have a medical practitioner in attendance at the birth whether there are likely to be complications or not). Some women stay in the capital city, Perth, for the last months of pregnancy and attend Perth hospitals. Medical advice is given over the radio-transceiver service every day by a medical practitioner.

Meat is a large proportion (up to 80 per cent) of the human diet and in winter all stations grow their own vegetables; summer vegetables are brought in from Carnarvon and from the southern region. Diets would not appear to be deficient and they are possibly lower than the Australian norm for carbohydrate and fat intake.

There are very few large families, that is with more than three children, amongst the pastoralists. Most of their station staff are single. Because a significant number or wives have been nurses and the predominant age group has been influenced by the contemporary changes in attitudes to reproduction and sexual mores, the values and attitudes tend to be more those of middle-class urban than of rural populations. These subjects can be discussed in open company and are not taboo as in the previous generation or in the present farming community.

The major health hazards include accidents to the males while handling animals; skin cancer is an occupational hazard. Back ailments are common due in part to lifting heavy materials, but also the product of sporting activities at school. Alcohol intake is substantial, particularly at social functions.

The School of the Air has one full-time teacher in both Carnarvon and Meekatharra. This school provides educational support for mothers of children of kindergarten and primary school age.

The socialization of children in these isolated and small family groups is aided by the radio-transceiver communication system; the children talk to their teacher and to other children in the region, but at the primary level it is difficult to convince them that other children in the world attend school.

There is a primary school at Gascoyne Junction with one teacher. Six children are resident in the township and six come from the nearest stations. The nearest secondary school serving the western end of the Basin is 180 km away in Carnarvon and station children attending this school live in a hostel. There is no bus service between Gascoyne Junction and Carnarvon.

The State Library Board supplies books and personnel for the library in Carnarvon but books can be obtained on an individual lender basis in the Basin. Distance and lack of communication are serious disabilities affecting women. In addition to the number of certificated nurses, wives have had previous occupational experience prior to marriage in teaching, secretarial and business sectors. By contrast, there are no graduates or diplomates amongst the men, few of whom have had previous business experience. The women's role is traditional, feminine and demanding, with responsibilities that include the management of the homestead system, all communications including letters, radio-transceiver, housework and where there is no governess, education of the younger children. The governess, a girl in her teens, usually stays for a year, often for the pastoral experience. Until the mid-1960s aboriginal women tended the children and worked around the homestead.

The husband is now foreman, labourer, mechanic and animal husbandryman.

As described already, the pastoralist's family is of the nuclear type without grandparents or other close relatives; these latter may holiday at the station in the cooler part of the year. The process of the station passing from father to son is not as common as before; the children prefer job opportunities within the urban system.

Kinship systems do not exist except in the case of the occasional family company with a number of stations in various Australian States.

Communications in terms of flows of information, agricultural products and merchandise impinge on many aspects of commercial and domestic life in the Gascoyne Basin.

The Telecommunications Commission, a statutory corporation responsible to the Federal Government, develops and maintains the nation-wide telephone system. The Gascoyne Junction telephone exchange has eleven station subscribers. These stations are either proximate to Telecommunication Commission lines or have erected their own private lines to the exchange.

The Royal Flying Doctor Radio Network gives each station contact with Carnarvon and Meekatharra several times each day and emergency contact at any time for both stations and portable transceivers. It transmits and receives telegrams for those stations not on the Government telephone network. This network may be used for contact between stations at certain times. The Network is a private organization maintained in large part by public subscription and its social role is highly significant in aiding the development of Girl Guides of the Air, Countrywomen's Association of the Air and Isolated Children's Parents Association.

Normal radio broadcasts (medium wave length) are available from one Australian Broadcasting Commission (a Federal Government Statutory Authority) regional station. Reception is poor during summer days. Broadcasts of particular interest to pastoralists would include The Country Hour (12 noon to 1.00 p.m.) daily, and Regional News Bulletins. However, the midday broadcast does not cater for the many pastoralists who work all day away from the homestead.

Another Federal corporation, the Postal Commission, maintains a letter and parcel service; the mail contract to deliver mail to station properties is let to the contractor by the Commission. The Post Office at Gascoyne Junction, as elsewhere, acts as a distribution and service agency for a wide range of Federal activities, including payment of various pensions, child allowances, savings bank agency, distribution of taxation forms, and information for Federal Government departments on matters such as migration, naturalization, census, quarantine and health regulations.  As an information service it is rudimentary.

State Government information is fragmented and issued by various departments and departmental officers wherever they are located.  The Shire Clerk and policeman receive material of public interest.

Carnarvon provides a wider range of information services derived from Federal and State governments, but such information tends to be for departmental use or public advise rather than consumer use.

Press releases are part of the modern mass media scene and these are issued in large numbers by many agencies.  Publication of these releases in whole or in abbreviated form depends entirely on the independent decision exercised by the editorial management of metropolitan and country newspapers, radio or television stations.  For pastoralists the radio is a more important and influential source of information than newspapers.

The newspapers and weekly journals available include *The West Australian* (published daily in Perth), *The Northern Times* (published weekly in Perth) and *The Countryman* (published weekly in Perth).  Two pastoral houses (large mercantile companies), Elders and Wesfarmers, each publish a weekly journal.  The *Journal of the Department of Agriculture* is published quarterly.

Surface communications rely on air and road services.  There is no railway to Carnarvon and the shipping service has been discontinued.  The Perth to Carnarvon route is serviced daily by jet aircraft.

In Western Australia, as is the case in other Australian states, transport of merchandise is a mix of State railways and private road transport with regulations, taxes, rebates and exceptions designed to keep the railway losses within acceptable limits, make the transport industry contribute to the maintenance of the roads, and assist industries with freight-cost problems.  In effect this arrangement favours the predominantly wool-growing regions not served by railways but with road haulage services which can obtain freight both to and from Perth.

Carnarvon provides a wider range of services than the usual rural centre and is the major commercial centre for the Upper Gascoyne; the contract mail service to the ten stations at the western end of the Basin reinforces this link.  Besides the mail carried under contract with the Postal Commission, the owner-driver of the 7-tonne truck conveys various station supplies and fuel.  Wool is back-loaded.  A few stations in the central Gascoyne are serviced by a mail-contractor operating from the railhead at Mullewa and the eastern end by a mail-contractor from the railway at Meekatharra.  In effect, the Basin is divided commercially and socially.

Charter aircraft of all configurations and size are available from Carnarvon at very short notice.

### PRESENT PHYSICAL AND BIOLOGICAL FACTORS OF THE ENVIRONMENT

*Climate*

The meteorological systems affecting the Gascoyne Basin produce an erratic and unreliable rainfall.  Approximately half falls in summer and half in winter.

The major meteorological systems operating in summer to produce rain are cyclonic disturbances which move into the area in a southern or south-easterly direction from the coast between Port Hedland and Carnarvon.  The accompanying rain is usually heavy (see Fig. 2) although cyclonic disturbances with no rain but with high winds have been recorded. Rain-producing cyclones cannot be relied upon every year.

Isohyet maps of the north-west of Western Australia have been prepared by the Australian Bureau of Meteorology for the 51 years 1909-1959 in which there were cyclonic depressions. Significant rain was brought to various parts of the Basin by forty-two of these cyclonic events. Some years had no such depressions, one had three and ten and two. Only five of these forty-two depressions brought rain (25 to 50 mm on average) to all the Basin, and there was a tendency for the centre and east of the Basin to have more depressions and heavier rainfall than the western end.

In the absence of cyclonic depressions a recurring pattern of high-pressure ridges and following troughs move inland over the Basin, bringing little or no rain to the region. Heavy sporadic rainfall from thunderstorm activity can be important locally.

In winter the southern anticyclonic systems reach their northern limit in the Gascoyne area and slightly to the north. These bring rain and high winds to the Basin. However, only intense depressions penetrate the Basin so that winter rainfall also is unreliable.

From September to November the rising temperatures further north in the tropics maintain low-pressure systems which develop as troughs towards the south and impede the movement northwards of late anticyclones from the south. The driest months of the year are recorded during this September to November period (southern hemisphere spring).

The reverse situation applies from March to early May, when the northern low-pressure systems relax and the southern anticyclones move north. During this period, rain from the northern systems becomes increasingly unlikely while the possibility of rain from the southern systems increases. As a general rule rainfall is usual during this March to May period (southern hemisphere autumn).

Evidence of climatic change in terms of past rainfall for the north-west is not convincing (see Tucker, 1975; Pittock, 1975).

High summer maximum temperatures and low winter minima characterize the thermal regime of the Basin. The diurnal fluctuations are between $11°$ and $17°$C. Table 1 shows the daily maxima and minina for each month at two stations, Peak Hill in the east and Gascoyne Junction in the west. The subdued topography and the magnitude of the climatic controls when set against the relatively small size of the Basin with its main east-west axis explains thermal similarities in the Basin.

Maximum daily temperatures exceed $38°$C on at least 45 and up to 60 days per annum. From November to March the daily temperatures are above the comfort zones acceptable to western-style living and working.

Frosts occur in winter, but are irregular and infrequent. The indigenous vegetation is seldom affected.

Humidity levels are low except immediately following rainfall.

The total radiation (cal/cm$^2$ day) is estimated at 650 in January and 350 in July. Evaporation, as measured in the standard Australian tank, is high with annual values of from 2300 to 2540 mm. In January, evaporation of up to 380 mm has occurred.

Table 1.  Mean Temperatures (°C) at Peak Hill (eastern Gascoyne Basin) and Gascoyne
Junction (western Gascoyne Basin)

|  | Jan. | Feb. | Mar. | Apr. | May | June | July | Aug. | Sept. | Oct. | Nov. | Dec. |
|---|---|---|---|---|---|---|---|---|---|---|---|---|
| **Peak Hill** | | | | | | | | | | | | |
| Mean max. | 37.5 | 36.7 | 34.5 | 29.6 | 23.5 | 19.6 | 18.9 | 21.1 | 25.2 | 29.5 | 34.1 | 37.3 |
| Mean min. | 23.5 | 23.3 | 21.2 | 16.9 | 12.0 | 8.6 | 7.5 | 8.6 | 11.6 | 14.7 | 19.1 | 22.5 |
| **Gascoyne Junction** | | | | | | | | | | | | |
| Mean max. | 40.3 | 39.1 | 36.7 | 32.9 | 27.5 | 23.6 | 22.4 | 24.7 | 28.0 | 31.6 | 35.2 | 37.8 |
| Mean min. | 23.3 | 22.9 | 21.9 | 17.8 | 13.5 | 9.7 | 8.9 | 9.7 | 11.7 | 14.9 | 17.9 | 20.3 |

The potential evaporation, a modification of Penman's evapotranspiration (see
Fitzpatrick, 1968), calculated for 5-day periods for Peak Hill gives mean values
exceeding 30 mm from November until the end of March, values less than 20 mm from
May until mid-September and less than 15 mm from June until mid-August. Rain
falling in winter will be more effective than the same amount in summer.

Rainfall data for the Basin are presented for four stations:  Bidgemia in the south-
west, Yarlarweelor in the south-east, Mount Augustus on the mid-north boundary and
Three Rivers in the far east of the Basin.

Average monthly rainfall data for the four stations are included in Table 2.

Table 2.  Average Monthly and Total Rainfall for Four Stations, varying years to
1972, 1973 and 1975 with Totals for January-March and May-July (mm)

|  | Jan. | Feb. | Mar. | Apr. | May | June | July | Aug. | Sept. | Oct. | Nov. | Dec. | Annual |
|---|---|---|---|---|---|---|---|---|---|---|---|---|---|
| Bidgemia (88 years) | 32 | 26 | 26 | 13 | 29 | 33 | 28 | 12 | 2 | 3 | 4 | 4 | 212 |
|  |  | 84 |  |  |  | 90 |  |  |  |  |  |  |  |
| Yarlarweelor (49 years) | 29 | 35 | 37 | 13 | 27 | 29 | 15 | 7 | 3 | 2 | 6 | 9 | 212 |
|  |  | 101 |  |  |  | 71 |  |  |  |  |  |  |  |
| Mt. Augustus (71 years) | 38 | 49 | 28 | 15 | 24 | 29 | 14 | 9 | 2 | 2 | 4 | 7 | 221 |
|  |  | 115 |  |  |  | 67 |  |  |  |  |  |  |  |
| Three Rivers (68 years) | 30 | 36 | 41 | 17 | 26 | 26 | 11 | 7 | 2 | 4 | 8 | 14 | 222 |
|  |  | 107 |  |  |  | 63 |  |  |  |  |  |  |  |

At Bidgemia the average winter (March-July) rainfall exceeds the average summer
(January-March) rainfall, but this is not so at the other three recording stations.
The variability of past rain as estimated from the decile levels of monthly rainfall
is set out in the section on desertification processes.

Deciles of annual rainfall in Australia for the years 1885 to 1965 given by Gibbs and Maher (1967) provide the context into which rainfall variability over the Gascoyne Basin can be fitted.


*Topography*

The topography of the Basin is subdued, with the plateau plain sloping gently from east to west. The river valleys are extremely wide and poorly defined. Although designated as the Gascoyne Basin, the Gascoyne River itself does not drain the whole Basin. A major tributary is the Lyons River which drains the northern part of the Basin. This west-flowing river was formerly part of the west-flowing Minilya River, but the rapid advance of the lower south-flowing Lyons through the soft Permian strata has resulted in the capture of the upper Lyons, leaving the present Minilya River as a diminished stream.

Both these rivers slowly descend to the sea at rates of about 1 m per km. They are fed by numerous streams and rivers, some of which are significant though, like the Gascoyne and Lyons, being quite intermittent. The Frederick and Edmund rivers and the Elliott and Kurubuka Creeks join the Lyons River, draining the divide on the north. The Gascoyne is fed by Dalgety Brook and the Daurie, Pells, Bush, and Dur-lacher Creeks.

In the east and north the watershed divides between the Asbburton, Minilya and Murchison Basins are clearly visible, but in the south-west the sandplain divide between the Gascoyne and the Wooramel rivers is indistinct, though the erosional divide between these two is quite clear in places.

The Basin is located principally on the Precambrian Yilgarn Shield with a small area of Permian origin in the west (Fig. 5). Relics of the Precambrian such as Mt. Augustus, Mt. Gascoyne and Mt. Egerton rise up to 760 m above the surrounding plain which itself reaches an elevation of 600 m above sea level in the east.

Six major geomorphological types occur in the Basin. These are:

  (a) The eastern tributary province - extensive depositional systems or drainage
      plains which discharge into calcreted drainages and the major rivers. Parts
      may have sheeted or gneissic- and quartz-covered surfaces, and can develop
      belts of sand banks or a patterned microrelief of the grove and intergrove
      type (Mabbutt *et al.*, 1963). Low hills rise up to 100 m above these plains.

  (b) The Bangemall province - high hills or uplands of Proterozoic (mid Precambrian)
      origin which exhibit severe dissection of the softer sediments of slates,
      shales and mudstones to produce a rugged terrain in which sharp cliffs and
      truncated bottle-necked canyons are common. Minor flattened uplands in the
      valleys in these rugged hills provide the only accessible pastures in this
      type.

      This Proterozoic series probably extended much further south to where only
      remnants are found today. Isolated massive remnants such as Mt. Augustus,
      Mt. Genoa and Mt. Isabella occur in the Bangemall Province and are now
      associated with the major drainage plains and not with the watersheds. These
      massive sandstone or layered monoliths arise abruptly to up to 750 m above
      drainage plains.

      The difference in erodibility of the sediments, quartzites and dolerites of
      the Proterozoic uplands has produced prominent residual quartzite ridges
      which have a major influence upon the direction of the major drainages.

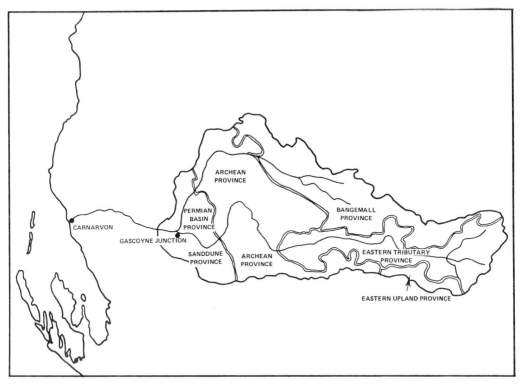

Fig. 5.  The six major geomorphological types which occur
in the Basin.

(c) The eastern upland province – a comparatively small area of metasedimentary
uplands is developed on extremely weathered, folded and intruded Archean
sediments and igneous rocks.  The low hills are rarely more than 100 to 150 m
above the plain.  Below the hills and intrusive quartz ridges, both of which
produce the stone mantle on the slopes which are common in this type, there
are undulating to flat, weathered, strew-covered slopes which ultimately
drain into the major river systems.

(d) The Archean province which is characterized by abundant, unweathered Archean
igneous rocks as hill belts and remnants.  These extend above the restricted
drainage plains and flatter areas.  The rivers lose their hitherto broad waterway pattern in this type and are reduced to deeply channelled rivers which
twist among the stony hills and plains.  A number of hills provide low relief
of up to 150 m above the elevated plains.  Large granite belts can be found
in parts of the area, though most of it is formed of more obviously metamorphic rocks such as gneiss and schist.

The flatter plans leading to drainage lines are characteristically covered
with a stony mantle which is predominantly quartz, but locally modified
with gneissic material.  In the granitic plains the strew is much reduced.
The lowest parts of the plans have a typically sluggish drainage which
increases salinity locally and thereby produces areas of halophytic pastures.
There are very extensive stony plains rarely broken by creeklines which are
often several km long and equally wide.

The flattened stony plains in places are characterized by extensive wind-sorted sandy banks and the mulga-grove pattern is found on the western edge of this Archean type where it discharges water into major stream lines.

(e) The Permian Basin province. The Permian geomorphological type is an area of very low relief, of flattened drainage plains with undulating stone-mantled areas between the hills and plains. The escarpment of the Kennedy Range is considered to form the western edge of the Basin because the sandplains and dunes on the Gascoyne cuesta (Jutson, 1934) contribute little if anything at all to the drainage.

Condon (1963) recognized three series in the Permian beds: the Sakmarian, Artinskian and Kungurian. In general terms, the Sakmarian series produce soils with an abundant surface strew which is absent in many of the Artinskian-based types. The folding of the strata has resulted in Sakmarian types predominating against the Archean block while the Artinskian series are found in the valley between the Archean block and the scarp of the Kennedy Range. The Kungurian series are present to a limited extent.

The soft rocks of the Permian have given rise to soils with a high clay content. Duplex soils are common. Soils are extremely alkaline, and very prone to water erosion. They are therefore quite unlike the soils of the Archean block and the Bangemall uplands, which are, in general, resistant to water erosion, if not to wind erosion.

The highest parts of the relief, up to 100 m, are provided by weathered or poorly weathered hill ranges, isolated hills and ridges. The tops are often capped with laterite of "billy" of Tertiary age which gives some hills a mesa-like appearance.

Undulating stone-covered slopes extend away from the hills. They are abruptly undulating, dissected with fine creeklines, and are found above the plains of the province. The flat plains show occasional low ridges of exposed sediments, sandy banks, and there may be stone-covered undulating sections.

In this area of low relief the tributary drainage plains are absent, but their place is taken by plains with sand dunes arranged along the direction of water flow. The interdunal flow areas frequently have duplex soils. The water flow is discharged into the major drainage channels which are well developed at this end of the Basin.

Massive sand dune-claypan complexes have developed towards the western edge of the Permian basin. The encircling dunes are presumed to have been derived from the sands behind the face of the Gascoyne cuesta.

(f) The sand dune province. The sand dune type is found above the Kennedy Range escarpment and in the south-west of the Basin where it forms a diffuse divide between the Wooramel and Gascoyne rivers. It consists of sandplain formed into stabilized dune fields. The dunes may be up to 12 m or more above the interdunal areas. The interdunes are alternatively sandy-bottomed or clayey. There is virtually no out-drainage and accumulated water evaporates in the occasional claypans.

Surface water is confined to a few pools along the major rivers. Ground water is readily available at depths of 30 m or less in small aquifers. These small aquifers have not been exhausted because a supply of 10,000 l per day is sufficient for one livestock watering point. There is only one strip of saline ground water in the Basin.

Although a comprehensive groundwater survey has yet to be attempted, there are known to be large reserves, for example, under the valley of the Gascoyne on the eastern side of the major Archean outcrop.

## Soils

Soils of the Basin (Fig. 6 modified from Bettenay *et al.*, 1967) occur widely in other parts of arid Australia. The classification and description that follows is based on Northcote *et al.* (1975).

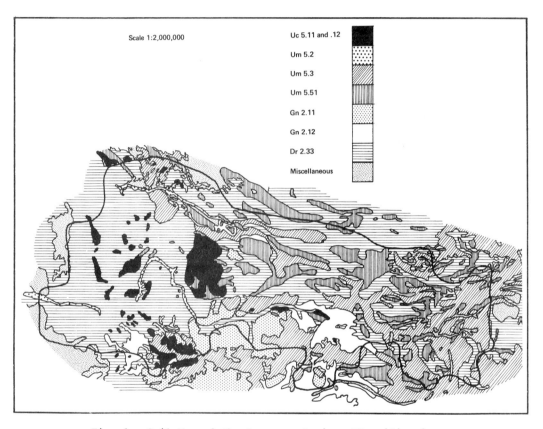

Fig. 6.   Soil Map of the Bascoyne Basin.  Classification
follows the scheme devised by Northcote (1975).

There are four categories of soils with uniform texture profiles.  The brownish sands, *Uc 5.11*, associated with the hills and the non-calcareous loams *Um 5.2* on depositional plains of low relief, are not common.  Substantial areas of earthy loams with red-brown hardpan *Um 5.3* are associated with low hills, ridges, undulating topography and denudational plains.  Shallow earthy loams *Um 5.51* are associated with hills in the vicinity of the Lyons River and the eastern end of the Basin.

Non-calcareous earths, massive, red and acid on *Gn 2.11* or neutral *Gn 2.12* are associated with denudational plains of relief less than 15 m.  The remaining soils have texture contrast profiles and are hard, pedal, red duplex soils, alkaline in reaction and with sporadically bleached A2 horizons.  These are associated with low

hills, ridges, and depositional plains at the western end of the Basin.  There are
smaller areas between the Gascoyne and the Lyons Rivers.

From the descriptions of these soils it will be appreciated that permeability and
water storage will be limited.


*Vegetation*

The vegetation of the Basin is an *Acacia* shrubland (Moore and Perry, 1970) and falls
within the Eremean Botanical Province (Aplin, 1975).  It is predominantly an
extensive high shrubland formation (i.e. shrubs over 2 m high) of the *Acacia aneura*
Alliance.  Associated with *A. aneura* are a number of other *Acacia* spp. and a low
shrub element of *Eremophila, Cassia, Bassia, Maireana* and *Rhagodia* spp.  Small trees
and tall shrubs of occasional significance include *Eucalyptus, Hakea* and *Grevillia*
spp.  Perennial grasses include species of *Monachather, Cymbopogon, Chrysopogon,
Themeda, Thyridolepis, Eriachne, Eragrostis, Plechtrachne* and *Triodia*.

Nine pasture groups have been defined and Table 3 summarizes the area occupied by
each group, a description of the site where the group is found and the dominant
trees, shrub and ground layer species with estimates of their density and height.
Representative pastures in the marked (x) groups have been selected for later
examination in the section on desertification processes.


POLITICAL, SOCIAL AND ECONOMIC HISTORY AND TRENDS IN LAND USE

*Settlement and Development*

In 1857 F. T. Gregory, the Assistant Surveyor of Western Australia, traced both the
Murchison River and the Gascoyne River for the greater part of their courses.  The
dominance of mining and the pastoral industry in the economy of the various
Australian colonies ensured that explorers, whether financed by colonial government
or by entrepreneurs, would assess the landscape in terms of these end uses.
Gregory noted the frequent occurrence of saltbush and grass flats along the
Gascoyne River but the overall impression of the Basin was not favourable.  Not
until the late 1870s and early 1880s, when Australia was immersed in an era of
unparalleled pastoral speculation and after the Murchison region was settled, was
there a limited amount of investment in the Basin.  Historical information on the
development of the pastoral industry in the Gascoyne Basin to the early 1930s is
scarce, but there is some relevant material from a station on the Minilya River
and this is used.

In 1863 regulations were gazetted in the colony of Western Australia to permit the
selection of up to 100,000 acres of pastoral land and the grazing of this crown
land rent-free for 3 years.  This lease could then be held for a further 8 years at
an annual rental of £1 per 1000 acres.  In 1872 the period of tenure was increased
to 14 years and in 1883 there were further amendments.  These later amendments were
controversial; the main criticism was based on the premise that a selector could
invest small amounts of capital in leases containing reliable water supplies and
in effect control vast areas of surrounding pastoral land.

Table 3.  Pasture Groups, Area Occupied, Site and Species

| Pasture group | Area (km²) | Site characteristics | Species |
|---|---|---|---|
| Hill pasture * | 14,500 | Partly inaccessible, particularly for cattle; stunted, sparse trees and variable shrubs; abundant strew on pockets of shallow soil; otherwise bald rock outcrop; short grass-forb pastures with minor halophyte plains below breakaways and in drainages | Tree layer of *Acacia aneura*, *A. linophylla*, *A. tetragonophylla*, *A. xiphophylla*, low sparse canopy 2–6 m high; shrub layer *Cassia*, *Eremophila*, *Solanum*, *Ptilotus*, *Kallstroemia* and some chenopods, 4–6 m apart and 0.5–1 m high; annual grasses and forbs |
| Stony short grass–forb pasture * | 22,200 | Undulating, sometimes dissected, strew-covered areas below the highest relief; flatter strew-covered plains carrying tributary drainage; stunted trees, sparse shrubs, short grasses and forbs in season; some rangelands with saline inclusions and halophytes; dense groves of vegetation in others | As for hill pasture with *A. pruinocarpa*, 6–8 m apart up to 5 m high; shrub layer *Eremophila*, *Cassia*, *Solanum*, *Maireana*, *Rhagodia*, *Scaevola*, *Ptilotus*, 5–10 m apart and 0.5–1 m high; annual grasses and forbs |
| Stony chenopod pasture * | 14,700 | Generally flattened strew-covered or bare plains and interfluves; undulating areas common in highest parts with abundant strew; saline soils common, either duplex or heavy clays both supporting halophytes and stunted trees. Run-off areas within each rangeland generally non-saline and with stony shortgrass-forb pastures with sparse stunted trees and shrubs. | Permian. *A. victoriae*, *A. aneura*, 6–12 m apart and up to 4 m high; shrubs *Maireana*, *Eremophila*, *Frankenia*, *Rhagodia* up to 140/ha; annual forbs *Bassia*, *Atriplex*. Non-Permian. *A. victoriae*, *A. tetragonophylla*, *A. aneura* 10 m apart, 2–3 m high; shrubs *Maireana*, *Cassia*, *Eremophila* |
| Chenopod pasture (a) all chenopod | 220 | Flat areas with very reduced slope and sluggish drainage often terminal locally; halophytic pastures | Sparse trees, *Eucalyptus microtheca*, *A. aneura*, *A. tetragonophylla*, *A. sclerosperma* up to 10 m high; shrubs *Chenopodium*, *Maireana*, *Phagodia*, *Cratystylis* 3 m apart; perennial grasses |

Table 3.  (cont.)

| Pasture group | Area (km²) | Site characteristics | Species |
|---|---|---|---|
| (b) with minor halophytes | 1730 | Minor halophytic pastures within these rangelands where short grass-forb pastures are common; principally tributary and minor trunk drainages | Stunted trees, *A. victoriae* or *A. sclerosperma* 6 m apart; shrubs *Maireana, Cratystylis, Enchylaena, Atriplex*; annual *Atriplex, Bassia, Pterigeron* |
| Total | 1950 | | |
| Wandarrie * pasture | 3900 | Sandy banks and larger sand areas on tributary drainage; perennial grassy pastures beneath a moderate canopy of low trees and shrubs | On banks and sandplain, dense to sparse *A. aneura, A. linophylla* up to 4 m apart, 5 m high; shrubs *Eremophila, Rhagodia, Cassia*, 4-5 m apart and 1 m high; perennial grasses *Monachather, Thyridolepis, Eragrostis, Eriachme*; annual grasses. Between banks and on shallow soils, mulga |
| Mulga, * short grass-forb | 6000 | Drainage plains tributary to main or confined flow areas; strew-covered or bare plains with areas of arcuate grove vegetation and sandy banks; segmented by concentrated flow lines | Drainage plains with scattered *A. aneura, A. tetragonophylla, A. craspedecarpa, A. pruinocarpa* 3-5 m apart and 3-6 m high; shrubs *Eremophila, Cassia, Maireana, Rhagodia, Ptilotus* up to 4 m apart; annual grasses |
| Sand dune-halophyte pasture | 1600 | Sand dunes with claypans, dunal flow areas with duplex soils. Drainage flow plains and dunes | Trees *A. tetragonophylla, A. linophylla, A. sclerosperma, Grevillea, Hakea*, 5-6 m apart and up to 4 m high; shrubs *Rhagodia, Hibiscus, Cassia, Verticordia, Prostanthera, Eremophila*, 3-4 m apart and up to 2 m high; sparse perennial grasses, *Monochather, Eriachme*. Interdune areas with *Frankenia, Ptiletus, Maireana*, 3 m apart |

Table 3. (cont.)

| Pasture group | Area (km²) | Site characteristics | Species |
|---|---|---|---|
| Sandplain pasture | 3200 | Sand plains with vegetated dunes in the east and west of the Basin | Dunes in east, *A. aneura* occasional, up to 4 m high over grass *Triodia basedowii*; scattered shrubs *Hakea, Grevillea*. In west, *A. sclerosperma*; shrubs *Eremophila, Calythrix, Scaevola* |
| River pasture * | 2300 | The major rivers and creeklines of the Basin, with associated islands and narrow plains marginal to rivers | *A. aneura, A. citrinoviridis, A. tetragonophylla, A. grasbyi* up to 8 m high under *Eucalyptus camaldulensis* 20 m high; shrubs, *Acacia, Eremophila, Cassia, Rhagodca* with invading perennial grass *Cenchrus ciliaris* |

* Selected for later detailed examination.

In 1887 new regulations incorporated features which were developed further in later legislation on land settlement and management.  The period that a lease could be held was increased to 21 years with a rental more appropriate to the district; leases were conditional upon specified improvements being undertaken.  These regulations attempted to correct the fault in the early legislation which set the same rental for leases in high and low risk districts and for good and poor-quality pastoral lands.  The peculiar property shapes seen in maps of the Gascoyne Basin (and elsewhere) are a legacy of the early land acts.  The first European settlers left the mountain ranges, scrublands and waterless lands to the later comers and to the aboriginals who had not yet moved down to camps near the homesteads where for 60 years they became the major part of the pastoral workforce.  In 1882 Magistrate Fairbairn reported on two visits to the Gascoyne to investigate native murders and noted the important role of aboriginal women in shepherding flocks distant from the homestead with supervision limited to a brief weekly visit.  Eventually a permit system to employ aboriginal labour was developed and permits had to be procured before aborigines could be employed or moved out of their home district. This system remained in force until the 1950s.

Merino sheep were brought in to the Gascoyne from the settled districts further south.  They were shepherded by aborigines and relied on water from natural springs and shallow wells.  The flocks were folded at night because of predation by the dingo; in dry periods the flocks travelled hundred of kilometres in search of food and water.

Although the first lessees could graze their flocks over areas of up to 400,000 ha, the absence of surface water, the dissected landscape with its mosaic of productive and unproductive vegetation types and a source of cheap labour for shepherding, favoured a semi-nomadic system in which small parts of the lease were severely used and large parts were unused.  These early nomadic practices continued for decades and, for example, prior to 1934 one station carried in excess of 100,000 sheep with no more than three wells and shallow soaks opened up in the river bed by one-horse scoops manned by aborigines.

A review of livestock numbers for the early 1900s suggests that the Merino sheep population built up rapidly, maintained itself and occasionally produced an excess for sale.  We estimate that by 1900 the number of sheep were already 60 per cent of the peak level attained immediately prior to the disastrous drought of 1936.

The Great Depression of the late 1920s and early 1930s generated great economic pressures in Australia.  In the Gascoyne Basin, an attempt was made to both maintain income levels and meet obligations to creditors by increasing sheep numbers.  The increase in numbers was aided by a run of good seasons.  Inevitably the lower prices for sheep led to retention of sheep on the stations (Fig. 7).

In Australia the classical investment pattern of heavy borrowings at high interest rates in boom periods is associated with the purchase and development of pastoral holdings.  This generally results in resource losses (desertification) and massive capital write-down because of a subsequent mercantile depression and drought, as for example in eastern Australia (Cain, 1962; Butlin and Jennings, 1970).  The drought which accompanies this painful process and which is generally considered to be the *raison d'être* merely advances the inevitable collapse in livestock numbers by a year or two.  The Basin, or probably less than 50 per cent of it, was carrying at least 650,000 sheep equivalents and a meat works in Carnarvon was nearing completion when this 1936 drought made the system (Fig. 7), that was already well on the way to collapse (see Fig. 8), crash.

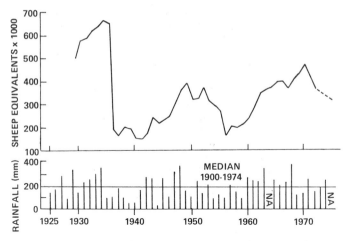

Fig. 7.   Sheep numbers in the Cascoyne Basin and rainfall
          pattern from 1925 to 1974.

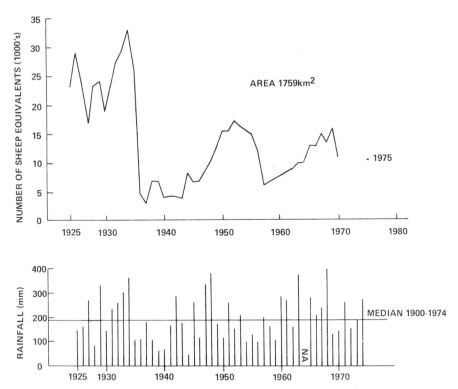

Fig. 8.   Sheep numbers and rainfall pattern on a Gascoyne
          station between 1925 and 1974.

In 1917 the Pastoral Appraisement Board (see later) was instituted with what appears in retrospect to be a limited house-keeping role. The Pastoral Inspectors' reports and maps of property inspections made in 1920 which describe and delineate range-land in terms such as "saltbush flats", light sandy flats" and "good open saltbush plains" are in marked contrast to the description and maps of these same rangelands in 1969-70, which refer to "none of which is present today", "now been stripped of their soil mantle" and "which does not exist in this area". Criticism of the early regulations and the comparatively short period of tenure has centred on their in-fluence in tending "to encourage exploitative stocking rates" (Humphries, 1951). However, the widespread and severe deterioration evidenced between 1920 and 1936 occurred under the later pastoral lease regulations as administered by the Pastoral Appraisement Board. During this latter period there was only one pastoral inspector for the whole State. This is in marked contrast to the present situation where the Pastoral Inspection Branch consists of the Chief Pastoral Inspector with two assis-tant inspectors, and additional Pastoral Inspectors located at Carnarvon, Port Hedland, Broome, Kalgoorlie, Geraldton and Meekatharra.

The function of the Pastoral Appraisement Board developed from the recognition that a supervisory agency was required in order to protect the interests of the State in the lands which it owned and leased for pastoral use under Pastoral Lease.

The Board comprises four members:

   (a) one shall be the person for the time being holding the office of Surveyor
       General who shall be Chairman of the Board;

   (b) one shall be the person for the time being holding the office of Director
       of Agriculture;

   (c) two shall be persons appointed by the Governor-in-Council, i.e. the Governor
       and at least two Ministers of the Government. Customarily one of these
       Board members is a nominee of the Pastoralists and Graziers Association.

The Pastoral Appraisement Board meets as and when required and meetings are not convened on a regular period basis; a certain degree of the work devolves on a sub-committee which investigate matters referred to them by the Board and which in turn report back to it. For example, each station must submit a 5-year improvement plan to the Pastoral Appraisement Board and these come up before the Developmental Sub-committee which consists of officers from the Department of Agriculture Rangeland Management Branch and the Department of Lands Pastoral Inspection Branch. All members are to have experience in the particular region. Only improvements approved by the Pastoral Appraisement Board should be proceeded with.

Unlike the professional staff of the Department of Agriculture which is appointed at university graduate level, pastoral inspectors have been recruited from various managerial positions within the pastoral industry where formal vocational training is rare. Because of rapid changes in rural employment relative to urban employment this supply of practical and experienced men is likely to diminish in the near future.

Research in the pastoral regions of Western Australia started with the pioneering ecological survey of the De Grey region to the north of the Gascoyne by Burbidge (1942, 1943) and with the reproductive aspects of animal production in the region south of the De Grey by Stewart and Moir (1943). Both of these ventures were under the aegis of the University of Western Australia. This was also true of the investigations by Melville (1939, 1947) on the nutritive value of *Acacia aneura*, and the effect of drought on the Murchison district to the south-east of the Gascoyne. The pastoralists' main problems at that time appeared to be drought and associated mortality, coupled with an inability to return to the high sheep numbers maintained for some years prior to the 1936 drought (see Fig. 8). In fact the livestock numbers were approximately half of those carried in the early 1900s.

Pastoral research started in 1950 in the Pilbara as a result of some stations being abandoned in 1946 because sheep numbers could not be maintained by breeding.

Chapman *et al*. (1973) have described the Australian wool industry and the operations on the wool-growing property, most of which are relevant to pastoral holdings in the Gascoyne Basin.

At the outset it is important to note that the wages of staff and contractors' employees are governed by awards fixed by arbitration tribunals or courts after hearing evidence in public from union advocates representing employees and advocates for the employer's association. These awards cover wages, conditions of work and holidays, and apply State-wide or nation-wide to specified categories of employees depending on whether the employees work under State or Federal awards. This "adversary" type of legal arbitration structure is universal in Australian industry and government. To the uninitiated this gives the impression of constant turmoil. Indeed on some occasions a dispute may need to exist in order that a conciliation and arbitration hearing take place. Under the Pastoral Award, a deduction of approximately 25 per cent of the gross wage is allowed where the employer provides housing and certain other defined benefits to his staff. The information on awards generally reaches the pastoralist in the form of a newsletter (example in Appendix 2). Staff tend to be versatile and skilled. Because they are single, mobile and employable they readily move from station to station or to cities and mining towns as they choose.

Contract labour is used extensively, not only for shearing and crutching, but also for cartage, mulesing, road-making, construction of buildings and other facilities, and livestock transport. Droving ceased in the mid-1950s following the introduction of large war-surplus trucks.

Water augmentation probably reached its full development of 1800 windmills (wind pumps) and associated works between 1950 and 1965. They generally pump from shallow wells and bores located in ground water aquifers. The sinking of bores was carried out by contractors and the small windmills of 3 m diameter were installed by station labour. Many unsuccessful wells were sunk in the past; these wells can either be dry or, more often, have water with a high salt content. Windmills generally pump directly into galvanized iron tanks of 22,500- to 45,000-litre capacity (for sheep) and 22,500- to 90,000-litre capacity (for cattle). Mill, tanks and drinking troughs require regular maintenance and frequent checking; this is an essential part of station routine.

Wells are unlikely to be drilled in future because there is little new country to be opened up. Ground water recharge has so far been sufficient to meet the present withdrawal via windmills in spite of drought. Engines are only used on wells near homesteads, and most homesteads are near streamlines.

There is no water conservation and surface storage because there is no need for it in a simple pastoral economy; water spreading is not feasible because of the rough terrain, and although the Three Rivers rangeland system has an ideal slope for water spreading, its soil is shallow, self-sealing and its vegetation is not of the type to respond in economic terms.

Boundary fences for sheep consist of five plain wires with steel posts (or pickets) at two to three per 70 m. Subdivisional fences consist of four plain wires. Near windmills, or where flocks congregate, steel "droppers" are clipped on to the wires. Where cattle are grazed, a top wire (barbed type) may be used. Old fences used wooden posts of mulga, but this timber is no longer available. The boundary rider, a horseman, whose job it was to check the fences and watering facilities has been replaced by four-wheel-drive vehicles and motor cycles operating from the homestead. Light aircraft are used on a number of stations. Checking one side of

Mt. Augustus station involves 280 km of arduous travel by vehicle and takes one day. This same task can be efficiently completed in a few hours by aircraft.

The homesteads range in size from small and compact with surrounding garden and nearby machinery sheds to a complex of buildings approximating a village, built when aboriginal help was abundant. Maintenance of these large establishments is impossible under present economic and labour conditions. Workers' cottages are provided. At the shearing shed there will be a set of dormitories and a kitchen provided for the shearers. The standard of facilities is negotiated nationally between the union and employers' representatives appearing before a Conciliation and Arbitration Commissioner.

Housing and storage structures differ little from those elsewhere in pastoral Australia. However, a characteristic building in north-western Australia is the bough or summer bush shed—a detached room constructed with walls and roof of two layers of wire netting between which is a layer of fibrous material (usually grass hay or spinifex grass); water trickles through the walls from a pipe with spaced holes; the floor is concrete. This shed, like the homestead buildings, represents the past rather than the present, and evaporative-type room coolers, powered by electric motors, are now used. This change mirrors the change from country leisure to the necessity for the family to continue in the suburban work mode.

Homesteads are built of natural stone and cement mortar or concrete blocks. Floors of the house and of the surrounding side verandahs are concrete. The roofs of all buildings are of corrugated iron (rolled, tinned sheet steel). This material is universally used for the cladding of sheds and other farm buildings. Most homesteads are large, with a floor area of from 3000 to 6000 $m^2$, and are set within a fenced area of 0.5 to 1.5 ha which has a small area of lawn, shade trees, a garden with a few fruit trees and a vegetable garden.

Shearing sheds are often very large structures which date from the days when the station flocks were two or three times their present size. The associated yards are appropriate for this large number. On some stations smaller sheds have been built in better locations for easy working and proximity to the homestead. The largest shed on the Basin now uses only eight "stands" (eight places with shearing gear for each shearer).

Out-of-season fruit and vegetables depend on visits to Carnarvon and the mail-contractor. The use of car-refrigerators for the transport of frozen foods is limited by the capacity of these units. Processed milk and canned foods are extensively used. Stations kill their own meat as and when it is needed. The kerosene (paraffin) refrigerator is favoured over the newer LP gas refrigerator because LP gas is expensive. However, spare parts for the discontinued lines of kerosene units are difficult to obtain. Deep-freezers are not generally used. Where a 240-V generator is installed the usual practice is for it to run for 3 hours in the morning and for the period where light is required at night. These hours are the  periods of maximum domestic use.

Much electricity generation equipment is 32 V and limited to lights and occasional domestic use. Appliances suitable for 32-V power are substantially more expensive than those produced for 240 V if indeed they can now be obtained.

LP gas is used for domestic cooking; smaller families, the absence of domestic staff, and cooler evening temperatures out-of-doors have led to the extensive practice of barbecue meals.

*Livestock and Fauna*

Rams are generally purchased from southern regions where the nutrition is good and climate less harsh.  This was the usual practice in the Pilbara 30 years ago, but poor ram performance and severe ram mortality allied to the expense of importing rams led to the production of locally bred rams.  The adoption of this practice has been discussed in the Gascoyne, where ram mortality is approximately 35 per cent per annum.

Rams purchased in southern regions and transported to the Gascoyne are unlikely to cost less than $100 each on the station.  Even with losses below the average the ram replacement bill for a viable sheep flock would exceed $5000.

The rams are generally joined with the ewes in the proportion of 3 to 5 per 100 in December and removed at shearing in May-June.  Rams are either shorn in October or jetted (treated with insecticide) to reduce the risk of fly strike.  The stations that recently changed from sheep to cattle (5 of 30) sold their sheep to neighbours and this conceals the true breeding position on stations, but not for the Basin as a whole.  On some properties lambings may be as low as 20 or 30 per cent.

Shearing in early winter removes the threat of blow-fly "strike" which results from winter rains, particularly those in May.  Sheep are not crutched because summer rains do not precipitate a fly "wave".  After shearing the sheep are spread over the station and left until the next shearing.  Even with low numbers of sheep per paddock this procedure in low-rainfall seasons puts pressure on desirable species and sensitive rangeland types.  In the event of drought, sheep can be sold to the southern farming areas, presuming that these areas are not overstocked or are also droughted.

Ewes, being survivors of the harsh nutritional environment, are well adapted. Weaners receive no preferential management and losses are heavy.  The undegraded chenopod shrubland upon which weaners once depended no longer exists.  Ewe weaners are commonly mulesed (skin removed from each side of the crutch) in order to reduce the risk of fly strike.

Drenching (oral administration) with anthelmintics for the control of intestinal parasites is not a regular feature.

Sheep lice are not a major problem, but a number of stations use an aqueous solution of insecticide ("dipping") after shearing to prevent infestations.

Supplementary or drought feeding is limited to that for the rams in the month before they are put with the ewes.  Horses receive occasional supplementation with oats purchased from the southern farming areas.

Although there are no declared reserves in the Gascoyne Basin for conservation of fauna, all fauna are protected and wildlife cannot be shot, poisoned or trapped at will.  The Gascoyne is included with the Murchison River district in System 10 in the classification drawn up by the Conservation Through Reserves Committee. Reports on fauna are issued through the Environmental Protection Agency.

The pastoral industry throughout Australia spends a great amount of time discussing the "competitors with sheep" and generally refers to kangaroos, dingoes, rabbits and feral donkeys, goats and raptorial birds as *vermin*.  Until recently most Australian States had regulations for the eradication and control of vermin, but the emphasis has shifted to the management of fauna.  Faunal research indicates that the effect on livestock production exerted by natural populations of indigenes is generally over-estimated by pastoralists and economic surveys show that expenditure by Western Australian pastoralists on "vermin control" is consistently less than 2 per cent of total station expenditure.  Animals known to be competitors with domestic livestock can be declared "managed species" and the numbers taken annually are prescribed.

Red kangaroos *(Megaleia rufa)* have been shot in large numbers (30,000 per year) in the Basin; about 40 per cent males and the turnoff was estimated at 10 per cent. In 1970 a scheme was devised to prevent exploitation and the reduction of breeding stocks to low levels in an environment subject to frequent drought.  Initially 4000 tags (to be affixed to carcasses) were allotted to each professional shooter. At prices then received the income was adequate to service the capital invested in a freezer (to hold 7 tonnes), guns and four-wheel-drive transport.  At present there are six shooters operating in the western portion of the Gascoyne Basin and three operating in the east.  All carcasses go to Perth for local use as pet food, but 90 per cent of the reprocessing and shipping of the hides to the United States takes place from the Eastern States.

The ratio of prices received by exporters to those received by shooters is 12:1 compared with 4:1 for domestic livestock and reflects the considerable amount of handling in the kangaroo trade.  Formerly this trade was of the cartel type with controlled low prices but there is now more competition.  Pressure to return to the cartel system is being exerted by the entrepreneurial sector of the industry. Pastoralists obtain no financial benefit from kangaroo harvesting, though they pay nothing for the harvesting.

There appear to be no answers to the questions "Is it necessary to kill more or less for pasture health?" and "At what levels do the kangaroo population reduce livestock production?"  However, the kangaroo uses water facilities maintained for sheep and hence depends on the continuing viability of pastoral enterprises.

Foxes *(Vulpes vulpes)* are rare but the numbers of dingo *(Canis familiaris dingo)* fluctuate, with the marauding dog of domestic origin they are a problem and may kill many sheep.  Men ("doggers") were employed by the Agriculture Protection Board and operated in the Gascoyne to track and trap these dogs and dingoes.  The Agriculture Protection Board still spreads baits by air on Crown land; these baits were made of strychnine-brisket fat mixture wrapped in paper.  Following severe local attacks some pastoralists make up meat baits from kangaroo, which are placed in the shade where they stay fresh for longer.

Emus *(Dromaius novae-hollandiae)* are uncommon and in any case do not compete with sheep.  Some faunal components have become extinct in the Basin either because of habitat destruction or change in food supply.  They are present elsewhere in Western Australia.  Purchase of leases specifically for wildlife conservation is unlikely to be worth while.

Rabbits *(Oryctolagus cuniculus)* are rare in the Gascoyne Basin, although there are suitable habitats.  Limits are inherent in high temperatures, rare open water in terms of dams or natural pools, and scarce food items.  Goats *(Capra hircus)* are less common than formerly; the 12,000 goats removed over 5 years from one station were in rough terrain in the Kennedy Ranges bordering the Basin.  Estimated stocks in the Basin would be 10,000 at least.  The meat works at Carnarvon processed 26,000 in 1972-73 and, together with meat works at Geraldton, processed 250,000 in one year, but few of these goats were from the Basin.

Wild horses are numerous in the upper reaches of the Gascoyne; the numbers are unknown, but a large station in the lower Gascoyne had 800 shot in the 1972-1974 period.  These horses are derived from the station populations, which prior to the introduction of the motor-cycle 15 years ago would have ranged from 100 to 200 horses per station.

Plants which poison livestock are uncommon.  An herbaceous annual, *Euphorbia boophthona* (Gascoyne Spurge) contains an alkaloid and can cause substantial losses if sheep feed on it.  This is most likely to occur after sheep have been held at the shed for shearing and are hungry.  Cyanogenetic plants such as *Melilotus* spp. can be a serious source of stock losses in some heavy rainfall years.

*Economic and Political Relationships with External Communities and Institutions*

The main link between the pastoralist and the market place is the "pastoral house" or "stock firm".  These are large pastoral finance companies.  The origin, development, mode of operation and importance to the Australian pastoral industry of these companies has been of considerable interest to economic historians (Butlin, 1962, 1964; Barnard, 1969; Cain, 1962).

Prior to the development and expansion of these pastoral houses, many pastoralists, both in the Gascoyne Basin and elsewhere, were forced to merchandise their own wool directly in the London market.  A number of pastoralists chose to continue this practice after the pastoral houses were firmly established and wool from the Gascoyne Basin appears to have been shipped to London through Carnarvon until the 1939-1945 war when government-to-government marketing arrangements known as BAWRA (British Australian Wool Realization Agreement) operated.  After the war, few wool growers anywhere returned to direct selling on their own account in London.

Recent changes in policies of these pastoral companies in rural financing in Western Australia, and the way that these companies now operate in borrowing, lending and merchandizing are well described by Hodan (1975).

In Western Australia there are now three major companies, Elder-GM, which is the dominant company in the Gascoyne Basin, Wesfarmers and Western Livestock.  The pastoral houses receive wool into storage, arrange for display to potential buyers and conduct the auctions at which the wool is offered.  The companies offer wool grading, cataloguing, interlotting and blending services, general livestock, stud livestock and property sales services, as well as credit and insurance facilities to pastoralists.  Elder-GM has resident managers in a large number of rural districts including Carnarvon, Meekatharra and Mullewa.

Sources of funds for Australian pastoral companies have changed during the period 1962 to 1973; the contribution from overseas liabilities has dropped from 25.7 to 13.8 per cent and shareholders' funds have diminished from 25.3 to 21.2 per cent. Credit balances of clients have fallen from 12.0 to 6.1 per cent and balances due to trading banks have decreased from 12.0 to 5.8 per cent.  Increased contributions have been made by various trade liabilities up from 18.3 to 20.9 per cent, a measure of attempts to diversify (for example into wineries, urban real-estate) debentures, notes and deposits up 9.5 per cent (6.4 per cent maturing within 12 months) to 32.1 per cent (22.1 per cent maturing within 12 months).  There is also a remarkable change in the uses of funds between 1962 and 1973.  Rural advances have fallen 49.2 to 32.3 per cent and fixed assets from 27.4 per cent to 20.0 per cent (some companies sold outdated woolstores and wholly owned pastoral stations).  Short-term assets rose from 2.0 to 18.3 per cent and Australian Government securities rose from 3.3 to 6.2 per cent, Hodan (1975) has pointed out that the fall in credit balances of clients and balances due to trading banks have reduced the ability of companies to advance money to pastoralists.  The uses of funds confirms the unpopularity of rural advances as an investment by the companies.

In the pastoral sector what the companies term the "handling and commission charges" to clients include costs and a profit component.  This profit component in interest charges on overdrafts, sales and purchase of livestock, wool transactions and sales of stations can mean that a pastoralist whose indebtedness is large is in effect

"tied" to a pastoral company for sales and produce.  As Hodan (1975) puts it: "Much
has been said about the insistence of some stock firms that clients purchase farm
goods and inputs from the trading department of the firm.  The findings here are
that farmers normally do reduce their credit balances, resulting from buying on
credit pending the sale of their produce.  However, there is no reason to suspect
exploitation of clients by stock firms in city and country towns as their list
prices, quality and terms are highly competitive.  In remote localities, the
situation may be different.  The farmer may have no alternative source of supply
and some complaints may arise, especially in cases of overspending before sales of
wool or stock are finalized.  'Hard-core' debtors are a problem, being virtually
'owned' by stock firms."

"Hard-core" debtors are those who have not been able to meet interest or capital
repayments and are responsible for about 25-35 per cent of debt to pastoral
companies in Western Australia.  In Western Australia the debt per property
increased from $1267 to $2381 between 1962 and 1973 compared with the Australian
average increase of from $823 to $1235.  This greater increase in Western Australia
reflects credit granted for investment, for purchase of property and land, for
short-term credit and for the "hard-core" debt.  This latter category is prominent
in remote pastoral areas and is associated with small pastoral enterprises.

In the Gascoyne Basin it is comparatively easy to sell a poor station.  Because
borrowing is out of the question for these stations and prices are low, the
purchaser usually pays cash.  The pastoral company that provided "carry-on"
finance by granting an overdraft to the vendor and probably arranged the sale, may
provide the same overdraft facility to the new lessee on the security of the
livestock by "Bill of Sale".  This cycle may be repeated in a few years time; one
Gascoyne station has already changed hands three times in 5 years.  In this way a
pastoral company may in practice control and make a profit in what appear to be
unprofitable areas of pastoral Western Australia.  Large stations are highly
priced and are difficult to finance.  These high prices reflect historical values
and a desire by vendors to cover their indebtedness which in some cases exceeds
$200,000.

A registered "Bill of Sale" is only rarely accepted as security by a bank.  Banks
seldom lend to pastoralists because the value of a pastoral lease is not considered
to be good collateral.

The seasonal limits to borrowings from a pastoral house can fluctuate, and depend
upon the estimated value of the product.  Pastoral houses endeavour to have their
clients' accounts cleared annually and when this is not possible they may insist
upon and exercise stringent budgetary control with the objective of obtaining such
a clearance in the forseeable future.

Permission to sell a station (the leasehold and improvements) is granted by the
Lands Department subject to the purchaser being acceptable to the Department,
i.e. they must not lease more than 404,685 ha or have indulged in Crown land
speculation.  For a non-viable lease, the lessee has to produce written evidence
that the property has been offered to neighbouring lessees.  Purchasers of
leasehold must sign that they are fully aware of the Land Act provisions and agree
to abide by them.  All leases in the Basin have the common expiry date of 2015.

Each year the lessee must notify the Lands Department as to the number of livestock
carried on the property as at 30th June.  The lessee also is required to spend on
new improvements a sum equal to 2.5 times the annual rental.  The annual rental
is based on the estimated carrying capacity (ECC) with allowances being made for
disabilities such as distance from markets and transport facilities.  Shire rates
on pastoral properties are based on the rental set by the Lands Department; where
an unimproved capital value equal to 20 times the annual rent is rated at about

6 cents in the $. The Shire rates and the rental are generally the same.

In terms of the Land Act the Minister can exercise considerable discretion in his decisions, but in practice decisions are made as proposed by his departmental advisers. However, it should be recognized that political pressures influence decision-making.

When the vendor and purchaser particulars have been checked and recorded at departmental level the material is forwarded to the Pastoral Appraisement Board which in due course makes a recommendation to the Minister. There are routine and internal management matters in which recommendations do not need to go to the Minister for decision.

There is yet no evidence from any part of pastoral Australia to suggest that either long-term or short-term leasehold types of conditional purchase, or even freehold, have had anything to do with whether or not the rangeland is degraded or eroded. Pastoral leasehold is best understood as *de facto* freehold, particularly when compared with State and Federal leases for grazing lands in western United States.

In Australia the agencies responsible for administering pastoral leases are now tending to use, albeit discreetly because of the inherent political sensitivity in rural matters, the supervisory powers given under the appropriate Land Acts in cases of extreme abuse by lessees.

There are remarkably few economic links between the Gascoyne and modern Carnarvon; the plantation and vegetable crops from 800 ha returns approximately $4 million and there is a substantial prawn fishing industry, a salt industry and a winter tourist industry with 600 occupied caravan places and up to 600 additional caravans at one time. Approximately $2 million was returned in the same year from the sale of wool from the 5.5 million ha of the Upper Gascoyne.

The economic significance of Carnarvon's industries can be seen to rank above that of pastoral interests. However, the political dominance of Carnarvon is not as apparent as this because of the statewide ramifications of pastoral organizations and their collective influence in Perth. In practice, a conflict of interests that threatened the viability of Carnarvon would be settled in favour of Carnarvon. This situation is reminiscent of the conflict between cattle men who leased the snow country of the Southern Alps in Australia and the farmers of the Murrumbidgee Irrigation Area who used the water from the Alps. The disparity in economic returns exceeded 5000 to 1 in favour of irrigation farming but this ratio bore little resemblance to the political odds.

Links between the pastoralist and the officers of various state government departments are regular in the case of Agriculture, Lands, Police, Wildlife and upon request in the case of labour inspectors and government medical practitioners. Contacts between the pastoralist and federal departments are of an information-gathering type and include Taxation, the Bureau of Census and Statistics, the Bureau of Agricultural Economics (BAE) and the Bureau of Meteorology. The BAE samples several stations in the Gascoyne as part of its Australia-wide economic and production monitoring programme, and the Bureau of Meteorology has several official recording stations, in addition receives rainfall records from all stations.

There is no monitoring of the mechanisms of social conditions in rural Australia. Even case studies are rare and this in a period when changes have been bewildering and rapid.

The economic history of the sheep industry in the Gascoyne Basin is a microcosm of the Australian wool-sheep industry from the 1890s to the present day. Both are predominantly export-orientated and differences, where they occur, are due

primarily to the occurrence of a drought in the Basin but not elsewhere, and vice
versa.

Three components external to the pastoralist have a major effect on profitability
and development.  These are the prices received for sheep and wool, prices paid
for inputs and the supply of feed for the sheep.  This latter is a function of the
type of vegetation and the characteristics of the rainfall.

Although we have no index of prices received or paid by Gascoyne Basin woolgrowers
over the period 1890 to 1976, Chua (1972) has calculated the time-trend 1861-1971
for the aggregate of wool, wheat and butter on an appropriately weighted basis,
together with a ratio which provides an estimate of the Australian farmers' terms
of trade    (Fig. 9).  Additional material has been incorporated to extend the
"terms of trade" ratio up to 1975-76.  Chua has noted the effect on these indices
of major Australian droughts, inflation and economic depressions, all of which
occurred in the period of 1905-1975, the period when the Gascoyne Basin was being
exploited, reached its maximum livestock population, declined and then rose to
present levels.

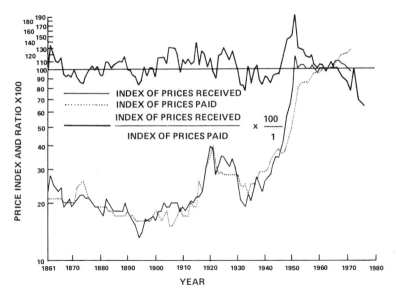

Fig. 9.    The terms of trade available to the Australian
farmer since 1860.

Assuming, not unreasonably, that farmers' and pastoralists' terms of trade are
similar, most of the period 1903 to 1929 appears favourable.  Serious drought in
the Basin (second decile of annual rainfall or less) occurred in 1911, 1924 and
1928 when prices received exceeded prices paid.  However, terms of trade changed
and were less favourable between 1929 and 1945.  This less-favourable economic
climate coincided with an unprecedented period of drought which persisted in
either part or all of the Basin for almost 6 years, commencing in 1935  (Fig. 10).
This drought caused a dramatic fall in livestock numbers which is evident at both
Basin and individual stations level (Figs. 7 and 8).  The two years 1944 and 1945
with annual rainfall in the lower deciles did not reduce what was still a small
livestock population.

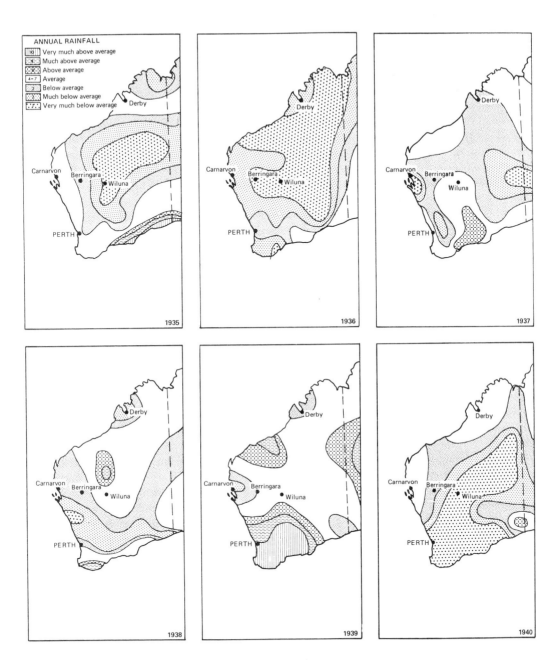

Fig. 10.  Distribution of decile ranges of annual rainfall
          1935-40.  (After Gibbs and Maher, 1967.)

In the post-war period from 1946 to 1958 the terms of trade were favourable, although the decline to the low 1975-76 level actually dates from 1950-51 and the reasons for concern over economic trends which began to affect the Gascoyne Basin in the mid-1960s can now be appreciated.  Annual rainfall entered the lower deciles in 1950, 1954-56 and 1959.  From 1958 the terms of trade for Gascoyne pastoralists would have progressively deteriorated and as at April 1976 approximately two-thirds of the stations in Upper Gascoyne Shire were understood to be for sale.  Possible reasons include: exceptionally good seasons, sheep numbers difficult to maintain because of poor reproductive performance linked to continuing depletion of the better quality rangeland types or their near-absence, as well as the continuing decline in the ratio of receipts to costs.

From 1970 until April 1976 the actual number of leases transferred (i.e. stations sold) was eighteen, but this included one station which was sold 3 times, four which were sold twice and thirteen which were sold once.

On the basis of past sales, many of the new lessees will have had little previous experience in pastoral enterprises; some come from commerce to use a station as a sinking fund or taxation benefit and some think that they would like to be pastoralists.

The similarity in the build up and collapse of sheep populations in widely separated parts of the Australian continent have been noted by many investigators (Williams and Oxley, 1977).  The Gascoyne Basin experience is certainly not unusual and, for example, Ealey (1967) has presented similar but more-detailed information for the Corunna Downs station in the eastern Pilbara district some 500 km distant from the Basin.  Although there is a marked similarity in the way that the sheep population fluctuates despite the substantial differences in district vegetation, it is the high level of sheep sales and ewe numbers at Corunna Downs for the 1908 to 1936 period compared with the purchase of sheep and the smaller numbers of ewes and lambs after 1936 that is noteworthy (Fig. 11).

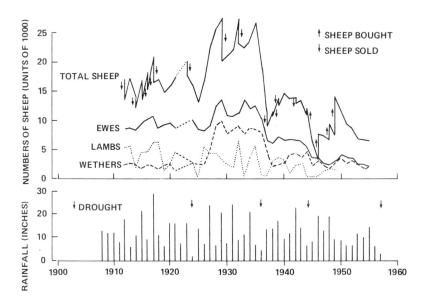

Fig. 11.   Changes in the sheep population at Corunna Downs
Station.  (After Ealey, 1967.)

High sheep numbers have already been noted for a Gascoyne station in the mid-1920s
(Fig. 8) and in Table 4 some figures for sheep shorn are given for a station
bordering the Basin.

Table 4.   Sheep Shorn in Various Years 1903 to 1968 on a
           Minilya River Station

| Year | Sheep shorn |
|------|-------------|
| 1903 | 20,000 (1500 cattle) |
| 1911 | 25,000 |
| 1930 | 22,759 (3.0 kg greasy wool/head) |
| 1935 | 30,000 |
| 1938 | 10,800 (3000 ewes purchased) |
| 1964 | 11,000 |
| 1968* | 14,100 (5.7 kg greasy wool/head) |

*In the preceding 6 years, twenty-six bores drilled and
 twelve equipped as watering points.

The wool production of adult sheep in the Upper Gascoyne Shire over the 15 years
1959 to 1973 has ranged from 4.3 to 5.6 kg (greasy wool) with a mean of 4.9 kg
(Fig. 12).  Variability is known to be high, both between years and between
individual stations, so that changes in productivity of sheep over time is
difficult to assess.  However, an overall increase of up to 1 kg between 1934 and
1973 is likely, with possible larger increases where breeding and culling
programmes have been possible.

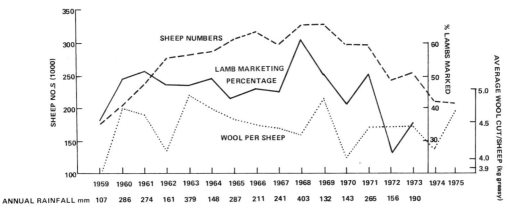

Fig. 12.   Sheep numbers, lamb marking percentages and wool
           produced per head in Upper Gascoyne Shire 1959-75.
           Annual rainfall (mm) for Dairy Creek.  (1900-1974
           mean is 205 mm, median is 187 mm.)

The level of wool production achieved in the Basin is high relative to other arid pastoral areas of Australia (Brown and Williams, 1970). The wool is free of burrs which lead to price penalties in many wools, and yields (ratio of scoured wool to greasy wool weight) are high.

The percentage of lambs "marked" (males castrated and all tails docked) at 2 weeks and older in relation to the number of ewes put to the rams has ranged from 27 per cent in 1972 to 62 per cent in 1968, with a mean of 46 per cent over the 15 years from 1959 to 1973 (Fig. 12). This mean is on the lower side of those for pastoral Australia and corresponds with estimates for the north-west of Western Australia and parts of northern Queensland (Brown and Williams, 1970). This contrast between substantial fleece weights of adult sheep and low mean lamb marking percentages is intriguing, particularly as high percentages can occasionally be attained.

Mortality of lambs, weaners and rams is thought to be high, but there are few estimates of losses. Ram mortality has reached 35 per cent per annum. If we assume that sales of sheep to markets outside the Basin are small, then we arrive at crude mortality rates for weaners and adult sheep which range from 4 and 5 per cent per annum to 16 per cent per annum. Weaners are thought to be more at risk than older sheep but there are marked differences between stations both at this stage and at lambmarking.

Cattle numbers have increased in the Upper Gascoyne Shire over the period from 1959 to 1971 when they reached their peak (Fig. 13). There has been a tendancy for a few stations to switch to cattle from sheep, rather than for sheep and cattle to be run together. This switch has been made without the modification of sheep fences or construction of cattle fences and livestock control is not particularly effective.

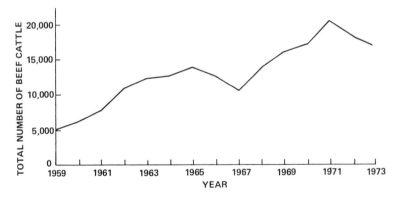

Fig. 13.   Cattle numbers in the Upper Gascoyne Shire, 1959-73.

Although there is no economic survey dealing specifically with the sheep industry in the Gascoyne Basin, a continuing economic survey of the Australian sheep industry in the pastoral zone is conducted by the Bureau of Agricultural Economics (BAE). Information has been published as statistics (Anon., 1973) and as reports (Hoogvliet, 1972) covering financial returns, costs, investment, interest paid, net farm income, changes in capital structure, rate of return to capital and observed changes in product-mix.

From this type of information and additional material appropriate to the Basin, the budget for a hypothetical station "Mt. Walkabout" has been constructed by J. Ripley and is set out in Appendix 2.

The challenge to the viability of pastoral enterprises can come from several directions in addition to income tax and poor seasons. For example, entrants to the industry often have too little capital and face failure as do those in the industry who decide, at the wrong time, to replace sheep with cattle, buy an aeroplane or purchase an adjoining lease.

State Probate and Federal Estate Duty can cause difficulties if not planned for, but major problems ensue when pastoralists want their estate to be shared by the family. Frequently only one individual wishes to continue the business and the viability of the enterprise is put at risk when the other family members request payment for their share.

In 1976 approximately 5000 sheep would be the threshold of viability for most pastoral enterprises in the Gascoyne Basin. Several stations with difficult terrain, including those with complex river-creek systems, would have substantially higher costs and the threshold could be 10,000 sheep. It would not be unreasonable to anticipate a flock size of 10,000 sheep in 1984 as a general level for viability. Properties tend to group into those which have reasonable prospects of meeting these viability criteria and those which cannot do so. There is no intermediate group. Lessees on several of the small stations have significant additional income from non-pastoral sources; this income allied to careful management and limited expenditure produces an anomalous and ungeneralizable situation in which capital can be accumulated over a short term for the acquisition of a more-productive station. The present cost-structure is such that some stations are being placed on a caretaker basis, i.e. one man at the homestead is responsible for keeping the watering facilities functioning and no fencing or general maintenance is undertaken.

On some stations the lessee now has little or no equity and under these conditions borrowing from the pastoral houses is not possible; these are the "hard-core" debtors. In 1975 shearing costs averaged $0.95 per sheep and it is estimated that it will cost in 1976 and 1977 $1.07 and $1.50 in 1976 and 1977, respectively. Sheep which cut 4.5 to 5.0 kg wool (greasy) will be uneconomic by 1977 at floor-level prices set by the Australian Wool Commission. Prices being obtained from the sale of stations are now equal to one or two times the purchase price of a well-built suburban house in a desired suburb of Perth, or the value of from five to ten suburban building allotments. At present the sale value of leases is calculated on the basis of $10 per sheep and $100 per bullock turned off annually.

Running costs per head are less for properties near the coast than for those well inland. For example, in 1973 the former were from $2.20 to $2.50, but 800 km east from Perth the lowest costs were $3.70 and transport costs of bullocks were $25 compared with $50. Even so, there is a large range in running costs within each district and in 1976 a range of $3 to $6 per sheep could be expected in the Basin.


DESERTIFICATION IN THE GASCOYNE BASIN

*Estimates of Erosion and Productivity—Procedures*

The scarcity of information on the vegetation and soils of the Basin and the inadequacy of the early (1918-1922) plans of each station in terms of rangeland have been noted already.

If desertification in the Basin is to be described so that the erosion and
rangeland condition anywhere in it can be classified and compared, formal
descriptions of the land forms will be needed.  On a base of this type parts of
the Basin could be related to each other and the areas of various land forms
subject to erosion on each station could be designated according to size, degree
of erosion and range condition.

The procedures adopted were similar to those developed by the CSIRO Division of
Land Research in surveys of land resources in Australia and New Guinea (Christian
and Stewart, 1964).  However, in the Gascoyne survey "rangeland types" replaced
land systems as the unit of mapping.  Land systems are areas or groups of areas
with a recurring pattern of land forms, soils and vegetation.  Rangeland types are
areas with recurring photo patterns of pastures and land forms in which the
patterns caused by local geology and soil characteristics merge together and are
often suppressed by the vegetation response.  In rangeland types two or more
distinct land systems may be united because of the similar vegetation.

Alternatively, large cohesive units of a land system may be described as separate
rangeland types because they are large enough to be significant pastures on
stations, where they are subject to distinct grazing pressures and to special
conditions of erosion.  In most cases, land systems and rangeland types are
identical because the genetic influences of land formation impose by far the most
outstanding pattern characteristics.

The initial interpretation of the area, using 1:63360 scale mosaics, was made in
August to October 1969 when three brief reconnaissance visits were made in order
to familiarize the survey party with the Basin.  At this time, a number of patterns
were delineated, sufficient for the interpretation of the 1:40,000 scale
photographs to be completed in the 1969-70 summer prior to the commencement of the
field survey.

The survey occupied the period April to October 1970 when a team from the
Departments of Agriculture and of Lands and Surveys worked throughout the Basin.
During the survey, the aerial photographs were examined in the light of field
experience and the boundaries of the rangeland types were altered according to the
results of the field examination.  The rangeland types were mapped subsequently
onto the 1:40,000 photographs for later transfer to the 1:40,000 clear acetate
compilation sheets which were available from previous mapping projects by the
Department of Lands and Surveys.  The finished 1:250,000 map sheets prepared by
the survey team were assembled from the above 1:40,000 sheets.

The rangeland types were established as reliable and repeatable mapping units by
a series of precise observations at range evaluation sites.  A number of these
sites were marked on the photographs for each of the rangeland types already
delineated and at each of these sites information on landform, geology, soils,
pastures, erosion and pasture condition was gathered.

The landform information notes included a brief description of the geology and of
the various components of the landscape.  The data included slope measurements,
channel descriptions, relief and the type of strew.  Soils data included texture,
pH and colour to 1 m, surface conditions and strew.  The vegetation data was
gathered according to the method described by Christian and Perry (1953) in which
the three levels of trees, shrubs and ground flora were described in terms of
species occurrence, dominance, height and density.  Quantitative measurements of
vegetation were made in a number of rangeland types using plotless methods
developed for shrubs by Cooper (1963) and by using an adaptation of the Tidmarsh
and Havenga (1955) wheeled transect marker.  This detailed information was
particularly valuable when taken on relic areas in good range condition because
these descriptions were made of the optimum or climax condition.  Each land system

on the Basin was thus capable of being ranked in terms of its condition as
encountered on each station, using the relic area as the guide to the optimum.

Although it is not suggested that climax conditions are always the most desirable
in the range situation, it can be assumed that optimum range condition in an arid
environment with generally less than 200 mm of erratic annual rainfall is most
commonly achieved close to the climax situation.  Inevitably, departures from the
climax condition are associated with increased instability of landscape and
lowered production.  The practical measure of deterioration or degradation of
pastures on the Basin is the extent of the departure of a rangeland type from the
climax, or if not climax, then the stable situation.

The above information provided the base for the description and the mapping of the
Basin into rangeland types.  Later the total area of each rangeland was determined
for the Basin and for each station.  From traverse data obtained on each station
the areas susceptible to or resistant to erosion were located and delineated.

The pasture and soil information was used to place the rangeland types in nine
pasture groups.  These were described earlier in this case study (Table 3).  The
allocation into pasture groups was based upon concepts of durability or ephemerality,
quantity of pasture available, acceptability and frequency of availability.  A
great number of different pasture types have been studied by the Department of
Agriculture personnel for over 20 years and have included pastures in the stony
short grass-forb, stony chenopod, mulga short grass-forb, chenopod, and wandarrie
groups which occur in the Basin.  During the course of these studies the various
levels of pasture condition have been defined in terms of species frequency and
distribution for each pasture group.  In this survey, five levels of condition were
established, each being large enough and sufficiently well defined to permit a
particular pasture condition to be allocated to every rangeland evaluation site and
traverse record site.  The levels are shown in Table 5.

Table 5.  Pasture Condition Classes

| Condition class | Pasture description |
|---|---|
| 1 | Pristine or original condition |
| 2 | Good condition, partly used, loss of some rare species |
| 3 | Vegetation degradation obvious, often reduction to unpalatable species or to ephemeral species—no erosion or very minor erosion |
| 4 | Vegetation degraded, with obvious wind and water erosion in parts |
| 5 | Vegetation degraded with major erosion, gullies and surface stripping over most of the area |

With this classification, areas of erosion hazard were defined.  Although pastures
in condition 3 are undesirable, they are currently stable and are not considered
in the assessment of erosion on the Basin.  Pastures in conditions 4 and 5 were
eroded.

The potential of the rangeland was assessed at each range evaluation site.  The
criteria of accessibility, durability, acceptability and availability were used.
Five levels of site potential were described for the Basin and are shown in Table 6.
Values of pasture condition and rangeland potential were assigned to each of the
range evaluation sites.

Table 6.  Rangeland Potential

| Potential class | |
| --- | --- |
| 1 | Palatable durable pastures, principally shrubby types with associated ephemeral species, e.g. saltbush plains |
| 2 | Palatable, partly durable pastures, with some drought-evading perennials, associated valuable ephemerals, e.g. wandarrie grass pastures |
| 3 | Shrubby pastures of mixed acceptability and palatability, with abundant ephemeral ground species in season, e.g. non-saline alluvial plains |
| 4 | Scattered shrubby pastures of mixed acceptability and palatability, sparse ephemeral ground species, e.g. rocky slopes |
| 5 | Pastures of low palatability, inaccessible and low productivity, e.g. spinifex (*Triodia basedowii*) or mountain summits |

Erosion was described at each range evaluation site in terms of the amount of wind
and water erosion present.  The classifications for each site are shown in Table 7.
The descriptions were clear enough to allow erosion, if any was present, to be
assigned with confidence to the particular class.

Table 7.  Classification of Wind and Water Erosion

| Erosion class | Description of site conditions | Erosion class | Description of site conditions |
|---|---|---|---|
| 0 | None | 0 | None |
| 1 | Slight surface sheeting or minor scalding | 1 | Sealing of the surface |
| 2 | Minor surface redis-tribution, small accumulations | 2 | Minor rilling of the soil surface in places but no deep gullies |
| 3 | Hummocking of sand beneath shrubs or into small banks | 3 | Surface stripping on even slopes in a terrace-like fashion |
| 4 | Major drift and dune activation | 4 | Erosion gullies, on the lower slopes only |
|  |  | 5 | Erosion gullies, on lower and upper slopes |

In this way each evaluation site was given a record of the landform, soils, vegetation present, erosion, condition and potential.  Over the Basin this information provided a picture of the range of conditions encountered in every rangeland type.

The exact location of each range evaluation site was marked on the 1:40,000 aerial photographs and ground photographs were taken at many of them.

The ground data and photographs taken at these points could provide the base for evaluating future trends in condition in the Basin.

These data for the 280 range evaluation sites, together with the prior knowledge of the ideal condition of each rangeland as determined from available ecological information, provided the base data for the evaluation of range condition and erosion in each of the rangelands on each station.

Information on erosion and range condition was also obtained on over 4800 km of vehicle traverse.  Traverse routes were plotted on the marked 1:40,000 aerial photographs.  Traverses were made across all rangeland types and in as many distinct locations on each station as possible.  Recordings of wind and water erosion, condition and capability were made of each rangeland type traversed, as it was entered, and left, and at 1.6 km intervals within the type.  In this way, 2426 recordings of condition were made on fifty-one rangeland types.  The standards used were those adopted for the range evaluation sites.  The field traverse record is shown on the maps that accompany the report and in the sample map (Fig. 14).

The recordings were always made by two experienced observers to eliminate bias. This role was always assumed by those concerned with research into the pastures of the area.

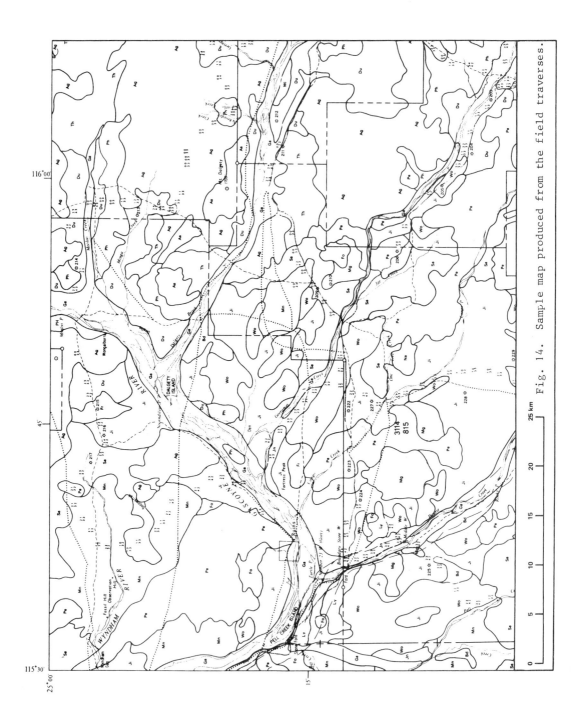

Fig. 14.  Sample map produced from the field traverses.

## THE RANGELAND TYPES

**Pe** — PELLS (1.12%)
Dissected Permian Hills; hill country pastures, degraded, no erosion.

**Wo** — WOORAMEL (0.72%)
Permian Uplands with sandy banks; chenopod pastures with wandarrie grasses, degraded, moderate erosion.

**Sa** — SANDIMAN (1.75%)
Undulating Permian Uplands, stony chenopod pastures, degraded, erosion on lower slopes.

**Ji** — JIMBA (2.62%)
Permian plains; chenopod pastures, degraded, moderate to severe erosion.

**Mn** — MANTLE (2.24%)
Stony Permian Plains; stony chenopod pastures, degraded, little erosion.

**As** — AUGUSTUS (11.62%)
Bangemall Series Pre-Cambrian Hills; hill country pastures, degraded, slight erosion lower slopes.

**Th** — THOMAS (3.78%)
Breakaways and plains on granite and gneiss; stony short grass-forb pastures, degraded, moderate erosion lower parts.

**Ph** — PHILLIPS (10.95%)
Undulating stony uplands; stony short grass-forb pastures, minor chenopod pasture, degraded, slight erosion lower parts.

**Du** — DURLACHER (7.07%)
Stony plains; stony short grass-forb pasture with major chenopod inclusions, degraded, moderate erosion.

**Ag** — AGAMEMNON (4.88%)
Pre-Cambrian Hills; crystalline rocks weathered and unweathered, hill country pastures, degraded, slight erosion lower parts.

**Ga** — GASCOYNE (3.20%)
Major river systems and associated plains and inclusions, river pastures, degraded, severely eroded.

**Na** — NADARRA (1.32%)
Recent (Pleistocene) stony plains; stony chenopod pastures, degraded, slight erosion.

**Jn** — JINGLE (0.29%)
Plains marginal to rivers with saline areas, short grass-forbs, wandarrie grass and chenopods, degraded, severe erosion.

**Fr** — FREDERICK (2.02%)
Stony outwash plains, with mulga groves; short grass-forb pastures, degraded, slight erosion.

**Ly** — LYONS (0.72%)
Sanddunes surrounding claypans; acacia scrub and minor halophytic pasture, degraded, slight erosion.

**Bd** — BIDGEMIA (1.59%)
Sanddunes with saline swales; acacia scrub and chenopod pastures, degraded, moderate erosion.

**Fo** — FOSSIL (0.45%)
Permian Hills; hill country pastures, degraded, no erosion.

**Mg** — MOOGOOLOO (0.71%)
Weathered Permian Hills, hill country pastures, degraded, erosion on lowest slopes.

**Wi** — WINMAR (1.28%)
Stony plains with sandy banks; stony short grass-forb pastures with wandarrie grasses on banks, degraded, no erosion.

**PH** — PEAK HILL (0.28%)
Pre-Cambrian weathered hills; hill country pastures, degraded, no erosion.

## TRAVERSE RECORD NOTATION

Wind Erosion Classification — 23 — Water Erosion Classification

Range Condition — 42 — Site Potential

**Wind Erosion**
0. None
1. Sheeted
2. Surface redistribution
3. Hummocking
4. Major drift

**Condition**
1. Pristine
2. Good — some use
3. Vegetation degraded — no erosion
4. Vegetation degraded — some erosion
5. Vegetation degraded — major erosion

**Water Erosion**
0. None
1. Sealing
2. Minor rilling
3. Stripping
4. Lower slope gullies
5. Upper and lower slope gullies

**Potential**
1. Good — durable shrubby pasture
2. Moderate — shrubby pastures, perennials and annuals
3. Fair — sparse shrubs, pastures and annuals
4. Low — very sparse shrubs, poor annuals
5. Poor — limited use from any part

Range Evaluation Site ....... ☆

The information was coded and the computer programme was written to provide a breakdown of the traverse record in terms of:

(a) the condition of each rangeland on each station;

(b) the condition of each rangeland on the Basin;

(c) the condition of the Basin as a whole; and

(d) the relationship of condition and potential (capability) to wind and water erosion in a series of two by two tables for each station and for the whole catchment.

The information from the traverses and range evaluation sites, together with the field notes, enabled a picture of erosion conditions on stations and on the whole Basin to be assembled. Information on the condition of each rangeland type for each station was available from the print out of the computer programme. Each rangeland type was ranked according to its erosion status and its condition. These statements were later modified on the plan of each station where the traverse data indicated a departure from the general view. An example of a modified print out is given in Table 8 to show part of the results for a particular station on the Basin.

The survey team attempted to traverse every part of the Basin that was in any way accessible and the traverse routes can be seen on the accompanying map where they are identified by the traverse record symbols. Some of the hill or stony short grass-forb pasture groups were omitted because they were inaccessible by vehicle. However, the records show that these pasture groups are not subject to erosion and could not have contributed to past and current erosion, whereas the lower rangelands are eroded, degraded and are of concern.

A number of conventions were used to partition the erosion information into three categories of condition, viz. acceptable, supervised and remedial condition.

*Acceptable rangeland condition* includes erosion classes of no wind or water erosion or erosion to the sealing or sheeting level with vegetation which has deteriorated to the unpalatable or ephemeral state. The hill pasture group and stony, short grass-forb pasture group are nearly always in the acceptable condition.

*Supervised rangeland condition* is that in which vegetation deterioration to ephemerals or to unpalatable species is associated with minor surface redistribution by wind or with minor guttering of the surface. Wandarrie pasture groups are frequently in this category.

*Remedial rangeland condition* is that in which there is pasture deterioration often associated with a *major reduction* in total plant cover, particularly of perennial shrubs, and with hummocking or drift, guttering, surface stripping or terracing, or with gullying on the slopes. Rangelands in this condition are frequently found in the stony chenopod, chenopod and mulga short grass-forb groupings.

These three classes of range condition were broad enough to be readily discerned in the field. Rangelands in the remedial condition were extensively eroded and were thus easily classified into this category, in contrast to the two former classifications which covered a much wider range of expressions of range condition.

Table 8. Erosion Assessment of Major Rangeland Types on a Gascoyne Station

Rangeland—Three Rivers  *Mulga shortgrass—forb pasture group*

| Rating scale | Wind no. | Per cent | Rating scale | Water no. | Per cent | Rating scale | Condition no. | Per cent | Rating scale | Capability no. | Per cent |
|---|---|---|---|---|---|---|---|---|---|---|---|
| 0 | 4 | 12.9 | 0 | 2 | 6.5 | 1 | 0 | 0 | 1 | 0 | 0 |
| 1 | 12 | 38.7 | 1 | 25 | 80.6 | 2 | 7 | 22.6 | 2 | 4 | 12.7 |
| 2 | 13 | 41.9 | 2 | 1 | 3.2 | 3 | 16 | 51.6 | 3 | 25 | 80.6 |
| 3 | 2 | 6.5 | 3 | 2 | 6.5 | 4 | 7 | 22.6 | 4 | 2 | 6.5 |
| 4 | 0 | 0 | 4 | 1 | 3.2 | 5 | 1 | 3.2 | 5 | 0 | 0 |
|  |  |  | 5 | 0 | 0 |  |  |  |  |  |  |
| Total 31 |  |  | Total 31 |  |  | 31 |  |  | 31 |  |  |

Rangeland—Warri  *Chenopod pasture group*

| Rating scale | Wind no. | Per cent | Rating scale | Water no. | Per cent | Rating scale | Condition no. | Per cent | Rating scale | Capability no. | Per cent |
|---|---|---|---|---|---|---|---|---|---|---|---|
| 0 | 2 | 12.5 | 0 | 4 | 25.0 | 1 | 0 | 0 | 1 | 0 | 0 |
| 1 | 7 | 43.8 | 1 | 6 | 37.5 | 2 | 0 | 0 | 2 | 10 | 62.5 |
| 2 | 6 | 37.5 | 2 | 3 | 18.8 | 3 | 5 | 31.3 | 3 | 6 | 37.5 |
| 3 | 1 | 6.5 | 3 | 1 | 6.3 | 4 | 9 | 58.3 | 4 | 0 | 0 |
| 4 | 0 | 0 | 4 | 2 | 12.5 | 5 | 2 | 12.5 | 5 | 0 | 0 |
|  |  |  | 5 | 0 | 0 |  |  |  |  |  |  |
| Total 16 |  |  | Total 16 |  |  | 16 |  |  | 16 |  |  |

Traverse records, range evaluation site information and field notes show that on the station given in Table 8, Sugarloaf and Warrie rangelands were degraded and eroded. The traverse record indicated that an area of Warrie in the east was not badly affected by erosion. Fifty-two $km^2$ were therefore placed in the supervised use category. No such partition was made of Sugarloaf because the record showed a complex mosaic of erosion and non-eroded areas on this rangeland. Therefore all of it was placed in the remedial use category.

Resistant rangelands with predominantly rocky surfaces of bare rock or heavy cobble and pebble strews were found to be in an acceptable condition. They are infrequently grazed by stock and have an inherent resistance to erosion. The remaining rangelands were placed in a supervised use category indicating the presence of patches of slightly eroded country associated with vegetation degradation. These rangelands are accessible to grazing animals and are prone to erosion with overuse. Careful management of these is essential if they are to remain stable.

Summaries of range condition and erosion status were given for each station by Wilcox and McKinnon (1972) together with the recommended stocking rate for each station where areas of rangeland in remedial condition necessitated withdrawal from grazing use. A sample station is described in the Appendix 4.

The computer sorting of the data also allowed estimates of the erosion status and range condition to be established for each of the fifty-one rangeland types. Tables and discussion for seven selected rangeland types are included later in this case study.

A realistic assessment of the sheep unit capacity for stations in the Gascoyne Basin cannot be built on either historical or current flock numbers because the wide fluctuations in both numbers and production characteristics which we described earlier, when taken into consideration with estimates of erosion and rangeland degradation, indicate rangeland use beyond the capability to produce on a continuous basis. The condition of the resource base is being lowered rather than being maintained. Estimates of carrying capacity which have been made in the past are primarily for rating for revenue purposes.

Survey procedures delineated the areas on each property which were eroded and which should not be grazed. It was then possible to measure the remaining rangelands and to allot them to their respective pasture groupings. Using information from investigations being undertaken in the general region, Wilcox and McKinnon proposed certain productivity levels for each class of pasture on the Basin. Table 9 summarizes the results of a number of production measurements made in various pasture groups in successive years. The stony chenopod estimates were the only values taken in the Basin.

In United States' rangelands, the management practice of equal levels of use and non-use by herbivores of annual dry-matter production appears to maintain rangeland productivity in the long term. More sophisticated systems have been developed, but these require a stronger data-base than exists for the Basin. Assuming 50 percent non-use, dry-matter production levels with median annual rainfall and an annual intake requirement for adult sheep of 450 kg of dry-matter, the acceptable stocking rates for each rangeland type can be calculated in sheep per $km^2$ or ha per sheep (Table 10). Information from the descriptions of rangeland types was used when the potential differed markedly from the bulk of those in the same group.

Table 9.   Dry Matter Production (kg per ha) in Various Pasture Types in Successive Years

| | Shrub component | Ground production | Total |
|---|---|---|---|
| Chenopod pastures | 560 | 11 | 571 |
| | 308 | 8 | 316 |
| | 114 | 0.6* | 115 |
| | 142 | 0.5 | 143 |
| | 39 | Nil | 39 |
| | 94 | Nil | 94 |
| | 234 | n.a. | 234+ |
| Mulga short grass-forb | *Acacia aneura* | 78 | 78 |
| | *A. terragonophylla* and | 34 | 34 |
| | *A. craspedocarpa* | 22 | 22 |
| | inaccessible or | 840 | 84 |
| | unpalatable | Nil | – |
| | | 112* | 112 |
| Stony chenopod | | 112* | |
| Gascoyne Basin | | 22 | |
| | | 227 | |
| Stony short grass-forb | Pasture reduced to | 11 | 11 |
| Meekatharra Western Australia | unpalatable | | |
| | *Eremophila* spp. | 134 | 134 |
| | to acceptable shrubs | 22 | 22 |
| | | 28* | 28 |
| | | 101 | 101 |
| Perennial grass (wandarrie) | 7.5 | 108* | 116 |
| Meekatharra | 32 | 18 | 50 |
| Stony chenopod | 6.7 | 16 | 23 |
| Meekatharra | 45 | 8.9 | 54 |
| | (Poor pastures) | | |
| Mulga short grass-forb | 11 | Nil | 11 |
| Meekatharra | 35 | 5.4 | 40 |
| | (Poor pastures) | | |

*Production levels attained at median annual rainfall.

Differences in productivity between adjacent rangeland types can be substantial and the mosaic of rangeland types in the Basin accentuates this patchiness which we suspect is more extreme than in eastern Australia where there are broad expanses of particular rangeland types, as for example with chenopod shrubland in South Australia and *Astrebla* grassland in north-western Queensland.

In terms of the Land Act, one cattle beast is equivalent to five sheep. This legal equivalence is different from the practical and experimental equivalents of one beast to seven or eight sheep but this difference reflects criteria for raising revenue rather than the capability of rangelands to support cattle or sheep.

Table 10.  Estimated Stocking Rates for Pasture Groups and their Rangeland
Types in the Gascoyne Basin (sheep/10 km$^2$ and ha/sheep)

| Pasture group | Rangeland type | Sheep per 10 km$^2$ | ha per sheep |
|---|---|---|---|
| Hills | Peak Hill | 22 | 40 |
| | Agamemnon | 23 | 40 |
| | Augustus* | 23 | 40 |
| | Glenburgh | 23 | 40 |
| | Diorite | 23 | 40 |
| | Mulgul | 23 | 40 |
| | Pells | 39 | 24 |
| | Moogooloo | 39 | 24 |
| | Fossil | 46 | 20 |
| Stony short grass-forb | Beasley | 39 | 24 |
| | Phillips* | 39 | 24 |
| | Collier | 39 | 24 |
| | George | 39 | 24 |
| | James | 39 | 24 |
| | Two Hills | 39 | 24 |
| | Thomas | 39 | 24 |
| | Jamindie | 23 | 40 |
| | Mabbutt | 23 | 40 |
| Stony chenopod | Woodlands | 62 | 16 |
| | Sandiman | 62 | 16 |
| | Horseshoe | 62 | 16 |
| | Durlacher | 62 | 16 |
| | Bryah | 62 | 16 |
| Stony chenopod | Yinnietharra* | 62 | 16 |
| | Sugarloaf | 62 | 16 |
| | Kurubuka | 62 | 16 |
| | Nadarra | 62 | 16 |
| | Mantle | 62 | 16 |
| | Jimba* | 124 | 8 |
| | Wooramel | 124 | 8 |
| Chenopod | Warri | 62 | 16 |
| | Peedawarra | 81 | 12 |
| | Jingle | 81 | 12 |
| | Biblingunna | 124 | 8 |
| Wandarrie | All types including Landor* | 62 | 16 |
| Mulga short grass-forbs | Frederick and all except | 39 | 24 |
| | Macadam* | 23 | 40 |
| Sand dune halophyte | Bidgemia | 124 | 8 |
| | Lyons | 62 | 16 |
| Sandplain | Divide | 23 | 40 |
| | Yalbalgo | 62 | 16 |
| River | Gascoyne* | 62 | 16 |

*Rangeland types to be described in detail later.

The area of each rangeland on each station, excluding the eroded area, was
estimated from planimeter measurements on the 1:40,000 maps and was used with the
appropriate stocking rate given in Table 10 to calculate the recommended rate or
sheep unit capacity (SUC) for each station.  The SUC was given in the station
descriptions (Wilcox and McKinnon, 1972) and in the sample description in this
case study (Appendix 4).

*Erosion and Rangeland Deterioration*

The eroded rangeland types and the extent of erosion as determined from the survey
are set out in Table 11.

Table 11.   Eroded Pasture Groups and Rangeland Types

| Pasture group | Rangeland type | Total area km$^2$ | Area eroded km$^2$ | Percentage eroded |
|---|---|---|---|---|
| Hill | Augustus* | 8266 | 0 | 0 |
| | Moogooloo | 508 | 34 | 6 |
| Stony shortgrass | Thomas | 2683 | 78 | 3 |
| -forb | Phillips* | 7770 | 269 | 3 |
| | James | 1686 | 300 | 18 |
| Stony | Sugarloaf | 313 | 137 | 44 |
| chenopod | Wooramel | 508 | 104 | 20 |
| | Jimba* | 1860 | 1194 | 64 |
| | Sandiman | 1241 | 199 | 16 |
| | Durlacher | 5017 | 1598 | 33 |
| | Yinnietharra* | 793 | 381 | 48 |
| | Bryah | 751 | 194 | 24 |
| | Nadarra | 938 | 70 | 7 |
| Chenopod | Jingle | 210 | 127 | 60 |
| | Warri | 1520 | 614 | 40 |
| | Peedawarra | 174 | 104 | 60 |
| Wandarrie | Doolgunna | 93 | 16 | 16 |
| | Winmar | 909 | 93 | 10 |
| | Blech | 114 | 109 | 95 |
| | Landor* | 1285 | 0 | 0 |
| Mulga | Three Rivers* | 4504 | 2787 | 62 |
| short grass | Frederick | 1435 | 197 | 14 |
| -forb | Clere | 119 | 78 | 65 |
| Sand dune | Bidgemia | 1134 | 609 | 53 |
| halophyte | Lyons | 518 | 122 | 23 |
| River | Gascoyne* | 2270 | ? | ? |

*Rangeland types to be described in detail later.

The total area of the twenty-three eroded rangeland types is shown and the
percentage of the eroded area is also shown for each type.  Gascoyne rangeland
type was included in the uneroded systems in the report because of difficulties
in assessing whether or not the changes in condition were merely temporal ones
caused by flash flooding or long-term changes caused by overuse and degradation.
We include it because of concurrent erosion and accession of sediment.  Augustus

and Landor rangeland types are also included in Table 11 although no erosion was evident on survey. They are discussed in Appendix 5.

Over three-quarters of the erosion on the Basin can be ascribed to six rangeland types. These are Three Rivers, 30 per cent of the eroded area, Durlacher and Yinnietharra, 21 per cent, Jimba, 13 per cent, Bidgemia, 7 per cent, and Warri, 6 per cent of the eroded area. The remaining rangelands contribute to erosion only marginally and then only on specific stations.

All twenty-three rangelands are readily accessible, have pastures which are acceptable to sheep and in most instances receive run-on water from areas up slope. They would be preferentially grazed by livestock, and at heavy rates, particularly where less acceptable rangelands surround them.

A substantial proportion of both the Jimba and Bidgemia rangeland types are eroded and degraded, indicating both over-use and a susceptibility to erosion. Mantle rangeland type is the sole accessible rangeland on the Permian with little or no erosion. Some of the more spectacular forms of erosion on the catchment are found in Three Rivers rangeland where 62 per cent is indicated as being eroded.

A full description of erosion status and rangeland degradation is set out for seven selected rangeland types in Appendix 4.

A summary of the status of wind and water erosion and range condition in the Basin has been calculated from the traverse information and is set out in Table 12.

Table 12.   Summary of Wind and Water Erosion and Range Condition in the Gascoyne Basin

| | Wind erosion | | Water erosion | | Condition | | |
|---|---|---|---|---|---|---|---|
| | Rating | Per cent | Rating | Per cent | Rating | Per cent | |
| | 0 | 27.0 | 0 | 35.7 | 1 | 0.5 | |
| | 1 | 26.4 | 1 | 30.7 | 2 | 5.8 | |
| | 1 | 38.5 | 2 | 12.6 | 3 | 65.0 | |
| Serious | 3 | 7.7 | 3 | 11.4 | 4 | 26.8 | Poor |
| erosion | 4 | 0.4 | 4 | 9.4 | 5 | 1.9 | condition |
| | | | 5 | 0.2 | | | |

Serious wind erosion occurred on 8.1 per cent of locations and a serious water-erosion problem existed on 21 per cent of the locations. Range degradation associated with serious erosion problems existed on 28.7 per cent of the sites visited on the survey.

In Fig. 15 we have prepared a map at a scale of 1:1,000,000 to show the vulnerability to erosion of the Gascoyne Basin. This map has been constructed from the nine 1:250,000 sheets which show the distribution of rangeland types in the Basin (example in Fig. 14) and three categories of vulnerability based on the percentage of eroded rangeland in each type (Table 11). The three vulnerability groups range from very slightly or not vulnerable, through slightly vulnerable (1 to 10 per cent eroded) to highly vulnerable (11 per cent and upwards). The numerals denote the actual stocking rate in sheep equivalents per 10 km$^2$ on each station in 1975.

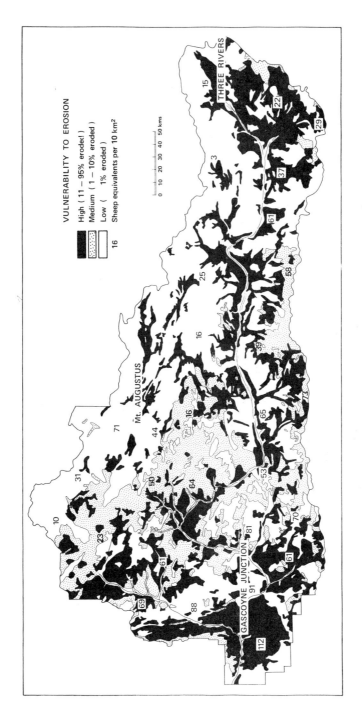

Fig. 15.   Erosion vulnerability in the Gascoyne Basin.

We made two basic assumptions.  First, that almost 80 years of intensive grazing use, combined with occasional severe drought and periodic torrential summer rain, is sufficient to allow erosion to be expressed on all rangeland types that have the potential to erode.  Second, that all stations were stocked to their capacity in 1975.

At this stage the map cannot be used to distinguish between the vulnerability and the current erosion status at a particular location.  However, the map is a general indicator of erosion status and grazing use.

At the western end of the Basin the stocking rates are high, even on the highly vulnerable (and eroded) rangeland types in contrast to the eastern margin where stocking rates are substantially less on highly vulnerable rangeland.  From an inspection of the rangeland maps at the 1:250,000 scale, records of the areas of various rangeland types on individual stations, the estimated stocking rates for these types (from Table 10) and the estimates of erosion vulnerability (from Table 11) it becomes obvious that the highly vulnerable rangeland types in the west are much more productive than their eastern counterparts.  The association of low and moderate vulnerability with low stocking rates and its expression in terms of low stocking rates at the level of the individual stations, can be seen in the north central part of the Basin.  In Table 13 the sheep-carrying capacity of a station from the productive but highly vulnerable (and eroded) western end of the Basin is compared with a station of similar size situated in the less productive but less vulnerable (less eroded) north central part.

Table 13.   Sheep-carrying Capacity of Two Stations which Differ in Rangeland Types with Respect to Vulnerability, Erosion and Productivity

|  | Western station | North central station |
|---|---|---|
| Area | 1513 km$^2$ | 1326 km$^2$ |
| Proportion supporting 1 sheep 25 ha | 81 per cent | 20 per cent |
| ECC* | 15,665 sheep | 9000 sheep |
| SUC** | 8850 sheep | 3980 sheep |
| Numbers 1972 | 14,300 sheep | 2625 sheep |
| Agreement*** | 12,000 sheep | 4500 sheep |
| Numbers 1974 | 12,000 sheep† | 2000 sheep |

* ECC   Estimated carrying capacity as determined by Department of Lands and Surveys for rating purposes.

**SUC   Stock unit capacity as determined by Wilcox and McKinnon (1972) for assessment of long-term productivity;

***       Agreement negotiated in 1974.

†         2000 sheep sold post-1972 when prices were high.

In general terms, all rangeland utilized between 1920 and 1939 is moderately to seriously degraded. The vegetation, composed of perennial saltbush (*Atriplex* spp.), blue bushes (*Maireana* spp.) and associated species upon which successful lambings had been achieved, changed to unproductive short-lived annuals. With more bare soil, and with removal of the sandy surface from duplex soils, the run-off into the rivers from the rangeland types bordering them was more rapid. The Jimba, Durlacher and Yinnietharra rangeland types exemplify this degradation. They were highly productive and are still amongst the most productive types even though extensive areas are severely eroded.

Desertification of the long-exploited rangeland types is proceeding, possibly at a decreased rate, but more precise rate measures than those given earlier are not available. Even after 30 years of non-use by travelling livestock, the major stock-routes can still be discerned on the ground and from the air. They appear to be no worse and little better for being grazed as part of the station through which they run. The initiation in March 1976 of a new extensive erosion network on recently unstocked rangeland when 150 mm of rain fell in 4 hours indicates the type of erosion potential that exists. Fortunately most of the soil is deposited elsewhere within the Basin and the alluvium is invaded and stabilized by *Cenchrus ciliaris*.

Undesirable changes in vegetation include the increase in *Acacia victoriae*, a spiny shrub which grows along narrow gullies and creeks, and *Hakea priessii*, another spiny shrub which grows on eroded duplex soils. Both species are normal components of the rangeland but increase under severe utilization. The ecological influence of fires, whether lit by aboriginals or by thunderstorms, was probably important in controlling these shrubs in the pre-European period. However, the amount of fuel which now accumulates under grazing is seldom sufficient to run a fire.

Desirable changes in vegetation include recent increases in perennial chenopod shrubs (*Rhagodia, Enchylaena,* and *Maireana* spp.) when sheep have been excluded from the appropriate rangeland types.

The evidence for rangeland deterioration and soil erosion is irrefutable because of the small isolated pristine or climax expressions of all rangeland types and the short time-span over which deterioration has occurred is known. Portions of some rangeland types escaped exploitation because of distance from water, but communities dominated by *Chenopodium auricomum* (northern bluebush) such as those on Mt. Augustus and Woodland stations were protected by annual flooding. Widespread but localized communities of this type were nutritionally significant in the reproductive phases of animal production in the early pastoral industry of northern Australia and were influential in allowing capital to be generated from sales of surplus livestock. Few areas now remain.

The upward and downward fluctuations in livestock numbers and in reproduction at both station and Basin level relate directly to rainfall and emphasize the dependence of pastoral enterprises upon annual plants. The remaining perennial plants are unable to maintain flocks, even with the additional areas that increased water supplies have made available since the 1950s. The great fluctuations in stock numbers also show that the rangelands are being exploited for maximum production with variations in rainfall having an immediate effect on livestock numbers.

A stable industry has not developed because patterns of use have been imposed without reference to the conservation of vegetation and soil and have led to the deterioration of both these resources. The present and past systems of use have demanded the utilization of all available vegetation to the exclusion of the needs of the pastures for maintenance or of the landscape for stability.

D.  C

Marshall (1970) has emphasized the importance of maintaining adequate shrub cover
in the arid environment because an adequate shrub population reduces the erosive
effects of wind, the principal eroding force. Unchecked wind continually causes
landscape deterioration through surface deflation, abrasion of the surface and
destruction of existing vegetation by sandblasting. The erosive effects of water
and the importance of maintaining a protective cover are recognized and appreciated
in most countries. Any consideration of erosion on the Basin must include not
only a description of the obvious signs of erosion such as hummocking or gullying,
but also recognition of the extent of pasture retrogression because this is an
associate, precursor and overt sign of soil erosion.

## Constraints and Aids to the Control of Desertification Processes

On the Gascoyne Basin under extensive grazing and with the economic constraints
described earlier, the building of structures to control gullying, the cultivation
and reseeding of the wind-swept alluvial plains or the construction of fences
around small highly productive rangelands set in large tracts of poor rangelands
are not feasible counters to desertification, although the first two programmes
may have a place in specific high-risk areas and so attract the necessary
governmental finance for their implementation. Indeed, many kilometres of fence
which crossed both small and large streamlines were washed away in the flash flood
of March 1976 will not be renewed because their replacement would strain the
financial resources of the pastoral enterprise.

In circumstances where investment is unattractive one is forced to consider an
ecological strategy. Such programmes appear to be low cost, but this is deceptive.
Ecological measures of value are long-term and load small annual costs but large
total costs onto individuals or communities in terms of immediate income foregone
or increased taxes.

On the Basin an ecological approach should aim at achieving "proper use" which, for
example, Dyksterhuis (1949) defined as the degree of grazing which will allow the
more desirable forage plants to maintain their stand and vigour and thereby prevent
undue run-off and erosion. He suggested that the four factors entailed in the
correct manipulation of rangelands for grazing use are proper numbers of livestock;
proper class and kind of livestock; proper season and sequence of use and proper
distribution of livestock.

On the Basin the major method of maintaining the resource base is to adjust
livestock numbers. This applies to all three categories of rangeland described
earlier as *acceptable*, i.e. presenting no problem, those requiring *supervised use*
because of degraded pastures with some erosion but with a potential erosion problem
of some magnitude unless grazing management is adopted, and *remedial use* with
removal of livestock because erosion is active.

The recommendations for stocking rates calculated according to the method previously
outlined, and apportioned according to individual stations (Appendix 4) apply to areas
of acceptable and supervised use rangelands and should permit continued use of these
pastures, with the adoption of range-management practices involving the deferment of
grazing for the rejuvenation of the stand if the resource is not to deteriorate. Such
treatments are of special significance after droughts have broken.

It is not possible to graze any pasture at a level which will minimize disturbance
to all the component species. The aim is rather to adjust numbers to a level at
which the stability of the pasture can be maintained. It is worth noting that
the reduction of sheep numbers to 237,290 proposed for the Basin by Wilcox and
McKinnon was not substantially different from the 290,000 actually carried from
1936 to 1969.

The 9400 km$^2$ of eroded and degraded rangelands in the remedial use category occur as a mosaic in the Basin with a major zone of concentration in the Permian and on the eastern alluvial plains. The destruction of the soil-surface conditions, the removal of vegetation and the current active erosion makes these areas highly unstable and of high erosional hazard. The complete exclusion of stock from these areas is the only effective means of achieving recovery. The process will in many cases be extremely slow since it will proceed through a number of seral stages. Grazing in the early seral stages of recovery is likely to impede regeneration and should not be attempted. When recovery is sufficiently advanced so that stability is guaranteed then grazing could be permitted provided that the pastoralist used discretion and did not remove all available feed. Young volunteer plants are particularly vulnerable in the early stages of growth and could easily be removed by stock.

Recovery of active gully head and terrace erosion will be an extremely slow process in this environment unless aided by a sequence of favourable seasons. Under normal rainfall any progress toward stability will be gradual and fitful. Unfortunately the sheetflow to gullying process is irreversible. This particular desertification process is active on the less-productive rangeland types which probably returned only the costs of their fencing.

A programme of reduced numbers and exclusion of stock from specified areas should halt the erosion process and stabilize the productivity of the Basin. In particular it should reduce the violent fluctuations in livestock numbers. Haskell (1945) reports the recovery of arid American range through stock reductions following heavy use and similar improvements should occur in the Gascoyne Basin.

General comments have been made concerning the scanty and variable rainfall. Specifically, using Bidgemia (median annual rainfall 212 mm) as an example, the rainfall for the individual winter months of May, June and July is 30 mm or less on 60 per cent of years and is 50 mm or less on 80 per cent of years. Approximately 10 mm rainfall or less occurs on 30 per cent of years.

In the summer months January, February and March the rainfall for individual months is less than 30 mm and 50 mm, respectively, on 70 and 80 per cent of years, with 10 mm rainfall or less being recorded on 50 per cent of years.

These two blocks of three summer and three winter months contribute 82 per cent of mean annual rainfall.

The highest rainfall in any month was 300 mm in March (50 per cent more than the median of annual rainfall) contrasting with the mean value for the ninth decile of only 94 mm. An examination of the daily rainfall records indicates greater but more erratic falls at more easterly stations, presumably as a result of cyclonic disturbances. Control of these tremendous volumes of water by earthworks is impossible. The random tracks which the cyclonic depressions take determine the stations that receive rain and the rivers that flood.

A further constraint to the control of desertification within the rainfall sector is rainfall effectiveness. Using the water-use model as developed by Fitzpatrick et al. (1967) and treating the daily rainfall in 5-day groups for four stations in the Basin, the duration of growth and non-growth or drought periods was calculated. The results for Bidgemia are set out in Fig. 16 as an example, showing the mean monthly rainfall as vertical bars and curves of monthly probabilities for rainfall to exceed the requirement for plant growth greater than 15 days and 30 days.

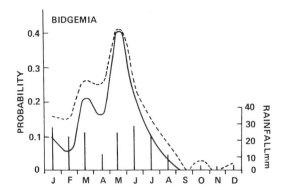

Fig. 16.    Probability of positive soil water store (less than
            15 bars) at Bidgemia, plotted for periods of more
            than 30 days in each month positive store (unbroken
            line) and for periods of more than 15 days positive
            store (broken line).  Rainfall is shown as vertical
            bars in mm.

The 15-day and 30-day growth period probabilities follow a closely related pattern.
However, in any consideration of rainfall effectiveness, the 30-day period is
probably the only significant one for the growth of grasses and adequate growth of
annuals.  The 15-30-day period is likely to be adequate for the growth of perennials,
but its effect on annual growth will be indifferent.  The importance of maintaining
and restoring perennial vegetation to stabilize production is therefore quite clear
since the 15-day rainfall growth occurs more frequently.  Further, areas which have
been denuded of perennial vegetation have less chance of production from annuals
than areas which have not been depleted.

In Table 14 the expected number of growth periods and non-growth periods during
summer and winter periods are set out for Bidgemia.  A growth period of 30 days or
more can be anticipated in each year, but growth periods of 60 days or more are
less frequent.  The longest drought period was 255 days, but five others lasted for
210 days.  By contrast, at Yarlarweelor (275 km ESE from Bidgemia) a drought period
of 465 days was recorded on one occasion, in 43 years there were two droughts which
lasted 285 days or more and four which lasted more than 250 days.  However, even at
Yarlarweelor there are growth periods of 30 days or more and 60 days or more,
though at a slightly lower frequency of occurrence than at Bidgemia.  It is these
good seasonal sequences which should be utilized to maintain and restore rangeland
productivity.  Further, the reliability of positive water storage for periods of
about 15 days makes it clear that management geared to perennial shrubs and grasses
should be adopted as these species are adapted to utilize smaller increments of
rain than are the more spectacular annual species which need prolonged wet conditions
to achieve their maximum growth.

The water use model used in this study, in common with others (e.g. Slatyer, 1960;
Nix and Fitzpatrick, 1969; Rose et al., 1972; Johns and Smith, 1975; Fleming, 1976),
assumes that surface run-off is negligible or that it occurs only after a defined
soil water storage has been filled.  These models over-estimate soil water storage
whenever the rate of precipitation exceeds the rate of infiltration and such is
often the case in summer in the Gascoyne Basin.  For this reason, the calculated
periods of summer growth are probably over-estimated on both eroded and non-eroded
soils but the calculated and actual values for winter growth are likely to be
similar, at least for the non-eroded soils.

Table 14.  The Number of Years and Expected Number of Occasions per year
          in which Growth Periods and Non-growth (drought) Periods occurred
          in Summer and Winter at Bidgemia

| | Summer<br>(Jan.-Mar.) | Winter<br>(May-July) | Annual |
|---|---|---|---|
| A.  GROWTH PERIODS<br>    (61 years to 1968) | | | |
| Greater than 15 days | | | |
| - No. of years | 35 | 49 | |
| - expected number | 0.57 | 0.80 | 1.37 |
| Greater than 30 days | | | |
| - No. of years | 22 | 44 | |
| - expected number | 0.36 | 0.72 | 1.08 |
| Greater than 60 days | | | |
| - No. of years | 11 | 37 | |
| - expected number | 0.18 | 0.61 | 0.79 |
| B.  NON-GROWTH PERIODS | | | |
| Greater than 15 days | | | |
| - No. of years | 45 | 18 | |
| - expected number | 0.74 | 0.29 | 1.03 |
| Greater than 30 days | | | |
| - No. of years | 32 | 12 | |
| - expected number | 0.52 | 0.20 | 0.72 |
| Greater than 60 days | | | |
| - No. of years | 15 | 6 | |
| - expected number | 0.24 | 0.10 | 0.34 |
| Greater than 90 days | | | |
| - No. of years | 6 | 5 | |
| - expected number | 0.10 | 0.08 | 0.18 |
| Longest drought period<br>- 255 days | | | |

The sensitivity of certain rangeland vegetation to changes in hydrology can be
exemplified by the effect of a small embankment produced by a road grader.  The
impounding of water on slopes of 1:1000 killed all the *Acacia aneura* trees on the
downslope side for a distance of 2 km in a period of 1 year.

Because the optimum temperature for germination of the desirable chenopodiaceous
shrubs of about 15°C occurs in the March to May period when rain can be anticipated
with some confidence, management schemes which will promote the germination and
establishment, and therefore regeneration of these important browse plants, will
necessitate the removal of livestock during this period and the following winter.
If winter rains fail, grazing must not recommence till a further season of
effective rain occurs.  Germination criteria are not known for all desirable shrubs

but field observation indicates a response situation similar to this.  Therefore,
while drought is the memorable and well-publicized characteristic of the
environment there is a somewhat neglected rainfall pattern which has the potential
to be utilized for the control of desertification.

An encouraging feature of desirable shrub species in the Basin is the apparent
longevity of individual plants.  Studies on the survivorship of semi-arid and arid
species in eastern Australia has indicated that a half-life (the period of time
over which half the number of plants entering the period die) exceeding 100 years
can be exhibited by some shrubs and up to 20 years by certain grass species
(Crisp, 1975; Crisp and Lange, 1976; Williams and Roe, 1975).  Conservation of the
rare to occasional substantial cohort of these species is likely to produce long-
lived (in excess of 500 years) rangeland.

We think that before the introduction of European livestock this longevity in an
erratic rainfall regime and in the presence of small populations of soft-footed
herbivores is sufficient to explain the precocious reproductive performance
(flowering, fruiting, germination and establishment of juveniles) of many
Australian trees and shrubs.  Although the plants can meet our demands for a long
life, they are not immortal and because they cannot surmount the grazing pressures
applied at the time when recruitment is possible we face the certainty of large-
scale mortality in what we can only describe as sparse geriatric communities.

Conversely, these same selection pressures enhance propulations of species which
are undesirable for domestic livestock.

Our optimistic analysis for recruitment of desirable species in the Basin rests on
the absence of the rabbit and possible control of domestic livestock.  However, in
those parts of arid and semi-arid Australia where the rabbit is now a normal
element of the fauna we do not expect recruitment and predict large-scale mortality,
precipitated but not caused by drought, as the pre-European cohorts senesce.


                    CURRENT MANAGEMENT PRACTICES

*The First Inspection, 1974*

The Wilcox and McKinnon report recommended that 9400 km$^2$ be withdrawn from grazing.
A further 32,800 km$^2$ in the supervised rangeland category were to require a
substantial management input over what was normally accepted.  The pastoralists in
the Basin were incensed when they heard of measures which they considered would
lead to a substantial reduction in both income and capital value of their
enterprise.  The authors of the report came in for vehement criticism.

A meeting of pastoralists at Gascoyne Junction in 1973 took place with
representatives of the Pastoral Appraisement Board, Departments of Agriculture and
of Lands and Surveys, and the Pastoralists and Graziers Association.  The meeting
agreed that a detailed inspection be made of all stations in the Basin.  The first
inspection started in 1974.

The two assessors appointed to this first inspection were experienced officers of
the Department of Agriculture and the Department of Lands and Surveys, long
resident in regions of arid Western Australia, who were conversant with the
Gascoyne Basin, who knew many of the pastoralists, but who were not involved
directly in the original survey.

The assessors lived and worked in a caravan office sited near each homestead for
the term of the 3-day visit.  Discussions with the lessee in this office were under
more discipline, albeit of an overt kind, than the free-ranging type which is

inevitable in the homestead office, the "territory" of the lessee.  The
appropriate maps and files were immediately accessible.

Following preliminary discussion on the scope of the inspection, the reasons for
it and the immediate objections of the lessee, the party of three visited all parts
of the station in the governmental vehicle.  Generally the pastoralist was in quiet
agreement with a comprehensive tour which covered, at Government expense, difficult
terrain that he was quite reasonably unable or unwilling to traverse in his own
vehicles.  During this tour the appropriate rangeland systems were identified and
discussed in relation to erosion, production, livestock management procedures used
by the lessee, and potential for improvement with *Cenchrus* sp. or deferment to
encourage regrowth of edible bush and scrub species.

After this arduous extension programme the final discussion sessions in the
caravan office integrated the survey assessments with the tour insights into a
property agreement.

Attitudes to the first inspection varied: some lessees did not become involved at
all and left their managers to carry it out, others had difficulty in appreciating
the reasons for, and the scope of, the inspection.  The remainder became interested
and participated fully.

Generally the most degraded paddocks on a station were the holding paddocks
associated with the shearing shed.  All the sheep on the property were brought here
to await the annual shearing and their subsequent return to the outer paddocks was
often delayed for months.  On some stations the holding paddocks were seldom free
of sheep.

It was agreed by pastoralists that the holding paddocks should only be used at
shearing.

The idea of keeping paddocks free of sheep did not meet with many objections
because pastoralists in discussion agreed that something needed to be done.
However, there were vigorous objections to the reduction in livestock numbers
presaged by the report.  These particular lessees had not caused the erosion and
the depletion, neither had they benefited financially from the "mining" programmes,
but they were the individuals to be penalized.

Although livestock watering facilities had been progressively developed since 1947
in hitherto ungrazed rangeland, little of this rangeland had become degraded because
of a combination of factors which included the inherently poorer productivity of
the new rangeland types, distance from shearing shed, homestead and sheep yards,
inability to expand flock size and increasing costs of labour and materials.  In
addition, lessees tended not to use these outer areas for breeding, supposedly
because of the dingo.  Assessors advised lessees to consider a heavier level of
usage; inordinate use was unlikely because the rangelands proximate to stream
frontages and homesteads were already degraded (dominated by annual plants) to the
extent that flock maintenance was difficult and sheep numbers could not be built
up either for heavy exploitation of these outer areas or for sale to raise the
capital that heavy exploitation would require.

The assessors had estimates of ECC (estimated carrying capacity—Department of Lands
and Surveys) and the SUC (sheep unit capacity—Wilcox and McKinnon).  These two
differed markedly; however, the combination of rangeland systems, the condition of
the rangeland systems, inspection of disputed and unsampled areas of the station,
an estimate of the realizable managerial input and vigorous bargaining resulted in
an agreed estimate (Agreement) which has to be reached 10 years hence (in 1984 and
1985).  In the Agreement a lessee also undertook to keep specified areas of
rangeland free of livestock.  In these areas the Department of Agriculture would

establish monitoring sites in order to determine the trend in rangeland condition.

In practice, properties with a good resource base were settled on the high side and properties with a poor resource base were settled on the low side because they already exhibited problems in maintaining sheep numbers and had approached or were approaching the threshold of economic viability. Examples are given in Table 13.

Although a substantial portion of the Western station has been severely degraded between 1920 and 1940, the large area invaded since 1961 by *Cenchrus ciliaris* should enable preferential treatment of the degraded and eroded Stony Chenopod rangeland group. Rangeland types on the North Central station are in good condition, but are of the unproductive Hill and Stony Short Grass-Forb groups. The eleven stations assessed to have the poorest resource base occupy 33.5 per cent of the catchment area and carry 40,450 sheep at a rate of 55 ha/sheep. Their Agreement total of 82,800 sheep is similar to their SUC, but these properties cannot be run at the Agreement level and superb management cannot aid them.

The ten stations assessed to have the better resource base occupy 40 per cent of the catchment area and carry 175,000 sheep at a rate of 16 ha/sheep. Their Agreement total is 166,000.

The overall picture of livestock numbers in the Gascoyne Basin in terms of sheep actually carried and assessments of carrying capacity for revenue rating and carrying capacity are summarized in Table 15.

Table 15.  Gascoyne Basin - Estimates of Sheep Numbers in
           Relation to Assessments of Carrying Capacity

| ECC | SUC | Agreement | Actual | Actual |
|-----|-----|-----------|--------|--------|
| Lands Dept. | GCSR | 1972 | 1972 | 1974 |
| 577,985 | 256,210 | 345,300 | 416,270 | 323,500 |

To cope with the margin given the first group, the assessors were depending on the application of technology and improved management practices in co-operation with the pastoralists, on the rangeland systems that were known to be capable of responding. The assessors thought that ecological studies elsewhere could provide a bonus in dealing with the regeneration of edible scrub species. Management plans and research appear to have value for this first group, but are possibly too late or of no use for the remainder.

Agreement was reached with thirty of the thirty-one lessees and an Appeal Committee was appointed to deal with the remaining case and with those that might eventuate in future. The Appeal Committee was constituted as follows under an independent chairman (a Commissioner from the State Rural and Industries Bank) with a representative of the Pastoral Appraisement Board and a representative of the Pastoralists and Graziers Association conversant with the district. In this first case the Appeal Committee upheld the agreement proposed by the assessors.

An example of agreement signed by the lessee is attached in Appendix 5. Each property has a separate agreement and these are confidential and vary considerably in their scope. Because they are based on incomplete information their structure permits interpolation and addition of new material. They cover both station and paddock.

Their first inspection and subsequent visits to the Basin have confirmed the extent,
activity, and severity of desertification as portrayed by the original survey.
In ecological and range assessment terms this original survey is still appropriate,
although some of the SUC estimates for poor rangeland types appear rather high.
The economic assessment implicit in the report appears realistic for the stations
with the poor rangeland types as several are now unable to maintain flock size in
spite of a series of good rainfall seasons and several more are in the "stalling"
phase which precedes the decline in sheep numbers.

However, the survey technique was inadequate in several respects, although its
overall assessments were reasonable. Access to rangeland systems on some stations
was difficult and observation sites were proximate to roads and tracks. In practice
entire rangeland systems on a station were evaluated on the basis of a small
section of road traverse. On a catchment basis an error of this type was not
important, but this was certainly untrue of property and paddock errors in the
maps which pastoralists received. The total of 2426 recording sites (or 1 per 39
$km^2$) for the Basin appears too low, even when allowance is made for the tendency
to place more sites in the vulnerable rangeland than elsewhere. The siting of
traverses in relation to fences is also of some significance because sheep tend to
use the eastern side of paddocks more heavily than the western side.

The calculation of SUC values depends on a small number of forage dry-matter
estimates which have been made in the Basin and elsewhere. These estimates have
the virtue of a probability element in them and this is rather unusual. Subsequent
estimates in the Basin suggest that the better rangeland types may be more
productive than the estimates given in the report. However, this apparent gain
does not affect the calculated SUC greatly because the 50 per cent usage cited in
the report includes forage actually consumed as well as weathering and trampling
losses. It is difficult to find levels of consumption per annum in excess of 20
to 25 per cent of total dry-matter production in semi-arid rangeland (Williams,
1974).

*Monitoring Programmes*

This monitoring programme uses large-scale aerial photographs and ground
measurements designed to determine if and when rehabilitation occurs on the areas
from which livestock have been removed. The technique closely follows that
described by Carneggie *et al.*(1971). A 70-mm aerial reconnaissance camera is used
in an aircraft flying at 150 m.

Already regeneration of desirable long-lived shrubs has been observed at several
of the sites and at one site, cattle subsequently gained entry to the paddock
completely removing all traces of these juveniles.

On "pillows" of surface soil remaining in one degraded but potentially highly
productive type, juvenile plants of a desirable species were unable to persist
because the soil moisture volume was inadequate. A substantial juvenile population
of the undesirable *Hakea priessii* remains.

*Educational Programmes*

Following the original report and first inspection, there have been requests from
pastoralists for field days and in 1975 a well-attended event included participatory
sessions on plant species identification and the estimation of range trend, as well
as the more usual animal husbandry demonstrations. Field days are to be held on

other stations at which research findings from the monitoring programme will be
applied to the recognition of vegetation change on station paddocks.  This
interest is in contrast to the poor support given to the previous field days held
in the western Gascoyne.

A side effect of the initial survey and its aftermath has been a more active local
branch of the Pastoralists and Graziers Association.  The combination of local
research and practice augurs well for fruitful rangeland management programmes on
stations with a reasonable resource base.

Formal educational levels attained by new lessees are likely to be higher than
those departing, but extension difficulties in the field of management may be
exacerbated should financial institutions and pastoral houses insist on more money
being paid than the station is worth in terms of the resource status and medium-
term economic conditions.


*Technological Adaptation*

The development of the Gascoyne Basin from its 1870 condition to that in 1976 has
involved the use of a wide range of European technology.  These innovations *per se*
have not caused the soil erosion and degradation of the rangeland although the
location-specific nature of structures such as shearing sheds, yards and wells
favours excessive concentration of livestock.  This phenomenon is aided by the
capital intensive nature of these investments.  Similarly, the inclusion of small
areas of sensitive rangeland types in the same paddock as rangeland types for which
sheep show little, if any, preference is due to the location of fencelines rather
than the construction of fences.  The philosophy which held that sheep be given a
variety of vegetation types to choose from often ran counter to dietary preferences.

Sowing of saltbush (*Atriplex* spp.) and blue bush (*Maireana* spp.) on eroded surfaces
has been attempted on an experimental basis using a browse plant seeder developed
by officers of the W.A. Department of Agriculture.  This machine cultivates, makes
a small pit into which a number of seeds are dropped and then covers the seed with
chopped hay.

Contour furrowing has been successful at Brickhouse station which is situated in
the more-reliable rainfall area in the Gascoyne delta.  Furrows 20 m apart were
made with a single-mould board plough; seed from the remnants of *Maireana aphylla*
and *M. pyramidata* was trapped in these furrows and an adult stand developed at a
spacing approximating 3 m along the furrows.  Although this procedure is
technically feasible on a wide range of soils, its application is likely to be
restricted to the most productive land systems where the aim of management is to
enhance reproductive performance in the sheep flock.

The most rapid method of vegetation improvement is limited to rangeland types such
as the Gascoyne where soils are sandy loams, and involves the introduction of
*Cenchrus ciliaris* by broadcasting seed and dragging a simple harrowing device
behind a vehicle.  A better stand of this grass has followed the more expensive
procedure of a single operation using disc cultivation seeding with a buffel grass
seed box in November-December on a suitable soil, that is one with a light-
textured surface.  In the western parts of the Gascoyne Basin, buffel germinates
and establishes in summer, but responds vegetatively to winter rains.  Land
adjacent to established pasture is colonized rapidly and dissemination of the seed
is assisted by the normal easterly wind system.  It is regrettable that no stands
have been established along streamlines in the eastern end of the Basin to take
advantage of these winds.  Even so, the grass is slowly but surely spreading
eastwards.  At the time of the first Gascoyne seeding in 1960 the desire to

innovate, the availability of risk capital and what are now seen to be reasonable cost levels happened to coincide.

The less-spectacular and less-predictable procedures of grazing management have yet to be implemented, although a start has been made on stations where sheep can be maintained on revegetated creek frontages and the remainder of the property given the opportunity to regenerate. Heavy utilization of these frontage buffel grass pastures is limited by the increase in the fibre content as plants mature. In the oldest (12 year) stand, plant size suggests that individuals are of the one age and that there has been no recruitment since establishment from seed sowing. The regeneration of edible shrub species is a practical ecological venture of immediate importance which cannot wait for research to be completed. Fortunately, recruitment into an old stand of a long-lived shrub species took place during 1975-76 in the absence of grazing by domestic livestock in several of the monitored sites. These observations confirmed the importance of deferments, their commencement at the time of seedling establishment and the choice of an appropriate rangeland type. Controlled grazing should be possible after several favourable seasons.

Technology of importance to animal health and production ideally involves the development of plain-bodied (i.e. non-wrinkled) and high-wool-producing sheep, the ewe portion of which is capable not only of maintaining optimum size of breeding flock but also of producing surplus sheep for sale.

This high aim is unattainable in the Basin because of the inadequate quantity and quality of forage on the present degraded and unproductive rangeland types. Importation of rams unsuited to this harsh pastoral environment merely accentuates the basic problem. Once again, financial returns from wool are insufficient to offset inputs and permit either ewes or wethers to be brought in from districts with a surplus.

The technology associated with ewe and ram selection for enhanced wool production and reproduction is well researched and its field application worked out more than 15 years ago. The literature is voluminous and all State Departments of Agriculture have skilled research and extension officers in animal husbandry.

An optimal reproductive programme would involve joining ewes in December before marked seminal degeneration occurred in the rams, with the hope that summer rain and subsequent vegetation response would initiate high levels of oestrus in the ewes.

Management aimed at increasing the chances of ewes being mated and restricting the lambing period includes the use of relatively small paddocks for several months at higher than normal stocking rates. These paddocks would be used in yearly rotation. Because of the distances involved, rams are transported to the mating paddocks by vehicle.

Rams might be bred in the Basin specifically for the harsh conditions, but in practice, small numbers of southern rams would still be purchased in order to preserve the reputation of a station whilst locally bred rams ensure production and profits. Lambing in the cool winter on rangeland types with a substantial component of edible shrubs would assist the ewes nutritionally in late pregnancy and lactation. Weaners should receive preferential treatment over the older ewes.

Particular difficulties in the application of technology in the Gascoyne Basin revolve around an inadequate nutritional base as already discussed as well as the naturally low stocking rates and the less-than-ideal terrain, which taken together can mean flocks of, say, 500 sheep in paddocks of 5000 to 10,000 ha. To these environmental constraints must be added the scarcity of risk capital.

In comparison with the wheat-sheep zone of Western Australia where technology has
enabled flock size to be increased over the past 10 years from levels of 1000 sheep
to 4000-5000 sheep/labour unit and exceptionally to 10,000 sheep/labour unit
(Fels and Hogstrom, 1973), the flock size in the pastoral zone generally and in the
Gascoyne in particular seems not to have increased greatly from around 4000 sheep/
labour unit.  There is very little unproductive land on a farm compared with the
non-productive area on some stations, and the numerous creek (watercourse) crossings
also keep station maintenance and transport costs high.

Major innovations on the Basin have perforce had to be limited to property and
sheep management.  Travelling time has been reduced by replacing horses with
motor-bikes (approximately 100), four-wheel drive vehicles (30-40) and aeroplanes
(14).  The use of 240-V power generators encourages the use of workshop equipment
such as welders, drills, power saws, earth-moving equipment; ancillary devices for
lifting and positioning heavy loads and road graders for maintaining station roads
(in inexpert hands a cause of serious erosion) all help to replace scarce and
expensive labour.  Large trucks owned by the station or by haulage contractors
are used to return shorn sheep to distant paddocks (cost 10c per sheep).  Sheep
handling can be made easier and cheaper by the use of laneways up to 200 m wide
which traverse the station.  Previously with abundant labour and horses a
"mustering" camp with cook and associated facilities was established 30 km from
the shearing shed.  Sheep were mustered in one paddock and passed through into the
next paddock which was also mustered.  The combined flocks would be brought in
through existing paddocks to the holding paddocks.  Lanes enable a paddock to be
mustered by a rider on motor-bike with occasional assistance by aeroplane in picking
up isolated flocks.  The sheep are put in the laneway and the musterers return to
the homestead at the end of the day, returning next day to commence a new paddock.
Laneways obviate the necessity to remuster flocks which disperse overnight.

Recently the sheep dog has been introduced after an absence of many years during
which sheep were moved by the riders on motor-bikes.  The dogs ride on a platform
behind the rider and make forays to form and control the flock.  For the first
time since large teams of aboriginal horsemen were used, it is possible to shift
sheep easily and efficiently, so increasing the potential for rangeland management.

Innovations adopted elsewhere to cope with the sheep blowfly are of limited value
in the Basin.  These include the crutching cradle and jetting equipment.  The
practice of mulesing the ewes, though of benefit, is not yet widely used.


*Social and Economic Adjustments*

The relative change in financial status of urban and rural families in recent
years has not gone unnoticed.  Almost 50 per cent of urban households have two
wage earners and combined husband and wife yearly earnings can range from
$10,000 to $30,000 with benefits such as sick leave, recreation leave and long-
service leave paid by the employer.  A pastoralist is fortunate to get to this
level.  Because urban values have already been assumed in the Gascoyne it is not
yet acceptable in practice to drop these to stay on the station.  By contrast,
evidence accumulating for eastern Australia suggests that urban values have
already been relinquished in order to remain on pastoral properties.

It is doubtful if pastoralists in the Gascoyne are investing outside the wool
industry in the form of urban real estate as was the case some years ago.

In the recent past, high incomes enabled the pastoralist's children to be sent to
a boarding school in Perth, but with fees now approaching $3000 per annum the
practice is beyond most of the present generation of lessees.

Education in Australia is seen as an avenue of advancement (upward social mobility) and recruitment of rural youth resident in farming regions has been pronounced in the fields of teaching, banking, public service and railways. In the case of pastoralist families the question is more one of maintenance of a former social position in a social milieu that has changed abruptly. We believe that the new pattern of redistribution of resources will intensify the disparity between rural and urban, with education the urban-based catalyst.

The global economic pressures now felt in the Gascoyne Basin and elsewhere cannot be met by the means adopted in the 1930s because the volume and cost of inputs have been increased substantially in recent years in an effort to maintain output by substituting capital for labour. In 1976 it is not possible to maintain income by increasing the flock size and grazing the rangeland more heavily as was the case in the 1930s.

Transport costs, in particular, are emerging as a crucial factor and one that is likely to increase in importance. Interest rates, currently in the vicinity of 12 to 15 per cent per annum compared with 4 to 5 per cent in the early part of the 30-year period, when set against current and foreseeable earnings are likely to militate against investment of the type that could lead to an acceleration in rangeland deterioration. The expected low level of new investment is a further reason for taking steps to conserve the historical capital that remains on stations in the Basin.

### FUTURE LAND USE

We expect little change from the present way of using the land. Although animal production can be improved by the adoption of various animal-husbandry techniques, the key to permanent improvement is in increased forage production from perennial rangelands and this improvement is more likely on the better, albeit degraded rangeland types.

The two major crops produced in the Gascoyne Basin are wool for export and water for the irrigation farms at Carnarvon.

We have described a biological and social environment in which wool is not easy to produce. The present and future economic environment also appears harsh. The simplest alternative land use is cattle production and this would reduce costs, but the biological, social and economic environment would still be unsatisfactory, except for those stations with the good resource base. However, these latter are profitable as sheep enterprises and are unlikely to move into cattle in the foreseeable future.

The new erosion networks, and the increased area of bare, compacted soil, have probably resulted in a greater and more rapid run-off, but this is impossible to quantify. Although the Gascoyne flow is measured there is only one official rain gauge per 2500 $km^2$ and an understanding of the hydrology in this region must await the completion of the proposed Representative Basin 7.4 in the Australian Representative Basins Program (Milne, 1975). However, we would anticipate no substantial reduction in river flows should a rangeland management programme concentrate on deferment and possible regeneration of the less-degraded parts of the better-quality rangeland types.

Tourism is, and will remain, an insignificant activity. Historically the Basin was less attractive for residence and development than the wheat-belt and, but for the investment boom in the 1950s fuelled by the extraordinary wool prices of that time, the Basin would not have been developed to its present level.

Large-scale mining of iron ore is concentrated too far to the north and north-east for financial benefits to flow into the Basin.  Mining within the Basin is now limited to talc.

The environment is too arid for forestry, but includes the limited production of sandalwood (*Santalum spicatum*) which is exported.

Finally, although statements are made from time to time that "if livestock are removed, the country will go back", there is no ecological evidence to corroborate this.  On the contrary, our observations suggest that, because of the absence of the rabbit in the Basin, the removal of livestock will effect an improvement in perennial cover and erosion resistance.  However, the statement would be valid if feral goats and cattle took the place of domestic livestock.


### COSTS AND BENEFITS IN DESERTIFICATION CONTROL

The cost of the original survey and the first inspection have been assessed at $35,000.  The cost of the monitoring programme and of field days can be assessed at $25,000 per annum.

The cost of the recommended reduction in livestock numbers from the average figure 1934 to 1973 period of 316,000 to 265,000 would increase stations costs by 20 per cent.  However, the Agreement total for the Basin was 326,000, the actual total in 1974 was 323,500, and so this cost would not apply.  The removal of livestock from the recognized over-utilized areas to under-utilized rangeland would be an additional cost that should be recouped in better animal production.

The cost of deferment routines on less-eroded, high-producing rangeland of the saltbush and bluebush types would be high initially, but this aspect of management at station level is essential for long-term stability in the pastoral enterprise. The cost of this programme should be recouped in terms of enhanced animal production. In practice we have noted elsewhere that benefits also accrue from the concomitant decisions made in adopting improved animal husbandry procedures.

A cost-benefit analysis for the Gascoyne Basin must stand on the economic base appropriate to its pastoral industry because regeneration of rangeland, viewed realistically, is unlikely to affect the flow of the Gascoyne River at Carnarvon in anything but a marginal way.

Present export earnings would approximate $1.5 million per annum and purchased inputs approximate $1.2 million with $0.6 million of this attributable to wages and expenditure with little or no import content.  These figures suggest that low-cost ecological research and station management, as outlined earlier in this case study, should be the major contributors to long-term resource maintenance.

A strict economic analysis is beyond our scope and may even be irrelevant.  As Waring (1973) points out, "Until recently, economists have been inclined to write off land as being indestructable. . . .  There has been little published discussion of the economics of using extensively, with minimal soil ameliorating inputs, a land resource that may unpredictably collapse—in contrast to being deliberately depleted, as by mining."

RECOMMENDATIONS AND LESSONS LEARNED

*The Rangeland Resource, Animal Production and Rangeland Management*

The original survey assessed the extent, severity and type of erosion on a property
and paddock basis. Apart from a small number of errors and omissions attributable
to an inadequate number of sampling sites and to the absence of traverses in some
areas of difficult terrain, there appears to be little disagreement over erosion
assessments.

Erosion is still proceeding actively in a number of rangeland types and in the
absence of range management is likely to continue. Evidence of new and extended
erosion networks is apparent after summer rain. Erosion has reached an irreversible
stage on some rangeland types. Rate measures as such have not been made, but series
of photographs taken over several years show recent and substantial increases in
gully formation. More of these series should be taken because of their high
information content about an unpleasant topic of importance to future pastoralists,
investors, land administrators and legislators.

The status of the rangelands and their present levels of animal production in
relation to their past and possible future is an area of dispute. However, the
remnants of climax vegetation in the Basin provide irrefutable evidence that
rangeland deterioration is a phenomenon of European pastoral settlement and directly
attributable to the introduction of domestic livestock with allied pastoral
technology. A low level of grazing by small numbers of soft-footed native
herbivores was replaced by a high level of continuous grazing maintained by large
numbers of hooved herbivores.

This statement is true for all of pastoral Australia, but in Western Australia the
key perennial plants appear to be more susceptible to  grazing or have fewer
opportunities to regenerate. Certainly progressive pastoralists and rangeland
research workers in Western Australia have a level of awareness and concern about
these plants which is uncommon elsewhere.

Production problems of the pastoral industry are largely in the field of
reproduction and have been defined as stemming from serious inadequacies in the
present degraded rangelands. Substantial improvement is unlikely in the absence
of a radical change in rangeland management which will ensure the regeneration of
long-lived perennial shrubs. Far too much attention is given to periods of
drought and not to the runs of good seasons when something creative can be done or
to the immediate post-drought period when the alleviation of grazing pressure is
critical. Regeneration does occur but our knowledge of its frequency is scanty
and once per human generation (25 years) is likely. On these rare occasions the
control of livestock is imperative. The least-eroded and the better-quality
rangeland types should receive priority. Similarly, exclosures for the study of
rangeland improvement should be located preferentially on these types rather than
following the more-usual practice of working on grossly eroded sites, and the
monitoring sites *are* grossly eroded.

Feasible regeneration programmes allied to improved rangeland management which may
retain a little more rainfall in the more-productive rangeland types appear to
offer no threat to continued irrigation from the Gascoyne River and no great
diminution in flood flows.

RESEARCH

The three linked programmes of monitoring, research and extension (education) in the Basin do not demand massive financial or manpower inputs of the type required for research stations and instrumented watershed studies. These comparatively low-cost and flexible programmes demand considerable expertise and should not be despised.

Because the Basin is leasehold there is guaranteed permanence of experimental areas (not to be confused with monitoring sites) on stations. Co-operation is good to excellent.

The structure of the Rangeland Management group in the Department of Agriculture which is responsible for the programmes favours an ecosystemic approach rather than separate soil conservation or animal husbandry studies. Because the departmental advisers located in the various pastoral districts are expected to combine an ecological research interest with their extension roles the institutional and vocational amalgam has resulted in a strong personal and applied arid-lands commitment with a bias toward management and resource maintenance. However, it has led to an admitted paucity of published information and a tendency for field data to be illustrative rather than quantitative. At the same time, the absence of economic and social considerations from rangeland management plans as occurred in the original Gascoyne Basin survey has been recognized and is being corrected.

Rangeland research in Australia is conducted by personnel from various State and Commonwealth agencies. Several universities have a sustained interest in arid-zone research. There is no formal Australian structure to accommodate these people, but many of them and some pastoralists are members of the Australian Rangeland Society. This society publishes a newsletter and a journal. An arid-zone newsletter, published annually by the Commonwealth Scientific and Industrial Research Organization, contains progress reports on field surveys and experiments which have relevance to the Australian arid zone.

*Financial Institutions*

In the past, financial institutions appear to have been slow to learn that past and contemporary production records for pastoral properties do not indicate future levels. No amount of skill, technological application and financial assistance can redress the situation in the Basin or elsewhere in arid Australia on grossly deteriorated and poor rangeland.

*Administration*

The Pastoral Appraisement Board has accepted the responsibilities entrusted to it under the 1963 Amendments to the Land Act and consequently has, in recent years, and since the inception of the Gascoyne Catchment Survey, implemented a policy aimed at determining the state at time of inspection of various regions embracing the pastoral industry; to date the Gascoyne Basin area, the West Kimberley Erosion Survey and impending surveys of the Ashburton Catchment, the Nullarbor region and the Pilbara are all part of that policy.

It is understood that the recommendations by the various inspection parties are somewhat unique so far as reports in Australia are concerned and it would be true to say that some lessons have been learned. One of the principle factors is that the initial report on the Gascoyne and also that for the West Kimberley provided the views of the initial inspection team as to what carrying capacities should be maintained on the areas in question. In the light of subsequent experience, the

Pastoral Appraisement Board considers that in future surveys of this nature, it
may well follow the policy of requesting the inspection parties not to recommend
any destocking rates but rather to leave the resultant stocking figures to an
inspection committee which would include the pastoralist concerned.

This viewpoint has been consolidated by the belief that any misconception of the
intentions of the Board or the Inspection group is largely due to differences of
opinion with the initial inspectors' findings.  In all of the examinations it is
imperative that public dialogue be maintained and that communications exist
between the Minister for Lands in this case, the Pastoral Appraisement Board and
the Pastoral Industry generally.  The actions now being pursued in the West
Kimberley and other regions have now proven this beyond all doubt.

Technological changes will no doubt result in some change in method, for example,
the initial surveys were accompanied by fairly substantial expenditure for aerial
photography.  In due course, it is felt that Landsat Imagery may well facilitate
the investigations with a reduced amount of ground truth cover.


PLAN OF ACTION

The Plan of Action for the Gascoyne Basin is short, simple and long term.

Research, extension and administration should be centred on a few critical aspects
of rangeland management.  These are regeneration of shrubs, livestock-control and
education.  Enthusiastic co-operation between pastoralists, their organization,
financial institutions and range management personnel is necessary for success in
this resource-limited area.

It may prove in the interests of the State to provide financial incentives and
compensation in order that an agreed co-operative rangeland programme be supported
at station level.

The key to any progress that can be made in the control of desertification in the
Gascoyne Basin lies not with improved animal production, animal husbandry, or more
development, but in that long-neglected resource, the perennial rangeland
vegetation.  Even here the emphasis must be on the important species within this
perennial component on the rare occasions when there is recruitment.

The relevance of the biological portion of this plan of action to other parts of
pastoral Australia depends on two factors.  These are the presence or absence of
the European rabbit and the occurrence of perennial shrubs which have or have had
the important potential of enhancing and stabilizing populations (and production)
of sheep and cattle, but have seldom been managed so as to express this potential.

From the theoretical viewpoint a massive death of important forage species across
the rangelands of southern Australia would be proof of our proposition concerning
geriatric communities.  We are sure that the inevitable commissions of enquiry and
advocates for the pastoral industry would then want "something to be done".
From the ecological and financial viewpoint such a massive death would be
devastating, but no doubt, as temporary inhabitants on this planet, we would
adjust to its inconvenience.

In fact, we expect an insidious, patchy mortality which is unlikely to attain the
necessary threshold of public awareness for action to be initiated.

This case study on the little-known Gascoyne Basin will have been worthwhile
preparing if, as a sensitizing agent, it lowers this threshold of inaction and
heightens research, extension and administrative awareness to the stage where such
a catastrophe is hypothetical and not probable.

ACKNOWLEDGEMENTS

It is a pleasure to acknowledge the support given us in this case study by
Mr. R.A. Perry, Chief, CSIRO Division of Land Resources Management, Perth,
Western Australia; Mr. E.N. Fitzpatrick, Director of Agriculture, South Perth,
Western Australia; Mr. J.F. Morgan, Chairman, Pastoral Appraisement Board, Perth,
and members of their staffs. Officers of the Commonwealth Bureau of Meteorology
in Perth were most helpful in providing weather information.

The Commonwealth Department of Environment, Housing and Community Development
provided financial assistance.

Mr. K.M.W. Howes, Divisional Editor, and Mr. M. Woodward of the CSIRO Division of
Land Resources Management, Perth, helped greatly in preparing the final document
and Mrs. Jeanette Prendergast, CSIRO Division of Land Use Research, Canberra,
typed the preliminary draft.

It is a pleasure to acknowledge the assistance and hospitality extended to us by
the pastoral families in the Gascoyne Basin.

REFERENCES

Anon. (1972) *The Australian Sheep Industry Survey 1967-1968 to 1969-1970*.
    Statistical Summary, Bureau of Agricultural Economics, Canberra, Australia,
    September 1972. Australian Government Publishing Service, Canberra.

Anon. (1974) *Arid Zone Newsletter 1974* issued by Arid Zone Liaison Officer,
    Commonwealth Scientific and Industrial Research Organization, Perth, 208 pp.

Anon. (1976) *Statistics, Quarterly Review of Agricultural Economics* 29, 53.

Aplin, T.E.H. (1975) The vegetation of Western Australia; being Part 3 of
    Chapter II represented with original page numbers from the *Official Year Book
    of Western Australia, 1975,* No. 14 (New Series) 66-81.

Barnard, A. (1969) Aspects of the economic history of the arid land pastoral
    industry. In *Arid Lands of Australia,* Slayter, R. O. and Perry, R. A. (eds).
    Australian National University Press, Canberra.

Bettenay, E., Churchward, H.M. and McArthur, W.M. (1979) *Atlas of Australian Soils,
    Explanatory Data for Sheet 6, Meekatharra Hamersley Range Area,* collated by
    Northcote, K.H. CSIRO Australia, Melbourne University Press.

Brown, G.D. and Williams, O.B. (1970) Geographical distribution of the productivity
    of sheep in Australia. *Journal of the Australian Institute of Agricultural
    Science* 36, 182-98.

Burbidge, N.T. (1942) Ecological notes on the De Grey - Coogan area, with special
    reference to physiography. *Journal and Proceedings of the Royal Society of
    Western Australia* 29, 151-61.

Burbidge, N.T. (1943) Ecological succession observed during regeneration of
    *Triodia pungens* R.Br. after burning. *Journal and Proceedings of the Royal
    Society of Western Australia* 2, 149-56.

Butlin, N.G. (1962) Distribution of the sheep population: preliminary statistical
    picture, 1860-1957. In *The Simple Fleece: Studies in the Australian Wool
    Industry,* Barnard, A. (ed.). Melbourne University Press, Melbourne.

Butlin, N.G. (1964) *Investment in Australian Economic Development, 1861-1900.*
    Cambridge University Press, Cambridge.

Butlin, N.G. and Jennings, J.N. (1970) Introduction. In *Atlas of Bundaleer Plains and Tatala* by Rothery, F.M. Australian National University Press, Canberra.

Cain, N. (1962) Companies and squatting in the Western Division of New South Wales, 1896-1905. In *The Simple Fleece: Studies in the Australian Wool Industry*, Barnard, A. (ed.). Melbourne University Press, Melbourne.

Carneggie, D.M., Wilcox, D.G. and Hacker, R.B. (1971) The use of large scale aerial photographs in the evaluation of Western Australian Rangelands, Department of Agriculture Western Australia, Technical Bulletin No. 10.

Chapman, R.E., Williams, O.B. and the late Moule, G.R. (1973) The wool industry. In *The Pastoral Industries of Australia: Practice and Technology of Sheep and Cattle Production*, Alexander, G. and Williams, O.B. (eds.). Sydney University Press, Sydney.

Christian, C.S. and Perry, R.A. (1953) The systematic description of plant communities by the use of symbols. *Journal of Ecology* 41, 100-5.

Christian, C.S. and Stewart, G.A. (1964) Methodology of integrated surveys. Conference on principles and methods of integrated aerial survey studies of natural resources for potential development. UNESCO: Paris.

Chua, T.K. (1972) A century of cost-price squeeze for agriculture? *Farm Policy* 12, 15-22.

Condon, M.A. (1963) Geological Report, Glenburgh four-mile sheet. Bureau of Mineral Resources, Canberra.

Cooper, C.F. (1963) An evaluation of variable plot sampling in shrub and herbaceous vegetation. *Ecology* 44, 565-69.

Crisp, M.D. (1975) Long term changes in arid-zone vegetation at Koonamore, South Australia. Ph.D. Thesis, University of Adelaide, Adelaide.

Crisp, M.D. and Lange, R.T. (1976) Age structure, distribution and survival under grazing of the arid-zone shrub *Acacia burkittii*. *Oikos* 27, 86-92.

Dyksterhuis, E.J. (1949) Condition and management of rangeland based on quantitative ecology. *Journal of Range Management* 2, 104-15.

Ealey, E.H.M. (1967) Ecology of the euro, *Macropus robustus* (Gould), in North-western Australia. 1. The environment and changes in euro and sheep populations. *CSIRO Wildlife Research* 12, 9-25.

Fels, H.E. and Hogstrom, A.W. (1973) Farm operations management. *Journal of Agriculture Western Australia* 14, 235-40.

Fitzpatrick, E.A. (1968) An appraisal of advectional contributions to observed evaporation in Australia using an empirical approximation of Penman's potential evaporation. *Journal of Hydrology* 6, 69-94.

Fitzpatrick, E.A., Slayter, R.O. and Krishnan, A.I. (1967) Incidence and duration of periods of plant growth in Central Australia as estimated from climatic data. *Agricultural Meteorology* 4, 389-404.

Fleming, P.M. (1976) Local variations in microhydrology. Australian UNESCO Committee for the hydrological decade on drought. University of New South Wales, Sydney.

Gibbs, W.J. and Maher, J.V. (1967) Rainfall deciles as drought indicators. *Commonwealth Bureau of Meteorology Bulletin* No. 48.

Haskill, H.S. (1945) Successional trends on a conservatively grazed desert grassland range. *Journal of the American Society of Agronomy* 37, 978-90.

Hodan, M. (1975) Rural credit operations of pastoral finance companies. *Farm Policy* 15, 17-25.

Hoogvleit, W. (1972) Recent developments in the Australian sheep industry.  A summary of BAE survey results 1970-71. *Quarterly Review of Agricultural Economics* 25, 245-54.

Humphries, A.W. (1951) The role of the saltbushes in the pastoral economy of Western Australia, B.Sc. (Agric.) Hons. University of Western Australia, Perth.

Ive, J.R., Rose, C.W., Hall, B.H. and Torssell, B.W.R. (1976) Estimation and simulation of sheet run-off. *Australian Journal of Soil Research* 14, 129-38.

Johns, G.G. and Smith, R.C.G. (1975) Accuracy of soil water budgets based on a range of relationships for the influence of soil water availability on actual water use. *Australian Journal of Agricultural Research* 26, 871-83.

Jutson, J.T. (1934) *The Physiography (Geomorphology) of Western Australia,* 2nd edn. Geological Survey of Western Australia Bulletin No. 95.

Lightfoot, L.C. (1961) Soil erosion on the Gascoyne River Catchment Area.  Report of the Gascoyne River Erosion Committee. Mimeo. Department of Agriculture, Western Australia, pp. 18, maps 2.

Mabbutt, J.A., Speck, N.H., Wright, R.L., Litchfield, W.H., Sofourlis, J. and Wilcox, D.G. (1963) Land systems of the Wiluna-Meekatharra Area.  In *General Report on Lands of the Wiluna-Meekatharra Area, Western Australia, 1958.* CSIRO Australia Land Research Series No. 7.

McGinnies, W.G., Goldman, B.J. and Paylore, P. (eds.) (1968) *Deserts of the World.* The University of Arizona Press.

Marshall, J.K. (1970) Assessing the protective role of shrub-dominated rangeland vegetation against soil erosion by wind. *Proc. XI International Grassland Conference,* Surfers Paradise, Australia, 19-23.

Melville, G.F. (1939) Nutritive value of mulga, a species of Acacia indigenous to arid Western Australia. M.Sc. Thesis, University of Western Australia.

Melville, G.F. (1947) An investigation of the drought pastures of the Murchison District of Western Australia. *Journal of the Department of Agriculture of Western Australia* 24, 1-29.

Milne, F.J. (1975) A descriptive catalogue of the Australian representative basins. Department of National Resources, Australian Water Resources Council, Australian Government Publishing Service, Canberra.

Moore, R.M. and Perry, R.A. (1970) Vegetation.  In *Australian Grasslands,* Moore, R.M. (ed.).  Australian National University, Canberra.

Nix, H.A. and Fitzpatrick, E.A. (1969) An index of crop water stress related to wheat and grain sorghum yields. *Agricultural Meteorology* 6, 321-37.

Northcote, K.H. (1975) *A Description of Australian Soils.* CSIRO Australia, Melbourne, 170 pp.

Pittock, A.B. (1975) Climatic change and the patterns of variation in Australian rainfall. *Search* 6, 498-508.

Rose, C.W., Begg, J.E., Byrne, G.F., Torssell, B.W.R. and Goncz, J.H. (1972) A simulation model of growth-field environment relationships for Townsville stylo (*Stylosanthes humilis* H.B.K.). *Agricultural Meteorology* 10, 161-83.

Slayter, R.O. (1960) *Agricultural climatology of the Katherine area, N.T.* CSIRO Australia, Division of Land Resources Ref. Survey Tech. Paper No. 13.

Stewart, A.M. and Moir, R.J. (1943) Fertility in Merino sheep in north-western Australia.  1.  Observations on the incidence of oestrus in merino ewes at Warralong Station.  2.  A survey of the fertility of Merino sheep in north-western Australia. *Australian Veterinary Journal* 19, 152-64.

Tidmarsh, C.E.M. and Havenga, C.M. (1955) The wheel point method of survey and
    measurement of semi-open grasslands and Karoo vegetation in South Africa.
    Memoir 29, Botanical Survey of South Africa, pp. 53.

Tucker, G.B. (1975) Climate: is Australia's changing? *Search* 6, 323-8.

Waring, E.J. (1973) Economic and financial constraints in the operation of livestock
    enterprises on arid shrublands. In *Arid Shrublands—Proceedings of the Third
    Workshop of the United States/Australia Rangelands Panel*, pp. 108-15. Society
    for Range Management, Tucson, Arizona.

Wilcox, D.G. and McKinnon, E.A. (1972) A report on the condition of the Gascoyne
    catchment. Department of Agriculture and Department of Lands and Surveys,
    Western Australia.

Williams, O.B. (1974) Vegetation improvement and grazing management. In *Studies
    of the Australian Arid Zone* 11. *Animal Production*, pp. 127-44. Wilson, A.D.
    (ed.). CSIRO Melbourne.

Williams, O.B. (1977) *Ecosystems of Arid Australia*. IBP Cambridge University Press,
    Cambridge.

Williams, O.B. and Oxley, R.E. (1977) Historical aspects of the use of Chenopod
    pastures. In *Studies of the Australian Arid Zone*. CSIRO, Melbourne (in press).

Williams, O.B. and Roe, R. (1975) Management of arid grasslands for sheep: Plant
    demography of six grasses in relation to climate and grazing. *Proceedings
    Ecological Society of Australia* 9, 142-56.

## Appendix 1

The following extract from a pastoralists' association newsletter indicates the detailed information which is circulated to members and to which they must adhere.


"NATIONAL WAGE CASE:

Changed Rates in Federal Pastoral Industry Award

To operate on and from Monday, 17th May 1976

1.  SHEARERS - Not Found

| (a) Machine - per 100 | Per 100 - $ |
|---|---|
| Flock Sheep | 51.55 |
| Stud Ewes, etc. (× 1¼) | 64.44 |
| Rams (× 2) | 103.10 |

(b) Learners:  Minimum Wage: Adult Shed Hand's rate + $1.75 per week

2.  CRUTCHERS - Not Found

| | Per 100 - $ |
|---|---|
| Crutching between legs | 10.31 |
| Full crutching | 14.95 |
| Wigging or ringing | 5.67 |
| Wigging or ringing in addition | 1.55 |
| Wigging and ringing | 9.28 |
| Wigging and ringing in addition | 2.58 |
| Cleaning bellies, etc. | 1.29 |

3.  SHED HANDS - Not Found

| | Per Week - $ |
|---|---|
| Adults | 147.90 |
| Juniors: under 18 years | 102.70 |
| 18 - 20 years | 135.30 |

4.  WOOLPRESSERS -

| | Per cwt | Per bale |
|---|---|---|
| By Hand | $1.02 | $3.05 |
| By Power | 68 cents | $2.03 |
| Weekly Wage Guarantee - Not Found $183.40 | | |
| Weighing and Branding - 7 cents per bale | | |

5.  FOUND DEDUCTION - Shearers, Crutchers, Shed Hands and Woolpressers

The rates shown in 1 to 4 less $24.97 per week.

6.  DAILY RATE - Shearers, Crutchers - per day

Not found $38.60        Found $32.25      "

## Appendix 2

*Budget and Financial Operations for "Mt. Walkabout" devised by*
*J. Ripley, Economist, Department of Agriculture, Perth, Western Australia*

J. L. Boots leases Mt; Walkabout Station 230 km NE of Carnarvon. The lease
expires in 2015. Mt; Walkabout is a 200,000-ha Pastoral lease operated by
J. L. Boots as sole trader. Rainfall is 200 mm per year.

Mr. Boots is married and has two dependent children, a boy of 12 and a girl of 7.

He is employed on the station on a full-time basis.

The station employs 3 casual, 2 permanent and one family (J. L. Boots) employee
with a total wages (including J. L. Boots) bill of $18,500.

The station carried 15,000 sheep and 200 cattle. The flock is made up of:

| | |
|---|---|
| 5000 ewes | 100 cows |
| 4500 wethers | 100 mixed-aged sex cattle |
| 2500 hoggets | |
| 2750 ewes | |
| 200 rams | |

Mr. Boots expects 2750 lambs annually in June-July from 5000 ewes. He shears
12,100 sheep each year in August. The wool cut is 4.2 kg for ewes, 5.0 kg for
wethers, 3.7 kg for weaners and 6 kg for rams. He anticipates wool prices to
hold at 1973/74 levels.

Each year 1000 to 2000 old sheep are sold and about 40 cattle are marketed as
steers.

Mr. Boots' assets and liabilities at the opening of the financial year were made
up as follows:

| Assets | $ | Liabilities | $ |
|---|---|---|---|
| Pastoral lease value | 90,000 | | |
| Urban land freehold | | | |
| 3 ha | 25,000 | | |
| Livestock | | | |
| Sheep | 62,150 | | |
| Cattle | 10,000 | | |
| Plant and Vehicles | 20,200 | | |
| Savings Bank a/c | 1,380 | | |
| Stock firm credit | 20,000 | Overdraft Carnarvon | |
| Life Assurance at | | Bank | 2500 |
| surrender value | 11,300 | Sundry Creditors | 1200 |
| | $240,030 | | $3700 |
| | | Equity | $236,330 |

Mr. Boots' assets under Plant and Vehicles and the improvement made in the year 1973/74 are set out below:

MT. WALKABOUT STATION

List of Plant

| | Date of purchase | Price | June 1974 Market value | June 1974 Tax value | 1973/74 Depreciation |
|---|---|---|---|---|---|
| Aeroplane | 1970 | 8000 | 6000 | nil | 2000 |
| I.H. truck | 1967 | 2500 | 1200 | nil | – |
| Landrover | 1964 | 2500 | 500 | nil | – |
| Yamaha motor-bike 250 cm$^3$ | 1971 | 700 | 400 | 485 | 105 |
| Yamaha motor-bike 250 cm$^3$ | 1971 | 700 | 400 | 485 | 105 |
| Yamaha motor-bike 250 cm$^3$ | 1971 | 700 | 400 | 485 | 105 |
| Holden utility | 1972 | 2900 | 1900 | 2030 | 435 |
| Holden utility | 1974 | 2600 | 300 | nil | 390 |
| Yamaha motor-bike | 1974 | 600 | 400 | 402 | 198 |
| Suzuki motor-bike | 1974 | 600 | 400 | 402 | 198 |
| Cat grader | 1974 | 6000 | 5000 | 5100 | 900 |
| Car holden* | 1974 | 3800 | 3300 | | 285 |
| | | | $20,200 | | $4721 |

*50 per cent personal use.

Improvements – mostly written down to nil in 1973/74.

| | | |
|---|---|---|
| Capital expenditure 1973/74 – shearing shed | 22,000 | 440 |
| Sheep yards | 2500 | 125 |
| Water supply piping (not metal) | 2500 | 125 |
| Water supply bores | 5000 | 375 |
| Water supply tanks (metal) | 2800 | 280 |
| Fencing | 8000 | 240 |
| | $42,800 | $1725 |

During the year 1974/75 Mr. J. L. Boots sold cattle in December and January, wool and sheep in August and September, paid income tax of $62,100 in February-March, purchased rams and a motor-bike. He also had his stock firm limit on finance raised from $20,000 to $50,000.

The Livestock Schedule shows the livestock changes from the beginning of the year to the end of the year.

## MT. WALKABOUT STATION

### Livestock Schedule - Sheep Cattle 1974/75

| Sheep | No. | $/hd | $ | Cattle | No. | $/hd | $ |
|---|---|---|---|---|---|---|---|
| Opening | | | | Opening | | | |
| Ewes | 5000 | | | Cows | 100 | | |
| Wethers | 4500 | | | Other | 100 | | |
| Weaners | 2500 | | | Bulls | 3 | | |
| Rams | 200 | | | | | | |
| Purchases | 40 | 40 | 1600 | Purchases | | | |
| Births | 2750 | | | Births | | | |
| Total Sources | 14,990 | | | Total Sources | 253 | | |
| Deaths | | | | Deaths | | | |
| Ewes | 500 | | | Cattle | 10 | | |
| Wethers | 250 | | | | | | |
| Rams | 40 | | | | | | |
| Weaners | 100 | | | | | | |
| Lambs | 250 | | | | | | |
| Ration | | | | | | | |
| Wethers | 100 | | | | | | |
| Sales | | | | Sales | | | |
| Ewes | 700 | 3 | 2100 | Steers | 40 | 50 | 2000 |
| Wethers | 850 | 4 | 3400 | | | | |
| Closing | | | | Closing | | | |
| Ewes | 5000 | | | Cows | 100 | | |
| Wethers | 4500 | | | Other | 100 | | |
| Weaners | 2500 | | | Bulls | 3 | | |
| Rams | 200 | | | | | | |
| Total Sources | 14,990 | | 5500 | Total Sources | 253 | | 2000 |

| Wool Production | No. | Kg/hd | Total | | No. | Kg/hd | Total |
|---|---|---|---|---|---|---|---|
| Ewes | 5000 | 4.2 | 21,000 | | | | |
| Wethers | 4500 | 5.0 | 22,500 | | | | |
| Weaners | 2500 | 3.7 | 9250 | | | | |
| Rams | 200 | 6.0 | 1200 | | | | |
| Total Production | | | | | | | |

| Proceeds | 53,950 kg @ 120c* |
|---|---|
| | $64,740 |

*150c in 1973/74.

The Cash Flow Budget for Mt. Walkabout for 1974/75 is set out below:

MT. WALKABOUT STATION

Cash Flow Budget for 1974/75

| INCOME | Budget Total | O/N | D/J | F/M | A/M | J/J | A/S |
|---|---|---|---|---|---|---|---|
| Sales: | | | | | | | |
| Cattle | 2000 | | 2000 | | | | |
| Sheep | 5500 | | | | | | 5500 |
| Wool 53,950 kg 120c | 64,740 | | | | | | 64,740 |
| Total | 72,240 | | 2000 | | | | 70,240 |
| OUTGOING | | | | | | | |
| Variable costs | | | | | | | |
| Fodder | 500 | | | 500 | | | |
| Fuel and oil | 3200 | 300 | 500 | 500 | 500 | 700 | 700 |
| Shearing - 12,200 @ 75c | 9150 | | | | | | 9150 |
| Bales 700 dip, etc. 800-stock medi & tags | 1500 | | | | | 1500 | |
| Stores | 2800 | | 700 | | 700 | 700 | 700 |
| Wages 2 persons | 10,000 | 1600 | 1600 | 1600 | 1600 | 1600 | 2000 |
| Other casual 30 wks | 3000 | | | | 1000 | 1000 | 1000 |
| | 4000 | 600 | 600 | 600 | 600 | 600 | 1000 |
| Stock purchases | | | | | | | |
| Rams - 40 | 1600 | | 1600 | | | | |
| Repairs & maintenance | | | | | | | |
| Vehicles | 3500 | 500 | 600 | 600 | 600 | 600 | 600 |
| Other | 3000 | 500 | 500 | 500 | 500 | 500 | 500 |
| General | | | | | | | |
| Accountancy | 600 | | 600 | | | | |
| Education expenses | 1500 | | 500 | | 500 | | 500 |
| Income tax | 62,100 | | | 62,100 | | | |
| Insurance | 950 | 950 | | | | | |
| Land rent P.L. | 1200 | | | | | 1200 | |
| Motor vehicle licence | 250 | | 250 | | | | |
| Rates & taxes | 1400 | 1400 | | | | | |
| Stamps, phone, telegrams | 1200 | 200 | 200 | 200 | 200 | 200 | 200 |
| Subscriptions | 200 | | | 200 | | | |
| Super. & life ass. | 1000 | | | | 1000 | | |
| Travelling exps. | 400 | 200 | | 200 | | | |
| Vermin control | 300 | | 300 | | | | |
| Finance | | | | | | | |
| int. working a/cs | 5000 | 600 | 700 | 800 | 1000 | 1200 | 700 |
| Capital plant & vehicles motor-bike | 800 | | | | | 800 | |
| TOTAL | 119,150 | 6850 | 8650 | 67,800 | 8200 | 10,600 | 17,050 |
| Account open $20,000 CR. | | +13,150 | +6500 | -65,300 | -69,500 | -80,100 | -26,910 |

Although Mr. Boots started the year well he ended in debt and with a severe liquidity problem.  The following actions could have improved the financial situation.

Income tax amounted to $62,000, but $31,000 of this amount is provisional tax against current income.  Mr. Boots could arrange for a reassessment of provisional tax and this would reduce his tax bill to $37,000.

Urban land could be sold and should realize $15,000.  Alternatively a mortgage for $10,000 could be arranged.

Deferment of accounts is unlikely to succeed, although the fuel company might be approachable.

Labour reduction is possible with casual employees but not on permanent employees because of difficulties in recruitment in the future.

Sale of cattle may involve heavy taxation if the timing of the sales is not chosen carefully.

Refinancing of the costs incurred in the property development programme of 1973/74 might be possible through a loan from the Commonwealth Development Bank.  It might also be possible to restructure the debts with the aid of the Rural Reconstruction Authority.

The motor-bike purchase planned in 1974/75 need not be proceeded with and the aircraft might be sold.  However, this latter move could make management of the station difficult in terms of stock water and fence inspection and mustering.

Off-farm income would be difficult to develop.  Because there is no town there is no opportunity for Mrs. Boots to obtain work in the way that wives have been able to do in some other pastoral districts.

Basically, Mr. Boots needed to be more aware of his expenditure and curtail it as wool prices went down below his estimate of 150c per kg, which would have given him a small operating profit, to 120c per kg which put him into a severe liquidity position.

Taxation, together with probate and estate duties, can cause problems, but early action generally achieves a satisfactory solution.

## Appendix 3

An example of an individual station assessment illustrating the area and condition of rangeland types, remedial rangelands to be withdrawn from grazing use, and the Stock Unit Capacity.

Rangelands were placed into three categories for the purpose of station assessment. These were acceptable (A), supervised (S), and remedial (R).

*Acceptable rangelands* were those which showed no signs of erosion although they could have deteriorated in respect of their pastures.

*Supervised rangelands* were those which showed some signs of erosion in parts though the record from traverse observations showed that this was not general. Pastures were degraded and the rangelands were in danger of deteriorating to an unacceptable condition if grazing pressure was continued. On different stations the same rangeland may be in supervised condition, or acceptable or even in remedial condition.

*Remedial rangelands* were those which showed areas of major erosion and pasture degradation. Their condition was such that further use was unadvisable since deterioration could only continue and reduce the rangelands even lower in condition. Some of these remedial rangelands were so badly degraded that recovery in even 25 years was considered to be unlikely. Some grassy rangelands such as Landor type were also profoundly degraded and ideally should have been placed in the remedial category. However, since they are not prone to water erosion and tend to resist wind erosion they were placed in the category for supervised use.

The allocation to these classes of condition was made on the basis of the traverse record, field notes taken on the survey and the data sheets for the rangeland evaluation sites. A summary of the condition of all rangelands was given as a short table.

The areas which should be removed from use were designated in respect of the rangelands in the table for each station and their general location on the station was also described. The suggested sheep unit capacity for each station was also given. These were the stocking rates that should apply until recovery was achieved.


*Gascoyne Station—Upper Gascoyne Shire*

Gascoyne station is wholly on the Basin.

Fifty-seven traverse recordings were made on eleven rangeland types and twelve range evaluation sites were selected on the property. The lease has been subjected to very heavy stocking rates in the past and this is reflected in its present condition. As Permian basin pastures form a large part of the area it is extremely degraded.

Two hundred and eighty-three $km^2$ should be withdrawn from use. These include parts of the Wooramel, Jimba and Jingle in the Permian Province and Thomas in the Archean block. All have suffered from surface stripping, gullying and gross changes in pastoral condition.

The remaining 1475 $km^2$ could be used under supervised use, but at much lower rates than the current ECC of 1:10 ha. A rate of about 1:15 is recommended to give a sheep unit capacity of 10,000 provided all the 1475 $km^2$ of available land is used. It should be noted that the property was supporting more sheep units than its ECC (i.e. 11,100 or 1:41).

Pastoral Inspectors' reports on previous occasions refer to the erosion on the property.

The area to be excluded from use extends from the shed to Western Creek.

Traverse Summary - Fifty-seven Observation Sites

| Wind erosion | %* | Water erosion | % | Condition | % |
|---|---|---|---|---|---|
| None | 17 | None | 30 | Pristine | 0 |
| Sheeting | 21 | Sealing | 17 | Good | 2 |
| Surface redistribution | 39 | Minor rilling | 19 | Vegetation | 56 |
| Hummocking | 23 | Stripping | 18 | Vegetation degraded; some erosion | 42 |
| Major drift | 0 | Lower slope gullies | 16 | Vegetation degraded; major erosion | 0 |
| | | Upper & lower slope gullies | 0 | | |

*Per cent of the fifty-seven observations.

84

STATION: GASCOYNE    1758 km$^2$

| Pasture group | Rangeland types | km$^2$ | Accept-able | Super-vised | Remedial |
|---|---|---|---|---|---|
| Hill | Moogooloo | 119 | | + | |
| | Pells | 163 | + | | |
| | Agamemnon | 101 | + | | |
| | Fossil | 62 | + | | |
| | Augustus | 3 | + | | |
| Stony short grass-forb | Thomas | 36 | | + | |
| Stony chenopod | Wooramel | 233 | | 130 | 104 |
| | Sandiman | 277 | | + | |
| | Mantle | 176 | | + | |
| | Nadarra | 18 | | + | |
| | Durlacher | 18 | | + | |
| | Jimba | 347 | | 189 | 158 |
| Chenopod | Jingle | 21 | | | + |
| Wandarrie | | | | | |
| Mulga short grass-forb | | | | | |
| Sand-dune halophyte | Bidgemia | 44 | | + | |
| | Lyons | 8 | | + | |
| Sandplain | Yalbalgo | 67 | + | | |
| River | Gascoyne | 65 | + | | |
| Total area on Basin | | 1758 | 461 | 1015 | 283 |

Area to be removed from use    283 km$^2$

Area available for grazing    1475 km$^2$

Stock Unit Capacity (SUC)    10,100
(in sheep equivalents)

Appendix 4

JIMBA RANGELAND TYPE   1860 km$^2$

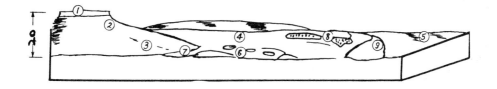

| Unit | % | Landform | Soils | Potential | Condition |
|------|---|----------|-------|-----------|-----------|
| 1 | 15 | Flattened low ridges and platforms | Red brown or brown clay of variable depth in P.M. pH 6-8 and with out-crop | Moderate; scattered useful shrubs | Vegetation degraded; erosion gutters and gullies |
| 2 | 10 | Pebble-strewn upper slopes | Brown gritty clay up to 60 cm, pH 8-8.5, scattered cobbles and boulders with pebble strew | Moderate; scattered useful shrubs | Vegetation degraded; erosion gutters and gullies |
| 3 | 10 | Lower slopes with drainage foci | Red-brown to brown gritty to fine clay, pH 7, of variable depth to 90 cm, pH 6-8 | Moderate; palatable shrubs | Vegetation degraded; erosion gutters and gullies |
| 4 | 30 | Diffuse drainage plains | Brown clay of variable depth, pH 7.5-9, with and without pebble strew | Good; many palatable, useful shrubs (chenopods) | Vegetation degraded; major erosion, sealing, gutters, gullies and truncation |
| 5 | 10 | Terraced tributary drainage slopes | Vegetated areas; brown fine clay to 90 cm, pH 7.5, bare areas; brown clay to fine clay with pebble strew | Moderate; good useful shrubs and grasses | Vegetation degraded; restricted erosion |
| 6 | 5 | Crab-holes and major drainage foci | Brown clay to more than 90 cm, pH 7-8 | Fair to moderate; useful shrubs and grasses | Vegetation degraded; little erosion |

| Unit | % | Landform | Soils | Potential | Condition |
|------|---|----------|-------|-----------|-----------|
| 7 | 5 | Tributary sheet flow drainage | Brown clay, pH 7–8 | Moderate; useful shrubs and grasses | Vegetation degraded; erosion gutters |
| 8 | 10 | Sandy banks | Red–brown loamy and greater than 90 cm, pH 6.5 | Moderate; useful shrubs and grasses | Vegetation degraded; hummocking of sand |
| 9 | 5 | Drainage lines | Up to 200 m wide, braided; incision to 1.2 m | Moderate; much good grass | Vegetation degraded; some banks consolidated, others with gutters |

Jimba rangeland type is an alluvial plain confined to the Permian basin west of the Precambrian block. The present pattern is very confused, a reflection of the sedimentary geology, over–use and regional topography. The plains are based on the Artinskian series of Permian sediments which are essentially free of boulders and pebbles, and which give rise to plains which generally have no pebble and cobble mantles. In this way, Jimba differs from Mantle, which is derived from the Sakmarian series Permian sediments, and in which tillitic, boulder and pebble-studded sediments are common. The absence of the pebble mantle has resulted in different erosion patterns in the two groups. Erosion is very severe in Jimba, and much reduced in extent in the stone–shielded pastures of Mantle rangeland type.

Flattened ridges and domes up to 15 m high above the drainage lines are characteristic. They are covered with cobbles and pebbles, and have outcropping areas which may be partially weathered. Stony slopes extend away from the ridges, sloping at 1:50 to 1:75, and frequently dissected by fine creeklines. Lower slopes with cobbles and pebbles, but with reduced regional slope and local drainage foci, unite these upper slopes with the diffuse drainage plains. The plains are frequently bare of stone cover and exhibit severe sheet and gully erosion. They slope at 1:250 to 1:750. Terraced, tributary drainage slopes, in which there are bands of stone-free clayey soils transverse to the slope, are separated from each other by long transverse stony areas. These drainage slopes occupy areas above the drainage plains in some instances and are common where the regional slope is about 1:100 to 1:250. The terraces are up to 1.6 km long and usually less than 30 m wide. Large crab–holes (gilgai) and other local drainage areas occur on the drainage plains. These may be up to 400 m in diameter. Discharge water from the drainage plains frequently collects in sluggish swamps which have very heavy clay soils. Sandy banks are found on the drainage plains. Some may be aggregated by wind to form minor sand–dune–claypan complexes which are up to 8 m high, but others may have resulted from water flows in the plains and here they are elongate with the flow, and merely 1 m high and up to 500 m long. Flowlines carrying the concentrated drainage may be up to 300 m wide with sand bedloads and are often incised to 3 m and up to 15 m across.

*Pasture Degradation*

The low ridges and platforms (1) have a sparse tree cover of *Acacia victoriae*,
*A. eremea* and *A. tetragonophylla* over a variable shrub layer. Where soil conditions
are suitable, halophytic shrub species such as *Maireana polypterygia* and *Arthrocnemum*
are common. Generally these have been depleted by severe over-use. Where the soils
do not suit halophytic species, *Cassia desolata*, *C. helmsii*, *Eremophila spathulata*
and *Solanum lasiophyllum* are common. With severe degradation *Hakea priessii* often
assumes dominance and *Ptilotus obovatus* and *Corchorus wolcottii* are the major mid-
storey species.

The upper and lower slopes (2 and 3) have a sparse overstorey of *A. victoriae*,
*A. eremea* and *A. tetragonophylla* over similar species to those on the ridges.
*E. cuneifolia* may be locally important, and halophytes such as *M. polypterygia* and
*M. pyramidata* can be found on non-eroded sites. Usually the more valuable species
have been removed by grazing and the pastures are restricted to annuals and species
such as *P. polakii* beneath the tree cover.

The diffuse drainage plains (4) are so frequently eroded and degraded that it is
difficult to reconstruct the original pastures. However, remnants indicate that
halophytic shrubs such as *M. pyramidata*, *M. polypterygia* and *Arthrocnemum* were
important species, occupying from 10 per cent to 15 per cent cover beneath
scattered, taller trees. Where the soil conditions are not so alkaline, species
such as *C. sturtii*, *C. desolata* and *S. lasiophyllum* are common. With degradation
but little erosion *H. priessii*, *E. pterocarpa* and *E. cuneifolia* are the dominant
species. Where severe over-use has reduced the pasture to annuals only, *Bassia*
and *Atriplex* form the basis of the pastures beneath very scattered and stunted
*Acacia*.

The terraced drainage slopes (5) in good condition carry a sparse tree cover of
*A. tetragonophylla* and *A. eremea* above *M. pyramidata* and *M. polypterygia* with
*Eragrostis setifolia* as the ground storey. Degradation reduced the vegetation on
the clay terraces to annuals and some perennial grasses. It is doubtful if
anything but sparse annuals grew on the stoney interterrace areas, and then only
after effective rainfall.

Crab-holes (gilgai) and major drainage foci (6) support a dense marginal vegetation
in which *Eucalyptus microtheca*, *Scaevola spinescens*, *A. tetragonophylla*,
*M. pyramidata* and *H. priessii* frequently surround a vegetated claypan dominated
with *Eriachne flaccida*. The tributary sheet flow drainage areas (7) with heavy
clay soils have a vegetation rather similar to that found in Bibbingunna rangeland
type.

The sandy banks (8) are very variable though this is, in part, due to their
derivation and partly to their degradation. Low elongate banks are usually very
degraded and carry *A. tetragonophylla* and *A. sclerosperma* with *H. priessii* above
worthless species such as *Eremophila maitlandii* and *E. margarethae*. Valuable
species such as *E. latrobei*, *Rhagodia* sp. and *M. polypterygia* are found infrequently
and then only on little-used sites.

Creeklines (9) in Jimba rangeland type are often colonized with Buffel grass
(*Cenchrus ciliaris*). This has prevented any extensive erosion of the banks and
incised drainage. In the absence of this resistant cover, severe gullying can
occur beneath the tree species which include *Eucalyptus camaldulensis*,
*E. microtheca* and *Acacia citrinoviridis*. The shrub layer is usually variable and
is suppressed when Buffel grass is dominant.

This rangeland type provides very valuable pastures on the western part of the
Basin. The halophytic sections are durable and acceptable to livestock, but almost

without exception have been severely degraded by over-use to the extent that the
valuable species have been removed.  The soils derived from the Permian deposits
are highly alkaline clays which are extremely susceptible to gutter and gully
erosion, particularly when surface cover is removed.  In many instances erosion
gutters are initiated by quite small surface disturbances upslope.

A dramatic increase in the spiny shrub *Hakea priessii* has followed over-use in
this rangeland type and the situation is particularly grave on the lower slopes and
drainage plains, where this unacceptable shrub now dominates very extensive areas.

Rehabilitation will only be effected by cessation of grazing for many years.  Areas
where the parent rocks have been exposed are incapable of restoration.  In some
areas rehabilitation through reseeding could be effected, but this will be a
tedious and costly procedure.  Jimba rangeland is particularly prone to over-use
and supervision would have been necessary from the time the area was first leased.
Alternatively, much of this type should have been excluded from leases.

Dominance of the pasture by *Hakea priessii* poses a separate problem.  Protection
alone will eventually aid its demise but this will take many decades.  The low
returns per unit area common in pastoral areas make it difficult to conceive of
any other management practise which would be feasible.

In summary this rangeland type is grossly degraded and eroded (Table 4.1) and
contributes in a major way to degradation on the Basin.

Table 4.1.   Jimba Rangeland Type.  Assessment of erosion and conditions
             at 141 observation sites on traverse

| Wind erosion | % | Water erosion | % | Condition | % |
|---|---|---|---|---|---|
| None | 2 | None | 11 | Pristine | 0 |
| Sheeting | 18 | Sealing | 34 | Good | 2 |
| Surface redistribution | 63 | Minor rilling | 21 | Vegetation degraded | 70 |
| Hummocking | 17 | Stripping | 10 | Vegetation degraded; some erosion | 28 |
| Major drift | 0 | Lower slope gullies | 24 | Vegetation degraded; major erosion | 0 |
| | | Upper & lower slope gullies | 0 | | |

AUGUSTUS RANGELAND TYPE    8244 km$^2$

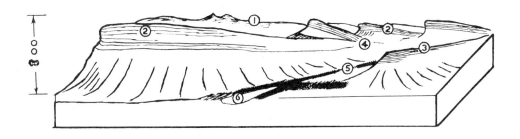

| Unit | % | Landform | Soils | Potential | Condition |
|------|-----|----------|-------|-----------|-----------|
| 1 | 40 | Mountains and summits with included slopes Northern divide | Rocks, isolated soils in pockets | Poor; inaccessible | Good |
| 2 | 25 | Ridges and rocky uplands; isolated massive hills, e.g. Mt. Augustus | Rocks, isolated soil in pockets, heavy boulder and cobble strew | Poor; partly inaccessible | Good |
| 3 | 10 | Quartzite ridges, e.g. Mt. George | Shallow rocky soils, boulder and cobble strew with prominent subconchoidal fracture | Poor; partly inaccessible | Good |
| 4 | 15 | Upper slopes and interfluves | Shallow soils with abundant stone mantle | Low, sparse scattered shrubs only | Good |
| 5 | 5 | Drainage floors | Some duplex red-brown soils, some grey clay of variable depth | Fair; some areas of good shrub pasture | Vegetation degraded; some gullies and sheet erosion |
| 6 | 5 | Incised drainage | Mostly incised into bedrock with heavy cobble bedloads | Poor | Good |

Augustus rangeland type forms the divide on the northern side of the Basin and is found in isolated monoliths penetrating almost as far as the Permian plains (Mt. Dalgety) in the south and west. The highest part of the catchment, Mt. Augustus, is 1322 m above sea level and about 721 m of relief above the plain. It is sandstone monolith standing freely in the drainage plain of the Lyons River.

Rugged mountain ranges, quartzite ridges and vast, rocky dissected uplands, all of middle Proterozoic age (Bangemall series) in the Precambrian era, form the basis of this rangeland type. Many of the sediments of the Bangemall series are comparatively soft, particularly the mudstones and lower dolomites. Geologic erosion of these strata has produced spectacular dissections and abrupt cliffs 50 to 100 m high in the divide area. These dissections are emphasized by the caps of diorite which as thin flows often surmount the Bangemall series. In some instances basaltic flows are found interbedded with the sedimentary rocks of the series.

Quartzite ridges up to 60 m high and several kilometres long on drainage plains influence the direction of major water flow. These ridges are almost completely unweathered, and the upper slopes are covered with massive boulders and large cobbles exhibiting typical subconchoidal fracture. Slopes of $6^{\circ}$ are not uncommon. Tributary slopes which descend to the plain from the ridges and lower slopes vary between 1:50 and 1:100. Flattened drainage floors which are often saline are common within the rocky uplands and carry distinctive vegetation. They are frequently strewn with flat angular "desert varnished" fragments. Major drainage within the type is incised into the bedrock and usually has cobble bedloads. This drainage is usually fine and dendritic, though major trunk drainage frequently traverses the type.

The rocky mountain summits (1) carry a stunted but moderate cover of *Acacia aneura* and *A. grasbyi* with *Grevillea nematophylla* prominent locally. *Cassia, Ptilotus* and *Eremophila* species above annuals occur beneath the low tree layer.

The ridges (2) are similar to the summits, but *Eremophila margarethae* and *E. compacta* may be characteristic of some locations, apparently the subject of some geologic control.

The quartzite ridges (3) are typically sharp and comparatively unweathered falling away steeply to lower slopes and plains. They carry a moderate cover of low *A. aneura, Solanum, Eremophila margarethae, E. freelingii, Halgania* sp. and annuals.

The upper slopes and interfluves (4) are rather similar to the foregoing, though it is noticeable that the vegetation is limited on the interfluves to scattered low shrubs such as *Eremophila freelingii* and *Acacia aneura*, but concentrated in the barely incised drainages.

The drainage floors (5) carry sparse halophytic pastures where saline conditions exist, but can also carry *Eremophila leucophylla*, perennial grasses and taller trees where the drainage is less sluggish and soil depth is above 45 cm.

The drainage (6) carries marginal vegetation where *A. aneura* is usually dense above dense *E. margarethae, E. freelingii* and *Solanum* spp.

Augustus rangeland type dominates the landscape over much of the Basin and is virtually worthless apart from the restricted areas of drainage flats where useful pastures are found.

Some of the drainage floors are badly eroded (Table 4.2) and should be rehabilitated. However, this could prove difficult as these are only found as small inclusions.

Table 4.2.  Augustus Rangeland Type.  Assessment of erosion and conditions
            at twenty-four observation sites on traverses

| Wind erosion | % | Water erosion | % | Condition | % |
|---|---|---|---|---|---|
| None | 79 | None | 76 | Pristine | 5 |
| Sheeting | 8 | Sealing | 8 | Good | 21 |
| Surface redistribution | 13 | Minor rilling | 4 | Vegetation degraded; some erosion | 67 |
| Hummocking | 0 | Stripping | 8 | Vegetation degraded; some erosion | 8 |
| Major drift | 0 | Lower slope gullies | 0 | Vegetation degraded; major erosion | 0 |
| | | Upper & lower slope gullies | 4 | | |

PHILLIPS RANGELAND TYPE   7770 km$^2$

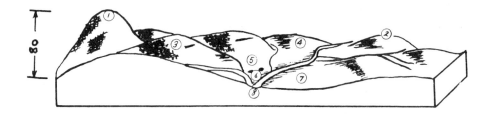

| Unit | % | Landform | Soils | Potential | Condition |
|------|---|----------|-------|-----------|-----------|
| 1 | 5 | High peaks and ridges | Rocky with pockets | Poor | Good; no erosion |
| 2 | 30 | Rounded summits | Shallow with o/c red-brown gritty clay to 38 cm on rock, pH 6, cobbles and pebbles | Low; shrubs have durability | No erosion; pasture deterioration |
| 3 | 1 | Dolerite dykes | Shallow soils with o/c and cobbles | Low; insignificant to total | No erosion; pasture deterioration |
| 4 | 30 | Rounded slopes and interfluves | Shallow soils of variable depth on rock, some o/c, pebble strew | Low; shrubs confer durability at low stocking rates | No erosion; pasture deterioration |
| 5 | 20 | Lower interfluves | Shallow brown gritty loam to rock at variable depth, pH 6-7 | Low; shrubs confer durability at low stocking rates | No erosion; pasture deterioration |
| 6 | 1 | Crabholes | Brown clay to > 90 cm, pH 6.5-7 | Fair; insignificant to total | No erosion; pasture deterioration |
| 7 | 5 | Drainage flats | Duplex soils of depths to >90 cm, pH 7-8 locally | Moderate; receiving run of; palatable pastures | Windswept and surface stripped; guttered in places, vegetation severely degraded |

| Unit | % | Landform | Soils | Potential | Condition |
|------|---|----------|-------|-----------|-----------|
| 8 | 8 | Channelled drainage | Sandy and cobbly bedloads | Moderate | No erosion; little pasture deterioration |

Phillips rangeland type occurs beneath hills and strike ridges.  The geologic erosional sequence has created extensive areas of Phillips which are unmarked by abrupt hills or violent dissection.

The high points in the type rise to about 76 m above the drainage tracts, and are usually found as quartz ridges and massive, bare, gneiss and schist-like residuals.  Rounded, cobble-strewn summits below the hills form the major part of this landscape.  Abundant low outcrop is characteristic, rising up to 30 m above the watercourses and slope at up to 5° away from the rounded summits.  Dolerite dykes up to 300 m wide traverse these summits and the elements below them.  They are often weathered in contrast to the generally unweathered rocks found in this type.

Cobble- and pebble-strew slopes extend below the summits towards the major drainage.  They are found as rounded interfluves dividing fine, channelled watercourses, and slope regionally at 1:70 to 1:90.  In the lower parts local drainage foci and minor crabholes occur above the sluggish drainage flats.  The low flats have a typically sluggish drainage discharging into more defined and dissected creeklines, or they may occur as minor deltas between more active streamlines.  The major drainages can be up to 60 m wide with 2 m of incision and carrying variable bedloads.  The bedloads are usually sandy, with minor areas of cobbles and pebbles.

The vegetation is the product of a shallow, rocky soil and on units 1 to 5 is characterized by stunted, sparse *Acacia aneura*, *A. kempeana* and *A. tetragonophylla* above a moderately sparse layer of *Cassia helmsii*, *C. pruinosa*, *C. charlesiana*, *Eremophila fraseri*, *E. cuneifolia*, *E. freelingii*, *Solanum* spp., *Ptilotus* spp. and *Rhagodia*.

On the duplex soils (7) *Arthrocnemum*, *Maireana polypterygia* and *Acacia victoriae* occur infrequently.

The larger creeklines and watercourses are lined by dense *A. aneura*, *A. eremea*, *A. tetragonophylla* and *A. sclerosperma* and dense shrubs (8).  Perennial grasses such as *Chrysopogon* occur on the non-saline alluvial flats associated with terminal tributary drainage.  Generally the ground flora is limited to annual grasses and forbs.

The drainage foci and crabholes (6) are ringed with *A. tetragonophylla* and *A. victoriae* which surround a central core of dense *Eriachne flaccida* or *Eragrostis setifolia* and sparse shrubs.

This rangeland type provides only ephemeral ground pastures and the shrubs provide only limited amounts of durable pasture in times of stress.  The sluggish drainage flats are overgrazed, and eroded, and contribute to the increased discharge of rivers on the Basin.  Without protection and remedial treatment they will continue to deteriorate and erode.  The duplex soils on which they are based are unstable and need careful treatment.

The eroded drainage flats contribute to erosion; those degraded ones would be impossible to rehabilitate.  Increased run-on due to sealing adds to erosion hazards downslope (Table 4.3).

Table 4.3.  Phillips Rangeland Type.  Assessment of erosion and conditions
           at 216 observation sites on traverses

| Wind erosion | % | Water erosion | % | Condition | % |
|---|---|---|---|---|---|
| None | 45 | None | 52 | Pristine | 1 |
| Sheeting | 29 | Sealing | 14 | Good | 7 |
| Surface redistribution | 24 | Minor rilling | 12 | Vegetation degraded | 71 |
| Hummocking | 2 | Stripping | 11 | Vegetation degraded; some erosion | 21 |
| Major drift | 0 | Lower slope gullies | 11 | Vegetation degraded; major erosion | 0 |
| | | Upper & lower slope gullies | 0 | | |

YINNIETHARRA RANGELAND TYPE   790 km$^2$

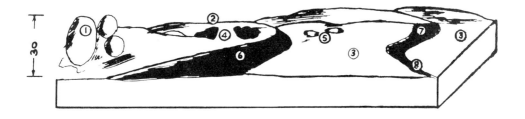

| Unit | % | Landform | Soils | Potential | Condition |
|------|---|----------|-------|-----------|-----------|
| 1 | 10 | Isolated domes and tors | None | Low; shrubs have use in stress periods | Good |
| 2 | 15 | Upper interfluves | Shallow soils, abundant out-crop | Low; shrubs have use in stress periods | Vegetation degraded |
| 3 | 40 | Flat plains | Some duplex soils, other with sparse pebbles on red-brown gritty clay to 40 cm | Low to moderate, depending upon vegetation | Vegetation degraded; gullied and sheeted |
| 4 | 3 | Low tors | None | Low | Good |
| 5 | 2 | Crab-holes | Brown clay 90 cm | Moderate, but insignificant to total | Vegetation degraded; some siltation deposits |
| 6 | 15 | Broad, braided drainage | Up to 180 m wide sandy bedloads | Fair | Vegetation degraded; gullies |
| 7 | 5 | Grove patterns | Groves—red-brown gritty clay 90 cm, pH 7, inter-grove—variable to 40 cm, red-brown gritty clay | Fair | Vegetation degraded |
| 8 | 10 | Concentrated flow lines | | Fair to moderate | Vegetation degraded; gullied and sheeted |

D. D*

Yinnietharra rangeland type is dominated by isolated granite domes and tors up to 30 m high. Where they are grouped together to form an area of generally higher ground, rounded, upper interfluves sloping at 1:50 regionally, with abundant surface outcrop, extend from their bases towards broad, flattened or slightly convex plains. These flattened plains may be up to 5 km long and 1.5 km wide between streamlines or watercourses. Low granite tors and crab-holes are found scattered on the plains which feed their run-off into broad flattened areas of concentrated flow and sandy watercourses up to 200 m wide in the lowest parts. Grove-intergrove situations are common where the regional slope approximates 1:250 and water flow is concentrated.

Around the tors and ridges (1 and 4) *Acacia tetragonophylla, Eremophila exilifolia* and *Solanum lasiophyllum* are common.

The upper interfluves (2) support stunted and very sparse *Acacia aneura, A. victoriae* and *A. eremea* over a variable sparse shrub cover of *Eremophila fraseri, E. freelingii, E. cuneifolia, Cassia helmsii* and *Rhagodia.* Cover ranges between 3 and 5 per cent.

The broad flattened plains (3) support a variable vegetation depending upon the flow of drainage. In the more saline or sluggish drainage sections *Frankenia, Maireana polypterygia* and *Maireana* spp. are found beneath *Eremophila pterocarpa, E. cuneifolia* and scattered trees. This situation was rarely found in the field due to severe over-use. With over-use the valuable *Frankenia* and *Maireana* spp. were absent.

Crab-holes (5) found on the plains have a characteristic ring of vegetation of dense trees such as *Acacia victoriae, A. tetragonophylla* and *A. sclerosperma* over a reduced shrub layer characterized by *Scaevola spinescens, Solanum* and *Rhagodia.* The central portion of the crab-holes carry variable amounts of *Eragrostis* and *Eriachne.*

Groves (7) marginal to or above the more concentrated drainage areas support a typical vegetation of moderately dense mulga over shrubs and grasses.

Broad, flattened, braided and sandy drainage lines (6) and areas of concentrated flow (8), characteristic of the pattern, support a variable cover of *Acacia aneura* and *A. eremea* over scattered shrubs and grasses. These areas are frequently degraded, especially where the inflow from upper slopes has caused recent incision and gullying.

Yinnietharra rangeland type provides valuable pastures on its plains and flow lines and these are usually degraded, gullied and sealed. Areas of outcrop and with low hills are poorly productive and carry shrubs and scattered ephemerals. Although the shrubs are durable under stress they cannot support many stock.

Where the lower plains are extensive this rangeland type contributes to erosion to a considerable degree (Table 4.4). Run-off can be expected to be high.

Table 4.4. Yinnietharra Rangeland Type. Assessment of erosion and conditions
at forty-one observation sites on traverses

| Wind erosion | % | Water erosion | % | Condition | % |
|---|---|---|---|---|---|
| None | 5 | None | 15 | Pristine | 0 |
| Sheeting | 51 | Sealing | 19 | Good | 0 |
| Surface redistribution | 39 | Minor rilling | 37 | Vegetation degraded | 76 |
| Hummocking | 5 | Stripping | 19 | Vegetation degraded; some erosion | 24 |
| Major drift | 0 | Lower slope gullies | 10 | Vegetation degraded; major erosion | 0 |
| | | Upper & lower slope gullies | 0 | | |

THREE RIVERS RANGELAND TYPE    4504 km$^2$

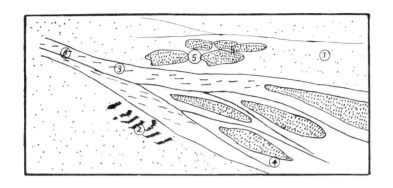

| Unit | % | Landform | Soils | Potential | Condition |
|------|---|----------|-------|-----------|-----------|
| 1 | 50 | Alluvial plains | Red-brown gritty clay on hard pan at variable depth, pH 6-7, extensive areas either sealed or have a stone mantle | Fair; shrubby pastures | Vegetation degraded generally eroded, major erosion in parts |
| 2 | 2 | Groves | Red-brown sandy loam to clay loam on hard pan at > 60 cm | Fair; shrubby pastures | As above |
| 3 | 20 | Alluvial plains receiving concentrated flow | Brown gritty clay on hard pan 60 cm, pH 6, extensive areas sealed | Fair; shrubby pastures | As above |
| 4 | 15 | Sandbanks | Red-brown sand to > 90 cm, pH 5.5-6 | Fair; some perennial grasses | As above |
| 5 | 10 | Interbanks | Red-brown clay on hard pan, pH 6 | Low | As above |
| 6 | 3 | Channelled drainage | | Fair | Vegetation degraded, some erosion |

Three Rivers rangeland type occupies 6.35 per cent of the Basin and is the dominant landscape form of the eastern tributary plains.  It is frequently sealed, guttered, scalded and stripped.

The type is commonly found as a large, non-saline, alluvial plain sloping at about 1:500, though occasionally less. The plains which carry sheet flow may be up to 11 km wide and 10 km long. They discharge their water into trunk or tributary drainage. Some areas of more concentrated flow may be braided, or may be marked by a locally dense shrubby vegetation cover. Sandbanks up to 0.3 m high and 1.6 km long are common on the plains. They extend, longitudinally with the slope, and mostly at the margins of sheet flow areas. Channelled areas may occur in the lines of concentrated flow. Down slope, the flat tributary plains become scalded and stripped, and present a different aspect in this condition compared to their original state.

The flat alluvial plains (1) carry sparse *Acacia aneura* up to 4 m high, and very scattered tall *A. pruinocarpa* up to 9 m high, above a variable shrub later dominated by *Eremophila fraseri* and *Solanum lasiophyllum*. Other shrub species such as *E. georgei, E. margarethae, E. freelingii, Ptilotus obovatus* and *Cassia* spp. are common. In the undegraded state *Maireana* species and *Rhagodia* are common, but these disappear with over-use. The herbaceous perennial *Ptilotus schwartzii* can be common in some situations and occurs with ephemerals after rains. Total perennial species cover on the alluvial plains lies between 5 and 8 per cent. Where the soil surface is pebble strewn, the vegetation is much sparser and more stunted. These areas are more prevalent upslope and tend merely to discharge water on the sealed areas below. The principal pastures on these are ephemerals.

The grove and intergrove complexes (2) are comparatively minor constituents of the total pasture and support *A. aneura* and variable shrubs.

The plains with concentrated flow (3) have pastures rather similar to those on the plains with more diffuse flow. Cover on these areas can be as high as 10 or 12 per cent and consists of *A. aneura, A. pruinocarpa* and *A. tetragonophylla* with *A. craspedocarpa* in the lowest parts. The shrub cover is little different, but as the soil is commonly deeper, the perennial grass *Chrysopogon latifolius* becomes common among denser annual grasses and forbs.

The sandy banks (4) carry *A. aneura, A. tetragonophylla, Canthium* sp. and sparse *Hakea lorea* above a shrub layer dominated by *Eremophila leucophylla, Cassia* spp., *Solanum* sp. and perennial tussock grasses. Under conditions of over-use the perennial grasses and useful shrubs disappear.

The interbanks (5) carry a very sparse cover of low shrubs; *Eremophila fraseri* and *Cassia* sp. predominate under very sparse and stunted *A. aneura*.

The channelled drainages (6) carry dense marginal vegetation similar to that found in the concentrated flow areas, though in the areas of deep incision *Eucalyptus camaldulensis* may be common.

This rangeland type produces fair ephemeral pastures with scattered palatable shrubs when it is in good condition. As it is a unit of tributary drainage it is subject to frequent run-on water and hence has the potential to produce ephemeral pastures when the total rainfall may be insufficient in less-favoured sites. For this reason the type has been severely over-used. The absence of a pebble strew and the particular soil type, combined with this over-use, have produced extensive sealing, gullying and erosion. In many instances soil stripping has reduced the alluvial plain to hard pan exposure which is quite incapable of producing pasture and incapable of rehabilitation. It is significant that those properties selected early in the settlement of the catchment and subjected to continuous and heavy use by sheep, have large areas of Three Rivers type, almost all of which are severely degraded. Rehabilitation will be extremely slow. No use is the only technique of regeneration likely to be effective.

The traverse record (Table 4.5) indicates that this type is severely degraded and eroded.  Over one-third shows moderate to severe erosion and must contribute, in a large measure, to the total erosion situation on the catchment.

Table 4.5.  Three Rivers Rangeland Type.  Assessment of erosion and conditions at 290 observation sites on traverses

| Wind erosion | % | Water erosion | % | Condition | % |
|---|---|---|---|---|---|
| None | 10 | None | 13 | Pristine | 1 |
| Sheeting | 29 | Sealing | 58 | Good | 6 |
| Surface redistribution | 52 | Minor rilling | 6 | Vegetation degraded | 51 |
| Hummocking | 8 | Stripping | 17 | Vegetation degraded; some erosion | 38 |
| Major drift | 1 | Lower slope gullies | 6 | Vegetation degraded; major erosion | 4 |
| | | Upper & lower slope gullies | 0 | | |

LANDOR RANGELAND TYPE    1285 km$^2$

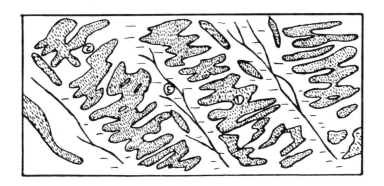

| Unit | % | Landform | Soils | Potential | Condition |
|------|---|----------|-------|-----------|-----------|
| 1 | 40 | Wandarrie banks | Red-brown sand to sandy loam with depth to 90 cm on hard pan, pH 6-7 | Moderate to good; perennial grasses and good shrubs | Vegetation degraded; marginal erosion |
| 2 | 30 | Interbanks | Shallow red-brown sandy or gritty clay on hard pan, pH 6.5, sealed surfaces | Low; annual pastures only and sparse shrubs | Vegetation degraded; sealing |
| 3 | 30 | Drainage floors | As above, often with locally higher areas with sparse mantles of weathered pebbles | Low; annual pastures only and sparse shrubs local benefits from run-on water | Vegetation degraded; some surface stripping on wide fronts down slope |

Landor rangeland type is associated with the alluvial drainage plains found in the east of the area and is rare on the Permian basin.

The type consists of low "Wandarrie banks" up to 1 m high, sometimes achieving a length of 3 km and up to 400 m wide. These banks are disposed on a drainage plain with marked through sheet flow. The banks and the associated interbanks occur on slightly higher areas between the lines of more concentrated sheet flow.

Landor rangeland type is characterized by the occurrence of "Wandarrie" grasses on the banks (1). These drought-evading perennial grasses *Monachather paradoxa, Thyridolepis mitchelliana, Eragrostis xerophila* and *Eriachne helmsii* occur beneath a moderate canopy of up to 10 per cent tree cover, of such species as *Grevillea nematophylla*, *Acacia aneura*, *A. pruinocarpa*, *A. grasbyi* and *A. tetragonophylla*. A variable shrub layer contributing to 10 per cent cover occurs beneath the tree layer. Species such as *Eremophila leucophylla*, *E. margarethae*, *Prostanthera*, *Solanum lasiophyllum*, *Cassia sturtii*, *C. helmsii* and *Rhagodia* sp. assume dominance in specific locations. Over-use in sheep-grazing country has reduced the pastures to sparse trees over the unpalatable *E. helmsii* and annual grasses such as *Aristida contorta* and *Eriachne aristidea*. Over-use by cattle appears to result in a loss of grass species only.

The interbanks and lines of through drainage (2 and 3) have very similar pastures in which *A. aneura*, *A. tetragonophylla*, *A. pruinocarpa* and *Grevillea nematophylla* occur as a sparse canopy (about 0.5 to 1.0%) over sparse shrubs such as *Eremophila margarethae*, *E. fraseri*, *Cassia sturtii*, *C. helmsii*, *Ptilotus obovatus* and *S. lasiophyllum*. Herbaceous perennials such as *P. schwartzii* may be common after good rains. The ground flora is never more than sparse grasses and forbs.

Landor rangeland type can provide valuable grass pastures which respond rapidly to rain. However, over-use has produced pastures which are ephemeral. Species such as *A. contorta* and *E. aristidea* which are of low value and acceptability have become dominant. In this degraded condition the pastures are of doubtful value. Rehabilitation involving rest after good summer rains is feasible and can be effected comparatively easily. Future use would then be dictated by species composition and vigour.

The areas of sheet flow are extensively sealed, the soil surface being stripped away in a "step-terracing" erosion form on wide fronts down slope. Where water flow rates are substantially increased the edges of the fringing banks are significantly eroded. With severe over-use by sheep, the sandy banks have become hummocked and are now subject to sand drift (Table 4.6).

Table 4.6.  Landor Rangeland Type.  Assessment of erosion and conditions at sixty-two observation sites on traverses

| Wind erosion | % | Water erosion | % | Condition | % |
|---|---|---|---|---|---|
| None | 18 | None | 60 | Pristine | 0 |
| Sheeting | 26 | Sealing | 31 | Good | 3 |
| Surface redistribution | 53 | Minor rilling | 6 | Vegetation degraded | 74 |
| Hummocking | 3 | Stripping | 3 | Vegetation degraded; some erosion | 20 |
| Major drift | 0 | Lower slope gullies | 0 | Vegetation degraded; major erosion | 3 |
| | | Upper & lower slope gullies | 0 | | |

GASCOYNE RANGELAND TYPE   2274 km$^2$

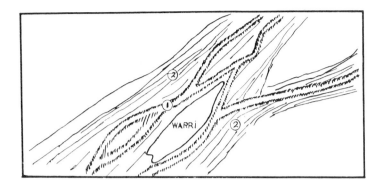

| Unit | % | Landform | Soils | Potential | Condition |
|------|---|----------|-------|-----------|-----------|
| 1 | 60 | River bottoms | Bedloads of sand and cobbles | None | Not applicable |
| 2 | 40 | Banks, islands and margins | Variable silty soils | Moderate, shrubs and perennial grasses | Vegetation degraded, margins and banks often gullied and eroded |

Gascoyne rangeland type consists of the major streamlines of the Basin, but
substantial creeks and rivers such as the Elliott, Edmund, Frederick, Daurie and
Dalgety also form part of this rangeland type.  The characteristic part of the
system is the wide, sand- or cobble-strewn beds of the major drainages.  The
channels may occur as single, deeply incised waterways, or they may occur as a
series of interlaced channels with a reduced, but still significant, incision.

As the major streamlines traverse a number of distinct rangeland types, the elements
which make up the pattern are confused.  Two major parts can be recognized.  These
are the river banks and within-pattern islands, and the river bottoms.

The banks and islands carry a dense marginal vegetation in which *Eucalyptus
camaldulensis* is found up to 20 m high.  *Acacia aneura, A. citrinoviridis
A. tetragonophylla* and *A. grasbyi* occur beneath the taller tree cover as trees up
to 8 m high.  The shrub layer is variable and consists of *A. pyrifolia, Eremophila*
spp., *Cassia* spp. and *Rhagodia* spp.  The ground flora is now frequently dominated
by *Cenchrus ciliaris* (Buffel grass), and particularly on the silty soils subject
to infrequent inundation found within the river systems and at its margins.  Buffel
grass and the above shrubs are also common on the islands and steep banks.

Gascoyne rangeland type provides good pastures on the banks, islands and margins.
Many are now colonized by *C. ciliaris* which has prevented erosion and increased

Productivity.  Where colonization has not been successful erosion has been very
severe and landscape deterioration has followed.  This is particularly noticeable
along the Gascoyne River and the Upper Lyons.  The lower and middle Lyons and the
middle Gascoyne flow through a rangeland type where plain development is
restricted.

Remedial treatment can only be expected after prolonged absence of grazing.
Structures to prevent erosion could not be used in this type.  It may be possible
to establish reseeding "nurse" plots to promote Buffel grass establishment in
areas not subject to current erosion and excessive flooding.

Erosion of Gascoyne is significant in many places and contributes in a major way
to the deteriorated condition of the range and its erosion status (Table 4.7).

Table 4.7.  Gascoyne Rangeland Type.  Assessment of erosion and conditions
            at sixty observation sites on traverses

| Wind erosion | % | Water erosion | % | Condition | % |
|---|---|---|---|---|---|
| None | 10 | None | 13 | Pristine | 0 |
| Sheeting | 7 | Sealing | 18 | Good | 9 |
| Surface redistribution | 63 | Minor rilling | 20 | Vegetation degraded | 37 |
| Hummocking | 18 | Stripping | 30 | Vegetation degraded; some erosion | 51 |
| Major drift | 2 | Lower slope gullies | 19 | Vegetation degraded; major erosion | 3 |
| | | Upper & lower slope gullies | 0 | | |

## Appendix 5

THE CHAIRMAN, PASTORAL APPRAISEMENT BOARD

*Gascoyne Sub-Committee*

ARUNDAL

1.  On the 13th, 14th and 15th of August, 1974, the Gascoyne Sub-Committee comprising Messrs. A. Pastoralist (the lessee), H. Suijdendorp (Senior Agricultural Adviser Rangeland Management Branch, Department of Agriculture) and A.D. Haldane (Pastoral Inspector Department of Lands and Surveys) inspected Station.

2.  Inspection proved the lease to be much better than the Gascoyne Report indicated. Of the 45,604 ha listed as in need of special attention, it was found that 26,142 ha were in reasonable order, leaving 19,461 ha requiring some attention.

3.  The areas requiring remedial attention are concentrated in the following paddocks:

| Paddock | Paddock area | Area affected |
|---------|-------------|---------------|
| Naggers | 11,093 ha | 259 ha |
| Hawker | 9514 ha | 1041 ha |
| Ram | 4878 ha | 2331 ha |
| House | 1554 ha | 338 ha |
| South Muscle | 8723 ha | 8623 ha |
| North Muscle | 24,493 ha | 829 ha |
| Shed | 809 ha | 809 ha |
| Dangars | 3208 ha | 1295 ha |
| Hamersley | 4635 ha | 518 ha |
| Jones | 6133 ha | 3368 ha |
| | 74,940 ha | 19,461 ha |

4.  This lease has made a remarkable recovery, chiefly due to the prolific growth of buffel grass in the past several seasons. It is the considered opinion of the Sub-Committee that nothing would be gained by closing up any one paddock.

5.  Therefore it is agreed that Dangars, Shed, South Muscle and Hamersley which in fact surround the shearing shed and are the main shearing paddocks should only be used during the shearing period. That these five paddocks will not be used for the balance of the year.

6.  That the remaining paddocks listed in para. 3 as affected, should be used, subject to normal approved pasture management in this area.

7.  The Sub-Committee considers that insufficient use has been made of the area north of the river (which includes North Muscle paddock 24,493 ha), that further fencing and, if possible, two waterpoints would improve the productivity of this area. Thus assisting to protect the "softer" country south of the river.

8.  It is agreed, that, subject to the proposals in para. 7 above being
    implemented, the total stock numbers carried should not exceed 12,500 sheep
    equivalents (grown sheep).


Signed

A. Pastoralist
A. D. Haldane
H. Suijdendorp

# China

# Combating Desertification in China

*Lanchow Institute of Glaciology, Cryopedology and Desert,*
*Chinese Academy of Sciences*

INTRODUCTION

The deserts in China (including gobi and sandy land* of the steppes) are situated
mainly in the north-western and northern regions, to a lesser extent in the north-
east, including the nine regions and provinces of Sinkiang, Kansu, Chinghai, Inner
Mongolia, Ningsia, Shensi, Liaoning, Kirin and Heilungkiang. They cover an area
of 1,095,000 square kilometres, about 11.4% of China's total area. Among them,
sand dunes (including wind-eroded land) make up 59%, and gravel gobi 41%. Since
the founding of the People's Republic of China, people of all nationalities in the
desert lands, under the leadership of Chairman Mao and the Chinese Communist Party,
embarked upon the socialist road. Under the guidelines of class struggle and the
Party's basic lines of revolution and production, they launched a concerted attack
on the problems of desertification and have achieved great successes.

DISTRIBUTION AND CHARACTERISTICS OF DESERTS IN CHINA

The deserts in China, of the temperate-zone type, are mostly situated in basins
among inland mountains, chiefly on the arid and barren lands west of $160^{o}$ east
longitude, which constitute 90% of China's total desert area. Due to their inland
location, annual rainfall in most desert lands is under 222 mm, and there are areas
where it is less than 50 mm. Annual evaporation is generally 2500 to 3000 mm, in
some areas as high as 3500 to 4000 mm. The climate is dry, aridity exceeding 4.0.
It is as high as 20 to 60 in the Tarim basin, Sinkiang, where vegetation is sparse
and shifting sand dunes dominate the scene, making up 75% of the total area of
sand dunes in this region. Only in the Uighur basin, along lake basins and
intermittent rivers inside the deserts, and on the front fringes of flood and
alluvial fans on the edges of the deserts are found stabilized and semi-stabilized
sand dunes. Irrigated oases are situated along the bank of rivers on the fringe
of the deserts and in the middle and lower parts of the flood and alluvial piedmont
plains. They are the principal agricultural centres. To the east of $160^{o}$ east
longitude are sandy steppes and semi-arid grasslands where there are only scattered
small areas of sand dunes and gobi land, making up only 10% of China's total area
of desert land. Due to their relative proximity to the oceans, they get the

---

*Sand dune areas of the steppes are referred to here as sandy land, to distinguish
 them from the deserts in arid and barren land.

effects of south-eastern monsoons. Annual rainfall is slightly higher, generally
between 200 and 450 mm. Aridity ranges from 1.5 to 4.0, and plants grow well.
Besides shrubbery, trees also grow on the sand dunes (for instance, on some sandy
land the western part of north-eastern China). Most of them are stabilized and
semi-stabilized, making up 80% of the total sand-dune areas of this region, while
shifting dunes are scattered here and there in small areas. Farmland and pastures
are located in the lake basins and along river banks in the western part of the
sandy area, often directly adjoining the sand dunes.

The deserts in China are distributed over a vast area between $35^{\circ}$ and $50^{\circ}$ north
latitude and between $75^{\circ}$ and $125^{\circ}$ east longitude, and due to their different
environmental factors such as water, heat and vegetation, they are also different
in their characteristics.

The Taklamakan desert in Sinkiang is the largest in China, with a total area of
320,700 km$^2$. It is noted for its big and tall shifting sand dunes (mostly 100 to
150 m high) and their complicated shapes (two-thirds of them are huge complex
dunes). Deep inside the desert, however, along the banks of rivers, due to the
intermittent floods and waters stored in the alluvial layers in river valleys,
there are dense forests of trees and shrubs, forming a natural green belt in the
desert. The Kurban-Tungut desert is characterized by its widespread stabilized
and semi-stabilized sand ridges. In its western part near the wind gorge, it has
features of wind-eroded topography. In the Baden Jiryn desert, the dominant
feature is its huge sand hills (200 to 300 m high, making up 68% of the total
desert area) with lakes and marshes criss-crossing among them. The Tyngeri
desert is a mixture of shifting sand and grass banks in the lake basins. The
Qaidam basin is a concentration of wind-eroded land (making up 67% of the desert
area in the basin) and sand dunes. It is China's highest desert (2600 to 3400 m
above sea level). The Maowusu sandy land on the steppes is a combination of
shifting, stabilized and semi-stabilized sand dunes and lake basins and river
valleys. The Lesser Tyngeri and the Huhunbal sandy land on the steppes to the
east consist largely of stabilized and semi-stabilized sand dunes, dotted here and
there with lakes and marshes. Among the plants that grow profusely on the sand
dunes are not only shrubs, but also big trees (several species of the pine family,
for instance). A clear knowledge of the various features of the deserts is
certainly a prerequisite to tackling the problem.

*Vis-à-vis* the particular features of the deserts in China, people of all
nationalities in the desert areas, in their long fight against the wind-sand
scourge, have developed the following measures to deal with the problem:

1. For deserts whose sand storms form a serious threat to the nearby oases, sand-
blocking forest belts on the periphery of the oases and farmland protective forest
networks within the oases are built, while on the fringe of the deserts are
constructed contain-sand-cultivate-grass areas to protect vegetation. At the same
time, in areas with the necessary conditions, full use is made of the surface water
resources near the oases to create farmland in the desert.

2. For deserts which consist chiefly of stabilized and semi-stabilized sand dunes
mixed with shifting sand, "grass kulun" are built to develop stock farming by
making rational use of the vegetation and grassland resources. In the meantime, a
mixed planting of trees, shrubs and grasses to stabilize the shifting sand and the
construction of protective forest belts and contain-sand-cultivate-grass areas
constitute an integrated programme to fight desertification.

3. On the vast expanse of land in the desert regions, full use is made of the
level land along the rivers and in the lake basins both on the fringe of the desert
and deep inside. Reservoirs are constructed to conserve waters from intermittent
floods and canals are built to bring down the melting snow from the high mountains.

In other cases, waters in the alluvial and lacustrine layers and ground water are used. Meantime, the land is levelled, soil improved, and protective forest belts constructed to reclaim the barren land and create new oases.

4. Along railroads and highways that pass through the deserts, engineering measures (such as sand shield) are taken to stabilize the sandy surface, followed by the planting of special varieties of plants to stabilize the shifting sand. In desert areas where it is difficult to stabilize the sand with plants, engineering technique is resorted to.

## ACHIEVEMENTS IN THE CONTROL OF DESERTS

Before liberation, the people of China had suffered from oppression and exploitation under imperialism, feudalism and bureaucratic capitalism. Its natural resources were subjected to destruction and plunder, and the land to irrational use. Vegetation in the desert areas was destroyed and wind and sand became a serious menace. Farmland, human dwellings, pastures and roads were often buried under the shifting sand. The deserts were constantly advancing. Take, for instance, the Maowusu sandy land situated in a corridor between barren grass plains and arid steppes. With an annual rainfall of 300 to 450 mm, it was originally a fertile piece of grassland, but as a result of the abuse of the land and its vegetation under generations of feudalistic rulers, the grassland and the stabilized sandy land were denuded of vegetation, turning the area into a land of shifting sand. Especially since the Opium War in the mid-nineteenth century, the imperialist forces made their inroad into the area, and their abuse of the land further aggravated the situation. On top of that, the Kuomintang reactionaries did their share in the further desertification of the area, until the areas of shifting sand made up 64% of the total area of sand dunes in Maowusu. The shifting sand along the Great Wall in the southern part of Maowusu was the result of human abuse for more than 250 years before liberation. The Ke-erh-hsin sandy land in the western part of the north-eastern plains suffered a similar fate. Originally a piece of grassland, it gradually degenerated, for over 200 years before liberation, into a land of shifting sand. It can therefore be concluded that the desertification of the land before liberation was the result of the destruction and plunder of natural resources by the feudalistic ruling class, the imperialists and the Kuomintang reactionaries.

Since the founding of the People's Republic of China, people of all nationalities in the desert areas got organized under the leadership of Chairman Mao and the Chinese Communist Party and, relying on the strength and wisdom of the masses and using their own hands, they launched an all-out war on the deserts. In particular since the Great Proletarian Cultural Revolution, people of all nationalities in the desert areas, under the guidelines of independence and self-reliance, were mobilized in a long and hard struggle. In the "In agriculture, learn from Tachai" mass movement, they adhered to the principle of class struggle and the basic lines of the Party, and with the heroic spirit of "man can conquer heaven", launched a stubborn struggle against the sand scourge, which had been encroaching upon farmland, pastures and highways. As a result, they created many new fields, pastures and forest lands. And in the course of the struggle, they constantly summarized and expanded the experience of the masses in combating desertification and finally won their great victory.

Today, great changes are taking place along the 10,000-li wind-sand strip in north China. In the western part of the north-eastern plains, a protective forest belt has been built that runs across the western parts of the three provinces of Liaoning, Kirin and Heilungkiang. It is an integrated protective system consisting of forest belts and networks. It is more than 800 km long, over 500 km

wide and provides protection to more than 45,000,000 mu of farmland. It is China's
largest farmland protection forest area and it has proved its efficacy in
protecting farmland against the wind-sand scourge. Take, for instance, the "East
Is Red Production Brigade at Chifeng, Liaoning, in the western part of the north-
eastern wind-sand region. Before liberation, it was a farmland subject to severe
wind-sand damage. After liberation, under the guidance of the revolutionary lines
of Chairman Mao and in a spirit of self-reliance, the masses were mobilized in
the construction of contain-sand-protect-field forests. Today, a forest cover
spreads over 36% of the area. In the meantime, land was levelled and sand removed
to create new fields, and flood waters were utilized for irrigation. As a result,
the once sandy barren land has been turned into a cropland of high and stable
yield. Since 1973, grain yield per mu has continuously exceeded 1000 catters.

In the Yuling area in Shensi Province in the southern part of the Maowusu sandy
land, 3,500,000 mu of prevent-wind-stabilize-sand forests and farmland protective
forests have been built since liberation, effectively blocking the southward
onslaught of the sand storms. Meanwhile, water resources were utilized to
rehabilitate the sandy land, and 350,000 mu of farmland have been created in the
depth of the desert. The Yangchiaopan Production Brigade in Chingpien County
levelled more than 1000 sand dunes and created over 11,000 mu of fertile farmland,
and every year since 1971 the grain yield per mu has exceeded the "Yellow River"
record. The Wo-tu-tsai-tang Production Brigade in Shenmu County, which was
surrounded by sand dunes, mobilized the masses during the "In agriculture, learn
from Tachai" movement, and in a spirit of self-reliance and under the guideline of
class struggle and the basic lines of the Party, constructed farmland protective
forest networks on the shoaly land and sand-blocking forests of shrubs, chiefly of
the sand willow variety, in the sand dune areas on the fringe of the shoaly land.
They have thus effectively conquered the sand scourge and have achieved spectacular
increases in their grain production. The Wushenchao People's Commune in Wushen
Banner, Inner Mongolia, in the northern part of the Maowusu sandy land, was in the
past a pastoral land subject to severe desertification. Shifting sand dunes
occupied 54% of the total area while available pasture land constituted only one-
third of the total land area, which was cut up by the shifting sand into scattered,
small pastures. Plant cover was sparse and the wind-sand malady was serious.
Before liberation, under the rule of the Kuomintang reactionaries, feudal lords
and herd owner classes, the stock farming industry suffered serious damage and the
people lived a miserable life. After liberation, under the leadership of Chairman
Mao and the Chinese Communist Party, the people launched their war on the deserts.
Especially since the "In agriculture, learn from Tachai" mass movement, imbued
with the spirit of "the foolish old man who moved mountains", and with a high sense
of self-reliance, they tackled the problem of 240,000 mu of shifting sand dunes and
100,000 of them have been transformed into pasture land. Today, grass kulun cover
a total area of 210,000 mu, of which 5000 mu are basic fodder cropland of high and
stable yield and 2000 mu of irrigated farmland. They have achieved great successes
in the control of the deserts and in the development of pasture land and the stock
farming industry. The cattle population today is more than five times the figure
during the early years of liberation. The total number of cattle contributed to
the state by this commune since the Great Proletarian Cultural Revolution is 142%
more than the cumulative total of the pre-cultural revolution years.

In the northern part of the Ulanpuhe desert in Inner Mongolia, a vast sand-blocking
forest belt more than 170 km long has been built since liberation which,
complemented by a contain-sand-cultivate-grass programme, constitutes a "Verdant
Great Wall", effectively blocking the encroaching sand and creating favourable
conditions for the development of agricultural production in the hinterland.

Great changes are also taking place along the wind-sand strip in the West-of-the-
River Corridor. Take, for instance, the Mingshan Production Brigade in Tunhuang,
Kansu. Surrounded on all sides by gobi sand dunes, it was in the past described

as a land where "the sand pushes man around and a mu of land produces 2 or 3 tou of grain". After liberation, under the guidance of the revolutionary line of Chairman Mao, the members of the Brigade threw themselves into the "In agriculture, learn from Tachai" mass movement. On their war on the wind and sand scourge, they adopted the strategy of "isolate them strip by strip, surround them plot by plot, use the wind to blow up the sand, and destroy them one by one" in their sand control and forest building programme. They have effectively brought the sand under control and their per mu yield of grain has exceeded the "Yangtze River" mark. Minching County is surrounded by deserts on three sides. After liberation, under the guidance of Chairman Mao's instruction to "Turn our fatherland into a green country", the people of the county have achieved great successes in controlling the sand and protecting the farmland through the building of forests and cultivation of grass.

In the desert areas to the south and north of the Tienshan mountain, the masses under the guidance of Chairman Mao's revolutionary line constructed a vast farmland protective forest network and have effectively tamed the wind-sand menace. Turfan, in Sinkiang Uighur Autonomous Region, was known as the "fire land" and "wind depot", and was subjected to severe wind-sand incursion. After liberation, people of all nationalities of the county, under the guidance of Chairman Mao's revolutionary line, threw themselves into the "In agriculture, learn from Tachai" movement, and with a high sense of self-reliance, constructed sand-blocking forests in the wind gorges and narrow forest belts and small forest networks within farmland areas. Together with the contain-sand-cultivate-grass belts on the fringe of the oases, they form an integrated system of protection which has effectively shielded the farmland from the wind-sand incursion. At present, 70% of the county's farmland is protected by forest networks. In the Five-Star Commune, the farmland has a 13% protective forest cover. Parallel to their efforts to check the wind and sand, they constructed canals to bring in water, created new fields out of sand land, and turned gobi into orchards. Today, the total area of its oasis is more than twice the size of pre-liberation days. In the Shache oasis situated between the Taklamakan and the Pukuli deserts, the people made an all-out effort to build farmland protective forest networks during the "In agriculture, learn from Tachai" movement. At present, their farmland has a 10% protective forest cover, which has enhanced farm production.

While engaged in fighting the wind and sand, the people of all nationalities in the desert regions made a parallel effort in developing the water and soil resources of the desert and created new oases out of barren land. On the fringes of the Taklamakan and Kurban-Tungut deserts, more than 11,000,000 mu of fertile land have been created. The Mosouwan reclaimed district to the south-west of the Kurban-Tungut desert, surrounded by deserts on three sides, used to be a vast expanse of barren sand. In the last 15 years, however, under the guidance of the revolutionary line of Chairman Mao, more than 250,000 mu of fertile land have been created, turning it into a new oasis with forest belts criss-crossing the fields like a checkerboard.

New oases and new pastures are not the only new phenomena in the deserts. New roads and highways have also made their appearance. In lands where few travellers would venture into and the only mode of transportation was the camel, railroads and highways have been constructed, notably the Pao-Lan railway and the Kan-Wu railway that pass through the southern part of the Tyngeri desert.

From the above facts, it can be seen that deserts, when we do not have an adequate knowledge of them, are something that inspires awe, but under the superior socialist system, people are ready to explore and tackle the unknown, and once ways and means are found to control the wind and sand, deserts can be transformed into orchards and farmland. Therefore, to review and sum up the experiences of the masses in dealing with the problem of desert will contribute significantly to the acceleration of the process of desert control.

### MEASURES OF DESERT CONTROL

In accordance with the different goals (such as farmland, pastures and roads and highways) in the control of deserts in different areas, the measures of desert control as practiced in China can be classified into the following categories:

*Sand-blocking Forest and Farmland Protective Forest Network to Combat Sand Scourge*

In many areas in north-western China, there are numerous oases situated on the fringes of deserts. Sand storms and shifting sand dunes created by high winds encroach upon the farmland (in the forms of wind erosion of the soil, crops damaged and cropland buried by sand, etc.). Therefore, the construction of forest belts on the fringes of deserts to block the sand, coupled with the building of forest networks within the oases to protect the farmland, provides the best means of combating desertification around oases in the desert regions.

1. *Sand-blocking forest on the fringes of oases.* On the basis of the natural characteristics of deserts on the fringes of oases, the construction of sand-blocking forest and the stabilization of the shifting sand take several forms as follows:

(a)   In desert areas on the fringes of oases which have irrigation facilities
       and where the height of the sand dunes is limited (under 10 m) and low
       land lies in between the sand dunes, the sand-blocking forest is usually a
       combination of forest belts and forest plots. First to be built is a
       forest belt 50 to 60 m wide along the main ditch on the fringe of the
       oasis, and then on the low-lying land in between the sand dunes, forest
       plot—consisting mainly of poplars (*Populus cupidata*) and sand dates
       (*Elaeagnus angustifolia*)—are built by making use of irrigation water or
       ground water. With the sand dunes thus separated and surrounded by the
       forest belts and forest plots (Fig. 1), the quantity of the sand source,
       which causes the sand dunes to shift, will be reduced, and the air currents
       not yet saturated with sand will blow away the dune tops. Under such
       conditions, sand dunes 4 to 5 m high will have lost 1 to 2 m in 3 or 4
       years. Under the levelling force of the wind, the sand dunes will
       gradually become a moderately undulating sandy land. The sand-blocking
       forests at Tunhuang, Lintse and Kaotai in the West-of-the River Corridor
       are mostly of this type. In a further step to stabilize the sand dunes
       among the forest plots, sand shields are built on the surface of the dunes
       and sand-stabilizing plants are planted inside the shields. The materials
       for building the shields are mostly local products (such as clay, wheat
       straw, reed, gravel, etc.). The purpose of all this is to increase the
       roughness of the sand surface and its resistance, and consequently to
       reduce the wind force (Table 1). Take, for instance, the clay shields at
       Minching: wind velocity inside the shields is reduced by 28 to 33% compared
       to outside the shields, which produces a stabilizing effect on the sand
       surface and is favourable to the growth of the young sand-stabilizing plants
       on the surface of the dunes. Next step is the planting of sand-stabilizing
       plants such as "susu" (*Haloxylon ammodendron*) in between the shields to
       stabilize the sand dunes. Such measures were taken at Shachingtze in
       Minching County. The once shifting sand there has become semi-stabilized
       dunes, and the plant cover on the dune surface has increased from the
       original 3 to 5% to today's 30 to 40% (Fig. 2).

Table 1.  Effects of Clay Shields on Surface Roughness and Wind
          Velocity (on the western fringe of the Tyngeri desert)

| Type | Wind velocity value | Wind velocity reduction inside shields (%) | Roughness (cm) |
|------|---------------------|--------------------------------------------|----------------|
| Shifting sand surface out- side shields | 100 | | 0.0025 |
| Square clay shields | 72 | 28 | 0.4923 |
| Belt-shaped clay shields | 67 | 33 | 0.4923 |

(b)  Around oases on the fringes of deserts which have level soil land as well
     as shifting sand and semi-stabilized sand dunes, the sand-blocking forests
     usually consist of both trees and shrubs (Fig. 3), with trees such as
     tamarisk (*Tamarix ramosissima*) planted on the side close to the desert,
     which have the effect of weakening the force of sand storms near the land
     surface.  It has been observed in the Pishan area south-west of the
     Taklamakan desert that, under conditions of medium wind velocity, the sand
     content of the air currents that have crossed the tamarisk and shrub forest
     is 80% less than that of air currents on the shifting sand surface.  The
     closer an area is to the sand source, the more shrubs can be added to the
     forest.  The sand-blocking shrub belts at Minching in the West-of-the-River
     Corridor is 300 to 500 m wide, and the purpose is to block the sand carried
     by the air currents at the edge of the shrub forests, to ensure a reduction
     of sand accumulation inside the tree forest belts, thereby facilitating
     irrigation.  Tree forests are built on the side close to the farmland,
     generally about 50 m wide, which will further reduce the sand content of
     the air currents.  This type of sand-blocking forests prevail around the
     oases to the south of the Taklamakan desert, in the new reclaimed areas in
     the lower basin of the Tarim River, and at Yumen and Minching in the West-
     of-the-River Corridor.  At the oases of Shache and Markit on the western
     fringe of the Taklamakan desert, the sand-blocking forest belts, about 180
     to 200 m wide, consist mainly of sand dates which, with their profuse
     foliage, constitute an effective means for weakening land surface wind
     velocity and reducing its sand content.  It has been observed that under
     conditions of medium wind velocity, the range of protection of the forest
     belts is 23 times the height of the forest, and within that range of
     protection, wind velocity is reduced by 40 to 47% on the average.  In the
     north-eastern part of the Ulanpuhe desert, wider forest belts (300 to 400 m
     wide) of less density are used along the side near the oasis, while on the
     side of the desert, the forest belts are complemented by shrubbery and the
     contain-sand-cultivate-grass belts.  It has been observed that within a
     range 30 times the height of the trees, wind velocity is reduced by an
     average of 50 to 60%, and about 70% of the sand content of air currents
     near the land surface (0 to 20 cm high) is blocked at the front rim of
     the forest belts.

(c)  For oases situated on the front edge of gravel gobi or wind-eroded land
where the principal menace is high winds and wind-sand erosion, the sand-
blocking forest belts usually consist of multiple strips of trees of
higher density and multiple ditches.  Take, for instance, the five-ditch
forest belt of the Five-Star Commune at Turfan, Sinkiang (Fig. 4).  The
particular feature of this belt is the combination of forest with irrigation
ditches and multiple belts.  Before the building of the forest, ditches are
dug, 1.5 m wide and 4 to 5 m apart.  This combination of forest and ditches
facilititates irrigation and the growth of the trees, and the controlled
use of water.  Ditch water is also used to wash away accumulated sand.  In
the choice of trees, those varieties with long life and fast growth are
preferred, and tall ones are blended with short ones.  Along the first
windward-side ditch are planted sand dates for their relatively high wind-
sand-resisting capacity and their salt-alkali tolerance.  Moreover, during
their early stages of growth, they serve as a shrubbery shield alongside the
forest.  Along each of the two ditches inside the forest are planted
homogeneous rows of different varieties, one row of Sinkiang poplar
(*Populus folleana*) and one of elm (*Ulmus pumila*).  Along each of the two
ditches on the leeward side are planted one row of Sinkiang poplar and one
row of mulberry (*Morus alba*).  This arrangement provides a stable structure,
gives the belt an undulating, almost saw blade-like surface, and increases
the unevenness of the forest top, thereby increasing its capacity to
diminish wind velocity.  It has been observed that under conditions of
medium wind velocity, within a range of 1 to 3H (multiples of the height of
the forest) behind the belt, the average wind velocity is only 26.7% of the
velocity in open fields, and 29% within a range of 7H behind the forest.
This kind of sand-blocking forest belt in the Turfan area is usually
complemented by the contain-sand-cultivate-grass belts and protective
forest networks within the farmland.  This integrated system of protection
has effectively shielded the farmland from the wind-sand encroachment.

In the choice of tree varieties, account must be taken of local conditions.  In
the sandy areas on the fringe of oases in Sinkiang, the forest belts consist chiefly
of Sinkiang poplar, sand date and elm, while tamarisk is the most important species
among the shrubs.  In the sandy areas in the West-of-the-River Corridor, white
poplar and sand date prevail, while "susu" is the dominant shrub.  In the Ulanpuhe
desert, it is mostly dry willow (*Salix matsudana*), small-leaf poplar (*Populus
simonii*) and sand date.  From years of experience, for the sake of the stability
of the protective forest, trees must be selected for their long life and fast
growth.  Homogeneous forest of one single variety is not advisable.

2.  *Farmland protective forest within oases.*  While sand-blocking forests are being
built on the fringes of deserts, farmland protective forest networks must be
constructed within the oases at the same time (Fig. 5).  The combination of these
two elements constitutes an integrated system of protection capable of effectively
preventing the wind-sand invasion.  From the experiences of the masses in tackling
the problem of desertification, the construction of  farmland protective forest
networks within the oases has the effect of progressively weakening the wind
velocity (Table 2).

Table 2.   Progressive Reduction of Wind Velocity within Farmland
Protective Forest Network

| Open field wind velocity value (%) | Average reduction of wind velocity within forest network behind various forest belts as compared with open fields (%) | | |
|---|---|---|---|
| | First belt | Second belt | Third belt |
| 100 | 38.0 | 42.0 | 51.1 |

In such areas as Markit, Shache, Pishan, Qira and the Turfan depression on the
fringe of the Taklamakan desert, they mostly use narrow forest belts complemented
by small forest networks.  It has been observed in the Turfan depression, where
the wind-sand threat is severe, that in small plots within the network, the
reduction of wind velocity is 7.4 to 26.7% more effective than in larger plots.
At the oasis on the fringe of the Taklamakan desert in southern Sinkiang, the main
forest belts are 200 to 400 m apart, the secondary belts 300 to 500 m apart.
They each consist of four to six or four to eight rows of trees of different
heights, presenting a two-level forest top, and they have proved their protective
efficacy against the wind (Table 3).

Table 3.   Protective Efficacy of Narrow Forest Belts against Wind
(on western fringe of Taklamakan desert)

| Distance in multiples of forest height (H) behind belts | 1H | 3H | 5H | 8H | 10H | 15H | 20H | 25H |
|---|---|---|---|---|---|---|---|---|
| Reduction of wind velocity behind belt as compared with open field, % | 18.92 | 61.11 | 61.11 | 50.0 | 46.3 | 25.5 | 15.7 | 15.7 |

In the southern part of the Maowusu sandy land in northern Shensi, the main forest
belts are 8 to 11 m wide, containing five to six rows of trees, while secondary
belts are 6 to 8 m wide with three to four rows of trees.  In all, the forest
belts occupy 7% of the total land area.  On the fringes of oases where the wind-
sand threat is serious, account must be taken of the wind force, and on that basis
protective belts are built with varying distances in between.  According to the
results of research carried out at Turfan, the best formula is as follows: for the
first row of network plots, the distance between tree strips is 15H (multiples of
height of forest), for the second row, 15 to 17H, and for the third row, about 30H.
The first and second strips must be complemented by shrubbery to add to the density
of the belt.

The protective range of the forest belts is usually expressed by the multiples of the belt height, and their wind-blocking efficacy is in direct proportion to their height. It has been observed that with forest belts comprising six rows of trees, under similar conditions of wind velocity and wind penetration coefficient, wind velocity is reduced by 33.2% within a range 1 to 30H behind the belt when the belt is 10 m high, and by 20.9% within the same 1 to 30H range when the belt is 6 m high (Table 4).

Table 4.  Wind-blocking Efficacy of Forest Belts of Varying Heights
(on the western fringe of the Kurban-Tungut desert)

| Height of forest belt (m) | Coefficient of wind penetration | Relative value of wind velocity as between areas behind belts and open fields (%) (open field wind velocity = 100) | | | | | | | Average reduction of wind velocity within range 1 to 3H behind forest (%) |
| --- | --- | --- | --- | --- | --- | --- | --- | --- | --- |
| | | 1H | 3H | 7H | 10H | 15H | 20H | 30H | |
| 6 | 0.54 | 84.4 | 51.1 | 57.8 | 77.8 | 86.7 | 95.6 | 100 | 20.9 |
| 10 | 0.52 | 67.5 | 47.5 | 47.5 | 60.6 | 70.0 | 80.0 | 95.0 | 33.2 |

The trees used in the farmland protective forest belts are usually selected among indigenous varieties for their fast growth and long life.  In the case of the Turfan depression, in view of the aridity, high temperature and strong winds of the area, several varieties of trees are used to form forest belts of multiple layers and sparse structure.  White elm and Sinkiang poplar, with their fast growth and long life, are the backbone of the narrow forest strips.  They are planted in the centre of the strips, giving them a high degree of protective capacity and endurance.  On the windward side are added sand dates which, with their profuse, low-hanging foliage, have the effect of shrubbery under the trees during their early stages of growth, and, when full-grown, provide the while elms with a side shield, thereby promoting the latter's growth in height and straightness.  Mulberries and apricots, varieties of economic value, are planted on the leeward side of the belts.  In addition to their economic value, theie extending tops add to the width of the belts.  In the oases in the West-of-the-River Corridor, white poplar and sand date are the principal varieties.  In the northern part of the Ulanpuhe desert, it is dry willow and small-leaf poplar, while within the oases on the fringe of the Taklamakan desert, such varieties of economic value as mulberries, apricots and walnuts are planted in addition to Sinkiang poplar, arrow shaft poplar and sand date.

Farmland protective forests are usually built alongside ditches (or roads), each ditch sandwiched between two forest belts.  Structurally, there are two major types: one is the sparse and penetrating type, and one is the ventilating type. On the basis of experience, the former is suitable for areas with serious wind-sand threat, while the latter with a low rate of ventilation is preferred in most oases. It has been observed in southern Sinkiang that, under conditions of medium wind

velocity, the coefficient of wind penetration of the forest belts is in the
neighbourhood of 0.5, the range of protection is 23.7 times the height of forests,
and within the range of protection, wind velocity can be reduced by 34 to 41%.
Near the land surface within the forest belts, the sand content of the air currents
is 60 to 70% less than outside the belts. All this shows the protective effect of
forest belts against the wind and sand. Take, for instance, the Mosouwan farm to
the south-west of the Kurban-Tungut desert where, under the protection of forest
belts, the farmland area damaged by sand has been reduced from 21% in 1961 to the
present 1%.

As to the scattered sand dunes within the oases, since the major source of sand is
the sandy riverbeds and the shifting sand caused by the destruction of vegetation
on the stabilized sand dunes within the oases, forests are built around the dunes
to prevent the shifting sand from encroaching upon the farmland, as has been done
at Shache in Sinkiang. In some areas, in addition to building forest around sand
dunes, clay is used to cover the dunes (for instance, in Jinta, Kansu) or clay
shields are built in which sand-stabilizing plants are cultivated (at Minching in
Kansu, for instance), in order to stabilize the shifting sand. At the oases in
Houtaohangchinhou Banner in Inner Mongolia, where the dominant feature is the slab-
shaped sand dunes, the Minchien Production Brigade launched a remove-sand-clear-
land-build-forest-stabilize-and programme, and as a result, the sand dunes now have
a 60 to 70% forest cover, and sand dunes once 5 to 6 m high have been gradually
levelled and stabilized.

*Trees, Shrubs and Grasses Combined to Stabilize Shifting Sand*

In sandy areas on the barren steppes and dry grassland, the more favourable
conditions of water, with annual rainfall from 200 to 450 mm, sometimes as much
as 500 to 600 mm, contribute to the success of sand stabilization through forest
building. Meantime, as most of the farmland is scattered in river valley terraced
land and shoaly land with moisture underneath and criss-crosses with sand dunes, a
combination of trees, shrubs and grasses is used to stabilize the shifting sand as
follows:

1. *"Block at the front and pull from behind" to stabilize the shifting sand.*
In the Maowusu area, sandy willow (*Salix cheilophila*) and dry willow or poplar are
planted on the low-lying land among the sand dunes in front of the leeward-side
slope of the crescent-shaped sand dunes and sand dune chines as a front shield to
block the sand (Fig. 6), and at the same time cut up and surround the shifting
sand dunes. On the windward side of the sand dunes, in areas below one-third of
the slope, are planted sand-stabilizing plants such as sand willow or "yukao"
(*Artemisia ordosica*) to increase the plant cover, reduce land surface wind velocity
(Table 5), and prevent the surface sand from being blown up by the wind, thus
producing a "pull from behind" effect. It has been observed that as the sand
content of air currents is reduced as wind velocity drops, the relationship of
direct cubic proportion between sand content and wind velocity quickly dissolves,
thereby reducing the sand source blown up from the windward-side slope, which is
the cause of the advance of sand dunes through sand accumulation on the leeward-
side slope. Meanwhile, advantage is taken of the stronger wind force at the top
of the dunes (Table 6) to level off their upper portions, and trees are planted as
soon as one section is levelled. Gradually, the whole area becomes one of
moderately undulating sand dunes, and the plant cover has increased from the
original 5% to between 50 and 60%, in some areas as much as 80%. The ultimate
goal of stabilizing the sand is thus attained.

Table 5.  Relative Value between Wind Velocity at Various Heights of Sand Dunes and Wind Velocity within 1.5 m of Tops of Shifting Sand Dunes after Application of Sand Stabilizing Measures

| Height (m) | Top of shifting sand dunes (%) | Sand dune tops after stabilized with planting of yukao, etc. (%) | Land among sand dunes planted with sand willows and other natural shrubs (%) |
|---|---|---|---|
| 1.5 | 100 | 90.0 | 52.8 |
| 0.5 | 87.1 | 57.1 | 34.2 |
| 0.2 | 72.8 | 54.2 | 30.0 |

Table 6.  Relative Value between Wind Velocity at Various Points of Crescent-shaped Sand Dunes and Wind Velocity at Sand Dune Tops (%)

| Part of sand dune | Low land in front of windward side slope | Foot of windward side slope | One-third of windward side slope | One-half of windward side slope | Top of sand dune | One-half of leeward side slope | Foot of leeward side slope | Land between dunes in front of leeward side slope | Low land in front of windward side slope of another dune |
|---|---|---|---|---|---|---|---|---|---|
| Wind velocity relative value | 76.7 | 77.9 | 91.5 | 94.7 | 100 | 8.4 | 27.0 | 45.2 | 67.3 |

Note: Height of observation is 20 cm; sand dune is 5 m high.

Generally speaking, this process will take 5 years.  In the experience of the Maowusu people, there are the following ways of tackling the problem:

(a)  "Pull from behind" only.  A shrub belt (sand dates) is planted on the lower part of the windward-side slope of sand dunes, and making use of the wind force, a moderately undulating sandy land is created in front of the shrub belt, on which another shrub belt is planted and similar sandy land is created in front of the belt.  This process is repeated again and again until the whole area becomes a shrub forest.  This method is used at Shenmu, Shensi, to solve the shifting-sand problem.

(b)  "Block first, pull later" method.  Tall tress (such as dry willow and small-leaf poplar) or shrubs like sand willow are planted on the low-lying land among sand dunes in front of the leeward-side slope of the sand dunes,

and the advance of the sand dunes will be blocked by the tall tree forest.
Within 2 to 3 years the top of the sand dunes will have been levelled.
When the height of the sand dunes has been adequately reduced, shrubs such
as sand willows are planted on the windward-side slope to stabilize the
sand surface. This method is used at Taikomiao in Ejinhoro Banner, Inner
Mongolia.

(c) In order to accelerate the stabilization of the shifting sand, trees and
shrubs are simultaneously planted on the low sand dunes (under 7 m) and
moderately undulating sandy land. Specifically, trees such as dry willow
and small-leaf poplar are planted on the low-lying land among the sand
dunes, while on the windward-side slope of the sand dunes, shrubs such as
yukao and sand willow are mixed with tall trees, with the former serving as
a shield for the latter. Yukao are removed (reasons explained below) in
2 or 3 years to facilitate the growth of the forest, and in due time the
sand dunes will be stabilized. This method is used at the "May 7" forest
farm in Ejinhoro Banner, Inner Mongolia.

(d) Combined use of trees, shrubs and grasses. The "block at front and pull
from behind" process of sand stabilization is complemented by the planting
of grasses on the low-lying land among the sand dunes, thereby forming a
tree-shrub-grass triple system of sand stabilization. This method is used
at the Chenchuan Commune in Otog Banner, Inner Mongolia.

From the "block at front and pull from behind" stabilizing strategy described
above, it can be seen that the central link is the "pull from behind" step of
planting sand willows or yukao, which forms in fact a living sand shield. It has
been observed in the northern part of Wushen Banner that 5 or 6 years after the
planting of yukao, wind velocity 20 cm above land surface is only about 74% of the
velocity above shifting sand surface. The relatively large volume of fallen leaves
of yukao, plus the growth of other plants, brings about changes in the sandy land
fertility. It has been observed in Dingbian, Shensi, in the southern part of the
Maowusu sandy land that 3 or 4 years after the planting of yukao, the land surface
becomes crusted, and 8 to 10 years later the content of organic matter within 0
to 50 cm of the sand layer has increased from between 0.17 and 0.33% at the time
of planting to between 1.42 and 1.48%. Meanwhile, due to the fact that sediments
between rows of yukao are no longer blown away by winds and new ones are similarly
stabilized, fine sediments in the sand layer are continuously on the increase. It
has been observed that the content of sediments of the 0.05- to 0.01-mm class has
increased from 1.28% in the year of planting to 7.46% 5 to 6 years later. It
should also be pointed out that the root system of yukao absorbs a large amount
of moisture, causing a corresponding decrease of moisture in the sand dunes. It
has been observed (in the later part of May) that the water content of sand dunes,
within a depth of 5 to 20 cm, has decreased from 5.56% before planting to 4.93%
after planting, and below 20 cm, the decrease is even more marked, a condition
obviously unfavourable to the growth of the forest. Therefore, it is essential to
build forest as soon as possible after the planting of yukao. The best arrangement
is to plant yukao in the fall (when the sand dunes have a higher water content,
wind force is less strong, and the rate of surviving is higher), to be followed by
forest building the following spring. In some areas, yukao are eliminated as soon
as they have performed their protective function and replaced by other species.
In Ejinhoro Banner, for instance, a mixture of yukao and sand willows is used on
the windward-side slope, with the former providing protection to the latter, and
once the sand willows are well established, yukao are eliminated and replaced by
pines, with the sand willows, in their turn, providing the pines with protection.
In some cases, purple-ear locust trees (*Amorpha fruticosa*) are used to further
improve the soil in addition to stabilizing the sand. It has been observed that
5 years after planting the content of organic matter in the sandy soil could
increase four-fold.

2. *Trees and shrubs combined to turn sand dunes into forest.* Sandy land in the
dry grassland areas, such as Ke-erh-hsin, is the best land in China's desert areas
as far as water is concerned (annual rainfall 300 to 600 mm), with an average water
content of 3 to 6% in its sand layer. Therefore, after trees are planted on the
low-lying land among the sand dunes and sand-stabilizing plants (chiefly shrubs)
planted on the dunes, a further step can be taken to build a pine forest on the
sand dunes, thus turning the whole area into a forest land. On the low-lying land
among the sand dunes, the trees planted are usually small-leaf poplar, small green
Poplar (*Populus pseudosimonii*), purple-ear locust (*Amorpha fruticosa*) and yellow
willow (*Salix flavida*). If the ground water table is 2 to 3 m deep and there is
no temporary water accumulation on land surface during the rainy season, a number
of varieties of the pine family can be added. In the Changkutai area in Changwu,
Liaoning, the sand-stabilizing process consists of two or three rows of man-made
sand shields about one-third from the top of the dunes on the windward side, in
order to level off the dune tops (no uncovered top is necessary for small dunes
under 3 m high), and below them rows of "chapayikao" (*Artemisia halodendron*),
yellow willow, "huchitze" (*Lespedeza davurica*) or "small-leaf pheasant" (*Caragana
microphylla*), etc. Once the sand-dune tops are levelled, sand-stabilizing plants
are again planted. Generally speaking, in 2 or 3 years, when the surface is
relatively stabilized, camphor pine (*Pinus sylvestris* var. *mongolica*), oil pine
(*Pinus tabulaeformis*), etc., can be planted between the rows of shrubs. If the
trees are planted too early when the surface sand is not sufficiently stabilized,
the young trees are vulnerable to wind erosion and could be buried by the sand;
if they are planted too late, the large amount of moisture absorbed by the root
system of the shrubs will have an adverse effect on the growth of the young trees.
The camphor pine is capable of building up an extensive root system in the shallow
sand layer, both deep and widespread, a favourable condition for absorbing moisture
and nutrient. It is therefore the most valuable species for forest building on the
sandy land in dry grassland areas. This method is used at Changkutai to the south-
east of the Ke-erh-hsin sandy land where the shifting sand is now stabilized under
a forest of pines, mainly of the camphor pine variety. The forest has an average
height of 7 m, in some parts as high as 10 m, and the trunk is 12 cm in diameter,
the biggest 24 cm. It has been observed that wind velocity inside the forest
(1.5 m high) is reduced by 78.4 to 81.2% as compared with forestless land outside.


*Contain-sand-cultivate-grass to Protect Vegetation*

This step is taken to grow a land surface cover and prevent wind erosion on the
one hand and, on the other, to block the shifting sand and protect the young
forest. On the desert land such as the northern part of the Ulanpuhe desert in
Inner Mongolia, this step is taken side by side with the construction of "block
sand protect farmland" forest. In places where contain-sand-cultivate-grass
measures are taken and water is brought in to irrigate the sandy land, plant cover
consisting of yukao, white thorn, etc., can reach 50 to 60%. In Tengkou County,
which lies between the Ulanpuhe desert and the oasis, as a result of the contain-
sand-cultivate-grass measures and the construction of farmland protective forest,
the original sand dunes with sparse vegetation have now become semi-stabilized sand
piles, with the plant cover increased to 20 to 30% from the original of less than
5%. In oases in the West-of-the-River Corridor and on the fringes of the
Taklamakan desert, the farmland protective forest is usually complemented by the
cultivation of tamarisks on the sand piles, turning them into an effective shield
against the wind and sand. It has been observed at Shache in Sinkiang that after
the contain-sand-cultivate-grass measures are taken, surface wind velocity above
the sand piles covered with tamarisks is reduced by 40 to 50% as compared with
shifting sand surface, and the sand content in the air currents reduced by 80 to
90%. In the sandy areas around the oasis in Turfan, Sinkiang, the initial contain-
sand-cultivate-grass measures have developed in recent years into irrigation with
winter water and manual cultivation of grass. As a result, the vegetation grows

by an average of seven young plants per square metre, and in 3 years will have
increased to more than 60%, as much as 80% in some areas. The principal species
for this purpose, planted on the undulating sandy land on the fringes of the oasis,
is camel thorn (*Alhagi pseudalhagi*) mixed with "plump maiden" (*Karelinia caspica*)
and deer horn grass (*Scorzonera divaricata tircz*). On sandy land with a higher
ground water table and a higher degree of mineralization, the chief varieties are
reed (*Phragmites communis*), tamarisk and some saline plants (*Halostachys
belangerina*, for instance), while mouse melon (*Capparis spinosa*) dominates the
scene on wind-eroded land. It has been observed that in contain-sand-cultivate-
grass belts with an 80 to 85% cover of camel thorns, the surface roughness is 40%
more than that of wind-eroded land and wind velocity near the land surface is
reduced by 50.5% (Table 7).

Table 7.  Changes in Surface Wind Velocity and Surface Roughness brought about by
          Contain-sand-cultivate-grass Measures (Lake Aidin Commune, Turfan)

| Land type | Land surface wind velocity (m/s) | Relative value (%) | Roughness (cm) | Relative value (%) |
|---|---|---|---|---|
| Wind eroded areas outside oasis | 9.0 | 100 | 0.0344 | 100 |
| Areas with 85% cover of camel thorns | 5.0 | 50.5 | 1.36 | 3953 |

The sand-carrying capacity of the near-surface air currents is correspondingly
reduced, causing the larger sediments to drop. Thus the contain-sand-cultivate-
grass area becomes an area of sand accumulation in front of the forest belts on
the fringe of the oasis, reducing the accumulation of sand inside the forest belts
themselves, and therefore protecting the young forest in its growth. A popular
saying among the masses sums up the situation in vivid language: "Forest stops the
wind, grass blocks the sand, together they cure the wind-sand malady" (Fig. 8).
On the barren steppes and dry grassland, due to their better water conditions, the
efficacy of the contain-sand-cultivate-grass belts in stabilizing the shifting sand
is even more conspicuous. On the sand dunes north-east of the Maowusu sandy land,
for instance, natural vegetation consisting mainly of yukao will reach 60 to 70%
in a matter of 4 to 5 years. Compared with sandy land, the amount of small sediments
less than 0.05 mm in diameter has increased by 50% and the content of organic
matter increased from the original 0.079% to 0.71%. On the sand dunes in the
northern part of Changwu, Liaoning, since the area was designated a prohibited area
and manual cultivation of plants started in 1971, a large number of gramineous and
leguminous plants have invaded into the area in addition to the original vegetation,
and by the following year, plant cover has increased to between 50 and 70%. With
the exception of individual areas where wind erosion is extremely severe, the sandy
surface of 70 to 80% of the area has been stabilized.

*"Grass Kulun" to Block Wind and Sand and Create Pastures*

On the barren steppes and dry grasslands, measures are taken, on the one hand, to block the wind and stabilize the shifting sand, while on the other, full advantage is taken of the water, soil and plant resources of the area to create pastures and develop stock farming. In the experience of the Wishenchao Commune in Wushen Banner, Inner Mongolia, the construction of the "grass kulun" is the most important step in dealing with the wind-sand problem, in the rational use, protection and management of grassland, and in creating basic pastures of high and stable yield (Fig. 9). It can be described as a perfect combination of desert control and the rational use of the natural resources of sandy regions. "Grass kulun" means the enclosing of sand dunes, natural grassland and low-lying land among sand dunes with barbed wire or mud fences and the cultivation of grasses and other plants inside the enclosures (or kulun).

As practiced at the Wushenchao Commune, three types of grass kulun are used, depending upon the natural conditions:

1. *Sand control kulun of trees, shrubs and grasses.* This type of kulun is built around areas of shifting and semi-stabilized sand dunes to control the sand, and eventually to build basic pastures. Specifically, for the shifting crescent-shaped sand dunes and sand dune chines less than 10 m in height, rows of sand willows are planted among the dunes in front of the leeward side slope, in some areas complemented by natural shrubs (*Salix microstachya, Hippophase rhamnoides,* etc.), forming a sand-blocking forest of dense structure as a front shield against the wind and sand. On the windward side and perpendicular to the wind direction, yukao are planted first on the lower half or one-third of the slope, which will enable the plants to survive and grow better. This increased degree of plant cover will reduce the sand-carrying capacity of the wind on the windward-side slope. Then every year more yukao are planted upwards on the slope to weaken the wind force at the dune top, and eventually to stabilize the sand, a process which normally takes from 3 to 5 years. In order to prevent the emergence of wind-erosion gaps due to the occasional death of yukao during the dry monsoon season, measures are taken to maintain the integrity of the protective system. Specifically, yukao and sand willows are planted in whole rows. In the first 2 years, dead or dying ones must be promptly replaced in order not to leave any gap. After 3 to 5 years, protective measures must be taken, such as prohibition of cutting and grazing, to facilitate their growth. The shifting sand dunes thus treated in the early stages of the programme have today a 50% plant cover-in some areas as much as 70 to 80%—as compared with the less than 5% cover before.

To control and "greenize" the moderately shifting sand dunes and level sandy land on the fringes of shoaly areas, dry willows are used to build forest. Seedlings of 3 to 4 years, about 3 m high, are preferred. They should be planted deep, about one-third of their height. If the ground water is more than 2 m below the surface, the seedlings should be soaked in water for 10 to 15 days, to prevent them from untimely death during the dry season. Adequate distance between individual trees and between rows is 5 by 5 or 3 by 4 m. With adequate density, they will form a closed, dense top in 3 years. The dry willows planted on the windward-side slope are subject to wind erosion which can result in the exposure of their root systems. Therefore, it is essential that shrubs such as sand willows be planted at the same time to protect the trees, and grazing grasses are planted at the same time to protect the trees, and grazing grasses are planted within the forest as a further step to prevent the sand from being blown up by the wind. In recent years, a mixture of dry willows, sand willows and yukao has been used, wherein yukao protect sand willows and sand willows protect the young tree seedlings, and it has proved effective in reducing the wind-sand force on the dune surface.

2. *Grass kulun for hay and for grazing.* Kulun of this type are usually built on
the low-lying land among sand dunes and on the shoaly land around lakes and
marshes with a low degree of salinity. The vegetation consists of a large variety
of grasses adapted to such an environment. Under conditions of adequate protection
and rational use, it has shown marked improvement in its range, density and height.
In pastures on shoaly land, grasses of an especially appetizing type increased
significantly, with the wind-dried matter showing a 137% increase per square metre.
Meanwhile, due to the density of the vegetation, fallen leaves cover the land and
shield the sand from wind erosion. The content of organic matter has increased
0.48 times as compared with degenerated pastures. These protective measures have
the same effect on sandy land pastures (Table 8). The increased range and height
of the vegetation enhances its capacity to resist wind erosion and prevent
desertification.

Table 8. Effect of Protected Cultivation of Vegetation on Sandy Land Pastures
(of Wushenchao Commune, Wushen Banner)

| Plant variety | Condition of pasture | Plant cover (%) | Height of shrubbery (cm) | Height of grass (cm) | Weight of wind-dried matter (g/100 $m^2$) | Number of years under protection |
|---|---|---|---|---|---|---|
| *Yukao* and *Hedysarum mongolicum* | Under protection | 60 | 66 | 4 | 6979 | 8 years |
| Annuals | Degenerated | 25 | 44 | 3 | 2031 | |

3. *Water-grass-forest-fodder four-element kulun.* This kind of kulun represents
the development from the initial stage of protection and cultivation to a stage of
integrated construction. They are usually built on level, low-lying land among
sand dunes, which has good soil with a higher content of organic matter and
adequate water supply. The process of building such kulun consists of the
following: (a) Development of ground water resources, by means of big-pit wells
and tube wells* for shallow ground water, and by means of mechanized wells and
artesian wells for deep ground water, for the purpose of developing irrigated land:
The area of land in the commune now under irrigation has been increased 1.7 times
as compared with the situation before the Cultural Revolution. (b) Construction,
perpendicular to the wind direction, tree-shrub protective forest belts of sparse
structure, usually consisting of, among shrubs, sand willows, and, among trees,
dry willows. Such belts not only provide the desired protection, but their
branches and leaves can be used as fodder. In forests close to the sand dunes are
also planted grazing grasses, and the combination of trees, shrubs and grasses
further enhances the belts' protective capacity. (c) Land levelling, including
the levelling of sand dunes and the filling of low-lying shoaly land: after

---

*
Big-pit wells are used in order to enlarge the areas under controlled irrigation,
and open-air reservoirs about 3 m deep are built to collect ground water. Tube
wells are constructed with concrete tubes, 50 cm in diameter and 20 to 30 m deep.
The tube walls permit water to seep through, but not the sand.

cultivation, marked changes take place in the soil.  The density of the soil drops by 0.38 g/cm$^3$, and its porosity increased by 14.3%.  (d)   The cultivation of superior grazing grasses and fodder crops: such grasses, notably the white sweet clover, purple alfalfa, etc., are not only high in nutritional value, but also capable of improving soil quality (Table 9).  In the meantime, fodder crops are planted and seedling beds created.  Take, for instance, a four-element kulun at the Chahanmiao Production Brigade.  The ratio of land utilization there is as follows: grazing grasses and fodder crops, 5%; natural grassland, 30%; pastures, 60%; forest and miscellaneous, 5%.  This kind of kulun is the focal point in the construction of pastures and the programme is gathering momentum.

Table 9.   Soil-ameliorating Effect of White Sweet Clover
(Wushenchao Commune, Wushen Banner)

| Land type | Organic matter (%) | Nutrients (%) | | | Porosity (%) | Density (g/cm$^3$) |
|---|---|---|---|---|---|---|
| | | Nitro-gen | Phos-phorus | Potas-sium | | |
| Land among sand dunes after 2 years of cultivation of clovers | 1.138 | 0.046 | 0.168 | 2.58 | 50.5 | 1.31 |
| Land among sand dunes without clovers | 1.018 | 0.040 | 0.074 | - | 44.0 | 1.48 |

The construction of grass kulun at the Wunschenchao Commune has achieved its desired effect in combating the wind and sand and creating pastures.  In addition, it has also brought about changes in the environment.

1. *Wind-sand activity reduced.*   After a series of sand-stabilizing measures are taken against the shifting sand, surface plant cover has increased and the wind-sand force reduced.  Results of observation show: land surface roughness has increased 290 times as compared with shifting sand surface; land surface (20 cm high) wind velocity and the sand content in air currents both show marked decrease (Table 10).  On the leeward side, on the land among sand dunes in front of the slope protected by forest, with a 75% plant cover, the surface roughness has increased 617 times as compared with shifting sand surface, and even more marked is the reduction of surface wind velocity and the sand content in the air currents.

Table 10.    Changes in Surface Wind Velocity and Sand Content
(Wushenchao Commune, Wushen Banner)

| Land type | Plant cover | Relative value of wind velocity (%) | Reduction of wind velocity (%) | Relative value of sand content in air current (%) | Reduction of sand content (%) |
|---|---|---|---|---|---|
| Unprotected shifting sand dunes | under 5 | 100 | | 100 | |
| Sand dunes protected by vegetation | 28-50 | 74.3 | 25.7 | 4.8 | 95.2 |
| Land among sand dunes protected by vegetation | 75 | 37.2 | 62.8 | 2.3 | 97.3 |

(Height of observation = 0-20 cm.)

2. *Changes in soil nature.* After sand-stabilizing measures are taken, changes take place in the nature of the soil. Take, for instance, sand dunes stabilized with sand willows and yukao. Compared with uncontrolled shifting sand, within a depth of 0 to 20 cm, sediments smaller than 0.05 mm in diameter have increased from 3.31% to 15.38%, soil density decreased by 0.12 g/cm$^3$, porosity increased by 4.4%, dry clusters larger than 1 mm increased by 7.6% (within a depth of 0 to 20 cm), and organic matter increased from 0.098% to 0.168%. Marked changes also take place in the nutrient content (Table 11).

3. *Improved pastures.* (a) Among the grasses in the kulun, graminous varieties now make up 42.7%, leguminous varieties 34.6%, toxic plants only 2.8%, in contrast to the situation of degenerated pastures, where toxic plants make up 84.6%, while graminous varieties only 6%. (b) The height of vegetation shows marked increase. Grasses of the reed family, for instance, are on the average 11 times higher inside the kulun than those outside. (c) The density of vegetation is also increased. Grasses of the reed family and those of the moss family, for instance, can reach 90% and 75% respectively inside the kulun, while only 15% and 20% respectively on degenerated pasture land. (d) Grass yield shows marked increase. In the case of the grass kulun consisting chiefly of moss varieties, built in 1964, grass yield has increased 19 times as compared to degenerated pasture land.[*]

From the above analysis, it is evident that the grass kulun has proved its effectiveness in stabilizing the shifting sand, improving the quality of the soil and grazing grasses, building the basic pastures and developing the stock farming industry.

---

[*]See "A new landmark in pasture building—the grass kulun". *Botany Journal* (ACTA BOTANICA SINICA), Vol. 18, No. 1, 1976, The Experiment Office, Wushenchao Commune, Inner Mongolia.

Table 11.  Changes in Surface Soil after Sand-stabilizing
Measures are taken at the Wushenchao Commune

| Content: | Particles <0.05 mm (%) | Density (g/cm³) | Porosity (%) | Dry clusters >1 mm (%) | Organic matter (%) | Nutrients (%) | | |
|---|---|---|---|---|---|---|---|---|
| Land type | | | | | | Nitrogen | Phosphorus | Potassium |
| Shifting sand dunes | 3.31 | 1.69 | 36.2 | 0.2 | 0.098 | 0.033 | 0.054 | 2.82 |
| Sand dunes stabilized with shrubbery | 15.38 | 1.57 | 40.6 | 7.8 | 0.168 | 0.063 | 0.060 | 3.00 |
| Sand dunes inside forest of tall trees | 6.33 | 1.61 | 39.2 | - | 0.141 | 0.040 | 0.087 | 2.90 |

Note:  Depth of sampling: organic matter and nutrients, 0-15 cm; dry clusters,
0-20 cm; density and porosity, 0-10 cm.  Time: 6 years after stabilization
of shifting sand.

*Engineering Measures in Addition to Sand-stabilization with Vegetation to Protect
Roads*

Following in the footsteps of our socialist development, a number of railroads and
highways have made their appearance on the desert land.  In order to ensure their
smooth running through the desert regions, besides the careful planning of the
layout, various engineering measures are taken in conjunction with the sand-
stabilization programme, which have changed the scene of the deserts along the
roads and highways.  Due to the fact that railroads and highways pass through
various kinds of deserts, the problems they encounter also vary, in some areas,
for instance, chiefly those of advancing sand dunes, in others those of sand drift,
while in still others combining both factors.  Consequently, the ways to tackle them
are also different.

1.  *Railroads that cross areas of shifting sand semi-stabilized and stabilized sand
dunes in dry grassland regions.*  Except for sections of shifting sand where at the
initial stage it is necessary to take measures of a temporary nature (such as sand
shields), other measures are taken to protect the side slopes of the roadbed (such
as using the grass cover on in-between sand dunes land as sod bricks to be paved
on the slopes).  Along both sides of the road, contain-sand-cultivate-grass belts
are built to protect vegetation, and sand-stabilizing plants planted on the sand
dunes.  In the case of the railroads that run through the Ke-erh-hsin sandy land,
various plants are used for various parts of sand dunes: "pheasant" for the top,
"huchitze" for the middle section (windward-side slope), poplars for the lower
section (and on the in-between dunes low land), and yellow willows as a curtain
(on the sand-dropping slope).  Due to the better water conditions, a variety of
trees, such as pines, can also be planted on the dunes.  Measures of sand

stabilization along the railroads include: sand shields are built on the sand dunes
to stabilize the surface; then sand-stabilizing plants (such as yellow willow,
pheasant, etc.) are planted inside the shields. In the case of the shifting sand
dunes to the north-east of Naiman in the middle of the Ke-erh-hsin sandy land,
less than 3 years after the above-mentioned measures were taken, plant cover over
the area has increased from 3% to the present 30 to 40%.

2. *Areas of undulating shifting sand dunes on the fringes of barren deserts.* On
the Chungwei-Kantang section of the Paotow-Lanchow Railway on the south-eastern
fringe of the Tyngeri desert, the roadbed is protected by side slopes of gravel
against wind erosion. On both sides are constructed gravel platforms to
facilitate the removal of sand and prevent the advance of sand dunes. Also on both
sides are built, according to the magnitude of the advance of sand dunes in the
previous year, a protective belt 500 m wide on the principal windward side and one
of 200 m on the secondary windward side. Within the belts are constructed large
areas of sand shields. It has been observed that with the construction of square
sand shields of 1 m by 1 m, the surface roughness has increased 220 times as
compared with shifting sand surface, wind velocity reduced by 23%, and sand content
in air currents also reduced markedly. Under conditions of 8 m/s wind force, for
instance, sand content is reduced by 84%. As sand shields can reduce the movement
of surface sand, sand-stabilizing plants planted inside the shields have a better
chance of surviving and growing. Meanwhile, a wet sand layer lies beneath the 3
to 20 cm dry sand layer on the windward side slope of the sand dunes. The rate of
water content there is 2 to 3%. With the wilting point at 0.7% of moisture, there
is a water content of 1.3 to 2.3% available to the plants. During the summer and
autumn rainy season each year, water content in the sand layers gets replenished.
Therefore, under conditions of stabilized sand surface through the sand shield
device, shrubs can still be used to stabilize the sand. In the experiences along
the Paotow-Lanchow lines, among the shrubs, "flower sticks" (*Hedysarum scoparium*)
have the highest rate of survival, and "pheasants" also do very well, followed by
sand dates (*Calligonum mongolicum*) and yellow willows. As a result of the sand
shields and sand-stabilizing measures described above, the once shifting sand dunes
have now become semi-stabilized and plant cover has increased from the original 3%
to 14.3%, in some areas as much as 25%, ensuring the smooth running of the Lan-Pao
line across the Tyngeri desert.

Since the Great Proletarian Culture Revolution, an irrigation project has been
undertaken to bring waters to the sand dunes from the Yellow River, in the forms
of spry and canal irrigation. In the meantime, sand dunes are levelled and
terraced fields created to facilitate afforestation through irrigation. From
many years of experience, the best pattern is an intermixture of tree belts and
shrub belts. Among the preferred tree varieties are locust (*Robinia pseudo-acacia*),
sand date, white poplar and Sinkiang poplar; among the shrubs are "flower sticks",
"pheasant", yellow willow, sand willow, etc. As waters from the Yellow River
contain a certain amount of muddy sand, the sand field surface will become crusted
after 1 year's irrigation, thereby stabilizing the sand surface. Irrigation
ensures an adequate supply of water for the growth of the forest and is a positive
factor in accelerating the process of sand stabilization along the railroads.

3. In gobi areas where wind and sand drift endangers the railroads, such as the
Yumen section on the Lan-Hsin railroad, besides the temporary measures of sand-
blocking ditches and dikes during the initial stage, canals are built to bring in
irrigation water for afforestation, in the form of sand-blocking forest belts of
trees and shrubs. Among the principal tree varieties are white poplar, sand date
and pussy willow, usually with the pussy willow on the windward side to block the
wind-sand drift. As the main purpose is to prevent the wind-sand drift from
burying the roadbed, the forest belts are of a dense structure. At wind gorges
where wind and sand drift is especially strong, two or three rows of sand shields
are built in front of the forest belts to stop the shifting sand there. The

process of forest building in this area consists of the digging of sand-blocking
ditches, planting of trees with "guest soil", intensive irrigation, loosening of
the soil and weeding.  To prevent seepage, irrigation canals are built with
concrete blocks.  As a result of these measures, the wind-sand threat to the
railroad has been successfully eliminated (Table 12).  Today the length of the
Yumen section of the Lan-Hsin railway subjected to the wind-sand menace has been
reduced from 94.7% of the whole length to 2.7%.

Table 12.    Effects of Sand-blocking Forest Belts along
Railroads on Wind Velocity

| Open field wind velocity (m/s) | Wind velocity at various points behind forest belt | | |
|---|---|---|---|
| | 2.5H | 7H | 10H |
| 11.4 | 6.4 | 7.7 | 9.0 |
| Relative value (%) | 56.1 | 67.5 | 79.9 |

4.   In desert regions crossed by highways where natural factors favour the
stabilization of sand by afforestation, road-protecting forest belts are
constructed along the roads, and shrubs (such as yukao, sand willow, etc.) are
planted on the sand dunes.  In areas of stabilized and semi-stabilized sand dunes,
contain-sand-cultivate-grass belts are built to protect vegetation.  Such measures
are taken along highways in the Maowusu sandy land.  In areas where it is
relatively difficult to stabilize sand through forest-building, in addition to
careful planning of the layout (such as selecting the narrowest area of sand dunes
in the river valleys and lake basins, or of areas in-between large sand hills
whose rate of advance is insignificant), a number of measures are taken to protect
the roads from sand drift, such as streamlining the vertical and cross sections
of the roadbed, building of level land strips of certain width on both sides of
the road, building of sand-removing roadbed sections consisting of shallow furrows
and wind-blocking dikes, raising the roadbed to a level above the average height
of the surrounding sand dunes and the paving of smooth, solid road surface to
facilitate the movement of the sand and reduce sand accumulation on the road
surface.  In the meantime, on the windward side of the road are constructed sand
shields, and local materials such as pebbles and salt blocks are used to cover and
bury the sand dunes, or sand shields are built with reed in checkerboard squares
to increase surface roughness and reduce wind velocity and the amount of sand
blown up by the wind.  Near the highway roadbed are also built sand-channelling
dikes (or wind-channelling shields) to prevent or reduce sand accumulation.  In
the case of the highways that run through the southern part of the Taklamakan
desert, it has been observed that streamlined road surface and wind-channelling
shields are effective in protecting the highways from being buried by the sand.
The former facilitates smooth circulation, while the latter heighten the surface
wind velocity (wind velocity at the lower opening of the wind-channelling shield
is 1.6 times the velocity in open field), which pushes the sand across and clear
of the road.  To prevent the advance of sand dunes, sand shields of reed and
pebbles are built to stabilize the sand dunes.

*Water and Soil Resources Utilized to Create New Oases*

There are always two sides to a coin: while the deserts constitute a serious menace
to farmlands, pastures and roads and highways, they also contain considerable
resources of water, soil, plants, heat and minerals which can be exploited and
utilized. Keeping in mind the natural conditions and resources of the deserts,
the following programmes can be undertaken for their exploitation:

1. *Creation of farmland by "bring water to level sand" method.* This method is
widely used in the Yulin area, Shensi, in the southern part of the Maowusu sandy
land, but the Yangchiaopan Production Brigade in Jingbian County is particularly
noted for its achievements in this area. "Bring water to level sand" means
utilizing the water resources of rivers, lakes and reservoirs, by means of artesian
channelling or mechanized pumping, using the force of water to level the shifting
sand dunes on shoaly land along river banks, and transforming the undulating land
into level sandy fields. Due to the large amount of water required for the
creation of fields, water resources must be developed on a large scale. In some
areas, flood waters are used to level the sandy land, each mu requiring an average
of 2450 cubic metres of water, each cubic metre of sand requiring an average of 2
to 2.5 cubic metres of water. In the meantime, measures are taken to improve the
soil, such as flooding the land, manual filling with soil, and planting of green
manure crops, and forest belts are constructed to protect the new fields thus
created. In the experience of the Yangchiaopan Production Brigade, marked changes
take place in the soil structure following irrigation, tilling, fertilizing and
cultivation. Before the irrigation and soil improvement programme was undertaken,
the shifting sand consisted mainly of fine sand grains 0.25 to 0.05 cm in diameter.
In the sand layer more than 25 cm deep, the content of fine sand reached 82.2 to
88.8%, while clay particles smaller than 0.001 mm in diameter constituted 4.4 to
6.4%. With the passage of time, the fine sand content in the soil has decreased
to 7 to 17% (Table 13), while powder sand 0.05 to 0.001 mm in diameter has
increased to 63 to 70%, and clay particles smaller than 0.001 mm in diameter
increased to 16 to 20%.

Table 13. Changes in Soil Composition brought about by "Bring Water, Level Sand"
Programme at Yangchiaopan Production Brigade

| Land type | Depth of sampling | Particle size (mm) | | | | | |
|---|---|---|---|---|---|---|---|
| | | $1\sim$ 0.25 | 0.25 $\sim$ 0.05 | 0.05 $\sim$ 0.01 | 0.01 $\sim$ 0.005 | 0.005 $\sim$ 0.001 | < 0.001 |
| | | Soil composition (%) | | | | | |
| Shifting sand dunes | $0\sim 5$ | 9.46 | 82.23 | 0.66 | 0.52 | 0.60 | 6.43 |
| | $5\sim25$ | 2.70 | 88.77 | 2.91 | 0.61 | 0.61 | 4.40 |
| 10 years under programme | $0\sim12$ | 4.13 | 17.14 | 47.59 | 9.83 | 5.49 | 15.82 |
| | $12\sim13$ | 2.42 | 7.38 | 54.70 | 23.69 | 2.29 | 9.52 |
| 20 years under programme | $0\sim15$ | 1.98 | 7.72 | 54.90 | 7.71 | 7.71 | 20.08 |
| | $15\sim40$ | 12.98 | 66.82 | 9.65 | 5.26 | 0.60 | 4.69 |

As for nutrients, they were very poor in the early stages of the programme, with the content of organic matter at 0.09 to 0.21% and pure nitrogen at 0.02 to 0.06%. After 10 years of improved use, the content of organic matter has increased to 0.7 to 0.8%, pure nitrogen increased to 0.04 to 0.08%, while other nutrients of quick effect have also shown corresponding increase (Table 14). As a result, grain yield per mu has increased from the original 50 to 60 catties to an unprecedented 650 catties.

Table 14.  Changes in Nutrient Content with Number of Years under "Bring Water, Level Sand" Programme (Yangchiaopan Production Brigade)

| Number of years under Programme | Depth of sampling (cm) | Organic matter (%) | Nutrients (%) | | | Fast effect nutrients (mg/100 g soil) | | |
|---|---|---|---|---|---|---|---|---|
| | | | N | P | K | Water-soluble N | $P_2O_5$ | $K_2O$ |
| 1 year | 0~13 | 0.214 | 0.026 | 0.064 | 1.57 | | 1.1 | 9 |
| | 13~24 | 0.086 | 0.063 | 0.042 | 1.07 | 3.79 | 1.1 | 7 |
| | 24~50 | 0.064 | 0.016 | 0.006 | 1.56 | 2.38 | 1.2 | 6 |
| 11 years | 0~26 | 0.706 | 0.042 | 0.076 | 1.66 | 3.70 | 0.9 | 17 |
| | 26~49 | 0.278 | 0.037 | 0.030 | 1.18 | 3.44 | 0.7 | 8 |
| 17 years | 0~14 | 0.814 | 0.071 | 0.088 | 1.86 | 5.82 | 1.3 | 21 |
| | 14~30 | 0.788 | 0.087 | 0.082 | 1.94 | 5.29 | 0.8 | 20 |

N - nitrogen;
P - phosphorus;
K - potassium.

This programme has taken on new dimensions in recent years when, in some areas in northern Shensi where there is adequate supply of clean water, rice is cultivated on the newly created sandy land. Long periods of flooding not only settle the sand and prevent further sand drift, but, due to the fact that irrigation water carries with it a small amount of mud and organic matter, have the effect of improving the quality of the sand field. It has been observed at the Yuhopao farm* in Yulin that when the land is used exclusively for dry crops, the density of the soil is 1.697 $g/cm^3$, and the porosity is 33.4%, while sand grains smaller than 0.05 mm in diameter make up 59%. But after 4 years of rice cultivation, and 1 year of dry crops, the density of the soil is 1.449 $g/cm^3$, its porosity 43.6%, and sand grains smaller than 0.05 mm in diameter make up 77%. Furthermore, due to the fact that large quantities of fertilizer are used during the years of rice cultivation, plus the decomposition of the roots, it adds to the organic content of the soil, facilitates its maturity, and turns the barren sandy land into fertile fields of high and stable yield.

*Water and Soil Conservation Bureau, Shensi Province: *Bring Water, Level Sand, Create Fields*. Water and Energy Press, 1974.

In the sandy regions in northern Shensi, the "bring water, level sand" programme
has in recent years further developed into a broad programme of building trenches
and dikes to accelerate the process of "greenization". Since the Great
Proletarian Cultural Revolution, many dikes have been built and many reservoirs
constructed. The Yutung canal, besides supplying water for irrigation, uses
surplus water to treat the sandy land and has achieved satisfactory results in a
matter of 6 or 7 years.

2. *Developing water resources, reclaiming barren land, improving soil, and
creating new oases.* Some of China's deserts are situated in the middle of basins
surrounded by high mountains, therefore they can make full use of the melting
snows from those great mountains. In the case of the many rivers which have their
sources in the Kunlun, Tienshan and Chilien mountains (such as the Yarkant, Khotan,
Adsu, Manas, Sule and Black Rivers), canals can be constructed on the mountain side
to bring water into the deserts. In the meantime, reservoirs can be built on land
in-between sand dunes, in lakes and marshes, and on shoaly land along the rivers
(Fig. 11) to collect and conserve flood waters, in order to make full use of the
water and land resources in the desert regions. The following measures may be
taken to improve the soil of newly reclaimed barren land:

(a) Flood waters for irrigation: flood waters contain large quantities of clay
particles and a definite amount of nitrogen. It has been observed, for
instance, at the No. 1 canal at Tengkow in the eastern part of the Ulanpuhe
desert that they contain 0.1 to 0.5 $g/m^3$ of nitrogen in the form of
ammonium compounds, 0.1 $g/m^3$ of nitrogen in the form of nitrate compounds,
and 0.1 to 0.148 $g/m^3$ of nitrogen in the form of nitrite compounds. These
nitrogen compounds can improve the sandy land soil, enhance its fertility,
and therefore contribute significantly to the successful reclamation of
desert land and to the amelioration of soil. In the Chungwei area to the
south-east of the Tyngeri desert, for instance, on the land of shifting sand
along the Yellow River, having gone through the process of flood irrigation,
fertilizing, tilling and cultivation, the content of organic matter has
increased from 0.077% to 0.657% in 8 years.

(b) Improving soil by adding sand: in using the method of flood irrigation,
attention must be paid to the depth of precipitation, for if the mud
accumulation is too thick, the soil will become crusted, its water-absorbing
capacity impaired, and evaporation will be strong, reaching a state of
"becoming saturated as soon as water pours in, and drying up as soon as the
sun shines", a situation definitely unfavourable to the growth of crops.
Furthermore, in some desert areas the soil is clay in itself, and it is
necessary to add sand to improve its structure. At one farm* to the south-
west of the Kurban-Tungut desert, for instance, experience shows that mixing
sand with clay prevents crustallization, causes the density of the soil to
drop by 0.14 $g/cm^3$, and its porosity to increase by more than 10%.
Furthermore, the salt content of the soil to a depth of 0 to 10 cm is
decreased by 0.7%, its water content increased by 3.5%.

(c) The cultivation of green manure crops such as alfalfa, sweet clover, etc.,
for the amelioration of soil is an effective means for the reclamation of
barren land and the development of agriculture and stock farming.
According to the results of an experiment conducted at a certain farm to the
south-west of the Kurban-Tungut desert, the fertility of the soil is greatly
enhanced after 3 years of alfalfa cultivation. Specifically, each mu can

*The "150th Corps Farm", Sinkiang: "Fifteen years of forest building and desert
combatting - A new chapter in a hard, bitter struggle", published in *Desert
Control*, Science Press, 1976.

accumulate 57.6 catties of nitrogen compounds, 10.9 catties of phosphorus, and 16.5 catties of potassium—the equivalent of 20,000 catties of animal manure in terms of nutrition.  The cultivation of alfalfa contributes significantly to the increase of crop yield, an increase of 2.14 times in the case of cotton, and 1.78 times in the case of winter wheat.  At the Pingchuan Commune, Lintze, in the West-of-the-River Corridor, the cultivation of alfalfa has had the same effect of controlling the sand and improving the soil (Table 15).  An analysis there shows that after the cultivation of alfalfa, the content of organic matter in the soil (at a depth of 0 to 12 cm) has increased from 0.038% to 0.901%.  The cultivation of alfalfa on newly reclaimed sandy land not only improves soil structure and enhances its fertility, but also adds to the fodder supply.  At a farm to the south-west of the Kurban-Tungut desert, the area of land devoted to alfalfa cultivation occupies 26% of the total area, a fact that reflects the importance of the green manure in the development of agriculture and stock farming and in the prevention of desertification.

Table 15.  Changes in Contents of Organic Matter and Nutrients in Soil after Cultivation of Alfalfa

| Land type | Depth of sampling (cm) | Organic matter (%) | Total nutrients (%) | | | Fast effect nutrients (mg/100 g) | | |
|---|---|---|---|---|---|---|---|---|
| | | | N | P | K | N | $P_2O_5$ | $K_2O$ |
| Land without alfalfa | 0∿15 | 0.038 | 0.045 | 0.086 | 1.16 | 1.62 | 1.12 | 22.9 |
| | 15∿60 | 0.557 | 0.033 | 0.138 | 2.05 | 1.74 | 0.50 | 57.6 |
| Land with alfalfa | 0∿12 | 0.901 | 0.051 | 0.128 | 1.63 | 1.51 | 1.76 | 40.0 |
| | 12∿35 | 0.523 | 0.045 | 0.158 | 1.93 | 3.51 | 1.62 | 51.8 |
| | 35∿85 | 0.564 | 0.042 | 0.172 | 1.54 | 3.89 | 1.68 | 63.1 |

(d)  Salination and alkalization is a problem frequently encountered in the reclamation of land in sandy regions, and the way to tackle it is using water to wash away the salt through a system of irrigation and drainage. The subject has been extensively discussed in many publications and therefore will not be dealt with here.

3.  *Improved use of gobi land.*  Gobi spreads over vast areas in China's desert land.  With the exception of a small part which consists of eroded stone segments, they are mostly piedmont flood or alluvial sand-gravel or gravel in nature.  With adequate irrigation, flood and alluvial gobi can be transformed into orchards or forest land.  In Turfan, Sinkiang, extensive gobi areas have been turned into vineyards.  The first problem to be solved is that of water.  Canals are built to bring down spring water or melting snow from the high mountains.  The canals are built with concrete to prevent seepage.  Along the canals and roads, trenches are dug to build protective forest, in the form of narrow forest belts and small forest networks.  Take, for instance, the Hungliuho Horticulture Farm in Turfan.  On the

windward-side fringe, the principal forest belts are 100 m apart, secondary belts
200 m apart, the inside principal and secondary belts are both 200 m apart.   The
belts are 10 m wide and the area of forest cover occupies 16% of the total orchard
area—a protective system that has proved effective against wind and sand drift.
In the meantime, under the protection of the forest belts, the land is levelled
and the soil ameliorated.   Fields are created by terracing alongside the slope.
First to be built is the terracing walls.   Then the soil is soaked with water.
Next is digging the planting ditches in the long strips of terraced field.   They
are 40 cm deep, 40 to 60 cm wide at the bottom, and the distance between ditches
is 5 to 10 m.   In case of salination, water is used to wash away the salt until
the main grape root layer is free of salt crust.   Then planting pits are dug on the
bottom of the ditches.   The pits are 90 to 100 cm deep, about 60 cm long and 40 cm
wide, which are then refilled with prepared, fertilized "guest soil" from the
farms.   Grape seedlings are planted in these pits.   This "guest soil" method has
proved its effectiveness in ameliorating the gobi soil (Table 16).   In the fields
thus created, as compared to the barren gobi, the amount of coarse matter has
decreased, while the amount of fine sand and clay particles has increased
(Table 17).

Table 16.   Changes in Organic Matter Content in Surface Gobi
Soil after Guest Soil Cultivation of Grapes
(at Hungliuho, Turfan)

| Land type | Organic matter content (%) |
|---|---|
| Gobi without grape planting | 0.44 |
| Area in-between rows of grape plants | 1.71 |
| Grape-planting pits | 2.35 |

Under normal conditions, the grape plants will begin to bear fruit in 3 years, and
in 5 years their expanding foliage will have provided an 80 to 95% plant cover,
thus effectively harnessing the wind and sand and converting the barren gobi into
a vast vineyard (Fig. 12).   Up to now, more than 29,000 mu of gobi land in Turfan
has been turned into orchards, and the area of gobi land now under grape
cultivation makes up 79% of the total area of vineyards in the whole county.

Table 17.   Changes in Gobi Soil Composition brought about by Guest Soil
Cultivation of Grapes (Hungliuho, Turfan)

| Land type | Depth of sampling (cm) | Soil particle composition (%) | | | | | | | |
|---|---|---|---|---|---|---|---|---|---|
| | | Over 1 mm in size | 1∿ 0.25 | 0.25 ∿ 0.05 | 0.05 ∿ 0.01 | 0.01 ∿ 0.005 | 0.005 ∿ 0.001 | < 0.001 | Loss due to HCl rinse |
| Grape-planting pits | 0–2.5 | 47.69 | 14.29 | 10.58 | 7.45 | 3.26 | 4.98 | 3.64 | 7.11 |
| | 2.5–41.5 | 64.95 | 3.87 | 20.79 | 4.30 | 0.31 | 0.50 | 1.22 | 4.06 |
| | 41.5–63 | 65.52 | 8.19 | 9.31 | 6.51 | 2.09 | 3.75 | 2.80 | 1.83 |
| | 63–100 | 50.93 | 21.16 | 18.45 | 2.29 | 0.25 | 2.13 | 2.99 | 1.90 |
| Gobi land surface | 0–4.5 | 67.75 | 18.20 | 3.71 | 3.53 | 0.51 | 0.83 | 0.96 | 4.51 |
| | 4.5–38 | 74.67 | 12.14 | 6.65 | 1.04 | 0.34 | 0.73 | 1.09 | 3.34 |
| | 38–47 | 46.40 | 32.16 | 10.34 | 2.13 | 0.99 | 1.91 | 1.95 | 4.12 |
| | 47–85 | 70.49 | 12.93 | 6.73 | 3.17 | 0.81 | 2.65 | 1.41 | 1.81 |
| | 85–100 | 76.90 | 6.08 | 8.10 | 1.12 | 0.78 | 2.31 | 1.35 | 3.36 |

Forest building on gobi land, while providing the oasis with protection against
the wind and sand, is also a valuable source of timber supply.  To build forests
on gobi land, in the experience of many areas in the West-of-the-River Corridor,
the process consists of digging ditches (in the northern part of Lintze, for
instance, the ditches are about 1.5 m deep and wide) to facilitate irrigation.
The accumulation of sand in the ditches is favourable to the growth of the trees
(Table 18).  In addition, the use of flood waters for irrigation has the effect of
enhancing soil fertility.  Again take, for example, the gobi area in the northern
part of Lintze.  Within a depth of 0 to 20 cm, the content of organic matter now
stands at 0.37 to 0.64%, representing a 400 to 500% increase as compared with
unirrigated areas.  Six-year-old white poplars can grow to a height of 5.6 m and
a waist diameter of 8.55 metres, clearly demonstrating that the old ills of poor
soil and slow growth of plants are over.  At the Hunan Commune, Tunhuan, in the
western part of the West-of-the-River Corridor, a vast expanse of gobi in the
northern part of the commune has been transformed into a forest land through
measures of "bring water, level sand" and flood irrigation.

From the above analysis, it can be seen that new oases are created out of deserts
in China through a scientific process that consists of the following elements:
comprehensive planning, development of water resources, levelling land to create
fields, planting trees to build forest, harnessing the wind and sand, and
ameliorating the quality of the soil.  The oases on the south-western fringe of
the Kurban-Tungut desert in Sinkiang have been increased 5.2 times in their total
area as compared with pre-liberation days (Fig. 13).  The total area of farmland
in Hotien on the south-western edge of the Taklamakan desert has also been
increased more than twice since liberation.

Table 18. Effect of "Dig Ditch, Plant Tree" on the Growth of Trees
(Pingchuan Commune, Lintze)

| Method | Age of seedling (year) | Age of forest (year) | Height (m) | | Waist diameter (cm) | | Average top spread (m × m) |
|---|---|---|---|---|---|---|---|
| | | | average | highest | average | biggest | |
| Ditch planting | 2 | 5 | 4.2 | 5.2 | 3.6 | 4.62 | 1.2 × 1.2 |
| Planting without ditches | 2 | 5 | 2.2 | 2.15 | 0.9 | 1.20 | 0.6 × 0.6 |

It should be emphasized that all these measures of sand control in accordance with local conditions represent the crystallization of accumulated experiences of the people of various nationalities in the desert regions in their long years of hard and bitter struggle against desertification. It illustrates the great truth enunciated by Chairman Mao that "The people, the people alone, are the moving force in the creation of the world's history". The labouring people, in their daily pursuit of production, are constantly creating new experiences in dealing with the problems of desertification, constantly enriching our knowledge about the deserts, and adding an infinite wealth to the science and technology required in this particular area. Therefore, it may be said that it is the strength and the wisdom of the masses and the mass spirit of self-reliance that have made it possible to win our battle against the deserts. In other words, we rely chiefly on the masses for this gigantic undertaking.

The measures of sand control described above, whether for the purpose of creating and protecting farmland, pastures, roads and highways, or of creating new oases, are the direct result of a process "from material to spirit, spirit to material, from practice to knowledge, knowledge to practice", a process which is repeated over and over again to improve itself. From a single measure for a single purpose, it has developed into a comprehensive, integrated system of protection and creation; from the prevention of the wind-sand scourge, it has gone on to exploit the natural resources of the desert, create new oases and expand pastures. This process also demonstrates the great truth that theories must go hand in hand with practice, and technical personnel must work side by side with the masses, in order to find a set of effective measures suitable to different local conditions. The key word is, therefore, "practice first".

CONCLUSIONS

Our success in the area of desert control has been won under the leadership of Chairman Mao and the Chinese Communist Party. It represents a great victory of the Mao Tsetung thought. It is an eloquent illustration of the great truth enunciated by Chairman Mao that "Socialism has liberated from the old society not only the labouring people and the material for production, but also the great world of nature that the old society had no way of utilizing". Before liberation, after generations of ruthless exploitation and oppression by the reactionary ruling class, and under the system of small-farmer economy where each family tilled the land for its own subsistence, it was altogether impossible to tackle the problems of desertification. Only today, under our socialist system, relying on the strength of our national and collective economy, and through the organization and participation of the people of all nationalities in the desert regions, is it possible to effectively harness the wind and sand and transform the barren deserts into productive land. In particular, under the guidance of Chairman Mao's revolutionary line, the people of all nationalities in the desert regions, adhering to the principle of class struggle and the basic lines of the party, and with a world outlook of dialectical materialism and historical materialism, are able to smash the shackles of the human spirit and reject the fatalistic theory that "the deserts are beyond control". On the basis of the collective strength of organized people's communes, we are able, in the course of our ceaseless struggle against the deserts, to reverse the man-desert relationship, from that of desert controlling man to that of man controlling desert. In fact, we have gone one step further: we transform the deserts. The deserts are, after all, limited in their scope, while man's knowledge and ability to fight them are unlimited, never standstill at any one level. Therefore, on the condition that the masses are fully mobilized, that we rely on the masses, that we believe in self-reliance and are ready for hard and bitter struggles and take the initiative to launch an all-out war against the deserts in the revolutionary spirit of "the foolish old man who moved mountains", we can "change the old face of the deserts into a new look". This tremendous change fully proves the correctness of Chairman Mao's conviction that "Correct thinking, that represents the progressive class, once grasped by the masses, becomes a material force which will transform society and rebuild the world". It is evident, therefore, that for our achievements in the area of desert control, what we have relied on is the leadership of Chairman Mao and the Chinese Communist Party, the proletarian revolutionary line of Chairman Mao, and our superior socialist system.

Chairman Mao teaches us: "In the area of struggle for production and scientific experimentation, man constantly develops, and the natural world also constantly develops, never standstill at any one level." From the pre-liberation situation of "sand advances as man retreats" to the war on deserts since the founding of the new China, through the knowledge about the deserts to the control of deserts, it is a process of our understanding the natural world, reforming the natural world, and finally liberating ourselves from the natural world. This process will go on developing; it has no end. Our deserts cover vast areas, and what has been done up to now is merely the first step in a Wan-li Long March. Much remains to be done. Further hard work, for a long time to come, awaits us. However, "There is nothing difficult in this world, as long as one is willing to climb". Under the guidance of Chairman Mao's revolutionary line, and with the kind of revolutionary impetus among the people, there is no difficulty or obstacle that cannot be overcome. We will, in our practice, constantly sum up and develop the experiences of the masses and continuously raise the level of scientific research, in order to make greater contributions to our socialist revolution and socialist construction.

Fig. 1.  Forest plots to isolate sand dunes.

Fig. 2.  Forest plots, sand shields and sand-stabilizing
         plants inside the shields to control shifting
         sand dunes.

Fig. 3.   Forest belts of trees and shrubs to block wind and
          sand.

Fig. 4.   Forest belts for protection against high winds and
          wind erosion.

Fig. 5.  Farmland protective forest network inside a
         desert oasis.

Fig. 6.  New look of once barren and dry grassland.

Fig. 7.  Shifting sand turned into forest land.

Fig. 8.  Contain-sand-cultivate-grass belts and farmland
protective forest network.

Fig. 9.  Grass kulun at Wushenchao Commune.

Fig. 10.  Checkerboard grass squares to stabilize shifting
          sand.

Fig. 11.   Reservoirs constructed on low-lying land.

Fig. 12.   Once gobi desert, oasis today.

# Control the Deserts and Create Pastures

*Wushenchao Commune, Wushen Banner, Inner Mongolia*
*Autonomoud Region, The People's Republic of China*

The Wushenchao Commune in Wushen Banner, Inner Mongolia Autonomous Region, is situated in the middle of the Ordos plateau in the northern part of the Maowusu sandy land, at a height 1300 to 1400 m above sea level. The commune covers an area of 1600 km$^2$, with a population density of 2.5 persons per square kilometre. The chief industry is stock farming. Shifting sand covers a wide area (Fig. 1), consisting chiefly of crescent-shaped sand dunes and sand-dune chiens, mostly less than 10 m in height. Shifting sand makes up 54% of the total area, lakes and marshes and alkaline shoaly land 10%, while usable pastures occupy only 34% (of which grass shoals and low-lying in-between dunes land make up 44.4%, stabilized sand dunes 37.8%, semi-stabilized sand dunes 17.9%), the rest being non-productive land.

Before liberation, under the ruthless exploitation of feudalistic lords, herd owners and the Kuomintang reactionaries, the grassland was seriously damaged. "Yellow sand pours down from the sky, and half of the grassland buried in sand" is a vivid description of Wushenchao in the old days. At the time of liberation, there were 18,000 head of cattle and 92 trees. After the founding of the People's Republic of China, under the enlightened leadership of the great leader Chairman Mao and the Chinese Communist Party and through the organization of co-operatives and communes, the pastoral people embarked upon the glittering road of socialism. In 1958, under the guidance of the general line of "Drum up your dogged spirit, fight upstream, and build socialism with speed", the Wushenchao people launched a battle to control the deserts, create pastures and reshape the mountains and rivers. A massive mass movement to fight desertification was soon in full swing. In 1964, when Chairman Mao called for "In agriculture, learn from Tachai", the Wushenchao people, under the guidance of Chairman Mao's revolutionary line and adhering to the principal of class struggle and the Party's basic lines of revolution and production, threw themselves headlong into an awe-inspiring "Learn from Tachai" movement, hitting a new high in the battle against desertification by means of the "grass kulun".* They adhered to the principle "With stock farming as our major interest, we will develop around it an enterprise of many facets" and have achieved significant successes in their task of controlling the sand, constructing pastures and developing animal husbandry. By 1975 the commune had brought under control

---

*A kulun is a stone wall - or fence - enclosed area for growing grass, though trees, fodder-grains and vegetables can also be grown. This is then transformed into stable, high-yielding grazing grounds which help to overcome deterioration of the pastures and the incursion of sand.

240,000 mu of desert land, of which 100,000 mu had been transformed into pasture land, and areas covered with grass kulun had reached 210,000 mu.  The number of cattle had increased by more than 5 times as compared with the figure at the time of liberation.  Since the great cultural revolution, the number of cattle the commune has contributed to the state is 142% more than the cumulative number before the cultural revolution.  Thus ended the tragic history of "the sand advances as man retreats", and began a new chapter in the control of the deserts and construction of pastures.  It is possible to have achieved all this only in the new socialist China under the leadership of Chairman Mao and the Chinese Communist Party.

Fig. 1.   Shifting sand dunes in the Wushenchao area

The rock formation under the Wushenchao area is red and blue-grey sandstone, topped with sandy sediment and wind-eroded sand.  Ground water resources are relatively abundant.  On shoaly land the ground water is only 1 m beneath the surface, while on higher land it is about 5 m deep.  The water is of good quality, mostly sweet water with a mineralization less than 1 g/litre.  At a depth of 300 to 600 m there is deep ground water in abundance.

Though the area is within the continental climate zone, it has the characteristics of monsoon climate.  The average annual air temperature is 6.4°C, average temperature in January is -11.4°C, while in July it is 22°C.  The lowest extreme temperature is -31.4°C, while the highest is 36.4°C.  There are 156 frostless days in a year.  The average annual range is 33.4°C, and the extreme range is 67.8°C.  The climate is arid.  Rainfall is scarce and concentrated, and sand storms are frequent.  Average annual rainfall is 377 mm, while annual evaporation is 2253 mm, about 6 times the rainfall.  Annual rainfall is unsteady.  It could vary considerably.  In one year (1961) it reached a record high of 715 mm, while in another year (1965) it was only 162.8 mm.  The seasons also involve drastic changes.  During the summer months, from July to September, the season of south-eastern monsoons, most of the rain, about 67.7% of the annual rainfall, falls, most of it in heavy rainstorms. The monsoons slacken off after September and strong north-western winds blow throughout the winter and spring.  The climate is dry and very little rain falls. From November to June, it sees only 25.7% of the annual rainfall, mostly precipitation of less than 10 mm which is practically useless, thus frequently creating drought in the spring.  It is also the season when the wind and sand play havoc, with an average wind velocity of 3.6 m/s, the highest reaching 25 m/s. The days of sand storms during this period make up 82.3% of the annual total. Under the strong north-western winds, the sand dunes advance south-eastward, and en-croach upon the grassland.

This is an area of temperate zone dry grassland, as reflected in its vegetation and soil. On the shifting sand, there are some sparse sand plants such as sand raspberry (*Agriophillum arenarium*), sand bamboo (*Psammochloa mongolica*), sand mustard (*Pugionium cornutum*), etc. On the stabilized and semi-stabilized sand dunes, they are chiefly, "yukao" (*Artemisia ordosica*), "hard grass" (*Poa spondy-lodes*), "Chinese grass" (*Cleistogenes chinensis*), sand onion (*Allium arenarium*), "bitter grass" (*Ixeris chinensis subspagramini folia*), "thorn grass" (*Chenopodium artistatum*), "heart-shaped thorn grass" (*Echinopsilon divaricatum*), etc. The soil is sandy soil of primitive castanozems. On the rocky ridges the plants are "Pheasant" (*Caragana korshinskii*), "lunkao" (*Artemisia frigida*), white grass (*Pennisetum flaccidum*), sand bean (*Oxytropis psammocharis*), "huchitze" (*Lespedeza davurica*), etc. The soil is sandy castanozems. On the in-between sand dunes shoaly land the ground water level is about 1 m deep and vegetation on the lower land consists chiefly of "inch grass moss" (*Carex duriuscula*), and the soil is ground water soil or swamp soil. On higher land it is chiefly reed (*Phragmites communis*) and "chichi grass" (*Achnatherum splendens*), and the soil is sand-covered ground water soil or saline ground water soil.

To control the sand, create pastures and develop stock farming against a background described above, the measures taken consist chiefly of planting trees and grasses to stabilize the shifting sand and create basic pastures.

*Plants to Control Sand*

The first step is the planting of "yukao" (*Artemisia ordosica*) which is arid-tolerating and grows with vigour, in rows perpendicular to the main wind direction on the lower one-third of the windward-side slope of the crescent-shaped sand dunes or sand dune chiens, in areas where the wind force is comparatively mild and moisture relatively adequate (Fig. 2). The plant cover thus created effectively reduces the land surface wind velocity. In the meantime, the stronger wind force at the top level of the sand dunes will level off the dune tops. As soon as a small section is levelled, it is planted and gradually the area becomes one of moderately undulating sand dunes. In 4 to 5 years they will be basically stabilized. As the sand dunes move south-easterly with the wind, sand-tolerating sand willows (*Salix michrostachya*) are planted on the in-between dunes land in front of the leeward-side slope to prevent the advance of the dunes. It has been observed that after the application of these measures, the plant cover on the windward-side slope of the sand dunes can reach 28 to 50%, surface roughness is increased 290 times as compared with shifting sand, and wind velocity within 20 cm of the land surface is reduced by 25.7%, thereby reducing the sand-carrying capacity of the wind by 21.5 times. On the in-between sand dunes land, due to the better moisture conditions, shrubs such as sand willow, black willow (*Salix microstachya*) and sand thorn (*Hippophae rhamnoides*) grow profusely, providing a plant cover of more than 70% and effectively checking the wind-sand movement. It has been observed that the surface roughness has increased 617 times as compared with shifting sand, surface wind velocity reduced by 62.8%, and the sand-carrying capacity of the wind reduced 44 times. Due to the growth of the plants and the activity of their root systems, the sand surface is gradually stabilized and changes take place in the structure of the soil. It has been observed that after 5 years, the surface of the sand dunes begins to show a fragile crusty structure, the density of the soil has reduced by 0.12 $g/cm^3$, its porosity increased by 4.4%, and dry clusters bigger than 1 mm increased by 7.6%. Meantime, the content of nutrients and clay particles has also shown increase (Table 1). As a result, some plants such as sand raspberry, "chungshih" (*Corispermum hyssopofolium*), "huangchih" (*Hedysarum mongolicum*), etc., begin to grow on the sand dunes. Changes in soil structure on the low-lying in-between sand dunes and are even more marked, soil density showing a decrease of 0.19 g/cm$^3$, porosity an increase of 7.2% and dry clusters bigger than 1 mm an increase of 30%.

Fig. 2. Yukao belts planted on the windward-side slope of shifting sand dunes.

Table 1. Changes in Soil Brought about by Sand-control Measures

| Land Type | Depth of sampling (cm) | Density (g/cm$^3$) | Porosity (%) | Dry clusters 1 mm (%) | Clay particles (%) <0.001 (mm) | Clay particles (%) <0.01 (mm) | Organic matter (%) | Nutrients (%) Nitrogen | Nutrients (%) Phosphorus | Nutrients (%) Potassium |
|---|---|---|---|---|---|---|---|---|---|---|
| Windward-side slope of sand dunes after measures taken | 0-15 | 1.57 | 40.6 | 7.8 | 3.31 | 3.51 | 0.168 | 0.063 | 0.060 | 3.000 |
| In-between dunes low-land with sand willows | 0-20 | 1.50 | 43.4 | 30.1 | 6.33 | 8.34 | 0.846 | 0.055 | 0.075 | 3.000 |
| Windward-side slope of shifting sand dunes | 0-20 | 1.69 | 36.2 | 0.2 | 3.31 | 3.31 | 0.098 | 0.033 | 0.054 | 2.820 |

It should be pointed out that because of the aridity and strong sand storms, even the hardy yukao could die sometimes and leave wind-erosion gaps, which would destroy the existing plant cover.  To prevent this, a "cultivate-plant-replace-protect" four-step measure is taken.  By "cultivate", it means the cultivation of yukao and sand willow at various parts of the shifting sand dunes; by "plant", it means the planting of plants such as "pheasants" in between rows of yukao on the windward-side slope in order to further strengthen the plant cover; by "replace", it means the urgent planting of yukao and sand willow wherever wind-erosion gaps occur in order to prevent the deterioration of the plant cover; by "protect", it means that once an area is planted with yukao and sand willow, the area will be declared a protected area in 3 or 4 years, prohibiting cutting and grazing.  All in all, it means "when one piece of land is controlled, that one piece is protected; when one piece of land lives, that one piece is consolidated and developed".

On this basis, it further develops into a tree-shrub-grass triple strategy.  While yukao and sand willow are cultivated on the windward-side slope of the sand dunes, sand willow and dry willow are planted on the in-between dunes land on the leeward side slope, and under the forest is planted a superior species of grazing grass - sweet clover.  In recent years, high-trunk dry willow is added to the sand willow and yukao on the windward-side slope (Fig. 3) forming a pattern where the grasses protect the shrubs and the shrubs protect the trees, thereby progressively slackening the wind-sand movement on the dune surface.  This strategy has the following merits: (a) Fast and effective stabilization of the sand:  at the Chahanmiao Production Brigade, for instance, in only 5 years, the in-between dunes land has been turned into a three-layer grassland of considerable density (Fig. 4).  The net result is the stabilization of sand, creation of new pastures and the levelling of sand dunes (the original 6-m-high dunes have been reduced by two-thirds of their height); (b) Changes in environmental conditions:  under the protection of the forest, it is not only possible to cultivate superior grazing grasses such as sweet clover on the low-lying in between dunes land, other plants such as "lai grass" (*Aneurolepidium dasystachys*), "huangchih" (*Astragalus adsurgens*), reed and "mongokao" (*Artemisia mongolica)* also grow, providing a 50% plant cover.  In the meantime, changes also take place in the density of the soil, its porosity and nutrient content (Table 2); (c) High economic value:  the high-trunk dry willows planted on the low-lying in-between dunes land on the leeward-side slope, favoured by light wind erosion, accumulated sand and adequate moisture, have a high rate of survival and grow very fast.  They can be cut for timber once every 6 to 8 years, with an average yield of 1300 trees per mu.  In addition, there is a per mu yield of 450 catties (wind-dried weight) of tender leaves and grazing grass.

At the Wushenchao Commune, in order to control sand storms and solve the problems of grazing grass and timber needs, timber forests and pasture protective forests are built over extensive areas on shoaly land with adequate moisture conditions (Fig. 5), consisting chiefly of dry willow and small-leaf poplar (*Populus simonii*).  They are usually planted in the spring, with an 80 to 90% rate of survival.  They can also be planted in the autumn, with a lower rate of survival.

The high-trunk dry willows chosen for this purpose are planted in rows 3 by 4 or 5 by 5 m apart.  Experience shows that, planted 4 by 4 m apart, they will provide a dense umbrella in 3 year's time.  As for the small-leaf poplars, 2-year seedlings are usually used, one seedling to each pit, in rows 2 by 3 m apart.

Under the protection of the forest, the shifting of the sand dunes is effectively checked, pastures grow profusely, and changes take place in soil structure (Table 3).  On sandy land where there was little vegetation before, now grow profusely a large variety of plants, such as "futzemao" (*Calamagrostis pseudophragmites*), "goose down grass" (*Potentilla anserilla*), reed "alkaline grass" (*Puccinelilla distans*), etc., providing a 60% plant cover.  Also planted are grazing grasses of the highest quality such as sweet clover and alfalfa.

Fig. 3.  Dry willow, sand willow and yukao planted on the
         shifting sand dunes.

Fig. 4.  Once land of shifting sand turned into a three-
         layer pasture of trees, shrubs and grasses.

Table 2.  Physical and Chemical Changes in Soil Brought about by Sand-control
          Measures

| Land type | Depth of sampling (cm) | Density (g/cm³) | Porosity (%) | Clay particles (%) | | Organic matter (%) | Nutrients (%) | | | Carbonate of lime (%) |
|---|---|---|---|---|---|---|---|---|---|---|
| | | | | <0.001 (mm) | <0.01 (mm) | | Nitrogen | Phosphorus | Potassium | |
| Land planted with sweet clover under sand willow forest | 0-22 | 1.62 | 39.0 | 5.33 | 7.34 | 0.344 | 0.055 | 0.057 | 3.18 | 0.452 |
| Unused sandy land | 0-15 | 1.70 | 36.0 | 3.92 | 4.93 | ---- | 0.025 | 0.052 | 2.70 | 0.251 |

Table 3.  Physical and Chemical Changes in Sand-dune Surface Brought about by
          Forest-building

| Land type | Depth of sampling (cm) | Density (g/cm³) | Porosity (%) | Clay particles (%) | | Organic matter (%) | Nutrients (%) | | | Carbonate of lime (%) |
|---|---|---|---|---|---|---|---|---|---|---|
| | | | | <0.001 (mm) | <0.01 (mm) | | Nitrogen | Phosphorus | Potassium | |
| Sand dunes inside dry willow forest | 0-15 | 1.61 | 39.2 | 5.33 | 6.33 | 0.141 | 0.040 | 0.080 | 2.900 | 0.904 |
| Shifting dunes outside forest | 0.20 | 1.69 | 36.2 | 3.31 | 3.31 | 0.098 | 0.033 | 0.054 | 2.820 | 0.150 |

*Protected Cultivation of Natural Pastures*

The natural pastures on the ridge, sandy and shoaly land in the Wushenchao Commune,
under conditions of rational use, can provide for stock raising a definite amount
of grazing grass without causing desertification.  Before liberation, however, as
a result of the ruthless exploitation by the reactionary ruling class, natural
vegetation was destroyed, pastures degraded, and desertification became a widespread menace.  Since 1958, the people of Wushenchao began taking measures to

protect some of the natural pastures by prohibiting cutting and grazing, and to cultivate them and improve their quality.  The natural pastures, once placed under protection, take full advantage of the moisture and heat during the growing season, and generate and store their own nutrients.  The net result is a significant increase in the density, height and range of the plant cover and increased productivity.  Tables 4 and 5 provide a good illustration of the effects of protected cultivation on shoaly land pastures.

Fig. 5.  Pasture protective forest belts built with tall-trunk dry willows.

Table 4.  Characteristics of Vegetation on Degraded Shoaly Land Pastures

| Plant species | Average height (cm) | | Coverage (%) | Spread | Vitality | Appearance and value |
|---|---|---|---|---|---|---|
| | Seed-ing | Foliage level | | | | |
| *Pycnostelma lateriflorum* | 30 | | 10 | not much | strong | fruit |
| *Aneurolepidium dasystachys* | 36 | 18 | 5 | fair | weak | nutrition-ear |
| *Agriophillum arenarium* | | 5 | 5 | fair | strong | nutrition |
| *Pennisetum flaccidum* | | 6 | 2 | not much | fair | nutrition |
| *Artemisia mongolica* | | 2 | 2 | not much | fair | nutrition |
| *Carex diriuscula* | | 12 | <1 | little | weak | nutrition |
| *Oxytropis glabra* | | 3 | <1 | single stem | weak | nutrition |

Table 5.   Characteristics of Vegetation on Protected Shoaly Land Pastures

| Plant species | Average height (cm) | | Coverage (%) | Spread | Vitality | Appearance and value |
|---|---|---|---|---|---|---|
| | Seed-ling | Foliage level | | | | |
| Aneurolepidium dasystachys | 46 | 28 | 15 | much | strong | ear |
| Phragmites communis | | 25 | 15 | fair | strong | nutrition |
| Pennisetum flaccidum | | 16 | 5 | not much | fair | nutrition |
| Artemisia mongolica | 23 | | 13 | fair | fair | nutrition |
| Lactuca tatarica | 20 | | 4 | not much | strong | flower |
| Euphorbia kaleniczenkii | 18 | | <1 | little | fair | fruit |
| Pycnostelma lateriflorum | 34 | | 2 | little | fair | fruit |
| Agriophillum arenarium | | | <1 | single stem | weak | nutrition |

From Table 5 it is obvious that the pastures, once put under protection, show marked improvement in the density, height and coverage of vegetation, especially the increase of the appetizing "lai grass".  In terms of quality, the wind-dried matter averages 213 g per square metre on protected pastures, of which the bad grass, "niu-hsin-pu-tze" (Pycnostelma lateriflorum), occupies only 3% (6.4 g), while on the degraded pastures, the wind-dried matter is only 90 g per square metre, of which 40% (36 g) is bad grass.

Changes in the vegetation bring about changes in the structure of the soil.  On the degraded pastures, due to the inadequate plant cover, wind erosion is more severe, desertification is in progress (Fig. 6), and the surface roughness and the nutrient content all show decrease.  On the protected pastures, on the other hand, the dense vegetation and the fallen leaves that cover the ground surface prevent desertification, and the soil is of a finer structure and has a higher nutrient content (Table 6) - all favourable factors for plant growth (Fig. 7).

Protection of pastures on ridge land and sandy land has the same effects (Table 7). The increased height and coverage of vegetation means higher resistance to surface wind erosion and prevention of desertification.

It should be noted that protection does not mean the disuse of the pastures for many years.  It means only the prohibition of grazing during the growing season, while they are open for grazing during other seasons.  Pastures, where tall grasses such as reek, lai grass, etc., prevail, are used for hay making in the autumn, and for grazing during winter and spring.  Shoaly land pastures, where grow mostly low grasses, and ridge and sandy land pastures, where shrubs and semi-shrubs dominate the scene, are used for winter and spring grazing.  On some of the in-between dunes shoaly land pastures which are favoured with better soil and moisture conditions, other measures (such as irrigation, draining, plowing, seeding and weeding) are taken for further improvement.  The Chahanmiao Production Brigade, for instance, experimented with plowing the shoaly land pastures of reed and weed, where the soil is sandy greysols.  As a result, plowed land, as compared with the unplowed land, showed a decrease in density from 1.53 g/cm$^3$ to 1.3 g/cm$^3$, and an increase in porosity from 42.2% to 49%, representing a physical improvement of the soil.

Fig. 6.   Degraded shoaly land pasture in the early stages
          of desertification.

Table 6.   Changes in the Content of Nutrients and Clay Particles in the Soil of
           Shoaly Land Pastures

| Pasture type | Depth of sampling (cm) | Organic matter (%) | Nutrients (%) | | | Clay particles (%) | |
|---|---|---|---|---|---|---|---|
| | | | Nitrogen | Phosphorus | Potassium | <0.001 (mm) | <0.01 (mm) |
| Degraded pasture | 0-10 | 0.275 | 0.015 | 0.050 | 1.670 | 7.34 | 8.35 |
| Protected pasture | 0-24 | 0.408 | 0.038 | 0.066 | 1.960 | 9.47 | 11.38 |

*Water-grass-forest-fodder Four-element Kulun*

All the measures of sand control and pasture building described above are for the
most part taken within the kulun at the Wushenchao Commune.  The enclosed kulun
(earthern walls and fences were used in the past; now barbed wires are used) form
the basis of pasture building.  The grass kulun, as now used by the Wushenchao
people, are the result of years of experiment and development, and their function
is now undergoing a change from that of providing winter and spring fodder to that
of seasonal, rotational grazing.  The kulun have also been growing in size, and the
big ones are sometimes subdivided into small ones to attain the maximum economy of
operation.  Consequently, the kulun are no longer merely a preventive measure; they
now constitute a positive step in the protection, management, rational use and
enlargement of the pastures.  In short, they provide the vital means of controlling
desertification and creating basic pastures of high and stable yield.

Fig. 7.  Degraded shoaly land pasture becomes a pasture of
         dense vegetation under the protection and cultiva-
         tion programme.

Table 7.  Effects of Ridge Land and Shoaly Land Pastures

| Pasture type | Plant species | Pasture condition | Coverage (%) | Average height* (cm) | Yield of wind-dried matter (g/100 m²) | Years under protection |
|---|---|---|---|---|---|---|
| Ridge land pasture | *Caragana korshinskii* – *Artemisia frigida* + *Pennisetum flaccidum* | Protected | 50 | 100/6 | 16124 | 7 years |
| | | Degraded | 30 | 64/7 | 5328 | |
| Sandy land pasture | *Artemisia ordosia* + *Hedysarum mongolica* – annuals | Protected | 60 | 66/4 | 6979 | 8 years |
| | | Degraded | 25 | 44/3 | 2031 | |

* The first figure under "average height" refers to the height of shrubs and semi-
  shrubs; the second figure refers to the height of plants of the grass family.

At the Wushenchao Commune, there are now four types of kulun:  fodder kulun, grazing
kulun, sand-control kulun and the water-grass-forest-fodder four-element kulun;
the first two are chiefly for the protection and cultivation of natural pastures;
the third type, as the name indicates, is for the control of desertification; the
fourth type, the most widespread in the Wushenchao area, is the focal point of the
creative activities at present (Fig. 8).

Fig. 8.  A water-grass-forest-fodder four-element kulun at Wushenchao.

The water-grass-forest-fodder four-element kulun are usually built on in-between dunes shoaly land in areas where water and soil conditions are favourable and operation is convenient. Their construction consists of the following elements:

(a)  Developing water resources:  As the annual rainfall varies greatly and is concentrated in the later part of the growing season, irrigation is essential in order to create pastures of high and stable yield, and with the lack of surface water, the development of ground water is the first step.  At present, big-pit wells (Fig. 9) and sand drift wells* are used to draw shallow ground water, and mechanized and artesian wells for ground water deeper than 100 m (Fig. 10).  Due to the highly sandy nature of the soil, which means a high rate of seepage, "sod bricks" are used to build the canals.  In recent years, plastic sheets are used to line the canals, and spray irrigation has also been introduced.

Fig. 9.  A big-pit well in a four-element kulan.

(b)  Protective forest belts of trees and shrubs:  in the process of the construction of the four-element kulun, protective forest belts of sparse structure are extensively built.  They consist chiefly of sand willows (Fig. 12), complemented by tall-trunk dry willows, in rows perpendicular to the main

*Big-pit wells are actually open air reservoirs, usually 1 mu to several mu in size and about 3 m deep.  Sand drift wells are built with concrete tubes about 52 cm in diameter, 20 to 30 m deep.  The concrete tubes allow water to seep through, but not the sand.

wind direction.  Under the protection of these belts, which are 3 to 4 m
high and 40 to 50 m apart, grazing grasses and other crops are safe from
wind-sand incursion, and the leaves are a supplement to the regular fodder.

Fig. 10.  Artesian well to draw deep ground water.

(c)  Levelling the land:  as the shoaly land is often cut up by sand dunes of
     different heights, the levelling of the dunes and filling of marsh land is
     an important step in the construction of the four-element kulun.  At the
     Patuerh Production Brigade, for instance, there is a piece of marsh land
     which becomes a muddy puddle in spring and a trap for the cattle.  They
     covered it with sand removed from the dunes nearby and, through a process
     of tilling, draining and fertilizing, turned it into a piece of fertile land.
     The soil, having gone through physical changes, is like neither the shifting
     sand, nor the mud (light grey gleysols).  As another example, may be cited
     the work of the Chahanmiao Production Brigade, where the soil matured after
     more than 10 years of levelling, tilling and fertilizing, showed marked
     changes in its physical structure (Table 9), thus providing favourable
     conditions for the high yield of crops.

(d)  Superior grazing grasses and grain crops for grazing and fodder:  the
     principal species of grazing grasses cultivated at present are the white
     sweet clover (*Melilotus albus*) and the purple alfalfa (*Medicago sativa*), both
     of which have an effect of soil amelioration (Table 10).  Grazing grasses of
     the legume family also have a beneficial effect on subsequent crops.  It has
     been observed that grain crops on land which has been cultivated with white
     sweet clovers or purple alfalfa previously shows a 50 to 100% increase in
     yield.  The fodder grains cultivated are chiefly "mitze" and "tsinkou" with
     a per mu yield of 250 to 300 catties and high potential for increased yield.

The Chahanmiao Production Brigade, for instance, planted grain crops on
irrigated land which had been cultivated with alfalfa and white sweet clover
previously.  Their summer and autumn biannual harvests give an average yield
of 814 catties per mu, which means a significant contribution to the fodder
needs for higher animal production.  Moreover, the stems and levels of the
grain crops are also a supplementary fodder during the winter and spring
months.  Therefore, the cultivation of grain crops, which provide both grazing grass and fodder, is a guarantee against the grass-deficient months of
winter and spring.

Fig. 11.  Spray irrigation.

Fig. 12.  Protective forest belt of sand willows in a four-
          element kulun.

D. F*

Table 8.  Physical Changes in Soil brought about by Tilling and Cultivation

| Land type | Depth of sampling (cm) | Density (g/cm³) | Porosity (%) | Clay particles (%) | | Carbonate of lime (%) |
|---|---|---|---|---|---|---|
| | | | | <0.001 (mm) | <0.01 (mm) | |
| Improved soil | 0-17 | 1.27 | 52.0 | 11.40 | 19.47 | 17.902 |
| Shifting sand | 0-20 | 1.69 | 36.2 | 3.31 | 3.31 | 0.150 |
| White muddy soil before improvement | 17-59 | 1.65 | 37.7 | 12.39 | 13.54 | 38.790 |

Table 9.  Physical and Chemical Changes brought about by Tilling and Cultivation

| Land type | Depth of sampling (cm) | Density (g/cm³) | Porosity (%) | Clay particles (%) | | Nutrients (%) | | | Carbonate of lime (%) |
|---|---|---|---|---|---|---|---|---|---|
| | | | | <0.001 (mm) | <0.01 (mm) | Nitrogen | Phosphorus | Potassium | |
| Wheat land | 0-22 | 1.57 | 40.6 | 5.34 | 7.35 | 0.033 | 0.089 | 2.650 | 0.654 |
| Unused in-between sand-dunes land | 0-15 | 1.70 | 36.0 | 3.92 | 4.93 | 0.025 | 0.053 | 2.700 | 0.251 |

(e)  Enterprise of multiple activities:  large-volume increase of grazing grass and high-quality fodder was the principal content and original purpose of the four-element kulun, but the people of Wushenchao did not stop there.  Having enriched the production content of the four-element kulun and contributed to the development of their major industry, the people of Wushenchao, determined to carry through the construction lines of the Party, branched into other spheres of activity.  They built nurseries inside the grass kulun, thus overcoming the difficulties involved in bringing seedlings from the outside.  They built ponds (Fig. 13) to raise fish.  They raise honeybees, and grow vegetables and fruits.  They have enriched the life of the people through such activities.

Table 10.  Soil-amelioration Effect of White Sweet Clover

| Land type | Organic matter (%) | Nutrients (%) | | | Porosity (%) | Density (g/cm³) |
| | | Nitrogen | Phosphorus | Potassium | | |
|---|---|---|---|---|---|---|
| After 2 years of cultivation of white sweet clover | 1.138 | 0.046 | 0.168 | 2.58 | 50.5 | 1.31 |
| Unplanted land | 1.018 | 0.040 | 0.074 | – | 44.0 | 1.48 |

Fig. 13.  Reservoir in a four-element kulun.

In the development of the four-element kulun, it has proved that they represent a tremendous advance in terms of actual production as compared with untreated natural pastures.  Take, for instance, a four-element kulun built by the Patuerh Production Brigade.  In 1974 land area devoted to irrigable grain crops made up 36% of the effectively used area of the kulun, irrigable high-quality pasture land 4%, high-quality wet land pasture 24%, and the rest are nurseries, protective forest belts and natural pastures.  This year, in addition to the natural hay, high-quality grazing grasses and grain fodder harvested, the kulun is open to grazing by sheep from December to April.  Just from the viewpoint of fodder production, it has increased more than 8 times as compared with the untreated natural pastures.

The great changes that have taken place in the Wushenchao desert have eloquently proved the irrefutable truth of Chairman Mao's teaching that "Social wealth is created by the labourers, peasants and labouring intellectuals themselves, and so long as these people grasp their destiny in their own hands, and, following the lines of Marxism and Leninism, face the problems squarely instead of avoiding them, any difficulty in the world can always be solved".  The success of the Wushenchao people in combatting desertification and creating pastures has once more proved that "the masses are the real heroes".  So long as you have the superior socialist system, so long as you adhere to the lines of Marxism and Leninism and the world outlook of dialectic materialism and historical materialism, you can smash the spiritual shackles of the theory of predestination that "the deserts are beyond control", and reverse the relationship between man and the sand.  In the spear-shield situation of "either man controls the sand or the sand controls man", man plays the active role.  The deserts are limited, while the knowledge and ability of man to combat then are unlimited and will never be at a standstill at any one level.  Therefore, as long as you believe in the masses, rely on the masses, and develop their wisdom and strength, determined to attain self-reliance through hard and bitter struggles in the revolutionary spirit of "the foolish old man who moved mountains", you can paint a most beautiful picture on the canvas of barren deserts. The great change from the "sand advances as man retreats" situation of yesterday, to today's creation of pastures out of the deserts at Wushenchao, illustrates with conviction that, for their achievements in desert control, what has been relied upon is the leadership of Chairman Mao and the Chinese Communist Party, the revolutionary line of Chairman Mao, and the masses of the people.  In fact, this is the basic factor in the success of our struggle against desertification.

Following Chairman Mao's teaching that "In the domain of struggle for production and scientific experimentation, man is constantly developing just as the natural world is constantly developing, never standstill at any one level.  Therefore, man must constantly sum up his experience, constantly discover, invent, create and advance", the people of Wushenchao regard their past achievements as a new starting point in their task of combatting desertification and creating new pastures.  They are now devoting themselves to the creation of a modern, scientific ranching industry in an effort to make a greater contribution to socialist revolution and socialist construction.

# Tame the Wind, Harness the Sand and Transform the Gobi

*Office of Environmental Protection, Sinkiang Uighur Autonomous Region,*
*The People's Republic of China*

NATURAL FEATURES AND ACHIEVEMENTS IN DESERT CONTROL

Turfan County is situated in the middle of the Turfan Depression in the Sinkiang Uighur Autonomous Region.  It is a basin in the Tienshan mountain range, its lowest point, at Lake Aidin, being 154 m below sea level.  Ninety-six per cent of the county's area is gobi, wind-eroded land (Fig. 1), sand dunes (Fig. 2) and arid-eroded hilly regions.  The present oasis lies between the flood and alluvial plains and the alluvial and lacustrine plains north of Aidin Lake.

Fig. 1.  Wind-eroded land.

Fig. 2.  Sand ridges.

The northern part of the basin is protected by the Tienshan mountain against the
damp and cold air currents, endowing the basin with features of temperate zone
arid desert.  The Tienshan mountain is perennially covered with snow, providing a
constant source of surface water and ground water in the basin.  The Tienshan
water system has an annual flow of 300 million cubic.*  The subterranean flow in
the flood and alluvial plains supplied by the Tienshan water system is blocked by
the Flaming mountain and the Salt mountain, thereby forming a spring-fed water
system with an annual flow of 200 million cubic.*  About 60 to 70 m underground,
along an east-west belt in the Aidin Lake area, exists a water regime which
provides artesian irrigation.

Due to its peculiar natural environment, the weather in the basin is characterized
by high temperature, aridity and frequent wind storms.  Average annual temperature
is 14°C, and the accumulated temperature of 10°C or above is 5454.5°C.  It is arid
and hot during the growing season, and there can be 35 to 40 days with temperature
above 40°C.  Each year has about 268.6 frostless days, and the sun shines 3096
hours annually.  Solar radiation is strong, with an annual volume of 139,000
calorie/cm².  Rainfall is scarce, only 16.6 mm annually, and evaporation is strong,
reaching an annual volume of 3003.1 mm.  It is extremely arid.  Due to the closed
topography of the basin, temperature builds up rapidly in the spring but dissipates
slowly, forming a pressure gradient of wide divergence with northern Sinkiang.
The Turfan basin, situated as it is in a low-pressure area, constantly draws the
high-pressure currents from northern Sinkiang which, passing through the wind
gorges of the Peiyang River and the Triple Springs, enter the basin as strong
north-westerners.  An average year experiences 36.2 days of winds above 8 on the
wind scale, some years as many as 68 days.  Winds above 10 on the wind scale
average 5 days a year, up to 10 days in some years.  Days of flying dust can
continue for 18 days at a time.  Strongest winds exceed 12 on the wind scale.

---

*Translator's note: This is the way the original text reads—presumably cubic metres.

Except for some camel thorns (*Alhagi canescens*), reed (*Phragmites communis*), tamarisk (*Tamarix ramosissima*), etc., along the front edge of the flood and alluvial plains and the salt-tolerating plants on the saline plains along the lake, vegetation in the basin is sparse, especially on the piedmont plains in the northern and north-western parts of the basin where there is no natural vegetation at all. Consequently, the winds blow up the sandy particles and erode the loose, sandy sediments on the flood and alluvial plains, thereby creating wind-eroded land. The winds also carry with them large quantities of sand and the consequent wind-sand drift and sand dunes constitute a serious threat to the oasis.

Turfan was an agricultural area in ancient times. Since as early as the Han and Tang Dynasties, it was one of the political, economic and cultural centres in western China. Before liberation, however, as a result of the ruthless exploitation and oppression of the labouring masses by generations of feudalistic rulers and by the Kuomintang reactionaries, the destruction and usurpation of natural resources, and uncontrolled use of the land and plants, the area had become desertified, and the people found themselves in a situation vividly described as:

> "When there is no wind,
> The land is covered with sand.
> When the winds blow,
> You can hardly see your own house.
> Soft soil is blown away by the wind
> And farms are buried under the sand."

After the founding of the People's Republic of China, the people of all nationalities of Turfan, under the enlightened leadership of Chairman Mao and the Chinese Communist Party, got organized to combat the wind-sand scourge. Especially since the great proletarian cultural revolution, in the "In agriculture, learn from Tachai" mass movement, adhering to the principle of class struggle and following the Party's basic lines of revolution and production, the people of Turfan have made outstanding achievements in combatting the wind and sand and in transforming the gobi land. Before liberation, irrigation by means of pit wells in the entire county amounted to only 13 cubic*/second. Today, in addition to digging new pit wells (Fig. 3), large canals have been built to bring the melting snow from the high mountains, reservoirs constructed to conserve flood water, and mechanized wells built to make use of ground water, bringing the total irrigation flow up to 30 cubic*/second. Before liberation, there were only a few scattered trees around houses. Today, there are more than 20,000 mu of land covered with forest, over 1400 km of protective forest belts, 170,000 mu of contain-sand-cultivate-grass areas, and 70% of the county's farmland is protected by forest networks, which have formed an effective, integrated system of farmland protection. During April and May in 1975, Turfan was repeatedly attacked by winds above 10 on the wind scale, sometimes continuously for 33 hours, but because of the protection provided by the forest networks, the damaged area was only 4% of the total seeded area. Moreover, as most of the damage was done in areas of no forest or little forest, the harvest of the year was little affected, with the grain and cotton yield, in fact, exceeding the target as envisaged in the national agricultural development programme. Before liberation, there were only 170,000 mu of scattered farmland. Today, as the protective forest belts have effectively reduced the wind-sand danger, farmland previously abandoned because of the wind-sand scourge have been rehabilitated and new farmland created. As a result, the area of the oasis is today more than twice the area of pre-liberation days, food production 3.2 times the figure of 1949, the year of the liberation, and the hide and cotton production tripled. All this is achieved under the leadership of Chairman Mao and the Chinese

---

*Ibid.*

Communist Party.  It represents a victory of the Mao Tsetung thought.

Fig. 3.  Big pit irrigation well.

MEASURES TO COMBAT THE WIND-SAND SCOURGE AND TRANSFORM THE GOBI

*Protect Farmland from Wind-sand Scourge*

To protect the farmland from the wind-sand scourge, contain-sand-cultivate-grass belts are created on the periphery of the oasis, behind them are built stop-wind-block-sand forest belts, and within the oasis itself a protective forest of narrow forest strips and small forest network.  This comprehensive programme of land protection (Fig. 4) has effectively dealt with the wind-sand problem.

1.  *Contain-sand-cultivate-grass belts.*  The vast areas of land on the periphery of the oasis, with their soft and loose surface structure, are extremely vulnerable to wind erosion and wind drift, and therefore to increase and strengthen the plant cover is of crucial importance (Fig. 5).  At present the arid, sandy land south of the Turfan oasis is 50 to 70% covered with vegetation.  The contain-sand-cultivate-grass areas are mostly along the edges of existing farmland, consisting chiefly of camel thorns, mixed with "plump maidens" *(Karelinia caspica)* and "deer horn grass" *(Scorzonera divaricata turcz)*.  Farther south, the ground water is close to the surface and the soil is highly mineralized.  Here the cover consists chiefly of reed, tamarisk, and "salt ear tree" *(Halostachys belangeviana)*.  In the area in between, it is camel thorns and reed, while "mouse melon" *(Cappavis spinosa)*, etc., cover other wind-eroded land (Fig. 6).

The initial stage of the contain-sand-cultivate-grass programme was limited to the protection of natural vegetation by prohibiting grazing and cutting in designated areas.  In recent years, the programme has advanced to the stage of winter irrigation and manual cultivation of grass.  With the constant supply of spring water and additional supply from pit wells for only 4 months during the winter, a total of 44 million cubic metres of water is available, which is a significant contribution to the cultivation of vegetation cover. Winter irrigation, depending upon topography, is either in the form of natural irrigation or by means of man-made canals. After the winter irrigation, plants within the belt begin to grow, adding an average of seven young plants to one square metre, and in 3 years the plant cover will have increased by 60%. Once the cover has increased to more than 60%, measures can be taken to permit rotational grazing and cutting in strip and plot patterns.

Fig. 4.   Protective system combining forest with grass.

Fig. 5.  Contain-sand-cultivate-grass belts.

Fig. 6.  Man-created grassland.

The contain-sand-cultivate-grass programme has the following effects: first, increase in the plant cover prevents wind erosion and the blowing up of sand.  It has been observed (Table 1) that, within the belt of camel thorns where the cover is 85%, wind velocity close to land surface is reduced by 49.5% as compared with wind-eroded areas.  The plants within the grass belt are relatively small (mostly under 1 m) and the wind shadow range is limited, but due to the width of the belt and the density of the vegetation, air currents passing through the belt are progressively reduced and weakened.  It shows that adequate width of the belt and density of vegetation are essential conditions for reducing wind velocity and preventing the blowing up of sand.  Secondly, the belt blocks the shifting sand and protects the young forest from being buried under the sand.  The wide belt (generally more than 300 to 500 m wide) not only reduces the surface wind velocity, but also increases the roughness of land surface.  In the belt of camel thorns where the cover has reached 85%, the surface roughness is almost 40 times more than in the wind-eroded areas.  This helps in reducing the surface wind velocity and weakening the sand-carrying capacity of the air currents, causing the rougher grains of sand to precipitate before they reach the protective forest belt.  A popular saying sums up the experience: "Forest stops the wind, grass blocks the sand, together they cure the wind-sand malady."  It explains the frontline role of the grass belt in blocking the sand and protecting the forest, and the merit of the grass-forest partnership.

Table 1.   Effects of Contain-sand-cultivate-grass Belt on Land Surface Wind
           Velocity and Land Surface Roughness

| Land type | Land surface wind velocity | | Land surface roughness | |
|---|---|---|---|---|
| Wind-eroded land outside oasis | 9.9 (m/s) | 100 (%) | 0.0344 (cm) | 100 (%) |
| Grassland with 85% cover of camel thorns | 5.0 | 50.5 | 1.36 | 3953 |

2.   *Stop-wind-block-sand forest belts on the fringe of oasis.*   The function of the stop-wind-block-sand forest belts on the fringe of the oasis is to further weaken the wind-sand velocity, causing the precipitation of the smaller grains of sand that have been carried across the grass belts.  Two types of forest belts are used to deal with different types of wind erosion and wind drift and the varying quantities of sand sources.  In wind-drift areas of abundant sand source, multiple-strip forest belts are constructed, with the strips 50 to 100 m apart.  In wind-eroded areas of lesser sand source are erected belts of large and tall trees of a fairly dense structure.  The former are still at an early stage of growth and their effect on the shifting sand is not yet conspicuous, while the latter, as exemplified by the five-ditch forest belts of the Five-Star Commune (Figs. 7 and 8), have the following features: irrigation ditches parallel to multiple forest strips, trees chosen for their quick growth and long life, and tall varieties blended with short ones.  Ditches are dug before the planting of trees.  They are 1.5 m wide and 4.5 m apart.  This arrangement has the advantage of controlled use of irrigation water, preventing salination and alkalization, and using the water to wash away accumulated sand.  As to the choice of tree varieties, two rows of sand date *(Elaegnus angustifolia)* are planted alongside the first windward-side ditch.  This variety is chosen for its wind-sand resisting capacity and its role as forest-fringe shrubbery during its early stages of growth.  Along each of the two ditches inside the belt

are planted one row of Sinkiang poplar (*Populus bollean*) and one row of elm
(*Ulmus pumila*).  Along the two leeward-side ditches are planted one row of
Sinkiang poplar and one row of mulberry (*Morus alba*).  This arrangement has the
merit of structural stability, and the belt presents at its top an undulating,
almost saw-blade-like surface, thus increasing its roughness and adding to its
wind-reducing capacity.  At present the five-ditch forest belts at the Five-Star
Commune have an average height of 16 m, a mighty "Verdant Great Wall" ringing the
oasis which has proven its wind-blocking capacity.  It has been observed that under
conditions of medium range of wind velocity, in areas 1 to 3H (multiples of belt
height) behind the belt, the average wind velocity is only 26.7% of open field
velocity, and 29% in areas 7H behind the belt.

Fig. 7.  Stop-wind-block-sand forest belts in wind-drift
         areas.

Fig. 8.  Stop-wind-block-sand forest belts in wind-eroded
         areas.

3.  *Farmland protective forest network within oasis.*   After the contain-sand-
cultivate-grass belts and the stop-wind-block-sand forest belts have effectively
weakened the force of the wind-sand onslaught, the task of further weakening the
remaining wind force falls upon the farmland protective forest network within the
oasis, which plays a central role in the elaborate system of protection (Fig. 9).
In the experience of the Turfan people in their long struggle against the wind and
sand, narrow forest strips coupled with small forest network provide the most
effective means of checking wind velocity and protecting the farmland.   It has
been observed that smaller plots within the network is more effective in reducing
wind velocity than larger ones (Table 2).

Table 2.  Size of Forest Network Plots and their Wind-reducing
          Effects

| Distance between forest strips | Metre | 70 | 92 | 175 | 250 |
|---|---|---|---|---|---|
| | H | 10 | 14 | 22 | 31 |
| Average reduction of wind velocity within plots (%) | | 52.8 | 50.2 | 38.4 | 29.8 |

Fig. 9.   Farmland protective forest network – narrow forest
strips and small network plots.

The wind-arresting effect of the narrow forest strips is very conspicuous.  It has
been observed that in the case of the narrow forest strips 12 m wide and 7 m high
in the Aidin Lake Commune, an open field velocity of 8.6 m/sec is reduced by more
than half within a 10H range (Table 3).  It should be pointed out that as the
forests grow and gain height, their protective capacity will correspondingly
increase.

Table 3.   Wind-reducing Effect of Narrow Forest Strips

| Open field wind velocity | Wind velocity at various points within network plots | | | | | | | Average wind velocity value within forest network |
|---|---|---|---|---|---|---|---|---|
| | 1H | 3H | 7H | 10H | 15H | 20H | 25H | |
| 8.6 m/s | 3.9 | 2.9 | 3.7 | 4.2 | 6.4 | 6.8 | 6.6 | 4.96 |
| Relative value (%) | 45.3 | 33.8 | 42.3 | 48.8 | 74.4 | 79.1 | 76.7 | 57.2 |

The choice of the right species and their proper arrangements are the essential conditions for the high efficacy of the narrow forest strips.  Strips of multiple layers, consisting of white elm, Sinkiang poplar, mulberry and sand date, have proved their value against conditions of aridity, high temperature and strong winds.

White elm, Sinkiang poplar and the arrow shaft poplar (*Populus nigra* L. var. *thevestina* Bean), due to their quick growth and long life, form the backbone of forest strips.  They are planted inside the strips, providing the necessary height for protective efficacy and long-lasting performance.  Sand-date, planted on the windward-side front line, is valuable because of its dense, drooping foliage, serving as a shrubbery shield alongside the forest during its early stages of growth.  As it grows in height, its top provides the white poplar with a side shield which promotes its growth in height and in its straightness.  Mulberry and apricot (*Prunus armeniaca*), planted on the leeward side of the strip, besides adding to the width of the strip by their extending tops, are plants of economic value.

The width of the forest strips varies between four to eight rows of trees or between 6 to 12 m.  To facilitate arrangement and selective cutting and replacement, each row is homogeneous and rows of different species run side by side.  Rows are 1.5 m apart and individual trees 1 to 1.5 m apart.  Up to now, forest strips around 10 years old have shown no sign of overcrowding or deterioration and still maintain their wind-reducing efficacy.  Forest strips of such width and density occupy less land, require less investment, facilitate management, and prolong their vitality. The existing strips would require consideration of selective cutting and replacement when they are 15 to 20 years old.

As to the size of the plots within the forest network, the decisive factors are whether the farmland is getting proper protection and whether irrigation and mechanized tilling and seeding and harvesting can be successfully carried out. Due to the severity of the wind-sand scourge, measures are taken to increase the density of the forest network and shorten the distance between the strips.  In the interest of land use economy and irrigation, generally two rows of trees sandwich every ditch and every road.

The farmland protective forest networks on the fringe of desert land are generally less than 200 mu in area.  The two belts facing and perpendicular to the wind direction are usually 150 to 200 m apart.  This is on the basis that Sinkiang poplar and white elm, the mainstay of the forest belts, reach a height of 15 to 20 m when full-grown, and 10 times of that height, or 150 to 200 m, is the most effective range of protection against the wind.

When the forest belts criss-cross into a network like a checkerboard, their effect on the wind is very different from the effect of isolated belts.  Table 4 shows the progressive reduction of wind velocity under conditions of a forest network.

Table 4.  Progressive Reduction of Wind Velocity in a Forest Network

| Relative value of open field wind velocity (%) | Average value of wind velocity in network plots behind different forest strips (%) | | |
|---|---|---|---|
| | First strip | Second strip | Third strip |
| 100 | 62.0 | 58.0 | 48.9 |

It is obvious from the above that the formula of forest strips and small forest networks in the oasis provides the most effective protection against the wind and sand.

The contain-sand-cultivate-grass belts, the stop-wind-block-sand forest belts and the farmland protective forest networks built by the Turfan people have not only brought the wind and sand under control, but have also successfully dealt with other lesser factors of climate. It has been observed that in the spring, the farmland soil temperature is generally 2°C higher than the soil temperature in forestless open field, and the earlier return of the warm temperature to the protected land is favourable to the early spring cultivation. In summer, the relative air humidity within the forest network is 7 to 21% higher than outside the network and its absolute humidity is 2.4 to 7.5 mb higher than in the open high land. Evaporation from water surface is 20 to 50% less than in open field. Summer temperature within the small forest network is 1 to 3.8°C lower than in the open field. During the hot and dry season, humidity in the forest network rises while temperature drops and evaporation decreases, conditions extremely favourable to the growth of field crops which result in high yield. It has been observed that under similar conditions, wheat germination on land protected by forest belts is 2.3 to 6.7% more effective than in forestless areas, and the weight per 1000 grains is raised by 10.7 to 15.5 g.

In addition to the building of protective systems, various measures are taken to improve agricultural technique, such as extensive planting of heat-loving kaoliang (*Sorghum vulgare* Pers.), cultivation of high-resistance crops, timely irrigation before wind storms, mixed cultivation of high-standing and low-standing crops, preparation of soil and protection of seedlings, and the digging of ditches for seeding.

*Turn Gobi into Vineyard*

The Turfan people, while engaged in cultivating grass and building forest to block sand storms, also started marching toward their ultimate goal of enlarging their oasis by creating new fields and transforming the gobi land. The most important part of this programme is the cultivation of grapes (*Vitis vinifera* L.) in the gobi (Fig. 10).

Gobi land occupies about 30% of the total area of Turfan County, 14 times of the area of the present farmland. The rebuilding of the gobi not only makes full use of its high temperature and its water and soil resources and extends the oasis, but is in itself an effective measure in combatting desertification. The successful cultivation of grapes in the gobi by taking advantage of its natural environment and the biological characteristics of grape cultivation represents an important experience of the local people in their development efforts. Since liberation, the Turfan people have reclaimed more than 19,000 mu of gobi land and the area cultivated with grapes constitutes 79% of the county's total vineyard area.

The following measures were taken in the cultivation of grapes in the gobi desert:

1. *Water resources*. To take advantage of the water resources of the area, canals were dug to bring down the melting snow from the Tienshan mountain, while full use was made of spring water. To prevent leaks, the canals were built with pebbles mixed with cement. The pit well irrigation, with its steady supply of water and an insignificant amount of leaking and evaporation, is especially suitable for the main grape-growing areas on the lower fringe of the alluvial fan.

Fig. 10.  Planting grapes in the Gobi.

It calls for special irrigation technique to grow grapes in the gobi.  Irrigation
is essential before germination and sprouting, before flowering, during the period
growth and during winter hibernation.  During the months from June to August when
high temperature prevails, irrigation every 7 days is essential.  During the
period of nourishment and growth, it calls for 20 to 30 times of watering, each
time requiring 60 to 80 m³/mu.  The canal system is mostly classes 3 to 4, and
the ditches for grape planting can substitute for canals of the smallest class.

2.  *Protective forest network*.  Because of the strong winds in the gobi area, it
is necessary to build protective forest shields (Fig. 11), usually in the form of
narrow forest strips (five to six rows) and small forest network.  In the orchards
at the front edge on the windward side, the main strips are 100 m apart, while
secondary and inside strips are 200 m apart.  The strips, 10 m wide, consist mainly
of the tall and fast-growing arrow shaft poplars supplemented by elms and
mulberries on the fringe.

3.  *Land and soil rehabilitation*.  The gobi land at Turfan is mostly in the
piedmont alluvial fan, and because of its steepness, it is necessary to reshape
the land before planting is possible, usually by terracing.  First to be built are
the terrace walls alongside the slope.  Then the soil is soaked with water and the
salt pan is removed.  Next is digging the planting ditches in the long strips of
terraced field.

The planting ditches are 5 m apart, 1.2 m wide at the top, 40 to 60 cm wide at the
bottom, 40 cm deep.  They have a 1:1 gradient, and less than 1% at the bottom.
When the ditches are ready, water is brought in again to wash away the salt until
the main grape root layer is free of salt crust.  Next is the digging of oblong-
shaped planting pits, 1 m deep, 60 cm long and 40 cm wide, which are refilled
with prepared, fertilized "guest soil" from the farms.  Each pit holds two plants.
In the first two years of cultivation, melons and leguminous crops can be planted
alongside the ditches to augment cash income and improve soil quality.  The use of
guest soil contributes significantly to the improvement of the gobi soil (Table 5).

Table 5.   Changes in Organic Matter in Gobi Surface Soil
           after "Guest Soil" Cultivation of Grapes

| Land type | Content of organic matter (%) |
|-----------|-------------------------------|
| Gobi without grape planting | 0.44 |
| Areas in between rows of grape plants | 1.71 |
| Grape-planting pits | 2.35 |

Fig. 11.   Bird's-eye view of Gobi vineyard.

4. *Strengthening the management.*  Due to the barrenness of the soil, it is
necessary to add farm fertilizer around the planting pits before sprouting.  The
way to do it is once a year digging a fertilizer furrow, 60 cm deep, on one side
of the pit, and using 50 to 80 catties of fertilizer per pit.  The fertilizer
furrow moves to a different side of the pit every year, in order to continually
add to the soil fertility.  The next important factor is the density of planting.
The guest-soil cultivation limits the area of nourishment, and per mu yield is
relatively low.  It is therefore necessary to increase the density of planting in
order to raise per mu yield, the proper density being 66 plants per mu.  The shape
of the grape plant also has a great deal to do with the yield.  The best type is
the fan-shaped plant with multiple main stems, from four to six main stems to each
plant, each main stem having a number of secondary stems, which in turn have a
fruit-bearing mother branch and a reserve branch.  Fan-shaped grape plants call
for small trellis and dense planting, and because of their low stature and density,
they have a high wind-resisting capacity.  The gobi area in Turfan County now under
grape cultivation is 2.9 times as big as it was before liberation, fruit yield 5.3
times and per mu yield 2.1 times, while the highest yield per mu is 9000 catties.
It shows that the gobi desert has great potential for grape growing.


CONCLUSIONS

The success of the Turfan people in combatting desertification and transforming the
gobi desert is an eloquent testimony to the fact that only under the leadership
of Chairman Mao and the Chinese Communist Party can be won such victories.  It
proves beyond doubt the great truth that "only socialism can save China".  Before
liberation, after generations of exploitation and oppression by the reactionary
ruling class, and under the system of small-farm economy where each family tilled
the land for its own subsistence, it was altogether impossible to combat the
desert.  Only today, under our superior socialist system when people of all
nationalities in the desert areas are organized and imbued with the revolutionary
spirit of "the foolish old man who moved mountains", and determined to attain
self-reliance through hard and bitter struggles, is it possible to conquer the
wind-sand scourge, transform the gobi and extend the oasis.  The history of "man
retreats as the sand advances" has been reversed into the present-day reality of
"man advances as the sand retreats".  The experiences of the Turfan people in
combatting the deserts have once more told us: "The masses are the real heroes."
From the protective measures of building earthen walls, preparing soil and
protecting seedlings on an individual basis developing into the present-day massive
programmes of building contain-sand-cultivate-grass belts, stop-wind-block-sand
forest belts and the narrow forest strips and small forest networks within the
farmland area and turning the gobi into a vineyard is a process from "material to
spirit, spirit to material, practice to knowledge, knowledge to practice", a
process which is repeated over and over again in a continuous effort to improve
itself.  It shows that man's ability to know and to deal with problems of
desertification is unlimited and will never stop at any one level.  It also
demonstrates that "the masses have an unlimited creative ability" and they are the
major force in the war against the sand.

The Turfan people have gained some initial experiences in combatting the deserts
and in transforming the gobi, but much remains to be done.  At present, under the
guidance of Chairman Mao's revolutionary line, they are continuing their efforts
to improve on the sand-combatting measures.  In the meantime, they are beginning
to attack the problems of yet unprotected wind-eroded land in an effort to further
enlarge the oasis and develop agricultural production, and to further contribute to
the socialist revolution and socialist construction.

# Iran

Maps 2, 3, 4 and Appendix 9 are
inserted in pocket at end of book.

# The Turan Programme

*Department of the Environment, Tehran, Iran*


INTRODUCTION

*Background*

The Iranian Plateau exhibits a long and varied history of desertification.
Comprising over 1½ million square kilometres of high arid country, it includes
most of Iran and extends into south-western Afghanistan and western Pakistan. It
lies between the major river systems of the Oxus and the Indus on the east and the
Tigris and Euphrates on the west, and has functioned historically as a crossroads
for population movements between central Asia and north-east Africa and Arabia,
and between the Indo-Pakistan subcontinent and Europe.  These movements have given
rise to relationships and affinities that are obvious both in the flora and fauna
and in cultural features.  Some ten millennia of human activity since the
domestication of plants and animals have in generally accepted opinion led to
serious reduction in the productivity of the Plateau's natural resources,
specifically in soil and vegetative cover.  However, though the decline may have
been continual, it has not been uniform and much can be learned from reconstruction
of the ecological history of the Iranian Plateau that will be of value in the
treatment of desertification problems elsewhere.

Although the Plateau is in many senses an ecological unit, many of its human use
systems extend beyond the high mountain ranges that define it and its history is
closely interrelated with that of the surrounding lowlands.  It is not yet possible
to produce a synthesis of the earliest land use patterns on the Plateau or to find
complete agreement on its pristine natural ecology, but there is evidence of human
activity for at least 100,000 years, and of agriculture and pastoralism for the
past 10,000 years.  The development of irrigation systems on the major rivers
around the outside of the Plateau, starting with Mesopotamia in the late fourth
millennium, gave rise to a qualitative differentiation between life in the denser
populations and more complex social systems of the lowland cities, and the sparser,
simpler structures of the Plateau, where no such technology that would allow the
development of large dense populations was yet feasible.

This type of ecological differentiation provides one of the themes of this study,
since it illustrates the role of exogenous factors in processes of desertification.
In many cases, and on smaller scales, it can be shown to lead to cultural
discrimination by large dense populations against the relatively small and
scattered populations of arid and semi-arid lands.

Changes in this ecological relationship between the Plateau and the Mesopotamian lowlands is not perceptible until over two millennia later when evidence appears of urban developments on the relatively meagre, largely seasonal rivers on the inside rim of the Plateau. These cities do not appear to have flourished until the period of economic and political expansion of the Achaemenian empire (sixth to fourth centuries B.C.) which coincided with the introduction of a new irrigation technology: the *qanat*.

The *qanat*—known east of Iran as *kariz*, and in North Africa as *foggara*—is an underground channel which brings ground water out onto the surface, where it is required for irrigation, by means of gravity flow. It is built and maintained by means of wells which give access to the channel every 10 to 50 m along its course. Qanats require considerable and long-term investment. Construction takes years, even generations, and regular maintenance is required to maintain the flow. Investment on this scale is not within the means of small sparse populations with simple economies. The investment required for the construction of major qanats could only be managed from within the economies of larger settlements. Qanat building was thus a major means of colonizing new areas, and constitutes a specific exogenous factor in the ecological history of many localities on the Plateau. It led to a new cultural differentiation—in this case, between the more fertile and better watered alluvial fans around the inside edge of the Plateau and the more arid interior.

The introduction of qanat technology revolutionized the settlement and land use patterns of the Plateau. The next comparable technological innovation was mechanization. During the long period of technological stability and consequent stability of land use patterns between these two processes—which may be dated arbitrarily at 750 B.C. and A.D. 1960, respectively—the surface water available from rivers and springs was probably constant except for variation between wet and dry years, and the quantity, quality and distribution of water sources on the Plateau could vary only along a single parameter: the varying ability at different times and in different places to make the investment necessary for the construction and maintenance of qanats and other largely ancillary irrigation works.

The greatest period of investment appears to have been under the Sassanian empire from the third to the seventh centuries A.D. The Arab conquest in the seventh century seems not to have had any permanent effect on investment, which began to deteriorate noticeably only in the period immediately preceding the invasion of the Mongols and then dropped significantly as a result of their invasion in the thirteenth century.

Investment is used here in the sense of the expenditure of labour and in some cases materials for the modification of the environment in order to increase the productivity of natural resources. Various forms of irrigation engineering require the most investment, dry farming requires relatively little, and pastoralism may require none at all unless it is necessary, for example, to increase the number of watering points by digging wells. It is possible to generalize that the greater the investment required by a particular technology the less likelihood of desertification because the population, having more at stake, monitors productivity more carefully.

There is also a sense in which pastoralists may be considered to have made and be maintaining an investment in their rangeland (beyond increasing the number of watering points)—if grazing has modified the vegetation, or maintains it in a subclimax condition, in such a way as to increase long-term pastoral productivity. The significance of fluctuation in levels of investment for understanding desertification is a second important theme in this study. It is important to note that this also is generally an exogenous factor, depending on the interest of urban populations.

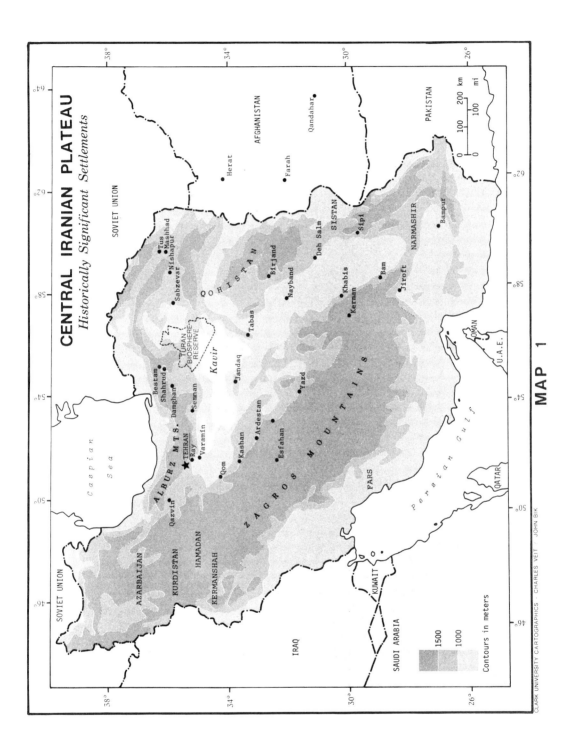

**CENTRAL IRANIAN PLATEAU**

*Historically Significant Settlements*

MAP 1

CLARK UNIVERSITY CARTOGRAPHICS · CHARLES VEIT · JOHN BIK

The ability and readiness to make such investments varied according to larger
political and demographic conditions. Qanats went out of use; villages moved.
The total number of villages and towns fluctuated. Variations in investment
corresponded with variations in the degree of pastoral activity compared to
agricultural activity. But the introduction of qanat technology had opened up the
Plateau to a set of human use systems based on a specific range of agricultural
and pastoral technologies which scarcely changed until very recently. The background to the present desertification problems in Iran was formed cumulatively
through that period of nearly three millennia.

During the 1960s the situation changed. The change in technology brought with it
a change in investment patterns. The most obvious cause for the change was
mechanization, though the role of other factors such as population growth should
not be ignored. Mechanization allowed the use of ground water for irrigation by
means of motorized pumps. Since it is cheaper to buy a pump than build a qanat,
but to keep the pump operating requires continuous expenditure for fuel and
maintenance, people tended to move from qanats to pumps and in so doing, to involve
themselves much more intimately in the larger economic system. Thus, the economic
dependence of marginal lands was increased by mechanization, which led in certain
areas to intensified use with lower investment. Increased desertification was
associated with this process.

The history of the areas vulnerable to desertification on the Iranian Plateau, and
probably elsewhere, since the "urban revolution" in Mesopotamia 3000 B.C. should be
studied in the context of larger social, economic and political developments, the
economic and administrative dependence of sparsely populated areas on the
populations of more densely settled land, and resultant cultural discrimination.
However, it is also necessary to bear in mind that this dependence is one aspect
of a symbiotic relationship. The intimacy of the relationship between the arid
centre and the fertile margins of the Iranian Plateau has increased considerably
as the result of the mechanization of transport and communications. The use of
arid rangelands by transhumant pastoralists who summer in the high mountain pastures
on the periphery has been greatly facilitated. The use of these rangelands is now
directly related to the urban meat and dairy markets. The compensation of shepherds
is now determined through competition with urban labour markets.

Of Iran's total territory of 165 million hectares, 125 million fall under the
heading of rangeland which includes the uncultivated and uninhabited land—forest,
mountain and desert. Iran's rural population in 1974 consisted of 18,800,000 which
is equal to 58% of the population. It was distributed among over 65,000 settlements
of which more than two-thirds have a population of less than 250, and almost one-
third has less than 50. These small scattered populations are a human resource,
without which the national resources of Iran's arid lands would produce less. The
figures alone are sufficient to show that the degree of interdependence between
arid and semi-arid and more fertile areas in Iran makes desertification a national
and a human problem. This problem is more critical now than ever before.

*Iranian Consciousness of Desertification*

This brief survey suggests a long period of equilibrium. However, there is
evidence to suggest that not only were there great fluctuations in population and
investment, but overall deterioration in soil and vegetative cover during this
period was considerable. The proportion of Iran affected was sufficient to create
the consciousness of a national problem already in the fifties. The disappearance
of wildlife and the severity of sand problems and dust storms were among the first
factors to attract general attention. The long drought at the end of the fifties
and the beginning of the sixties ensured that desertification would receive
comprehensive attention in the future. It was at this time that Iran began to

embark on a programme of intensive economic development and, a little later, of administrative revolution.

Towards the end of the fifties specialized departments were formed in the Ministry of Agriculture and the University of Tehran, which embarked on long-term programmes of sand stabilization, watershed management, range improvement, wildlife conservation and general programmes of desert research. In 1962 a programme of land reform was begun; in 1963 all forests and rangelands were nationalized, and in 1967 the nationalization programme was extended to the country's water resources. These administrative and legislative measures—once again exogenous factors—had far-reaching effects on man-land relationships throughout those parts of Iran vulnerable to desertification. In combination with the effects of the drought and increasing availability of motorized equipment, they set the scene for significant changes in settlement and land use systems.

These measures were radical and far-sighted but their effects have not always been restricted to the benefits that were planned. For example, certain details of the Land Reform Law combined with the availability of tractors allowed the extension of dry farming onto unsuitable soils (including vertical ploughing of hillsides), which led to increased soil erosion. Nationalization of rangelands, although it had definite social benefits, has reduced the pastoralists' flexibility, and perhaps also their sense of ecological responsibility—essential features of efficient land use in arid zones—and removed an element of personal investment. It is noteworthy that one result of both of these measures was to reduce the need for investment as a basis for exploitation, and that degradation ensued.

Interest in the deserts generally increased through the sixties among intellectuals and planners, and in the seventies a number of government institutions have established special departments or programmes responsible for the desert areas. The responsibilities of these agencies vary in their emphasis on natural and human factors, and suffer generally from the lack of an overall coordinating and planning authority, specifically and actively concerned with vulnerable areas.

The Department of the Environment, which was established in the Prime Minister's Office in 1974, has shown a special interest in desertification as part of its general programme for the conservation and study of representative ecosystems. This programme includes the establishment of a network of parks and reserves which presently totals 8 million hectares and is divided into four categories of which two are important here: (1) Protected Areas, which are lands of strategic conservation value set aside for management, and (2) Wildlife Refuges, which, in addition, support significant wildlife populations (IUCNNR, 1976). Nine of these areas have recently been designated Biosphere Reserves for the purpose of participating in the coordinated worldwide programme of conservation and research organized under the Man and the Biosphere Programme. Concern for the human factor in these areas set aside for conservation in the more arid parts of the country led the Department in 1975 to institute a programme of research aimed at the development of management and monitoring programmes paying special attention to the problem of maintaining a balance between conservation, productivity and socio-cultural viability.

*The Turan Programme*

In order to concentrate this research effort a pilot programme was started in an area chosen for its representativeness. The Turan Protected Area, which includes a Wildlife Refuge, and has now been formally declared a Biosphere Reserve, covers 1.8 million hectares on the north-eastern margin of the central deserts. Historically it has formed a no-man's-land between two major provinces (Khorasan

and Qumis) and was selected for protection because the potential richness of its
vegetation was judged an excellent basis for the development of alternative
methods of conservation.  In May 1971 it was assessed as severely degraded, partly
as the result of an excessive population of domestic animals which were in
relatively poor condition.  Shrubs were heavily browsed and there was an almost
total absence of ephemeral and perennial forbs and grasses.

In order to deal appropriately with the human factor, the human populations outside
the Biosphere Reserve, which have traditionally made use of the area, and the
human use systems that overlap its boundaries were included in the study.  It is
these systems, as much as the range of representative habitats in the Reserve, that
make this choice of study area particularly significant, since they demonstrate the
close economic interdependence of urban, mountain and desert habitats on the Iranian
Plateau.

The Turan Programme sought to bring together representatives of all the academic
disciplines that could be brought to bear on the history of the interaction of
human activity and the natural resources of the area, and formulate a theoretical
framework or set of criteria that would integrate their work and lead them to
focus on problems of long-term management.  Specifically, it was aimed to generate
a dialogue between representatives of the natural, human biological, and the social
sciences.  From the beginning it was decided to seek out scholars both in Iran and
abroad whose personal research interests and experience fitted into the developing
framework of the Programme and to facilitate their work, rather than hire "experts"
for limited periods.  In this way it has been possible to build a research team
with long-term interests in the Programme and long experience in addressing the
problems it deals with, without cutting them off from normal communication with
their disciplines.

This policy has the disadvantage that it does not produce predictable results at
predictable times.  Nevertheless, the Programme is gathering momentum, and an
outline of the components that are in progress and those that are still sought is
given in an appendix.  The present study has been produced out of current work,
mostly preliminary field reports with little time depth of recording.  Despite the
obvious drawbacks of this type of data, it has been deemed valuable to produce this
study from it at this stage because of the comprehensive ecological character of
the Programme and its emphasis on the problems of the human component.


*Description of the Study Area*

The Turan Programme for Integrated Ecological Research and Management in the Central
Deserts of Iran covers the Turan Biosphere Reserve, neighbouring populations that
have traditionally used the area and adjacent land forms that have direct relevance
to the Reserve such as the sand sea on its eastern boundary.  The Reserve presents
a variety of habitats, including three extensive plains at different altitudes,
varying from 700 to 1400 m, a saline river system, three mountain systems rising
to a maximum of 2200 m, large areas of broken country and some 200,000 hectares of
sand including moving dunes, and a vast expanse of barren playa.  Climatological
information is incomplete both in time depth and geographical coverage.  Published
syntheses of existing data show the 200-mm isohyet passing through the northern
part of the area.  The southern plain probably receives less than 100 mm.  A light
snow covering appears on the higher mountains for 2 to 4 months of the year and
snow lies on the higher northern plains for short periods.  Only the central salt
river (*Kal-e Shur*) flows at least intermittently throughout the year.  Rainfall of
several millimetres at a time generates sheet run off and wadi (arroyo) flooding.
Springs occur on the southern slopes of the mountain ranges.  Soils are generally
light and sandy except for solonchak in the playas.  Vegetation varies according
to land form, and, secondarily, according to human activity patterns.  Woody shrubs

predominate with ephemerals and annuals growing largely in their protection.
Perennial cover over most of the plains varies between 5 and 40%.  Flora and
mammalian fauna generally show great affinity to the Kara Kum in Soviet Turkmenistan
to the north.  Vegetation is heavily modified by human use in the vicinity of
permanent settlement and winter sheep pens, and has been characterized as anti-
pastoral throughout the area.

The dominant form of land use is pastoralism of various types, sedentary and
transhumant.  At present some 150,000 sheep and goats (1975-6 figures, see
Appendix 5 for earlier figures) winter in the area from November to May, of which
25,000 belong to the local settled populations and remain in the area through the
summer.  Local populations also keep camels, donkeys and cattle.  Apart from the
125,000 sheep and goats that spend the winter only in the area, most of the local
populations move their animals in and out of the area seasonally and according to
general conditions.  Agriculture is also important around settlements and is
conducted by means of irrigation, from qanats, springs, diversion of run off and
by direct rainfall.  The total human population that has at least a potential
interest in some part of the area may be estimated at 20,000.  Of these, some 2000
in the two groups of villages known as Khar and Tauran on the eastern margin of
the area are intimately involved with it.  There is a close relationship of
interdependence between the settled and transhumant populations.


*Desertification Problems*

Preliminary surveys suggested that the natural resources of the area are
deteriorating and the quality of human life is falling further behind that of
neighbouring less arid areas.  The vegetative cover has been judged to be degraded
and possibly still deteriorating in quality and quantity as the result of
excessive exploitation by both settled and transhumant populations, which was
causing gradual elimination of the more palatable components, increase in wind
erosion, and sand accumulation and movement.  The human population itself appeared
to be declining, and threatened in the long term to cease to be viable owing to
the migration of the youth to the cities.  Transhumant pastoralists find it more
and more difficult to recruit shepherds.  Medical and other social services are
almost non-existent.


*Criteria of Relevance*

This study makes use of preliminary results from the investigation of these
problems.  However, it is recognized that evaluation of conditions and trends in
these complex and interlocking ecosystems and human use systems can be made only
according to certain criteria, not according to absolute standards.  The criteria
implicit in this study derive from the view that since Iran can cultivate only 10%
of its total 165 million hectares in order to support a population of 35 million
presently growing at 2.8 - 3.0% per year, and counts 100 million hectares as arid
rangelands, it must plan for maximum sustainable productivity from the natural
resources throughout its total territory.  The problem is how to achieve this aim
while also developing the highest possible standard of living for the total
population.  An example of alternative methods would be strategies to concentrate
the population into settlement centres large enough to support the full range of
services and facilities recognized necessary to civilized life, *versus* relatively
homogeneous distribution of the rural population in order to facilitate the most
efficient use of resources.  A second example lies in the alternatives of maximum
diversification of land use *versus* zoning of specialized land use patterns.

*Biases*

Besides the short history of the study and the preliminary and incomplete nature of the results so far, the possibility of certain biases must be recognized. The most significant of these derives from the recent pattern of precipitation. The year 1970-1 is known to have been an extra dry one, but the actual precipitation is not known from anywhere inside the area. Since 1971 there has been a succession of relatively good years. The one professional ecologist who saw the area in spring 1971 and in the subsequent years states that the vegetation now presents a different impression, but it is not possible to quantify this difference in terms of either biomass or precipitation.

The second bias could be more serious. It derives from the effects of legislation concerning use of natural resources generally, and in the area particularly, and of its implementation. Specifically, although no holdings were large enough to be affected by Land Reform, all rangeland was nationalized as an integral part of the Shah-People Revolution that was begun in 1963. Since then there has been no free market in grazing. Secondly, the fact that Turan was given the status of Protected Area, that part of it was reclassified as a Wildlife Refuge in 1976, and the whole was declared a Biosphere Reserve in 1977, held implications for the local populations of protection from or restriction of grazing, and is known to have affected their pastoral and agricultural strategies. These legislative influences are exogenous factors whose effects are difficult to evaluate or quantify, and to the extent that they do not derive from market forces and are due to factors that do not derive from the relationship between the populations of the deserts and the more fertile margins, they are different from the exogenous factors emphasized in this study.

In what follows, the vegetation structure of Turan is first described. This description serves as a basis for an account of the main productive technologies in the area and their distribution. Then the arguments for desertification are given and these arguments are given historical perspective in a section that assembles the evidence for the ecological history of the area. Finally, the situation is assessed from the point of view of economic efficiency and the quality of life of the existing local populations. Throughout it is to be remembered that the data derive from preliminary reports of studies that are still in progress.


        VEGETATION

The Vegetation Map shows five basic vegetation types in the Turan Biosphere Reserve:

1. *Salsola-Zygophyllum* communities generally in the plains with 5-40% cover up to about 1300 m;

2. *Artemisia-Ephedra-Amygdalus* communities, usually above 1300 m;

3. *Astragalus-Cousinia* communities on the higher mountains, descending to about 1400 m on northern slopes;

4. *Stipagrostis-Calligonum* communities on fixed or shifting sands in some cases up to 40% cover;

5. Halophytic vegetation on playa margins, sometimes with dense annual cover up to 90%.

This is a first tentative categorization formulated before the final tabulation of field inventories and comparison with data from similar areas such as the Kavir National Park (a similar reserve approximately 300 km to the west in which all human activity ceased 6 years ago, and which in the continuation of the Turan Programme will be used as a control area). It is based on identifications made for *Flora Iranica*, but some names are only provisional and further identification is required.

A list of species so far collected and identified is given in Appendix 1. It is worth mentioning that no new species have been discovered in Turan, and so-called narrow endemics are poorly represented even in the mountainous parts of the area. Species rather largely distributed through the most arid parts of the Iranian highlands prevail and larger genera are usually represented by their hardier representatives.

The categorization on the map is simplified both because of the demands of presentation at this particular scale and because of the basic theme of this study—vegetation as the most significant interface between human activity and natural processes. Simplified to this degree the Vegetation Map conforms usefully with the variation in human land use. It also fits the variation in the degree of vulnerability to desertification processes. For example, types 1, 2 and 4 are used as rangelands by transhumant flocks, except in the close vicinity of villages where they are used as pasture for village flocks and in some cases historically for dry farming.

In fact the vegetation is considerably more complex, and as work is continued it is expected that finer cartographic differentiation of vegetation types will be desirable. In the present map dominant communities are somewhat over-emphasized. In fact throughout the area the various plant communities are arranged in a mosaic according to a combination of geomorphological features and variations in the history of human use, which in turn is based on the variation of natural features. For instance, in areas where rock outcrops predominate, such as the predominantly limestone ranges, only the vegetation of that particular habitat is indicated, and the different communities on the slopes with deeper soil accumulation or in the valleys with better water supply, do not appear. Even the comparatively homogeneous vegetation of the extensive plains is interspersed by specific variant communities in the deeper runnels, along the sides of dry rivers and on the gravels of the larger dry river beds. Similarly, small-scale variation due to concentration of human exploitative activities could not be shown, for example, around winter sheep pens, spring and early summer milking stations and the immediate environs of the smaller settlements. Finally, because of the vastness of the area it was necessary in several cases to resort to extrapolation, based mainly on contours, and broken lines were used in some cases to indicate uncertainty of border lines between communities.

*Population and Dispersion Studies of Dominant Species*

Some researchers prefer to classify the Turan vegetation as degraded steppic rather than sub-desertic. Some of their reasoning will be given later in the discussion of the effects of human activity on the vegetation (Chapter 4). As part of an investigation of the basis of this classification, a series of studies of the population structure and dispersion of dominant species was planned. *Zygophyllum eurypterum* was chosen for the first study since its dominance over large areas gives the vegetation of Turan one of its most characteristic features. An understanding of the interaction between human activity and the population structure and distribution of this species would be an important breakthrough.

Because of the height of the shrub and the deep green colour of the leaves between
March and July it gives an exaggerated impression of dominance.  One researcher was
struck by the regularity both of the distribution and of the size of the plant.
The subjective impression that small plants were scarcer than larger ones was
tested by measurements made upon the 532 plants of this species within a 1-hectare
exclosure on the plain 9 km south-east of Delbar.  Height, maximum diameter and
diameter at right angles to maximum diameter were measured for each plant (see
Appendix 2A).  Frequency distribution histograms were constructed for height
measurements which confirmed the initial impression that large plants are more
abundant than small ones.  A frequency peak occurs between 70 and 90 cm, and few
plants were found below 40 cm in height.

These data imply either a low germination success of the species or a very high
seedling mortality which could pose a threat to the continued survival of this
important species.  Several possible explanations of the observed data present
themselves:

1.  Succession.  The community may be unstable in the long term and in the process
of transition to a different vegetation type.  If this were so, one might expect
some other species to be regenerating beneath the *Zygophyllum* cover which will
eventually replace it.  No such contender for dominance was found.

2.  Changing physical environment.  New climatic stresses, such as drought or
temperature, may have reduced the capacity of the species to reproduce efficiently.
If this were so, one might also expect reduced productivity and this could be
checked by annual growth ring measurement.  Viable seed is formed, but appears to
be heavily predated on falling from the bush, probably by rodents and other seed
eaters.

3.  Intra-specific competition.  If the environment is effectively saturated by the
current population of *Zygophyllum*, i.e. the carrying capacity has been attained,
then it is possible that further recruitment is discouraged by intraspecific
competition pressures.  These could take several forms, such as toxic exudates in
the leaves or roots of the adult plants, or depletion of a resource such as water
or minerals by the adults, thus excluding seedlings.  If such intra-specific
competition pressures exist one might expect a tendency to regular spacing in the
population.

4.  Changing biotic environment.  Some new predatory or pathological pressure may
be causing seedling failure.  This could result from:

   (a)  A "natural" predator or pathogen increase.  About 34% of bushes have their
        rooting areas burrowed by rodents.  Direct physical damage and seedling
        (and seed) predation could increase mortality.  An unidentified organism
        bores into the wood of *Zygophyllum*, apparently invading the roots and
        boring its way through aerial stems eventually to emerge via a small hole.
        Several small fungi are found to infect the woody parts.  None of these
        organisms appears to have reached epidemic proportions.

   (b)  Increased grazing pressures, mainly from sheep and goats, may be causing
        increased juvenile mortality, thus causing population instability.

The third hypothesis above can be supported or eliminated by a simple test of
dispersion in the plants.  Two techniques were employed to make this test.  Random
bushes were selected on the basis of proximity to random points (determined by
random coordinates within the hectare exclosure) and the distance to the nearest
neighbour was measured.  Results (50 measurements) have been subjected to
preliminary analyses and the implications are that dispersion is non-random and
tends toward regularity.  Secondly, density and cover measurements were taken

within 128 5 x 5-m quadrats, arranged in a linear sequence outside the exclosure.  In
a Poisson (random) distribution the variance of such data should equal the mean.
So far density data only have been analysed, but this shows a strong departure from
randomness towards regularity.  If further analysis and research upholds this
hypothesis the implications for management of the use of the vegetation are
interesting.  The population and distribution of this species are not significantly
modified by human activity.  However, it is possible that human activity has
allowed it to establish this dominance, possibly at the expense of better forage
species.  The nature of the competitive factors remains to be demonstrated.

Mean weight was also calculated and came to 4.86 kg with a standard error of
0.14 kg.  The total biomass amounted to 2581.9 kg/ha—a figure which, given the
validity of the above hypothesis, is probably representative for this shrub
throughout those parts of the area where it dominates.

## Dendrochronological Studies

Dendrochronological studies have also begun.  The first project was done on the
trunks of *Zygophyllum* shrubs harvested from an area 25 x 25 m adjacent to the
exclosure and six samples from elsewhere in the area.  Preliminary results give
indications of the climatic record back to 1889 (see Appendix 2B) and demonstrate
the potential of this type of study on desert shrubs, but the sample must be
enlarged to allow reliable reconstruction of the climatic record.

## Support for the Hypothesis of Intra-Specific Competition

It was noted that the age of the harvested shrubs showed no relation to any other
measured parameter.  This is probably due to the degeneration in height and general
size and weight of senile shrubs.  A small shrub, therefore, may be very young or
very old—which reinforces the hypothesis of intra-specific competition, since the
small end of the frequency distribution is inflated by senile members, and young
plants are even scarcer than appears from the data on size.

## Studies of Germination and Establishment

The clearance of a quadrat adjacent to the exclosure will allow a long-term study
of the germination and establishment of *Zygophyllum* at a site where according to
the hypothesis of intra-specific competition an increased rate of recruitment
would be expected.

## Palynological Studies

Further assistance in the reconstruction of the climatic record will come from
palynological studies that have been commenced in the playas.  Results so far
demonstrate that pollen is recoverable from these sediments, but further work
awaits the formation of a reference collection of pollen.

TECHNOLOGIES

## Pastoralism

The key to an understanding of the interaction between human activity and the
vegetation lies in the repertoire of productive technologies. It has been argued
already that this repertoire remained unchanged for over 2000 years up to 1960.
In Turan there has been little technological change since that date (except that
certain subsidiary technologies have disappeared), but there has been considerable
socio-economic change as the result of mechanization of transport and legislative
developments in the country as a whole. Throughout, the human populations have
depended on a network of different pastoral and agricultural technologies,
interrelated through the social structure and linking the area with the larger
socio-economic system of Iran in various ways.

## Transhumant Pastoralism

The dominant technology in the area is a transhumant form of pastoralism. A group
of pastoralists, based on the small town of Sangsar, just north of Semnan, 400 km
west-north-west of the area, summer in the high mountain pastures of the Alborz
and send some 125,000 of their animals into the area for the winter. The animals
enter the area in October-November in flocks of 400 with four to five shepherds
for every two flocks, and settle in at sheep pens constructed of dung and brush.
The shepherds may also bring along a score or so of their own animals. The pen
may belong to the owner of the animals or may be rented from a local resident. A
certain amount of repair is required from year to year. Until recently, each pen
would be burned and rebuilt regularly to destroy vermin, but since the introduction
of insecticides, this is no longer necessary. A large proportion of the shepherds
are from the local population for whom shepherding for the transhumants represents
a valuable alternative resource. The pens are commonly located about 4 hours'
grazing slow walk from a spring or well (which in some cases is used by two or more
pens) so that the animals will water at midday in the cold weather. Pens are
commonly built in twos in order to allow the shepherds more flexibility. The
minimum distance between pens is 6 km. If the minimum grazing area for two flocks,
therefore, is a circle with a radius of 3 km, then the densest stocking ratio in
the area would be about 3.5 hectares per animal. Apart from investment in a pen,
shepherds, a watering point, and a dog, the expenses of the flock owner (who may
own any number from one to more than ten flocks in the area) may include payment
for someone to keep local flocks off his grazing during the summer. During the
last 12 years, it has become customary to supplement the grazing with barley from
January until the spring makes this superfluous, usually early in March. Lambing
takes place in late February. Typical flock structure before lambing is 220
pregnant ewes, 100 female yearlings, 10 rams, 50 pregnant goats, 20 female
yearlings, 5 males. A certain admixture of goats in the flock is technologically
important because goats fulfil some of the functions of the sheep dog in other
parts of the world. (Here dogs only protect the flock from pedators.) They also
give more milk for a longer period. However, the Sangsari are primarily concerned
with meat production and use a breed of sheep that is adapted to the long migration
but is a relatively poor producer of wool and milk. This Sangsari form of
pastoralism is very closely related to market forces—for meat, barley and labour.
The economics of this system are discussed below (p.209).

## Sedentary Pastoralism

Three other technologically distinct forms of pastoralism are currently practised
in the area, all of which are on a smaller scale and less directly related to
market changes because they are, to a greater or lesser extent, concerned with

producing also for their own consumption. One of these three is practised by
sixty families from a tribal group of nomadic pastoralists, called Chubdari, who
gave up their black tents, built a village and settled in the area 15 years ago.
Previously they had moved seasonally as nomads with all their families and
belongings between winter grazing in the vicinity of their present village and
summer grazing some 50 miles to the north. Animal losses incurred in the 1958-1963
drought constituted a major factor leading to their decision to settle but since
the 1970-71 drought their flocks have grown again steadily and now approximate
10,000. They appear unwilling to limit further growth—which has already led to
conflict with neighbouring Sangsari. The Chubdari keep a different breed of sheep,
which is an all-round producer of wool, milk and meat, with a small admixture of
goats, and practice a rotational system within a maximum of 15 km of the village.

The Chubdari also keep about 200 camels which they sell for meat. Most camels in
eastern Iran are no longer herded but are left to find their own forage and come
to water when they will. They are usually branded in spring but otherwise left
alone except when individual owners decide to take one or more for sale as meat.
Camel meat (the cheapest available) sells in the towns for Rls 100=$1.40 per kg
and a healthy adult animal fetches Rls 30,000 or $425 in meat value. The Chubdari,
however, herd their animals. This practice is to some extent a carryover from the
pre-1960 system when camels were important to their mobility. But it is also
conditioned by official discouragement of camel herding. There has been pressure
on pastoralists to reduce the numbers of browsers—both camels and goats. Free
ranging camels have the further disadvantage that they tend to monopolize isolated
water sources in the summer and inhibit wildlife.

The other two forms are practised by the villages of Khar and Tauran and emphasize
goats. Villagers who have very few animals—less than 20—keep them in the vicinity
of the village throughout the year, while those who have more make special
arrangements for spring grazing in more favorable areas away from the villages. A
few families in Salehabad in Tauran have as many as 1000 or more, and need to make
special arrangements for the entire year. The size of these flocks appears to be
effectively limited by the number of women available to milk and to convert the
milk into storable products.


*Ecology and Ethology of Domesticated Animals*

The technology of traditional forms of pastoralism has been little studied and is
inadequately understood. In cases like Turan, where pastoralism has probably
been the dominant form of land use for many thousands of years, the mechanisms of
co-adaptation between the vegetation and the domesticated animals may repay careful
attention. The Turan Programme includes a project for this type of study. It was
begun during the summer of 1976 in the summer grazing area of 1000 animals, mostly
goats, belonging to a family from Salehabad in Tauran. A brief account of this
project is included here because, even though it has scarcely begun, it is
theoretically innovative and promises to answer some of the basic questions about
traditional forms of pastoralism in relation to desertification.

The basic premise of the study is that it should be possible to study human
ecology in the same manner that the socio-ecology of other primates and other
species is studied in ecology and ethology. Thus, hunting and gathering populations
might be treated as part of a predator-prey system and a herbivore system, and
pastoralists could be seen as the attendant predators on herds of ungulates grazing
in arid zones. It is possible that human groups with particular subsistence
patterns are arbitrarily located with respect to their environment; that their
presence in any particular case can be adequately understood historically, and
their cultures purely the results of social forces. The introduction of such

concepts as evolution, selection and adaptation may be superfluous. For example, while it is well accepted that hunter-gatherers are ecologically adapted in at least certain ways, it is often maintained that nomads—perhaps pastoralists, in general—merely live in the arid environment and not from it. In fact, it is frequently claimed that traditional pastoralism is extremely destructive to the environment that supports it. However, sheep and goat pastoralism in the Middle East is an ancient subsistence pattern. Its long history and widespread use for converting primary productivity of arid zones into milk, meat and wool suggests that it is significantly adapted—even co-adapted—to its environment. This adaptation in the context of progressive degradation raises questions that require careful ecological investigation. In fact, it is necessary to ask why traditional forms of pastoralism in the Middle East are so widespread and enduring. The following hypotheses should be tested:

1. Middle Eastern pastoralism in its nomadic, transhumant and sedentary permutations is an ecologically co-adapted system in which deterioration of the range has been matched by physiological adaptation in the animals and changes in herding strategy.

2. Cultural practices—the technology—including control over herd movement and reproduction, maximize production, without regard to the condition of the basic resource—the vegetation.

3. Steady range deterioration over long periods during which pastoralism has exerted greater pressure on the vegetation than a wild herbivore population with its endogenous regulating mechanisms has led to a situation where exogenous factors, such as climatic change, or national, economic or legislative developments, such as the closing of national borders across traditional migration routes, cause permanent disruptions of the system.

4. The long-term coexistence of plants and domesticated animals has resulted in co-adaptation in which the plants have developed toxins and other defences, and the animals have developed detoxifying physiologies and specialized foraging strategies which allow them to subsist at the price of continuous reduction in efficiency. Furthermore, the domesticated animals, if of more than one species, may be niche-differentiated as a result of human selection for the broadest environmental exploitation.

If a significant co-adaptation of animals and plants exists in spite of a general downward trend, it follows that an understanding of the ecology of the flocks is essential for an understanding of the ecology of pastoralists, which in turn could be an important component of any programme designed to correct the situation. In hypotheses 1, 2 and 3 it is assumed that natural selection, particularly "K" selection, works on cultural systems and that cultural practices can be regarded as normally adaptive, with or without equilibrium. The 4th hypothesis simply requires that the normal relationship between plants and their herbivores has had sufficient time to develop in the case of domesticated herds.

Only this type of study can answer the essential question: whether traditional forms of pastoralism, which is still the only productive technology that can feasibly be employed over vast areas of the world's arid rangelands, should be facilitated and improved or actively discouraged as part of the struggle against desertification. For example, the methods of quantitative ecology will yield the following types of information: what species and quantities do different types of animal choose to graze or browse in different conditions and at different times of the year?; how do these preferences and requirements plus the formation of "goat paths", general trampling, urination, and defaecation interact with other natural and cultural factors to affect the quantity and quality of vegetation?; what ethological factors affect the general impact on the vegetation on the one hand,

and the technology and life of the pastoralists on the other?

Data are being accumulated on the details of sheep and goat behaviour in relation to choice of grazing, social interaction, expenditure of energy, and productivity. Preliminary results suggest that co-adaptation of flocks and vegetation is at an advanced stage. An average of fifty feeding events per 20-minute observation period was recorded among goats—which would maximize their ability to digest toxic material. Further, the animals were in acceptable condition, but it is expected that comparison of biological productivity data with data from less degraded arid rangelands will show lower rates of conversion efficiency.

## Agriculture

With the exception of the Chubdari all the settled populations in the area also depend to a greater or lesser extent on agriculture. (The Chubdari attempted agriculture when they settled, but were unsatisfied with the results and have long since reverted to an exclusive interest in pastoralism.)

## Principal Crops

The most important crops are wheat, barley, cotton, tobacco and grapes. Subsidiary crops include vegetables and fruits. Wheat is grown primarily for domestic requirements but in some years a surplus is produced and sold. Barley and other grains such as millet were also grown for human consumption until the sixties but are now used only as animal feed—presumably an indication of an improved standard of living, as well as the spread of urban values and improved access to markets. Cotton is a cash crop grown for sale in Sabzevar as a result of the motorization of transport. Tobacco is a government monopoly and grown under licence. Grapes cannot be moved to the city markets quickly and carefully enough to be competitive, and the excess is rendered into syrup, which is a staple item of diet through the winter.

## Irrigation

Except for wheat and barley, all these crops are grown by irrigation from qanats or springs on cycles of 12 to 16 days. Ground water is abundant in good years but fluctuates annually with levels of precipitation. The historical importance of qanat technology has already been discussed. The principal advantage is that once the investment has been made, the water continues to flow, requiring only a minimum of maintenance. In comparison with mechanized irrigation technologies, this is now seen to be a disadvantage: much of the water is wasted because it cannot be turned off when not required. In Tauran qanat water runs to waste for much of the winter and is often in short supply in the summer. A further disadvantage consists of the vulnerability of qanats to natural events such as earthquakes and floods. The abandonment of the village of Yakarig in 1973 was probably due to the destruction of its qanat by a flood.

## Dry Farming

Wheat and barley are also cultivated by direct rainfall. Most of the surface area of central Tauran shows evidence of having been dry farmed in the past. If rainfall is promising in early spring, large areas are sown with wheat and barley on the chance that further rain will bring it to maturity.

*Bund Farming*

The most interesting agricultural technology for the reconstruction of the
ecological history of central Tauran is a form of irrigation that may have the
longest history of any irrigation technology in this part of the world.  Run off
is diverted into prepared fields, trapped by an earthwork and allowed to
infiltrate and deposit its sediment.  This method will be discussed further below
in the section on the ecological history of the area.

*Flexibility and Interdependence*

This ends a brief description of the major productive technologies currently
practised in Turan.  As might be expected in an arid area, in order to cope in the
long term with the irregularity and unpredictability of precipitation, users of
the area maximize their options.  Individuals either keep different species of
animal or types of land and irrigation supply and different employment possibilities
available, or maintain a network of relationships with others who have access to
different resources.  The Chubdari, for instance, whose cultural identity involves
them closely with one specific technology, cultivate a network of relationships
in the villages of Khar and Tauran and the town of Sabzevar for the trade of
animals and pastoral products.  Interdependence of local residents and transhumants
appears to have been particularly important in recent years, but the transhumants
are now finding it difficult to compete as employers with the labour market in the
towns.

To conclude this section, it should be noted that there are no essential elements
of the primary food production technologies in the history of Turan that lead
inevitably to degradation or desertification.  The causes of desertification
therefore must be sought in the factors that determine how these technologies are
applied.  But first the evidence for present and past desertification in the area
will be examined.

EVIDENCE OF DESERTIFICATION

Data collected so far provide no quantitative evidence of continuing deterioration
of the vegetative cover in Turan.  It is expected that such evidence will appear
as the Programme proceeds.  In the meantime, however, there are a number of
indicators that deterioration has occurred in the past and that primary productivity
in the area has suffered as a result of the history of human activity.  In this
section these factors are discussed and related to the technologies described above.

*Disturbance Vegetation*

A number of features of the vegetation of Turan can only be explained as the result
of disturbance.  Perhaps the most interesting of these features is the association
of *Goebelia pachycarpa* with the dry-farmed areas of central Tauran (for plant list
see Appendix 1).  *Goebelia pachycarpa* is a perennial herb of 15-35 cm with widely
creeping subterraneous stem systems causing the formation of large colonies, which
often cover thousands of square metres continuously.  It is highly unpalatable
when green, but is grazed by village flocks when dry.  Apart from being very common
and often dominant in the dry farmed or irregularly irrigated areas around Baghestan,
it also invades the sand dunes to the north and effectively contributes to the
stabilization process, but it is seldom seen in less disturbed habitats.  This
plant is now dominant or characteristic over some 1000 hectares in central Tauran,
where the original vegetation has been replaced or modified by cultivation, although
probably less than 20% of this area is ever farmed now.  However, although the
drainage appears to be in a down-cutting phase, there is no sign of serious soil

erosion, possibly because of the binding qualities of this species' root systems.

Other disturbance vegetation is particularly conspicuous within a varying radius of villages and winter sheep pens. The most conspicuous and characteristic species of this disturbance vegetation are *Peganum harmala*—the wild rue, the seeds of which are burned to ward off the evil eye throughout much of the Mediterranean and the Middle East—and *Alhagi camelorum*, "camel thorn". The distribution of the following Species in relation to human activity is also interesting:

*Cousinia congesta*, a monocarpic perennial of 30-60 cm found on deeper soils up to altitudes of 1300 m, is very common around permanent settlements and indicates heavily disturbed habitats. It is never seen in more natural vegetation.

*C. eryngioides*, another monocarpic perennial or biannual of 40-70 cm, replaces the former in medium altitudes from about 1350 m upwards and often penetrates further into less disturbed rangelands, but is also absent from natural rangelands.

*C. piptocephla* differs from the foregoing by much longer involucral bracts and an almost globular shape is scattered throughout the area in lower to medium altitudes from about 1050-1300 m on sandy or gravelly soil. It has a distinct subruderal tendency and grows preferably around settlements and along roads and ravines, often in degraded *Artemisia-Ephedra* communities.

*Hulthemia berberidifolia*, a creeping dwarf shrub of 5-15 cm which forms dense communities in high altitudes of 1300 m upwards, is found especially in *Artemisia-Ephedra* and *Stipa-Cousinia* communities on deeper soil, and becomes a dominant weed under strong human influence around villages.

*Ephedra intermedia* is especially common in areas with a high degree of human influence. It is a shallow-rooting dwarf shrub of 20-40 cm, which often covers several square metres and sometimes forms almost complete cover. It is very common on all non-saline soils and in most plant communities from 1150 to 1300 m upwards, except north-exposed slopes of more than 1900 m. It contains an alkaloid and is poisonous to young goats.

*E. strobilacea*, which is similar to the foregoing but 30-70 cm tall, is very common in the plains and rocky hills up to 1100-1300 m. It is a major component of *Salsola-Zygophyllum* communities and also contains an alkaloid poisonous to young animals.

*Anabasis setifera*, a weak dwarf shrub of 10-35 cm, very common and locally dominant up to 1150 m on almost any soil except strongly saline ones, is particularly common in disturbed habitats.

*Salsola tomentosa*, a dwarf shrub of 5-25 cm, common in almost any habitat except sand and saline soils, and particularly on plains around settlements and sheep pens, is a typical component of *Salsola-Zygophyllum* communities and its dominance generally indicates strong degradation.

The distribution of *Zygophyllum* and the two species of *Artemisia*, the most common dominants in the area, may also prove to be anthropogenic (see above, Chapter 2). *Artemisia* and the seeds of *Zygophyllum* are important forage and both are used for fuel and construction. The distribution often following also appears to have been affected significantly, especially by use for fuel and construction:

*Pistacia khinjuk*, a tall shrub or more rarely a small tree, rising to 3 m, with the shrub habit caused either by regeneration from stumps following cutting or extremely dry periods, is common in all the mountains in the southern part of the area, and is highly valued as fuel—which has undoubtedly resulted in a strong reduction of the population and probably in its disappearance from many suitable habitats which are more accessible and productive.

*P. atlantica* is a rarer species reaching 4 to 6 m. The surviving individuals are isolated and sometimes protected—almost certainly remnants of former, much larger populations in medium altitudes.

*Certoides latens*, a dwarf shrub of 15-35 cm, sometimes collected for fuel, is found in normal density only at some distance from villages.

*Haloxylon aphyllum* is one of the most valuable fuel species. It is found as a shrub or small tree of 0.3-3 m, and is very common throughout the area up to 1200-1300 m on fine-textured soils of plains and valley bottoms (often with a sand layer) and only there the dominant species, but scattered also on rocky slopes except limestone; it often penetrates salt marsh communities of Seidlitzia and sometimes is found even in open *Tamarix* stands. It is evidently favoured by medium to rather high concentrations of soluble salts and the most important stands are adjacent to Seidlitzia marshes. Though it does not depend upon ground water, the tallest specimens are seen in river beds, along runnels or at playa shores. In other habitats it usually reaches only 1.5-2 m and is often brownish in appearance. In certain depressions, e.g. in the west of the area near Chahjam, it reaches only 0.2-0.5 m with a habit resembling *Halocnemum strobilaceum*. It is a typical species of *Salsola-Zygophyllum* communities and on some sites develops a variant of its own or even a distinct association. Its distribution has been heavily reduced because of its desirability for charcoal burning and probably also small-scale metallurgy (see below Chapter 5)—despite its ability to sprout from stumps. It is also an important forage species for camels and is browsed by smaller stock when the ground is covered by snow. Undisturbed stands with aged individuals and are extremely rare. Since the recent cessation of charcoal burning *Haloxylon* is rapidly expanding, and judging from its high competitive vigour and high seed production it should soon reoccupy lost areas.

*H. persicum* is also a favourite fuel, but seems to be regenerating only very slowly, if at all. The potential range and density of this species is intimately related to the problem of sand in Turan.

*Halimocnemis pilifera* is a late developing annual of 3-15 cm—a typical component of *Salsola-Zygophyllum* communities, especially in the *Haloxylon* variant where it often dominates the herbaceous ground layer. As this species is intimately associated with *Haloxylon*, it may serve to indicate sites of previous *Haloxylon* communities.

*Salsola orientalis*, a dwarf shrub of 15-45 cm, like the foregoing, little browsed and of minor use as firewood, may similarly indicate sites of former *Haloxylon* populations.

*S. arbuscula*, a shrub of 0.4-2 m common in low to medium altitudes, thrives best in sand but is never dominant. It is little browsed, but the wood of older individuals is collected for fuel.

*Calligonum comosum*, a tall shrub, occasionally in the form of a tree, was exploited on a large scale for fuel and has reportedly recovered remarkably since the cessation of charcoal burning.

*Amygdalus lycioides*, a very common shrub in medium and higher altitudes traditionally in great demand as fodder and fuel.

*Tamarix* spp.—tall shrubs of 2-4 m common throughout the area, along all river beds with shallow ground water, has been important for construction.

This listing shows how important the role of woodcutting has been in the formation of the present vegetation. Firewood is needed for a number of different purposes and ideally different species are used for different purposes according to the intensity and duration of heat required. Bread ovens, general cooking and heating are three different domestic functions that require a continual supply of firewood. Paraffin has now replaced wood for the latter two in most cases, but so far bread ovens have not been adapted to paraffin. Traditional village baths also require firewood but are gradually being replaced with oil-fueled baths. Outside the village all the fuel requirements of winter sheep pens of transhumants and the spring-summer milking stations of local pastoralists must still be supplied by firewood.

Another important use of the ligneous vegetation and of brush generally outside the villages is for construction. Although the effects of this have been mitigated since the introduction of insecticides, which make it no longer necessary to burn and rebuild pens regularly, nevertheless the use of brush for construction must still be the single most important factor controlling the vegetation around pens. Brush is also cut or uprooted to form temporary milking pens on migration. A final relatively minor human impact on the vegetation comes from the gathering of certain other species for use as medicines, tanning agents and foods.

## Arguments from the Distribution of Faunal Species

Other arguments concerning the history of the vegetation and present trends have been offered on the basis of the distribution of fauna (see Appendix 2). For example, elsewhere on the Plateau *Gerbillus cheesmani* is typical of sandy areas and tends to predominate in areas of shifting sand. It was therefore expected to occur in the Khar sand dunes in high numbers, if not to the exclusion of other species. However, it proved to be absent. Instead, very high numbers of *Meriones meridianus*, relatively high numbers of *Rhombomys opimus*, and numerous *Dipsus sagitta* were found. These three species predominate in sands of the Kara Kum and until recently *Meriones meridianus*, the most abundant species, was only known from extreme north-east Iran. While *M. meridianus* and *D. sagitta* occur occasionally on shifting sand, *P. opimus* is not a species one would immediately associate with such sites. Its occurrence in the Khar sand dunes suggests that it is filling a niche recently vacated by another species, or a niche which only recently emerged. One possible explanation is that the sands of Khar were relatively stable until recent times, and *G. cheesmani* has not yet pioneered them, but, given sufficient time, could do so. A study of interface populations of *G. cheesmani* and *M. meridianus* may shed further light on this question.

A second significant feature is the existence of *Ellobius fuscocapillus* in high numbers. This species requires a soft, moist sub-strate in which to burrow. It typifies the steppic portions of Northern Iran and is absent from the more arid parts of the central Plateau. This suggests two important conclusions: (1) that precipitation is more reliable in Turan than elsewhere in the Plateau, and (2) that much of Turan represents degraded steppe, rather than climax sub-desert flora.

Supporting these conclusions are data on the distribution of other species. *Vulpes vulpes*, a fox unknown in the sub-desert parts of the central Plateau, occurs throughout Turan. *Vulpes ruppelli*, which typifies the sub-desert, is known from only one observation in Turan. Similarly, where one would expect to find only the coronated sandgrouse for similar reasons, only the black bellied sandgrouse is abundant.

Finally, preliminary data from a study of gazelle populations in Turan (reproduced as Appendix 9) suggest that densities are only one-ninth to one-quarter those of comparable habitats in the Kavir National Park, which has been protected from grazing for over 10 years.

Each of these factors suggests on the basis of comparison with other parts of the
Plateau that Turan has undergone relatively recent degradation but can be
substantiated only through further investigations of the climate and the vegetation.
Nothing can yet be said of the complementary effects of wild herbivores—rodents,
ungulates, birds—and insects on the vegetation.

*Grazing Pressure*

That overgrazing has been an important factor in the history of the vegetation of
Turan has been demonstrated by comparison with experience from ecologically
similar Protected Areas immediately to the north (Miandasht and the central and
eastern parts of Khosh Yeilaq).  Shepherds and flock owners alike in Turan today
deny that overgrazing can occur in the long term because it would automatically
reduce their profits.  However, there is evidence that overgrazing is occurring
in the Chubdari area, west of Rezabad, as a conscious strategy.  After the Chubdari
settled at Rezabad with much reduced flocks in the early sixties, the Sangsari took
advantage of the situation and used the new nationalization law and their close
contacts with the central administration of the province to obtain permits to graze
the areas left vacant by the Chubdari and other nomads.  Because of the commercial
nature of their pastoralism the Sangsari were able to adapt more efficiently to the
drought conditions and build up their flocks more quickly afterwards.  During the
recent succession of good years, the Chubdari flocks have finally grown again to
the point where they are forced to challenge the Sangsari for rights to their old
grazing areas.  In order to make their challenge effective, they are forced to
overgraze as a calculated risk.

The degree of overgrazing appears therefore to have varied historically in response
to particular sets of circumstances but derived from exogenous factors.  An
underlying constant has been the orientation of the pastoralist towards his basic
resource—the vegetation.  The primary concern of the traditional pastoralist appears
always to be in the condition of his animals, which he considers to be his basic
capital, not the vegetation which he believes will always recover.

An extremely important but secondary danger to the vegetation comes from wood
collection—which could be obviated by management programmes that would include
provision for alternative fuels and construction materials, possibly by plantation
in the area—that is, by investment.


### HISTORICAL RECONSTRUCTION

Information on the history of Turan is scanty since no settlement in the area was
ever large enough to develop a literary tradition.  Historical reconstruction
depends on the following types of information:

   1.  archaeology,
   2.  circumstancial information in historical writings from neighbouring regions,
   3.  occasional traveller's accounts,
   4.  oral history.

Because of the nature of these sources, it is not possible to interpret them
without relying on a high degree of speculation.  Nevertheless, at least two
significant themes show through unmistakably: Turan has been subject to continual
population movements and (probably closely related) fluctuations in the level of
investment.

*Archaeological Evidence of Settlement*

Although no excavation or scientific survey has yet been undertaken, archaeological evidence appears to be confined to the regions of Khar and Tauran and consists of settlement sites, burial sites, industrial sites (slag deposits and kilns) and engineering sites (dikes, dams, qanats). The major problem in the interpretation of the evidence so far available is dating. Only the presence of certain types of pottery so far allows fairly reliable dating and this indicates a climax of settlement and economic prosperity and investment in both Khar and Tauran in the late Sassanian and early Islamic periods which coincides with investment history on the Plateau as a whole as outlined in the introduction.

The following historical outline is suggested by the evidence available so far and fits generally with possible reconstructions of the vegetation history. There is no direct unequivocal evidence for human activity in Turan before the introduction of irrigation engineering, which need not have been earlier than the fifth to third centuries B.C. However, there is evidence that could relate to earlier periods and since there is evidence of human activity from other parts of the central Plateau from periods predating the domestication of plants and animals in the Middle East (at least 10,000 years ago), early human activity may reasonably be posited for Turan also. A hunting and gathering adaptation based on the springs in the mountains and the abundant wildlife in the mountains and intervening plains must have been perfectly viable and may very well have lasted here into later times when it had been replaced elsewhere by food production. This pattern may not have changed before the introduction of qanats into the area which—judging by the pottery sample—could have happened at any time between their introduction on the Plateau in the mid-first millennium B.C. and the middle of the Sassanian period (fifth century A.D.). It is likely, however, that irrigated cultivation by the diversion of run off—a simpler form of engineering that is known to have been introduced much earlier elsewhere on the Plateau in combination with other strategies—might have supported significant pre-qanat populations. Study of the land forms of central Tauran so far suggests that a large percentage of the arable land is composed of sediments formed by this technology, which has been practised long enough to modify significantly the surface drainage and topography of hundreds of hectares. However, probably only the introduction of qanats could have brought settlement out into the centre of the plains, but at the same time qanats introduced a dependence on a system that was expensive and fragile in that it was vulnerable to earthquakes and floods, and made imperative the maintenance of a certain level of investment. This may explain why no mounds developed in the area and there appears to be very little accumulation of cultural deposits, even under existing settlements. The densest and most extensive sherd scatters are around Baghestan, the ruins of Khar in the sand and Hizomi—which suggests that in early Islamic times up to the eleventh century these settlements might have been large and diversified enough to be called cities. At the least they represent a larger and more complex society than the present 2000 people dispersed among thirty-five settlements.

Did the present situation develop as a result of over-exploitation of natural resources by the medieval cities of Khar and Tauran? This explanation at first seems obvious, especially since in the case of Khar the site is now surrounded by sand and was in fact finally abandoned completely in 1940 primarily because of the sand. However, a number of other pieces of evidence suggest that the interaction between human history and natural processes in the area has been more complex and that degradation cannot simply be explained as Nemesis. This evidence includes the fact that prosperity and decline in Turan appear to have coincided with prosperity and decline over the Plateau as a whole.

*Industrial Activity*

Another piece of evidence that is difficult to interpret is the existence of
industrial sites, and especially of slag. Slag heaps are the most common type of
archaeological site in the southern part of Turan. Nearly forty were located in
3 weeks of survey. They occur in foothills, in the mountain passes between plains,
in the open expanses of the plains themselves, close to modern villages, sheep
pens, natural springs and seeps or isolated from any detectable source of
permanent water or settlement. One slag deposit was found very close to the edge
of the *kavir*.

These sites are all very similar, generally consisting of low piles of black glassy
slag (up to half a metre in height and 1-3 metres in diameter), dumped in rough
concentric ridges around a slight central depression. The total scatter of slag
generally ranges between 15 and 20 m in diameter, and the maximum dimension of the
pieces of slag varies from a few centimetres and fist-sized, although piles of
"pea-sized" pieces, perhaps the result of trampling by animals, were occasionally
observed. Fragments of malachite are evident on most sites. No azurite,
chalcopyrite, bornite, or other copper minerals have been found. Sherds are usually
rate to absent, and the few that were found were undiagnostic and may not have been
contemporary with the slag. Flakes were found on several of the slag heaps, the
majority of which were large, of igneous or volcanic rock, with pronounced bulbs
and cones and flat striking platforms. Some of them resemble spalls from stone
hammers. One site yielded twenty chalcedony artefacts, which included one side-
scraper, one steep nosed scraper, eight core fragments and ten retouched flakes.
All had flat platforms and pronounced bulbs and cones.

The combination of malachite and slag indicate copper-smelting activities. The
type of ore and the absence of any signs of crucibles, furnaces, or tools suggest
the simplest form of pit-hearth smelting, but without excavation or laboratory
testing of the slag, any reconstruction must be provisional. Malachite is one of
the carbonate copper ores, an easily smelted type often available in accessible
surface deposits. (Many other kinds of copper ore require much more elaborate
methods of mining and smelting.) From comparable ethnographic and archaeological
sources, the process could be reconstructed as follows: malachite, probably in
ground form, mixed with charcoal and flux, was added to a pit-hearth dug in the
ground, which might have been lined with clay, gypsum, or stones (one site had
burnt rocks). The required temperatures were maintained by some kind of *tuyere*—a
fireproof blow pipe inserted directly into or over the fire. As the mixture melted,
the copper sank to the bottom, and the slag, made up of the rest of the ore, plus
perhaps a flux and any residual fuel, floated on top. The cooled slag had then to
be dug out and broken away from the copper ingot. Since any kind of crucible or
furnace would probably have been destroyed in the process, one would expect to find
fragments nearby if they had been used. The materials of the process itself would
include fuel, ore, flux and tools, in addition to food, water and transportation
for the workers, the raw materials, and the product. The best fuel source would
have been charcoal. Brushwood is an alternate possibility—it was and is used for
pottery kilns—but probably would not have held the higher temperatures required for
smelting. Shallow surface mines of malachite ore were located on survey, but
without slag heaps or other signs of smelting activity nearby. Identifying flux
is extremely complicated and must await laboratory analysis, but lime, iron ore,
and sand are common fluxes for copper smelting (flux facilitates the separation of
the metal from the rest of the ore.) The very glassy state of the slag suggests that
the flux may have had a high silicon content (the mineral malachite itself has no
silicon), so that sand is a likely candidate. The location of the smelting sites
was probably determined primarily by fuel supply (brushwood or charcoal) but their
distribution relative to sand cover must also be considered.

If it were possible to date and predict the location of slag sites relative to resources, it might be possible also to reconstruct soil and vegetation patterns in earlier periods. It is important to remember that the primitiveness of the method does not in itself imply antiquity (although it is true that in many areas high-grade, easily accessible and reducible ores were probably exhausted long ago, forcing metallurgical techniques of increasing sophistication). Dating on the basis of existing information alone is difficult, though several factors suggest that the workings are comparatively recent. First, the piles of slag have not been severely eroded or scattered by surface run-off; second, piles occurring next to drainages that are beginning to undercut their banks have not been badly damaged, and sites in areas of heavy alluviation do not appear to be deeply buried (although without excavation this is speculative). The sites are old enough, however, to be attributed by local informants to the activities of a mythical ancestor.

Slag sites in the area are numerous, but it is difficult to assess their effect on the landscape without knowing how long such a practice continued, its intensity (how many sites were in use in a unit of time) and what the fuel requirements were. It is sometimes suggested that the metal technology of the Iron Age dealt the final blow to the forests and brush cover in other parts of Iran, and certainly the requirements of the Parthians and Sassanians (as well as more recent periods) for metal were enormous compared to earlier periods. Unfortunately, precise estimates of fuel use in pre-industrial metallurgy are not available, except that according to one source (Caldwell, 1967) silver workers at Nakhlak and Muteh (in Kerman) reported that they use 35 kg of charcoal, 30 kg of lead ore, and 30 kg of iron ore (flux) in a single day's smelting charge. Copper smelting does not require as much fuel as iron smelting, but the quantities are still great compared to other pre-industrial activities. Furthermore, the smelting in Turan was wasteful, since the oven was probably opened and the metal removed after a single firing. More elaborate systems permit the tapping of the copper from the bottom of the furnace, and therefore a continuously operating fire—a much more fuel-efficient process.

Presumably, then, smelting was carried on relatively near but not at ore sources, and in close proximity to fuel supplies, rather than at the site of the next stage in production (probably casting). It might be possible to speculate on the market for this copper if we knew more about the dates involved. For example, most of the Samanid mints (tenth century) were located in Khorasan and nearby provinces; one of these mints was at al-Biyar (presently, Biarjomand, see Miles, 1975:374). Perhaps the Turan smelters were providing copper for coinage.

As far as sources of ore are concerned, a number of discontinued surface workings are evident but undatable. The best explanation for these data would seem to be that sometime in the historical period there was a relatively short period of intense small-scale mining and smelting activity in the area, which is likely to have had a crippling effect on the ligneous component of the vegetation.

A similar industry which has only recently stopped and may have been practised continuously since early historical times is the production of charcoal. Once again no precise figures are available but charcoal was the favourite fuel for many purposes, not only here but in the towns, until the relatively recent prohibition and rise of paraffin. Travellers' accounts during the last 150 years suggest that charcoal production was a major occupation of males in Turan until as little as 10 years ago.

Once again it is significant that both these industries presumably rose and fell in response to the needs of an urban population on the edge of the Plateau which avoided investment in the improvement or conservation of the resources they were exploiting. The local populations who did the work were taking advantage of the full range of resources available to them. Charcoal burning has been replaced with migrant labouring.

*Historical Evidence*

Documentary evidence for the ecological history of Turan is sparse. The place
names Biarjomand, Khar and Tauran are attested since the tenth century in a
somewhat ambiguous position between the two provinces Khorasan and Qumis, but it
is difficult to tease any ecological details out of the incidental mentions that
have survived. Khar disappears from the record from the fifteenth century until
the visit of an Austrian traveller in 1933 (Gabriel, 1935). According to oral
tradition it had been hit by an earthquake around 1860 and was finally abandoned
in 1940. Tauran, however, is mentioned by each of the four European travellers
who actually went through the area and published accounts of their journeys.

The reasons for inattention to this region could be varied: both European and
Persian historians have traditionally found the city and its monuments to be more
interesting than rural areas, and Tuaran has most probably been a backwater
territory since the Mongol invasions; the rise of Isfahan and the Safavid dynasty
in the sixteenth and seventeenth centuries drew interest and travellers to the
south and centre of the Plateau; this desert alternative to the more heavily
travelled mountain and piedmont routes to the north was not very popular. In the
words of General Petroosevitch (in Marvin, 1881:434), the route from Astrabad to
Meshed "via Shahrood, Biyar, Tavroon, Toormeez, and Toorbet-i Hyderi" was "said
to be fit only for caravans; runs alongside the great salt desert; lacks water,
fuel, and forage. Did not traverse it myself, but heard nothing but bad about the
route." In spite of these disadvantages (or perhaps because of them), George
Forster, a civilian Englishman who worked for the East India Company, on returning
home from India in 1783, chose the route through this area. His interests were
humanitarian rather than scientific or commercial, and his disguise was to conceal
his Christianity rather than to secure secret information or safe passage of
valuable goods. As he himself describes his encounter with an Armenian (who
remained convinced that he had unmasked a jewel-merchant or a spy),

> "I endeavored to explain, that, among the natives of Europe, it was a common
> usage to visit foreign countries, where an observance of the manners and
> arts of various people improved the understanding, and produced a more
> extensive knowledge of mankind; and that a frequent intercourse with nations
> of different customs and religious opinions, taught them to shake off
> domestic prejudice, and to behold all men with the eye of common affection"
> (p. 152).

Forster's journal, unfortunately, suffers from this need to conceal his identity (the
had to take notes furtively for fear of exposure) and his dependency on commercial
travel which often moved by night. Nevertheless his account remains, except for
Clerk's even briefer notes, the only eyewitness Western account of the Shahrud-
Turshiz route (which led on through Torbat-e Heidariyeh to Herat). "Few roads",
he says, "are of more dangerous passage than that from Turshiz to the Caspian Sea
(p. 185)", a condition that had persisted since the Afghan destruction of Meshed
some 50 years earlier. His own trip, however, was uneventful. On 31 December he
arrived at Doruna, south-east of Tauran. Between Turshiz and Doruna he comments
that "the country is open and well cultivated, but like the eastern division of
Khorasan, scantily supplied with wood and running water". The area between Doruna
and Tauran is described as "a desert, interspersed with low hills and a thin
smattering of wood (p. 190)", for which he provisioned himself well ahead of time.
Judging by the distances given (probably obtained through informants rather than
direct observation), he must have come up to Tauran through what is now Talkhab;
but he mentions no settlement between Doruna and Tauran. "Towrone", he says, is
a "small fortified village, situate in the districts of Ismael Khan, an independent
chief, who also claimed the desert, extending from Derrone to this place; nor is it

probable that the property will ever be disputed. Many travellers, it is said,
have perished in this track, from the intense heats, and scarcity of water, which,
in the course of the first stage, is procured but in one spot, by digging small
wells (p. 194)." Unfortunately he describes nothing more until he reaches
"Khanakhoody" ("fortified and populous") and the Biarjomand plain ("a wide extended
plain, thickly covered with villages and arable land").

In summary, the area near the end of the eighteenth century was, in the stretch
between Turshiz and Biar, but sparsely populated, without caravanserais (except at
Turshiz) and with scanty provisions for food, water and fuel for travellers. There
were only five or six in Forster's party.

Seventy-five years later Captain Claude Clerk travelled across Persia to Herat,
returning, like Forster, by the Turshiz-Shahrud route. His notes are abbreviated
but he finds the following features of interest: a group of tents pitched at a
pool of rainwater; a few small villages on the way to Tauran, which is itself a
small village with a fort, but few provisions. He notices water and ruins at
Tauchah, but says nothing of inhabitants. At Hizomi, however, besides water,
trees and ruins, were a few inhabited dwellings. When he reached the pass at
Zughdi between the present Ahmadabad and the *Kal-e Shur* he comments that firewood
was abundant.

Otherwise the situation had changed little since Forster's day; he also talks
constantly of terror from the Turkmen, though his own trip across the desert route
was undisturbed. The area itself remains unimportant, with small villages
scattered in the more hospitable regions. In fact the area was unknown enough that
on his earlier trip east across the high road to the north he comments that,
"between Abbasabad and Mazinan, the desert stretches away to the south and
south-west without a break. A region entirely uninhabited til near Tubbes  Tabas
and Yezd." Neither Clerk nor Forster mention pastoralism, tent settlements, milking
stations, or in fact any economic activity except agriculture in the area, though
almost certainly such activities were present as is indicated by the reference to
a group of tent-dwellers.

The only other nineteenth-century traveller who approached the area and wrote
anything was Lt. H.B. Vaughan, an English officer of rather more adventurous
nature, who struck off from Torud close to the edge of the *kavir* in an easterly
direction. Vaughan's closest approach to the Tauran plain was at Nur, on the
southern side of the mountains. Nur was then called Sheikh 'Abdu'l Hosein Nuri and
was a place of pilgrimage at a height of 1440 m.

Further on Vaughan met the only other group of travellers he had seen since leaving
Semnan—"a caravan of tobacco from Tabbas" headed for Tehran. Unfortunately he did
not note the route it would take.

Finally, in 1933 Alphons Gabriel, a physical geographer from the University of
Vienna, travelling by camel with local guides and collecting flora and fauna,
meteorological and geological information, entered the area, as did Vaughan, from
Torud. In June he picked up the Shahrud-Turshiz route followed by Clerk at the
Zoghdi pass (where he records the saltiness and temperature of the water). Here
his guide returned from a trip for provisions, having been forced to go all the
way to Biarjomand since he could buy nothing in either Qal'a Bala or Khanehodi.
Between here and Hizomi were many abandoned ruins with their cemeteries nearby.
Hizomi was then, as now, a summer milking station.

*The Last Years of Khar*

At Hizomi the road forked and Gabriel took the north branch, "over drifting sands",
to Khar rather than continuing on to Tauran.  In order to escape the stares of the
villagers, who had never seen a foreigner, he camped in the dry bed of the Kal
Tauran cut (which was then also surrounded by dunes).  The contemporary settlement
at Khar consisted of more than 100 houses, the first of which were built about 20
years earlier (that is in the early 1910s) near the abandoned fort.  The 500
inhabitants were primarily farmers, but he adds that some men burned charcoal or
herded, and comments on the number of women and children in the village.  In the
gardens at the north of the village grow grapes (which he says ripen in June there),
pomegranate and *Zizyphys vulgaris*.  Barley and wheat stretch out to meet the dunes.
Malaria was reported to be a serious problem, especially in the fall, with a high
mortality rate.  Fresh water came by qanat a distance of 18 km from "the mountain"
to the south, but the supply was dwindling, and there were no resources for
restoring the system.  The villagers were desperate—the sand was taking their
fields, and they knew they must leave (as indeed they did, some 8 years later).

*The Use of Outlying Settlements*

Darbahang is mentioned as a small summer grazing station where people from Khar
pasture goats and raise wheat.  The area nearby had been "seriously altered by
firewood collecting".  (Ahmadabad, which is not mentioned, would probably have
had a similar function.)  The wind had exposed the clay floor beneath the sand,
furrowing it into terraces on the slopes.  However, the area generally was
excellent camel-grazing, "among the most richly overgrown in the Persian arid
zones" (Gabriel, 1935), consisting of tamarisk, saxaul, *Calligonum, Salsola* and
*Atraphaxis*.  Surprisingly, then Gabriel states that "Khar has few animals now,
and imposes a stiff water tax to keep camel owners out of its district, so that
the pasture goes unused for the most part".

*Predators*

Besides the sand, an additional menace were wolves—hardly a night passed without
loss, in spite of the dogs.  Hyenas, on the other hand, would avoid humans and
dogs, but if a herd scattered or strayed, they would move in and slaughter the
whole group or at least all those who did not escape to the rocky heights, where
the hyena could not follow.  Wolves are still a problem, though less so.  Hyenas
are no longer reported.

*Nomadic Pastoralists*

Gabriel moved on north, recording black tents of a tribe from south-west Iran in
the vicinity of the present Rezabad.  (They do not, he says, weave much, since
the demand for rugs and saddlebags is light and wool has become valuable.)  Further
on, he runs across two tents of impoverished nomads from Baluchistan.  The land
around Mazinan is, except for the cultivated portions, barren of the rich
vegetation that the dunes support to the south.  Returning south, further east the
dune plants began again—especially thick bands of grass (*Aristida pennata*).  Here
there were scattered tents of Baluch nomads.  Just north of Talkhab, the "once often
used" caravan route from Sabzevar to Tabas joins his track.  At Talkhab (where the
Shahrud-Turshiz road leads eastward out of Tauran) he found eighteen tents of
another Baluch tribe.

## Fortified Villages

To our great loss, Gabriel now changed his pace considerably, speeding up in order
to move out of the desert as quickly as possible to avoid the summer heat.  But
before he left the Tauran plain he stayed at the small settlement of Fath Hava,
which is now an exclusively pastoralist colony of Salehabad, and records that
there were fifteen villages in Tauran, and that most of them were behind
fortifications.  None of them had more than twenty households, with Eshqvan, Barm,
Zamanabad, Baghestan, Kariz, and Nahar being the largest.  The area was well
watered and the land fertile; the harvested wheat in a good year met the villagers'
own needs, while the surplus from animal husbandry and charcoal was exchanged for
tea, sugar and woven goods.  The dunes to the north were stable and full of
vegetation.

Khar and Tauran appear to have been less hospitable then than now.  The mention of
problems with fodder and firewood suggest that the vegetation was certainly not
better then than now but we know that three settlements have been abandoned because
of sand since 1940.  This general historical picture can be filled out with the aid
of oral history.

## The Sand

The most conspicuous feature of the landscape around Khar and Tauran is the sand.
Khar was abandoned in 1940 because the labour required to keep the qanat free of
sand from year to year was leading more and more people to migrate, until the
point was reached where the whole population decided to cut their losses and leave.
The cause for the abandonment about 1960 of Baba Kuh, a much smaller settlement on
the Hojjaj River, appears to have been similar.  Another small settlement, Yaka Rig,
also on the Hojjaj River and at the southern edge of the high sand, was abandoned
in 1973.  However, although the abandonment of Yaka Rig is generally said to have
been due to the sand, further investigation suggests that an unusually severe flood
in the river damaged the qanat, and the sand was simply a factor making it more
than usually difficult to organize the investment needed to repair it.

This interpretation fits well with the statements of other informants about the
sand, which suggests that since the prohibition of charcoal production finally
became effective in the late sixties, there has been significant increase in
vegetation on the margins of the sand and decrease in sand movement.

## The Impact of Camel Grazing

In this context the travellers' report that the people of Khar had outlawed camel
grazing in their territory is interesting.  They were after all continuing to
produce charcoal—a practice that may have been more lucrative but was probably a
more serious threat to the environment.  It is difficult to assess the impact of
camel grazing on the vegetation historically since it is impossible to know how
many camels might have grazed the area on the average, and whether given a much
higher population than at present and possibly therefore a somewhat different
vegetation, their forage preferences would have been the same.  Since camels formed
the basis of the transportation system in the area until 20 years ago or less, it
is safe to assume that they must have been present in much larger numbers, that
their presence over a long period must have constituted an important factor in the
history of the vegetation, and that the recent drastic reduction in their numbers
must similarly have had a significant impact.  Testable hypotheses for the
investigation of these processes are not easy to formulate, but should presumably
concern the ratio of browse to grazing—an important consideration in determining
the current carrying capacity of the rangelands.

## The Effects of Motorization

The change from camels to motorized transportation has affected Turan in other
ways that may have greater ecological impact in the long term.  Before
motorization, under the camel-based system of communications Khar and Tauran were
at the crossroads of a number of desert routes that linked the cities on the
northern rim of the Plateau, and towns to the east and south of the central playas
(kavir).  Much of this traffic was in fact organized by men from Anarak, a
settlement on the southern side of the kavir, some 450 km west-south-west of Tauran.
As the mode of transportation changed, the routes also changed, and Khar and Tauran
lost contact with areas to the south and east, ceased to be a crossroads and became
a cul-de-sac served only from Shahrud and Sabzevar.  The most serious result of
this change in relations with the outside world is the reduction in the number of
exploitable resources: the loss of the opportunity to provide services to through
traffic.

## The Establishment of Security

As already outlined, this change in the mode of communications coincided with
several other changes.  Villages used to be fortified, and the area was controlled
by leaders who sought to concentrate the ownership of resources in their own hands.
At certain periods, especially it seems during the forties and early fifties,
security was very poor, which further enabled local leaders to expand their power,
usurp official authority and exploit local populations.  Turan took on the
character of a "refuge area", attracting refugees from the effects of economic
decline in more fertile parts of the country.  Apart from the Kurdish and Baluch
nomads which wintered in the area until the 1960s, the population of Turan became
a mosaic of tribal and non-tribal groups from origins as diverse as Tabas, Birjand
and the south-west of Iran.  The most wealthy and influential members of the
population of Tauran in the fifties had been exiled from the south-western
province of Fars in the last century.  A rival group were outlaws from the same
area.

At that time all the local resources were owned by local residents, including the
winter sheep pens, which were rented by transhumant pastoralists.  It is somewhat
surprising that there is no mention in the historical sources of the Sangsari
transhumant pastoralists, although there is circumstancial evidence that the area
has been used by transhumants for many centuries at least, and seasonal pastoral
movement between the Alborz mountains and the arid rangelands along the edge of
the central deserts constitutes a niche that, given the patterns of land use
throughout the Middle East, is unlikely to have remained empty for long.  The
Sangsari appear therefore to have risen in importance in recent decades.  They
benefited from a combination of the drought and the administrative revolution,
which allowed them to buy or otherwise take over many of the pens they use in
Turan, to acquire permits to grazing vacated because of the misfortune of other
pastoralists, and adapt to the rising meat market generated by the growth of an
urban middle class and the expanding national economy and increased security.

This survey of the evidence so far for the history of Turan supports the hypotheses
suggested in the introduction.  Industrial technologies, which expanded and
contracted according to market conditions outside the area, have probably had
serious impacts on the primary productivity of the area at certain periods, and
the greatest period of prosperity the area has known depended on a higher level
of investment (in irrigation) than has been made in the area at any time since.

ECONOMICS

*The National Context*

If the hypothesis is valid that there is a correlation and even a causal relationship between desertification and levels of investment, then exploitation—without desertification—in areas like Turan requires a firm economic basis. It is necessary therefore to look at Turan in the context of the national economy. Since the various types of pastoralism are economically the most important technology in the area, it is necessary here to review briefly the economics of pastoralism in the country as a whole.

Iran has a total human population of about 34 million and an average *per caput* GNP (1975) equivalent to U.S. $1650. In terms of volume, domestic product (GDP) in recent years has been growing at between 10% and 15% per annum. When changes in international oil prices are taken into account, national product (GNP) has been growing at a rate in excess of 35%, but there is great variation of growth in successive years. Some 40–50% of GDP originates in the petroleum sector and only about 10–15% in agriculture. But 58% of Iran's human population live in rural areas; and their *per caput* expenditure is only about 25–50% of that of the average in urban areas. As might be expected the emigration rate from rural areas is high.

In contrast to the economy as a whole, agricultural output has grown at only 3–4% per annum in recent years, and the output of the livestock sector at only 1–2%. As a consequence of the slow growth of livestock output in relation to that of national income and consumption expenditure, there has been a very rapid rise in the importation of livestock products. For example, recorded imports of meat and livestock for slaughter increased, in volume terms, by a factor of 2 between 1970 and 1974, amounting to 65,000 tons (about 12% of total meat consumption) of meat-equivalent in the latter year.

Statistics on the size and composition of the Iranian livestock population, and on its economy and modes of production are incomplete. The best recent estimates (relating to 1974) for the size of the national herd give the following range of estimates:

| Type | Head in millions[a] | Female animals (millions)[b] |
|------|---------------------|------------------------------|
| Sheep | 31.3 | 19.6 |
| Goats | 14.5 | 9.0 |
| Cattle | 6.6 | 3.1 |
| Camels | 0.3 | NA |

[a]Excluding the year's products.  [b]Females of reproductive age.

Of this total national ruminant livestock population of 53 million (87% of which are sheep and goats), it is estimated that 50–60% are involved in major seasonal (nomadic or transhumant) migratory movements between grazing areas. A recent estimate puts the number of tent dwelling nomadic pastoralists in Iran at 700,000. Some 25% of all sheep and goats and 18% of cattle are thought to belong to nomads and 13% of the remainder belong to people without land. Among farmers, small land-owners (less than 10 ha) control 42% and 54%, respectively, of the national total

of small ruminants and cattle. This confirms the impression gained when
travelling around the country that extensive animal husbandry for meat is in the
hands of small landowners, landless and transhumant or nomadic pastoralists. The
average holding among settled pastoralists is 24 head (sheep and cattle). Herds
of more than 50 head make up only 32% of non-nomadic small ruminants. Among non-
nomads, ownership of cattle is fairly evenly distributed (90% of all cattle being
owned in holdings of less than eleven in number, and 55% in herds of less than
five). The ownership of sheep and goats by non-nomads is rather more concentrated,
32% being owned in holdings of more than fifty in number. The degree of
concentration of ownership of the flocks of nomads is not known but is likely to
be more concentrated because nomads are generally more specialized.

Available figures, which may be used as a guide to the main production parameters
of the national herd as a whole, are as shown in Table 1.

Table 1

|  | Sheep | Goats | Cattle |
|---|---|---|---|
| Calving/lambing rate[a] | 80% | 92% | 65%[b] |
| Mortality—lambs | 15% |  |  |
|   Up to 1 yr incl. lambs/calves | 20–25% |  |  |
|   Adult | 5% |  |  |
|   Average incl. lambs/calves[c] | 13% | 11% | 10%[b] |
| Offtake rate[c] | 26% | 30% | 18%[b] |
| Meat tonnage produced (carcass) in thousand tonnes | 180% | 60 | 80 |
| Average carcass weight in kg | 18% | 12.7 | 87 |
| Milk (1000 tonnes) | 500 | 250 | 800 |
| Wool (1000 tonnes) | 48 | – | – |

[a]Live young born as % of breeding females.

[b]Includes specialized dairy herds.

[c]Expressed as % of total population including those born in
current year.

The value of extensive animal husbandry production is in the order of Rls 80 billion,
of which 55.4% is from sheep, 28.8% from cattle and 15.8% from goats. The average
gross product per female animal is around:

- Rls 7500 ($106) for local cattle,
- Rls 2300 ($32.50) for sheep,
- Rls 1400 ($20) for goats.

Prices of meat and milk products have risen sharply in recent years, probably
doubling in the last 4 or 5 years (a period during which retail prices generally
rose by 50%). Meat prices—at or near the "farm-gate"—are in the following range:

Live sheep:  US $1.1—1.4 (Rls 80—100) per kg live weight,

Ghee (clarified butter): US $7—10 (Rls 500—700) per kg,

Cheese: US $2.4—3.5 (Rls 170—240) per kg.

If we assume that it takes 28 litres of milk to make 1 kg of ghee, and from this quantity an additional 1 kg of cheese-like products are made, this gives a value to raw milk (without labour) of about US $0.34—0.48 (Rls 24—33) per kg.

Seventy-five per cent of the total territory of Iran is classified as rangeland or desert.  The proportion of total livestock feed contributed by these areas has recently been estimated at 63.5%, the remainder coming from cereals and fodder crops (11.8%), agricultural by-products (23.3%), and industrial by-products (1.4%).

This situation—the combination of the distribution of animal holdings and the importance of "free" grazing—suggests that unless there is an extraordinary rise in the price of meat, animal husbandry for meat and in particular sheep and goat rearing, is likely to continue to be based on the exploitation of wild rangelands, even if they continue to be of poor quality.

The most feasible way for the income of pastoralists to rise in the coming decades is for pastoral production to become steadily more integrated with agriculture. This would allow the continuation of the use of complementary wildlands by means of transhumant adaptations, as with the Sangsari in Turan, but would introduce another factor in the integration of the use of range and farm land in a single human use system, and so allow a degree of intensification, as well as the continued economic use of the country's arid rangelands.  This will have another advantage—the need for which is a subsidiary theme of this study—that it will encourage forms of organization that will integrate traditional and industrial forms of land use, and rich and poor areas.
It is beyond the scope of this study to go into more detail concerning the overall national value of the resources of marginal land and their populations.  In summary, rangeland makes up a large proportion of the value of Iran's marginal lands, but marginal agricultural areas are equally important: they cover approximately 30% of the area under cultivation and contribute more than 10% to the production of cultivated land.  These resources thus constitute a large amount of capital, particularly for the production of red meat (rangeland and small isolated irrigated areas associated with grazing areas) and for the production of cereals (dry crops, extensive irrigation).  A means of conserving these resources is thus indispensable as a means of reducing the country's food deficit.


*Pastoralism in Turan*

Turan exports substantial quantities of livestock and livestock products, cotton and tobacco.  It imports paraffin, consumer durables, clothes, sugar, tea, small amounts of other foods, fertilizers and feed barley.  Although 80% of the animals that use the area belong to non-residents, some 30—40% of the proceeds of the sales from these animals returns to residents in the form of shepherds' wages; and a further small proportion may return as payment for feed barley grown or bought in the area.

Compared to areas of traditional pastoralism in other parts of the world, Turan appears to have quite a healthy economy.  Standards of housing, health and hygiene are relatively high.  Wage rates for hired shepherds run at US $1200—2400 (80,000—170,000 Rials) per annum, plus food, and most shepherds also make some additional income from the farming activities of their families.  However, shepherding as an occupation has a low cultural value because it implies an arduous and uncomfortable life without modern facilities. Very tentative estimates of net income from one village in Turan, on the basis of an average livestock and land holding, suggest a possible family income in that village from livestock and cultivation averaging about US $325 (23,000 Rials) per year. Such farm income could be supplemented by employment or craft earnings (e.g. in carpet weaving).

Although this figure is considerably below the *per caput* GNP indicated above, it must be remembered that GNP figures include much expenditure on government services, investment, etc., not applicable to family income and expenditure. A more meaningful comparison can be made by looking at figures for annual private expenditure per head. In 1973 this amounted to about US $490 (34,000 Rials) per person for Iran as a whole, the total being an aggregate of US $210 (15,000 Rials) per head in the rural sector. On the basis of these figures, and those given in the previous paragraph, and assuming that family size is about five persons in Turan, then it appears that incomes in Turan are at least equal to, and may be considerably in excess of, those for rural incomes in Iran as a whole, and may approach the level of the working class in urban areas, whose total consumption is only about 50—70% of the average figure for all urban classes. It is necessary also to bear in mind that in statistical comparisons of this kind the real value of housing, water supplies and domestic fuel tends to be underestimated in published figures and that such figures, therefore, give an unduly poor impression of rural life.

## *The Transhumant Flocks*

The major economic activity in Turan is the winter grazing of the Sangsari transhumant flocks. Besides many that pass through Turan to areas further to the south-east, between 300 and 400 of these flocks enter the area between mid-October and mid-November. The flocks average 400 head, consisting of approximately 90% sheep and 10% goats. They lamb in late February, take full advantage of the spring in Turan till mid-April to mid-May, and then slowly follow the spring back up into the mountains to the west, taking some 6 weeks to cover 450-600 km. The animals are milked in the summer pastures only. Lambing percentages (live births) average 85% of which in turn 85% probably survive to weaning, and in the case of males to sale. Of the combined sheep and goat pre-lambing flock some 70% are breeding ewes, 3% sires and 27% replacement females. The general opinion is that flock size and animal population throughout the area among the Sangsari is constant from year to year. Variation occurs in the amount of barley consumed. This information suggests the model of income and expenditure for a transhumant flock as shown in Table 2.

## *Sedentary Pastoralists*

While holdings of transhumant pastoralists tend to a normal size of 400, the holding of the area's residents vary widely in size. On average, breeding ewes form a lower proportion, since some holdings are primarily "fattening" rather than breeding operations. Lambing percentages in resident flocks appear to be slightly higher (reflecting genetic as well as managerial differences). Mortality may be lower as may be feed costs because of the availability of crop stores to supplement barley grain. The value of milk production per ewe/doe is higher than in the case of transhumants, in reflection of the fact that the animals are milked for a longer period. The estimated value of milk output per annum per ewe/doe is US $14 (Rls 1000). The proportion of the flock sold is slightly lower (since animals on average are kept longer) but the unit value heightens in reflection of higher weights at sale. A local resident who gives roughly equal emphasis to pastoralism and agriculture in his economic strategies is likely to have a minimum holding of thirty animals, mainly goats. On the basis of a 35-head flock of sheep of which 60% are breeding females, sales and expenses might be as shown in Table 3.

Table 2

| Sales | US $ | Rials |
|---|---|---|
| Sale of male offspring 100 @ US $35 (Rls 2500) each | 3546 | 250,000 |
| Sale of females 70 @ US $50 (Rls 3500) each | 3475 | 245,000 |
| Sale of milk products @ US $8.50 (Rls 600) for 220 breeding ewes | 1872 | 132,000 |
| Total Sales | 8893 | 627,000 |
| Costs | | |
| One chief shepherd @ US $220 (Rls 14,000) per month | 2383 | 168,000 |
| One assistant shepherd @ US $100 (Rls 7000) per month | 1191 | 84,000 |
| Feed barley at 37.5 kg/head (300-750 g/day/head/for 75 days @ Rls 10 kg) | 2234 | 157,500 |
| Miscellaneous expenses - food | 681 | 48,000 |
| Total Costs | 6489 | 457,500 |
| Profit Margin (Total Sales less Total Costs) | 2404 | 169,500 |

The rate of profit as a % of capital employed (400 head @ US $50 each) is about 12%— rather a modest return.

Table 3

| Sales | US $ | Rials |
|---|---|---|
| Sale of milk products—19 ewes @ 1000 Rials | 270 | 19,000 |
| Sale of 5 male lambs @ US $35 (Rls 2500) | 177 | 12,500 |
| Sale of 4 1-year-old males @ US $57 (Rls 4000) | 227 | 16,000 |
| Sale of 7 cull ewes @ US $50 (Rls 3500) | 348 | 24,500 |
| Total Sales | 1021 | 72,000 |

Costs per head are lower than in the case of transhumant flocks and possibly 50–60% of sales will represent profit—say US $600 (Rls 40–45,000) per flock of 35 head.

*Agriculture*

Agricultural crops in general appear to be more important for supplying domestic needs than generating income, with the exception of cotton and tobacco which are cultivated explicitly as cash crops, and surplus grains from dry farming in good years. Current "farm-gate" prices per kg for these crops are:

| | US $ | Rials |
|---|---|---|
| Cotton | 0.70 | 50 |
| Tobacco | 0.60 | 42 |
| Cereals | 0.17 | 12 |

The amount sown per year by individual families fluctuates according to several factors. The ability to command labour at the right time is one of the most critical of these, and severely restricts the opportunities of some families. But the possibility of adding several hundred dollars to the annual family income by these means is always there.

*Obstacles to the Development of the Economy of Turan*

Livestock development can be thought of in terms either of the value and volume of total output or of livestock output per inhabitant. They may, but need not necessarily, be the same thing, for a constant livestock output coupled with a declining human population may lead to a rising *per caput* output. What then are the factors limiting the total value and volume of livestock output from Turan? Prices of livestock and livestock products, relative to the prices of other goods, are not, at present, unfavourable in comparison to relative prices elsewhere in the world.  It is unlikely that in the foreseeable future the value of livestock output will be raised by government policies designed, as in Europe, to bolster (pastoral) producers' incomes by raising prices to consumers.  There may be some scope for reducing costs and margins in the marketing chain, but high costs or margins are not conspicuous in the present system.

Losses from livestock diseases, while not yet quantified, do not appear to be serious.  Fertility, especially of sheep, is somewhat low in comparison to some countries, but this appears to be as much due to the low incidence of twinning as to absolute infertility.  More twins may not be desirable with present levels of feeding.  In Sangsari flocks wool yields are very low, and milk yields, at an apparent 25-45 kg per lactation, rather low.  Proper data on weight gains do not exist but it would appear that male lambs can be sold off at 6 months without supplementary feeding at about 25-35 kg live weight, and that with feeding a live weight of 50 kg at 11 months old can be achieved.

Livestock specialists tend to stress the importance of performance per animal (e.g. milk yield per lactation per ewe, daily rate of live weight gain per head).  Where the most important costs (of labour, mainly, or of medicines, housing, etc.) are proportioned to the number of head kept, this emphasis on productivity per animal is useful.  Where the most critical scarce resource is feed, however, it may be more useful to emphasize conversion efficiency (feed into milk or meat or wool) and not on performance per head per day.  Conversion efficiency is hard to measure, and livestock specialists argue that performance per head per day is very closely correlated with conversion efficiency; that selecting in terms of productivity per head is tantamount to selecting for conversion efficiency.  It is possible to demonstrate this under conditions where ample feed is available in front of the animal's nose, but where feed is scarce and difficult to find (hidden away in crevices and under thorny bushes), it may not be so since eight legs (two small animals) may gather more food than four legs (one large).  The conversion rate applicable is then not "product per feed consumed" but "product per feed available if looked for".

The last two paragraphs argue that, while the present performance of livestock in Turan is not impressive, it may not be very easy to improve it without a radical change in the level of feeding.  Whether such improvement in feeding can be obtained by "managing" (protecting, rotating, reseeding, etc.) the range, or whether it will require a complete change from "range resources" to "intensive feedstuffs" (implying an abandonment of the range resources to wildlife) is obviously a matter for discussion.  But the focus of such discussion should always be the need to determine the most productive use of the resources of arid lands in the long term.  In any case, it is not clear whether "feed" is the critical constraint on livestock production at the moment.  The high level of barley fed (an innovation dating from the sixties) suggests that it is.  On the other hand, the low level of "rents" paid for sheep pens (rent for grazing is illegal since nationalization in 1963), a mere 3% of the value of output from an area, suggests that it is not.  Livestock owners and shepherds, in discussing reasons for limiting holdings, put the emphasis on shortage of labour not of feed.  On the other hand, the last few years may have been exceptionally favourable climatically.

The main pressure on existing systems of livestock keeping in Turan appears to come from a growing labour scarcity (and consequent high cost of shepherding) arising from strong competition from urban industries.  The present profitability of transhumants' livestock operations is low.  Costs of production appear to come to 70% of the value of output, and 55% of total cash costs are labour costs. There are other non-cash costs involved in the labour required for milking herds, although abandonment of milking in favour of concentration on meat production might not be very serious for transhumants since there would be some compensatory gains in heavier weights of lambs at sale.  There appears to be some scope for

increasing labour productivity in shepherding, with the implication that, unless
total livestock numbers in Turan can be increased (for example, by "range
management"), a lower human population would be supported by livestock activities.
There may be valid technical reasons determining 400 as the optimum flock size
among the Sangsari, but output per head of sheep could be improved, and even if
this meant no greater total output per unit area, it might mean more output per
shepherd.  Undoubtedly, additional equipment and communication devices, and more
frequent watering points, could lead to reduction in the need for "assistant
shepherds", and probably a 50% gain in labour productivity could be achieved in
this way, although at the expense of some capital investment and higher equipment
costs.

This economic review suggests that the outlook for transhumant pastoralism in Turan
is uncertain unless productivity can be increased and shepherding be made more
attractive.  Economically, the self-employed resident mixed farmer does relatively
well.  However, the viability of this latter adaptation during the coming decades
will depend on the interest of the younger generation and the rate of migration
to the cities.  Apart, therefore, from arguments concerning the ecological
efficiency of these two adaptations, there is room for serious doubt about the
survival of either unless they are included and encouraged in long-term management
and development programmes.


                    THE QUALITY OF LIFE

The vital question that has not yet been posed concerns the quality of life in
Turan, and in what ways it may have been related historically and potentially to
processes of desertification.  The only historical information comes from sources
such as those that have been quoted above.  They are generally unfavourable, but
they are written exclusively by outsiders and foreigners.  Similar appraisals of
the quality of life in Turan today are also invariably unfavourable, but the
opinions of local residents tend to vary with their age.  Many young people,
especially youths who have served their statutory term in the armed forces and
therefore travelled extensively outside the area, tend to seek ways of moving to
the city permanently.  The reasons they give fall under the headings of variety
of social life and economic opportunities.  Other age groups often argue for the
advantages of life in Turan.  Many of their reasons are negative, deriving from
general conservatism, and fear of failure in a new social and economic niche, but
positive reasons are also voiced.  Freedom to organize their own work and lives,
even though the work may be arduous, obviously carries weight, as well as the
knowledge that so long as they have land and water they need never depend on others
for a livelihood, but can produce for themselves their basic food supply.  They
are well aware that the food they produce for themselves is generally superior in
quality to what they would have to buy at what seem to them inflated prices in the
towns.  But however definite an informant might be about advantages of life in
Turan, he is likely to complain about the lack of medical facilities, and the
disadvantages of the lack of good roads and public transport.  Studies of drinking-
water supplies, nutrition and general public health are in progress.  Preliminary
results do not indicate any major problems, but relevant comparative data are not
yet available.

These views come from people who live in some of the more isolated villages in the
country, but are aware that during the last 20 years the conditions of life of
their community have changed almost beyond recognition.  Oral accounts are unanimous
that conditions were particularly difficult during the forties and early fifties,
and that symptoms of desertification in the form of poorer vegetation and more sand
movement were conspicuous—which demonstrates again that conditions in Turan, despite
its isolation, are intimately connected with conditions in the country as a whole.

To recapitulate, the principal changes that have come about in Turan since the
early fifties are the establishment of basic security, the cessation of charcoal
production, the change from camels to motorized transport and the resulting
commercialization of pastoralism and agriculture. It is noteworthy that these
are all exogenous changes.

Another fundamental change that is less often noticed has occurred in the structure
of the society. The families that provided the leaders of the society up to the
sixties no longer fulfil that function, and have either migrated, become impoverished,
or are now scarcely distinguishable from the average family.

All these changes—and the list could be extended—lead to a feeling of uncertainty
about the future, which unfortunately has been increased by speculation about the
implications of the special interest of a government department such as the
Department of the Environment, and uncertainty is bad for investment.


CONCLUSION

Desertification is not new. In Turan it has probably been more serious in the
recent past than now. But from a national point of view it is more critical now
than ever before. Old problems are now exacerbated by the increasing differentiation
between rates of socio-economic change in city and desert, which leads to a growth
in cultural prejudice, that in turn reinforces both neglect and abuse of the
deserts and their margins. In Turan social decline, decrease in investment and
desertification have been intimately interrelated.

Government intervention is often characterized by a tendency toward solutions with
a patronizing or charitable flavour. They are often authoritarian, and always
technocratic. This is above all the result of distrust for the traditional, rural
world. It is also due to a certain ignorance of this rural world.

Desertification processes in vulnerable arid and semi-arid areas have been
inseparable from social and economic processes in neighbouring, more fertile areas.
In order to counteract them large-scale planning and long-range management
procedures are required that would include desert and related non-desert areas, and
apply the same ecological and economic standards to both.

Lack of interest in marginal areas is dangerous for two essential reasons: it
encourages their abandonment, even though they have an important contribution to
make to present and future production; and it allows continued deterioration of
fragile areas which are also necessary for the reduction of the country's food
deficit—deterioration that could be contained or reversed by monitoring, planning,
management and investment. An example of the way satellite remote sensing
materials can be used to improve the data base and monitor ecological change over
vast inaccessible areas is given in Appendix 7. It is hoped to extend this project
considerably within the framework of the Transnational Project to Monitor
Desertification Processes and Related Natural Resources in Arid and Semi-Arid Areas
of Southwest Asia (also prepared for the United Nations Conference on Desertification)
for which Turan will serve as a pilot area.


*Recommendations*

In the light of these conclusions, it is recommended that the struggle against
desertification should be conducted through management programmes based on the
reconstruction and evaluation of the ecological history of vulnerable areas. Such
programmes should be fully comprehensive and integrated on three levels. They
should integrate:

(a)   the theoretical and field orientations of the physical, biological and
      social sciences;

(b)   the functions of research, experimentation and management;

(c)   the participation of the research team, the local population and relevant
      decision makers.

Careful attention should be given to building on existing technologies, supporting
innovation within existing traditions, and introducing modern or exotic technologies
only where the payoff and the risk are well defined.  Emphasis should always be
given to increasing the interdependence and range of interlocking systems, and to
encourage livelihood diversification and flexibility.  In more specific terms, in
order to prepare for and plan human exploitation of vulnerable areas in the future,
and reduce the risk of desertification to the minimum, it is necessary to monitor
natural resources, prepare for the effects of predictable desertification processes,
and finally by provision of facilities, including public education, and
communications, to seek generally to reduce the basis of cultural discrimination
between urban and rural living in arid zones.

The most important theme that issues from this study and from the experience of the
Turan Programme so far is the importance of investment.  In order to provide an
element of personal investment in the human use systems of arid rangelands in Iran,
and induce the population generally to recognize the value of these renewable
natural resources, it has recently been decided at government level to embark on a
programme of long-term leasing of the country's rangelands to individual
pastoralists.  It is hoped that the introduction of an element of personal
investment and responsibility in this way will play an important part in Iran's
struggle against desertification.

REFERENCES

Adle, C. (1971) Contribution a la Geographie Historique du Damghan.  *Le Monde
    Iranien et L'Islam* I: 69-104.

Aubin, J. (1971) Reseau Pastoral et Reseau Caravanier Les Grand'routes du
    Khurassan a l'epoque mongole.  *Le Monde Iranien et L'Islam* I: 105-130.

Bobek, H. (1959) *Features and Formation of the Great Kavir and Masileh.*  Arid Zone
    Research Centre, University of Tehran, Publ. No. 2.

Caldwell, J.R. (ed) (1967) *Investigations at Tal-i Iblis.*  Illinois State Museum
    Preliminary Report No. 9.

Clerk, Capt. C. (1861) Notes on Persia, Khorassan, and Afghanistan. *Journal of the
    Royal Geographical Society* 31: 37-65.

Forster, G. (1970) (1808) *A Journey from Bengal to England.*  Punjab Languages
    Department, Vols. I and II.

Gabriel, A. (1935) *Durch Persiens Wusten.*  Stuttgart: Strecker Schroder.

International Union for Conservation of Nature and Natural Resources (1976)
    *Ecological Guidelines for the Use of Natural Resources in the Middle East and
    South West Asia.*  Morges, Switzerland.

Krinsley, D.B. (1970) *A Geomorphological and Paleoclimatological Study of the
    Playas of Iran.*  U.S. Geological Survey, Final Scientific Report, Contract No.
    PROCP70-700.

Markwart, J. (1931) *A Catalogue of the Provincial Capitals of Eran-Shahr.*  Rome:
    *Analecta Orientalia 3.*

Marvin, C. (1881) *Merv. The Queen of the World*. London: W.H. Allen.

Miles, G.C. (1975) Numismatics in the *Cambridge History of Iran*, ed. by R.N. Frye. London: Cambridge University Press, pp. 364-377.

National Statistics Center (1973) *Statistical Handbook*, Tehran.

Pabot, H. (1967) *Report to the Government of Iran on Pasture Development and Range Improvement through Botanical and Ecological Studies*. Rome: FAO No. TA 2311.

Rechinger, K.-H. (ed.) *Flora Iranica*. Vienna.

Spooner, B. (1974) City and river in Iran: Urbanization and irrigation of the Iranian Plateau. *Iranian Studies* VII: 681-713.

Vaughan, Lt. H.B. (1893) A journey through Persia. *Royal Geographical Society Supplementary Papers* III: 89-115.

Zohary, M. (1963) On the geobotanical structure of Iran. *Bulletin of the Research Council of Israel*. Vol. 11D, Supplement.

PLANTS OF THE TURAN BIOSPHERE RESERVE

PTERIDOPHYTA
*Cheilanthes persica*


GYMNOSPERMAE –
Ephedraceae
*Ephedra strobilacea*


ANGIOSPERMAE –
Dicotyledones
ANACARDIACEA
*Pistacia khinjuk*


BORAGINACEAE
*Arnebia decumbens*
*A. linearifolia*
*A. minima*
*Asperugo procumbens*
*Caccinia macranthera*
*Gastrocotyle hispida*
*Heliotropium acuti-*
*florum*
*H. erembium*
*H. nodulosum*
*H. popovii*
*Heterocaryum irregulare*
*H. macrocarpum*
*H. rigidum*
*Lappula ceratophora*
*L. sessiliflora*
*L. sinaica*
*L. spinocarpas*
*Myosotis minutiflora*
*Nonnea caspica*
*N. caspica* subsp. *zygo-*
*morpha*
*N. turcomanica*
*Onosma johnstonii*
*Paracaryum calathi-*
*carpum*
*P. intermedium*
*P. platycalyx*
*P. salsum*
*P. stellatum*
*Rochelia bungei*


CAMPANULACEAE
*Campanula khorasanica*

CAPPARIDACEAE
*Capparis spinosa*
*Cleome coluteoides*


CARYOPHYLLACEAE
*Acanthophyllum diezianum*
*Cerastium*
*Holosteum glutinosum*
*Lepyrodiclis holo-*
*stereoides*
*Silene affinis*
*S. bupleuroides*
*S. chaetodonta*
*S. coniflora*
*S. conoidea*
*S. nana*
*Stellaria blatteri*
*St. media*


CHENOPODIACEAE
*Aellenia auricula*
*Ae. subaphylla*
*Ae. glauca*
*Agriophyllum latifolium*
*A. minus*
*Anabasis eriopoda*
*Atriplex dimorphostegia*
*A. griffithii*
*A. leucoclada*
*Ceratocarpus arenarius*
*Ceratoides latens*
*Chenopodium vulvaria*
*Corispermum lehmannianum*
*Esfandiaria calcarea*
*Gamanthus gamocarpus*
*Girgensohnia oppositi-*
*flora*
*Halimocnemis longifolia*
*H. pilifera*
*Halocharis sulphurea*
*Halocnemum strobilaceum*
*Halopeplis pygmaea*
*Halostachys belangeriana*
*Haloxylon aphyllum*
*H. persicum*
*Horaninowia platyptera*
*H. ulicina*
*Hypocylix kerneri*
*Kochia stellaris*
*Londesia eriantha*
*Noea spinosissima*

CHENOPODIACEAE (cont.)
*Petrosimonia glauca*
*Salicornia herbacea*
*Salsola aucheri*
*S. dendroides*
*S. incanescens*
*S. leptoclada*
*S. cf. nitraria*
*S. orientalis*
*S. praecox*
*S. richteri*
*S. sclerantha*
*S. tomentosa*
*S. turcomanica*
*Seidlitzia rosmarinus*
*Suaeda arcuata*


COMPOSITAE
*Acantholepis orientalis*
*Achillea tenuifolia*
*A. wilhelmsii*
*Aegopordon berardioides*
*Amberboa turanica*
*Anthemis austro-iranica*
*A. odontostephana*
*Artemisia herba-alba*
*Carduus pycnocephalus*
*Centaurea pulchella*
*Chardinia orientalis*
*Chrysanthemum gaubae*
*Cirsium arvense*
*Cousinia congesta*
*C. eryngioides*
*C. lachnosphaera*
*C. lasiandra*
*C. meshhedensis*
*C. onopordioides*
*C. piptocephala*
*C. prolifera*
*C. turkmenorum*
*C. sancta*
*Echinops robustus*
*Epilasia hemilasia*
*Gnaphalium luteo-album*
*Gymnarrhena micrantha*
*Heteroderis pusilla* var.
*pusilla*
*H. pusilla* var. *leucoce-*
*phala*
*Jurinea carduiformis*
*J. radians*
*J. ramosissima*

COMPOSITAE (cont.)
*Koelpinia linearis*
*K. tenuissima*
*Lactuca glauciifolia*
*L. undulata*
*Launaea acanthodes*
*Microcephala lamel-*
*    lata*
*Oligochaete albispina*
*O. minima*
*Phagnalon nitidum*
*Picnomon acarna*
*Pulicaria crispa*
*Scariola orientalis*
*Scorzonera litwinowii*
*S. paradoxa*
*S. pusilla*
*S. raddeana*
*Senecio desfontainei*
*Taraxacum pseudocalo-*
*    cephalum*
*T. pseudodissimile*
*Thevenotia persica*
*Tragopogon jezdianus*
*T. montanus*
*Varthemia persica*
*Zoegea purpurea*


CONVOLVULACEAE
*Convolvulus eremo-*
*    philus*
*C. erinaceus*


CRASSULACEAE
*Pseudosedum multicaule*


CRUCIFERAE
*Aethionema carneum*
*Alyssum dasycarpum*
*A. lanceolatum*
*A. linifolium*
*A. marginatum*
*Arabidopsis pumila*
*A. wallichii*
*Brassica deflexa*
*Cardaria draba*
*Chorispora tenella*
*Cithareloma* cf. *regis-*
*    tanicum*
*Clypeola aspera*
*C. dichotoma*
*Crambe kotschyana*
*Descourainia sophia*
*Erysimum crassicaule*
*Euclidium syriacum*
*Fortuynia garcinii*

CRUCIFERAE (cont.)
*Goldbachia laevigata*
*Isatis buschiana*
*I. emarginata*
*I. minima*
*I. trachycarpa*
*Lepidium vesicarium*
*Leptaleum filifolium*
*Malcolmia africana*
*M. africana* var. *tricho-*
*    carpa*
*M. grandiflora*
*M. strigosa*
*Matthiola chenopedii-*
*    folia*
*Moriera spinosa*
*Octoceras lehmannianum*
*Sameraria armena*
*S. elegans*
*Sisymbrium septulatum*
*Spirorrhynchus sabulosus*
*Sterigmostemon acantho-*
*    carpum*
*Tauscheria lasiocarpa*
*T. lasiocarpa* var. *gymno-*
*    carpa*
*Tetracme recurvata*
*Torularia aculeolata*
*T. torulosa*


CUSCUTACEAE
*Cuscuta brevistyla*


DIPSACACEAE
*Scabiosa olivieri*
*S. rotata*


EUPHORBIACEAE
*Chrozophora gracilis*
*Euphorbia buhsei*
*E. bungei*
*E. cheirolepis*
*E. densa*
*E. gedrosiaca*
*E. microsciadia*
*E. turcomanica*
*E. Turczaninovii*


FUMARIACEAE
*Fumaria parviflora*
*F. vaillantii*


GERANIACEAE
*Biebersteinia multifida*

GERANIACEAR (cont.)
*Erodium glaucophyllum*
*E. pulverulentum*
*Geranium rotundifolium*


LABIATAE
*Chamaesphacos ilicifolius*
*Hymenocrater elegans*
*Eremostachys hyoscya-*
*    moides*
*E. molucelloides*
*Lallemantia royleana*
*Lamium amplexicaule*
*Marrubium alternidens*
*Nepeta bracteata*
*N. ispahanica*
*N. micrantha*
*N. persica*
*N. pungens*
*N. sewerzovii*
*Perowskia abrotanoides*
*Salvia leriifolia*
*S. macrosiphon*
*Thuspeinantha brahuica*
*Th. persica*
*Ziziphora tenuior*


LEGUMINOSAE
*Alhagi camelorum*
*Astragalus (Ammodendron)*
*    podolobus*
*A. (Ammodendron) squarrosus*
*A. (Chronopus) spinescens*
*A. (Erioceras) ulothrix*
*A. (Falcinellus) bakali-*
*    ensis*
*A. (Harpilobus) campy-*
*    lorrhynchus*
*A. (Harpilobus) corrugatus*
*A. (Harpilobus) hauarensis*
*A. (Harpilobus) hauarensis*
*    var. glaber*
*A. (Malacothrix) comosus*
*A. (Mirae) mirus*
*A. (Myobroma)*
*A. (Oxyglottis) ammophilus*
*A. (Oxyglottis) oxyglottis*
*A. (Oxyglottis) tribuloides*
*A. (Xiphidium) argyroides*
*Goebelia pachycarpa*
*Hedysarum micropterum*
*Medicago lupulina*
*Onobrychis tavernieri-*
*    folia*
*O. Aucheri* subsp. *teher-*
*    anica*
*Smirnovia turkestana*

LEGUMINOSAE (cont.)
*Trigonella noeana*

MALVACEAE
*Malva neglecta*

OROBANCHACEAE
*Cistanche fissa*
*C. laxiflora*
*O. mutelii*

PAPAVERACEAE
*Glaucium elegans*
*Hypecoum pendulum*
*Papaver decaisnei*
*P. paveninum*
*Roemaria dedecandra*
*R. hybrida*

PLANTAGINACEAE
*Plantago evacina*
*P. lanceolata*

PLUMBAGINACEAE
*Acantholimon acmostegium*
*Limonium iranicum*

PODOPHYLLACEAE
*Bongardia chrysogonum*

POLYGONACEAE
*Atraphaxis spinosa*
*Calligonum* cf. *comosum*
*C. leucocladum*
*C.* cf. *turkestanicum*
*Polygonum afghanicum*
*P. polycnemoides*
*Pteropyrum aucheri*
*Rheum* cf. *ribes*

PRIMULACEAE
*Androsace maxima*

RANUNCULACEAE
*Anemone biflora*
*Ceratocephalus falcatus*
*Clematis songarica*
*Consolida rugulosa*
*Nigella integrifolia*
*Thalictrum isopyroides*

RHAMNACEAE
*Rhamnus pallasii*

ROSACEAE
*Amygdalus lycioides*
*Hulthemia berberifolia*

RUBIACEAE
*Callipeltis cucullaria*
*Galium ceratopodum*
*G. setaceum*
*G. spurium*
*Leptunis trichodes*
*Rubia florida*

RUTACEAE
*Haplophyllum furfuraceum*
*H. pedicellatum*
*H. perforatum*
*H. robustum*

SCROPHULARIACEAE
*Scrophularia leucoclada*
*S. striata*
*Veronica anagallis-
 aquatica*
*V. anagalloides*
*V. arguteserrata*
*V. campylopoda*
*V. macropoda*

SOLANACEAE
*Hyoscyamus leucanthera*
*H. pusillus*
*Lycium depressum*
*L. ruthenicum*

TAMARICACEAE
*Reaumuria fruticosa*
*Tamarix brachystachys*
*T. hispida*

THYMOLAEACEAE
*Dendrostellera lessertii*

VIOLACEAE
*Viola occulta*

UMBELLIFERAE
*Bunium cylindricum*

UMBELLIFERAE (cont.)
*B. persicum*
*B. rectangulare*
*Bucrosia anethifolia*
*Eryngium* cf. *nigro-
 montanum*
*Eryngium* cf. *bungei*
*Ferula foetida*
*Prangos latiloba*
*P.* cf. *pebularia*
*Psammogeton canescens*
*Ps. brevisetus*
*Scandix*
*Schumannia karelinii*
*Zozimia absinthifolia*

VALERIANACEAE
*Valeriana ficariifolia*
*Valerianella dufresnia*
*V. oxyrrhyncha*
*V. szovitsiana*
*V. triplaris*

ZYGOPHYLLACEAE
*Peganum harmala*
*Zygophyllum eurypterum*

ANGIOSPERMAE –
Monocotyledones
ALLIACEAE
*Allium borszczowii*
*A. caspium*
*A. scotostemon*
*A. umbilicatum*

AMARYLLIDACEAS
*Ixiolirion tataricum*

CYPERACEAE
*Carex diluta*
*C. divisa*
*C. physodes*
*C. stenophylla*

GRAMINEAE
*Astenatherum fors-
 skahlii*
*Boissiera squarrosa*
*Bromus danthoniae*
*B. tectorum*
*Eremopoa persica*
*Eremopyrum bonae-
 partis*

GRAMINEAE (<u>cont</u>.)
*E. orientale*
*Henrardia persica*
*Mordeum glaucum*
*Nardurus subulatus*
*Pennisetum orientale*
*Phalaris minor*
*Phragmites australis*
*Piptatherum microcarpum*

GRAMINEAE (<u>cont</u>.)
*Poa bulbosa*
*Stipagrostis pennata*
*Taeniatherum crinitum*

IRIDACEAE
*Iris kopetdaghensis*
*I. songarica*

JUNCACEAE
*Juncus gerardi*

LILIACEAE
*Colchicum robustum*
*Eremurus inderiensis*
*Fritillaria* sp.
*F. gibbosa*
*Gagea gageoides*
*G. reticulata*

DIMENSION AND AGE DATA FOR *ZYGOPHYLLUM EURYPTERUM*

January 1977

from 1-ha exclosure 9 km ESE of Delbar

| Bush No. | Height (cm.) | Maximum diameter | Diameter at right angles | Weight (kg.) | Age |
|----------|--------------|------------------|--------------------------|--------------|-----|
| 1  | 107 | 200 | 199 | 9.57  | 43 |
| 2  | 79  | 177 | 119 | 5.15  | 22 |
| 3  | 57  | 149 | 135 | 2.65  | 51 |
| 4  | 76  | 183 | 151 | 3.41  | 51 |
| 5  | 30  | 68  | 68  | 0.72  | 58 |
| 6  | 107 | 268 | 222 | 11.10 | 52 |
| 7  | 48  | 90  | 73  | 0.31  | 48 |
| 8  | 82  | 160 | 116 | 3.98  | 46 |
| 9  | 35  | 76  | 75  | 0.37  | 17 |
| 10 | 78  | 187 | 163 | 2.48  | 38 |
| 11 | 120 | 205 | 198 | 10.08 | 33 |
| 12 | 94  | 215 | 200 | 7.57  | 21 |
| 13 | 58  | 170 | 167 | 3.78  | 17 |
| 14 | 43  | 141 | 109 | 2.21  | 32 |
| 15 | 48  | 126 | 121 | 1.39  | 19 |
| 16 | 91  | 211 | 206 | 9.98  | 76 |
| 17 | 100 | 232 | 157 | 12.44 | 80 |
| 18 | 115 | 220 | 191 | 5.91  | 58 |
| 19 | 40  | 108 | 59  | 0.66  | 26 |
| 20 | 82  | 139 | 126 | 1.05  | 16 |
| 21 | 104 | 200 | 200 | 7.71  | 47 |
| 22 | 88  | 173 | 144 | 3.15  | 54 |
| 23 | 39  | 49  | 28  | 0.08  | 6  |
| 24 | 31  | 34  | 29  | 0.08  | 8  |
| 25 | 25  | 39  | 36  | 0.05  | 9  |
| 26 | 42  | 50  | 39  | 0.12  | 10 |
| 27 | 47  | 72  | 68  | 0.23  | 12 |
| 28 | 52  | 46  | 39  | 0.21  | 8  |
| 29 | 50  | 75  | 47  | 0.35  | 21 |
| 30 | 27  | 30  | 25  | 0.03  | 6  |
| 31 | 34  | 50  | 46  | 0.11  | 8  |
| 32 | 57  | 107 | 79  | 0.46  | 20 |
| 33 | 67  | 111 | 67  | 0.59  | 19 |
| 34 | 130 | 272 | 260 | 17.15 | 55 |

## Appendix 2B

SUMMARY OF RESULTS OF RING ANALYSIS OF TWENTY-FIVE *ZYGOPHYLLUM EURYPTERUM*
BY POSITIVE AND NEGATIVE YEARS BASED ON THE MEAN: (I) BY INDIVIDUALS,
(ii) GENERALIZED

Plant Number

Year

Plant Number

Year

## Appendix 2B

| | | | | | |
|---|---|---|---|---|---|
| 1976 | + | 1946 | + | 1916 | − |
| 75 | + | 45 | m | 15 | m |
| 74 | + | 44 | − | 14 | m |
| 73 | − | 43 | m | 13 | m |
| 72 | + | 42 | − | 12 | |
| 71 | − | 41 | m | 11 | m |
| 70 | − | 40 | m | 10 | m |
| 69 | + | 39 | m | 09 | m |
| 68 | + | 38 | − | 08 | m |
| 67 | − | 37 | m | 07 | + |
| 66 | + | 36 | m | 06 | m |
| 65 | − | 35 | + | 05 | − |
| 64 | − | 34 | − | 04 | − |
| 63 | − | 33 | + | 03 | + |
| 62 | + | 32 | − | 02 | + |
| 61 | m | 31 | m | 01 | + |
| 60 | m | 30 | + | 1900 | − |
| 59 | − | 29 | − | 1899 | + |
| 58 | − | 28 | m | 98 | + |
| 57 | − | 27 | m | 97 | + |
| 56 | m | 26 | m | 96 | + |
| 55 | m | 25 | + | 95 | − |
| 54 | − | 24 | + | 94 | + |
| 53 | + | 23 | + | 93 | + |
| 52 | + | 22 | − | 92 | − |
| 51 | + | 21 | − | 91 | + |
| 50 | − | 20 | m | 90 | − |
| 49 | − | 19 | m | 89 | + |
| 48 | m | 18 | + | | |
| 47 | − | 17 | − | | |

Six trunks collected from other parts of the area (with one exception collected approximately 20 km north of Biarjomand) show similar values.

MAMMALS OF THE TURAN BIOSPHERE RESERVE

ORDER INSECTIVORA

FAMILY ERINACEIDAE
 *Hemiechinus auritus*
 *Paraechinus hypomelas*

FAMILY SORICIDAE
 *Crocidura zarudnyi*


ORDER CHIROPTERA

FAMILY RHINOPOMATIDAE
 *Rhinopoma muscatellum*

FAMILY RHINOLOPHIDAE
 *Rhinolophus ferrumequinum*
 *Rhinolophus bocharicus*
 *Rhinolophus blasii*

FAMILY MOLOSSIDAE
 *Tadarida teniotis*

FAMILY VESPERTILIONIDAE
 *Myotis blythi*
 *Myotis mystacinus*
 *Myotis emarginatus*
 *Vespertilio murinus*
 *Eptesicus nasutus*
 *Nyctalus leisleri*
 *Pipistrellus savi*
 *Miniopterus schreibersi*
 *Otonycteris hemprichi*
 *Plecotus austriacus*


ORDER CARNIVORA

FAMILY CANIDAE
 *Canis lupus*
 *Canis aureus*
 *Vulpes vulpes*
 *Vulpes cana*
 *Vulpes ruppelli*

ORDER CARNIVORA (cont.)

FAMILY MUSTELIDAE
 *Martes foina*
 *Vormela perequsna*

FAMILY HYAENIDAE
 *Hyaena hyaena*

FAMILY FELIDAE
 *Felis catus*
 *Felis margarita*
 *Felis manul*
 *Lynx caracal*
 *Panthera pardus*
 *Acinonyx jubatus*


ORDER PERISSODACTYLA

FAMILY EQUIDAE
 *Equus hemionus*


ORDER ARTIODACTYLA

FAMILY BOVIDAE
 *Gazella subgutturosa*
 *Gazella dorcas*


ORDER LAGOMORPHA

FAMILY OCHOTONIDAE
 *Ochotona rufescens*


FAMILY LEPORIDAE
 *Lepus capensis*

ORDER RODENTIA                 ORDER RODENTIA (cont.)

FAMILY HYSTRICIDAE
     *Hystrix indica*

FAMILY DIPODIDAE
     *Allactaga elater*
     *Allactaga hotsoni*
     *Allactaga euphratica*
     *Allactagulus pumilio*
     *Jaculus blanfordi*
     *Dipus sagitta*
     *Paradipus ctenodactylus*
     *Salpingotus* sp.

FAMILY GLIRIDAE
     *Dryomys nitedula*

FAMILY MURIDAE
     *Apodemus sylvaticus*
     *Rattus norvegicus*
     *Rattus turkestanicus*
     *Mus musculus*
     *Nesokia indica*

FAMILY CRICETIDAE
     *Calomyscus bailwardi*
     *Cricetulus migratorius*

FAMILY GERBILLIDAE
     *Gerbillus nanus*
     *Gerbillus cheesmani*
     *Meriones persicus*
     *Meriones zarudnyi*
     *Meriones libycus*
     *Meriones crassus*
     *Meriones meridianus*
     *Rhombomys opimus*

FAMILY MICROTIDAE
     *Ellobius fuscocapillus*
     *Microtus (Blanfordimys) afghanus*
     *Microtus socialis*

CLIMATOLOGICAL DATA FOR TOWNS OF THE NORTH-EAST OF THE IRANIAN PLATEAU
(1961-1973)

| Station[a] | Altitude | Mean maximum temperature (°C) | Mean minimum temperature (°C) | Absolute maximum temperature (°C) | Absolute minimum temperature (°C) | Mean annual temperature (°C) | Precipitation (mm) | Mean relative humidity 6.30 a.m. | Mean relative humidity 12.30 p.m. | No. of frost days |
|---|---|---|---|---|---|---|---|---|---|---|
| Sabzevar | 944 m | 23.9 | 9.0 | 44.5 | -19.8 | 16.4 | 160 | 54 | 29 | 74.0 |
| Semnan | 1138 m | 24.3 | 11.0 | 44.5 | -12.5 | 17.7 | 129 | 52 | 32 | 42.9 |
| Shahrud | 1366 m | 20.9 | 7.4 | 40.0 | -14.0 | 14.2 | 149 | 64 | 37 | 84.7 |
| Tabas | 691 m | 29.1 | 12.8 | 48.2 | - 9.3 | 20.9 | 73 | 54 | 25 | 38.1 |

[a]See Map 1.

CENTRAL TAURAN: POPULATION, RESOURCES, SERVICES
1966 CENSUS

| Village | Families | Sheep and goats | Cattle | Arable[a] land (ha) | School | Public bath | Mosque | Co-operative | Village Council | Headman |
|---|---|---|---|---|---|---|---|---|---|---|
| Barm | 30 | 1500 | 6 | 38 | | | | | 1 | 1 |
| Eshqvan | 50 | 5300 | 20 | 13 | 1 | | 1 | | 1 | 1 |
| Faridar | 20 | 1200 | 9 | 2 | | | 1 | | | |
| Baghestan | 32 | 400 | 8 | 39 | 1 | | 1 | | 1 | 1 |
| Ja'farabad | 18 | 700 | 4 | 1 | | 1 | 1 | | | |
| Kariz | 25 | 1000 | 6 | 2 | 1 | | | 1 | 1 | 1 |
| Nahar | 13 | 40 | 3 | 4 | | | 1 | | 1 | 1 |
| Nauva | 11 | 200 | 5 | 3 | | | | | | |
| Ravazang | 7 | 1500 | 2 | 6 | | | | | | |
| Salehabad | 25 | 7300 | 25 | 19 | 1 | | 1 | | 1 | 1 |
| Taghmar | 6 | 200 | 5 | 4 | | | | | | |
| Yakarig | 3 | 300 | | | | | | | | |
| Zamanabad | 46 | 1500 | 10 | 8 | | | 2 | 1 | 1 | 1 |
| Zivar | 12 | 300 | | 6 | | | | | | |
| Central Tauran Total | 298 | 21,440 | 103 | 145 | 4 | 1 | 8 | 2 | 7 | 7 |

[a]The 1966 figures for arable land are incomplete and should be treated as minima only.

OUTLYING TAURAN VILLAGES: POPULATION, RESOURCES, SERVICES
1966 CENSUS

| Village | Families | Sheep and goats | Cattle | Arable[a] land (ha) | School | Public bath | Mosque | Co-operative | Village council | Headman |
|---|---|---|---|---|---|---|---|---|---|---|
| Asbkeshan | 12 | 500 | | 2 | | | | | | |
| Chah-e Mer'i | 4 | 500 | | | | | | | | |
| Derazab | 17 | 300 | | 4 | | | | | | |
| Div | 7 | 600 | 5 | | | | | | | |
| Farinu | 9 | 200 | 2 | | | | | | | |
| Garmab-e Bala | 5 | 300 | 4 | 6 | | | | | | |
| Garmab-e Pa'in | 9 | 500 | 3 | 2 | | | | | | |
| Hojjaj | 18 | 500 | 2 | 4 | | | | | | |
| Jorjis Peighambar | 1 | | | | 1 | | | | | |
| Kalagh Zili | 1 | 250 | 2 | 2 | | | | | | |
| Kalata-ye Rei | 7 | 600 | 8 | 2 | | | | | | |
| Kalata-ye Reza Qoli | 1 | 400 | 2 | 5 | | | | | | |
| Mer'i | 5 | 100 | | 6 | | | | | | |
| Narestana | 8 | 50 | | 6 | | | | | | |
| Nur | 11 | 20 | 5 | 1 | | | | | | |
| Posht-e Asman | 2 | 50 | | 6 | | | | | | |
| Salamrud | 8 | 200 | 3 | | | | | | | |
| Tejur | 1 | 40 | 1 | | | | | | | |
| Talkhab | 11 | 900 | 7 | 1 | | 1 | | | | |
| Tauchah | 3 | 450 | 4 | | | | | | | |
| Outlying Tauran Total | 140 | 6460 | 48 | 47 | 1 | 1 | 0 | 0 | 0 | 0 |
| Khar: Population, Resources, Services 1966 Census | | | | | | | | | | |
| Ahmadabad | 95 | 800 | 80 | 9 | 1 | 1 | 1 | | 1 | 1 |
| Darbahang | 42 | 1000 | 80 | 5 | | 1 | | | | |
| Rezaabad | 44 | 1500 | 4 | | | | | | | |
| Khar Total | 181 | 3300 | 164 | 14 | 6 | 3 | 9 | 0 | 1 | 1 |
| Khar Tauran Total | 619 | 31,200 | 315 | 206 | 6 | 3 | 9 | 2 | 8 | 8 |

[a] The 1966 figures for arable land are incomplete and should be treated as minima only.

CENTRAL TAURAN: POPULATION, RESOURCES, SERVICES
1973 CENSUS

| Village | Families | Sheep | Goats | Cattle | Camels | Arable land (ha) | School | Public bath | Store | Mosque | Paraffin distribution centre | Co-operative | Village council | Headman |
|---|---|---|---|---|---|---|---|---|---|---|---|---|---|---|
| Barm | 30 | 100 | 100 | 10 | | 31 | 1 | | | 1 | | | | 1 |
| Eshqvan | 50 | 200 | 550 | 12 | | 19 | 1 | | 3 | 1 | | | 1 | 1 |
| Faridar | 20 | | 100 | | | 25 | 1 | | 1 | 1 | | | | 1 |
| Baghestan | 34 | 200 | 400 | 20 | | 95 | 1 | | 1 | | | | 1 | |
| Ja'farabad | 20 | 70 | 380 | 6 | | 11 | 1 | | 3 | 1 | | | | |
| Kariz | 24 | 120 | 1200 | 10 | | 46 | 1 | 1 | 1 | 1 | | | | 1 |
| Nahar | 15 | 40 | 400 | 4 | | 14 | | | | | | | | |
| Nauva | 12 | 50 | 300 | 5 | | 27 | | | | | | | | |
| Ravazang | 5 | 100 | 500 | 3 | | 12 | | | | | | | | |
| Salehabad | 30 | 1500 | 5000 | 20 | | 32 | 1 | 1 | 1 | 1 | | | 1 | |
| Taghmar | 8 | 150 | 250 | 6 | | 24 | | | | | | | | |
| Zamanabad | 45 | 100 | 400 | 17 | 6 | 30 | 1 | 1 | 3 | 1 | 1 | 1 | 1 | 1 |
| Zivar | 15 | 30 | 200 | | | 3 | | | | | | | | |
| Central Tauran Total | 308 | 2660 | 9780 | 113 | 6 | 369 | 8 | 3 | 12 | 6 | 1 | 1 | 4 | 5 |

OUTLYING TAURAN VILLAGES: POPULATION, RESOURCES, SERVICES 1973 CENSUS

| Village | Families | Sheep | Goats | Cattle | Camels | Arable land (ha) | School | Public bath | Store | Mosque | Paraffin distribution centre | Co-operative | Village council | Headman |
|---|---|---|---|---|---|---|---|---|---|---|---|---|---|---|
| Abol Hasani | 3 | 100 | 150 | | | 10 | | | | | | | | |
| Asbkeshan | 10 | 100 | 300 | | | 1 | | | | | | | | |
| Chah-e Mer'i | 3 | 100 | 500 | | | 4 | | | | | | | | |
| Cheshma Mer'i | 4 | 70 | 130 | | | | | | | | | | | |
| Derazu | 18 | 50 | 850 | | | 12 | | | | | | | | |
| Farinu | 15 | 120 | 1200 | 5 | | 9 | | | | | | | | |
| Garmab-e Bala | 6 | 45 | 200 | 2 | | 6 | | | | | | | | |
| Garmab-e Pa'in | 11 | 100 | 1400 | 1 | | 7 | | | | | | | | |
| Hojjaj | 18 | 200 | 700 | | | 36 | | | 1 | | | | | |
| Kalagh Zili | 2 | 30 | 200 | 2 | | 2 | | | | | | | | |
| Kalata-ye Rei | 8 | 57 | 500 | 6 | | 6 | 1 | | | 1 | | | | |
| Kalata-ye Reza Qoli | 1 | | 2 | | | 1 | | | | | | | | |
| Mer'i | 3 | 40 | 310 | | | 1 | | | | | | | | |
| Nur | 12 | 30 | 600 | 8 | | 7 | | | | | | | | |
| Salamrud | 5 | 10 | 200 | 2 | 3 | 4 | | | | | | | | |
| Tejur | 1 | 25 | 150 | 2 | | 2 | | | | | | | | |
| Talkhab | 14 | 200 | 700 | | | 115 | | | 1 | | | | | |
| Tauchah | 6 | 44 | 500 | 1 | | 4 | | | | | | | | |
| Outlying Tauran Total | 140 | 1321 | 8592 | 29 | 3 | 227 | 1 | 0 | 2 | 1 | 0 | 0 | 0 | 0 |
| Ahmadabad | 95 | 300 | 1700 | 200 | 50 | 73 | 1 | 1 | 4 | 1 | 1 | 1 | 1 | 1 |
| Darbahang | 30 | 100 | 700 | 45 | 3 | 6 | | | 1 | 1 | | | | |
| Rezaabad | 45 | 1700 | 800 | 200 | | 4 | | | 2 | | | | | |
| Khar Totals | 170 | 2100 | 3200 | 445 | 53 | 83 | 1 | 1 | 7 | 2 | 1 | 1 | 1 | 1 |
| KHAR TAURAN TOTAL | 618 | 6081 | 21,572 | 587 | 62 | 679 | 10 | 4 | 21 | 9 | 2 | 2 | 5 | 6 |

# Appendix 6

## COMPONENTS OF THE TURAN PROGRAMME

| Studies in progress | Studies planned |
|---|---|
| Climatological recording | Hydrology |
| Geological mapping and geomorphology | Plant productivity and succession |
| Soil mapping and analysis | Endoparasitology |
| Sand accumulation and movement | Ecology of avifauna |
| Vegetation mapping and botanical taxonomy | Ecology of reptiles |
| Use of LANDSAT data to improve mapping and monitor ecological change | Ecology of insects |
| Vegetation history | Range ecology |
| Plant physiology | Systems analysis |
| Plant population structure and distribution | |
| Palynology | |
| Dendrochonology | |
| Wildlife ecology | |
| Ethology and ecology of domesticates | |
| Dietary studies of all herbivores by means of faecal analysis | |
| Prehistory and history of human activity by means of the study of land forms, archaeological evidence and historical materials | |
| Pastoral and agricultural technologies | |
| Economics, demography, health, nutrition, social organization and values of the present populations | |
| Comparative economics and ecology of different pastoral and agricultural technologies | |

PRELIMINARY LANDSAT ANALYSIS OF SAND AND SETTLED AREAS
TURAN BIOSPHERE RESERVE

This appendix presents an illustration of preliminary satellite data analyses
carried out in the Turan Biosphere Reserve. These data are derived from one
LANDSAT scene. Detailed application of ground truth has not been made in
preparing the thematic map which accompanies this appendix; when this is done
(following geometric correction to the LANDSAT scene) further refinements to the
classifications will be possible.

The material includes: (1) a grey-scale printout of band 5 showing the area in
question, and (2) a thematic map illustrating the distribution of the signatures
indicated below. The area takes in cultivated land, a portion of a sand sea,
mountainous terrain, and settlements. Flocks are grazed on much of it.

These data are being used in the development of a dynamic picture of edaphic and
vegetative resources in the Turan Biosphere Reserve. Subsequent work will produce
time series showing major short- and long-term trends in the area.

The map has been created on the basis of multispectral radiometric scanner data
ERTS-1 (LANDSAT 1) scene 81382062035 (quality "8" in all bands).

*Characteristics:*

|  |  |
|---|---|
| Date: | 9 August 1973 |
| Centre point of scene: | N35 59 38, E56 49 31 |
| Altitude: | 921.4 km |
| Area mapped: | 512 × 512 pixels |
| Geometric correction applied: | none |
| Approximate scale of printout: | 22000:1 |

The image has not been enhanced in any way, nor has it been destripped.
Destripping will be applied to future maps.

In cases of parallelopiped overlap, more inclusive signatures were processed before
less inclusive signatures (see below).

The themes are represented by eight symbols. These are:


          *    #    @    %    $    &    ?   and   &lt;


The spectral characteristics and ground truth correspondence are:


(1)  *  B4:47-51; B5:57-61; B6:53-56; B7:22-24
       Six-pixel area within sand sea.

(2)  #  B4:46-50; B5:54-61; B6:51-56; B7:21-24
       Five-pixel area deeper within sand sea.

(3)  @  B4:47-51; B5:54-58; B6:53-56; B7:22-23
       Eight-pixel area of high homogeneity in sand sea.

(4)  %  B4:39-49; B5:39-54; B6:62-71; B7:33-35
       Small areas within two villages.

(5)   $   B4:40-56; B5:38-67; B6:63-71; B7:30-35
          Village peripheries and outliers.

(6)   &   B4:55-57; B5:68-70; B6:62-66; B7:27-30
          Eleven pixels to east of village:
          peganum (four-pixel area).

(7)   ?   B4:53-55; B5:65-66; B6:58-61; B7:26-27
          Abandoned field between Kariz and Zamanabad.

(8)   <   B4:56-59; B5:70-70; B6:66-66; B7:28-29
          Trampling and sparse vegetation between Kariz and
          Zamanabad.


Geometrical distortion: Apart from rubber sheet distortion, which is uncorrected, the printout map format contains a consistent exaggeration of the vertical dimension of 9.812% above the true dimensions of the bulk CCT.

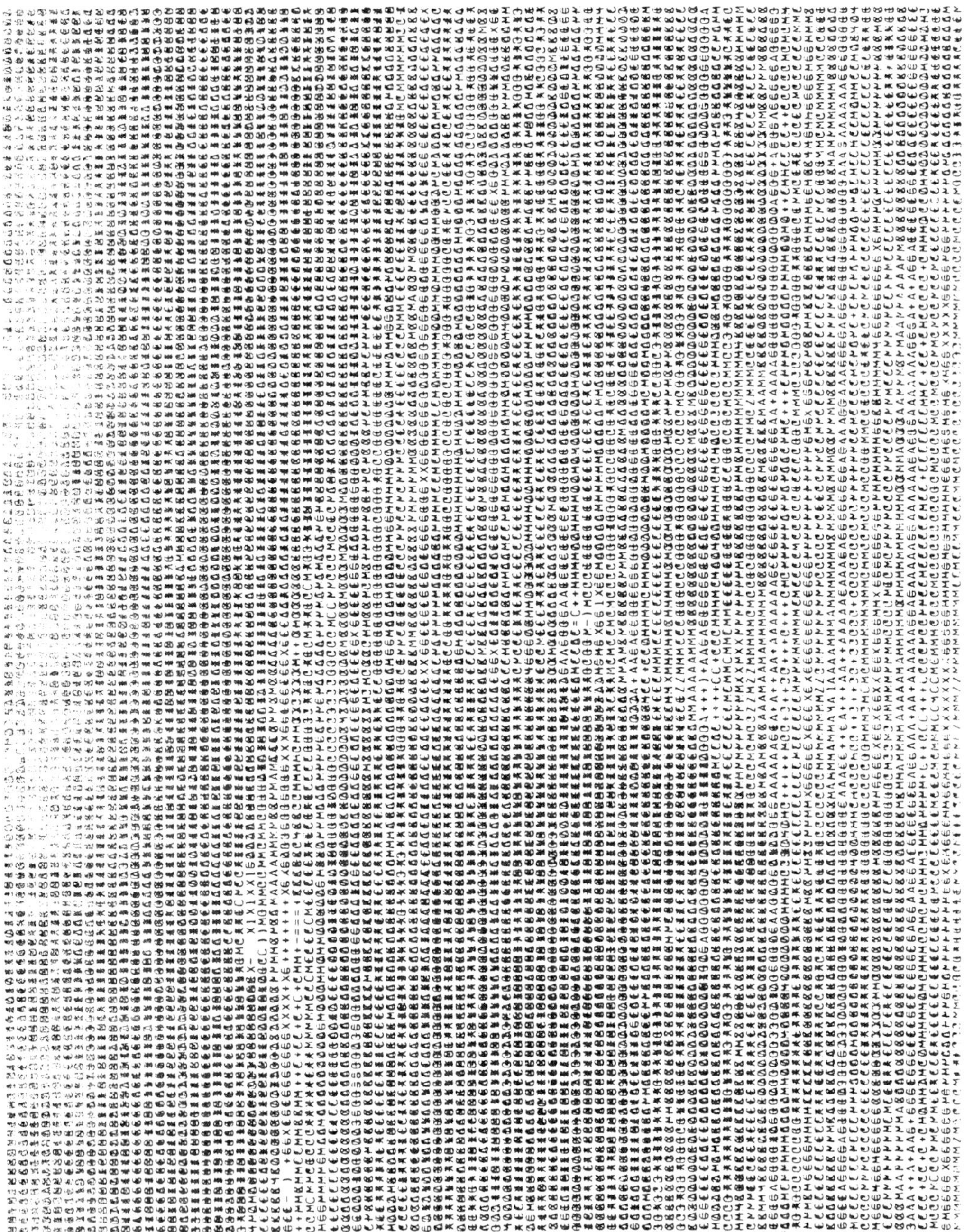

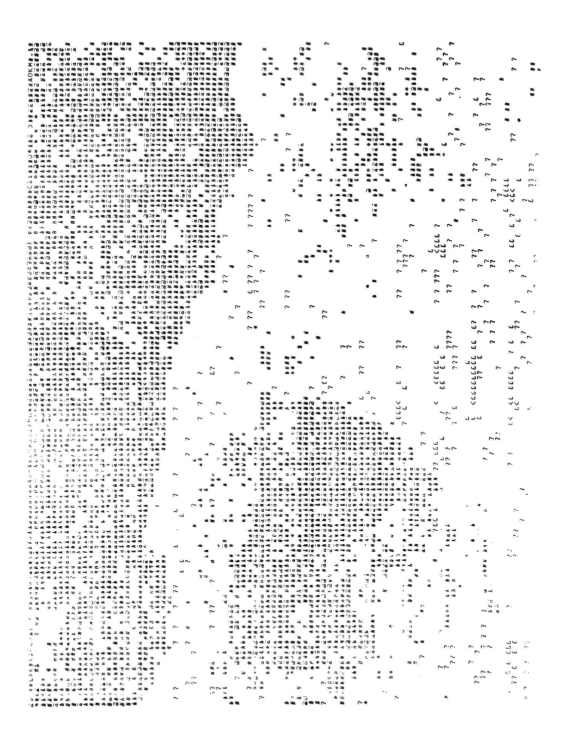

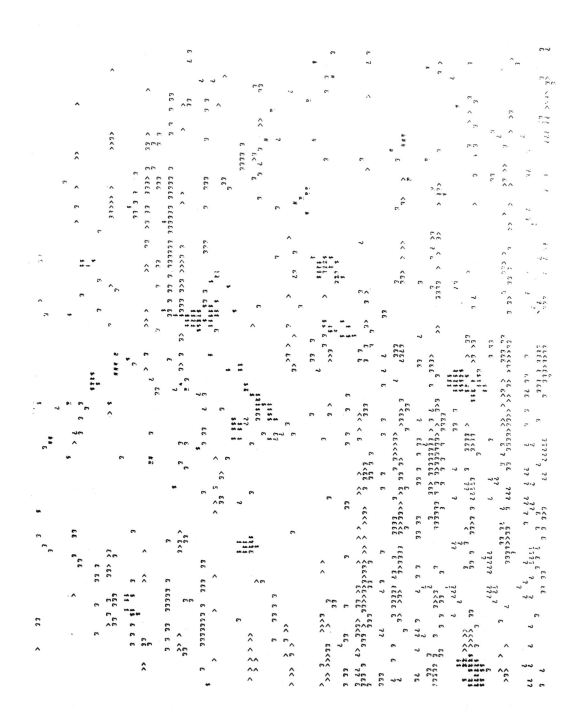

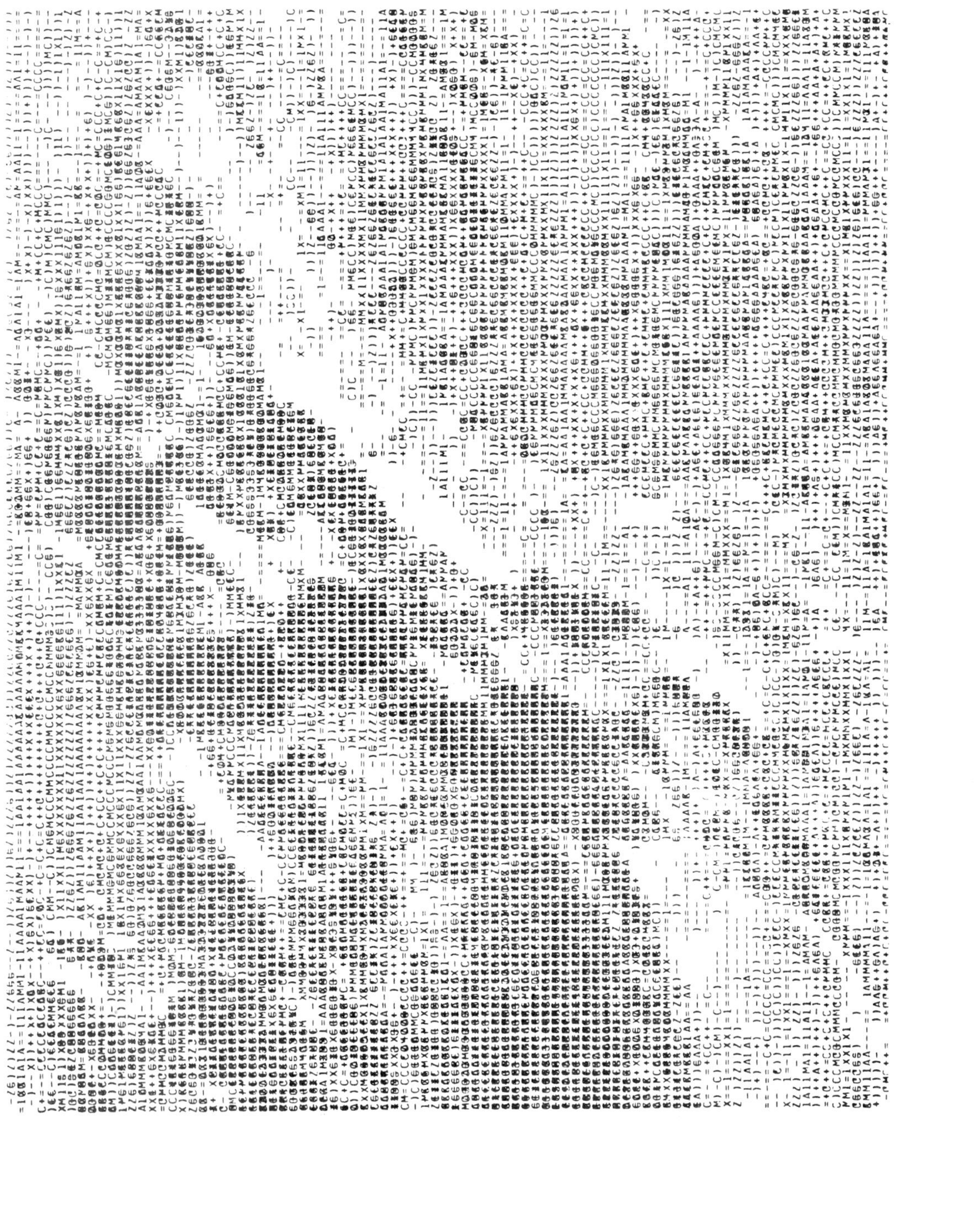

TURAN BIOSPHERE RESERVE

PRELIMINARY VEGETATION MAP

*Expanded Legend*

1a  *SALSOLA - ZYGOPHYLLUM* COMMUNITIES:
hot desert and semidesert vegetation types up to about 1300 m, usually
developed in the plains; plant cover ranging from 5 to 40%. Most important plant
species:

    *Zygophyllum eurypterum*
    *Salsola tomentosa*
    *S. orientalis*
    *Aellenia subaphylla*
    *A. auricula*
    *Anabasis setifera*
    *Fortynia garcinii*
    *Ephedra* cf. *strobilacea*
    *Haloxylon aphyllum*
    *Artemisia aff. herba-alba*
    *Gymnarrhena micrantha*

1b  Variant of *Haloxylon aphyllum* usually with mass development of *Halimocnemis
pilifera.*

1c  Dominated by *Zygophyllum eurypterum.*

1d  Dominated by *Salsola tomentosa* (indicating higher degree of disturbance).

1e  Variant of *Aellenia glauca,* typical for rocky areas.

1f  Variant of *Gamanthus gamocarpus,* typical for tuffites and other materials
highly vulnerable to erosion, characterized by extremely thin vegetation cover
with high proportion of annuals.

1g  Variant of *Cousinia turkmenorum,* characterized by continuous and rather dense
layer of psammophilous annuals.

    *Cousinia turkmenorum*
    *Lepidium vesicarium,* etc.

and a few psammophilous perennials, especially

    *Astragalus squarrosus*
    *Acanthophyllum* cf. *bracteatum*

on plains with a continuous sand layer, usually on the northern foot of
mountain ranges.

*ARTEMISIA AFF. HERBA-ALBA — EPHEDRA INTERMEDIA — AMYGDALUS* cf. *LYCIOIDES*
COMMUNITIES: more mesic semidesert communities, usually from about 1300 m,
2a  mainly on rocky slopes.

Most important plant species:

> *Cleome coluteoides*
> *Ceratoides latens*
> *Amygdalus* cf. *lycioides*
> *Astragalus glaucacanthos*
> *Cousinia* cf. *neurocentra*
> *C. piptocephala*
> *Ephedra intermedia*
> *Acanthophyllum* div. spec.
> *Acantholimon* div. spec.
> *Stipa arabica*
> *Artemisia "recta" (Darmaneh-e-K hi)*
> *Noea spinosissima*

2b   *AMYGDALUS LYCIOIDES—ATRAPHAXIS SPINOSA* COMMUNITIES:
on limestone rocks, in fissures only, vegetation extremely sparse, usually
dominated by *Amygdalus, Astragalus podolobus* or *Atraphaxis*    3-15%.

2c   *AMYGDALUS—HYPOCYLIX* COMMUNITIES:
on shales, conglomerates, porphyrs and coarse-textured pediment plain usually
dominated by *Amygdalus, Hypocyclix kemeri*.

2d   *AMYGDALUS—HYPOCYLIX* COMMUNITIES IN COMPLEX WITH *SALSOLA—ZYGOPHYLLUM* COMMUNITIES:
the former on rocky slopes and outcrops, the latter on deeper soil in the
plains, proportion about 50:50.

2e   Variant of *Cousinia* cf. *neurocentra*, on marly or other fine-textured soil, often
dominated by *Hypocylix*, without *Amygdalus* or *Amygdalus* very sparse.

2f   Variant of *Gamanthus gamocarpus*, on highly eroded marl hill tops and slopes, in
complex with the former.

2g   Variant of *Ceratoides latens*, on deeper soil, usually dominated by *Artemisia*
aff. *herba-alba*

3a   *ASTRAGALUS STROBILIFERUS—COUSINIA MESHHEDENSIS* COMMUNITIES:
mostly mesophytic communities in summit regions of the higher mountains, but on
north-exposed slopes descending to 1400 m.

Most important plant species:

> *Astragalus strobiliferus*
> *Artemisia "recta" (Darmaneh-e-Kuhi)*
> *Cousinia meshhedensis*
> *Ephedra intermedia*
> *Acantholimon* div. spec.
> *Stipa caucasica*
> *St. turkestanica*
> *Piptatherum molinioides*

3b   *ASTRAGALUS STROBILIFERUS—AMYGDALUS* COMMUNITIES:
usually on rocky slopes, dominated either by *Astragalus* or *Amygdalus*; in the
highest north-exposed slopes of the *Kuh-e-Peighambar* by *Onobrychis cornuta*
(forming a community of its own); further typical species are *Cotoneaster*
*kotschyi, Jurinea stenocalathia, Stipa turkestanica, Hymenocrater elegans*.

The community grows in a mosaic-like complex with *Stipa caucasica-Cousinia meshhedensis* communities on slopes or plateaus with deeper soil, but dominates usually.

4a  *STIPAGROSTIS—CALLIGONUM* COMMUNITIES:
on fixed or shifting sands.

4b  *STIPAGROSTIS PENNATA—CALLIGONUM* COMMUNITIES:
on fixed sands, with dense shrub and herbaceous vegetation summing up to 40%, dominated by

   *Stipagrostis pennata*
   *Calligonum leucocladum*
   *C.* cf. *comosum*
   *Haloxylon persicum*
   *Artemisia eriocarpa*

besides a rich annual vegetation, with

   *Agriophyllum minus*
   *A. latifolium*
   *Euphorbia cheirolepis*

4c  *STIPAGROSTIS KARELINII—SMIRNOVIA* COMMUNITIES:
on shifting sands, cover up to 5% only, dominated by

   *Stipagrostis karelinii*
   *Smirnovia turkestanica*
   *Heliotropium* cf. *acutiflorum*

5a  BARREN KAVIR or clay flats without vegetation or vegetation only in and along runnels.

5b  Dense annual halophilous vegetation (cover up to 90%) on clay flats, dominated by *Petrosimonia glauca, Cressa cretica,* etc.

5c  SHRUBBY SALT MARSH COMMUNITIES:
along Kavir borders, in some depressions and river beds; differentiated in some communities:

   *Seidlitzia rosmarinus* community, the most common one, usually in contact with *Haloxylon* variant of the *Salsola-Zygophyllum* units.

   *Halocnemum strobilaceum* community, common as the outermost vegetation belt against the barren flats.

   *Halostachys belangeriana* communities, more rare than the former and requiring more moisture.

   *Tamarix* communities, requiring permanent water supply.

ECOLOGY OF *GAZELLA DORCAS* (JEBEER) AND *GAZELLA SUBGUTTUROSA*
(GOITERED GAZELLE) IN TURAN BIOSPHERE RESERVE
PRELIMINARY REPORT

1. *Introduction*

This report combines the results of two field trips in June and July 1976 of 10
days and 6 days, respectively. Since these were the first two trips in the area,
this must be regarded as a preliminary report. The figures presented—population
size, densities, biomass, food intake, etc.—will almost certainly change as work
progresses and sample error decreases. Nevertheless, these figures are presented
to give an indication of the expected final result.

2. *Methods*

Road transects were set up in the area and divided into nine separate strata to
simplify sampling and accommodate the varying habitat of the region. The criteria
for dividing the strata were somewhat arbitrary, being based on topography, habitat
and convenient boundaries such as tracks. Turan is too large to sample extensively,
and so only a part of the area was selected in order to allow repeated sampling in
the time available.

During repeated driving of the transects, at 10-km intervals, topography, soil, and
dominant vegetation were recorded in order to provide an indication of the
distribution of different habitat types; at the same time the ground was inspected
on foot to see what plants were present, and to determine from tracks and chewed
shoots which plants were eaten.

Sightings of gazelle were recorded, with the number, sex, age, date, time of day,
location and habitat and distance away. Distances up to 400 m can be estimated
accurately and were periodically checked by pacing, and so the transect width was
800 m. This was multiplied by the distance driven on a transect in order to arrive
at the area sampled, and hence densities. For estimating densities, only those
gazelles cited within the 800-m transect width were used.

Two whole days were spent observing gazelle movements from fixed observation points,
one at Abul Yahya spring (south-east of Majrad) and one in the open foothills
overlooking the spring, both in stratum 6.

Weights of gazelle and domestic sheep and goats have been taken from specimens
collected elsewhere. Ecological efficiencies are from studies on the Mountain
gazelle in Israel, a species closely related to the Jebeer, and studies on
ungulates in East Africa. From these studies, the values shown in Table 1 have
been used.

Table 1

| | |
|---|---|
| Average weight of Goitered gazelle | 22 kg |
| Average weight of Jebeer gazelle | 17 kg |
| Average weight of domestic sheep | 30 kg |
| Average weight of domestic goat | 25 kg |
| Calorific value of wild ungulates | 1400 kcal/kg |
| Food intake by Mountain gazelle | 100 kcal/kg/day |
| Assimilation efficiency | 67% of intake |
| Production | 2% of assimilation |

3. *Results*

*1. Distribution.* The southern limit of the Goitered gazelle range is along
the southern edge of the Biarjomand plain where it meets the mountain, the
southern edge of the Delbar plain where it meets the Majrad mountain, and from
Ahmadabad northwards along the western edge of the sand dunes. The greatest
numbers are seen in the plain between Abbasabad and Kuh Do Shakh, and just west
of Ahmadabad.

The northern limit of the Jebeer gazelle range is the southern edge of the
hills extending from Majrad westwards, the bridge over the Kal-e Shur between
Ahmadabad and Delbar, and the southern edge of the Ghariba range of hills.

Individuals are occasionally seen outside this normal range. For instance, in
December 1973 some Jebeer gazelle were sighted on the Kal-e Shur north of
Abbasabad and in June 1976 one Goitered gazelle was seen south of Ghariba
spring. No gazelle were seen in the vicinity of the concentrations of villages
in the Biarjomand and Tauran plains or the plantless solonchak by the Kal-e Shur.

Jebeer do occur out into the solonchak in the south of the area in dominant
*Tamarix* and *Seidlitzia*. Their densities here appear to be very low but this
part of the area has been insufficiently surveyed.

*2. Habitat characteristics.* Habitat categories were defined according to
topography, soil and dominant vegetation. The habitat categories and the
strata in which they occur are shown in Table 2.

Table 3 lists the different strata and the gazelle densities for each habitat
category within each stratum.

For Goitered gazelle, preferred habitats are dominant *Haloxylon*, *Zygophyllum*,
and *Artemisia*, and for Jebeer *Zygophyllum*, *Zygophyllum/Artemisia*, *Haloxylon*,
and *Seidlitzia*. The very high density of Jebeer in *Haloxylon* in stratum 6 is
due to the fact that this is the habitat of the open foothills, and during the
middle of the day the Jebeer move into these foothills. This particular area
was always sampled in the late morning. Gazelle do not occur in habitats
where one plant superdominates, such as the *Zygophyllum* in strata 5 and 9.

Jebeer will enter foothills where the gulleys are broad and flat, and in effect
a continuation of the plain habitat. In rocky hills where they have to step up
and down they do not occur unless chased. Jebeer are noticeably absent from
dominant *Artemisia*.

Table 2

| Topography | Soil | Dominant vegetation | Stratum |
|---|---|---|---|
| 1.  Plain | sandy/coarse | *Dorema* | 1 |
| 2.  Plain/open foothills | sandy | *Haloxylon* | 1,6,7,9 |
| 3.  Plain | coarse | *Zygophyllum* superdominant | 5,9 |
| 4.  Plain/open foothills | coarse/ stony | *Zygophyllum* dominant | 1,3,5,6,7,9 |
| 5.  Plain/open foothills | coarse/ stony | *Artemisia* dominant | 1,2,3,5,6,7 |
| 6.  Plain | sandy/coarse stony | *Peganum harmala* | 2 |
| 7.  Plain | sandy | *Ephedra* | 2 |
| 8.  River gulleys | sandy/coarse stony | *Pteropyrum* | All |
| 9.  Plain/open foothills | coarse | *Zygophyllum/ Artemisia* codominant | 2,5,6,7 |
| 10. Plain | halophytic | *Seidlitzia* | 4,6,7 |
| 11. Plain/gulleys | halophytic | *Tamarix* | 4 |
| 12. Plain | solonchak | *Tamarix/Haloc-nemum* | 4 |
| 13. Plain | sandy | *Stipagrostis* | 3 |
| 14. Plain | solonchak/ mudflats | *None* | 1,4 |

Table 3

| Stratum | Habitat category | % of area sampled | Density Jebeer | Density Goitered |
|---------|------------------|-------------------|----------------|------------------|
| 1. | 1. *Dorema* | 10% | | |
| | 2. *Haloxylon* | 10% | | 1.6/10 km$^2$ |
| | 4. *Zygophyllum* | 30% | | 3.6/10 km$^2$ |
| | 14. *Solonchak/mudflats* | 30% | | |
| | 5. *Artemisia* | 20% | | 1.6/10 km$^2$ |
| 2. | 5. *Artemisia* | 30% | | |
| | 6. *Peganum harmala* | 25% | | |
| | 7. *Ephedra* | 25% | | |
| | 9. *Zygophyllum/ Artemisia* | 20% | | |
| 3. | 4. *Zygophyllum* | 50% | | 2.2/10 km$^2$ |
| | 13. *Stipagrostis* | 25% | | |
| | 5. *Artemisia* | 25% | | 1.5/10 km$^2$ |
| 4. | 10. *Seidlitzia* | 20% | | |
| | 11. *Tamarix* | 20% | | |
| | 14. *Solonchak/mudflats* | 60% | | |
| 5. | 5. *Artemisia* | 20% | | |
| | 9. *Zygophyllum/ Artemisia* | 20% | | |
| | 4. *Zygophyllum* | 30% | | 0.6/km$^2$ |
| | 3. *Zygophyllum* superdominant | 30% | | |
| 6. | 4. *Zygophyllum* | 50% | 2.8/10 km$^2$ | |
| | 5. *Artemisia* | 10% | | |
| | 2. *Haloxylon* | 10% | 14/10 km$^2$ | |
| | 10. *Seidlitzia* | 10% | 1.0/10 km$^2$ | |
| | 9. *Zygophyllum/ Artemisia* | 20% | 3.0/10 km$^2$ | |
| 7. | 4. *Zygophyllum* | 25% | 2.75/10 km$^2$ | |
| | 9. *Zygophyllum/ Artemisia* | 60% | 0.7/10 km$^2$ | |
| | 5. *Artemisia* | 5% | | |
| | 10. *Seidlitzia* | 5% | 1.5/10 km$^2$ | |
| | 2. *Haloxylon* | 5% | 1.5/10 km$^2$ | |
| 8. | Insufficiently sampled | | | |
| 9. | Insufficiently sampled | | | |

*3. Biomass and production.* By extrapolation from comparable studies (see Table 1), it is possible to give the figures for the ecology of gazelle in Turan as shown in Table 4.

Table 4

| Stratum | Density biomass (kg/10 km$^2$) | Density energy content (kcal/ 10 km$^2$) | Food intake (kcal/ 10 km$^2$) | Assimil- ation (kcal/ day/10 km$^2$) | Production (kcal/day/ 10 km$^2$) |
|---------|---------|---------|---------|---------|---------|
| 1. | 28.6 | 40,040 | 2860 | 2000 | 330 |
| 2. | 0 | | | | |
| 3. | 33 | 45,000 | 3300 | 2200 | 450 |
| 4. | 0 | | | | |
| 5. | 4 | 5500 | 400 | 250 | 50 |
| 6. | 42.5 | 60,000 | 4250 | 2800 | 570 |
| 7. | 18.7 | 25,000 | 1850 | 1250 | 250 |
| 8. | 0 | | | | |
| 9. | 13.2 | 18,500 | 1300 | 880 | 175 |

In order to give some idea of the extent of competition with domesticates, a survey was made of the sheep and goat population in the strata 2, 5 and 9 (excluding transhumant flocks). The values as described in Section 2 will probably not be the same for domesticates, since their efficiencies generally are less than for wild populations. Therefore, they probably have a greater food intake per kilogramme live weight. The domestic sheep, for instance, contains a lot of fat, deposited in the tail, and the production of this fat requires three times as much energy per unit weight as the production of protein. Nevertheless, the figures shown in Table 5 are given for the purpose of preliminary comparison.

Table 5

| | Density biomass (kg/10 km$^2$) | Density energy content (kcal/ 10 km$^2$) | Food intake (kcal/ 10 km$^2$) | Assimil- ation (kcal/ day/10 km$^2$) | Production (kcal/day/ 10 km$^2$) |
|---------|---------|---------|---------|---------|---------|
| Sheep | 7200 | | | | |
| Goat | 5800 | | | | |
| Combined | 13,000 | 18,000,000 | 1,300,000 | 870,000 | 175,000 |

4. *Behaviour*. Breeding on the Jebeer takes place in early November and in the Goitered gazelle at the end of November, beginning of December. Fawns are dropped after a 5½-month gestation at the end of May and in mid-June respectively. Goitered gazelle usually seek out sheltered habitat to drop their fawns, and in Turan appear to move to the western edge of the sand-dune area and the low foothills in stratum 3. In the fawning season, the sexes are separate. The males of both species are normally territorial in the breeding season, but this has not yet been established in Turan. Sometimes where densities are low there is not enough interaction to bring about this behaviour.

No seasonal movement has been observed for the Jebeer.

In summer both species have a peak of inactivity in the middle of the day when they either bed down or rest standing and ruminate. The Jebeer commonly move into the springs between 10.00 and 13.00, and remain in the foothills and springs until afternoon when they disperse back onto the plain. Neither species require water in winter and spring, although if it is readily available they will drink.

Jebeer gazelle have been observed to eat heavily the following plants:

> *Pteropyrum*
> *Artemisia*
> *Seidlitzia*
> *Ephedra*
> *Salsola arbuscula*

They are very delicate eaters, taking only the succulent parts of the plant. Other species are undoubtedly also eaten.

5. *Population structure*. The Jebeer gazelle commonly occur in groups of one to four individuals. The largest group sighted contained eleven. Average group size was two to four. The population comprised 25% male, 46% female and 27% fawns. Female-fawn rates were 1:0.6. The Goitered gazelle occurred in groups of one to seven, the average being 1.8. The population comprised 30% male, 40% female and 30% fawn. The female-fawn ratio was 1:0.73.

## 4. *Discussion*

The densities of both species are very low. In the Kavir National Park 300 km to the west the densities are 4 to 9 times greater in equivalent habitats. The Kavir has been protected from grazing for over 10 years and the population is expanding. This would suggest that competition from domestics reduces the Jebeer population and therefore there is competition for food and space. The populations of Jebeer and Goitered in Turan are probably stable. The female-fawn ratios of 1:06 compare badly with the figure of 1:1 for the Kavir at the same time of year. Similarly with the Goitered gazelle, the ratios of 1:0.73 compare unfavourably with the ratio of 1:1.2 in the Shahrud area at the same time of year. It is possible that the populations may even be declining in the long term.

Competition with the Wild ass is probably not as critical, at least for food, since the Wild ass represents the roughage browser/grazer, and can take much woodier parts of the plants which would not be eaten by gazelle.

# Israel

# The Negev - a Desert Reclaimed

## Yoel Schechter and Chaya Galai

*Environmental Protection Service, Israel Ministry of the Interior*

INTRODUCTION

The purpose of this case study, stressing recovery in the Negev desert, is to present a general description of the policies and technologies used in the development
of Israel's arid and semi-arid southern regions.  The history of this region is
well-documented, both in written records and archeological sites.  It is an especially interesting area from several points of view.  Firstly, it is the meeting place
of several ecological systems.  The Saharo-Indian desert belt extending across
North Africa and Asia passes through the southern Negev.  The Irano-Turanian steppic
vegetation extends down from the North, and the Mediterranean region borders the
desert on its northern coastal fringe.  Due to this conjunction of systems, the
Negev is rich in flora and fauna, each belonging to its individual ecosystem.  Topo-
graphically, the region presents a large variety of land forms, from wide loessial
plains to sand dune formations and rugged rocky hills. Elevations vary from 1000
meters above to 400 below sea level, the lowest elevation on earth.  Climate is
varied, with rainfall levels decreasing rapidly from about 300 mm in the semi-arid
northern Negev to less than 25 mm in the south of the region.  All these changes
occur in a land area of only 10,000 square kilometers, presenting the planner and
developer with a wide variety of environmental problems, and requiring for its
development the concerned efforts and skills of a large number of scientists and
engineers.

The Negev forms a natural land connection joining Africa, Europe and Asia.  The
history of human settlement in this area presents a panorama of settlement and
migration, conquest and reconquest, invasion and withdrawal, with large armies
passing through to reach more prosperous regions to the north, south and east.  The
negative human contribution to desertification is clearly evident, but conversely,
man's ability to overcome adverse environmental conditions and to build a civilizat-
ion with rich cultural and spiritual values has been demonstrated throughout the
historical saga of the Negev.

Today the Negev represents a large proportion of Israel's land area.  Since the
establishment of the State of Israel an intensive program of research and development, coupled with resettlement projects, has transformed large sections of this
region into vitally important productive areas, contributing to the progress and
well-being of the entire nation.  This case study, prepared for the United Nations
Environment Program Conference on Desertification, will present Israel's experience

in regeneration of the Negev Desert in the hope that others in similar situations will be able to build upon it and utilize the lesson of Israel's successes and failures.

### GENERAL DESCRIPTION OF THE AREA

*Borders*

The precise limits of the area known as the Negev are disputable, and almost every scholar who has studied the subject has formulated his own definition (Fig. 1). In the distant past the Negev and Sinai were no-man's-land, separating the inhabited Nile Valley from the Judean Mountains and the coast. Until the arrival of the British in the area, Sinai and the Negev constituted one region. The political boundaries of the latter were first fixed only in the twentieth century; its border with Sinai was created in 1906, as the result of an agreement between Britain and Turkey, and its eastern border with Jordan was demarcated in 1922 by the British government. The northern border is no clear-cut line, but rather a transition-zone between the cultivated lands and the desert. The 300 isohyet, which passes some 20 km north of Beer Sheva, is often taken to represent the northern demarcation line (though it should be recalled that isohyets fluctuate and can only constitute a rough gauge). The Turkish and British authorities accepted this demarcation, since it usually marked the borderline of the Bedouin northward migration. It also more or less conforms to the northern administrative boundary of the Beer Sheva Sub-District of the Southern District, as delineated by the Israel Ministry of Interior. The region encompasses approximately 12,000 square kilometers, which constitute 62% of the entire area of Israel within the pre-1967 boundaries.

*Geomorphology of the Negev*

The Negev may be subdivided into five regions: Eilat Hills in the south, the Paran Plateau, the Negev Hills, the Beer Sheva region and the Arava Valley (see Fig. 1).

Eilat Hills. This region lies on the fringe of the ancient Arab-Nubian Massif, which builds both flanks of the Red Sea, and displays a Precambrian core of plutonic and metamorphic rock. It is characterized by a great variety of rocks and morphological features, enhanced by fractures and fault lines of geological antiquity. The crystalline rocks contain such minerals as quartz, orthoclase, mica and minerals of the Nubian sand-stone series. The intermingling of varieties of rocks, sometimes separated by fault lines, sometimes interbedded with each other, results in variegated forms: sharp crests, canyons and steep narrow valleys. Some mountain peaks rise to 800-900 m. There are numerous gorges, often only a few feet wide, hemmed in by rock walls over 300 m high.

Paran Plateau. This plateau, inclined from southwest to northeast, descends from 600 m above sea level at the Sinai border to 100 m where Nahal Paran (which passes through it) enters tha Arava Valley. Nahal Paran, originating southwest of Eilat, is the largest stream in the country (240 km course) with a large drainage basin and numerous tributaries from the south, west and north. It is dry most of the year and is partly (and sometimes entirely) flooded by occasional rainstorms. Parallel to it to the south runs Nahal Hiyon. Most of the Plateau is flat or slightly undulating, its bedrock formed by limestones, chalks and marls of the Turonian and predominantly, the Senonian. The flint intercalated in the Senonian chalk accumulates on the surface when the soft chalk erodes; it is a major element in forming the hard "hamada" surfaces of the Paran Plateau. The small, closely grouped hilltops of Mt. Senifim extend from southwest to northeast of the plateau, forming the watershed between Wadis Paran and Hiyon. Near the northern outskirts of the Plateau lies the Meshar plain, where phosphate deposits have been located.

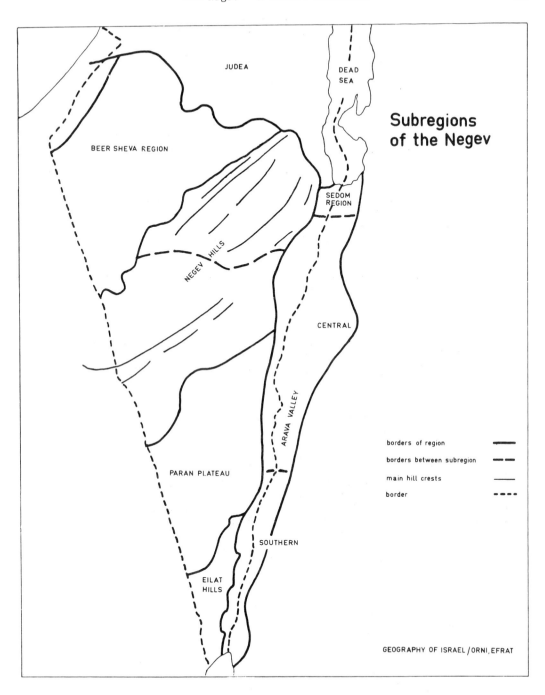

Fig. 1.

Negev Hills. This region occupies more than half the Negev area and is divided by
the deep Nahal Zin Valley into a higher southern and lower northern half. It was
created in the Miocene period, and was comparatively little affected by faulting
and erosion. Geological structure and topography are therefore substantially identical; most anticlines are still present as hill ridges and synclines as valleys.
Some hills are over 800 m above sea level (Har Ramon and Har Saggi). In the synclines Senonian and Eocene chalks have been preserved while harder limestones of
Cenomanian and Turonian are exposed in the anticlines.

Variety is added to the area by the craters (makhteshim) or erosional cirques, of
which there are three: Makhtesh Qatan (Small Makhtesh) on the Hazera ridge, Makh-
test Gadol (Large Makhtesh) on the Hatira ridge and the long Makhtesh Ramon on the
Ramon ridge.

In most years dry wadis carry flood water several times for a few hours each time.
Their drainage pattern mirrors the morphology and rock types of the region: a
coarse stream network typifies permeable limestones and dolomites, a finely meshed
one - impermeable chalk and marl. Nahal Paran, Nahal Zin and other wadis descending to the Northern Arava possess great erosional power and capture tributaries of
the western wadis (Nahal Nizzana and Nahal Besor). Thus the watershed is gradually
pushed westward.

Beer Sheva region. This region rises nearly imperceptibly from 50-100 m above sea
level in the west to approximately 250 m near Beer Sheva and attains 600 m at its
eastern extremity. The region subsided with the opening of the Jordan and Dead
Sea Rift in the Miocene and Pliocene. The region is thickly covered with loess
soil, which in the Beer Sheva area is frequently 30 m thick or more. Certain of
its physical properties contribute to sheet erosion and badland formation. Sand
dunes cover some 500 sq. km in the western and southwestern section of the region,
with strips of loess separating the dunes into smaller units. Vegetation is often
richer here than on adjacent loess, because the thinness of the sand layer cover
permits rainwater to filter swiftly through to the loess, where it is trapped,
feeding the plant roots.

Almost the entire region is the drainage basin of a single stream, Nahal Besor,
running down from Har Haluqim in the Negev Hills, and receiving tributaries en
route.

Arava Valley. This is the southernmost section of the Great Rift Valley in Israel.
It is thickly covered with alluvial sand and gravel, and hemmed in by rock walls
on both sides. It is 165 km long and divided into: the Southern Arava (77 km
long and 5-15 km wide); the Central Arava (74 km long and up to 32 km wide) and the
Northern Arava or Sedom salt swamps, some 14 km in length and almost rectangular.
The Edom Mountains to the east, border it for 120 km, with precipitous rock walls
rising in places to 1,000 m (i.e., up to 1,600 m above the bottom of the valley),
exposing crystalline rocks and reddish Nubian sandstone. To the west lie the
Negev Hills.

The rare flash floods which descend into the Valley carry vast amounts of detritus
and build up alluvial fans at the foot of the mountains on both sides. The Edom
mountains are steeper and higher, with consequent greater erosive force of flood-
waters, and have a high rainfall. Hence alluvial fans are much larger on the east
side, and the base level of the Arava has been pushed gradually westward to the foot
of the Negev Hills. The high rainfall in Edom also accounts for the relatively
strong, fresh springs on the eastern rim of the valley, while those to the west are
brackish.

The southern Arava rises from the Eilat shore to 230 m above sea level, forming the

watershed between the Dead Sea and the Red Sea.  The drainage pattern, however, is
not continuous since many streams are blocked by alluvial fans.  The water which
seeps into the subsoil is drawn up by capillary action during the hot summer, forming playas or salt flats.  These are often covered with a halophytic vegetation.

In the Central Arava, Nahal ha-Arava is formed by the confluence of Nahal Paran,
Nahal Hiyon and several other wadis.  This area slopes toward the Dead Sea, descending to 210 m below sea level.  The southern region is covered with coarse gravel and
sand, but northward from the Hazeva oasis (one of several in the area) whitish or
yellowish lissan marl appears.  Wide deep courses have been carved in the soft
sediment by wadis.

Towards the Sedom region the valley bottom descends precipitously, 140 m in less
than 3 km.  Since the ground is almost flat and only slightly above Dead Sea level,
the flats are frequently flooded by water from Nahal ha-Arava.  There are several
strong springs here, those on the eastern side fresher and move abundant than on
the west.  Raised water levels of the Dead Sea in rainy winters increase the salinity of the Sedom swamps.  The Dead Sea shore area consists of mud and salt patches, with dark loam to the south.

*Climate*

Aridity in the Negev is caused mainly by two closely related factors.  The first is
the formation of dry, stable air masses that resist convective currents.  These air
masses are associated with the descending branches of the sub-tropical semi-perman-
ent high pressure cells (Hadley circulations) which exist around the globe.  The
second factor is the lack of storm systems.  The deserts of the sub-tropical latitudes are particularly sensitive to the climatology of cyclones.  The Arabian and
Australian deserts and the Sahara are examples of regions positioned between major
wind belts with their associated storm systems.  The position of the descending
branch of the sub-tropical high pressure belt not only leads to stability and dryness in the Negev, but also acts to block cyclones farther north from penetrating
the region, especially during the summer.

The Negev climate is characterized by winter rainfall and summer dryness (Fig. 2).
The average annual rainfall varies between 300 mm in the north and 25 mm in the
south.  The rainfall is related to the occurrence of barometric lows in the Mediterranean and in the Red Sea, but is very variable in space (spotty) and in time.
These characteristics of desert rainfall detract from the "average" as a valuable
statistic.  The basic physical system that produces local rainfall is a small-scale
convective cell, which develops in unstable, warm and moist air.  In arid areas, a
convective cell can maintain a rain-producing process only if it is large and powerful enough to draw in the necessary energy and water supply from over a wide area.
Thus cells are larger (5-10 km in diameter) and well separated from each other both
in space and time.  To illustrate the "spottiness" of desert rainfall, measurements
using 20 rain-gauges in a 10 hectare area at Avdat during a single rainstorm (1
March 1960) showed a maximum of 7-8 mm, which was 3.5 times the minimum of 2.2 mm
recorded for the same day.  On year-long averages, there are 16 rainy days per
year in the Negev hills, with over 80% of the rainfall occurring in light showers
(less than 10 mm).  The frequency of days with precipitation of less than 1 mm is
relatively higher in the Negev than in the north (though this may have little value
for agriculture).  During the summer (August), average minimum and maximum temperatures range from $19°C - 32°C$ at Beer Sheva, to $27°C - 40°C$ at Eilat.  Temperature
differences of more than $17°C$ between day and night have been recorded in a single
24-hour period in the Negev.  During the occurrence of *hamsin* (*sharav* in Hebrew),
temperatures may reach $42°C$ and higher at Avdat, and $48°C$ in the Arava.  The *hamsin*
occurs when the dry desert wind passes over Israel from the Arabian or Sinai desert

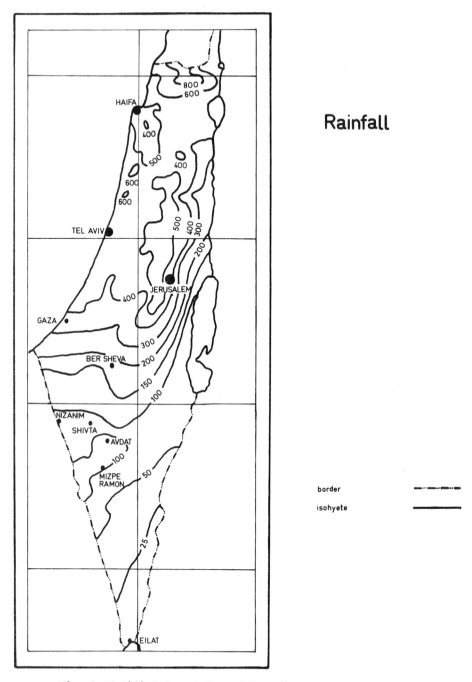

Fig. 2. Modified from Atlas of Israel.

peninsulas. Relative humidity usually drops below 10%. Potential evapotranspiration in the Negev is between 1700 and 2700 mm annually, compared to 1300-1600 in
northern Israel, and relative humidity averages 40-60%, as against 65-75% in the
north. Solar radiation is 195-201 kcal cm$^{-2}$ yr$^{-1}$ in the Negev and 182 kcal cm$^{-2}$
yr$^{-1}$ in the north. The dew average at Avdat for 1963-1966 was 33 mm at a height of
0 cm, and 28 mm at a height of 100 cm. Yet, in 1962-63, the annual dew amount
exceeded the annual rainfall, 28.4 mm vs.25.6 mm.

The above data indicate that the Negev is a desert with very low rainfall, low
relative himidity, high solar radiation, and high evaporation potential. Rainfall
is scanty and highly irregular, with a variation quotient (i.e., ratio of maximum
annual rainfall to minimum) of 5 or more. The Negev's variation quotient is 5-8,
as against 3.4 for Haifa and 2.8 for Greenwich. One index which gives a fairly
good measure of the degree of aridity of a region is the Penman Index

$$P_1 = (\frac{P}{ETP}) \text{ winter}$$

where P is precipitation and ETP is potential evapotranspiration. Values of $P_1$
range from 0.02 in the southern Negev to 0.24 in the northern Negev. Comparison
values of $P_1$ are 0.37 for Baghdad, 0.44 for Teheran, 0.54 for Amman. The limit of
$P_1$ for dry-land farming is 0.75. The value for Kameshlieh, situated in northern-
most Syria in one of the agricultural districts of the whole area, is 1.16.

The climatic fluctuations in the Middle East during the period of instrumental
measurement show fairly good agreement with those of southern Europe. Changes of
precipitation and temperature, as expected in an arid or semi-arid region, are
opposed. The main deviation of the trend in the Middle East from that in southern
Europe occurs when spells of low precipitation occur in the Middle East, without
apparently being based on changes in circulation on a world-wide scale, as for
example in the 1950's. These deviations may be connected with anomalous conditions
in the monsoon belt. During this period, the average temperature in the Middle
East actually increased (in fact, the rise continued until the early 1960's),
while the average precipitation dropped. From the early 1960's until the early
1970's, the average temperature dropped, while the precipitation increased. These
results were obtained from selected Middle East stations, so that they do not
necessarily apply to the Negev. Continental stations seem to be more directly subject to variations in the circulation pattern of the atmosphere, whereas maritime
stations seem to depend more on fluctuations of sea temperature, which reflect
changes in air circulation patterns more slowly. This would seem to imply that the
continental Negev may be more closely tied in with world-wide circulation changes
than was hitherto thought to be the case.


*Flora and Fauna*

Flora. The variegated Negev landscape supports some 1,200 plants. Small fluctuations in water balance, which is the dominant factor in the area, produce great
changes in vegetation.

The Negev highlands, which cover some 90% of the region, can be divided into several main habitats:
a)  the hilltops, which are very dry, with shallow soils, are dotted with a dwarf
    shrub, the bean caper (*Zygophyllum dumosum*), an extreme xerophyte with woody
    stems and succulent leaves which drop off during the dry season;
b)  the hammadoid slops, with a maximum of 50 mm water available, are dotted either
    with the *Zygophyllum* association or by an association dominated by the gray-
    leaved sage brush (*Artemisia herba alba*), another dwarf shrub;
c)  the loessial plains receive only rainwater, with no runoff, so that moisture
    does not penetrate below 30-50 cm. Here the jointed saltwood (*Hammada scoparne*),

a leafless dwarf shrub, prevails.  In depressions in these plains, were runoff
accumulates and penetrates deeper layers, plant growth increases;

d)  the loessial wadis display dense, contracted vegetation, since they can store
water in the upper three meters of soil.  Here one finds saltbush (*Atriplex
halimus*), with salty edible leaves; sparrow wort (*Thymelaea hirsuta*) and
white broom (*Retama raetam*);

e)  the gravelly wadis display the same vegetation at their edges.  In their centers,
however, plant cover is scant because of the erosive action of floodwater.
Trees such as the Atlantic pistachio or various species of acacia grow here.

Another factor of vital importance to plant growth is the salt content of the soil.
Salinity is negligible in wadis, low in loessial plains and extremely high on hilltops and slopes.

There are several other smaller plant habitats in the Negev.  The sand-field between
Dimona and the Arava is dominated by white broom, *Calligonum comosum*, and two plants
with leafless stems: *Anabasis articulata* and glasswort saltwood (*Hammada salicorn-
ica*).  The reg plains of the southern Negev, with their saline soil and scant available water, support single plants, such as Fagonia or the rose of Jericho (*Anastat-
ica hierochuntica*) which feed on accumulations of runoff water in depressions. In those
areas of the Arava where the water table is fresh or only slightly brackish, there
occur oases with tropical vegetation.  Where the table is highly saline, salt marshes exist, with tamarisk trees, sea blite (*Suaeda*) and bearberry bushes (*Nitraria
retusa*).

Fauna.  Israel lies at the meeting place of three zoogeographic units:  the Mediterranean, the Irano-Turanian and the Saharo-Arabian, a fact which accounts for the
high variety of animal species which adapt successfully, in many different ways,
to the extreme climatic conditions.  The region supports some 45 varied species of
reptiles, 56 kinds of fowls, and approximately 40 mammalian species.  The variegated topography and changing water conditions which, as noted, have created varied
plant habitats, have also provided a number of biotypes for animals of widely-
ranging ecological requirements.  Their density and the mobility of the animals
make it difficult to demarcate distribution areas, and the sole clearcut line runs
near the northern ridge of Makhtesh Ramon northward to the Hazera anticline and to
Zohar in the North.

*Population*

The Negev's current population (figures for end of 1974) is 228,900, or 6.7% of the
entire Israeli population, consisting of 191,800 Jews and 37,100 Bedouins.

An analysis of the population growth rate in the Negev since the establishment of
the State of Israel, as compared with other parts of the country during the same
period, reveals a significant growth rate in the former until 1965.  In 1950, only
2% of the Israeli population lived in the Negev, and in 1965, 6%.  During the past
decade the relative weight of the Negev has increased by only ½%.  According to
forecasts by the Planning Division of the Ministry of the Interior, the country's
population will reach 5 million in 1992, the Negev then accounting for 7.4% of the
total, or 370,000.

The Negev's Jewish population consists mostly of families who arrived in Israel
after the establishment of the State, particularly from North Africa and Middle
Eastern countries.  This population is distinguished by large families and relatively lower levels of education and income than the national average.  The percentage
of veteran residents of European origin is much lower than the national average.

The majority of the inhabitants (85%) reside in urban areas and are employed mainly in industry. The number of residents in agricultural settlements, such as kibbutzim (communal settlements) and moshavim (small-holders cooperatives) is small in comparison to other parts of Israel. The Bedouin live mainly in the Beer Sheva-Dimona-Arad triangle. Many of them have given up their migratory way of life, and work in urban settlements in the region. A conspicuous phenomenon in the area is the high rate of employment in industry and low percentage in services and commerce. The ional average (8%), while among the Bedouin population a higher percentage work in agriculture.

*Desertification Processes*

The processes associated with desertification of the Negev have been in progress for many millenia. It is generally considered that there has been no ecologically significant climatic change since 7000 B.C. or possibly even 8000 B.C. It would be simple to attribute any increase in desert area to the influence of man alone. However, there is evidence demonstrating that on the northern marginal areas of the Negev between approximately the 150 mm to 400 mm isohyets, even seemingly insignificant fluctuations in precipitation create an ecological response causing the northern border of aridity to fluctuate and the desert to expand or contract. The northern Negev border area has an extremely sharp rainfall gradient ranging from 400 mm 50 km north of Beer Sheva to 100 mm only 20 km south of the town, a gradient of over 4 mm per km. Any slight climatic change or variation causes a northward or southward direction of this isohyetal gradient with consequent significant changes affecting the population of these fringe areas.

The pattern of the distribution of settlement in the Negev provides some evidence of this shifting borderline. For example, I. Blake has suggested the following chronology:
    6000 B.C. - Settlements mostly in the Rift Valley (Arava) with several in Negev
                south of Dead Sea and Beer Sheva.
    5000 to 4000 B.C. - Previous settlements abandoned; settlement does not exist
                south of the Dead Sea but only on oases north of Dead Sea and on
                agriculturally favourable lands further north.
    3500 to 3000 B.C. - Settled area again extended towards south, mostly on
                loessial soils around Beer Sheva. Abandoned again around 3000 B.C.

These expansions and regressions of settlement correspond broadly to rainfall maxima suggested by Butzer. They undoubtedly demonstrate the crucial effects of climatic variation over periods of thousands of years. However, they do not provide much insight into desertification processes during the last one thousand years. These patterns of settlement indicate that during this period there were cycles of more or less precipitation, but that despite these fluctuations there were few ecologically evident changes in the environment. For example, it is thought that there was more abundant rainfall than today during the period from 1185 to 1255 A.D. and from 1540 to 1625 A.D. and much less rainfall from 1625 to 1790 A.D. These climatic changes undoubtedly had a strong impact on the prosperity of the region. However, over the centuries there has been little net ecological change caused by fluctuation in climate. On the contrary, the archeological evidence shows that the woody species prevalent today have been substantially the same for several millenia. *Tamarix aphylla, Acacia radiana* and *Phoenix dactylifera*, which are common species today, are found at Beer Sheva, Tel Arad, Ein Gedi and other archeological digs.

Extermination of some natural plant communities has occurred due to use of wild plants for fodder, fuel and building materials. Archeological investigation at Ein Bokeq, an oasis on the shores of the Dead Sea, showed that *Populus enphratica* was a commonly used building material around the 4th century A.D. This species

was probably very prevalent at the time but has been eradicated by extensive use.
Useful trees with low growth rates in arid and semi-arid areas have a tendency to
disappear at a fast pace.  The last wave of deforestation swept the Negev (as well
as a large part of present-day Isreal and Jordan) during World War I when the
Turkish armies needed wood for fuel, railroad construction and transportation.  This
massive felling operation completely destroyed the forests in the coastal area and
decimated the spare woodlands of the Negev.  Subsequent grazing by goats, which
tend to destroy seedlings, has not allowed much natural growth of forested areas,
even where climatic conditions are suitable for regeneration.

Overgrazing has been one of the most destructive influences leading to desertification.  The Negev has been intensively grazed for many thousands of years and some
botanists believe that many palatable and nutritious plant species have been
completely eradicated over the millenia.  Some research has indicated that the
eradication of natural vegetation increases the albedo of the ground by exposing
the light colored soil.  These aldebo alterations could bring about changes in the
heat balance of the area leading to increased air subsidence with correspondingly
less rainfall.  This would constitute a positive feedback mechanism whereby less
rainfall would result in less vegetation and even higher albedo, further reinforcing
the tendency for subsidence.  Statistical studies are under way to test this hypothesis of a vertical velocity-albedo relationship for an area as small as the Negev.

Study of the pressures of the Negev's ecosystem leading to desertification must take
into account several vital geographical and economic factors relating to the history
of the region.  Situated between the river valleys of Egypt and Mesopotamia, it was
meeting place and often battleground of the two political powers.  Both coveted the
highways which crossed the country, hence the Negev repeatedly changed rulers.  Circa
the 12th century B.C., the tribes of Israel appeared in the area from Egypt and
Sinai, no longer as nomads but as soldiers and peasants, occupying the Negev as
part of a strong, expanding kingdom.  Vestiges of villages and farmland dating from
this period have been found in the Negev hills.  It was in this period that the
centralized Judean kingdom devoted attention to the South, where Solomon constructed
the port of Etzion Gaber on the Red Sea.  A network of fortresses aimed at safe-
guarding commercial routes from marauders was established on hilltops and near
water sources, with small farmsteads nearby and limited livestock herding.  When
central government again weakened in the 6th century B.C., nomads took over the
the Negev and agriculture was abandoned.  Judea was never again stron enough to
regain permanent control of the Negev, except for a brief period under the Hasmoneans
(end of 1st century B.C.).

The area flourished again in the Nabatean-Roman-Byzantine era from the 3rd century
B.C. continuously for 900 years.  According to Deodorus, the Nabateans "bring
incense, myrrh and most previous perfumes that they received from Arabia Felix to
the ocean".  They built six fortified towns to service their vital caravan routes -
Avdat, Shivta, Khalutza, Kurnub, Nitzana and Rehovot.  Roman competition and new
trade routes weakened the Nabatean empire though the population remained.  The Negev
lost its importance as a commerce route and became a Roman frontier province where
legions guarded the Empire's borders, at times unsuccessfully, against nomads and
enemy infiltration.  During Roman times the population of Israel and Jordan reached
at least three million and, according to the writings of Josephus Flavius, even
five million.  In 392, the Negev fell under the jurisdiction of East Rome, and its
commercial importance again increased as ships reached Eilat from as far away as
India.  The Byzantines used the area as a buffer against nomads, and established
garrisons with local residents who farmed and performed military duties. building
numerous churches and thousands of kilometers of terrace walls.  Intensive farming
was initiated with sophisticated water-collecting techniques, all runoff water
being fully exploited.

From the 7th century on there began a rapid decline of agriculture and apart from
a few hundred nomadic Bedouins, no settlement existed in this area.  Wars and
internal instability, as well as increased pastoral nomadism, led to destruction
of terracing with resultant erosion and depopulation.  The breakdown of central
authority institutionalized land use systems whereby land was exploited without
regard for conservation.  The result was a rapid deterioration of this sensitive
ecosystem.

## WATER - A MAJOR FACTOR IN RECOVERY

*Water Sources*

The obvious direction for recovery of arid areas is the supply of additional water
and more efficient use of already available supplies.  This is essentially the
major policy which has guided Israel in bringing its arid areas into productive
use.  This task was undertaken as a concerted effort, combining technological means
with social and economic methods and remarkable results have been achieved over the
last 25 years.

As can be seen from the rainfall map (see Fig. 2), most precipitation occurs in the
northern areas of Israel and it is there that the national water reservoirs (both
surface and subterranean) exist.  All water in Israel is derived from rainfall,
which occurs only during the winter season.  A large proportion of this precipitation simply runs off to the Mediterranean or the Dead Sea, or evaporates from the
soil.  The remainder seeps into underground aquifers or drains into Lake Kinneret
(Sea of Galilee) and is stored (minus evaporation loss) until needed, which is
generally during the long, dry summer season.  These storage basins are relatively
far from the arid Negev, which has no reservoirs of good quality water.  They are
also situated at low elevations, hence water must be pumped up several hundred
meters in order to reach those elevations where it can be used for agricultural
purposes.  The costs of pumping and of drilling wells render Israel's water supply
costly even before it is transported to agricultural districts and to the fields.

Israel utilizes today over 95% of its potential water supply.  This amounts to only
about 1,600 million cubic meters per year, which is the annual rate of replenish-
ment of all water sources.  In years of poor rainfall, aquifers are not sufficiently
replenished and this can lead to difficulties in suplying the needs of agriculture.
The present and projected water demands for the entire country are as follows:

Table 1.  National Water Consumption in 1974 and Forecast
          for 1979 and 1985 (millions of cubic meters)

|                                     | 1974  | 1979  | 1985      |
|-------------------------------------|-------|-------|-----------|
| Urban and Industrial consumption    | 410   | 550   | 700-800   |
| Agricultural consumption            | 1,170 | 1,170 | 1,170     |
| Losses and miscellaneous            | 60    | 100   | 130       |
| TOTAL                               | 1,640 | 1,820 | 2000-2100 |

Source: Guidelines for the determination of water Policy,
        Ministry of Agriculture, Water Commission, Tel
        Aviv, 10.9.1974.

As can be seen from the table, the water potential could become severely over-exploited in the near future. It is intended to eliminate this deficit by the treatment and use of municipal and industrial waste effluents, the use of saline water resources and possibly, in the future, by desalination of ocean water.

In order to convey surplus water potential from the North to areas which lacked it, and to facilitate coordinated control of water sources, several regional schemes were carried out in the 1950's. These schemes were integrated by the construction of the National Water Carrier in the mid-sixties. In the early fifties, pipelines with a yearly capacity of 15 million cu.m. replaced older, smaller pipeline systems from Nir Am in the Southern Coastal Plain to the Northern Negev. By 1955, with the completion of the first stage of the Yarkon-Negev project, more water was reaching the Negev. The National Water Carrier, which issues from Lake Kinneret, carries over 300 million cu.m. water per year. From there it is conveyed through a network of canals, reservoirs, pipes and pumping stations, which interconnect the secondary regional schemes, integrating the whole water-supply network into a centrally-managed supply system.

It is this system which conveys water from the northern, more humid areas to the agricultural areas of the south, where it is used as a basis for settlement and revitalization of this formerly inhospitable, arid region.

The factors described above, namely high pumping costs, long-distance transportation of water, lack of sufficient reservoirs and general overall water shortage, have forced Israel to relate to water as a scarce and precious natural resource.

*The Legal and Economic Status of Water*

Shortly after the establishment of the State it was realized that water would have to become a nationalized commodity, owned and regulated by the Government in accordance with a centralized plan for its production and use. The Government needed to be legally empowered to transport water on an inter-regional basis, despite possible objections of vested interest groups. Hence, the Israel "Water Law" was legislated in 1959, and stated:
> "Israel's water sources are public property, controlled by the State, and devoted to the needs of its residents and the country's development. ... A person's right in land does not grant him rights in a water sources located on that land or passing through it or within its boundaries."

The law further empowers the Government to set up an administrative system to allocate water quotas to various regions and municipalities and to individual farmers. It is this law that constitutes the legal basis for the inter-regional transport of water to the arid Negev.

The Water Law also takes into account economic factors of water use. It provided for an "equalizing" fund to regulate the price of water in such a way as to reduce the differences in water charges among the various consumers. This fund, as well as the water quota allocation system, stemmed from a desire to attain an equalitarian division of this vital resource. At the same time, it imposed upon the Government the responsibility of administering a complex economic and social organization whose ramifications extend into almost every aspect of the Israeli economy. The provision that "every person is entitled to receive and use water, subject to the provisions of the law" has prevented preferential treatment.

The advantages of the law can be summarized as follows:
a. It allows more equalitarian distribution of water among the farming population.

b.  It has led to the development of an overall water plan based on rational fact-
    ors.
c.  It permits encouragement of regional specialization, and hence positive exploit-
    ation of local differences of climate and soil.
d.  It acts as a tool for regulation of agricultural production to meet the demands
    of the local market and to establish export markets.
e.  The quota system limiting the amount of water to each farmer is an incentive for
    efficient use of water.
f.  The water price differential, albeit relatively small, can be used to encourage
    rational use of water.

Some disadvantages are:
a.  In many cases, the subsidized pricing system permits the use of expensive water
    for uneconomic crops.
b.  The water quota system does not react sufficiently rapidly to changes in market
    demands or new developments in agricultural technology.
c.  The entire administrative system is sensitive to changing political outlook and
    to organized pressure groups.
d.  Since each family farming unit can receive a water allocation, the system does
    not provide incentives for large farming units where "economy of scale" would
    lead to more efficient water use.

## Technology of Water Use

Because water is the limiting factor for agricultural products in arid zones,
every effort has been made to exploit each unit of costly water transported from
the North as efficiently and effectively as possible.  The use of advanced agricultural techniques and the development of technological innovations have contributed,
more than any other factor, to the high productivity of Israeli agriculture.  Income
from agricultural produce is measured per unit of water input as well as per unit
of land.  Decreasing the amount of water used per unit of production not only
reduces production costs and raises the farmer's profit but also frees water for
additional production.  In the framework of a tight water quota the farmer has
ample incentive to utilize his allocation as productively as possible.

High capital investments have characterized Israeli agricultural technology.  The
major system of irrigation used is sprinkling.  This technique gives good uniformity
in water distribution and allows the farmer excellent control of the quantity of
water to be delivered to any particular area.  Water is brought to the fields in a
closed system of pipes, thereby reducing problems of loss by evaporation or leakage.
This system is relatively simple to operate even by inexperienced farmers and
requires less labor than surface irrigation methods.  In reality, the capital
investment required for a sprinkler irrigation system is little more than for
surface irrigated fields if those fields are properly graded and levelled.

In the last few years the use of drip or trickle irrigation systems, an original
Israeli development, has been expanded.  Plastic tubes with tricklers inserted at
desired intervals are placed in the field.  The great advantage of this system is
reduced evaporation, since only a small area of the soil is wetted and the water is
not sprayed into the air.  Here too, excellent control of water quantities delivered
to the field is attained.  Fertilizers are usually injected directly into the irrigation water, resulting both in their effective utilization and in reduced costs.
The tricklers are run almost continuously so that the soil root volume is continuously wetted.  Prevention of the wetting and drying cycles in the soil has resulted in
exceptionally high yields per unit of water and of surface.

Table 2.   Water Consumption in Agriculture, 1948/49 - 1973/74

| | Water consumption (millions of cubic meters) | Area under irrigation (thousands of hectares) | Water per irrigated hectare | |
|---|---|---|---|---|
| | | | Cubic meters | Index change 1948/49 = 100 |
| 1948/49 | 257 | 30 | 8570 | 100 |
| 1950/51 | 413 | 47 | 8790 | 103 |
| 1955/56 | 830 | 95 | 8690 | 101 |
| 1958/59 | 990 | 124 | 7980 | 93 |
| 1962/63 | 1140 | 147 | 7740 | 90 |
| 1968/69 | 1235 | 166 | 7430 | 87 |
| 1970/71 | 1245 | 172 | 7240 | 84 |
| 1972/73 | 1390 | 176 | 7900 | 92 |
| 1973/74 | 1150 | 180 | 6390 | 75 |

Source: Statistical Yearbook for 1973 and Agriculture and
        Settlement Planning and Development Center,
        Ministry of Agriculture.

The table shows average figures on a national basis.  Much better results have been
achieved, however, indicating that still much more can be accomplished to increase
water efficiency.

It was understood that installing a modern irrigation system affording good distribution and regulation of water must be accompanied by other technological inputs in
order to optimize agricultural yields.  This meant the development of a highly
intensive farming system utilizing the most modern cultivation methods.  The intensive use of technology ensures the maximum output for each unit of water applied to
the field.  A modern irrigation system must go hand in hand with a modern agricultural technology including such factors as an efficient extension service, research,
marketing facilities, etc.  The *kibbutz* sector of Israeli agriculture has the additional advantage of achieving further economies of water due to the large scale of
the communally-cultivated fields.  In recent years in the *moshav* (where fields are
cultivated by each family individually), progress has been made towards achieving
"economy of scale" by pooling orchards or other production units.  In addition,
crops are chosen on the basis of their water requirements as well as for their
other characteristics.  By use of these methods Israel has increased its agricultural production on the whole *more than ten fold during the past 25 years*.  Many
crops have shown increased efficiency with water use.  For example, cotton has
shown a 50% increase in yield over a period of 6 years, as shown in Table 3.

*Run-Off Water*

Some of the rains in the Negev occur as torrential downpours of relatively high
intensity, usually over a very restricted area.  A large amount of this precipitation runs off the hills and slopes and collects in the wadis, resulting in floods,
sometimes of several days' duration.  These flodds represent a loss of potential

irrigation water.  The Ministry of Agriculture has made long-term loans available to
settlements for the building of dams to catch these waters and use them for irrigation purposes.  The major problem is that while rains occur only in winter, irrigation water is needed mostly in summer.  The storage of water from winter to summer
results in substantial losses due to evaporation, leakage and infiltration.  The
solution to this situation was to use the water immediately for supplementary
irrigation of rain-fed winter grain crops in areas of the Negev with marginal rainfall.  For example, in a region of 300 mm rainfall another 100-200 mm of collected
run-off water is applied.  This additional water will often raise yields by over
50% and ensure a grain crop even in years of abnormally low precipitation.  Pumping
the water to the fields as soon as possible after it has accumulated in the dam
ensures minimal losses.  It also frees the dam for collecting water if additional
floods occur during the season.  Where used, this technique has resulted in average
grain yields of 3.5 tons per hectare, and yields of five tons per hectare are not
uncommon.

Table 3.  Raw Cotton Yield per Unit of Water in Irrigated
          Areas, 1955/56 - 1971/72.

|  | Water consumption (cu.m/Ha) | Yield (kg. per Ha.) | Yield per water unit (kg/cu.m) | Index |
|---|---|---|---|---|
| 1965/66 | 6140 | 3120 | 0.51 | 100 |
| 1966/67 | 4620 | 2940 | 0.64 | 125 |
| 1967/68 | 4720 | 3240 | 0.69 | 135 |
| 1968/69 | 4580 | 3380 | 0.74 | 145 |
| 1969/70 | 4890 | 2970 | 0.61 | 120 |
| 1970/71 | 4460 | 3170 | 0.71 | 139 |
| 1971/72 | 4620 | 3550 | 0.77 | 151 |

Source:  "Profitability of Cotton Growing in 1971/72".  The
         Institute of Farm Income Research, September 1973,
         Tel Aviv (Hebrew).

Another form of utilization of run-off water collected behind dams is to pump it to
infiltration basins where the collected water will infiltrate and enrich a subterranean aquifer.  This form of underground storage again reduces evaporation losses and frees the dams for additional flood collection.  The water can then be pumped out of shallow wells and used for irrigation of summer crops.  Obviously, this
technique is limited only to those situations where natural underground storage is
possible with minimal losses.

A further method of utilizing run-off water has been experimented with by Professor
Evenari at Avdat, in order to test techniques of ancient desert agriculture.  This
site represents the remains of an ancient Nabatean town whose inhabitants cultivated
the low areas of the wadis about 200 B.C.-400 A.D.  These wadis are terraced and
rainwater falling on the hillsides was collected by a series of long channels, each
channel bringing water to a specific area of the wadi terraces.  Although the
region's total annual precipitation amounts to only 100 mm, this usually includes
at least one rainfall heavy enough to result in a flood that will wet the wadi soil

sufficiently to yield a good crop.  The Nabateans were skilled hydraulic engineers and succeeded in constructing thousands of these farms with efficient water collection and distribution systems.

The Evenari team reconstructed two of these ancient Nabatean farms and succeeded in obtaining excellent yields of grain, fruits, vegetables, pasture and other crops. Some of the yields were exceptionally high, as can be seen by Table 4.

This method of runoff farming, while very effective under extremely adverse conditions, is not yet economically feasible due to the high investment costs.  The same group of scientists also developed a system of individual microcatchments.  In one corner of each plot a single tree or bush was planted and the plot graded so that the runoff water would accumulate around the plant itself.  The optimal size of the microcatchments had to be determined experimentally for each of the various species that were tried.  The advantage of this system is that mechanized equipment can be used for the construction of the microcatchments.  Depending on the plot size, it is estimated that investment costs will be in the range of $20 per hectare.  Yields of 400 kg of dry matter per hectare have been obtained, which is a considerable increase over the original dry matter production in the area.  On the basis of this work a large area is now being established for wider scale experimentation.

Table 4.  Yields of various field crops and vegetables at
          Avdat obtained in comparatively good years.

| Crop | Use | Yield (t/ha) | Year |
|------|-----|--------------|------|
| Wheat "Nanasit" | grain | 4.4[a] | 1966 |
| Wheat "Florence" | grain | 2.7[b] | 1966 |
| Barley | grain | 4.8 | 1966 |
| Peas "Perfection" | seed | 5.6 | 1966 |
| Peas "Dunn" | whole plant | 48.4[c] | 1966 |
| Radishes | seed | 0.62 | 1964 |
| Carrots | seed | 0.75 | 1965 |
| Onions | seed | 0.65 | 1966 |
| Sunflower | grain | 2.4 | 1965 |
| Safflower | grain | 2.3 | 1965 |
| Artichokes | | 9.5 | 1965 |
| Asparagus | | 2.0 | 1965 |

a.   Straw, 3.7 t/ha.
b.   Straw, 3.0 t/ha.
c.   Fresh weight; dry weight 12.9 t/ha.

Source: Professor Evenari

*Water Desalination*

Another source of water can be obtained by desalination of brackish water or of
ocean water. Israel has spent considerable sums for research and development in
this field. The techniques experimented with include electrodialysis, reverse
osmosis and ion exchange for desalination of underground brackish water, and various distillation processes for desalination of ocean water. Today there are several desalination plants operating in the Negev and the manufacture of desalination
units for export has become a very lucrative industry.

Two large size pilot plants of Israeli design were constructed in the Negev for
brackish water desalination. In addition, a unit for testing imported equipment
was set up in order to determine the best method for the process. In general, it
has been found that saline water rich in chlorides is best desalinated by electrodialysis methods, while water rich in sulfates responds best to reverse osmosis
methods. Both methods are still much too expensive for use in agriculture. However, they certainly could be used for supplying potable water to population centers
at a reasonable price. Several reverse osmosis plants are now under construction
in the Arava to supply drinking water to the agricultural settlements there. This
area has fairly large supplies of underground brackish water of the sulfatic type.
It is feared that this type of water could have undesirable effects on the health
of the settlers who use it for drinking purposes. The high magnesium content possibly causes damage to the adsorptive capacity of the intestines while the sulfate
lowers the pH of the urine, thereby increasing the tendency to develop kidney
stones. Excess fluorine could have deleterious effects on the skeletal development
of children raised in this region. Desalination of these brackish waters would
reduce or eliminate these dangers to the health of the local population.

As will be shown below, brackish water irrigation can prove almost as effective as
irrigation with good quality water when proper techniques are employed. However,
in many areas there is a slow but gradual rise in water salinity. Water in an
aquifer usually drains into a river or into the sea, carrying its salt with it.
This is a natural process which removes salt from the hydrological system. However,
when water is removed from the aquifer for irrigation purposes this process largely
ceases. The salt draining into the aquifer now accumulates and salinity rises. In
some Negev aquifers salinity is rising by 3-4% per year. At some point desalination
processes will have to be used to remove salt from the hydrological system, even
though this is not yet necessary.

Another future use for brackish water desalination methods is for desalination of
municipal and industrial effluents. This water, if properly treated, could be used
for industrial or agricultural purposes. At present a large proportion of these
wastewaters is being infiltrated into the coastal aquifers. The water is purified
in the process with resultant recharging of the aquifer.

It is more difficult to desalinate sea water, which is more saline than brackish
water and often has a higher organic matter content which can cause fouling of
desalination equipment. The use of vapor-compression methods for distilling sea
water has been successful in Eilat and other settlements in the south. Recently,
construction has begun on large size plants of this type with a new process developed by Israel Desalination Engineering Ltd. Again, the price of desalination is
still too high for normal agricultural use but is cheap enough for municipal or for
many industrial uses.

The combined use of nuclear power plants with sea water desalination equipment has
been extensively studied in Israel. By combining the operation of these two plants,
the price of the electricity-water could be considerably reduced. However, the
economics of this method still were not good enough to justify such an investment.

Recently, with the development of new distillation processes in Israel which can utilize lower temperatures, interest in a combined water/electricity plant has been revived. Undoubtedly, as agriculture becomes more sophisticated and as the price of desalinated water is reduced, these methods will become economical for producing water for irrigation. This development might take place sometime toward the end of the next decade.

*Rainfall Enhancement*

Another experimental method for increasing water supply is rainfall enhancement by cloud seeding. Most clouds suitable for seeding are found in the rainier northern region of Israel and not in the Negev. However, since a large part of the Negev's irrigation water originates in Lake Tiberias in the north, increased rainfall in that area has direct significance for the Negev.

The Israeli experiments were launched with the purpose of investigating the possibility of increasing the water potential of the country. The first experiment was performed in 1961-1967. The second Israeli experiment, 1969-1975, was designed with the explicit purpose of exploring the potentialities of rainfall in the catchment area of Lake Tiberias. This lake is Israel's main water reservoir, and is the source of the National Water Carrier. Thus, rainfall enhancement in the Lake Tiberias Catchment could have important consequences for the Negev. Despite difficulties in interpretation of complex statistical data, results show the following:
1. The rainfall increases, due to seeding, are 17% in the Lake Tiberias Catchment. This figure is statistically significant at the 3.8% level.
2. Analysis of the effects of seeding with data obtained from recording rain gauges indicates that the increases in rainfall can probably be attributed to an increase in the number of rain periods, on any day, and to a similar increase in total duration of precipitation during any seeded rainy day.

The cloud physics studies conducted in conjunction with the seeding projects have contributed greatly to the understanding of, and confidence in, the statistical results.
1. Since "cold" winter continental clouds have a low ice content and high liquid water content, conditions exist for the artificial addition of ice crystals for the formation of additional solid precipitation particles on practically all rain days.
2. The increases in precipitation can mainly be attributed to effects produced in clouds that otherwise would not have precipitated and to the formation of a more efficient prolonged rain process in clouds that are already precipitating naturally.
3. Cold winter cumuli of a continental origin have, by virtue of their droplet size distribution, as ideal a potential for cloud seeding as stratiform clouds (contrary to maritime cumuli).
4. The consistency and magnitude of the positive effect on rainfall due to seeding in Israel are also a result of the relative predominance of clouds in the -12 to -15 deg. C range on the majority of rain days.

These experiments are continuing. The seeding is performed from aircraft flying at cloud base altitudes from a line-source upwind from the target areas. Recently, the "dynamic Seeding" technique, in which pyrotechnics of silver iodine are released into cloud tops, has been used with great success in Florida. If Negev clouds prove to have the correct properties, it may be possible to enhance rainfall from them by dynamic seeding.

*Arid-Zone Irrigation with Brackish Water*

Brackish water reservoirs occur in most deserts of the world, and in the Negev desert, south of the 200 mm rainfall line, most of the underground aquifers are saline. Two large deep brackish water aquifers underlie the Central and Northern Negev, and shallow saline aquifers exist in the Western Coastal areas. All the settlements in the Arava use local brackish water with salt concentration between 700-3,000 ppm total dissolved solids (TDS) for irrigation of their out-of-season vegetable and flower crops. Most of the brackish waters in the Central and Western Negev, however, are not being fully exploited at present. Recent developments in agricultural technology, irrigation methodology and plant selection have made possible the utilization of brackish water for modern agriculture, and thus these large resources can provide a major water source for future development.

Irrigation Technology. The breakthrough in brackish water agriculture was brought about by the development of trickle irrigation. This technique, developed in Israel in the early sixties, lifted the "salt tolerance" levels of most crops and made possible the cultivation of many plant species (onions, green peppers, cucumbers, citrus) which grew poorly when irrigated with brackish water (2,000-3,000 ppm TDS) by other irrigation methods. The advantages of this irrigation system for brackish water use are as follows: a) The leaves are not wetted with salt water, as in the sprinkle irrigation method (salts were found to penetrate leaves, causing severe burning, chlorosis and leaf distortion); b) Continuous leaching of excess salts from the root zone; c) Maintenance of very low soil matrix potential, the soil water potential thus being largely composed of the osmotic component; d) Wetting of a relatively small soil surface area (as compared with sprinkler irrigation) thus creating a much higher salt leaching capacity for a given amount of water applied.

Methodology of Irrigation. Most plants are especially sensitive to salt during the germination and establishment stages. Overcoming salinity hazards at these stages will be necessary to ensure successful yields. With the conventional methods of irrigation in the Negev, the soil is wetted prior to sowing to a depth of $\sim 150$ cm (pre-irrigation), and light irrigations are given after sowing to keep a moist soil surface for the germinating seed (post-sowing irrigation). However, recent experiments have shown that frequent irrigations being about rapid accumulation of salt around the germinating seed, reducing germination, and inhibiting growth of those seedlings which do germinate.

To prevent salt accumulation around the germinating seed, salts must be leached continuously out of this zone. This has been achieved by changing the irrigation practice. No pre-irrigation is given, but very large quantities of water are applied during sowing-to-emergence period, exploiting the water which was "saved" from pre-irrigation together with the water normally applied at post-sowing irrigation. Results achieved with this method are very favorable compared with those of the conventional method.

The quantity of salt removed by plants is very small in comparison to amounts introduced via the irrigation water. In areas of moderate to heavy rainfall (in Israel, the 300 mm rainfall line) the accumulated salts are leached by rain. In more arid areas, water in excess of evapotranspiration (Et) must be added to prevent year-to-year salt accumulation. This requirement is a function of the salt concentration in the irrigation water, the irrigation frequency and the salt tolerance of the cultivated crop. Salt tolerance depends on many factors, i.e., variety, atmospheric conditions, soil temperature and aeration.

Salt-sensitive plants require a more rigid control of salt in their root zone during the growth season and more leaching water than salt-resistant species. Table 5

shows the salt concentration at the root zone in salt-sensitive (tomato) and salt
resistant (cotton) crops at the beginning and at the end of the growing season.
Tomatoes were irrigated every seven days with 25 to 35% water in excess of evapotranspiration. Cotton was watered every two weeks with quantities only slightly
exceeding evapotranspiration.

Table 5.  Mean electrical conductivity of saturated soil
extracts (EC$_e$) in tomato and cotton fields at a
depth of 1-150 cm.  (Ec of water = 4.4 mm·cm$^{-1}$)

| Crop type | Canning tomatoes | Cotton |
|---|---|---|
| Total water applied | 1070 | 817 |
| Percentage water in excess of Et | 25-35% | 0-5% |
| Irrigation intervals | 7 days | 14 days |
| Initial EC$_e$ (millimhos·cm$^{-1}$) | 1.0 | 1.2 |
| Final EC$_e$ (millimhos·cm$^{-1}$) | 3.1 | 5.9 |

Source: Division of Plant Introduction and Applied Ecology,
        Research and Development Authority, Ben Gurion
        University of the Negev, 1972.

Whenever large quantities of leaching water are given, it is necessary to ensure
drainage of this excess water.  In rhe Negev, the water is drained into the dry
river beds (wadis) and/or percolates through deep soils and permeable rocks.  There
are no significant underlying fresh water aquifers and hence no danger of salt contam-
ination of underground water.  In many places in the world the natural drainage
system cannot carry the excess water and artificial drainage must be provided to
avoid water logging and salt accumulation at the soil surface.

Selection of salt resistant species and varieties.  Plants differ greatly in their
resistance to salt in the root zone.  Where possible, salt-resistant species such
as cotton, wheat and sugar beet are being used, yields of which are normally un-
affected by the salt concentration in the brackish water of the Central and Northern Negev (2,500 ppm TDS), provided irrigation, drainage and fertilization regimes
are correct (Fig. 3).  There exist genetic variations in resistance to salt within
many species.  Selection of the most salt-resistant varieties is most important in
those species which are only moderately salt-resistant.  Table 6 illustrates genetic
variation in salt resistance in canning tomatoes.

Fodder plants are more resistant to salt than other field crops.  The limits of
resistance of Bermuda grasses (*Cynodon dactylon*) or Rhodes grass (*Chloris gayana*)
are yet to be determined. The *Atriplex* genus contains species rich in protein which
grow well in soils of an electroconductivity of 30 millimhos cm$^{-1}$.

A summary of five years experimental results is given in Table 7.

The introduction and selection of salt- and drought-resistant species for desert
landscaping and gardening is being carried out at Ben-Gurion University in Beer
Sheva.  Suitable seeds are collected from deserts all over the world, and sown in
the nursery.  Those which germinate and grow well for at least one season are transferred to experimental fields.  Plants which grow successfully in the field are

selected for repropagation in the nursery.  New seedlings are distributed to various
locations, representing different climatic regions, and their progress is recorded.
Plants can now be recommended for all regions of the Negev.  A garden has been
planted at Sodom on the shores of the Dead Sea, irrigated with local underground
saline water, and landscaping is being develop in the town of Eilat and along the
Red Sea shore under similar irrigation.

Fig. 3.  Wheat grown with brackish water irrigation.

Table 6.  Yield of seven varieties of canning tomatoes sprin-
          kle-irrigated with fresh and brackish water.

| Variety | Yield (Kg·10 m$^{-2}$) | | % yield reduction |
| | Brackish water (2,300 ppm TDS) | Fresh water (400 ppm TDS) | Fresh water = 100% |
|---|---|---|---|
| Mecheast-22 | 57.1 | 78.5 | 27 |
| VF 198 | 59.1 | 86.5 | 31 |
| Napoli | 73.5 | 107.7 | 32 |
| VF 154B7879 | 43.6 | 75.6 | 42 |
| VF 317 | 49.6 | 87.4 | 43 |
| VF 134-1 | 37.6 | 65.9 | 43 |
| VF 145F$_5$ | 38.8 | 72.0 | 46 |

Source: Division of Plant Introduction and Applied Ecology,
        Research and Development Authority, Ben Gurion
        University of the Negev, 1976.

Table 7. Yields of various vegetable, field and fodder crops irrigated with brackish water in the Central Negev Highlands. (Soil - sandy to loess. Brackish water - 2,300 ppm TDS. Fresh water - 400 ppm TDS).

| Crop | Irrigation method | Yield (Kg/ha) | | Comments |
|------|-------------------|---------------|-----------|----------|
| | | Brackish water | Fresh water | |
| Cotton | Sprinkler | 5,400 | 4,250 | Average 2 yrs |
| Sugar beet | " | 18,000 | 19,000 | Sugar yield |
| Wheat | " | 6,700 | 6,700 | -- |
| Sorghum | " | 8,400 | 10,000 | -- |
| Rhodes grass | " | 33,000 | - | Dry weight |
| Bermuda grass | " | 33,000 | - | " |
| Canning peas | " | 17,000 | 19,000 | Green pods |
| Canning tomatoes | " | 70,000 | 100,000 | |
| Table tomatoes | Trickler | 113,000 | - | |
| Melons | " | 48,000 | - | |
| Watermelons | " | 62,000 | - | |
| Cucumbers | " | 42,000 | - | |

Source: Utilization of Brackish Water Resources for Development of the Negev Desert, Research and Development Authority, Ben Gurion University of the Negev, June 1975.

## AGRICULTURAL TECHNOLOGY IN THE SEMI-ARID ZONE

Farmers in Israel's arid and semi-arid zone have a wide range of management options open to them because of the availability of external inputs. These inputs include fuel, machinery, fertilizer, plant protection chemicals and sometimes water. The type of farming system adopted and its economic viability are determined, as everywhere, not only by the constraints imposed by biological and environmental conditions but also by economic and social considerations. Among the economic factors that influence management decisions are commodity prices and stabilizing factors like government-sponsored drought compensation. Sociological considerations include farmer's preference for more convenient types of work as well as the availability and acceptability of hired labour. For instance, integration of livestock and cropping systems is dependent on social constraints because of the great and continuous demands on specialized labour required for handling livestock. These constraints can, of course, change with time.

The elements of the system that are directly managed to maximize profit are the crop cultivar, the moisture regime, soil fertility, weed population and disease incidence. The crop management operations include soil cultivation, crop rotation, irrigation, herbicide and fungicide applications. Commodity prices and drought compensation influence the choice of management options. Livestock integration adds more management variables related to the animals and to the crops and pastures. A study of these management variables as practiced in the semi-arid regions of Israel has been

the subject of much research and some of the results are included in the following
discussion.

## Crop Cultivars

The crops cultivated in semi-arid regions of Israel include wheat, barley, vetch
for hay, cotton and sorghum. Other crops cultivated on a much smaller scale include
watermelons, oats, sunflowers and safflower. As a result of an extensive wheat
introduction and breeding program there are about a dozen wheat cultivars in current
use. Barley varieties available are much fewer because of the decline in barley
culture over the past fifteen years, due to higher wheat prices coupled with the
introduction of new varieties of high-yielding wheat varieties. The actual area of
hay has dropped drastically over the past decade and the dominant remaining species
used is a locally bred vetch variety ("Assor"). Sorghum breeding has been fairly
active and a number of sorghum species are currently available.

Wheat: Originally, all local wheats were hard wheats (*T-iticum durum*), the main
cultivars being Noursi and Ettit. During the early thirties, selection from local
varieties was introduced, but the main elements in increasing yields was improved
agrotechnical practice, crop rotation and chemical fertilization. From 1930 to 1945
the yields in the new agricultural system increased from 700 to 1200 kgs per ha,
with occasional record yields of 3,500 kgs per ha. At that time new varieties of
*T. aestivum* were introduced and began replacing the *T. durum*, mainly because of
better baking quality and higer yield potential. The cultivar Florence was introduced from Morocco in 1937, but because of its sensitivity to rust, was replaced by
Florence/Aurore (F/A) from Algeria. Under good conditions F/A yielded as much as
5,000 kgs/ha.

In 1957/58, the new Mexican dwarf cultivars were introduced. These were high-yielding but had poor baking quality. In 1962/63, new dwarf and semi-dwarf cultivars
were introduced, also with high yielding potential, but with better baking quality.
Trials at the Lakhish Experimental Station (with 380 mm mean annual precipitation)
showed that these varieties considerably outyielded F/A.

Subsequent yields (with supplementary irrigation) reached 7,000 kgs per ha. The
dwarf and semi-dwarf cultivars rapidly replaced F/A, which accounted for only 10% of
the total area in 1972 and was not sown at all after 1973.

Wheat breeding took on added momentum and many new local dwarf and especially semi-
dwarf cultivars were developed. These are being used both in the humid and semi-
arid regions, but a recent survey of wheat yields, over the past fifteen years,
suggested that the effect of the new semi-dwarf varieties on actual yield on the
farm was much more prominent in the humid region. Those more frequently used are
the earlier maturing cultivars.

Barley: Until 1961/62, barley yields were 11-78% higher than wheat yields. Subsequently, with the introduction of the new wheat varieties, barley yields became
relatively smaller, about 79% of wheat. As a result of the lower yield, and the
lower price per kg, barley cultivation decreased steadily and now covers only a small
area. Barley breeding has received much less attention than wheat and the number
of cultivars used is, as a result, much smaller. The main barley varieties are
listed in Table 8.

Sorghum: In the semi-arid region sorghum is sown only when sufficient soil moisture
has been stored from the winter rains. The area is thus variable and confined mainly to the northern margins of the semi-arid zone (Table 2). In years when winter
rains are less than 350 mm, farmers sometimes sow sorghum instead of leaving the

land fallow.  Bird damage is often a serious problem.  New hybrid varieties are being bred.

Table 8.  Some crop cultivars currently used for dry-land farming in the semi-arid zone in Israel (1975/76).

| Crop cultivar | Bred by | Characteristics |
|---|---|---|
| Wheat (*T. aestivum*) | | |
| Lakhish | Ephrat (ARO) | Medium ripening; very high yield potential; high baking quality; tends to lodging |
| Miriam | " " | Early ripening; high yield potential; very high baking quality; tolerance to septoria |
| Ceeon | Hazera Seed Co. | Early ripening; very high yield potential; poor baking quality |
| Wheat (*T. durum*) | | |
| Inbar | Ephrat (ARO) | Germ plasm ex-CYMMIT (Ulorico).  Late maturing; high potential yields (early maturing being bred) |
| Barley (*H. vulgare*) | | |
| Dvir (six-row) | | Selection from local variety |
| Omer " " | Ephrat (ARO) | High yield potential; susceptible to rust, septoria |
| C.K. | Weizmann Inst. | High yield potential (new CV) |
| Esperance-Volla (two rows) | | Early maturing |
| *Sorghum vulgare* | | |
| Various hybrid varieties, rapidly changing | Hazera Seed Co. | |
| Vetch (*Vicia sativa*) | | |
| Assor | Arnon & Blum (ARO) | Late maturing; high yield potential |
| "Purple" (*V. atropurpurea*) | | |

Source: J. Ephrat, B. Rettig, Leshem, 1967.

Table 9.  Relative importance of various dry-land crops in
          the semi-arid zone in Israel

| Crop | Area | | Comment |
|------|------|---|---------|
|      | ha x $10^3$ | % | |
| Wheat | 36.0 | 65.2 | Of which 10,000 ha with supplementary irrigation |
| Barley | 4.0 | 7.3 | |
| Hay | 4.0 | 7.3 | Mainly seed production in wetter margins |
| Fallow | 6.0 | 10.9 | Mainly in drier margins |
| Sunflower | 3.0 | 5.4 | In wetter margins |
| Sorghum | 1.0 | 1.8 | " |
| Safflower | 0.5 | 0.9 | " |
| Oats (seed grain) | 0.3 | 0.5 | " |
| Cotton (dry land) | 0.3 | 0.5 | " |
| Total cultivated area | 55.1 | 98.2 | |

Source: D. Ariel, Extension service, Ministry of Agricult-
        ure, Tel Aviv.

Table 10.  Comparison of yields between dwarf varieties and
           Florence/Aurore at Lakhish (kgs. grain per ha).

| CV | Dry-Land | Supplementary irrigation |
|----|----------|--------------------------|
| Dwarf CVS (mean) | 4370 | 6120 |
| F/A | 2480 | 4240 |

Source: J. Ephrat, 1972, Wheat and Barley Trials at the Gat-
        Lakhish Experiment.

Hay crops:  The major hay crop is vetch, which is cultivated mainly in the more
humid regions.  A considerable part of the vetch in the semi-arid region is grown
for seed, yielding 500 to 600 kg/ha$^{-2}$ in a good year.

Others:  Most of the remaining crops are summer growing species.  As a result, they
can produce economic yields only in relatively good years, or with supplementary
irrigation.  These are mainly "opportunistic" crops in the sense that they are sown
as an alternative to leaving the land fallow on wheat rotation, whenever soil
moisture at sowing time is sufficient to ensure a crop.  Among that group sunflowers

D. K

(local dwarf CV) have been prominent. Safflower (*Carthamus tinctorious*), is also grown on a scale that varies with local market conditions. Dryland cotton is becoming more common as cotton prices continue to rise. Watermelons are occasionally grown too.

Table 11. Effect of new varieties on wheat yields - results of regression analysis on data from farms covering the years 1957-1974.

| Region | Mean Precip. (mm) | Mean yield (kgs/ha) | Regression Coeff. for "new varieties" | U-test value |
|--------|-------------------|---------------------|----------------------------------------|--------------|
| Humid | 500 | 3000 | 170 | 4.5 |
| Semi-arid | 250 | 1600 | 51 | 2.1 |
| Pooled | - | - | 129 | 8.3 |

Source: M. Hoffman, 1974, Technical Progress and Economic Returns from Wheat Research, M.S.Agr. Thesis, Hebrew University Faculty of Agriculture, Rehovot (Hebrew).

*Management of Cultivated Semi-Arid Ecosystems*

The erratic nature of the weather, especially rainfall, results in wide fluctuations of yield from year to year and as a result, management decisions are difficult. In Israel, prices are usually guaranteed and government-supported drought compensation removes part of the economic hazard in the wetter part of the semi-arid zone. The main management objective in the field is thus to produce economically the maximum amount of marketable products under conditions of climatic uncertainty. The agro-technical practices available to the farmer can be applied so as to improve the moisture regime, to increase soil fertility, to reduce competition from weeds and to control plant disease. The practices themselves include soil cultivation, fertilizer application, crop rotation, use of herbicides, pesticides and fungicides and, where possible, supplementary irrigation. Additional practices are related to the crop itself and include the use of growth retardants, like CCC to produce shorter and sturdier plants under conditions where lodging may be expected, i.e., with supplementary irrigation in the more humid regions.

Cultivation. Seed-bed preparation for both winter and summer crops includes subsoiling, discing and fertilizer application, levelling and rolling. This phase accounts for 25% of the production costs, the most expensive practice being ploughing. Different methods, such as deep ploughing, ordinary ploughing, deep and shallow subsoiling and no ploughing were compared. The test crops were wheat, sorghum and hay. There were very small, and generally insignificant differences between methods, except for no ploughing which resulted in yields between 20-25% lower than in the ploughing treatments.

Fertilizer applications. The wheat crop is regularly fertilized with nitrogen and phosphorus. No response to potassium has been recorded as yet. Nitrogen fertilizer, on the other hand, is given according to standard extension service recommendations. These have changed over the years as follows:

| Year | Recommendation (kgs N per ha) |
|------|-------------------------------|
| 1949 | 20 |
| 1959 | 30 |
| 1969 | 70-80 |
| 1972 | 80-100 |

The increased use of nitrogen has been made possible by the introduction of the stiff-stemmed semi-dwarf wheat cultivars that resist lodging, which is common when heavy dressings of nitrogen are applied.

In recent years a biological test for determining the soil nitrogen status has been developed. The amount of nitrogen available for plant growth is determined by measuring the amount of nitrogen taken up by test plants (originally wheat, later maize) from a 8 kg soil sample grown for 60 days under optimum soil moisture and temperature. As a rule, fertilizer application was not necessary when the method indicated more than 100 kgs available N per ha. The method is not a rapid one and is rather cumbersome, and these characteristics limit its wider application. However, its use has shown that response to nitrogen fertilizer is strongly influenced by the amount of available soil nitrogen. This is generally low after a wheat crop; higher after a leguminous hay crop.

Analysis of actual farm data from the semi-arid region that cover an 8 year period from 1966 to 1974 showed a marginal response to added nitrogen equal to (7.5-0.6 N) kgs grain per kg N, resulting in a maximum response at 125 kgs N per ha. However, the economic optimum is between 60 and 70 kgs N per ha. As the ratio between the price of 1 kg of nitrogen and 1 kg of wheat is about 3 and has remained so for many years, this result should be relatively insensitive to price changes in the near future.

The response of the wheat crop to nitrogen depends also on the amount of rainfall. As a rule, there is no response to nitrogen when total annual precipitation is below 200 mm.

It is, however, clear that the main difference between the traditional cropping systems and the new is the introduction of nitrogen fertilizer. Clearly, grain yields of 600 kgs per ha with 250 to 300 mm of rainfall are limited by nutrient deficiency and not by moisture. The increase in yields to 1,500-3,000 kgs per ha under the same rainfall is almost completely accounted for by better nitrogen nutrition. The use of nitrogen in semi-arid conditions where cropping is still possible is thus the key to increased production. It also raises questions that are specific to arid regions. These relate mainly to the nature and extent of nitrogen loss from the system. It has been pointed out that under arid conditions, anaerobic soil conditions necessary for denitrification seldom occur. The low rainfall wets only the top 50-250 cm soil layer so that leaching below the rooting zone (in deep soils) is negligible. Nitrogen applied to the soil and incorporated into it is thus trapped and can be withdrawn only by the plant roots. It is quite likely then, that nitrogen applied but not taken up in a dry year is available for plant growth in a subsequent wetter year. As a result, utilization of fertilizer nitrogen in semi-arid ecosystems may be more efficient than in more humid ecosystems, when calculated over a number of years. In principle, every kg of nitrogen applied should, in the long run, produce 6.25 kgs of plant protein. However, this has not yet been conclusively proved.

In conclusion, it appears that the strategy of nitrogen application in deep-soil, semi-arid, cultivated ecosystems should be reviewed and investigated accordingly. Even though increased yields in Israel are clearly due to better plant nutrition, there is still some confusion as to the optimum amounts of fertilizer and frequency of application, especially in the semi-arid rainfed regions.

Crop rotation. Till the early sixties, a fairly standard 3-year crop rotation was followed, even in the semi-arid region: wheat or barley, sorghum, hay. With the introduction of new, disease-resistant varieties of wheat and the increased use of nitrogen fertilizer, attempts were made to increase the proportion of wheat in the rotation. In many cases continuous wheat for a number of years proved feasible, provided soil fertility was maintained and disease control was effective. The higher wheat yields and better price compared to barley have made wheat the dominant crop in the dryland farming region. Hay is still grown but only on a small scale and mainly in the wetter parts where at least 350 mm of rainfall are ensured. Sorghum is used as a break in the continuous wheat cropping especially when the winter was wet - above 300 mm.

In the drier part of the region (less than 300 mm), hay and sorghum are seldom grown under dry-land conditions and continuous wheat is not always successful because of the occurrence of dry years when the yield of wheat is to small to warrant harvesting. Under these conditions the wheat-fallow system is common.

In a regression analysis of yield data from the region for the period 1967-1973, the yield increase due to fallow was equal to $0.29 \times 0.29 \times$ (mm rainfall in the fallow year). It was shown that about half the rainfall above 120 mm was conserved in the soil for the subsequent wheat crop.

$$\text{Conserved water} = 0.5 \times (\text{mm rainfall in a fallow year} - 120)$$

If the fallow is replaced by a hay crop which is harvested while green and before all the available soil moisture is removed, approximately one-quarter of the rainfall above 156 mm is available for the subsequent wheat crop:

$$\text{Conserved water} = 0.22 \times (\text{mm rainfall in hay year} - 156)$$

The wheat-fallow rotation is more profitable than continuous wheat when rainfall is below about 320 mm. This rotation is indeed practiced in the drier part of the region. The fallow affects the subsequent yield not only by water conservation. During the fallow year, plant growth is prevented by periodic cultivations, and as a result, there is mineral nitrogen buildup in the soil. Weed infestation and plant disease are also reduced.

Weed control. The old 3-year rotation system was fairly effective in reducing weed-infestation to relatively low levels, but continuous wheat has necessitated the use of weed killers. The prominent weeds in the early sixties were crucifers (e.g., wild mustard - *Sinapis alba*), which were easily controlled with 2-4D, as were other broad-leaved species. As a result, the gramineous weed species became more common. *Phalaris* spp. and *Avena* spp., which are tall plants and prolific seed producers, were particularly difficult to control. New selective herbicides have been applied, generally with considerable success. "Avenge" (1,2 dimethyl - 3,5 diphenyl pyrasolium) is used to control *Avena*, and "Tribanil" (1,3 dimethyl 3-(2-benzothiozalyl urea) to control *Phalaris*. Use of increasingly expensive herbicides is becoming prohibitive, however, and may force a return to a rotation system with less continuous wheat.

Disease and pest control. Here the situation is similar to that with regard to weeds except for the fact that disease-resistant wheat varieties are continuously being bred. Nevertheless, it is sometimes necessary to control outbreaks of fungal diseases, especially septoria and rusts. Maneb (manganese ethylene bis dithiocarbamate) is currently being used for this purpose.

The main pests in dry-land farming are field mice and birds, mainly starlings, to which sorghum is especially vulnerable. When mice populations become prominent, poison bait is distributed, generally with considerable effectiveness. Unfortunately uncontrolled use of such poisons can cause secondary poisoning of predator birds, thus weakening the natural control of the mouse population.

Bird damage is generally tolerated. For valuable seed crops, especially sorghum, fine thread nets are drawn over the crop to prevent access by birds.

## Economic and Social Factors

Management of semi-arid ecosystems in Israel is strongly influenced by several economic and social factors.

Drought compensation is an important consideration in managing the semi-arid region, causing land that would otherwise not be cultivated or be less intensely cultivated, to be worked regularly. On the other hand, the stability provided by the promise of such aid removes the incentive to seek systems and practices that would be viable in the region even without drought compensation.

Another example of support for the semi-arid agriculture is the policy of water prices, alluded to in the previous section. Underlying the economics of all new settlement in the semi-arid region is the fact that considerable capital is diverted from public funds to establish the settlements and provide them with means of production sufficient to maintain an acceptable standard of living. Utilization of the resources within the region then becomes geared to these standards.

Social factors that influence management of land resources are associated with the type of settlement in the region. These are mainly communal settlements (*kibbutzim*) or small-holders cooperatives (*moshavim*). In both types, dry-land farming is practiced cooperatively on relatively large areas. The area is managed as an independent, specialized branch of the settlement, with its own manpower and machinery. Livestock husbandry is yet another specialized, independent branch. There is, of course, coordination between branches, generally through the central settlement institutions, but often on a direct basis as well. Integration of livestock and dry-land farming into a single management system has proved to be extremely difficult due to economic considerations, lack of experience with integrated systems, and social and organization restrictions.

## Livestock Husbandry

General. Livestock husbandry systems in the semi-arid region of Israel can be divided into the following groups:

a. Intensive dairy farming, based largely on imported concentrate feed, and supplemented with locally-grown hay and a small amount of irrigated green forage. Where available, residues of other agricultural crops are also utilized. These include peanut hay, low-grade vegetables, potatoes and sugar beet tops. This system is managed as an oasis, creating its own conditions, and virtually independent of the surrounding semi-arid conditions. The main adaptation to the environment is effected through the locally-bred animals (Israeli-Friesian) that produce well in a hot climate and through the building installations that are usually light and open, as very little protection from the elements is necessary.

b. Intensive sheep-farming, which is divided into two main directions: milk production for the cheese industry, based on improved locally-bred Awassi fat-tail

sheep; and mutton production, based on the imported German Meat Merino. Both systems rely heavily on imported concentrate feed, the mutton-raising system almost
wholly so. The milk sheep utilize green winter pasture when this is available, no
further than two or three kilometers from the milking shed. There is also some
utilization of stubble fields in the summer. Recent price restrictions on sheep
milk have made the branch less profitable than previously. This, coupled with the
fact that available trained manpower to manage such intensive systems is becoming
increasingly scarce as more lucrative and less demanding alternative employment
becomes available, has resulted in many herds being disbanded, especially in the
*kibbutzim* (communal settlements). In the *moshav* (small-holders cooperative), the
tendency has been to develop mutton raising, based on the German Meat Merino. Only
seldom do these go out to pasture so that they, too, are managed virtually indepen-
dently of the environmental restrictions around them.

c. Extensive beef raising, based on a mother herd, maintained mainly on range and
stubble fields and on a feed lot for fattening young stock after weaning until marketing. As there is very little pasture that is sown for the use of the beef-herd,
its viability depends on the extent of range-land available for winter, spring and
early summer grazing. As such land is limited in the main small-grain region, but
is more common in the east (southern Judean hills) and in the Northern Negev, such
herds are indeed to be found on the fringes of the cultivated region. Stubble lands
for summer grazing are available in excess and as a result are not fully utilized
by the beef herds. These stubbles are hired out to Bedouin herds or burnt as a
phytosanitary measure.

The carrying capacity of the hill range in the southern Judean hills is between 5 to
8 ha per cow. The range is generally fenced into paddocks of 100 to 300 ha per cow.
The grazing system is a loose rotation movement of cattle from one paddock to another dependent on the judgement of the herd manager. The herds are mixed breeds based
on the local Baladi cattle, other Mediterranean breeds (Yugoslav and Turkish land
races), Hereford, Siementhal, Brahman, Friesian and other breeds. Crossing with
Charolais bulls is common as well as with other European breeds. As a result the
local types as well as the earlier Brahmans are hardly evident any more.

Supplementary feeding of the mother herd is practised in summer and especially in
fall. The summer supplementation is often limited to chicken droppings which are
fed at the rate of 2-5 kgs per cow per day. This is cheaper than the more common
oilcake protein supplement and is sufficient for summer maintenance on stubble and
dry native range. In fall and especially after the first rains when the pasture
is particularly poor, supplementation is increased by feeding either barley or
concentrate, up to 4 kgs per cow per day. On the average about 100-150 kgs concentrate and up to ½ ton of chicken manure per cow per year is given. Weaning weights
are between 200 to 250 kgs and the number of live calves weaned is generally above
80%.

The beef herds are maintained on rangeland with an average of more than 200 mm rainfall. Beef production is then between 20 and 40 kgs per ha of rangeland plus the
supplementary feed detailed above and about 4 to 5 months of stubble grazing.

Range improvement is limited to fencing and water development. Fertilizer application has been applied on small areas of hill range with variable results. It is
seldom practiced today in the semi-arid region, but is fairly common in the wetter
regions (above 400 mm) where nitrogen fertilizer is commonly used to obtain abundant green grazing two to four weeks earlier than in unfertilized range.

In the fifties and early sixties, some areas of pasture shrubs, mainly *Atriplex
halimus*, were planted. These became established and provided some green summer feed
for the beef herds. But the benefit did not appear to warrant the cost of

establishing these shrubs and the practice has been discontinued.  Subsequent research on the palatibility and feed value of pasture shrubs indicated that other species
like *Atriplex nummuluria*, *Cassia sturtii* and others should be superior to *Atriplex
halimus*.  But it is not clear that these would materially change the carrying capacity of the range or improve the profitability of the operation.  Experimentation is
continuing since they may prove to be of value, especially in drought years.

Small areas of cultivable land have occasionally been sown with annual legumes,
mainly *Medicago polymorpha*, *Medicago truncateula*, *Vicia dasycarpa* and others.  Some
stands have been maintained for a number of years, providing nutritious winter
grazing.  Some have been turned back to wheat cultivation, with *Medicago* reseeding
itself from hard seed in a fallow year.  However, as pointed out previously, there
is virtually no integration of livestock and crop husbandry in the new settlements
and the use of cultivable land in a ley-rotation has not become an established
practice even though a number of observations have indicated that it should be superior to the present non-integrated system.

d.  Bedouin herds, mainly composed of sheep and goats and based on nomadism.  These
herds are also part of the new cropping system even though they belong to separate
communities.  Winter grazing is mainly in the hill and fallow pasture in the southern and central, more arid parts of the region and summer grazing is on grain stubble in the main cropping region.  The stubble grazing is generally leased to herd
owners on a per head, or more generally, per unit area basis.  Animal density on the
stubble lands is on the average approximately 1 sheep per ha for 4-6 months of the
year, but in some areas it is two to three times higher.  These are not very high
animal densities and as a result much of the grain stubble is not grazed.

Integrated cropping and livestock systems.  Ley-farming rotations based on sown
medic and small-grain cultivation, resembling that practiced in similar regions
in Australia, have been advocated for the region.  Preliminary investigations have
been undertaken and have indicated that such systems have economic advantages over
current practice.  The advantage has not been great enough, however, to make wide-
scale change attractive, especially as the present system is supported by a number
of fiscal measures, such as the drought compensation mentioned in a previous section.
Current research is concerned mainly with separate cropping and livestock systems,
with possible integration being kept in mind for the future.

Intensive experimental pasture utilization.  At the Migda (Tadmor) experimental
farm, pasture improvement and utilization has been investigated since 1960.
Originally, the experiments were planned on current practice, and animal densities
of 1 to 2 sheep per ha appeared to be realistic stocking rates.  Some pastures were
sown with annual legume species.  In a grazing trial that continued for five years,
2½ sheep per ha were maintained without any supplementary feed.  Lamb production was
around 60 kgs per ha on the average.

In 1970, a series of experiments on potential primary production were initiated
in order to determine the dry matter production of a pasture in a semi-arid region
when plant nutrients in the soil are non-limiting.  It soon became clear that when
rainfall was higher than 200 mm per annum, it was nitrogen and not soil moisture
that limited plant growth.

In addition, it was found that the production from native pasture plants (e.g.,
*Phalaris minor*, *Hordeum murinum*) was equivalent to that from sown wheat.  The land
in the Migda farm has been cultivated over centuries and the native vegetation is
actually a weed vegetation of cultivated land.  Nevertheless, it was clear that
with selected sown pasture species it would be extremely difficult to improve on
the dry matter production potential *per se* of the native vegetation in cultivable
land (Fig. 4).

Fig. 4.  Sheep grazing on introduced fodder shrub at Migda

Where the pasture was fertilized with phosphorus but not with nitrogen, legume species, mainly *Trigonella arabica*, increased and in the fourth year dominated the vegetation, only to drop to a small fraction of the vegetation in the fifth year.
However, when the legumes did dominate, the dry matter production at the peak of the
season was similar to that of the nitrogen fertilized native grasses, 6.6 tons per
ha compared to 7.2 tons per ha.  During that year, total annual rainfall was 275 mm.
As the annual dry matter intake of a ewe with lamb in season is about 650 kgs, it
should be possible to maintain up to 10 productive ewes per ha.  This is considerably more than was previously thought possible and raises questions about the effect
of grazing on primary production.

Experiments were conducted in the 1975/76 season to determine the effect of heavy
grazing on pasture growth and dry matter intake by the grazing animal.  In particular, attention was paid to the relationship between growth rate of the pasture and
intake rate of the animals.  As would be expected, on theoretical grounds, the
pasture continued growing even with 12 ewes per ha as long as the sheep entered the
pasture after the growth rate exceeded the intake rate.  As this was a relatively dry
year (199 mm) overall dry matter production was low even in the control plots (4.4
tons per ha), and grazing was discontinued before the end of the season.  However,
it did appear that it should be possible to attain near potential primary production
even under grazing conditions.

Prospects. The integration of livestock and cropping in the new agricultural systems of the semi-arid zone in Israel demands an intensive grazing system that will
provide an attractive alternative to the wheat-fallow rotation. This is possible
only if the return per unit area from pasture in a ley rotation is of the same
order of magnitude as that from the crop-land. The work at Migda does point to
possibilities in that direction. Sheep maintained at a stock density of one ewe
plus lamb per ha could give a greater return than wheat, provided they could be
maintained only on pasture. It has been demonstrated that this is possible in the
green season, even in a dry year. If one hectare of crop land was associated with
the pasture, then the crop residues would suffice for summer and autumn maintenance
of the flock in most years. In drought years, when the grain crop is too small to
cover costs of cultivation, it would be grazed to advantage, as in such years total
dry matter production is much less seriously affected than is grain yield.

Lamb yields should also be high so as to cover the heavy investments in livestock.
Fecund breeds (Merino, Finnish land race crosses) or hormone-induced twinning in
the local adapted breeds could provide above 1.6 lambs per ewe per year. Mutton
production should be greater than 300 kgs per ha. Such an intensive pastoral
system would considerably improve the productivity and profitability of the present
system, and may be a viable system for the future, especially if subsidies such as
drought compensation or support for irrigation water prices are reduced in real
value.

In the uncultivated ecosystems, the hill pastures in the east and the more arid
pasture in the south, no major changes in present day practice are envisaged. In
the wetter part of the region, above 300 mm of rainfall, it is possible that
fertilizer applications on suitable sites could alter the present production levels.
In general, the hill soils are shallow and the potential for primary production is
certainly less than in the deeper soils. Where such soils cover areas too small to
be cultivated, they could profitably be fertilized and used to supplement the more
productive animals in the herd. Unless there are major changes in the ratio of meat
prices to fertilizer prices, it is unlikely that such practice will be possible on
any more than a small fraction of the hill pasture.

In the more arid zone, south and south-east of the cultivated belt, the use of
nitrogen fertilizer is unlikely to be economical for most of the area. However,
there are considerable areas here that receive additional water from flash floods
or which could be irrigated with such water. Here primary production with fertilizer can be higher than that of the surrounding pasture by more than an order of magnitude. Such areas could be used to supplement productive animals in a similar way
to that suggested for the deeper soils in the hill pastures.


*Greenhouse Agriculture*

In deserts which are situated near the sea, water need not be a limiting factor,
since sea water could, in theory, be desalinated and transferred inland for irrigation purposes. This is feasible, however, only if the return for the crops irrigated
is high enough to cover the high costs of desalination and/or the water consumption
by the plants is drastically reduced. It is possible that these two conditions could
be set by development of greenhouse agriculture based on out-of-season crops.


Greenhouse agriculture offers the following advantages:
1. It permits the utilization of the desert's advantages, namely high radiation,
clear winter days and, in locations close to the sea (such as the Western Negev),
relatively warm winter nights.
2. The return per unit of water applied is three to four times higher than the

D. K*

return for convential agriculture (a farmer uses only some 1,500 m$^3$ water per annum to irrigate 0.2 hectare of greenhouses).

3. It is an industry which requires a high degree of specialization so that, in the case of Israel, it permits the exploitation of the skills of local farmers and of advanced farming services, including research institutes, extension services, packing houses and marketing.

4. It provides the opportunity for controlling the environment of plants.

If greenhouses could be sealed during the daylight hours without resultant excess overheating, then evapotranspiration losses would be markedly reduced. This would result in drastic economy in irrigation water. A system is being developed which will economically collect excess solar radiation during the daylight hours, store it in the greenhouse soil and release it during the cold hours of the night. This system, in principle, a "closed system," could bring about significant water conservation and thus meet the second requisite for the efficient utilization of desalinated sea water.

The first greenhouse in the Western Negev was constructed in 1971 and there are now 40 acres, mostly devoted to tomato cultivation. The majority of the greenhouses are located in Sdeh Nitzan, a *moshav* (small-holders cooperative), established by immigrants from English-speaking countries, mostly with academic, white-collar backgrounds and no previous experience in agriculture. Each settler has 0.2 hectare of greenhouses in which tomatoes are cultivated. After two years of settlement, the more successful farmers have attained yields of 250 tons per hectare. It is planned to establish a large number of new settlements in the Western Negev by the end of the century (some planners speak of as many as 100), based on the greenhouse industry.

## SETTLEMENT AND DEVELOPMENT OF THE NEGEV

### *Population Dispersal Policy*

The process of settlement and development of the Negev since the establishment of Israel must be viewed in the context of the overall national settlement policy. The planning authorities were faced, in the early days of statehood, with a settlement pattern characterized by medium and large urban centers in close geographical proximity, on the one hand, and numerous small rural settlements widely scattered through the country, on the other, with hardly anything between the two extremes. In 1948, 67% of the population was concentrated in the three large towns of Tel Aviv, Haifa and Jerusalem, and 43.2% in Tel Aviv alone. Various factors had contributed to this structure: immigrants had always tended to prefer larger towns, with their wider range of employment possibilities; rural sectors traditionally maintained direct contact with large towns so that there was no need for intermediate small service towns; and finally, because of the "back to the soil" ideology of early Jewish immigration to Palestine, rural settlement enjoyed much greater attention and allocation of resources than urban planning.

The planning authorities regarded this uneven population distribution pattern as highly inefficient and unsuited to a rapidly developing country with a constant influx of immigration and with limited resources, both natural and financial. They recommended dispersal of the population through the establishment of a network of small and medium-sized urban centers, adding the missing link between village and large town, and supplying services to rural hinterlands. It was thought essential to achieve the following aims:

- settle the sparsely populated regions (mainly in the north and south) in order to create a more even population distribution pattern and reduce the population density on the coastal strip;

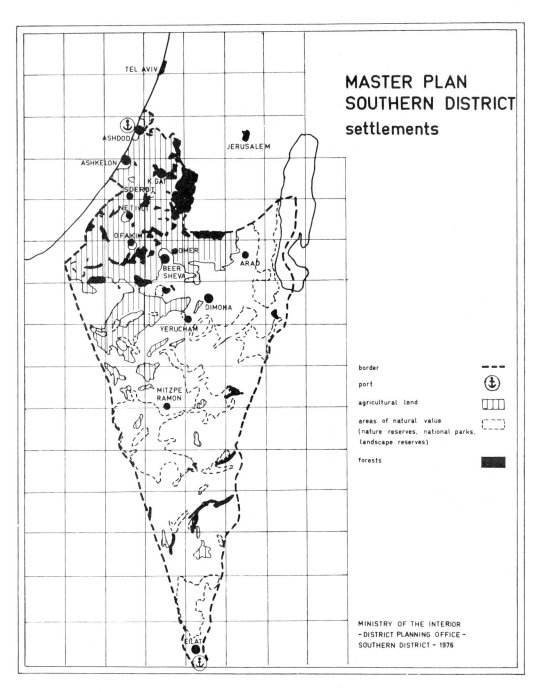

Fig. 5.

- exploit the resources of peripheral regions, particularly the desert areas of the south, which constituted approximately two-thirds of the country's land area;
- settle border areas for security reasons;
- create integrated, almost self-contained regional systems, each with its distinctive identity, for more efficient service distribution and easier absorption of immigration.

This dispersal policy has been implemented in stages by a series of national plans. The first phase, ending in 1956, was directly connected with the establishment of new rural settlements in a hierarchical pattern (village, local service center, rural town, regional town). From 1956 on, efforts were concentrated more on encouraging industrial investment in the new towns, promoted and subsidized by the Government. Measures included granting development loans to investors and special tax relief measures for both investors and settlers.

Particular effort had to be invested in encouraging settlement in the Negev because of the hot, dry climate and the scarcity of natural resources. A vigorous program of road-building, extension of the electric power grid and, most important of all, development of local water resources and import of water from the north was undertaken. Hydrological surveys were carried out, wells were drilled and the construction of the National Water Carrier (see p.266 ) helped convert large unproductive tracts of arid land into productive areas.

Along with the establishment of population centers, cultural, educational and health facilities were set up. The dearth of primary school teachers was made up by volunteers who fulfilled their army service requirements by teaching in the settlements and cities of the Negev. High schools and vocational schools were established and oriented to meet the industrial and professional requirements of the area. A modern hospital and health care service was established to serve the entire southern area of Israel.

Two scientific research institures were founded in the South in the nineteen fifties, attracting a large number of scientists and engineers. One of them was especially oriented to the solution of problems of the arid zone. Aside from the direct benefit resulting from their research, these two institutions at a later date formed the nucleus for the establishment of the Ben-Gurion University.

The dispersal policy has achieved a considerable measure of success, but much remains to be done since the coastal belt remains heavily crowded. Some 87% of Israelis still live in towns of over 10,000 inhabitants and 50% in towns of over 50,000. Density reaches over 5,500 persons per sq. km in parts of the coastal plain (Tel Aviv conurbation) while in the Beer Sheva sub-district it is only 18.5 per sq. km (29.3 in the Southern District as a whole). The fact that the policy has been noticeably more successful in the south than in the north is indicated by the following table:

Table 12.  Population distribution by %

| Region | 1948 | 1961 | 1974 |
|--------|------|------|------|
| Jerusalem | 10.2 | 8.8 | 11.2 |
| North | 16.8 | 15.5 | 15.3 |
| Haifa | 20.5 | 17.0 | 15.1 |
| Central | 14.3 | 18.7 | 18.8 |
| Tel Aviv | 35.7 | 32.0 | 27.8 |
| South* | 2.5 | 8.0 | 11.8 |

* Figures relate to the entire Southern region, i.e., both
  Ashkelon and Beer Sheva sub-districts.

Source: Settlement in Israel, Environmental Protection
        Service, Isreael Ministry of the Interior,
        Jerusalem, 1976.

The primacy of Tel Aviv has been reduced, and the establishment of small and medium-
sized new towns in the north and south has achieved considerable success (nearly 20%
of the total population now live in these towns), though as will be seen below, some
are too small to function effectively without continuing government assistance. It
was decided at an advanced stage not to found any more settlements but to concentrate
on increasing the size of existing new towns.

The present plan for a target national population of 5 million by 1992, follows the
same general goals as its predecessors and envisages a slow but steady increase in
the population of the south.

Table 13.  Planned Population Distribution

| Region | Population distribution in 1974 | Target for 1981 (or population of 4 million) | Target for 1992 (or total population of 5 m) |
|--------|------|------|------|
| Jerusalem | 11.2 | 12.5 | 12.8 |
| North | 15.3 | 15.6 | 16.0 |
| Haifa | 15.1 | 15.0 | 15.4 |
| Central | 18.8 | 17.4 | 17.4 |
| Tel Aviv | 27.8 | 26.6 | 24.3 |
| South (Ashkelon & Beer Sheva sub-districts) | 11.8 | 12.1 | 12.8 |

Source: Settlement in Israel, Environmental Protection
        Service, Israel Ministry of the Interior, Jerusalem,
        1976.

*Agricultural Settlement of the Negev*

Of a total population of some 230,000 in the Negev (which, as noted above, can be roughly defined as corresponding to the Beer Sheva administrative sub-district), only a relatively small sector is occupied with agriculture. Some 26,000 Jewish inhabitants live outside urban areas, about 16,000 of them in villages and *moshavim* (small-holders cooperatives) of various types, and approximately 8,000 in *kibbutzim* (communal settlements). It was agriculture, however, which pioneered the settlement of the desert. In 1943, three observation settlements were set up in different climatic regions (east, south and west of Beer Sheva) to study the possibilities of developing agriculture on loess soils, and in 1946, eleven *kibbutzim* were established in a planned simultaneous operation in different parts of the Northern Negev. The valuable experience they accrued facilitated the founding of numerous settlements in the Negev after the establishment of the state. There are (1975 figures) 33 *kibbutzim* and 37 *moshavim* in the Negev, and 6 *kibbutzim* and 6 *moshavim* in the Arava, a total of 82 agricultural settlements. These may be grouped into three general areas with their own specific conditions:

Northern and Western Negev - where the great majority of the settlements are located. Many of the *moshavim* in the area were settled in the early years of statehood by planned direction of new immigrants from Asian and North African countries with no previous experience in agriculture. The immigrant villages were planned as regional clusters with rural service centers, and two development towns (Ofakim and Netivot) were built as service centers for their hinterlands (see next section). These settlements utilize water brought from the North by the National Water Carrier, and have some rainfall which enables them to grow winter grains. The outstanding irrigated crop is cotton. Deep loessial soils are prevalent.

Negev Hills - in this area rainfall is insufficient for winter crops. Water is available from the National Water Carrier, but in small quantities. Underground brackish water resources have recently been developed from deep drillings. Soils are loessial and sandy. There are three *kibbutzim* in the Negev Hills, established by volunteers (one of them was among the three observation settlements founded in 1943), and a *moshav*, established in recent months by a group of young ex-towndwellers, motivated by the desire to "return to the soil" and develop the area. No rural immigrant villages were established in this area, though the town of Yeruham originally planned to be based on agriculture (utilizing the waters of a dammed wadi). Since plans for an agricultural base were unsuccessful, it gradually developed an urban character. Other towns in the area are Dimona and Arad (see below), both based on industry.

Arava Valley - this area has only brackish water available and an average rainfall of about 25-50 mm. The settlements here, as in the Negev Hills, were all established by groups with high pioneering motivation. The exceptionally warm climate permits cultivation of vegetables during the entire winter season. The only town serving the area at present is Eilat, at the southernmost point. A second town is being planned south of the Dead Sea.

A considerable amount of research and development had to be undertaken in order to establish and consolidate successful agriculture in these areas. In each area, a separate branch of the Agricultural Research Organization was established because of the great differences in physical and climatic conditions. The stations work in coordination with the main agricultural research station and have contributed substantially to the success of agriculture in the south.

Although some emphasis was placed on preparation of new areas for cultivation, the major research thrust has centered upon the efficient and economical use of irrigation, utilizing both good-quality imported water and highly saline subterranean water.

Agricultural settlers in these areas, especially in the Arava, attempted to find those crops which would lend some advantage to their economy. Off-season crops, expecially vegetables, have been a major source of income for them. The warm winters and lack of frost enable them to grow vegetables and flowers which are not available in Europe or in the rest of Israel during that season, and this has proved an excellent source of income. The Negev Hills settlers have been successful with cultivation of deciduous fruit trees which flourish, due to the cold frosty winters. They too are able to go to market before the remainder of the country, and hence enjoy higher prices for their produce.

An impetus to the successful development of desert agriculture was provided by the availability of long-term, low-interest development loans. The necessity for such loans is, of course, a well-known factor in regional development.

The unique communal structure of agricultural settlements in Israel was undoubtedly a key element in the rapid development of these settlements under adverse environmental conditions, especially in the southern part of the area. This structure permitted more efficient use of both material and human resources. It gave the settlers a greater sense of security and encouraged a bolder, innovative approach. Together, the farmers could exert more effective political and economic pressures on the Government and its various agencies. The regional structure of marketing transport and storage services further strengthened the economic position of the communes.

Efficient agricultural research organization, closely linked with a wide-ranging extension service, converted new immigrants with no previous agricultural experience into modern farmers within a few years. To do this it was necessary to control the main factors of production and income so that the new farmers rapidly learned that industrious effort resulted in profit. In such a manner, the farmer has been encouraged to invest maximum effort, and in so doing, has not only overcome the adverse conditions of his environment but has utilized them to his advantage.


*Urban Development*

Of the 30 new towns built throughout the country as part of the overall population dispersal policy, eight are in the Negev: Beer Sheva, Arad, Dimona, Ofakim, Netivot, Mitzpe Ramon, Eilat and Yeruham. There were three possible ways of creating new towns: development of existing rural settlements, expansion of small towns, and founding of new ones. The first possibility was not applicable in the Negev, and the second was applicable only to Beer Sheva, the sole urban settlement in the Negev, which was, in fact, expanded. Hence, all other urban settlements in the Negev were new towns, literally built up from the foundations.

Of the nine new towns established throughout the country in 1952, one, Yeruham, was in the Negev. It suffered from all the flaws which characterized these first-stage towns: very low standard of infrastructure and public services which made rapid growth difficult, and poor locations for industrial development. When the second generation of new towns was built in the mid-fifties, the planners had learned from their errors, and sites were carefully chosen to meet the needs of regional development. At this stage, Dimona, Netivot, Ofakim and Mitzpe Ramon were built. Since 1957, only two new towns have been established in Israel, one of them, Arad, in the Negev. They represent a significant shift in policy in that they were not specifically designed for immigrants but were planned to attract, from the beginning, middle class, native-born Israelis.

Though some of the new towns have remained too small to be economically viable without continuing government support, sometimes on a very large scale (Mitzpe Ramon,

Yeruham), they have, in qualitative terms, achieved a fair degree of success.  They
have played a vital role in immigrant absorption, particularly in the light of what
could have been the alternative, i.e., crowding of the newcomers into large cities.
Settlement in small towns gave immigrants the opportunity to participate in the
administration of local affairs and the political life of the community and to develop a sense of local identity.  Over the years, the immigrants gained experience
in local government and are now a vocal group in the country's affairs.  Veteran
Israelis from the north of the country are being attracted to the more successful
of the new towns of the Negev (Arad or Dimona, for example), which offer an alternative life-style - urban life in a small community.

The towns which have met with the greatest success have been those with a healthy
economic base, particularly those with a strong industrial infrastructure (Fig. 6).

Dimona - Its economy is based currently on the textile industry, which provides
employment for about half the town's workers.  This industry is particularly suited
to the area, as it need not be located close to sources of raw materials or to its
market, and requires mostly non-skilled labor.  The Government has given preference
to the promotion of this industry in several geographically remote development towns
with large populations of unskilled workers.  A ramified metal industry has been
developing in recent years in the town and will probably soon outstrip textiles.  A
large number of inhabitants are employed in the nearby nuclear research center, and
production of Dead Sea potash for fertilizers at the Dead Sea Works (45 minutes
journey away) is a further source of employment.

Arad - Founded in 1963, Arad is considered one of the most successful new towns in
Israel.  The majority of its population consists of veteran Israelis, mainly with
professional or technical qualifications, who came to the town by choice after
selection, and the number of new immigrants is relatively small.  The town attracts
a constant stream of new settlers.  Its employment structure is based on the Dead
Sea Works and chemical plants located in the vicinity.  Since Arad enjoys a dry,
clear climate and municipal by-laws forbid the planting of pollen-producing plants,
it attracts people who suffer from asthma.  It has a number of large hotels catering
to tourists and vacationers drawn by the scenery, climate and nearby Dead Sea
therapeutic facilities.

The towns established as regional service and market towns did not succeed in ful-
filling these functions because of the tendency of rural settlements to sidestep the
intermediary link and make contract directly with the larger towns.

Netivot and Ofakim - Located north-west of Beer Sheva, these towns were established
in 1955 and 1956, respectively.  Their economy is based mainly on the textile industry.  It is thought that the geographical proximity between them, and their proximity to Beer Sheva and Ashkelon were planning errors, restricting their growth.
Ofakim seems to be developing into a dormitory town for people commuting to Beer
Sheva.

The most problematic of the new towns have been Yeruham and Mitzpe Ramon because
insufficient attention was paid to their economic infrastructure.

Yeruham - Yeruham was founded with the intention of using the waters of a dam,
built in the wadi of Nahal Revivim, for agriculture.  Non-implementation of this
plan caused total stagnation, with resultant social and economic problems.  For a
number of years permanent employment could be found in the Oron phosphate works,
south of the town.  Yeruham now has one of Israel's largest soft drink plants and
an adjacent glass works, based on sand from the Makhtesh.  There is also a ceramics
industry and further plans for local industry are under consideration.

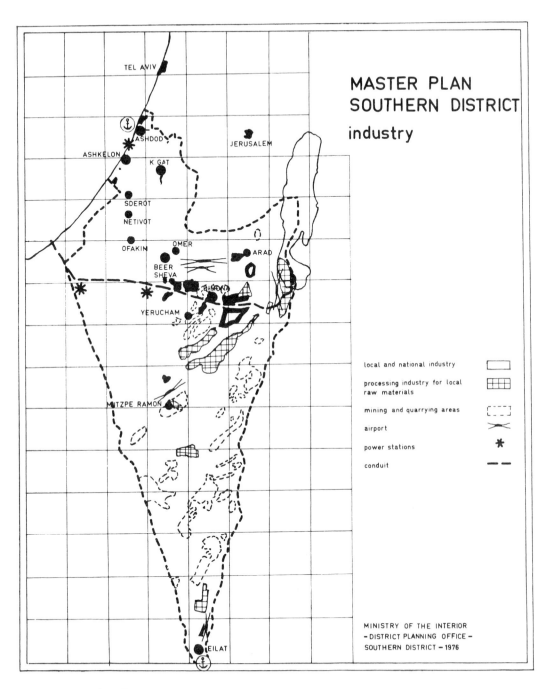

Fig. 6.

Mitzpe Ramon - This is an isolated settlement on the old road to Eilat. Construction of the new road, which by-passes Mitzpe Ramon, increased the population's psychological sense of isolation. Lately, a massive government aid program has revived
its development and it has begun to attract new settlers, attracted by the magnificent scenery and positive ecological conditions. The basis for the town's employment
are the various metal works, and there are plans to build rest-homes and to nurture
desert tourism.

Eilat - Founded in 1951, it is Israel's southern gateway, the port town at the head
of the Gulf of Eilat. Most of its working population is employed in the port and in
the extensive hotel and tourism services. A quarter of the entire labor force was
employed until recently in the Timna copper mines, and the closing of these mines
created an employment crisis. Some of the Timan staff have been employed in constructing the new international airport and a metal-works in the town. Most of the oil
imported to Israel arrives at the port of Eilat and is conveyed from there by pipeline to the center of the country, and a considerable percentage of phosphate and
potash is exported through Eilat. Water supply problems have been mainly overcome
by the construction of desalination plant (Fig. 7). The extreme summer heat is
combated by the use of "desert cooler" fans, which also raise the moisture content
of the air. One of Eilat's main disadvantages, however, remains its distance from
the rest of the country, despite the construction of the Arava road in 1966. Transport and supplies are expensive and labor costly, since workers are given free
flights northward and a special desert allowance. Hence, the town's growth has been
slower than ancitipated and no industries, except those based on local factors, have
been set up in the town. Tourism, however, has expanded rapidly in recent years,
and the town now attracts large numbers of visitors from abroad, particularly from
Northern Europe.

## The Role of Beer Sheva as a Regional Center

The development of Beer Sheva has been a direct function of the development of the
Southern District as a whole. The reciprocal relations between the town and its
region are stronger than in any similar case in Israel and result from its geographical distance from other large urban centers.

Beer Sheva, with 110,000 population, is the eighth largest town in Israel. It has
a higher rate of growth than the national urban average, although it has slowed down
in recent years, and it is now 4% annually, the fourth highest in the country.

Beer Sheva is the most important city of the region, being several times larger than
any of the other towns. It supplies important services to the surrounding population, which consists of:
    - the urban population living at an average of 30 to 45 minutes travel from
the capital (which also includes, to some extent, Kiryat Gat in the Ashkelon sub-
district, with a population of 20,000);
    - the Bedouin population, concentrated north and east of the city, a large
proportion of which is in the stage of permanent settlement, for whom Beer Sheva is
the chief administrative, economic and social center;
    - the agricultural population, which has need of administrative services but
often sidesteps the city for economic services, in favor of communal purchasing
organizations located for the most part in Tel Aviv.

Fig. 7.  Desalination unit at Eilat built by Israel Desalination Engineers, (Zarchin Process) Ltd.  Photograph by Keren-Or.  Provides 50% of Eilat's drinking water

As capital of the Southern District, Beer Sheva fulfills numerous vital administra-
tive functions.  Almost all government ministries are represented here:  the
Ministries of the Interior, Social Welfare, Trade and Industry, Housing, Justice,
Absorption, Education, Tourism, Health and Labour; the Regional Income Tax office;
Ministry of Agriculture instructors and regional veterinary services.  The Soroka
Medical Center, including the Central Negev Hospital and its outpatient clinics,
serves the entire area.  The Municipal Theatre and Music Conservatory draw their
audiences from the entire region, and often go out to give performances in more
distant settlements.

Ben Gurion University of the Negev at Beer Sheva has made a considerable contribution to the region.  Founded in 1968, it now has an academic staff of 900, and
4,500 students.  Granting of tenure to staff is conditional on residence in the
Negev.  Before its establishment, all the students from the Southern District studied either at Jerusalem, the Haifa Technion or Tel Aviv University.  Now 50% of the
District's students attend their local university; 75% of Beer Sheva students are
studying in Beer Sheva.  Before Ben Gurion University came into existence, students
from the south, among whom a high percentage are African- and Asian-born, accounted
for only 2.4% of the country's student population.  In 1975, 7% of Israeli students
were attending Ben Gurion University alone.  An indicator of the University's impact
on the life of the region is the fact that 26% of the students are of Asian and
African origin, a percentage twice as high as in any other Israeli institution of
higher learning.

The most prominent industry in Beer Sheva is the chemical industry, utilizing raw
materials extracted from the Dead Sea to produce pesticides and fertilizers for
agricultural use.


*Housing and Town Planning*

An aspect of desert life for which few satisfactory solutions have been found is
the relationship between housing and climatic conditions.  In most desert areas
this problem has found a satisfactory answer only in those societies which are
either extremely primitive or economically very advanced.  The Bedouin tent, for
example, deals with many aspects of climate quite adequately, and modern air
conditioning provides comfortable living conditions for those societies that can
afford it.  There does not yet seem to be a viable solution for middle income groups
in the desert areas of developing nations.

Housing in the desert has often been planned and built with little consideration for
climatic conditions.  This has resulted in excessive heat loads on apartment units
and factories.  Whereas mechanical air conditioning is becoming more common, heat
loads on buildings are so high as to make this type of cooling unattainable for the
majority of the population.  Even if it were to become economically feasible to
introduce widespread mechanical air conditioning, the increased electric generating
capacity needed for such a system raises other problems such as air pollution,
thermal pollution, an expanded power grid and power failures, that leave the desirability of such a system an open question.

In large parts of the Negev, winters are chilly.  While there are few hard freezes,
low night temperatures of $1°-5°C$ are not uncommon in some areas in December, January
and February.  This means that housing solutions suitable for tropical areas cannot
be simply transplanted to this region.  Indeed, many inhabitants consider the problem of cold, damp winters as important as the stresses of the hot dry summer.

The original towns built in the Negev scarcely took into account the specific climatic conditions of the region.  Their design, like that of other new towns in the north

of the country, reflected the influence of the British school of civic design of
the thirties and forties. They followed the "garden city" pattern, stressing low
densities and a spread-out pattern, with self-contained neighborhood units separated from the town center by wide strips of open spaces and cultivated areas (this is
particularly evident in Beer Sheva). Allotments and gardens were included in the
plans as a quasi-economic basis for towns suffering from limited employment opportunities. The generous allocation of "green spaces" proved of very limited practical
value in the Negev. The low-density layout exposed inhabitants to excessive solar
radiation, causing high heat loads on the buildings. Little shelter was provided
from the desiccating winds and dust storms. Futhermore, distances within the townss
were considerable, costs of infrastructure high, and the towns lacked both physical
and social "urbanity".

Some of the lessons of this failure were quickly learned, and from the late fifties
onward existing towns began to fill in their empty spaces with apartment blocks of
three to four storeys. New planning called for higher population densities with
sheltered areas sandwiched in among the buildings. Experiments have been made with
patio-style housing, which offers shade and privacy, though conventional apartment
houses still dominate the urban landscape.


*Industry and Mining*

Till quite recently, the potential for settlement in the arid and semi-arid areas
of the country was linked with the potential for agricultural development. It is
now realized that agriculture alone cannot supply employment and sustenance for
large numbers of inhabitants in this area. The attention of planners has now turned to more specialized and intensive forms of agriculture and to industry and
tourism as additional sources of employment.

The Negev is poor in major natural resources. Some years ago the Israel Geological
Institute undertook a large-scale prospecting program in order to draw up an inventory of existing mineral resources, and on the basis of this work, mining operations
were undertaken. These include copper in the Eilat area, phosphates, clays and sand
in addition to various minor building materials. The Dead Sea has proved to be a
major source of raw materials, the largest being potash fertilizer. In addition,
bromine and magnesia are being extracted. Though mining and export of minerals
were important activities during the early phases of industrialization, development
of more sophisticated products based on these minerals is envisaged as the basis
for future industrial development. This type of activity gives employment to more
workers, with added income and profits. Development of a chemical industry was
planned and steps were taken to get it started. Government and Histadrut (Labour
Union) investment companies were established to manufacture products based on local
natural resources, including bromine compounds, ceramics, refractories and various
pesticides. At a later stage phosphoric acid production was started, utilizing
Negev phosphate deposits and magnesia produced from Dead Sea minerals. A large
glass bottle plant was set up as well as various plant producing wall and floor
tiles and other building components. In this way a second generation of industry
was developed, based on the original mining operations.

In addition, as noted, the Government extended special incentives to investors who
set up their own manufacturing facilities in the developing towns of the Negev.
The incentives included grants, long-term low-interest loans and various tax
advantages for both workers and investors. Large housing projects were undertaken
to house the needed labourers. In general, industrialization was a success, although hindsight now affords planners a view of past errors in policy and execution.
Government controls and bureaucracy often resulted in the withdrawal of foreign

investors; too much confidence was placed on foreign technology, and only limited resources were expended on local research and development; the program for the development of secondary products based upon the raw materials of the region was not sufficiently bold or imaginative and industry could have played a greater role in developing the Negev.  In fact, future plans for the Negev place considerable emphasis on expanding industrial output.


*Tourism and Recreation*

The desert is becoming an increasingly important recreation area where people can escape, at least temporarily, the pressures and stresses of the crowded urban centers.  The need for parks and nature preserves is acute.  There have been some attempts in this direction but the lack of water has impeded progress.  A new approach to planning and maintenance of recreation areas is needed.  Several plans have been drawn up and the awareness of the necessity for allocating large tracts of land for this purpose is becoming more generally felt.  At Ben Gurion University, experimentation has been underway for several years in introduction of salt- and drought-resistant plants for landscaping of arid areas for the benefit of the local population and to improve facilities for tourism.

Tourism, with its attractive economic potential, has made rapid advances.  The shores of the Dead Sea and Eilat are dotted with hotels, bathing centers and other facilities to attract tourists.  The warm winters in these areas are especially attractive to tourists escaping from the rigours of the European winter.  Possible therapeutic effects of the Dead Sea bring many visitors wishing to obtain relief from various skin ailments.  Tourism can be a lucrative branch of the economy and a force for desert development, even though it is very sensitive to world-wide economic recessions.


*Future of Settlement*

In December 1975, the Southern District Administration of the Ministry of the Interior submitted to the National Council for Planning and Building a development plan for the entire Southern District (Ashkelon Sub-district and Beer Sheva Sub-district).  The central aim of the plan is to create the physical conditions necessary for expansion of the population of the District from the present 400,000 to one million by the end of the nineteen nineties.  The demographic goal for the Beer Sheva Sub-district (or Negev, by our definition), is a population of 615,000 as against the present 230,000.  Within the framework of this general trend, efforts will be made to shift the center of balance of the District southward.  This means that emphasis will be placed on accelerated increase in the urban population with parallel efforts to expand agricultural settlements (as Table 14 shows).

The plan will contribute significantly to the consolidation of existing development towns without earmarking areas for new towns, with the exception of a small town near Ein Yahav in the Arava Valley, planned as a service center for the entire Arava.

In order to provide increased employment opportunities, the planners envisage a new National Industrial Area spanning the area between Beer Sheva to the west and Arad to the east, the Dead Sea Works and Yeruham.  This area is earmarked for industrial enterprises which need large expanses of land or which, for ecological reasons or for considerations of safety, cannot be located in densely populated areas.  These enterprises, which include science-based industries and a petrochemical industry, will draw workers from Arad, Beer Sheva, Dimona and Yeruham, all within commuting distance.  An industrial area is also planned for the area north of Eilat.

Table 14.  Estimated population - 2000

| Local Councils | 1974 | 2000 |
|---|---|---|
| Beer Sheva | 93,400 | 235,000 |
| Dimona | 26,900 | 65,000 |
| Eilat | 14,900 | 65,000 |
| Netivot | 6,650 | 20,000 |
| Ofakim | 10,600 | 24,000 |
| Arad | 8,050 | 35,000 |
| Yeruham | 6,350 | 25,000 |
| Mitzpe Ramon | 1,530 | 25,000 |
| Omer | 1,690 | 5,000 |
| Ein Yahav | 337 | 5,000 |
| Merhavim | 6,304 | 10,000 |
| Azata | 5,632 | 9,000 |
| Eshkol | 4,641 | 10,000 |
| Bnei Shimon | 5,906 | 7,000 |
| Tamar | 1,262 | 2,000 |
| Ramat Negev | 1,504 | 8,000 |
| Eilot | 837 | 2,000 |
| Arava | 10 | 3,000 |
| Bedouin | 36,213 | 60,000 |
| Total | 232,716 | 615,000 |

Figures:  Ministry of the Interior, Southern District
          Administration.


At the same time, large areas of the Western Negev, the Halutza area, the Arava
Valley and the Negev Hills will be allocated for agricultural settlement.  In the
last two areas it is hoped to double the number of existing settlements, and in the
first two there are plans for numerous new settlements, some planners speak of as
many as 100, to be based on intensive, specialized agriculture.

The plan proposes two sites, one in the Halutza area and the other 25 km south-west
of Beer Sheva, for power stations.  It also proposes a route for a salt-water pipeline to link the Mediterranean and the Dead Sea, possibly providing a solution to
the problem of supply of cooling water for power stations and removal of industrial
wastes.  It allocates clearly defined corridors for technical infrastructure:  roads,
electricity, waterpipes and oil pipelines.

The planners emphasize the importance of improved communications, and have called
for a second international airport east of Beer Sheva (with related industries located nearby), a larger airport at Eilat, extension of the railway to Eilat and

relocation of the port so as to facilitate its expansion.

While focusing on the vital need for industrial development, the planners have also stressed the importance of preservation of the unique desert landscape and have allocated a half million hectares as nature reserves and parks.

## SEDENTARIZATION OF NEGEV BEDOUINS

*General Survey*

The twentieth century has witnessed a widespread process of sedentarization of nomads in the Middle East, and fundamental changes in the overall framework of the Bedouin pastoral nomadism culture. Technological development, modern communication networks and the existence of a strong central government have undermined the basis of several of the main economic branches of the nomads and reduced their political and military strength. The establishment of new political units and boundaries, particularly in the Middle East, has restricted the seasonal nomadism of the tribes. The development of agriculture, particularly that based on irrigation, has increased the profitability of farming, and modern technology has brought industrialization to semi-arid and arid zones. Nomadism, therefore, is no longer the sole ecological alternative in these regions. Throughout the Middle East, pastoral nomads are settling to practice agriculture or to become wage laborers. In some countries this process of settlement is encouraged and/or enforced by the state authorities. In others, it is a spontaneous process which occurs through the pastoral nomads' adaptation to their changing ecological environment.

In the Negev, sedentarization of Beduoins has occurred as a result of changes in the ecological and political environment. It started under the British Mandate, and is still in progress today. Initially, it took the form of spontaneous settlement, with clusters of flimsy, temporary structures lacking adequate services. It was only in the second half of the nineteen sixties that the Israeli authorities began to centralize the settlement by establishing planned areas and villages with modern facilities: water, electricity and schools.

The Negev tribes have lived under the indirect rule of a strong, central government since 1870. They apparently entered the region, mostly from Sinai and some from Transjordan, after Ibrahim Pasha's wars in 1835, and subsequently fought among themselves for territory and waterholes, and clashed with villagers. In 1870, they were pacified by the Turks, who established fluid tribal boundaries. By 1946, it was estimated that there was a total Bedouin population of about 70,000-90,000 in the Negev. The end of the British Mandate period and the subsequent political upheavals were a time of great turbulence and uncertainty for the Bedouin and many left. In 1953, it was estimated that some 11,000 remained and the 1973 census estimated the Bedouin population of the Negev at 30,000. The figure is now taken to be 36,000.

Many of the changes in the sociological and economic structure of Bedouin life in the past 25 years can be attributed to the new pattern of access to and distribution of land, which is quite different than that which existed during the Turkish, British and early Israeli administration. For example, the tribe is no longer a fighting unit defending territorial rights, nor a significant territorial unit because of increasing state control over land and the spread of individual ownership and activity. It remains the main administrative unit and is regarded as such by the Israeli government (like the Turkish and British authorities before then), which sanctions the appointment of sheikhs and pays them a salary. The Government was particularly dependent on the sheikhs from 1948-1964, when the 19 tribes left in the Negev lived in a limited area in the north-east of the region and were governed by a military administration. The sheikhs then enjoyed great influence

as sole intermediaries with the authorities, controlling distribution of resources
such as land, work, movement and food.  Since the end of military government in
1966, however, the power of the sheikhs has waned and individual Bedouin enjoy freedom of movement and tend increasingly to maintain contacts with the authorities on
a personal, face-to-face basis, rather than through the sheikh's intercession.

The decline of semi-nomadism as the dominant way of life in the last few years can
also be attributed to the scarcity of land due to new patterns of distribution.
Before 1948, land was individually owned and landless Bedouin (usually of peasant
origin) sharecropped.  It is now possible to lease land from the state.  The Negev
Bedouin use approximately 40,000 hectares for cultivation, about half their own
land and the remainder leased to them by the Land Administration.  The latter is
distributed from July through September; rent is low and more symbolic than for
profit - 10 agorot per dunam (one-tenth of a hectare) for cultivation land and 5
agorot per dunam for grazing land.  Individual families are allocated a minimum of
100-200 dunams according to the following criteria:
- individuals over 40 with no other form of employment are entitled to more
  than 100 dunams;
- persons employed by the army or government;
- those living in planned villages or who have bought plots there;
- every sheikh is entitled to 500 dumans.

These criteria reflect current government policy of encouraging Bedouin to settle
in planned government villages and work for wages, with land being cultivated only
for subsistence.  The landless sharecropper can now lease his own land if he no
longer practices semi-nomadism.

The State is at present negotiating a settlement of compensation for land expropriat-
ed for industrial and agricultural development.  According to the settlement presently being considered, the State is prepared to accept less legalistic proof of ownership than is provided by the official Land Register, such as proof that the land was
worked by the family in the past, or evidence from the 1946 aerial survey that the
land was then being cultivated.  When the issue is settled, the State will be able
to utilize the area defined as State land freely.  The Bedouin will retain access
to land partly through leasing and partly through inheritance of land recognized
by law as their own, and by sharecropping of both.

Negev Bedouin, as noted, are undergoing a process of economic transition common to
many Bedouin elsewhere in the Middle East (and to pastoral tribes in Africa).  In
the traditional phase their livelihood was based on animals and access to pasture
land, with a balance between population and land resources.  After 1870, access to
land was limited by the various administrations, and population pressures increased
so that an imbalance was created.  The last decade has seen the increasing influence
of proximity to modern society.  There are 17 elementary schools, one high school
and two vocational high schools serving Negev Bedouin children.  Some 6,500 children
(80% of the boys and between 40-65% of the girls) are now attending school, from
kindergarten to twelfth grade.  Of the 255 teachers, one-third are local Bedouin
including one young woman, and 16 of the school principals are Negev-born Bedouin.
The school attendance has doubled in the past three years alone.  Growing numbers
are going on to higher education.

As a result of these factors and of others mentioned above, the wage labour market
has developed and a certain amount of agricultural modernization has also taken
place.  Few Bedouin now live solely from flocks and agricultural land as in the past.
Most either live from wage labour alone or from a mixed economy of wage labour plus
flocks or land.  Hence, agriculture and flocks have become supplementary sources of
income.

The semi-nomadic Bedouin moves with, and lives from his livestock, wandering according to their needs but returning to the area of his land at the time of sowing and
harvesting of his winter crops.  These crops consist of wheat and barley, the former
providing his family's bread and the latter supplying fodder for his flock.

The settled Beduoin lives from wage labour and hence is not mobile.  In the Negev,
many Bedouin now work in guarding and tracking, driving and construction.  There
are, for example, five agencies in Beer Sheva employing an average of seventy
Bedouin each to guard various institutions and installations.  Others are tile
layers, road surveyors, roof layers and independent labour contractors, and some are
trickling into the professions.  In 1974, the Histadrut, Israel's trade union movement, had 2,800 Bedouin members all over Israel, and by 1975, 3,500.  The Ministry
of Agriculture employs a young Bedouin to advise on new techniques in crop and flock
management, the trade union movement has a Bedouin representative and there is a
qualified Bedouin doctor.

The transition from semi-nomad to wage-earner sometimes takes a generation.  At
first, wage labour is a supplementary, intermittent source of income which does not
interfere with crop and flock management.  It then gradually becomes the primary
source of income; as fewer family members are available, the flock becomes smaller.
For the Bedouin in the transition stage, living from a mixed economy, the flock may
be regarded as capital to be used only when wages are not available or in times of
crisis.  His crops are increasingly sold rather than being used for home consumption.  Eventually the family sells off its flock and stops moving, pitching a tent
or building a hut near relatives, a water source and the road.

As noted, in the mid-sixties the government initiated planned settlement for the
Negev Bedouin (and Bedouin elsewhere in the country).  It was hoped that such
inducements as planned modern facilities and services and very favourable financial
conditions for purchase would attract them and reduce scattered, hapazard construction of buildings dotted throughout the North-eastern Negev.  The first planned
Bedouin village in the Negev was Tel Sheva, which did not meet with the success
anticipated.

*Case Study:  Tel Sheva*

The village, established in 1968, lies 6 kilometers to the north-east of Beer Sheva.
It has electricity, running water, an asphalt road linking it to the main Beer
Sheva-Arad road and bus service to Beer Sheva.  Forty-three houses were built around
a center consisting of two shops, a community center and a clinic, and a mother-and-
baby clinic is located in one of the houses.  Each house consists of a guest room,
sleeping room, kitchen, shower and separate W.C.  An open porch between the rooms
can be roofed to make a third room.  The design, with two entrances, allows for the
segregation of men and women.  On all sides of the village, up to a distance of 4
kilometers, there are clusters of tents and huts of several tribe groups who have
in the area since the early fifties.  They utilize all the village facilities except
water, but continue living outside and are reluctant to move into preconstructed
houses despite official encouragement.  In fact, only 25 of the houses are owned and
lived in by Bedouin families.

Analysis of the characteristics of the village householders reveals that almost all
live solely from wage labour, whereas most of the outsiders earn their livelihood
from a mixed economy; that villagers are young and moved in when they had few
children; and that the majority live in nuclear family units.  Living in a house
imposes certain patterns of spending and regular financial commitments which can
only be met by those with regular income.  The mixed economy household may enjoy
the same total annual income, but this will fluctuate widely over the year.  In

addition, age is an important factor influencing the individual's capacity to integrate into the wage labour economy, and the older men tend to prefer a mixed economy,
thus rarely integrating into the wage labour economy. Some of the outsiders have
refused to move into the village for social rather than economic reasons. They are
reluctant to live among "strangers". Bedouin society is stratified into three
groups: Bedouin (*badoo*), peasants (*fellaheen*), and slaves (*abeed*). The economic
differences between them, based on Bedouin monopoly of access to land, no longer
exist, but social distinctions remain, interaction is minimal with an element of
fractionalism in the relationship, and there is no intermarriage.

In 1974, the Government officials responsible for Bedouin planning decided, in the
light of the reluctance of the outlying population to move in, to modify their
original plans. The decision was taken to build no more houses and instead, to
parcel off plots of land which families could buy to build on themselves. The
present plan is to develop neighbourhood clusters based on the existing "shanty
town" groups where plots will be sold to related individuals who will build their
own houses. No houses will be preconstructed. There is already one such area near
the village with twelve occupied plots. Only two houses have been built, however,
and other families have constructed huts. A dunam of land costs 2,500 lira, a
symbolic price, and a mortgage between 45,000-60,000 is available from the Ministry
of Housing, repayable over twenty years at an interest rate of 10%. 40,000 of this
load is cancelled after ten years.

The mistakes made at Tel Sheva were taken into consideration when subsequent settlements were planned. It was realized that social structure and kinship ties are
an important factor in Bedouin settlement. Furthermore, the fact that Tel Sheva
had attracted mainly wage-earners able to undertake regular financial commitments
suggested that future villages should be constructed with their own industrial areas
or near potential sources of employment. A village has been established at Shuval
in the Western Negev at the request of the Bedouin themselves, based on a central
nucleus of the Huzeil tribe with all its components. Occupying an area of 7,000
dunam, it is planned to absorb 5,000 inhabitants over the next few years, and
thousands more by the end of the century. Emphasis has been placed on separate
neighbourhoods for each sub-unit of a tribe, and each neighbourhood has its own
services, such as kindergarten, school, store, etc., with more complex services
located in the center. Green areas have been planted, enabling movement of flocks
and agricultural implements from homes to fields.

A third village is now being established north of Beer Sheva and in coordination
with tribes, another three are to be established in the region before 1980. It is
also planned to expand Tel Sheva.

*Conclusions*

The recent development of Israel's arid and semi-arid areas clearly indicates that
given sufficient human resources, determination and capital, modern technology can
be successfully utilized to regenerate desertified areas on the fringes of the
desert. Barring long-range climatic shifts, these regenerated areas can serve as
a barrier to desert expansion until such time as the desert itself succumbs to
man's constructive efforts. Organized into a suitable economic and social framework, these regenerated areas can support a population at economic and social levels
comparable to those of more humid regions. That such endeavors can prove successful
is undoubtedly the salient lesson to be learned from the Israeli experience.

It should, however, be recognized that countries involved in the effort to contain
or reverse desertification should not always embark upon the same paths or utilize
identical technologies. There is a fairly wide range of physical conditions within

the semi-arid and arid regions and an even wider spectrum of cultures, customs and political and social organization. Because of cultural and historical discontin-uities, Israel has been able to effect a quantum jump directly into the most modern technologies. This may not be possible or even desirable, at least at an early stage, in other newly-developing nations. Each country has its unique social struct-ure and physical characteristics, and the practices and techniques utilized for generations by indigenous agriculturalists should not be lightly dismissed. These practices often represent valuable experience gained over the years by trial and error, and should be improved and modified in the light of modern knowledge to a point where optimum productivity and resource conservation is obtained. However, when new settlement or development is undertaken in relatively unpopulated regions, a more radical approach may be feasible. It is especially in this latter case that the Israeli experience can be of direct consequence.

The rational exploitation, on a national basis, of all potential water resources has been the foundation of Israeli planning and implementation for regeneration of the nation's arid and semi-arid regions. For this purpose, laws have been promulgated nationalizing all water resources, and a national program for distribution and utilization has been put into effect. An equitable system of water quotas and water prices was instituted, requiring institutional forms of far-reaching cooperative nature. The establishment of suitable political and social organization, coupled with national ownership of all water resources, was the basic factor without which the national water distribution scheme could not have been implemented. This is, perhaps, among the most important considerations for any developing nation contemp-lating large-scale projects for water resource development and utilization.

When irrigation systems are already in operation, much can be done to increase the efficiency of water use and to prevent deterioration of valuable farm land through water-logging and salinization. Israeli farmers have demonstrated that by use of modern agricultural technology, productivity per unit of water can be increased manyfold and damage to the soil can be eliminated. This technology includes the use of fertilizers, pesticides, better plant varieties, drainage and other inputs. In many situations it would be more effective to modernize existing water-use syst-ems than to use scarce capital resources for new water development construction. In addition to doubling and tripling yields, more efficient water use with existing facilities can be of far-reaching ecological value by controlling erosion, saliniz-ation, water logging and disease. New water projects could be undertaken at a later stage at appropriate locations.

Dry-land farming for the production of grain has also undergone extensive develop-ment in Israel's arid and semi-arid zones. The use of nitrogen fertilizer in areas with at lease 200 mm of winter rainfall has been shown to be vital in raising yields to a high level. Wheat has become the major grain cultivated and it responds well to additional nitrogen and phosphorous fertilization. Dwarf and stiff-stemmed varieties are used to prevent lodging of the wheat crops. In the arid and semi-arid zone, only small amounts of nitrogen are lost by denitrification and leaching. Hence, fertilizer applied to plants and not utilized because of drought will still be available for the following year's crop. Experimentation to determine optimum fertilization in different crops and varieties seems to constitute a never ending process. In most areas the stubble is allowed to remain till late summer and is usually grazed by sheep. The maintenance of high fertility and high productivity has been an effective barrier to erosion and soil degradation.

Supplementary irrigation of grain crops has proved exceedingly effective. The avail-ability of moisture in addition to the natural rainfall ensures a minimum yield even in dry years and an excellent yield in normal or rainy years. Wherever water and irrigation facilities are available this practice has been profitable for the farmer. In all cases modern agricultural technology is utilized, and great stress is placed on weed and pest control.

Drought compensation has been the cornerstone of Israel's dry farming policy. By insuring the farmer against inordinate losses due to natural calamities, optimum use of land resources is obtained. Compensation is, of course, limited to those areas in which "normal" rainfall would produce an economically feasible yield. In Israel this compensation covers areas having at least 200 mm of winter rainfall. The knowledge that compensation is available enables the Israeli farmer to utilize high-yielding varieties which are perhaps not as drought-resistant as lower yielding ones but which guarantee a far higher low-range aggregate yield. The farmer can work his land more intensively, aiming at maximum yields, in the knowledge that all will not be lost because of drought. The result is greater stability and incentive for the farmer to achieve high productivity.

A distinctive feature of Israeli land settlement is its communal character. The benefits of larger-scale operation are apparent, but these forms of organization also increase the political power of the farmers. In Israel, an extensive system of production quotas, price controls, compensation and credits ensures the hard-working competent farmer of an income commensurate with his efforts. There are strong incentives for efficient production and farmers comprise an advanced and prosperous sector of Israeli society.

Applied research and development have played a vital role in development of the Negev. Considerable effort has gone into the adaption of known technology to Israeli conditions, and into local innovation. An efficient extension service brings the results of research to the production system. Experimental stations and research institutions, especially of an applied nature, have much to contribute, from the technological, educational and sociological viewpoints. These experimental stations are working today on new technologies for the continuing productivization of the desert. Included in their research programs are such unconventional subjects as water harvesting, pasture shrubs, new industrial crops, closed cropping systems, new energy sources, desert landscaping and basic physiological studies of adaptation of plants, animals and man to the conditions of the arid zone.

Town planning in the arid Negev unfortunately followed traditional forms, at least during the early settlement stages. However, lessons were learned from the mistakes of the past and planners have begun to utilize more suitable architectural forms. Higher population densities are planned with enclosed protected courtyards and public areas. The sociological preferences of nomads and other ethnic groups have been taken into consideration in settlement schemes.

Present and future development of the Negev is oriented towards intensive industrialization, founded on existing raw materials and on technology and science-based industries. Israel is poor in major natural resources so that this type of development is dependent upon the education and training of large numbers of scientists, engineers and technicians. Transfers of industry to the large open spaces of arid and semi-arid areas could help relieve population pressures on the presently overcrowded metropolitan centers whose outskirts now constitute deprived slum areas. Utilizing desert areas for industrial development would also reduce pressures on more cultivable land in the more humid areas. In order to encourage industry to move south the Israeli Government undertook an ambitious program which included the following measures:
a. Establishment of research institutions in the Negev area.
b. Allocating priority for new housing construction in the Negev and awarding low-interest mortgages to settlers.
c. Large reduction in income taxes for Negev settlers.
d. Special incentives for establishment of industrial enterprises and for tourism.

These measures have been effective, but it seems that even greater efforts will have to be made if demographic distribution is to be significantly changed. Since an educated and skilled population is a key factor for industrial development, education remains the most important activity with which governments should be concerned.

ACKNOWLEDGEMENTS

The following authors have contributed to this case study:

Dr. Yehuda Gradus of the Geography Department, Ben Gurion University - the sections on borders, populations and Beer Sheva.

Professor Louis Berkofsky of the Desert Research Institute of Ben Gurion University, Sde Boker - climate and rain enhancement.

Dr. Dov Pasternak of the Plant Introduction and Applied Ecology Division, Research and Development Authority, Ben Gurion University of the Negev - Water - A Major Factor in Recovery.

Dr. Noam Zeligman of the Vulcani Institute of Agricultural Research - Agricultural Technology in Semi-Arid Zones. Thanks also to Professor J. Ephrat and Dr. B. Rettig for their helpful suggestions, and to Mr. D. Ariel and Mr. M. Hoffman for placing unpublished material at the disposal of Dr. Zeligman.

Ms. Gillian Lewando-Hundt - Sedentarization of Negev Bedouins - based on field work for a Ph.D. thesis.

The editors of this case-study would like to thank the following for their advice and assistance: Mr. Yosef Dehan, Southern District Administration, Ministry of the Interior, Beer Sheva; Mr. Mahmoud Diab, Inspector of Bedouin Education, Ministry of Education, Beer Sheva; Mr. Zvi Raz, Mapping Division, Ministry of Agriculture, Tel Aviv; the staff of the Planning Unit, Settlement Department of the Jewish Agency Beersheva; and the Advisor on Arab Affairs, Prime Minister's Office.

The editors are grateful to Professor D. Amiran and Professor M. Evenari for reading the manuscript and offering helpful comments.

# The U.S.A.

Figures 2, 4, 6, 7, 15, 16, 24, 27,
48 and 60 are inserted in pocket
at end of book.

# The Vale Rangeland Program
# The Desert Repaired in Southern Oregon

## Harold F. Heady and James Bartolome

*Department of Forestry and Conservation, University of California, Berkeley, USA*

## INTRODUCTION

This report evaluates a large-scale rangeland rehabilitation program on lands administered by the Vale, Oregon, District of the Bureau of Land Management (BLM). Analysis goes beyond a biological-physical characterization because the program cannot be fully understood without knowledge of the many factors surrounding its initiation. The report presents the history of land use in the district, some practical politics of land management, multiple use relationships, impacts of range rehabilitation on many parts of the rangeland ecosystem, community reactions to the program, and economics of rangeland rehabilitation. The Vale Program exemplifies these national land use issues. Program evaluation should be useful in a broader context than just Malheur County, Oregon. We have two principal objectives in this report: (1) to make the lessons learned in the Vale Program available for land rehabilitation programs elsewhere and (2) to present a large and practical example of successful cooperation among land users of different kinds, including their supporting political and social institutions.

A resource management program, such as the Vale Program, aims to accomplish good deeds. The kinds of products which are good, the quantities of each, and where they arise may be indicated in the plans for the program; but society, economics, and political necessities change. Competition and controversies develop, so the managers of public lands must answer changing multiple use questions as time goes on. The public now asks for more consideration of environmental impacts, deeper analysis of alternatives in land use, better informed resource allocation, and more multiple resource planning on a long-term basis than was considered when the program started. Congress has established by law a long-term planning process in the Forest and Rangeland Renewable Resources Act of 1974. Although the program planning part of that act does not apply to the lands administered by BLM, additional resource planning on those lands will probably be required. This case history of the Vale Program should be helpful in future planning efforts both locally and on other districts.

The Vale Program started without full inventory and analysis of the landscape conditions. Little or no continued monitoring of effects was done beyond estimates and evaluations needed for further on-the-spot decisions. Therefore, the data base for this report varies in accuracy and quantity. File materials, mimeographed reports, opinions of persons interviewed, and early photos have been used. Data were obtained from other agencies and we collected considerable measurements of vegetation in the many treated areas. Therefore, our conclusions are based on a variety of sources and impressions gained on a part-time basis extending from April 1975 to September 1976.

Several terms are defined briefly to clarify their use within this work. Rangeland refers to the land and its resources of soil, vegetation, and wild animals. Rangeland management means land management for all purposes. Livestock management principally concerns the movement and husbandry of domestic animals. Wildlife includes game, fish, and other wild animals. Animal unit month (AUM) refers to a mature cow, with or without a calf, grazing for 1 month, or its equivalent in other kinds and classes of livestock. Any cow or horse over 6 months old is counted as an animal unit (AU) by BLM. We use "program" throughout to encompass the whole operation and "project" to be specific, as the "Chicken Creek seeding project."

THE VALE DISTRICT

*Location and Extent*

The Vale District of the Bureau of Land Management occupies the southeastern corner of Oregon, approximately within latitudes 42 and 44 degrees north, and longitudes 117 and 118 degrees west. The boundaries of Malheur County, Oregon, nearly coincide with those of the district. In addition, a small area in Idaho southwest of the Owyhee River and another piece to the south in Nevada are included in the district. At the time the Vale Program was begun in 1962, the district enclosed 6.5 million acres (2.6 million ha). Several boundary adjustments resulted in a shift in location and a slight reduction in area. The Vale District forms a rough rectangle approximately 175 by 60 miles (280 by 100 km) (Fig. 1). To avoid extensive redrafting, the maps presented in this report are based on boundaries as they existed in the 1960's.

*Physiography*

As shown in Fig. 2, elevations in the district range from 2,000 to nearly 8,000 feet (600 to 2 400 m). The higher elevations in the Trout Creek Mountains to the southwest and the upper reaches of Bully Creek in the northwest drain toward the Snake River along the northeastern edge of the district. Main drainages are the Malheur River which flows from the west and the Owyhee River which flows northward through the district from its origins near the corner of Oregon, Idaho, and Nevada.

The most extensive land form is a gently sloping to rolling lava plateau with elevations above 4,000 feet (1 200 m). This plateau has been extensively dissected into canyons with vertical cliffs by branches of the Owyhee River and Succor Creek (Fig. 3) (Kittleman 1973). Mesas of several thousand acres, the remnants of earlier plateaus, are important as topographic features and as management units. The variety of physiographic prominences such as the rugged Owyhee Breaks along the east side of the Owyhee Reservoir and the Rome Colosseums, Mahogany Mountain, and Three Finger Rock contrast with the broad flat expanse of Barren Valley in the west-central region of the district. Numerous closed basins indicate the existence of ancient lakes. Recent lava flows, some probably between 500 and 1,000 years of age, in the central region still remain devoid of soil and vegetation. The Jordan craters and caves in the lava flows appear as if they were formed only yesterday. The older lava has varying degrees of soil development. Basaltic and rhyolitic lava and tuffs, ranging in age from Miocene to Recent, underlie extensive areas in the district.

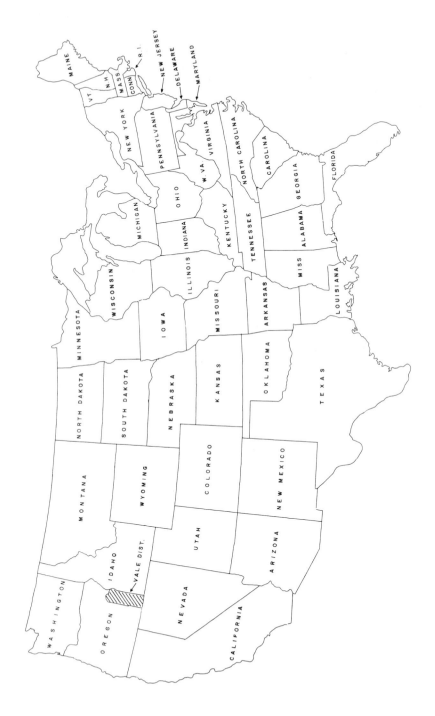

Fig. 1. The Vale District occupies the southeastern corner of Oregon.

Fig. 3.   The Owyhee River and its branches cut this and other
          canyons across the Vale District (Bureau of Land
          Management photo).

*Climate*

The semiarid climate of the Vale District is in a transition zone between continental and Pacific coastal types, with wide variations in rainfall and temperature
between seasons.  The district typifies the Great Basin region and is called a cold
desert.  Most of the district receives an average of 7 to 12 inches (180 to 300 mm)
of precipitation annually (Fig. 4).  Average annual precipitation strongly corre-
lates with elevation, but only the higher mountains receive more than 15 inches
(380 mm).

Most precipitation falls during the winter (November-March) in the form of snow;
however, May is the wettest month of the year (Fig. 5).  Thunderstorms contribute
rain in early summer, but significant moisture for plant growth comes almost
entirely in winter precipitation.  At Vale, Oregon, the crop year precipitation
varied as much as 70 to 140 percent of the 22-year average of 9.3 inches (236 mm)
from 1955 through 1976 (Table 1).  During the 11 years (1962-72) of major vegetational manipulation in the Vale District program, 7 received more than average
precipitation and only 1 year was exceptionally dry in the spring.

Temperatures vary greatly by season and are markedly influenced by elevation.
Danner, Oregon, at 4,000-foot (1 200-m) elevation near the center of the district,
showed a range of mean monthly temperatures from 68.5°F in July to 25.6°F in
January (20.3 to -3.7°C).  All mean monthly temperatures for November through
March were below 40°F (4.6°C) (Fig. 5).

Table 1.  Precipitation at Vale, Oregon, on a crop year
basis, July 1-June 30, 1975-76[1]/

| Year ending | Total | July-December | January-June |
|---|---|---|---|
| | | Inches | |
| 1976 | 8.98 | 5.69 | 3.29 |
| 1975 | 9.44 | 3.40 | 6.04 |
| 1974 | 6.98 | 4.11 | 2.87 |
| 1973 | 7.29 | 4.19 | 3.10 |
| 1972 | 7.91 | 4.16 | 3.75 |
| 1971 | 9.80 | 5.52 | 4.28 |
| 1970 | 10.27 | 3.54 | 6.73 |
| 1969 | 12.59 | 5.90 | 6.69 |
| 1968 | 6.79 | 2.63 | 4.16 |
| 1967 | 11.13 | 5.37 | 5.76 |
| 1966 | 6.57 | 4.36 | 2.21 |
| 1965 | 10.12 | 5.43 | 4.69 |
| 1964 | 11.19 | 4.12 | 7.07 |
| 1963 | 10.54 | 5.40 | 5.14 |
| 1962 | 9.39 | 4.38 | 5.01 |
| 1961 | 7.68 | 4.56 | 3.12 |
| 1960 | 10.96 | 4.39 | 6.57 |
| 1959 | 6.23 | 1.99 | 4.24 |
| 1958 | 10.74 | 2.75 | 7.99 |
| 1957 | 12.47 | 4.68 | 7.79 |
| 1956 | 10.01 | 4.90 | 5.11 |
| 1955 | 8.01 | 3.01 | 5.00 |
| Mean | 9.31 | 4.28 | 5.03 |

Source: U.S. Weather Bureau.

[1]/ To convert inches to millimeters multiply by 25.4.

The cold winters and lack of summer moisture limit the actual growing season to a
short period in spring and early summer.  The frost-free season is less than 90
days in areas above 4,500-foot (1 375-mm) elevation, which limits agriculture to
the harvesting of hay in valleys south of the Malheur River.  The low-elevation
lands along the Malheur and the Snake Rivers produce sugar beets, onions, potatoes,
feed grains, hay, and many other crops under irrigation.  Grazing use is restricted
by the ephemeral nature of watering places as well as the short green-feed season.
Little permanent, undeveloped water exists over much of the district, especially
outside of patented land.  Water development for livestock has been a major range
management practice.

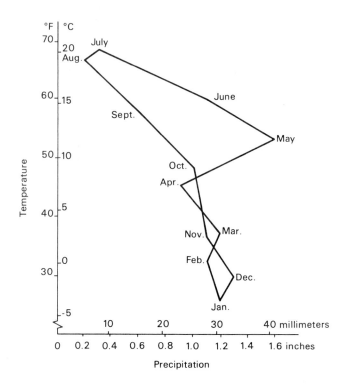

Fig. 5.   20-year mean monthly temperature and precipitation
          for the Danner, Oregon, Weather Station, 1944-64.
          Danner is approximately 15 miles (24 km) west of
          Jordan Valley.  Yearly mean was 11.5 inches
          (290 mm) (U.S. Weather Bureau.  Climatological
          Data, Oregon).

## Soils

Soils of the Vale District fall into five of the great soil groups (Fig. 6).  Of
the mapped groups, only three, numbers 2, 3, and 5, are of major importance on
rangeland.

Group 1 soils are deep alluvial sierozem calcisols which underlie the irrigated
cropland in several areas of the Vale District, mainly in the northeast on low-
elevation terraces and flood plains of the Snake and Malheur Rivers.  These soils
are only used as grazing land where they cannot be irrigated.

Group 2 soils of the sierozem desert group were formed from alluvial deposits.  They
constitute a significant portion of the rangeland soils on the Vale District.
These soils occur on old fans and as high terrace remnants.  They are loamy, well-
drained soils with cemented hardpans about 10-20 inches (250-500 mm) below the
surface.  The texture varies from gravelly loam to silt loam.  A coarse gravel and
cobble pavement characterizes many soils of the group.  Native vegetation is
dominated by big sagebrush (*Artemisia tridentata*),[1] low sagebrush (*Artemisia*

---

[1] Common and scientific names follow Hitchcock and Cronquist (1973).

*arbuscula*), bud sage (*Artemisia spinescens*), rabbitbrush (*Chrysothamnus* spp.),
saltbush (*Atriplex* spp.), needlegrasses (*Stipa* spp.), Sandberg bluegrass (*Poa
secunda*), and squirreltail (*Sitanion hystrix*) (Lovell *et al*. 1969).

Soils in Groups 3 and 5 differ primarily in type of volcanic origin; Group 3 soils
developed from rhyolites and Group 5 from basalts of Miocene age.  Soils on both
are lithosols or brown chestnuts, and they occur on gently sloping to rolling lava
plateaus.  Typically these soils are fine loamy to clayey, light colored, very
stony, and usually less than 20 inches (0.5 m) above bedrock.  Often a thin silica-
cemented hardpan is present just above bedrock.  Areas of Group 3 and 5 soils with
18 inches (45 cm) or more of soil depth are major areas for rangeland reseeding.
Native vegetation is bluebunch wheatgrass (*Agropyron spicatum*), Sandberg bluegrass,
big sagebrush, and low sagebrush.  Idaho fescue (*Festuca idahoensis*) is present on
more mesic sites (Lovell *et al*.1969).

Soils of Group 4 are lithosols confined to a small area in the extreme northwest
of the district.  They developed from granitic parent material and have little
potential for range production.

*Vegetation*

Brush dominates Vale District vegetation (Table 2).  Of the six vegetational types
in Fig. 7, big sagebrush is by far the most common (Fig. 8).  The species occurs
in all the other types.  Vegetation of the whole district has a strong shrub
component.

Table 2.  Area of vegetational types on Federal lands
          administered by Bureau of Land Management, 1961-64

| Types | 1,000 acres | 1 000 hectares |
|---|---|---|
| Grass | 274 | 111 |
| Halogeton and larkspur | 7 | 3 |
| Sagebrush-grass | 4,068 | 1 648 |
| Ponderosa pine | 5 | 2 |
| Barren, inaccessible, and waste | 17 | 7 |
| Juniper | 53 | 21 |
| Desert shrub | 211 | 85 |
| Total | 4,635 | 1 877 |

The map in Fig. 7 was generalized from Range Reconnaissance Surveys made in 1963-64,
shortly after the rehabilitation program was started.  The type numbers and names
follow the system of standard symbols used in that survey.

At high elevations near the extreme northern edge of the Vale District, sagebrush-
grass intergrades into the ponderosa pine (*Pinus ponderosa*) type typical of the
Blue Mountains to the north.  Few pine trees actually grow within the district.

Fig. 8.  Big sagebrush with a mixture of perennial grasses
characterizes a large part of the district.

Western juniper (*Juniperus occidentalis*) occurs at high elevation throughout the
Vale District.  These areas are mapped as type 9 (Fig. 7).  The juniper type is
essentially sagebrush-grass with the addition of scattered juniper trees.  The
shrubs and grasses are typical of adjacent areas without trees.

Lower elevational vegetation with rainfall of less than 10 inches (25 mm) and with
alkaline soils of the sierozem desert type also intergrades with the sagebrush-grass
type.  Shadscale (*Atriplex confertifolia*), budsage, and spiny hopsage (*Grayia
spinosa*) characterize the desert shrub, type 16 (Fig. 7), in a mosaic with big
sagebrush (Fig. 9).  Principal grasses are squirreltail and Sandberg bluegrass.
This vegetation constitutes a desirable winter range on the district because of the
many palatable browse species.

The vast area described as sagebrush-grass is characterized by complex, intergrading
mixtures of several dominant plant species, depending on prior treatment and varying
microsite.  Climax vegetation of much of the region is a mosaic of sagebrush and
native bunchgrasses.  Forbs and the annual cheatgrass (*Bromus tectorum*) are ever
present.  Excellent range may contain up to 25 percent sagebrush.  The mix of
bunchgrasses and sagebrush at the start of the Vale Program had been strongly tipped
toward high brush density and few palatable bunchgrasses as a result of a century of
often exploitive grazing.  In some locations, a perennial grass understory was almost
absent with annuals or bare soil occurring between the shrubs.  In 1961 only 1 percent of the Vale District was described as excellent, or near climax range.  Ninety-
nine percent reflected varying degrees of range deterioration as exemplified by a
reduction in palatable perennials in the understory and an increase in brush density.

Fig. 9.  The low sagebrush type with scattered grasses grows
         on thin, rocky soils (Bureau of Land Management
         photo).

Shrub species characteristic of the sagebrush-grass type in addition to big sagebrush are low sagebrush, rabbitbrush, bitterbrush (*Purshia tridentata*) and mountain
mahogany (*Cercocarpus ledifolius*) (Fig. 10).  Understory plants in good to excellent
range are mainly bluebunch wheatgrass, giant wildrye (*Elymus cinereus*) on lowland
sites, and Idaho fescue on north-facing slopes and at high elevations.  Common
perennials in the understory, especially where the range is in fair to poor
condition, are the less desirable grasses, squirreltail and Sandberg bluegrass.
Cheatgrass may be the only common understory plants, reflecting past extreme use
which eliminated the perennials.

The grass type in Fig. 7 includes large burned areas where the sagebrush was missing
and either cheatgrass, Sandberg bluegrass, or both dominated Halogeton (*Halogeton
glomeratus*) and larkspur (*Delphinium* spp.) also indicate poor condition ranges and
were located in small areas southwest of Rome and near McDermitt.  They were much
reduced in size since the map was drawn in 1963-64 because of their replacement
through plant succession and range rehabilitation.

Streamside woody vegation, too small in area to be mapped but highly important
habitat for wildlife and control of erosion, includes willow (*Salix* spp.), cotton-
wood (*Populus trichocarpa*), hawthorn (*Crataegus* spp.), and wild cherry (*Prunus* spp.).
In the alkaline areas, greasewood (*Sarcobatus vermiculatus*) dominates the riparian
community.

Fig. 10.  Bitterbrush and mountain mahogany often occupy the
          north-facing slopes and coves near the tops of
          mountains.

DEMOGRAPHY AND ECONOMIC PROFILE OF MALHEUR COUNTY, OREGON

*Population*

All but a few of Vale District permittees reside in Malheur County which is
essentially the same area as the BLM District.  Therefore, census data as presented
here for Malheur County accurately describe the Vale District.  The population of
23,380 in 1970 was highly concentrated in the irrigated crop region in the north-
east.  Fewer than 850 persons resided in the remainder of the county, giving that
part an average density of one person per 6,000 acres (2 400 ha), and making it one
of the most thinly populated areas of the United States.  Total county population
has remained relatively constant since 1950, showing a net increase of only 175
from 1950 to 1970.  During that period, rural populations declined; the major city
of Ontario grew from 4,465 in 1950, to 7,140 in 1972, and 7,710 in 1975.  The
number of people in the age group 20 to 40 years declined, and the number of
persons older than 40 increased during 1950 to 1970.  These trends in distribution
and age structure approximate similar trends in the United States.

*Economy*

The economic base of Malheur County is primarily agriculture and related industries
with livestock raising, the largest single component, contributing about $15 million
or 22 percent of the total annual county income.  Nearly 100,000 acres (40 000 ha)
of privately owned irrigated land depend on the Owyhee Reservoir for water.  Additional lands are irrigated from waters in the Malheur River and Bully Creek.  Other

major economic inputs into the county are from hunting and other forms of recreation.

Malheur County livestock trends since 1920 typify those observed in many parts of the Intermountain West (Table 3). Cattle numbers nearly tripled between 1920 and 1970 with a correspondingly dramatic decline in horse, mule, and sheep numbers. Overall forage consumption, as indicated by AUM's of livestock use in the county, was only slightly less in 1970 than in 1920. Peak forage consumption occurred in 1960 with a low in 1940 at barely half of the peak. Public lands contributed 22 to 37 percent of the total forage provided to county livestock. Approximately 64 percent of the ranchers have had grazing permits on public lands since 1934.

Table 3. Numbers of livestock and forage provided by public lands in Malheur County

| Year | Cattle | Horses and mules | Sheep | County | Public land | Forage from public lands |
|------|--------|------------------|-------|--------|-------------|--------------------------|
|      |        |                  |       | AUM's[1] | | Percent |
| 1920 | 62,265 | 22,740 | 403,685 | 1,988,904 | [2] | [2] |
| 1930 | 37,149 | 13,608 | 342,264 | 1,430,518 | [2] | [2] |
| 1940 | 65,234 | 12,901 | 131,300 | 1,132,812 | 418,592 | 37 |
| 1950 | 114,672 | 7,327 | 50,874 | 1,586,086 | 463,935 | 29 |
| 1960 | 153,753 | 4,268 | 55,744 | 2,030,038 | 451,537 | 22 |
| 1970 | 152,352 | [3] | 23,000 | 1,893,295 | 442,974 | 24 |

Source: Bureau of Land Management (1974).

[1] Animal unit months.

[2] Unknown before BLM District was established.

[3] Combined with cattle numbers.

Ranches in the Vale District are typically small with an average herd size of 280 head in 1961 and 320 head in 1974. A trend toward consolidation into larger operations is shown by the frequency distribution in Table 4. This increase in ranch size reflects a reduction in the number of ranches in Malheur County from 719 in 1964 to 419 in 1970. Sheep ranches with permits on the public lands declined from 14 in 1961 to 1 in 1975. A shortage of skilled labor in handling sheep appears to be an important cause in their decline.

Employment in Malheur County totaled 9,418 in 1970 and services and trades contributing 47 and agriculture 21 percent of the total work force. Food processing employed 19 percent of the county's workers in 1970. Increased farm mechanization, with a resulting decrease in employment directly in agriculture, has been compensated by rapid expansion of food processing. In 1950, 48 percent of the county workers were employed in agriculture with only 2 percent in food processing. Services and trades, which increased from 36 to 47 percent of the work force between 1950 and 1970, will likely continue to expand as Ontario becomes increasingly the trade center for the region.

Table 4.   Frequency distribution of grazing licenses and permits, Vale District, Bureau of Land Management, 1961 and 1974

| Animals | No. of permittees | Percent | No. of head | Percent |
|---|---|---|---|---|
| 1961 GRAZING YEAR | | | | |
| Cattle and horses: | | | | |
| 1-    25 | 21 | 6.6 | 418 | 0.5 |
| 26-    50 | 23 | 7.2 | 938 | 1.1 |
| 51-  100 | 62 | 19.5 | 4,994 | 5.5 |
| 101-  200 | 81 | 25.5 | 12,591 | 14.1 |
| 201-  350 | 50 | 15.7 | 13,872 | 15.5 |
| 351-  500 | 27 | 8.5 | 11,374 | 12.7 |
| 501- 1,000 | 42 | 13.2 | 27,539 | 30.9 |
| Over 1,000 | 12 | 3.8 | 17,547 | 19.7 |
| Total | 318 | 100.0 | 89,273 | 100.0 |
| Sheep and goats: | | | | |
| 1-  100 | -- | -- | -- | -- |
| 101-  250 | -- | -- | -- | -- |
| 251-  500 | 2 | 14.3 | 900 | 2.2 |
| 501- 1,000 | 2 | 14.3 | 1,317 | 3.3 |
| 1,001- 2,000 | 8 | 57.1 | 15,050 | 37.6 |
| 2,501- 5,000 | 1 | 7.2 | 4,810 | 12.0 |
| 5,001-10,000 | -- | -- | -- | -- |
| Over  10,000 | 1 | 7.1 | 18,000 | 44.9 |
| Total | 14 | 100.0 | 40,077 | 100.0 |
| 1974 GRAZING YEAR | | | | |
| Cattle and horses: | | | | |
| 1-    25 | 30 | 12.8 | 466 | .6 |
| 26-    50 | 16 | 6.8 | 636 | .8 |
| 51-  100 | 30 | 12.8 | 2,257 | 3.0 |
| 101-  200 | 45 | 19.2 | 7,209 | 9.5 |
| 201-  350 | 40 | 17.0 | 11,466 | 15.1 |
| 351-  500 | 25 | 10.6 | 10,705 | 14.1 |
| 501- 1,000 | 37 | 15.7 | 26,116 | 34.4 |
| Over 1,000 | 12 | 5.1 | 17,038 | 22.5 |
| Total | 235 | 100.0 | 75,893 | 100.0 |
| Sheep and goats: | | | | |
| 5,001-10,000 | 1 | 100.0 | 8,000 | 100.0 |

Median income per household in Malheur County was the lowest in Oregon at $5,903 in 1971. The average payroll per worker ranked second lowest in Oregon at $5,672. Unemployment in 1970 was 6 percent in the county compared with the eastern Oregon average of 7.1 percent.

In summary, the ranching population is small and most jobs stem from crop-related industries. Malheur County has lower levels of income and higher rates of unemployment than most urban communities in the Intermountain area. Significant

outmigration, except from Ontario, foretells continuing problems such as scanty
social services and cultural amenities. Diversification and industrialization have
little chance because the primary production depends on land, which cannot be changed.
The rangeland rehabilitation program and the continuing inflow of new monies to
manage the rangeland resources have helped to stabilize the community. Reconstitu-
tion of the BLM District Advisory Board to include persons with a wide spectrum of
interests should further stabilize land use and community *esprit de corps*.


## HISTORY OF LAND USE AND ITS EFFECTS

*Prior to 1934*

When Captain George Vancouver arrived on the Washington coast in 1792, he recorded
the presence of cattle, sheep, goats, pigs, and poultry belonging to Spaniards.
Cattle raising spread up the Columbia and Snake River systems to Fort Boise and
Fort Hall in Idaho as early as 1834. The first of a flood of people traveling
by covered wagons passed through Vale and the northern part of the district
beginning about 1843. All these early travelers and settlers maintained livestock,
on which they depended for food, power, and clothing. Hanley and Lucia (1974) and
Oliphant (1968) gave particularly good historical accounts of land use, much of it
directly applicable to the Vale District.

The rush for gold in California intensified the need for animals and resulted in
the beginning of an animal industry throughout the Western States. Between 1850 and
1865, every creekbed and likely geological formation was searched for gold and
silver. In 1863, Michael Jordan discovered gold in Jordan Creek and others opened
mines at Silver City in the Owyhee Mountains not far away to the east. People came
to the area by the thousands, including miners, Chinese laborers, freighters, stage-
coach operators, roadbuilders, saloon keepers, bawdy house madams, ranchers, and
roustabouts. Many used the route from McDermitt to the Rome crossing of the Owyhee
River and through the Jordan Valley. All needed horses for travel and beef to eat.

Occasional raids by Indian parties until 1878 restricted travel except along the
roads but hardly reduced the use of extensive rangeland areas by livestock. The
district, as well as adjoining regions, received many herds from 1865 onward and
rapidly became fully stocked with cattle owned by a few ranchers who controlled
large land areas. Between 1876 and 1882, as many as 150,000 cattle per year
trailed eastward from Oregon and Washington to Denver and the northern Great Plains.
It was also a time of great losses from poisonous plants, blackleg and other diseases,
and dependence on the chinook winds to melt the snow so cattle could graze in the
winter. The long and severe winter of 1889-90 reduced many cattle herds to near
zero thus ending an era of control by the western cattle barons. Sheep were completely eliminated. In the following years, many herds and bands were brought from
southern ranges to fully stock the Owyhee ranges again.

Sheep raising and farming began in the Owyhee country about 1865. Many sheep were
in migrant bands which traveled over "free" range, as the land claims of the
cattlemen were ignored. Homesteaders gradually fenced the water, further complicating the use of the rangeland. Although resident cattlemen, sheepmen, and farmers
often remained helpful to each other, the migrants of all three types caused great
conflicts. They took all the grass and water, plowed some land, and moved to
greener pastures. The catastrophic winter of 1889-90 altered the balance of use
toward more sheep on the rangelands. For example, the largely Basque community in
the valley of Jordan Creek controlled an estimated 200,000 sheep in the 1920's and
early 1930's. Cattle now dominate again; in 1975 only 7,400 sheep were permitted
to graze in the whole of the Vale District.

Horses arrived in eastern Oregon about 1750, and most people who came also owned horses (Jackman and Long 1964). The well-known trappers, Donald MacKenzie in 1818 and Peter Skene Ogden in 1824-29, searched for beaver in the Owyhee, Malheur, and Snake River drainages. Each party had 30-50 men and well over 200 horses (Cline 1974). Indians stole some of the horses. Few became feral until after the last Indian war in 1878 when horse numbers increased rapidly. Thousands roamed the ranges of the Owyhee country from 1900 to the mid-1940's. During that time, gathering mustangs (from the Spanish *mestengo* meaning wild horse) provided income for ranchers in the area. Herds were reduced to low numbers following World War II.

No doubt exists that cattle, sheep, and horses occupied the grazing lands of the Vale District in large numbers for about 60 years beginning in 1875. Little hay or other winter feed was available so the use was yearlong. Grazing on farm-raised feeds and haying increased after the winter of 1889-90. Probably, range deterioration had reached severe proportions by 1900. Lack of livestock controls on the public domain until 1934 permitted continued rangeland deterioration and erosion.

Between 1863 and 1866, 3 alternate square miles of land were granted for building each mile of the Oregon Central Military Road from Silver City through Jordan Valley to Fort Smith and westward through central Oregon (Preston 1970). These land grants preceded similar ones for building railroads across the West some 5 or more years later. Although the road was not well constructed, the land was appropriated and shows today as a checkered landownership pattern (Fig. 2).

In response to popular demand, Congress passed the Homestead Act in 1862 providing title to 160 acres (64.8 ha), if the person lived on the land and used it over a 5-year period. This act and later versions, the Desert Land Act in 1877, Enlarged Homestead Act in 1909, and the Grazing Homestead Act in 1916, influenced landownership in the district. The State of Oregon received sections 16 and 36 to support schools, an Indian reservation was established near McDermitt, and lands have been withdrawn for public reserves of various kinds. Table 5 shows the result of these factors in terms of landownership. Differences between 1961 and 1976 reflect changes in the boundaries of the Vale District and changes in ownership. Land trades and sales are gradually consolidating the crazy-quilt ownership pattern which developed before 1934. The Vale District has been approximately 75 percent Federal land since it was formed.

*1934 to 1962*

Until 1934, the public domain was free to be claimed by the user whether the purpose was to graze it or to "prove a claim" and actually be granted a deed or patent. The land belonged to all and yet no one was responsible for sound land use. A 1642 Virginia law, upheld for the Northwest Territory in 1792, stated: "The open woods and uninclosed grounds within the Territory shall be taken and considered as the common pasturage or herbage of the citizens thereof saving to all persons their right to fencing" (Oliphant 1968). This law was interpreted to mean free range and a lawful fence. Such practices as yearlong grazing, branding, and the cooperative roundup developed as a result. Free range and the right of transit between States without taxes favored nomadic herds of livestock, mainly sheep. These customs received sanction in an 1890 U.S. Supreme Court decision which stated that English common law did not prevail because it was ill-adapted to the nature and conditions of the country. The English law stated "that every man must restrain his stock within his own grounds, and if he does not do so, and they get upon the unenclosed grounds of his neighbor, it is trespass for which their owner is responsible."

Many conservationists, ranchers, farmers, politicians, and members of the general public recognized that rangelands were deteriorating but accepted this in order to develop the West. Livestock overgrazed, miners prospected everywhere, and homesteaders made their own choices of land to plow. They not only did these things but also were encouraged to do so by the laws of the land, court decisions, and the overall public attitude. Some activities of cattle kings, migrant sheepmen, and homesteaders were regrettable in hindsight but destructive land use was the level that was maintained at the time. In effect, political decisions directed social forces to destroy the range vegetation and to retard its recovery because of "crazy-quilt" landownership patterns. It would seem that the public as well as private interests contributed to rangeland deterioration; the Vale District was just a small example from the whole West. It would also seem appropriate as the price for opening the West for the public to shoulder a part and perhaps all of the rehabilitation of deteriorated public rangelands. The costs to repair the land and the costs of maintenance should be public costs, otherwise the bearer of the cost develops a vested interest.

Table 5. Landownership in the Vale District, Bureau of Land Management, 1961 and 1976

| Land administered by | 1961 | | 1976 | |
|---|---|---|---|---|
| | Acres[1] | Percent | Acres[1] | Percent |
| Bureau of Land Management: | | | | |
| Public lands | 4,578,311 | 70.01 | 4,604,878 | 71.12 |
| BLM reserved lands | 6,833 | .01 | 58,438 | .90 |
| Other Federal | 53,674 | .83 | 21,778 | .34 |
| Non-Federal | 304,900 | 4.66 | 298,920 | 4.62 |
| Total | 4,943,718 | 75.60 | 4,984,014 | 76.98 |
| Other: | | | | |
| Federal lands | 128,465 | 1.97 | 27,560 | .42 |
| Private and State | 1,466,633 | 22.43 | 1,463,191 | 22.60 |
| Total | 1,595,098 | 24.40 | 1,490,751 | 23.02 |
| Total | 6,538,816 | 100.00 | 6,474,765 | 100.00 |

Source: Bureau of Land Management.

[1] 1 acre equals 0.405 hectare.

With passage of the Taylor Grazing Act in 1934, a major step was taken to rectify the land use problem on the public domain. The purpose of the act was "to preserve the land and its resources from destruction or unnecessary injury, to provide for the orderly use, improvements, and development of the range." This act followed the various homestead acts, and technically marked the end of that era. Cattlemen, sheepmen, and farmers had been fighting over land for 50 years. Submission to the new law was difficult. Regulations, such as issuance of permits, determinations of grazing capacities, setting of allotment boundaries, improvements to be constructed, formulas to set grazing fees, and other administrative ground rules came in to play gradually.

Allocation of grazing privileges quickly became the principal issue. Final preference was to be given to those with commensurate property but the demand outstripped the supply of AUM's of grazing. Therefore, in practice, first priority grazing privileges went to those with commensurate property and prior use during a 5-year period before passage of the law.

The new Grazing Service depended on advisory boards elected by the permittees to set grazing capacities and priorities of use. Persons most influential in the community became board members, thus assuming positions of power. Migrant sheepmen were out; the permittee's grazing rights were not always proportionally reduced when cuts had to be made; correct data on base properties were not marshalled; Federal expenditures were supervised; and advisory boards selected and determined tenure of Federal employees. These were a few of the powers rightly or wrongly exercised by some of the advisory boards. The one in the Vale District was notable for its independence and power. Its principal purposes were to maintain the status quo of range use and lowest possible grazing fees.

An example of the dispute was described by Foss (1960) as the "Battle of Soldier Creek." Soldier Creek is a grazing unit near Jordan Valley in the central part of the district. In 1935 the commensurate base for the unit was set at 77,419 AUM's, but the advisory board set grazing capacity at 43,260 AUM's. A range survey in 1951 set the grazing capacity at 31,284 AUM's; but the permittees continued to demand 77,419 AUM's, although many fewer AUM's were being used. In 1956 a careful study that marshalled data on base property indicated an eligibility for 31,000 AUM's. After numerous meetings that number was accepted and the dispute was over. Many more details may be found in the publication by Foss (1960).

The ranchers in the Soldier Creek unit were anxious to maintain their ranges and to stay in business. They built fences, developed additional water and, in a few instances, controlled sagebrush. Migrant sheep were eliminated in 1934 and 1935. Throughout the period, the ranchers were improving their stewardship of the land as well as attempting to protect their positions in arguments with the Federal agencies over permitted livestock numbers. It is incorrect to describe either side as totally right or wrong in the "Battle of Soldier Creek."

## Vegetation before Grazing by Domestic Animals

Although a few head of horses may have grazed in the district as early as 1818 when Donald McKenzie sent trappers to follow the Owyhee River, heavy stocking probably began with the discovery of gold in 1863. Evidence from many sources, most of it circumstantial, contributed to the development of our visualization of the pristine climax vegetation in 1863.

Oliphant (1968) cites writings of Harvey H. Hines, a Methodist minister, who stated, in 1882, that the lower Malheur River plains were covered with sage, but that was nearly 40 years after people crossed from Snake River to Vale as a part of the Oregon Trail. The surveyor-general of Idaho reported some lands in Oregon and Nevada as grazed-out in 1871. Vale (1975) reviewed 29 journals and diaries of early travelers who mainly followed river routes in the sagebrush-grass region - none of the 29 travelled extensively in the Vale District. They reported abundance of sagebrush on lower slopes and terraces and large amounts of grass at upper elevations. Hines also described the higher country south of Vale, Oregon, in 1882 as mostly covered with bunchgrass.

In addition to grazing influences, range fires were set by Indians both before and after white men arrived (Oliphant 1968). Lightning caused fire then as it does today. Introduced plants, such as Russian thistle (*Salsola kali*), Halogeton, and cheatgrass had not arrived. In the last 20 years, plant succession has moved rapidly toward climax as a result of managed grazing, according to the data now available. Exclosures, one as old as 40 years, have been studied. Plots of various ages also gave us information on successional trends. We pieced together this information as our best guess of the original climax vegetation in the Vale District. Excellent publications by Daubenmire (1970) and Franklin and Dyrness (1969, 1973) include discussions of stable vegetation as it was before the advent of Caucasian man. We found that those publications contained accurate descriptions of the vegetation in the district.

There are two major types of pristine vegetation in the Vale District. One type was dominated by big sagebrush and bluebunch wheatgrass (Fig. 11). Shrub cover remained less than 25 percent and may have been near zero following fires. We have no evidence that big sagebrush can be eliminated from this vegetation nor that it covered as much area as grass did. Other species characterized the type according to elevation, soil, and rainfall. Sandberg bluegrass and squirreltail were in dry areas; low sage replaced big sage on shallow stony soils; Idaho fescue and bitterbrush reached codominance with bluebunch wheatgrass and big sagebrush at upper elevations. This combination composed the understory in juniper and ponderosa pine. Other minor species included Thurber needlegrass (*Stipa thurberiana*), prairie junegrass (*Koeleria cristata*), needle-and-thread (*Stipa comata*), and several shrubs. This grassland with shrubs scattered or in moderately thick stands, but always variable, extended over at least 90 percent of the district. At any one time, the landscape probably showed a mosaic of sagebrush densities, with low density following fire and a gradual increase until the next fire occurred.

The second major vegetation type grew on alkaline soils and was composed primarily of shrubs. Shadscale dominated; and others included spiny hopsage (*Eurotia lanata*), budsage, and greasewood. Bluebunch wheatgrass occurred in the type but larger amounts of squirreltail and Indian ricegrass (*Oryzopsis hymenoides*) characterized the landscape. The grass dominated if the soil was sandy. This type occupied about 6 percent of the district.

Fig. 11.  Bluebunch wheatgrass and big sagebrush.

We offer several other descriptive points about the pristine vegetation. Grasses
occurred between widely spaced shrubs as well as under their canopies. Without
grazing or fire, large amounts of litter accumulated in the centers of some of the
bunchgrasses. Grazed or burned bluebunch wheatgrass plants often appeared more
vigorous than those left untouched for years. The pristine vegetation, of course,
did not contain several introduced species, which are present in today's climax
vegetation. Riparian communities, wet meadows, lakebeds, and rocky and barren areas
occupied small acreages in the district. The native grasses did not burn as readily
as cheatgrass.

## Destruction of Cover

Reconstruction of the pattern of range deterioration as shown by vegetation can only
be done in general terms. Exploitive grazing after 1878, and perhaps locally before
that date, probably reduced the perennial bunchgrasses from the interspaces among the
shrubs. Annuals may have invaded the bare ground; but one must keep in mind that
Russian thistle, cheatgrass, and other introduced plants had not arrived. Therefore,
the invading species probably were the unpalatables such as poisonous species and
shrubs, including big sagebrush and rabbitbrush. Many more animals were lost to
poisonous plants before 1934 than afterwards. Also, the sagebrush thickened, in
some examples becoming monocultures with few other plants (Fig. 12). A temporary
halt, or a couple of years of rest and recovery, occurred following the livestock
die-off in the winter of 1889-90. The lowest point in the vegetational destruction
and bare soil probably occurred between 1900 and 1920. Griffiths (1902), following
his observations between Winnemucca, Nevada, and Ontario, Oregon, in 1901, reported
finding large areas of bare soil and traveling 1-3 days across deteriorated ranges.
Sandberg bluegrass, which matures in early spring, probably remained in the openings;
but the dominant grasses were found only in the protection of shrubs and rocks.
They may have disappeared altogether from sizable acreages, especially those burned.
Russian thistle arrived about 1900 and was followed by mustards (*Brassica* spp.,
*Sisymbrium* spp.). Invasion by cheatgrass about 1915 and its spread over large areas
of rangeland during the 1920's (Stewart and Hull 1949, USDA Forest Service 1914)
increased ground cover and provided a flash fuel and scanty forage, but more than
had been produced for a few years. Fires which were common in the 1860's to 1880's
again became common. Stands of pure sagebrush burn only with high winds.

It seems to us that plant succession toward increased cover, less erosion, and at
least some grass forage production was underway by 1934 and continued thereafter.
Stages of succession as suggested by Piemeisel (1938, 1951) for big sagebrush-grass
in the Burley BLM District in Idaho apply here. The climax appears to be similar,
and the same species are present. Russian thistle is the first on bare soil. Next
come the mustards and other annual forbs; cheatgrass soon follows (Fig. 13).
Cheatgrass and Sandberg bluegrass may last for years as pure stand where burning
removes the sagebrush, or the combination may be closely associated with brush
stands (Fig. 14).

## Pattern of Range Deterioration

In the Vale District, as elsewhere, ranges suffer most near water and centers of
human population. The first area overgrazed occurred along the Oregon Trail, which
crossed the northeast corner of the district from the mouth of the Boise River into
Snake River to Vale and north to Farewell Bend of the Snake River. The trail was
broad, and livestock were moved outward to find feed. Even today that belt has
some of the poorest condition ranges in the district. Other points of population
concentrations and high livestock pressures include those around Westfall, Harper,
Rome, and to a lesser extent near Jordan Valley and McDermitt. The areas where
damage occurred latest and perhaps not to a serious extent because of lack of water

are exemplified by bits of country near Skull Springs south of Harper and Antelope Creek northeast of McDermitt.

Fig. 12.  Severe grazing resulted in monocultures of big sagebrush on these sites (Bureau of Land Management photos).

Fig. 13.  Big sagebrush and rabbitbrush with a complete stand
          of cheatgrass.

Fig. 14.  Big sagebrush and Sandberg bluegrass precedes the
          climax.

Until permanent stock water was developed after 1934, the remote areas were grazed in the spring and the livestock removed to the creeks, rivers, and other permanent waters as temporary water failed. Nomadic bands of sheep moved through the district, repeatedly grazing in the spring as one band followed another. In short, the uncontrolled grazing led to centers of destruction concentrated around the villages. These destroyed areas were located at the lowest elevations where temperatures were hottest, rainfall least, and the dry season longest. They remain the areas of rangeland in the district needing the greatest repair and at the same time they are the hardest to fix. Unfortunately, the destroyed areas are the first and most often seen by the population, resulting in a widely held belief that the Vale Rehabilitation Program has largely failed. As will be shown later in this report, the opposite is true.

*Wild Animals 1776-1962*

During October 1776, Father Escalante, a Franciscan friar, led a party westward across northern Utah to Utah Lake and southward to Arizona. He made no mention of deer and elk, seen earlier in Colorado, and experienced difficulty in finding food (Utah State Fish and Game Commission 1948). In 1826, Peter Skene Ogden found deer in abundance along the Snake River near the mouth of the Malheur River; but they were scarce across Oregon to the west, occurring locally. Also he reported antelope in places (Davies *et al.* 1961). Apparently, buffalo, antelope, elk, and deer were present near Salt Lake, in southeastern Idaho (Williams *et al.* 1971), and in eastern Oregon. In March 1826, Ogden's men found elk near the present site of Twin Falls in southern Idaho; but 3 months later the party was eating horsemeat during their travels along the headwaters of the Bruneau and Owyhee Rivers (Cline 1974). Clearly, the populations of elk, deer, antelope, and buffalo were small in the northern intermountain region when the fur trappers crisscrossed the Owyhee region from 1818 to 1830. Beaver, the objective of the expeditions, varied in density from stream to stream.

Wild animal species reach their highest populations in relation to abundance of food and water, which supplies individual needs, and to sufficient cover and space, where the species finds its needs for reproduction and running room (Thomas *et al.* 1976). Preceding sections described probable vegetational characteristics in 1863 and the likely changes which followed. This section characterizes the changing food and cover for wildlife just as it does for livestock. For example, nearly all accounts of mule deer described them as scarce in the early climax vegetation and abundant in the shrub stage of succession from the 1920's to the mid-1960's. Poor or fair cattle range would provide excellent browse for deer. Sagegrouse also do well in sagebrush but antelope reach peak numbers in grasslands. Each species has its own best habitat, but these may be difficult to define.

The migrating species use selected sites and vary in density seasonally as well as by location. The trapping expeditions may have missed the migrations, but as with livestock, the centers of concentration should have been near water. Beaver were not plentiful on all streams. It seems fair to suggest that man's use of the range has affected the different species to various degrees. The habitat may have improved for some species and deteriorated for others. Causes for changes in numbers of wild animals are not clear.

Several points need to be kept in mind when wildlife is considered in references to rangeland changes brought about by livestock and rehabilitation practices. Grassland may be the best for some species, sagebrush-grass for others, and sagebrush with bare ground between plants for others. The rangeland manager must know these ideal habitats for individual wild species, know how to attain them, evaluate which species the public wants, and judge the situation long enough in advance to finish the work project. None of these four requirements can be determined sufficiently

for any wildlife species on the Vale District, although the rehabilitation program
has considered them.  The situations for a few of the 294 animal species in the
district will be given in a later section as an evaluation of the rehabilitation
programs.  Data on individual species numbers before 1962 are too nebulous to
warrant further discussions (Bureau of Land Management [n.d.]).


*Range Rehabilitation Prior to 1962*

No more than 0.1 percent of the rangeland in the Vale District had received a range
improvement treatment prior to 1962.  This included about 30,000 acres (12 000 ha)
of brush control by spraying, plowing and seeding, and seeding after wildfires.
Approximately 582 livestock watering points had received attention by ranchers and
BLM personnel.  Several drift fences had been constructed, but pastures had not been
enclosed nor seasonal grazing plans established.  The scatter of the projects prior
to 1962 is shown in Fig. 15; but at the map scale used, only groups of water
developments could be shown.

The negative side or lack of management prior to 1962 needs to be mentioned in order
to emphasize conditions at the beginning of the Vale Program in the fall of 1962.
No grazing systems were in effect beyond stipulation of allotment boundaries and
dates of grazing.  Permitted numbers of livestock and AUM's of grazing may or may
not have been the same as actual use because BLM personnel were too few to make
effective checks on trespass livestock.  Erosion control with gully plugs, fire-
breaks, and construction of recreational sites had not been done.  Resource surveys
had covered approximately 30 percent of the public land, and adjudications to determine commensurate property qualifications had been completed for less than half the
permittees.

Contributions to rangeland management by the permittees was perhaps in the same
order of magnitude as by the BLM.  Ranchers, either cooperatively with BLM or at
their own expense, constructed almost 500 miles (800 km) of fence and developed
numerous watering facilities.  Ranchers did the fence repairs and maintenance.
The start toward range rehabilitation before 1962 came as a cooperative effort
between the BLM and the permittees - contrary to many stories in the public press
which condemned the ranchers for being interested only in range destruction.

Range research at the Squaw Butte Experiment Station near Burns, Oregon, and in the
sagebrush-grass type added still another factor that made the Vale Program feasible.
The station superintendent emphasized in talks to ranchers and BLM personnel that
a twofold increase in AUM's could be attained.  Six management practices were
needed: (1) more water to improve animal distribution, (2) more riding to scatter
the cows, (3) sagebrush control by spraying, (4) seeding of crested wheatgrass
(*Agropyron cristatum* and *A. desertorum*), (5) adjustments in opening and closing
dates of grazing, and (6) providing sufficient winter feed.  These practices had
increased annual meat production per cow on the Squaw Butte Station from 150
pounds (70 kg) in 1946 to approximately 400 pounds (180 kg) in 1960 (Bureau of Land
Management [n.d.]).

Thus, the district was ready in 1961 for a range rehabilitation program: (1) Range
condition was poor and, if not deteriorating, certainly not improving; (2) open
controversies indicated that a new program was needed; (3) a start at cooperation
had been made; (4) information on what to do and how to do it was available;
(5) local people, politicians, and the BLM were anxious to accomplish a land
management program in place of wasting resources on disagreements over adjudication
of grazing permits.  The need for funds forced all parties to turn to Congress for
help.

THE VALE REHABILITATION PROGRAM

*The Original Proposal*

The original proposal was prepared as a 28-page document by personnel of the Vale
District of the Bureau of Land Management.  It gave concrete suggestions for halting
range deterioration in southeastern Oregon.  A paragraph quoted from a letter
written by three members of the Oregon State BLM Advisory Board on February 19,
1962, indicates the praise and enthusiasm by people in Oregon for the proposal:
    The Bureau has had inadequate funds to improve the range and has, therefore,
    been forced to evaluate carrying capacities with little hope of improvement.
    This plan provides for positive improvement and continuous evaluation while
    improvement is underway.  It also provides for adjudication on the basis of
    actual use supported by observations of range condition and trend.  These
    things can be accomplished with adequate money and personnel.

Contingent upon funding by Congress, the project proposal specifically offered
". . . a solution to the national problem of depleted and deteriorating public
rangelands.  It proposes to do so without seriously impairing the livestock
industry and supporting local economies.  The Vale District would be a practical
demonstration of the government's ability, through the BLM and the Department of
the Interior, to solve a critical national problem."  The objectives were ". . .
a seven-year development program with emphasis on rehabilitation measures designed
to protect and improve the soil, conserve and utilize the water, and increase
forage for livestock and wildlife.  It also considers the needs for recreational
development and construction of service roads and related measures that will
strengthen and improve the local economy" (Bureau of Land Management [n.d.]).

The Vale proposal specifically listed eight objectives:
1.  To correct erosion and accompanying downstream sedimentation - and prevent
    further soil losses.
2.  To increase the forage supply for wildlife and livestock.
3.  To stabilize the livestock industry at the present or an increased level of
    production.
4.  To facilitate fire control by replacing high hazard cheatgrass and sagebrush
    with low hazard perennial grasses and improving detection and suppression
    facilities.
5.  To prevent the encroachment and spread of noxious and poisonous weeds.
6.  To accomplish necessary land tenure adjustments.
7.  To safeguard public lands from improper recreational use.
8.  To provide for the development of access roads and service roads in the vast
    areas of untapped recreation potential.

The procedures to carry out these eight objectives were not specifically stated,
although particular methods such as brush eradication, range seeding, and water
development plans were mentioned in the proposal.  The proposal encouraged the
development of a particular plan or project for each specific area to satisfy the
objectives.  The program needed to be flexible as lessons were certain to become
apparent from mistakes during the first few years.  In fact, the Vale Program
could be a model for other land treatment programs in addition to the direct
results of the program itself.

Contrary to earlier range improvement programs, this one emphasized wildlife,
recreational facilities, and watershed values.  People expert in these subject areas
contributed to the proposal and to the individual projects from the beginning.

*Passage through Congress*

Easy passage of the Vale Program proposal through Congress resulted from the emergence of several coincidental factors. First, the early 1960's marked the end of the bulk of legal action by Federal range users to delay implementation of cuts in permits as a result of adjudication. Second, this period marked a re-emphasis on conservation by the Federal government. Third, Senator Wayne Morse of Oregon, a long-time critic of BLM policy, was a candidate for re-election in 1962. With Congressman Al Ullman, Morse became an ardent supporter of the Vale proposal. These two men guided the passage of the special appropriations bill funding the Vale Program. Local support for the proposal and little opposition gave both Morse and Ullman direction to help southeastern Oregon, an area that had been troublesome to them for several years.

Certain specific recommendations, such as seeding to crested wheatgrass and the priority of various land treatment activities raised questions. A proposal on such a large scale caused many to wonder at its feasibility, but the obvious and real local benefits of such a program were never in doubt. The unwavering support of congressional sponsors, strong local encouragement, and a clearly written and well-planned proposal for implementation made possible the passage and funding of the program as a special appropriation in the Federal budget in the summer of 1962. Some money was spent before allocation of the funds occurred in September 1962. The first large-scale projects in the Vale Program began in the Cow Creek unit in summer of 1962.

*Budget*

The original proposal for the Vale Program estimated the total cost at $16,230,460 for 7 years. Cost for the first 2 years was to be $2,505,000, but Congress appropriated $2,071,789. From the beginning, the concepts, scheduling, and funding frequently changed from the original proposal. For example, an extensive 2-year range survey to identify suitable sites for treatment was immediately modified at the requests of Ullman and Morse. They wanted more money and more efforts put immediately into land treatment than the BLM had planned. Further, congressional backing apparently was in jeopardy without immediate on-the-ground results from rehabilitation efforts. Thus the range survey extended for 3 years, and several treatments were undertaken prior to thorough site evaluations. The program extended over an 11-year period and used total funds of about $10 million.

*Land Treatment Projects*

Land treatments were accelerated early in the program, and later slowed considerably due to receipt of less funds than requested. One hundred and sixty-four land treatment projects were finished (Fig. 16). Table 6 lists them by name, year, acreage, treatment, and the location number in Fig. 16, providing an easy reference for location of results mentioned throughout this report. At the end of the formal Vale Program in 1973, some aspects of the program goals were exceeded; others were not met (Table 7).

The number of projects, acreages, miles of pipelines, number of new watering points, and magnitude of other improvements are subject to considerable interpretation. For example, a few areas underwent several treatments on the same acreage following failures. We treated these as separate projects. In other situations, we were seldom certain whether an acreage was for a pasture or for a treatment that nearly filled a pasture; or if the acreage given was the contracted rather than the completed acreage. Sometimes assumptions of size had to be made in order to evaluate costs, benefits, and grazing capacity. Wherever possible we have chosen to evaluate the overall Vale Program, thereby minimizing, but not eliminating, the importance of accurate data on individual projects.  Although some of our data varies from that of others, we have selected what appears to us to be the best available.

Table 6.  Land treatment projects in the Vale District,
Bureau of Land Management, 1952-73

| Year | Number[1] | Name | Acres[2] | Treatment |
|------|-----------|------|----------|-----------|
| 1952 | 1 | Ten Mile seeding | 2,700 | Plow/seed |
| 1955 | 2 | Soldier Creek seeding | 2,015 | Plow/seed |
| 1960 | 3 | Mud Flat seeding | 400 | Plow/seed |
|      | 4 | Beulah seeding | 1,150 | Fire/seed |
| 1961 | 5 | McCain Springs seeding | 2,675 | Fire/seed |
|      | 6 | Jordan Valley seeding | 1,575 | Fire/seed |
|      | 7 | Downey Canyon seeding | 1,429 | Fire/plow/seed |
|      | 8 | Brickey Springs seeding | 2,744 | Plow/seed |
|      | 9 | Gluch seeding | 3,567 | Spray/seed |
|      | 10 | Whitehorse brush control | 10,400 | Spray |
| 1962 | 11 | Mormon Basin seeding | 919 | Fire/seed |
|      | 12 | Tableland brush control | 2,500 | Spray |
|      | 13 | Hooker Creek seeding | 2,292 | Fire/plow/seed |
|      | 14 | Jordan Valley brush control | 1,098 | Spray |
|      | 15 | Rock Creek seeding | 1,800 | Plow/seed |
|      | 16 | Monument brush control | 1,800 | Spray |
|      | 17 | Monument seeding | 1,800 | Fire/seed |
| 1963 | 18 | Mormon Basin brush control | 360 | Spray |
|      | 19 | Horse Flat brush control | 2,773 | Spray |
|      | 20 | Poverty Flat brush control | 1,050 | Spray |
|      | 21 | Mesa brush control | 4,047 | Spray |
|      | 22 | Drip Springs brush control | 4,003 | Spray |
|      | 23 | Tunnel Canyon brush control | 5,920 | Spray |
|      | 24 | Bas brush control | 3,800 | Spray |
|      | 25 | Owyhee Butte seeding | 9,265 | Plow |
|      | 26 | Schnable Creek seeding | 2,015 | Fire/plow/seed |
|      | 27 | Rome seedings | 7,785 | Plow/seed |
|      | 28 | Sheep Springs seeding | 685 | Plow/seed |
|      | 29 | Starvation brush control | 20,098 | Spray |
|      | 30 | Indian Canyon brush control | 2,650 | Spray |
| 1964 | 31 | Love seeding | 375 | Plow/seed |
|      | 32 | Vines Hill seeding | 1,800 | Fire/seed |
|      | 33 | Chicken Creek seeding | 4,464 | Plow/seed |
|      | 34 | Page seeding | 4,400 | Fire/seed |
|      | 35 | Warm Springs brush control | 7,713 | Spray |
|      | 36 | Winter Springs seeding | 2,222 | Plow/seed |
|      | 37 | Sand Hollow seeding | 3,300 | Plow/seed |
|      | 38 | Granite Creek brush control | 3,550 | Spray |
|      | 39 | Top brush control | 9,560 | Spray |
|      | 40 | Rockville seeding | 3,600 | Plow/seed |

continued

See footnotes at end of table.

Table 6. Continued

| Year | Number[1] | Name | Acres[2] | Treatment |
|------|-----------|------|----------|-----------|
| 1964 | 41 | Lodge brush control | 6,500 | Spray |
|      | 42 | Old Maid seeding | 1,900 | Plow/seed |
|      | 43 | Sticky Joe seeding | 700 | Plow/seed |
|      | 44 | China Gulch seeding | 2,116 | Fire/seed |
|      | 45 | Jaca seeding | 2,650 | Spray/seed |
|      | 46 | Chimney Creek brush control | 12,180 | Spray |
|      | 47 | Indian Canyon seeding | 2,350 | Spray/seed |
|      | 48 | Starvation seeding | 13,910 | Spray/seed |
|      | 49 | Frenchman Creek seeding | 1,480 | Plow/seed |
| 1965 | 50 | Agency Ridge seeding | 294 | Plow/seed |
|      | 51 | Hope Butte seeding | 2,622 | Plow/seed |
|      | 52 | N.G. Creek seeding | 4,593 | Plow/seed |
|      | 53 | Harper seeding | 1,155 | Plow/seed |
|      | 54 | North Chicken Creek Maintenance seeding | 1,000 | Follow up seeding |
|      | 55 | Cottonwood seeding | 4,465 | Plow/seed |
|      | 56 | Lower Clover Creek seeding | 1,459 | Plow/seed |
|      | 57 | Lava Ridge seeding | 1,000 | Plow/seed |
|      | 58 | Juntura seeding | 589 | Plow/seed |
|      | 59 | Juniper Basin seeding | 692 | Plow/seed |
|      | 60 | Little Valley seeding | 691 | Plow/seed |
|      | 61 | Callahan brush control | 11,070 | Spray |
|      | 62 | Double Mountain brush control | 8,400 | Spray |
|      | 63 | Creston brush control | 3,100 | Spray |
|      | 64 | Blue Canyon brush control | 10,000 | Spray |
|      | 65 | Little Sandy seeding | 2,900 | Plow/seed |
|      | 66 | China Gulch "B" seeding | 3,700 | Plow/seed |
|      | 67 | Greeley seeding | 4,000 | Plow/seed |
|      | 68 | Bull Creek seeding | 3,000 | Plow/seed |
|      | 69 | Beber seeding | 870 | Plow/seed |
|      | 70 | Battle Creek seeding | 8,800 | Plow/seed |
|      | 71 | Steer Canyon seeding | 6,100 | Plow/seed |
|      | 72 | Oregon Canyon brush control | 3,186 | Spray |
|      | 73 | Andy Fife brush control | 3,540 | Spray |
| 1966 | 74 | Mormon Basin "B" seeding | 740 | Spray/seed |
|      | 75 | Farewell Bend seeding | 1,045 | Plow/seed |
|      | 76 | Bierman Springs seeding | 1,440 | Plow/seed |
|      | 77 | Beulah seeding | 460 | Plow/seed |
|      | 78 | Radar Hill seeding | 1,005 | Plow/seed |
|      | 79 | Westfall seeding | 340 | Plow/seed |
|      | 80 | East Cow Hollow seeding | 800 | Plow/seed |
|      | 81 | Needham Well seeding | 995 | Seed only |
|      | 82 | Slaughter Gulch brush control | 12,376 | Spray |
|      | 83 | Mosquito Creek seeding | 1,910 | Plow/seed |
|      | 84 | Squaw Creek seeding | 980 | Plow/seed |
|      | 85 | Rye Field seeding | 3,400 | Seed only |
|      | 86 | Board Corrals brush control | 4,350 | Spray |
|      | 87 | Owyhee Canyon brush control | 14,000 | Spray |
|      | 88 | Owyhee Butte "B" seeding | 300 | Plow/seed |

continued

See footnotes at end of table.

Table 6. Continued

| Year | Number[1] | Name | Acres[2] | Treatment |
|------|-----------|------|----------|-----------|
| 1966 | 89  | Pascoe seeding             | 1,950  | Plow/seed       |
|      | 90  | Field Fire brush control   | 4,600  | Spray           |
|      | 91  | Dry Creek seeding          | 3,195  | Plow/seed       |
|      | 92  | Greeley brush control      | 2,000  | Spray           |
|      | 93  | Rock Creek brush control   | 2,500  | Spray           |
|      | 94  | Black Butte brush control  | 2,000  | Spray           |
|      | 95  | Overshoe Pass seeding      | 7,345  | Spray           |
|      | 96  | Sheep Corrals brush control| 2,785  | Spray           |
|      | 97  | Oregon Canyon seeding      | 4,950  | Spray/seed      |
|      | 98  | Schoolhouse seeding        | 3,855  | Spray/seed      |
|      | 99  | Flat Top seeding           | 2,864  | Spray/seed      |
| 1967 | 100 | Bully Creek seeding        | 691    | Spray/seed      |
|      | 101 | Willow Creek seeding       | 2,180  | Spray/seed      |
|      | 102 | Swamp Creek seeding        | 1,150  | Plow/seed       |
|      | 103 | Lincoln Bench brush control| 1,700  | Spray           |
|      | 104 | Antelope Flat seeding      | 1,313  | Plow/seed       |
|      | 105 | Spring Creek seeding       | 2,040  | Plow/seed       |
|      | 106 | Big Ridge seeding          | 3,000  | Plow/seed       |
|      | 107 | Field Fire seeding         | 4,600  | Spray/seed      |
|      | 108 | Soldier Creek "B" seeding  | 280    | Plow/seed       |
|      | 109 | Antelope seeding           | 4,500  | Plow/seed       |
|      | 110 | Black Butte seeding        | 1,655  | Plow/seed       |
|      | 111 | Basque seeding             | 3,200  | Spray/seed      |
|      | 112 | Cascade brush control      | 7,950  | Spray           |
|      | 113 | Mine Creek seeding         | 4,846  | Fire/plow/seed  |
|      | 114 | Bretz seeding              | 2,631  | Plow/seed       |
|      | 115 | Angel Canyon seeding       | 4,247  | Plow/seed       |
|      | 116 | Old Jaca seeding           | 3,874  | Spray/seed      |
| 1968 | 117 | Hope Flat seeding          | 1,100  | Plow/seed       |
|      | 118 | Meeker Flat brush control  | 2,520  | Spray           |
|      | 119 | Saddle Butte seeding       | 4,106  | Spray/seed      |
|      | 120 | Sheepheads seeding         | 4,392  | Plow/seed       |
|      | 121 | Turnbull Lake seeding      | 7,430  | Plow/seed       |
|      | 122 | Shellrock brush control    | 5,235  | Spray           |
|      | 123 | Frank Maher Flat seeding   | 2,820  | Spray/seed      |
|      | 124 | Bankofier seeding          | 3,610  | Plow/seed       |
|      | 125 | Haystack Butte brush control | 3,388 | Spray          |
|      | 126 | Red Butte brush control    | 8,340  | Spray           |
| 1969 | 127 | Buckbrush seeding          | 850    | Plow/seed       |
|      | 128 | North Harper seeding       | 2,687  | Fire/seed       |
|      | 129 | Hunter brush control       | 10,350 | Spray           |
|      | 130 | Quicksand Springs brush control | 5,400 | Spray        |
|      | 131 | Upper Meadow seeding       | 540    | Plow/seed       |
|      | 132 | Stockade brush control     | 3,122  | Spray           |
|      | 133 | West Crater brush control  | 11,637 | Spray           |
|      | 134 | Spring Basin seeding       | 1,740  | Plow/seed       |
|      | 135 | Spring Mountain seeding    | 616    | Plow/seed       |

continued

See footnotes at end of table.

Table 6. Continued

| Year | Number[1] | Name | Acres[2] | Treatment |
|------|-----------|------|----------|-----------|
| 1969 | 136 | Falen seeding | 395 | Plow/seed |
|      | 137 | Barlow brush control | 2,833 | Spray |
|      | 138 | Twelve Mile seeding | 2,015 | Plow/seed |
|      | 139 | Sheepline brush control | 1,345 | Spray |
|      | 140 | Upper Whitehorse brush control | 891 | Spray |
|      | 141 | Lazy T Pasture brush control | 1,315 | Spray |
|      | 142 | Rim Basin seeding | 1,510 | Plow/seed |
|      | 143 | Arritola Reservoir seeding | 400 | Plow/seed |
| 1970 | 144 | Rufino Butte brush control | 10,321 | Spray |
|      | 145 | Rabbit Farm seeding | 2,093 | Plow/seed |
|      | 146 | McIntyre brush control | 1,050 | Spray |
|      | 147 | Sulfur Springs seeding | 1,437 | Plow/seed |
|      | 148 | Summit brush control | 3,208 | Spray |
|      | 149 | Jackson Creek brush control | 4,750 | Spray |
|      | 150 | Mud Springs brush control | 2,013 | Spray |
|      | 151 | Pole Creek Seeding | 3,010 | Spray |
|      | 152 | Wildcat brush control | 6,115 | Spray |
| 1971 | 153 | Needham Well seeding | 995 | Reseed |
|      | 154 | Freezeout Lake seeding | 475 | Plow/seed |
|      | 155 | Carter Creek seeding | 3,600 | Plow/seed |
| 1972 | 156 | Freezeout Butte brush control | 3,535 | Spray |
|      | 157 | Willow Butte seeding | 3,310 | Plow/seed |
|      | 158 | Buckskin seeding | 4,960 | Plow/seed |
|      | 159 | Fish Creek seeding | 5,000 | Plow/seed |
|      | 160 | Boulevard seeding | 175 | Fire/seed |
|      | 161 | Baker Creek brush control | 4,760 | Spray |
| 1973 | 162 | Brassy Mountain seeding | 1,675 | Fire/seed |
|      | 163 | Tunnel Canyon seeding | 2,500 | Fire/seed |
|      | 164 | Bogus Creek seeding | 7,415 | Fire/seed |

[1] Numbers refer to locations in Figs. 15 and 16.

[2] 1 acre equals 0.405 hectare.

## THE RANGELAND REHABILITATION OPERATION

*District Planning*

Planning in the Vale District contributed to the success of the program.  Division
of the district into three management areas, called resource areas, with separate
managers spread the workload and responsibilities.  The resource areas were further
divided into 14 planning units, which continued to be the basis for planning.
Area managers proposed and developed improvement plans, projects, and grazing
systems with considerable autonomy.  Thus, the mixture of management practices and

land treatments differed among the three resource areas.  Various differences among
the divisions exist today, and they will be discussed in later sections of this
report.

Table 7.  Original goals and actual accomplishments of Vale
          District Program, Bureau of Land Management,
          through 1973

| Treatment or management aid | Unit[1] | Program goal | Units completed as of 1973 | Percent of goal |
|---|---|---|---|---|
| Brush control | Acres | 730,000 | 506,570[2] | 69 |
| Seeding | Acres | 410,000 | 267,193 | 65 |
| Fencing | Miles | 2,000 | 1,994 | 100 |
| Reservoirs | Each | 400 | 583 | 146 |
| Springs | Each | 500 | 440 | 88 |
| Wells | Each | 100 | 28 | 28 |
| Pipelines | Miles | 120 | 462.9 | 385 |
| Water troughs | Each | 640 | 538 | 84 |
| Cattle guards | Each | 500 | 360 | 72 |
| Test plots and exclosures | Each | 79 | 69 | 87 |
| Costs | Million dollars | 16 | 10 | 63 |

[1] 1 acre equals 0.405 hectare; 1 mile equals 1.6 kilometers.

[2] Total brush control acreage; 280,407 acres were control of
    brush only, not seeded.  Some 41,000 acres were seeded with-
    out brush control.

Area managers initiated planning and site selection which was consolidated into
district plans.  The final authority for the coordinated program rested with the
district manager who supervised staff personnel responsible for range conservation
and development, wildlife management, engineering, watershed protection, land
tenure problems, administration, public information, and program coordinations.
District personnel include about 75 persons on a permanent basis and another 75
during the field and fire season.

*Site Selection*

The original program proposed a 2-year survey of 2,660,000 acres (1 000 000 ha) and improvement planning for 4,000,000 acres (1 620 000 ha) to aid in location of land treatments (Bureau of Land Management [n.d.]). Plowing, spraying, seeding, fencing, water development, and other practices were to follow careful planning. Shortly after funds became available, the congressional supporters of the program expressed alarm that the first appropriations of more than $2 million would not show in visible results on the land and that any delay in initiation of rehabilitation could jeopardize future funding. BLM responded by immediately beginning land treatments but with fears that poor site selection would generate habitat damage and ineffective treatment, concerns not supported by the results obtained. Starting in the 2nd year of the program, a resource survey enabled site selection to proceed according to plan as modified by the level of funding.

Wisely, the Vale Program proposal required selection of sites for treatment based on their potential for improvement. Sites with greatest potential for improvement were treated first. As funding continued, progressively poorer sites were treated. Local needs for additional forage to satisfy obligated animal numbers did not play a major role in site selection. Likelihood of success determined site selection, not degree of range deterioration.

Although several early Vale Program reports stated that the first land treatment projects, due to pressures for immediate results, directed efforts at the most depleted ranges, records do not bear out that conclusion. Sites treated from 1962 to 1964 had an estimated grazing capacity before treatment of between 21 and 24 acres/AUM (8.5-9.7 ha/AUM), higher capacities than lands treated in later years (Fig. 17). The poorest land to be rehabilitated, averaging more than 40 acres/AUM (16 ha/AUM), received treatment in 1967 and 1968. Most areas requiring seeding (preceded by plowing or spraying) and with high site potential had been treated before 1968.

An increased pretreatment grazing capacity in projects after 1968 resulted in part from improved range condition. Native perennial grasses on untreated sites recovered more rapidly than expected, reducing the need for seeding and increasing the effectiveness of spray-only treatments. Two-thirds of the pre-1969 projects (64 of 95) but only one-third (9 of 25) of the post-1968 projects included seeding. Thus, successful early treatment and improved livestock management resulted in a shift in emphasis from plow-and-seed to spray-only. Lack of suitable sites for spraying did not limit the projects from 1969 to 1972. The criteria for site selection and type of treatment changed in 1969 in response to improving range conditions.

The selection of a specific site for treatment and the determination of treatment specifications involved a complex set of factors and criteria, many of which were never formalized or recorded. Primarily, site selection necessitated building the level of judgment by range conservationists to a degree that recommendations were correct biologically and effective managerially. Some of the value judgments that proved effective were: Adequate native perennial grasses as an understory in sagebrush required only a spraying and livestock control to improve the grass stand; but "adequate perennial grasses" was a value judgment through the early program years. Steeply sloping areas, shallow rocky soils, vegetation with substantial browse for wildlife range, and riparian vegetation were not plowed, seeded, or sprayed.

Range sites with few native perennial grasses and with big sagebrush plants over 3 feet tall indicated high site potential for plowing and seeding. Several criteria of potential success emerged from experiences in the first few projects; (1) Plowing and seeding should be done in areas where few or no perennial grasses occur and where mature big sagebrush is at least 3 feet tall. (2) Spray-only should be done where numerous perennial grasses occur in the sagebrush stands. (3) Spraying in the district should not be combined with plow-seed treatments. (4) Drilling of seed after spraying and without plowing proved effective on some rocky soils and moderately steep slopes. (5) Contract specifications for seed bed preparation are more important than stipulations for percent kill of brush.

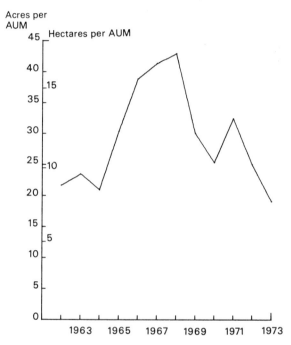

Fig. 17.  Estimated grazing capacity for the project areas immediately prior to treatment (source: project site inspection reports).

Misapplied treatment served to establish these criteria. The native bunchgrasses returned faster than expected. Therefore, some sagebrush sites selected for plowing and seeding could have been sprayed to preserve existing native bunchgrasses. Treatments on old lakebeds frequently failed, and treatments of alkali soils proved unsuccessful.

Considerations of other possible land uses strongly influenced site selection. Beginning in 1963, all land treatment sites were evaluated by the district wildlife biologist and rehabilitation projects were approved by representatives of the Oregon State Game Commission. A few treatments were altered and 11 projects were cancelled to preserve wildlife habitats. Some projects, when executed, did not preserve small areas designated as wildlife habitat due to contractor error and inadequate supervision by BLM personnel. As the program progressed, compatibility between site selection and wildlife habitat requirements improved.

Sixty-nine test plots and exclosures, built before and during the early years of the Vale Program, played a strong role in site selection and stipulation of treatments. Some of the exclosures continue to provide useful vegetational information. Many areas, alkaline soils for example, on which plot responses to treatment were poor, did not show promise for large-scale success and were cancelled from the projects. Conversely, success in plots led to successful projects on areas originally rejected. Test-plot results did not guarantee success. Their use, however, demonstrated the value of pilot tests, a highly important lesson for any large rangeland rehabilitation program.

Uniform distribution of projects (Fig. 16) over the district complemented untreated range throughout. Perhaps land treatment projects were concentrated in certain areas and years. At the beginning an extensive rehabilitation program was already underway in the Soldier Creek Management Unit, southwest of Jordan Valley. As additional funds became available in 1962, BLM concentrated its efforts in the Soldier Creek area. Units without significant improvements are Barren Valley in the west-central region of the district, and Star Valley in the remote southeastern portion of the district. Barren Valley has poor potential for improvement, being primarily winter range. The northern part of the district needs additional rehabilitation.

This program shows that rehabilitation on 10 percent or less of the area will result in rapid improvement of the untreated areas through proper management. Thus, the Vale Program dealt with improvement of the whole district, not just the areas plowed, seeded, and sprayed.

Overall, site selection in the Vale District Program was excellent. Problems with particular areas and combinations of treatments did not materially detract from the excellent job of site selection and rehabilitation. Intimate knowledge of the field situations formed the best basis for selection of land for treatment. Even areas treated in the 1st year of the project were successfully improved because of the familiarity of BLM personnel with the range.

*Brush Control*

Methods to reduce the density of shrub species included plowing, spraying, burning, or some combination of treatments. Although not used as a planned treatment, the *Aroga* moth thinned extensive areas of big sagebrush through defoliation.

Plowing with a disk-plow (Fig. 18) as a method of brush control became standardized early in the Vale Program, and contract specifications changed little once a few projects showed the relative effectiveness and costs of various treatments. As finalized and used, contracts required plowing to a depth of 4-6 inches (10-15 cm), and an estimated 90 percent kill of brush, which often required two passes over the land. Rangeland plowing generally commenced in late summer or fall immediately prior to seed-drilling time and at the direction of BLM personnel. Timing of plowing operations was not particularly important as a factor in percentage brush kill, but it may have been critical in preventing brush seedling establishment. Plowing after seed of big sagebrush had matured probably fostered big sagebrush regeneration. Primary factors in the success of plowing operations were degree of rockiness, slope percentage, and species of brush. Low sagebrush and rabbitbrush resisted plowing. Plowing contracts were closely supervised, well executed, and generally effective.

Plowing contracts went to the low bidder. If all bids were judged excessively high, budget specifications enabled direct land treatment by BLM. A successful contractor furnished labor, the power for pulling government-owned brushland plows, and all necessary maintenance of equipment. Costs of plowing varied greatly due to site and increased from the low figures during early years of the program.

Fig. 18. Removing big sagebrush with a disk-plow (Bureau
of Land Management photo). Inquiries concerning
design and availability of the latest models of
the brushland plow should be addressed to the
USDA, Forest Service Equipment Development Center,
San Dimas, California 91773.

Effects of spraying herbicides to control brush varied much more than plowing.
Contractors applied the specified spray mixture at certain rates over designated
areas (Fig. 19). Although BLM personnel closely supervised most spray operations
and aided in field applications, contractor compliance with specifications was less
easily accomplished and policed than plowing.

The herbicide used, 2,4-D, and the rate, 2 lb acid equivalent per acre (2.2 kg/ha),
did not change throughout the program. Many successful controls of big sagebrush
had been obtained in other places, so experiments with types of herbicides and rates
of application were not required. The herbicide carrier and timing of application
significantly affected percentage kill and hence, the effectiveness of particular
spray operations. In most cases, 2,4-D with a diesel oil carrier killed big sagebrush. Environmental considerations caused substitution of water for diesel oil in
1965, which made accurate timing of application critical. Poor kills of big sagebrush resulted from spraying in 1965 and 1966; however, the water-based herbicide
killed brush even better than herbicide with diesel oil base when specifications
were followed. Applications of 2,4-D was usually made by fixed-wing aircraft, but
occasionally by helicopter.

Every contract for spraying specified that the timing of the operations was to be
regulated by BLM. Soil moisture and plant phenology, as originally recommended on
the Squaw Butte Experiment Station by Hyder and Sneva (1955), were used to indicate
the season for spraying. Heading of Sandberg bluegrass and rapid spring growth

indicate onset of effective spraying conditions. Sufficient soil moisture (more
than 8 percent) for an adequate kill of big sagebrush remains until half the bluegrass leaves have dried. The officer in charge controlled the day-to-day progress
of the operation. Spraying was halted any time that winds exceeded 10 miles per
hour (16 km/h). The timing of operations for maximum kill of big sagebrush often
resulted in unsatisfactory kill of rabbitbrush.

Fig. 19.  Spraying long strips of big sagebrush tends to
cross steep slopes and streams, which should not
be sprayed (Bureau of Land Management photo).

Several spray projects suffered from inadequate compliance with contract specifications, such as the West Crater brush control in which inadequate overlap of spray-
runs resulted in alternate strips of killed and unkilled brush.

The Lodge brush control project in 1964 serves as an example of the procedures in a
spraying operation (Irons 1964). District personnel were in charge and monitored
both spraying the site and loading the aircraft. Three flagmen marked the spray-
runs, and they used two-way radios and four-wheel drive vehicles to keep in line.
The contractor used two converted TBM torpedo bombers of World War II vintage, each
capable of carrying 700 gallons (3 100 liters) of spray. He also furnished the
spray mixture consisting of 2 lb acid equivalent 2,4-D in 3 gallons of diesel oil
per acre (2.2 lb in 11 liters/ha). Thus, each aircraft covered approximately 233
acres (95 ha) per trip. Samples of the spray mixture were taken by BLM personnel
at the airport for analysis. Each trip involved 20 minutes of flying time from
the Homedale airport and 3 minutes for loading. The aircraft flew at an altitude
of 50 feet (15 m), and spray-runs were 190 feet (58 m) wide. Spray extended over
a strip 400 feet (120 m) wide, giving excellent herbicide overlap. This operation

covered 6,500 acres (2 630 ha) between 4:45 a.m. and 4:20 p.m. on May 15, 1964, at
a cost of $2.10 per acre ($5.20/ha).  Winds stayed below 10 m/h (16 km/h), otherwise the operation would have been halted.  Temperature rose from 29°F (-2°C) in
the morning to 65°F (18°C) in the afternoon.  Soil moisture was 12 percent.  The
resulting kill of brush was excellent.

Wildfires frequently followed land treatments, especially sprayings; and all or
part of several projects were swept by fire.  Burning further increased the effectiveness of brush control and left no detectable detrimental effects on forage for
livestock after the 1st year.  Removal of grazing for a year following treatments
permitted fuel to accumulate, thus favoring fires.  Wildfires which burned independ-
ently of brush control treatments also effectively killed sagebrush.  Burned areas
have the lowest average density of sagebrush of any treatment.

An outbreak of *Aroga* moths killed sagebrush in several areas during the early 1960's
just as the Vale Program began.  They did not kill significant amounts of sagebrush
(Fig. 20).  A single project located in the Cherry Creek drainage was cancelled as
a result of *Aroga* kill of sagebrush.  The moth may strip parts of the brush of
leaves, but kill seldom exceeds 10 percent of individual shrubs.

*Seeding*

Seeding followed a variety of land treatments.  All plowed land and some of the
sprayed areas were seeded (Fig. 21).  The plowing, mostly for brush control, also
reduced cheatgrass and other herbaceous competitors and prepared a seed bed.
Seeding usually followed wildfire and failures from previous rehabilitation attempts
without site preparation by plowing.

Fig. 20.  The moth *Aroga* seldom kills the whole bush of big
          sagebrush plants.

Fig. 21.  Top, drilling crested wheatgrass (Bureau of Land
          Management photo).  Bottom, a poor stand of crested
          wheatgrass in cheatgrass after a burn and broadcast
          seeding.  The good stand from the single pass of
          the drill demonstrates the need for drilling.
          Inquiries about the rangeland drill should be
          addressed to the USDA, Forest Service Equipment
          Development Center, San Dimas, California 91773.

Decisions concerning particular practices and whether or not to seed at all
depended on test plots and ocular site evaluations.  Species tested in plots
included crested wheatgrasses, pubescent wheatgrass (*Agropyron trichophorum*), tall
wheatgrass (*A. elongatum*), western wheatgrass (*A. smithii*), yellow sweetclover
(*Melilotus officinalis*), and other clovers (*Trifolium* spp.).  Crested wheatgrass
seldom failed in the plots, and the other plant species seldom succeeded.  The
standard seeding became 7 lb/acre (8 kg/ha) of crested wheatgrass with a rangeland
drill – specifications not significantly modified throughout the program.  The seed,
purchased annually in large commercial lots, consisted of mixed Standard
(*Agropyron desertorum*) and Fairway (*A. cristatum*) crested wheatgrass; at least that
was the appearance of most stands in 1975.

Alkaline soils, shallow rock soils, and a vegetative cover of low sagebrush indicated marginal sites for seeding of crested wheatgrass.  Other species of grasses
and legumes were also planted on such sites.  On a mud flat or dry lakebed, for
example, pubescent wheatgrass at 1.5 lb/acre (1.7 kg/ha), western wheatgrass at
2.6 lb/acre (2.9 kg/ha), tall wheatgrass at 0.75 lb/acre (0.85 kg/ha), crested
wheatgrass at 2 lb/acre (2.3 kg/ha), and strawberry clover (*Trifolium fragiferum*)
at 0.33 lb/acre (0.37 kg/ha) constituted the seed mixture.  Immediately after that
treatment, the seeding contained mainly crested wheatgrass; but by 1975 pubescent
wheatgrass dominated, with only about 5 percent crested wheatgrass.  Nomad alfalfa
(*Medicago sativa*) was seeded on 56,340 acres (22 800 ha) by air in the spring
following fall drilling to crested wheatgrass (Fig. 22).

Fig. 22.  A stand of nomad alfalfa and crested wheatgrass
          (photo, courtesy of R. Kindschy, Bureau of Land
          Management, Vale, Oregon).

Seeding practices drew heavily on methods developed during the 1950's at the Squaw
Butte Experiment Station near Burns, Oregon, and limited experience in range seeding
on the Vale District before the start of the Vale Program.  An early seeding, the
Soldier Creek project (Fig. 15, Number 2), which was plowed with a Wheatland disk-
plow in the fall of 1955 and broadcast seeded with crested wheatgrass at a rate of
6.25 lb/acre (7.1 kg/ha) in the fall, failed because of cheatgrass competition.
The Soldier Creek project cost $13.58/acre ($33.53/ha) for seeding, plowing, water
development, and fencing.

Contract procedures for seeding became standardized in 1962.  An example is the
Sheep Springs project which was plowed twice with Wheatland plows in the fall of
1962 and seeded to crested wheatgrass at 8.5 lb/acre (9.6 kg/ha) in November of
1962 on partially frozen soils.  Costs averaged $14.94/acre ($36.89/ha) for 605 acres
(245 ha).  A second example is the Gluch project which was sprayed with 2,4-D in
diesel oil at 2 lb/acre (2.2 kg/ha) from a helicopter in April 1961.  Areas in the
project lacking in grass cover were drilled with crested wheatgrass at 5.5 lb/acre
(6.2 kg/ha) in November 1961.  Fencing enclosed 9,107 acres (3 688 ha) of which
5,450 (2 207 ha) had been sprayed and 3,567 acres (1 445 ha) seeded.  Average cost
was $5.77/acre ($14.25/ha).

*Fire*

Fire, as an ecological and historical factor, has been mentioned repeatedly in this
report without discussion of its role in the district operations.  The original
program budget included $314,000 for fire protection.  The Vale District fire
control program became large, effective, and the headquarters for widely used hot-
shot crews - the Snake River Valley firefighters - which service other areas.
Planning and preparation for control take place in the winter and additional personnel are hired in the summer for detection and suppression of fire.  When fires pose
threats to valuable resources, structures, livestock, habitations, etc., they must
be suppressed.  After a wildfire, rehabilitation becomes an emergency project to be
accomplished with haste.

The goals of the Vale Program stipulated that fire control, specifically the
replacement of highly flammable cheatgrass with less hazardous perennial grasses,
would be increased in effectiveness.  Other benefits to fire suppression would
include access roads, reduction of big sagebrush cover, and additional water sources.
The Vale Program would incur costs for fire control because of needs to protect
investments in land treatments, specifically seedings.  Fire control was not considered a management tool nor the burned areas opportunities for rehabilitation.

Rangeland fires have persistently caused controversy over costs, damages, and
benefits of burning.  The ready availability of funds for wildlife suppression and
rehabilitation, and conflicting goals in land management contribute to continuing
disagreements.  To illustrate, hundreds of thousands of dollars are spent annually
in the Vale District for fire suppression (Table 8); yet burned and rehabilitated
lands produce as much forage as the acceptable but more expensive plowed-and-seeded
areas.  Perennial grasses are encouraged because they reduce the high fire hazard
of cheatgrass, yet an abundance of perennial herbage with rest from grazing creates
high fuel volumes on some pastures.  These and other conflicting situations do not
yield to simple solutions in planning for proper rangeland rehabilitation and use.

In hindsight, the dismissal of fire from the Vale District Program as a land treatment was a mistake.  The district's present emphasis on fuel management in brush
types of vegetation and the recognition of the natural role of fire in the big
sagebrush-grass ecosystems have established the development of prescribed fire as
a legitimate land management practice.  At the beginning of the Vale Program,
however, fire was considered both harmful and dangerous, which it is if uncontrolled.

Table 8.   Costs for fire protection and fighting fire on the
           Vale District, Bureau of Land Management, 1972-76

| Fiscal year | Protection | Firefighting |
|---|---|---|
| | Dollars | |
| 1972 | 66,500 | 523,700 |
| 1973 | 67,467 | 924,555 |
| 1974 | 88,540 | 786,963 |
| 1975 | 105,178 | 707,558 |
| 1976 | 89,840 | 470,478 |

Historically, fires in the Vale area were a result of lighting strikes or were set
by Indians.  Peter Skene Ogden mentioned fires along Bully Creek which Indians set
in 1827 (Williams *et al.* 1971).  Such fires did not eliminate big sagebrush nor the
perennial bunchgrasses (Uresk *et al.* 1976), but they created a mosaic of big sagebrush and grass of varying proportions, densities, and ages.  The big sagebrush at
any given time probably did not exceed 25-percent cover.  Due to overgrazing, the
unrehabilitated range now has the introduced cheatgrass, much more big sagebrush,
and less perennial grass than the vegetation before livestock grazing.  The addition
of cheatgrass caused the flammability and fire hazard to increase (Fig. 23).

Where the bunchgrasses are abundant, especially where their density exceeds an
average of three plants/yd$^2$ (3.6 plants/m$^2$), cheatgrass is reduced or nearly eliminated, thus reducing a major source of fuel for range fires.  Big sagebrush alone
will burn and so will the bunchgrasses; but fires in vegetation without cheatgrass
spread less rapidly and are easier to control.  Therefore, fuel management should
aim for reduction of cheatgrass and an increase in the perennial grasses with less
big sagebrush.  This reduction is in harmony with proper range management for other
purposes.

Where native perennial bunchgrasses remain, even as scattered as 10 yards (9 m)
between plants, proper livestock use will encourage establishment of thick stands
which will reduce fire hazards.  Where extreme overuse has eliminated perennial
grasses, reseeding will be needed.

A well-designed management plan for large areas will have a few strategically placed
perennial grass seedings which will allow other areas to rehabilitate through natural
succession to perennial grass codominance with big sagebrush.  When wildfires occur,
any necessary seeding can be done.  A wildfire should be viewed as a land treatment
or site preparation and as an opportunity for range rehabilitation.

Fuel management aims to make fire suppression more effective than at present and to
facilitate other uses.  In big sagebrush-grass, fuel management must be coordinated
with changes in botanical composition caused by defoliation, grazing, and wildfire.
Cheatgrass, a high fire-hazard fuel, is not sufficiently defoliated by grazing
animals to reduce the hazard.  Cheatgrass can be reduced in most areas through proper
grazing management which favors perennials.  Fires which reduce big sagebrush also
can favor the succession to perennial grass.  Big sagebrush and perennial grasses
should be managed as fuels and as forage in the integrated system.  The pasture,
then, is the logical management unit for both as it is already under controlled
grazing use.  Roads as fuel breaks should be used only where pastures do not make
adequate fuel management units.

Fig. 23.  Top, a fire burned this area in 1975; bottom, the
same area in 1976.  Crested wheatgrass did not
burn as readily as the annual cheatgrass.
Apparently cheatgrass and crested wheatgrass
survived the fire with little damage.

Ideal management of big sagebrush-perennial grass takes advantage of all alternative types of manipulations and uses. Fuel management affects the vegetation and the uses made of that vegetation. Grazing management, mechanical brush control, spraying, and seeding also affect vegetation *and* fuel management. The original Vale District Program considered fires as catastrophes. A fuel management program would risk perpetuating that attitude if people from all disciplines were not included from the beginning of planning. Fuel management, including the use of prescribed fire, has much to offer as an effective tool for rangeland rehabilitation, especially as a replacement for spraying with berbicides. Ecosystem considerations are essential.

## Water Developments, Fences, and Roads

Most range rehabilitation operations should include provisions for improvements in livestock management by increasing water, fences, and roads (Fig. 24). Roads were difficult to evaluate because much of their utility was neither measured nor described. If an unimproved road existed and was graded, the access improved for only certain types of vehicles, perhaps cattle trucks; yet large areas in the district need no roads for accessibility for some types of vehicles. The permanence of a road constructed in conjunction with a range improvement project varied from quick abandonment after a project to one improved and maintained for general use.

Newly constructed fences and watering points, even though they benefited uses other than livestock grazing, facilitated use of all the rangeland. Seedings required fencing to insure their protection and use as special pastures, and seasonal grazing systems needed pastures. That usually necessitated new watering points. Location of fences depended on the characteristics of the pasture and the needs for animal management. A typical pattern utilized natural barriers and existing fences as outer allotment boundaries and the new fences as cross-fences. Usually, a large crested wheatgrass seeding would be divided in anticipation of an alternating spring turnout grazing system. In this system, a pasture would be grazed first in one year and second the following year. Seldom did the occurrence of free water fit the needs of livestock in these pastures. A total of 2,081 miles (3 348 km) of fences on the Vale District were built by the BLM to standards which allowed antelope passage under the lowest wire. Since 1971, users have maintained the fences. Six hundred miles (960 km) of fence were constructed, largely by ranchers, before the program began.

Two basic types of water development were used. One created reservoirs in suitable locations within pastures (Fig. 25). During the course of the Vale Program, 624 such reservoirs were constructed. They had a high probability of failure to hold water for the full grazing seasons. Many were planned as sources of water for spring use of crested wheatgrass turnout pastures. This limited summer and fall use; consequently much effort went into the second type of development - reliable sources of year-round water, specifically wells, pipelines, and troughs. During the Vale Program (Table 9), 28 such systems were built. A typical system used a well drilled at a location to produce sufficient water and in a place where gravity feed could be used to supply water to troughs. Propane-powered pumps, maintained by the BLM, kept water in an 18,000-gallon (65 000-liter) tank in each well system. From each centrally located tank, water flowed through buried plastic pipe by gravity to fill individual stockwater troughs. Many such troughs were made from discarded jet engine shipping containers (Fig. 26). Spring developments numbered 448 during the Vale Program (Table 9). The 2,000 miles (3 200 km) of fence and 1,600 watering points, plus those installed before the program started, fulfilled the original project goal.

D.—M*

Table 9. Wells, pipelines, other water developments, and
fences in the Vale District, Bureau of Land
Management, 1940-75[1]/

| Years | Wells | Pipeline | Reservoirs | Springs | Troughs | Total | Fences |
|---|---|---|---|---|---|---|---|
| | | Miles | | Number | | | Miles |
| 1940-60 | 12 | 0.2 | 413 | 119 | 1 | 533 | 596.7 |
| 1961 | 0 | 0 | 41 | 8 | 0 | 49 | 87.7 |
| 1962 | 0 | 21.4 | 9 | 11 | 28 | 48 | 108.2 |
| 1963 | 2 | 12.8 | 24 | 17 | 20 | 61 | 80.5 |
| 1964 | 2 | - | 13 | 62 | - | 75 | 181.0 |
| 1965 | 1 | 9.0 | 54 | 49 | 13 | 116 | 175.9 |
| 1966 | 1 | 28.7 | 44 | 43 | 35 | 122 | 56.2 |
| 1967 | 1 | 38.4 | 52 | 30 | 39 | 121 | 277.3 |
| 1968 | 0 | 142.0 | 169 | 59 | 152 | 380 | 461.3 |
| 1969 | 7 | 28.6 | 69 | 52 | 44 | 165 | 269.8 |
| 1970 | 5 | 82.5 | 36 | 44 | 85 | 165 | 141.1 |
| 1971 | 3 | 28.6 | 31 | 11 | 39 | 81 | 87.3 |
| 1972 | 5 | 30.6 | 16 | 32 | 41 | 89 | 64.0 |
| 1973 | 1 | 10.9 | 15 | 2 | 11 | 28 | 35.6 |
| 1974 | 0 | 7.7 | 33 | 19 | 11 | 63 | 42.8 |
| 1975 | 0 | 21.7 | 18 | 9 | 20 | 47 | 12.6 |
| Total, 1961-75 | 28 | 462.9 | 624 | 448 | 538 | 1,610 | 2,081.3 |
| District total | 40 | 463.1 | 1,037 | 567 | 539 | 2,143 | 2,678.0 |

[1]/ 1 mile equals 1.6 kilometers.

*Errors and Lack of Compliance with Contracts*

An undertaking with the scope in acreage and treatments of the Vale District Program cannot be without errors. Errors resulted from lack of knowledge, lack of experience, and lack of compliance to job specifications. A discussion of these problems may be useful for other rehabilitation programs.

One benefit was that plowing left patches of brush, irregular borders, and a mosaic of vegetation, because the machinery could not operate on steep slopes and rocky areas. Spraying by air, however, covered the landscape completely. Spraying tended to convert larger and more continuous blocks than plowing. Aerial brush control requires more careful attention to siting and ground flagging than does plowing. Such control was not always accomplished in the Vale Program.

Fig. 25.  Commonly, one type of water system starts with a
reservoir (top), water piped to a storage tank
called a noodle-bowl (middle photo by Bureau of
Land Management), and buried pipeline to troughs
(bottom photo by Bureau of Land Management).

Fig. 26.  A second type of water system uses a well and
butane-operated pump, a metal storage tank on the
hill (top), and pipeline to troughs (middle).
The large shallow trough (bottom) stores water
and permits cattle to escape if they fall into
the trough.

Although contracts were carefully written, they were not always carefully followed. Some examples serve to illustrate the need to have continuous field supervision. Sprayings in a few instances killed big sagebrush in strips because of improper flagging or cheating on the contract. Some sprayings extended over areas that should not have been sprayed. In one instance the seed of intermediate wheatgrass was used when the contract called for crested wheatgrass.

Siting and developing of watering points did very well for livestock, but these same developments variously affected wildlife habitats. Before development, many small springs had wet areas, small meadows, and associated fauna that were destroyed when all the water was collected into tanks and troughs. The smaller animals find watering at a trough difficult or impossible. Even though chukar partridge, sagegrouse, and quail can water at properly built troughs, their foods provided by the meadows are gone. Overflow water should be piped to fenced sites to create new meadows. A few of these new meadows in the Vale District have produced larger wildlife sites than the original meadows.

Provision for watering and safety of small animals at livestock watering troughs need imaginative engineering. Few troughs have satisfactory designs for smaller animals. The design of troughs for livestock and the large game animals also needs consideration.

Fence design and construction show few errors. The standards used, a four-strand wire fence with the bottom wire 18 inches (46 cm) and the top strand 42 inches (107 cm) above the ground, allow the free movement of antelope and mule deer. A new fence should be flagged with a white cloth between every post to make it obvious to antelope. Fence surrounding study exclosures should have two additional wires with stiles substituted for gates.

*Continued Upkeep after the Vale Program ended*

The users pay fuel costs to operate the water systems; maintenance of pumps, tanks, troughs, and pipelines is BLM's responsibility. BLM also maintains reservoirs and springs on public lands. Maintenance personnel and the permittees continually monitor water supplies; many of the water systems are examined from low-flying aircraft every 2nd or 3rd day during the grazing season. Much of the maintenance budget is used to keep the water systems operating. Since livestock are critically dependent on water, the systems must be continually monitored. A failure in 1972 resulted in cattle dying of thirst, controversy over responsibilities, and unfavorable publicity.

The permittees maintain fences but BLM replaces them. Fences last many years before they need replacement. BLM repairs the roads. Since 1973, the Vale District has concentrated on maintenance of the facilities developed during the program and continued vegetational improvement, essentially through management of livestock grazing. For the most part, the action has been aimed at the holding of gains, protection from fire, and some rehabilitation after wildfires, rather than new and expanded projects.

The costs of the Vale Program go beyond initial establishment. Maintenance of improvements continues to be expensive. Thus, any cost-benefit evaluation of the program on a long-term basis must include continuing costs. Imperfect data are available for those costs, even for investments in the program itself, because accounting has not separated costs of rehabilitation projects, maintenance, and other operating expenses. Rough estimates of these costs are possible when funding of the Vale District is compared with that of the adjacent Burns BLM District. The largest single annual allocation for range improvement to the Vale District was $1,406,000 in 1965, but funding was over $1 million annually from 1964 to 1968.

During that period, the Burns District received approximately $200,000 per year (Table 10). The Vale Program formally ended with fiscal year 1973, by which time funding for the district had dropped to $538,875. The budgets for 1974 and 1975 were $503,081 and $530,025, respectively. In contrast the Burns District received only $120,000 for range improvements in fiscal year 1973 and $270,000 in 1975. Thus, the difference of $260,000 between Vale and Burns Districts, adjusted downward by 25 percent because of the size difference in the districts, yields an estimate of $195,000 per year in added maintenance costs which must be attributed to the Vale Program. BLM resource lands in the Burns District total 3,500,000 acres (1 400 000 ha) which support 265,000 AUM's; in the Vale District they total 4,600,000 acres (1 860 000 ha) which support 420,000 AUM's.

Table 10.  Estimated costs of the Vale Program, fiscal years 1962-73

| Fiscal year | Range management, soil, and watershed | | Base budget for Vale | Program funds for Vale |
|---|---|---|---|---|
| | Vale District | Burns District | | |
| | $1,000 | | | |
| 1962[1]/ | 107.5 | 103.2 | 107.5 | 0 |
| 1963 | 918.7 | 149.0 | 155.0 | 763.7 |
| 1964 | 1,116.0 | 195.0 | 205.0 | 911.0 |
| 1965 | 1,159.3 | 241.0 | 245.0 | 914.3 |
| 1966 | 1,332.3 | 283.0 | 295.0 | 1,037.3 |
| 1967 | 1,406.9 | 273.6 | 285.0 | 1,121.9 |
| 1968 | 1,369.3 | 284.0 | 292.0 | 1,077.3 |
| 1969 | 1,079.2 | 209.2 | 215.0 | 864.2 |
| 1970 | 1,072.4 | 224.3 | 234.0 | 786.4 |
| 1971 | 794.9 | 251.1 | 260.0 | 534.9 |
| 1972 | 792.5 | 211.5 | 208.0 | 584.5 |
| 1973 | 666.9 | 200.3 | 205.0 | 461.9 |
| Total | 11,656.4 | 2,521.7 | 2,599.0 | 9,057.4 |

Source: Bureau of Land Management State and District Office records.

[1]/ 1962 gives pre-Vale Program funding level and is not included in the total.

GRAZING MANAGEMENT

*Permitted Grazing Load*

Animal unit months of forage provided on the Vale District are largely the outcome of customary practice. There is little accurate analysis of either the ultimate capacity of the land to produce forage or of the forage-producing capacity of dependent property. Before 1934, unfenced public domain was free to anyone who ran livestock. After the passage of the Taylor Grazing Act, a user of the public domain had to establish a right to obtain a permit and to pay for the grazing use. Two categories of permits were established by the act. Class I permits for a certain number of AUM's depended on use of the public lands during the 5 previous years, and the number of animals which could be supported by local private property for 5 winter months. Class II permits were to be granted after all Class I permits had been filled. Class II permits required the independent private property commensurability but did not require the establishment of prior use on public land. In 1934 there was no way of knowing how much actual forage could be provided by the public domain; thus, all Class I and most of the Class II applications were granted. In the beginning, the Vale District provided the amount of forage to permittees with commensurate property that they had historically used. It took 2 years for all permits to be issued; therefore, permitted numbers increased from 146,193 AU's in 1935 to 122,322 AU's in 1936 (Table 11).

Forage provided in AUM's increased from 255,900 in 1935 to 412,618 in 1936 and continued to increase, reaching a maximum of 504,024 in 1955. The peak in 1955 was approximately a 20-percent increase from the late 1930's. As described earlier in this report, the advisory board on the Vale District in effect regulated permitted animal numbers until the late 1950's. At that time, the BLM won a series of battles with livestock users and began to assert control over livestock use on the Vale District and elsewhere. Range surveys conducted during the 1950's showed that the range was overobligated to the point that proper use of some areas on the Vale District would require 50-percent cuts in permitted use. To avoid this reduction by restoring forage production was the principal motive for the Vale Program.

The first districtwide estimated grazing capacity, 285,000 AUM's, was made in 1961. In that year, 427,476 AUM's were licensed (Table 12). Cattle and horses consumed 96 percent of the forage, sheep only 4 percent.

As the Vale Program developed, grazing capacity increased. Within the separate projects, the permittees took temporary nonuse in lieu of a permanent reduction of permitted grazing and the promise that temporary nonuse would be restored. Estimated grazing capacity for the district as a whole first exceeded actual use in 1972 (Table 12).

Although these data are the best available, they can be misleading. First, as mentioned above, demanded forage or permitted numbers stem from the historical granting of permits which was largely determined through negotiations and not by measurement of the capacity of the land. Thus, increased grazing capacity from 1961 to 1974 signifies that the rangeland now has the capacity to produce what has been used throughout that period. Area range conservationists provided the grazing capacity data in Table 12, and they based the estimates on impressions of overuse and underuse. No planned grazing capacity surveys were made.

Second, district data mask variations. Forage beyond that being used exists in the southern part of the district while parts of the northern resource area received heavy use each year. Therefore, former cuts in Class I permitted numbers are being restored in the south but not in the north. Some range users are still operating under reductions in Class I permits while others are not able to use all the forage produced.

Table 11.  Licensed numbers of animal unit months of grazing
          and animal units, Vale District, Bureau of Land
          Management, 1935-75

| Year | Animal unit months | Animal |
|------|--------------------|--------|
| 1935 | 255,900 | 146,193 |
| 1936 | 412,618 | 122,322 |
| 1937 | 346,980 | 114,113 |
| 1938 | 457,360 | 111,972 |
| 1939 | 424,231 | 106,662 |
| 1940 | 418,594 | 90,638 |
| 1941 | 424,070 | 90,446 |
| 1942 | 406,649 | 110,091 |
| 1943 | 414,718 | 108,595 |
| 1944 | 399,903 | 109,110 |
| 1945 | 442,454 | 113,070 |
| 1946 | 468,121 | 117,678 |
| 1947 | 459,751 | 105,891 |
| 1948 | 489,718 | 122,717 |
| 1949 | 458,294 | 121,032 |
| 1950 | 448,895 | 118,854 |
| 1951 | 484,800 | 107,439 |
| 1952 | 458,124 | 102,969 |
| 1953 | 468,728 | 110,416 |
| 1954 | 467,111 | 108,474 |
| 1955 | 504,024 | 111,695 |
| 1956 | 491,311 | 114,249 |
| 1957 | 483,539 | 181,673 |
| 1958 | 489,971 | 107,708 |
| 1959 | 415,737 | 88,811[1] |
| 1960 | 439,013 | 100,920 |
| 1961 | 427,476 | 98,559 |
| 1962 | 400,663 | 92,743 |
| 1963 | 399,386 | 86,435 |
| 1964 | 409,726 | 85,676 |
| 1965 | 411,285 | 87,024 |
| 1966 | 419,567 | 88,166 |
| 1967 | 392,481 | 75,698 |
| 1968 | 422,414 | 80,910 |
| 1969 | 426,024 | 83,829 |
| 1970 | 407,152 | 72,805[1] |
| 1971 | 418,010 | 72,676 |
| 1972 | 416,248 | 77,640 |
| 1973 | 417,207 | 75,504 |
| 1974 | 432,394 | 77,493 |
| 1975 | 415,383 | 75,868 |

[1] The drops in licensed use resulted from Vale District
boundary changes.

Table 12.  Licensed grazing use by livestock and estimated
           grazing capacity in the Vale District, Bureau of
           Land Management

| Year and class of livestock[1] | Licensed numbers | Licensed AUM's of use | Estimated grazing capacity, available AUM's |
|---|---|---|---|
| **1961:** | | | |
| Cattle and horses | 89,624 | 409,691 | |
| Sheep | 44,679 | 17,785 | |
| Total | 134,303 | 427,476 | 285,000 |
| **1962:** | | | |
| Cattle and horses | 81,461 | [2] | |
| Sheep | 56,409 | [2] | |
| Total | 137,870 | 400,663 | 343,000 |
| **1963:** | | | |
| Cattle and horses | 79,963 | 389,306 | |
| Sheep | 32,518 | 10,080 | |
| Total | 112,481 | 399,386 | 285,000 |
| **1964:** | | | |
| Cattle and horses | 79,016 | 399,211 | |
| Sheep | 33,301 | 10,515 | |
| Total | 112,317 | 409,726 | 300,000 |
| **1965:** | | | |
| Cattle and horses | 78,456 | 401,201 | |
| Sheep | 42,841 | 10,084 | |
| Total | 121,297 | 411,285 | 350,000 |
| **1966:** | | | |
| Cattle and horses | 82,061 | 410,316 | |
| Sheep | 30,525 | 9,251 | |
| Total | 113,586 | 419,567 | 300,000 |
| **1967:** | | | |
| Cattle and horses | 68,332 | 384,895 | |
| Sheep | 36,828 | 7,586 | |
| Total | 105,160 | 392,481 | 331,000 |
| **1968:** | | | |
| Cattle and horses | 75,160 | 417,180 | |
| Sheep | 28,748 | 5,234 | |
| Total | 103,908 | 422,414 | 340,000 |
| **1969:** | | | |
| Cattle and horses | 79,584 | 419,237 | |
| Sheep | 21,225 | 6,787 | |
| Total | 100,809 | 426,024 | 373,000 |
| **1970:** | | | |
| Cattle and horses | 67,904 | 400,858 | |
| Sheep | 24,505 | 6,294 | |
| Total | 92,409 | 407,152 | 383,000 |
| **1971:** | | | |
| Cattle and horses | 67,646 | 411,729 | |
| Sheep | 25,050 | 6,281 | |
| Total | 92,696 | 418,010 | 414,000 |

continued

Table 12. Continued

| Year and class of livestock[1] | Licensed numbers | Licensed AUM's of use | Estimated grazing capacity, available AUM's |
|---|---|---|---|
| 1972: | | | |
| Cattle and horses | 74,160 | 411,374 | |
| Sheep | 17,400 | 4,874 | |
| Total | 91,560 | 416,248 | 419,000 |
| 1973: | | | |
| Cattle and horses | 73,264 | 413,361 | |
| Sheep | 11,200 | 3,846 | |
| Total | 84,464 | 417,207 | 423,000 |
| 1974: | | | |
| Cattle and horses | 75,893 | 429,623 | |
| Sheep | 8,000 | 2,771 | |
| Total | 83,893 | 432,394 | 435,000 |
| 1975: | | | |
| Cattle and horses | 74,388 | 411,873 | |
| Sheep | 7,400 | 3,510 | |
| Total | 81,788 | 415,383 | 438,000 |

[1] Excludes wild horses.

[2] Data not available.


Many reasons exist for the differences, including less rainfall in the north, a longer history of rangeland abuse, allotment herds composed of mixed dairy and beef animals, common use allotments with animals from several owners, failures in cooperative management by numerous permittees with few animal units, frequent changes in permittees, and a more complicated mixture of landownerships in the north than in the south. Individuals find herd improvements difficult to attain, and the group allotments remain difficult to manage. Allotments with large pastures, however, require less fencing, fewer water developments, and are easier to administer than small areas. Some reallocation of grazing has been done, but redistributing grazing use to fit available forage remains one of the critical problems facing Vale BLM administration.


*Season of Grazing Use*

Most of the Vale District is generally considered spring range. Water and green forage are then abundantly available and animals put on the best gains. Wildlife, however, use rangeland at all seasons, and livestock can use it whenever weather permits (Fig. 27 shows actual use). Few areas are used yearlong. Areas well supplied with palatable browse, especially the desert shrub type, are used in the winter by livestock. The area of sagebrush-grass, which encompasses most of the public lands, is used in spring, summer, and fall. The typical permitted grazing season on Federal lands is 7 months long, April through October. Within that grazing season, the grazing period in any pasture follows a particular management system.  For example, many areas are not grazed in the fall to preserve browse for wintering wildlife.  Lack of water restricts use to spring and early summer.  In other places elevation restricts fall use, and convenience to the home ranch results in repeated seasonal use of a few pastures.


*Grazing Systems*

Within the season of grazing use – that time during which grazing is feasible – animals often graze different pastures.  The grazing period is defined as the time when livestock actually graze a pasture.  It may be as long as the grazing season, or it may be considerably shorter.  The pattern of grazing one to several pastures within the grazing season constitutes a seasonal grazing system.  The term "grazing system" implies many possible combinations of grazing periods during which grazing is systematically regulated and controlled.  Grazing systems require an organized framework for understanding.  Table 13 shows the wide variety of seasonal grazing treatments practiced with 144 pastures in 29 systems.  The Vale District has many more pastures and systems not formalized in allotment management plans.

The simplest grazing system keeps the animals in one pasture throughout the grazing season.  This season-long use has been the historic pattern of livestock use on public lands in the West and continues on many areas today.  Much overuse and range deterioration have been blamed on season-long grazing with little thought being given to other faulty range management practices.  Thus, efforts toward improvement of range livestock management have usually started with elimination of season-long grazing.  The initiation of an allotment management by BLM in recent years has been almost synonymous with the establishment of some kind of grazing system other than season-long grazing.  Yearlong grazing is not practiced on Vale District lands.

Repeated seasonal grazing describes use that occurs at the same season each year.  On the Vale District, repeated seasonal grazing may be spring, late spring, after seed ripening, fall, winter, or some combination of these times.  About 15 percent of the pastures studied received only repeated seasonal grazing.  Nine were native range and six were crested wheatgrass.  Of the 15 pastures so grazed, 8 received repeated grazing at more than one time each year (Table 13).  Reasons for repeated seasonal grazing included adequate stock water only in the spring season, crested wheatgrass grazed early to defer native range, need to facilitate animal husbandry practices, and proximity to the home ranch.  Repeated fall grazing reduced trailing and permitted gathering of animals before winter storms.  In a few instances early fall removal preserved bitterbrush for wildlife.  An additional 47 pastures received repeated grazing after seed ripening as well as some form of rotational grazing before seed ripening.  None of these pastures failed to improve in range condition during the program.

The third main category of grazing systems involved rotation of seasonal grazing – the modification of the pattern of grazing in succeeding years (Fig. 28).  Patterns took a wide variety of designs with all seven seasonal periods of grazing rotated in innumerable combinations (Table 13).  Rotational grazing is said to avoid damage to vegetation caused by repeated grazing at the same time each year.  We found the pastures grazed in same season every year to be in as good range conditions as those grazed on a rotational basis.  The systems aim to improve range conditions by fostering seedling establishment of desirable species.  Rotational systems will not be described in all combinations but a typical example would be a native range allotment which is divided into several pastures.  A different pasture would not be grazed until after seed ripening each year.  Another system would begin with grazing on a pair of crested wheatgrass pastures, which would be followed by a rotation on native ranges.  The crested wheatgrass pastures would be alternated in consecutive years.  This sytem delays turnout onto native ranges and rotates early use of the seeded pastures.  Rotational grazing was practiced on 129 pastures.

Table 13.  Number of pastures for 29 grazing systems by type
of management and season of use, Vale District,
Bureau of Land Management

| Type of seasonal use | Native | Seeded | Total |
|---|---|---|---|
| Summary of 29 grazing systems: | | | |
|     Number of pastures[1] | 105 | 39 | 144 |
|     Turnout to 6 weeks into season | | | |
|       (about Apr. 1 to May 15) | 63 | 39 | 102 |
|     Spring until seed ripening | | | |
|       (about May 15 to July 15) | 89 | 31 | 110 |
|     After seed ripening, deferred | | | |
|       (about July 15 to Sept. 1) | 75 | 24 | 99 |
|     Fall | | | |
|       (about Sept. 1 to Oct. 31) | 59 | 21 | 80 |
|     Winter (Nov. to March) | 4 | 0 | 4 |
|     Rest (no grazing in a year) | 40 | 5 | 45 |
|     2 consecutive years of rest | 6 | 3 | 9 |
| Pastures with repeated seasonal | | | |
| use, no rotation at any season: | | | |
|     Number of pastures[1] | | | |
|     Turnout to 6 weeks into season | | | |
|       (about Apr. 1 to May 15) | 4 | 6 | 10 |
|     Spring until seed ripening | | | |
|       (about May 15 to July 15) | 1 | 0 | 1 |
|     After seed ripening, deferred | | | |
|       (about July 15 to Sept. 1) | 1 | 4 | 5 |
|     Fall (about Sept. 1 to Oct. 31) | 2 | 4 | 6 |
|     Winter | 1 | 0 | 1 |
| Pastures with repeated seasonal use | | | |
| in at least one season, rotation in | | | |
| some other season: | | | |
|     Number of pastures[1] | 27 | 20 | 47 |
|     Turnout to 6 weeks into season | | | |
|       (about Apr. 1 to May 15) | 0 | 0 | 0 |
|     Spring until seed ripening | | | |
|       (about May 15 to July 15) | 0 | 0 | 0 |
|     After seed ripening, deferred | | | |
|       (about July 15 to Sept. 1) | 27 | 20 | 47 |
|     Fall (about Sept. 1 to Oct. 31) | 20 | 4 | 24 |
|     Winter | 0 | 0 | 0 |
| Pastures with rotation of seasonal use | 96 | 33 | 129 |
| Pastures with "switchback"[2] system of | | | |
| turnout on crested wheatgrass and | | | |
| deferment of native range (two grazing | | | |
| systems with 11 pastures) | 7 | 4 | 11 |
| Pastures with crested wheatgrass treated | | | |
| the same as adjacent native range (seven | | | |
| grazing systems with 45 pastures) | 24 | 21 | 45 |

[1] Not a total of seasonal treatments because some pastures are used
more than once.

[2] Alternating forest grazing among two pastures in succeeding years.

Fig. 28.  Top, cattle entering a stand of bluebunch wheat-
          grass (big sagebrush reduced by spraying) about
          June 20.  The middle photo shows proper use of
          bluebunch wheatgrass in June without big sage-
          brush, and bottom, with big sagebrush.

Allotment management plans early in the program established deferred-rotational
systems on native range. Many of these systems have changed. At the inception of
the Vale Program it was envisioned that crested wheatgrass seedings would primarily
serve for deferment of native ranges. Turnout onto crested wheatgrass every spring,
with a switchback between two pastures in alternate years, would permit late spring
use of native range. In 1975 that arrangement persisted in only 2 of 29 sampled
allotments. Although all crested wheatgrass seedings are still used for turnout,
at least in some years, most are treated like native bunchgrass range. Twenty-one
of 39 seeded pastures were managed identically to adjacent native range. Another
recent modification involves the use of identical treatments for 2 years rather
than 1 in the rotational cycle. Resting, or no grazing at all, for 2 consecutive
years occurred on nine pastures, six native and three seeded, about 6 percent of
the pastures in our sample. The most notable change in seasonal grazing practice
has been the tendency to use the seedings and the native ranges in the same manner.

All grazing systems provide for flexibility in dates of grazing and numbers of
animals to deal with variability in water supply, forage quantity, and inclement
weather. Large variations from the written plans indicate day-to-day decision-
making in the grazing of the national resource lands, as should be the case. A few
plans which include large proportions of private land in mixture with public land
give the users responsibility for management of animals, and the BLM range conserva-
tionist serves only in an advisory capacity. This arrangement encourages user
responsibility for the range and it should be encouraged as the range improves.

The grazing systems originally established aimed to protect and use the crested
wheatgrass seedings, to rehabilitate the native ranges, and to preserve browse for
wildlife. For those objectives yearlong rest and little early grazing on the
native bunchgrass were effective practices. Many ranges are now in good to excellent condition and the permittees have learned to manage the vegetation as well as
the livestock. Some of the seasonal plans could be improved. We see little need
and some disadvantage in yearlong resting of pastures with good to excellent stands
of bluebunch wheatgrass. The bunches accumulate dead material in their centers,
causing increased fire hazard and less vigor in the plant.

Some grazing each year in the mature bunches promotes greater vigor than no grazing
at all. Deferred and rotational treatments must be maintained. Season-long use
should be included in some systems. This is the most flexible method of livestock
use, involves a minimum disruption of livestock, takes less labor, reduces animal
diseases related to crowding, and allows animals to exercise natural selectivity of
forage. With proper regulation of animal distribution and numbers, season-long use
of ranges in good to excellent condition can be a highly satisfactory grazing
treatment. The time has arrived to take a new look at seasonal grazing systems on
the basis that the ones needed for rehabilitation are not necessarily the best,
especially not for using excellent condition range.


*Control of Animal Distribution and Management*

Any effective modification of forage production must include provisions for control
of animal numbers and distribution. Improvements such as fences, gates, roads, and
water furnish the attractions and boundaries needed to control animal distribution.

Water controls animal distribution more than fencing but both could have been used
more effectively in the Vale Program. A few pipelines terminate in troughs
located near the bottoms of drainages, where livestock naturally congregate.
Perhaps these locations were selected by compromise between engineering and
managerial requirements. Not only must the systems function for entire grazing
systems; they must be continually maintained, at a substantial cost. In 1975,
maintenance of the district's water systems required 15 full-time employees.

Maintenance of water has been critical for livestock survival. Minimized installation costs and engineering considerations led to high maintenance costs in a few
instances.

Water, to the ranchers, was the first priority for development. Lack of water on
large land tracts in the districts had prevented grazing abuse, and abundant
forage was going unused. The ranchers argued that more drinking water would make
use of that feed possible.

The BLM rightly resisted development of water without an overall plan which included
the needs for protection and encouragement of wildlife as well as the use of all
feasible range management practices. Livestock water also improves wildlife
habitat, particularly around fenced reservoirs, and even provides new wildlife
habitat. Where livestock are uncontrolled, water developments can be ineffective
for wildlife. Overall, the water systems on the district operate with high efficiency as managerial devices.

Supplementary feeds other than minerals are not allowed on Vale District lands,
and none are needed. Uneven use of salt and mineral supplements results in poorer
than expected distributional control of livestock. Often salt blocks are dropped
near water, along roads, and in other undesirable locations. Allotment management
plans need to specify appropriate locations for placement of salt.

Ranchers, for the most part, practice herding of animals for animal husbandry
requirements. Unfenced seedings that did not have protective boundaries and fire
rehabilitation areas within large pastures required herding to prevent concentration
of livestock. Riders have been cooperatively employed between the Advisory Board
and BLM to keep animals out of such areas. Herding is an expensive and necessary
measure for proper range management. Herding does not substitute for the lack of
properly placed fences and watering points. Several allotment management plans
specify that a rider be used to influence animal movement where natural drift does
not achieve desired grazing use. Any system for the control of animal distribution
must also allow for flexibility in order to accommodate animal husbandry requirements.

*Monitoring of Grazing*

A management plan, no matter how sophisticated, cannot function properly for long
periods without continual checks for compliance. BLM grazing policies and allotment
management plans require monitoring even with stated acceptance by the user. Plans
or policies may not be followed automatically, especially where memories of historic
conflicts still exist.

Monitoring of livestock numbers and movement of animals from one pasture to another
are a time-consuming but necessary part of the BLM managerial role. Thinly available manpower requires that most of the control rest with the users. Several
management plans require that the user (1) limit livestock numbers and season of
use to those specified in the written plan, and (2) submit certification of actual
use at the close of the season. Ideally, this should be the method on all allotments as it fosters user responsibility.

Table 14 lists the number of formal trespass actions by year between 1961 and 1976.
No trespass at all existed prior to 1934; the public range was free to all. Lack
of data from 1934 to 1961 prevents evaluation of trespassing during that period.
The increase in number of court cases to a maximum in 1966 resulted from increased
surveillance. Afterwards, compliance with stocking rate restrictions improved and
the cases declined.

Table 14.  Number of livestock trespass cases in the Vale District, Bureau of Land Management, by fiscal year

| Year | Trespassing cases | Year | Trespassing cases |
|------|-------------------|------|-------------------|
| 1961 | 35 | 1969 | 32 |
| 1962 | 41 | 1970 | 24 |
| 1963 | 47 | 1971 | 18 |
| 1964 | 47 | 1972 | 8 |
| 1965 | 66 | 1973 | 16 |
| 1966 | 81 | 1974 | 5 |
| 1967 | 38 | 1975 | 18 |
| 1968 | 42 | 1976 | 32 |

Proof in animal trespass requires two witnessed observations and counts of the same animals at different times.  Even so, trespass is extremely difficult to prove in common use allotments where ownership of animals can change.  In a sample of 22 cases, each involved an average of 75 cattle or 13 horses and only one action implicated more than 135 head.

To ease administration of the monitoring program, the BLM started an ear-tagging procedure in 1975.  Tags were issued for only the permitted number of animals. Licensee objected because of the added cost of labor to the tags.

Monitoring of grazing systems enforces regulations on animal movements between pastures and the length of time animals spend in the various pastures.  Typically, BLM personnel observe compliance with animal movement dates by checking opening and closing of gates.  A small number of trespass cases were due to grazing on areas which should have been either deferred or rested.  Our observations during the course of field studies and the data in Table 14 suggest that compliance was good over the district as a whole.  Noncompliance was more likely to be caused by difficulty in gathering every animal from rugged terrain rather than from deliberate noncompliance with grazing schedules.

Small but important enclosed areas on the Vale District were built for scientific studies, plot tests, protection of riparian vegetation, protection of reservoirs, and for wildlife habitat.  Evidence of trespass animals was occasionally observed in these enclosures.  Although the probable impact on the vegetation was not great. The high and specific values of these enclosures make any grazing in them intolerable.


VEGETATIONAL CONDITION IN 1975

*Methods*

The methods of vegetational sampling used in this study provide information on the results of the Vale Program, and they also suggest a need for more efficient and accurate sampling of range vegetation than has been accomplished in the past by the district.  The parameters measured were density of selected species and

percentage of botanical composition by foliage cover.  Time restraints limited the
sampling methods to those which yielded data rapidly.  Large representative sections
within each project area and in adjacent untreated brushland were selected as the
general locations of the samples.  Of the 164 projects listed in Table 6, 153 were
sampled.  Many rehabilitation projects resulted in relatively uniform vegetation
with adjacent untreated brush stands relatively homogeneous in density and cover.
Therefore, a single or a few large samples were taken in each project, placing
the emphasis on variable results among projects rather than within them.

Major species in paced belt transects, each 18 inches wide and 200 yards long
(46 cm by 183 cm), were tallied to obtain densities.  A hand-carried T-shaped
sampling form established the transect width.  Plants with more than 50 percent of
their base within the belt were tallied on hand counters.  Infrequent species were
tallied directly.  Only major categories of brush and desirable grasses were
included in this type of sample.  The recorded grasses included as desirable were
crested wheatgrass, bluebunch wheatgrass, basin wildrye, Idaho fescue, Thurber's
needlegrass, and Indian ricegrass but not Sandberg bluegrass, squirreltail, and
cheatgrass.  Coefficient of variation among transects was about 50 percent.

After completion of the transects, the surveyor estimated botanical composition on
a basis of foliage cover.  His notations at each site included the presence of
seedlings, dead plants, erosion, grazing use, and other characteristics.  Many
sites were photographed.  Thus, counts and reconnaissance evaluations provided the
data for vegetational analysis.

In June of 1976, 50 sagebrush plants were collected in each of six project areas to
determine age through ring counts, density on the ground, and size of plants.

*Untreated Areas*

Sampling of adjacent treated and untreated areas provided data for comparisons and
evaluations of projects.  Results from the untreated areas do not apply to the Vale
District as a whole but only to those sites which have undergone brush control,
seeding, and fire.  Projects were concentrated in the big sagebrush-grass vegetational type so all untreated samples came from that one type.

Overall vegetational composition of untreated rangeland is related to elevation
and rainfall.  Since these two factors correlate on the Vale District, rainfall will
serve as the basis for comparison.  Samples from 65 untreated sites were divided
into 4 rainfall categories, 6-8, 8-10, 10-12, and 12-14 inches (152-203, 203-254,
254-305, 305-357 mm) of annual precipitation with 5, 27, 28, and 5 samples per
category, respectively.

Brush density averaged 1.05 plants/yd$^2$ (1.25 plants/m$^2$) (Fig. 29).  Big sagebrush
remained consistent and rabbitbrush increased in density with increased rainfall.
Lack of significant correlation between brush density and desirable grass density
fails to show a consistent relationship.  This suggests that the density of brush
does not determine density of grass, but instead, that the grass is related to
rainfall (Fig. 30).

Density of desirable grasses was greater at higher rainfall (and elevation) than
at lower rainfalls (Fig. 29).  In areas with annual rainfall of less than 8 inches
(203 mm), the desirable grasses were almost entirely bluebunch wheatgrass.  At
8-10 inches (203-254 mm), bluebunch wheatgrass still dominated but the stand
included basin wildrye on low-lying areas.  Idaho fescue and needlegrass were
present in significant numbers above 12 inches (305 mm) of rainfall.  Bluebunch
wheatgrass was the most common desirable grass at all rainfall categories.

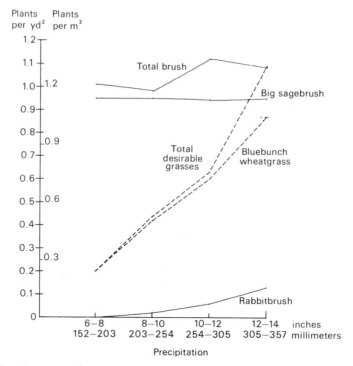

Fig. 29.  Density of brush and grasses on 65 untreated areas
          in 1975 in relation to mean annual precipitation.

When related to precipitation, brush species showed the same trends in relative
percent species composition as they did in density; big sagebrush remained constant
at 50 percent of the stand, and rabbitbrush became more important as rainfall
increased (Fig. 31).  Rabbitbrush formed less than 1 percent of the vegetation in
areas with rainfall of less than 10 inches (254 mm), and about 5 percent with more
than 10 inches (254 mm).  Bitterbrush, present in areas with more than 12 inches
(305 mm) of precipitation, never exceeded 1 percent of the cover.  Relative percent
of brush cover declined with increased precipitation.

Desirable grasses, when analyzed, revealed the same trends for relative cover as
they did for density (Fig. 32).  Cheatgrass decreased in importance as rainfall
increased, squirreltail followed the same trend as bluebunch wheatgrass, and
Sandberg bluegrass reached its greatest percentage of the stand at middle amounts
of rainfall.  Annual forbs in the season sampled averaged 1 percent or less of the
cover for all rainfall groups.

Estimates of percentage species composition provided a basis for comparison with
step-point data taken prior to treatment in the 1963-68 period.  Interpretation of
the differences directly pertains to plant succession and range trend.  Plant groups
compared include big sagebrush, rabbitbrush, bitterbrush, total brush, bluebunch
wheatgrass, desirable grasses, squirreltail, Sandberg bluegrass, cheatgrass, and
annual forbs.  Interpretations must be evaluated in the context that different
sampling methods were used.  Seasonal and yearly variability also undoubtedly
contributed to the differences, especially where cheatgrass and annual forbs formed
a significant part of the vegetative cover (Fig. 33).

Fig. 30.  Neither the monoculture of the big sagebrush on
          the left nor the sagebrush-bluebunch wheatgrass
          mixture on the right received a brush control
          treatment.  The differences in botanical composi-
          tion are due to livestock management.

Samples in the years 1963 to 1968 contained more cheatgrass and annual forbs than
those in 1975.  This may be either improvement in the range condition or yearly
variability.  On the other hand, the increased percentage of brush and desirable
grass in 1975 may indicate a real decrease in percentage of annual grasses and
forbs.  Changes in composition within the group of perennial grasses, 28 percent of
the vegetation, suggest that range improvement has occurred.  The small increase
from 8.5 percent desirable grasses in 1963-68 to 11.1 percent in 1975 masks important changes (Fig. 34).  Bluebunch wheatgrass increased from 8.1 to 10.2 percent
and squirreltail from 3.5 to 6.9 percent, whereas Sandberg bluegrass decreased from
16.1 to 9.7 percent.

These modest changes in percentages portray significant ecological effects.  The
taller grasses now occupy more space between the sagebrush plants than they did in
1963-68, hence there is less room for Sandberg bluegrass and cheatgrass.  These
results substantiate the description given earlier for the climax vegetation and,
in fact, contribute to that description.

An additional point needs emphasis.  Little ongoing increase in the density of
bluebunch wheatgrass was actually observed.  Sampling disclosed few seedlings of
this species.  Perhaps none were needed to maintain many of the stands because the
bluebunch wheatgrass plants on grazed untreated areas were growing vigorously with
no dead plants and few dead centers of plants.  The only plants of bluebunch wheatgrass in poor condition individually in relation to livestock grazing were some of
those in an exclosure west of Jordan Valley which had *not* been grazed by livestock
for several years.  Resting an area for a year or more without grazing promotes

accumulation of litter and dying in the centers of bluebunch wheatgrass. Many areas
without brush control are in much improved range condition in 1975 over what they
were in the early 1960's. Several allotments in the northern part of the district,
however, will take decades to improve significantly because of the virtual absence
of desirable grasses.

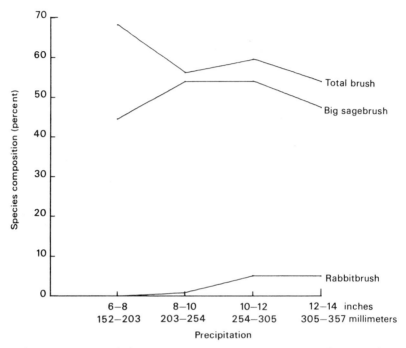

Fig. 31.  Composition of brush on untreated areas in 1975 in
          relation to average annual precipitation.

Methods previously used by BLM personnel for evaluating range condition on the Vale
District were inadequate for our purposes. A few key sites were selected for
permanent plots, each consisting of a photo point and a staked yard-square
(0.836 m$^2$) plot on which vegetation was mapped. Proper evaluation of an entire
management unit could not be made from examination of one to a half dozen of these
small plots. Photos yielded valuable information and should be continued. Mapping
of the small plots, however, is time consuming and of questionable accuracy because
of infrequent sampling by a wide spectrum of individuals, some with little interest
in the assignment, and none with adequate instruction. A more reliable method for
collecting adequate condition and trend data should be found. A second fault with
the present plots is that most were located close to water and other places of
livestock concentration, hence they do not represent entire management units. A
third problem with these plots stems from the practice of including cheatgrass in
the trend sample, thus confusing high yearly variability in cheatgrass stands with
long-term trends in range condition. Annuals should be included in the analysis
as important parts of the vegetation, but their small and ephemeral nature makes
them difficult to map and the maps of doubtful meaning. A fourth problem is
inadequate plot size. A yard-square plot included less than one big sagebrush
plant and about three of the desirable perennial bunchgrasses on the average. A
large number of these plots would be needed on each site in order to obtain an
accurate estimate of range condition and trend.

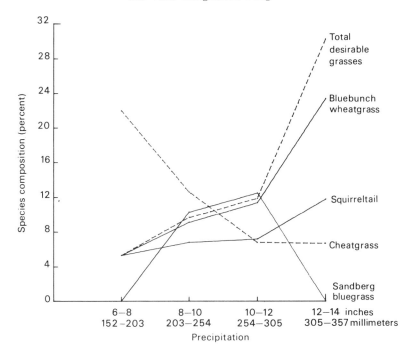

Fig. 32.  Relative percentage species composition of grasses
          on untreated areas in 1975 in relation to average
          annual precipitation.

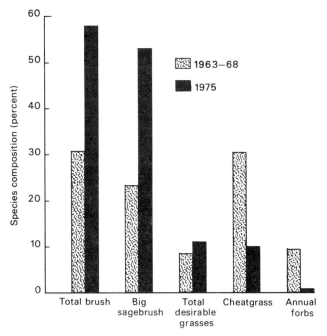

Fig. 33.  Species composition, 1963-68 and 1975.

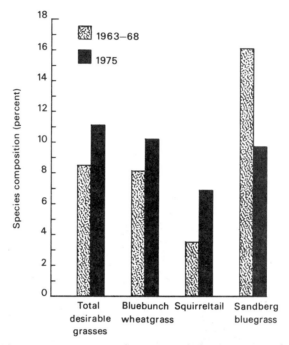

Fig. 34.  Percentage species composition of perennial
grasses, 1963-68 and 1975.

New procedures need to be established for monitoring changes in vegetation on the
lands administered by BLM.  The technique should apply to large managerial units,
give reasonably pertinent and accurate data on vegetational changes, and be useful
to nonresearch-oriented personnel, who have many other assignments.

*Brush Control and Seeding Treatments*

Seedings followed four pretreatment practices: plowing, spraying, wildfire, and no
preparation prior to planting.  A few reseedings followed unsuccessful prior
attempts - as many as three or four tries.  This section of the report examines
the vegetation that returned following brush control and seeding.  All seedings
were to crested wheatgrass, unless stated otherwise.

In general, similar big sagebrush kills were obtained with either spraying-and-
seeding or plowing-and-seeding.  Many well-executed and planned operations resulted
in kills exceeding 95 percent (Figs. 35 and 36).  The relationship between sagebrush kill and longevity of projects, however, is not at all clear.  Brush density
on untreated areas averaged 1.05 plants/yd$^2$ (1.25/m$^2$), 0.95 (1.14) big sagebrush,
0.04 (0.05) rabbitbrush, and 0.06 plant/yd$^2$ (0.07/m$^2$) of other species (Fig. 37).
Big sagebrush was dramatically killed by all treatments, with wildfire the most
effective in reducing its density.  Burned areas averaged only 0.09 big sagebrush
plant/yd$^2$ (1.08/m$^2$).  Areas sprayed and seeded showed the lowest sagebrush density
of any nonburned section with 0.17 plant/yd$^2$ (0.20/m$^2$).  Plowing reduced big sagebrush density to 0.24/yd$^2$ (0.29/m$^2$); spraying alone was least effective with 0.26

plant/yd$^2$ (0.31/m$^2$) (Fig. 38). Lowest sagebrush densities were observed where seeding followed spraying, rather than with no seeding.

Fig. 35.   Top, N. G. Creek seeding site dominated by big sagebrush and cheatgrass before treatment in 1963 (Bureau of Land Management photo). Middle, grazed crested wheatgrass with little apparent big sagebrush in 1969 (Bureau of Land Management photo). Bottom, big sagebrush appears as a scattered stand in 1975.

Fig. 36.  The spray-only treatment (top) released bluebunch
          wheatgrass which developed into a thick stand.
          Most spray and seed treatments also developed
          grasslands (bottom).  Big sagebrush invaded areas
          receiving either treatment.

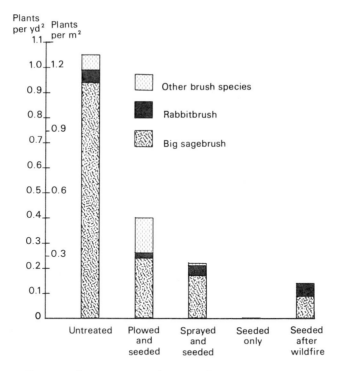

Fig. 37.  Density of brush in 1975 in seeded areas, by
          treatment.

Rabbitbrush was more common on treated areas than untreated, averaging $0.04/yd^2$
$(0.05/m^2)$.  Plowing effectively reduced rabbitbrush to $0.02/yd^2$ $(0.024/m^2)$.
Spraying resulted in higher density, 0.05 and $0.08/yd^2$ (0.06 and $0.09/m^2$) for
seeded and nonseeded sprayed areas.  Rabbitbrush was strongly correlated with
particular soil and elevational types, complicating interpretation of the results.

Brush control projects which were without seedings used aerial application of
2,4-D to kill big sagebrush.  This practice was used most often.

Spraying had variable results.  Sprays before 1965 used diesel oil as a carrier for
the active agent, and they more effectively killed brush than the water-based sprays
used beginning in 1965.  Applications were timed more accurately by 1967, making
the water-based sprays as effective as the earlier results with diesel oil (Fig. 38).
In paired treated and untreated samples, the untreated areas adjacent to sprays
averaged 0.98 big sagebrush plant/$yd^2$ ($1.17/m^2$), and spray-treated samples averaged
0.26 plant/$yd^2$ ($0.31/m^2$) (Fig. 39), half of which became established after treatment
(see next section).  Estimated initial overall percentage kill by spraying was
80-90 percent.

Desirable grass density increased in unseeded sprayed areas.  Paired treated and
untreated adjacent transects had 1.02 desirable grasses/$yd^2$ ($1.22/m^2$) on treated
areas versus 0.81/$yd^2$ ($0.97/m^2$) on untreated areas, a 25-percent increase in grass
density due to spray treatment.

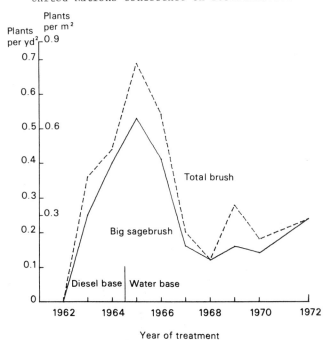

Fig. 38.   Density of brush in 1975, averaged for the year of
spray treatment with 2,4-D at 2 lb acid equivalent
per acre (2.2 kg/ha).

When crested wheatgrass is grouped into four categories of areas with 6-8, 8-10,
10-12, and 12-14 inches (152-203, 203-254, 254-305, 305-357 mm) of average precipitation, little difference is noted between success at the various rainfall levels.
Plow-and-seed operations resulted in crested wheatgrass densities of 3.19, 3.11, and
3.38 plants/yd$^2$ (3.82, 3.72, and 4.04/m$^2$) for the three lowest levels of rainfall.
However, the dry years reduced seedling success. The 2 years with the least rainfall
during the Vale Project, 1966 and 1968, resulted in poor seeding success with average
densities of 2.82 and 2.11 plants/yd$^2$ (3.37 and 2.52/m$^2$) for plow-and-seed and spray-
and-seed operations compared with the overall average success of 3.15 plants/yd$^2$
(3.77/m$^2$). Generally, plowing was the most successful preseeding treatment, giving
an average crested wheatgrass density of 3.22 plants/yd$^2$ (3.85/m$^2$) (Fig. 40).
Spraying, fire rehabilitation, and no pretreatment, in that order, resulted in 2.99,
2.77, and 2.17 plants/yd$^2$ (3.58, 3.31, and 2.60/m$^2$). The two sampled attempts at
reseeding without site preparation following initial failure were judged unsuccessful with only an average of 1.61 perennial grass plants/yd$^2$ (1.93/m$^2$).

Percentage compositions of species on seeded areas generally parallel these for
density. Plow-and-spray reduced brush composition of 59 percent for untreated areas
to 12 percent, and burning lowered the composition to 9 percent. Notable, however,
was that the highest average percentage composition of desirable grasses occurred
on spray-and-seed areas. The slightly lower percentage composition of crested
wheatgrass in sprayed areas compared with plowed areas (49 vs. 55 percent) was
balanced by the presence of desirable native grasses in the sprayed areas. Although
sprayed-and-seeded areas were among the poorest ranges on the Vale District at the
beginning, the presence of remnant native grasses resulted in an average of
60-percent desirable grasses (11-percent native and 49-percent crested wheatgrass).
Spraying, by not killing native grasses, resulted in significantly better mixtures
of perennial grasses than plow-and-seed.

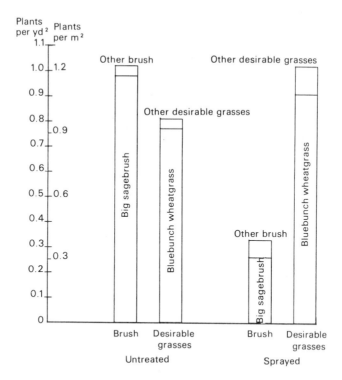

Fig. 39.  Comparison of sprayed areas and adjacent untreated
          areas, 1975.

Trend in grass composition on treated areas was closely related to the rate of
change in the brush population, not to changes in their own density.  Since the
grasses displayed little evidence of decrease or change in density, downward trend
would be the result of brush reinvasion.  A widely accepted proposition in many
evaluations of range improvement by means of brush control stipulates that the
improvement has a finite lifespan due to return of brush.  We disagree with this
proposition in the Vale District.  Few areas on the district which were successfully treated will require retreatment to maintain a substantial portion of their
forage productivity.  Brush will invade but not to the degree that grasses will be
greatly impaired - as long as overgrazing does not destroy the grasses.

*Big Sagebrush Reinvasion*

To further investigate the structure of controlled sagebrush and seeded stands, we
obtained 300 plants of big sagebrush in lots of 50 from six project sites (Table 15).
All big sagebrush plants within a 1-meter-wide belt were measured for crown diameter
and height and were cut at ground level for ring counts to estimate age.  The
sample ended when 50 plants had been measured.  Although rotten centers and incomplete rings reduced the accuracy of age determination, the number of annual rings in
any stem younger than approximately 20 years gave a good estimate of the age of the
plant.  Estimates of actual age were not possible in 29 plants, or about 20 percent
of the samples, because of missing centers.

Table 15.  Age in years and density of big sagebrush on six
treated areas, Vale District, Bureau of Land
Management, 1976

| Project name | Number of project | Age at time of treatment | Age | | | | Plants per square yard[1] |
| | | | Mean | Median | Min. | Max. | |
| --- | --- | --- | --- | --- | --- | --- | --- |
| | | | Years | | | | |
| Ten Mile seeding | 1 | 24 | 17.7 | 19 | 5 | 24 | 0.35 (.42) |
| Brickey Springs seeding | 8 | 15 | 12.6 | 13 | 6 | 21 | .24 (.29) |
| Rock Creek seeding | 15 | 14 | 12.2 | 12 | 5 | 26+ | .63 (.75) |
| Big Ridge seeding | 106 | 9 | 9.3 | 9 | 1 | 18 | .24 (.39) |
| Antelope seeding | 109 | 9 | 11.2 | 10 | 7 | 23 | .33 (.39) |
| Basque seeding | 111 | 9 | 15.4 | 11 | 3 | 38+ | .54 (.65) |

[1] Figures in parentheses are plants per square meter.

Areas sampled were chosen primarily for convenience and thus do not constitute a
representative sample of the Vale District as a whole.  However, the data point to
important facts concerning treatments, their effectiveness, and sagebrush reinvasion in general.

Size of plant and age were poorly correlated (Fig. 41).  The best regression
coefficient for age on size of plant was obtained in the Basque brush control but
it was only r = 0.482.  The Big Ridge, Antelope, and Rock Creek seedings all had
correlations of less than 0.13 or no relation at all between size and age.  The
practice of making inferences about age-class distribution of sagebrush stands
based on size classes is highly inaccurate and in fact may lead to erroneous
conclusions.  Often, apparent seedlings less than 5 inches (1 dm) tall may be more
than 10 years old.  As an example, the Big Ridge seeding yielded sagebrush plants
within a few meters of each other, both with nine growth rings, one with a crown
2.5 by 1.5 inches (6 by 4 cm) and the larger 32 by 36 inches (80 by 90 cm).
Brickey Springs had two adjacent plants, one with 14 rings and 8 by 4 inches
(2 by 1 dm) in size; the other 15 rings and 36 by 50 inches (9 by 12.5 dm) in size.

A common assertion is that big sagebrush invades rapidly following land treatment
and that most seedlings become established at that time.  In general, the results
of the age-class survey substantiate that claim.  On three of the treated areas the
most numerous age class occurred the year after the treatment.  This effect was
particularly pronounced in the Big Ridge seeding where 32 of the 50 plants in the
sample apparently established in the 2 years following treatment in 1966 (Fig. 42).
All treated areas showed evidence of continued establishment in the years following

treatment except that the Antelope and Brickey Springs seedings had no plants younger than 6 years (Figs. 43 and 44).

The Brickey Springs seeding had large and obvious big sagebrush, whereas the Antelope seeding appeared relatively free of big sagebrush plants because they were small (Fig. 45). Densities of big sagebrush plants in the two areas were similar. Big sagebrush crown cover in Brickey Springs was 5.7 percent, but only 1.6 percent in Antelope; yet median ages were similar - 13 years in Brickey Springs and 10 years in Antelope. The only real difference was that the big sagebrush plants in Brickey Springs were larger and hence covered more area.

Only the Ten Mile seedings displayed complete kill of big sagebrush by initial treatment (Fig. 46) - no plants older than the treatment were found. In all other projects sampled, ample big sagebrush plants remained after treatment to allow reinvasion from seed produced. Invasion is by establishment of seedings immediately after treatment from seed on the site and from seed produced later. Little evidence was found that particular years were more favorable for sagebrush establishment than others. Individual areas showed groups or cohorts of seedlings, but they were of different ages. From 1970 on seems to have been unfavorable for sagebrush establishment.

This sample, encompassing many years of treatment, resulted in some conclusions concerning the life expectancy of crested wheatgrass seedings and the rate of big sagebrush reinvasion. First, older brush controls did not show more sagebrush invasion than younger projects. Degree of big sagebrush invasion related to the type and effectiveness of the particular treatment rather than year of treatment. Plowing, spraying, and burning are all effective methods of big sagebrush control when used properly.

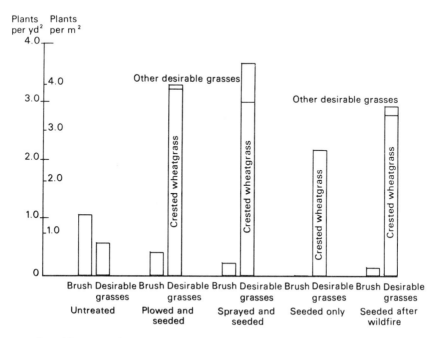

Fig. 40. Density of brush, crested wheatgrass, and other desirable grasses in 1975 according to treatment before seeding.

Fig. 41.  Both these plants of big sagebrush, growing side
          by side, were 9 years old.

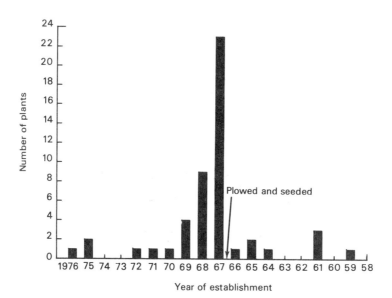

Fig. 42.  Age-class distribution of big sagebrush, Big Ridge
          seeding project.

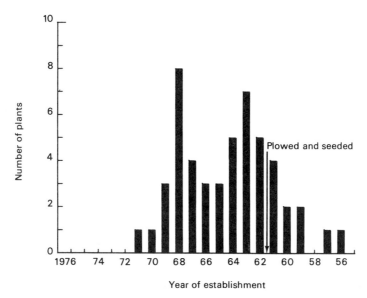

Fig. 43.  Age-class distribution of big sagebrush, Brickey
Springs seeding project.

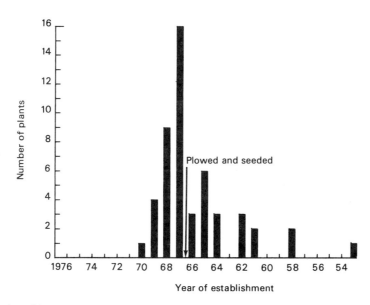

Fig. 44.  Age-class distribution of big sagebrush, Antelope
seeding project.

Fig. 45.  Antelope seeding on the left and Brickey Springs
          seeding on the right.  Small plants of big sage-
          brush in the Antelope seeding are about the same
          number per unit area as the larger plants in
          Brickey Springs.

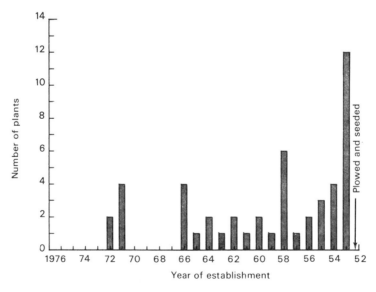

Fig. 46.  Age-class distribution of big sagebrush, Ten Mile
          seeding project.

A reasonably effective brush kill can be expected to last indefinitely if properly managed and if a certain degree of big sagebrush cover is tolerable. Stands of grass usually appear to be deteriorating rapidly in the first few years following treatment. Most of the apparent reinvasion of big sagebrush, however, is actually the recovery of unkilled plants and the growth of seedlings established in the first few years following treatment. Seedlings established shortly after treatment generally remain small as adult plants. Growth of big sagebrush seedlings in stands with either well-established crested wheatgrass or excellent native bunchgrass is very slow, and many brush seedlings do not reach maturity. We believe that big sagebrush stands composed of less than 25-percent brush do not significantly lower the grazing capacity of associated crested wheatgrass or native grasses. If properly used, seedings containing big sagebrush should not significantly deteriorate unless brush cover increased beyond 25 percent.

Areas with nearly complete big sagebrush kills, especially those doubly treated - as spraying followed by wildfire - will return to brush slowly or not at all during a reasonable management timespan. Although a complete big sagebrush kill will result in an essentially permanent absence of big sagebrush, kills of between 90 and 95 percent allow seedlings to become established and significant mature plants to survive. We contend that the mixture of brush and grass will also be expected to have a long lifespan. Once the brush reaches equilibrium, generally within a few years, proper use will result in ample grass on a long-term basis.

Areas sprayed and then seeded to crested wheatgrass had much less brush than areas sprayed and not seeded, 0.22 and 0.33 plant/yd$^2$ (0.26 and 0.39/m$^2$), respectively. Before spraying, the spray-and-seed sites supported the heaviest brush stands and the fewest perennial grasses. The drilling operation certainly killed some brush plants, but higher density of perennial grasses following seeding resulted in less re-establishment of big sagebrush.

## Summary Comments on Vegetation in 1975

Condition and trend of the treated and untreated areas varied as did the rangeland itself. An argument can be made that thickening of stands and reinvasion by big sagebrush are causing a decline in range condition for domestic livestock. Although this is happening, we believe that management through control of stocking rates, animal distribution, and seasonal grazing systems will prevent the return of the big sagebrush to its pretreatment density. Stands of the large perennial grasses between the bushes will cause the invasion to stabilize at a probable brush cover of less than 25 percent, whereas it frequently was 50- to 60-percent cover before treatment. Few areas sampled showed concrete evidence of a downward trend. Plant vigor was excellent, and only one project area had significant numbers of dead desirable grasses. Sheet erosion was minor, and both erosion and pedestalling of plants were less in grazed areas than in the ungrazed exclosure west of Jordan Valley. Pedestalling of as much as 1 inch (2.5 cm) is normal for the perennial bunchgrasses in this area. Although we do not have survey data, we believe that at least 50 percent of the district is in good or excellent condition and that the trend of nearly all the district is either stable or improving.

Crested wheatgrass is stable or increasing in density in seeded areas. Only in China Gulch "B" seeding were any dead crested wheatgrass plants noted. Reproduction of crested wheatgrass over much of the Vale District was related to the present stand density. Seedings with more than four plants per square yard (4.8/m$^2$) rarely contained crested wheatgrass seedlings. Less successful initial seedings often contained seedlings, indicating stand thickening. Apparently, the maximum density of crested wheatgrass beyond which the stand does not thicken is about one plant for 2 square feet. Management practices intended to foster plant reproduction in these well-established stands wastes forage and are not needed.

Crested wheatgrass shows little evidence of dying out, even under heavy use.  We
found none of the many seasonal patterns of grazing harmful to crested wheatgrass.
It should be used in whatever pattern overall management requires.

Bluebunch wheatgrass also appears stable on treated areas.  Not one seedling was
found during sampling in the summer of 1975.  Small plants occurred commonly, but
none was unequivocally a seedling and not part of a broken larger bunch.  Bluebunch
wheatgrass has been reported to establish only in summers of higher than average
rainfall (Harris 1967).  Paired treated and untreated samples showed density to be
0.75 plant/yd$^2$ (0.90/m$^2$) in the brush and 0.96 plant/yd$^2$ (1.15/m$^2$) with little
brush.  Following spraying, large bunches which had grown under big sagebrush plants
often broke into several smaller plants.  The evidence, as observed in the field,
suggests that bluebunch wheatgrass, although a bunchgrass, primarily increases by
this vegetative means rather than by seed.  We believe that moderate grazing helps
this process.  Bluebunch wheatgrass appears to be stable under the intensities of
grazing practiced on the Vale District.  The potential for further increase is not
clear.  Many areas, both with and without brush control, support excellent stands
of bluebunch wheatgrass.  Less well-stocked stands will slowly increase in grass
density.  Sprayed areas with densities of bluebunch wheatgrass of less than one
plant per square yard (1.20/m$^2$) appear to have more big sagebrush seedlings with
the shrubs more actively invading than do treated areas with denser stands of
native grasses.  The eventual density of big sagebrush in the climax stands was
discussed above.  The dense stand of big sagebrush with numerous plants of bluebunch wheatgrass responds dramatically to a treatment of spraying and no grazing
for 2 years.  Two years of resting unsprayed areas also brings dramatic response.
Perhaps spraying alone has been overrated as a treatment of sagebrush-grass.
This point will be explored later in conjunction with costs and benefits of
spraying.

The relationship between crested wheatgrass and the annual cheatgrass must be
discussed.  Some areas have little cheatgrass and others have dense stands.  This
pattern, obvious on a large scale, also occurs within small areas (Fig. 47).
Seedings with crested wheatgrass densities of less than three plants per square
yard (3.6/m$^2$) were patchily infested with cheatgrass.  Seedings with more than
four plants per square yard (4.80/m$^2$) rarely had significant amounts of cheatgrass.
This annual formed dense stands where crested wheatgrass density was less than
1.5 plants/yd$^2$ (1.79/m$^2$).  The mechanism of establishment of this pattern is not
at all clear since cheatgrass seed occurs everywhere, and the periods of growth
of both species differ significantly.  A research study is needed on this point.
Cheatgrass does fill a useful role in the poorer seedings, providing forage in
some years, which rivals total production in successful seedings, and protecting
the soil from erosion.

From a vegetational standpoint the Vale Program has been highly effective.  Formerly
dense and nearly pure stands of big sagebrush have been converted to grasslands on
about 8 percent of the district.  The additional forage provided by improvement of
range conditions gave the opportunity for flexibility in grazing use and further
improvement in the untreated ranges.  The district now produces more range forage
than livestock harvest.  The excess, however, provides stability against drought
and needed cover and feed for wildlife.  Some of the relationships with other uses
of the land are examined next.

Fig. 47.   Patches of cheatgrass occur and remain ungrazed
where crested wheatgrass is in thin stands.


## MULTIPLE USES AND RELATIONSHIPS IN THE VALE DISTRICT

### *Livestock*

The Vale Program began with major emphasis on rehabilitation of soil and vegetation,
conservation of water, and increased forage for livestock and wildlife.  Clearly,
the rangeland resource needed repair, regardless of the use to which it might be
put.  In 1962, that use was grazing by livestock and, in fact, major emphasis in
the program aimed to improve livestock forage resources and livestock management.
The accomplishments for 1962-75 are listed briefly as follows:

| | |
|---|---|
| Big sagebrush plowed and seeded to crested wheatgrass | 164,000 acres (66 400 ha) |
| Big sagebrush sprayed with 2,4-D | 280,000 acres (113 400 ha) |
| Big sagebrush sprayed and seeded to crested wheatgrass | 53,000 acres (21 500 ha) |
| Seedings for wildlife (legumes and browse) | 58,000 acres (25 500 ha) |
| Seeded only and reseeded | 8,000 acres (3 250 ha) |
| Fencing | 2,000 miles (3 200 km) |
| Deep wells and water storage tanks | 28 |
| Pipelines | 443 miles (709 km) |
| Reservoirs | 574 |
| Spring developments | 428 |
| Cattle guards | 360 |
| Roads | 500 miles (800 km) |

In addition to rehabilitation and construction of physical improvements, 28 grazing management plans have been formally accepted by livestock permittees and the BLM. All the remaining national resource grazing lands are in less formally controlled seasonal grazing plans.

The estimated grazing capacity of the whole district increased from 17 acres (6.9 ha) per AUM to 10.4 acres (4.2 ha) between 1962 and 1975, largely through removal of big sagebrush and increases in crested wheatgrass and the native perennial bunchgrasses. The task is not finished because large portions, mainly in the northern part of the district, remain in big sagebrush and cheatgrass. If all the vegetation were changed to something near the climax types, the overall grazing capacity might be 5-6 acres (2-2.5 ha) per AUM. The final result of the Vale Program, we estimate, will be about 8 acres (3.2 ha) per AUM.

The purposes for which the Vale District Program was established have been met in large measure. Livestock grazing caused the range deterioration in the first place, and the rehabilitation has restored much of the land into its once fully vegetated condition. The economy of the community depends on livestock, about a third of which grazes the public lands. Livestock grazing exceeds all other uses, the situation for over a century and one likely to continue.

To recognize that livestock is the principal use does not suggest that others of the multiple uses should be eliminated or reduced. Many are compatible with grazing by domestic animals, especially where fences, water, and riding permit manipulation of when, where, and how much grazing takes place. Grazing by domestic animals may be used as a tool to enhance the habitats for other species. Actually, other users, particularly wildlife, received increasing attention as the program proceeded. In addition to the seedings mentioned above, deep reservoirs provided permanent fish habitats. Goose nesting sites, fenced water, fence designs, and other practices favored wildlife. Eleven of the originally planned projects were eliminated because of probable damage to browse. Areas within projects were eliminated from treatment, including streambanks, canyons, deer winter ranges, sagegrouse concentration areas, and most of the low sagebrush vegetational type.

Although multiple use decisions from 1962 to 1973 may not suffice for 1975 or 1980 situations, the Vale Program attempted to be accountable to all users. The following sections examine the multiple use situations, as we found them. Mainly because few data were collected before and during the program, these analyses are inconclusive, and they depend largely on value judgments.

*Wild Horses*

Thirteen horse management areas on the Vale District supported 2,416 wild horses according to counts made from an airplane on April 19, 1975 (Fig. 48, Table 16). Average band, family, or harem size was 7.6 head which ranged from about 4 to 11 mares per dominant male. Younger males may be in the band and single males may be found. About 15 percent of the horses were young foals. It is estimated that 10 percent of the colts are born in the fall and 90 percent in March, April, and May.

Table 16.  Counted numbers of wild horses in the Vale
District, Bureau of Land Management, April 1975

| | Number[1] and name of horse management area | Acres[2] | Number of horses | | | Percent foals | Average band size |
|---|---|---|---|---|---|---|---|
| | | | Adults | Foals | Total | | |
| 1 | Hog Creek | 18,120 | 64 | 6 | 70 | 8.6 | 6.2 |
| 2 | Lake Ridge | 2,720 | 11 | 1 | 12 | 8.3 | 6.0 |
| 3 | Pot Holes | 3,840 | 19 | 3 | 22 | 13.6 | 7.3 |
| 4 | Basque | 7,570 | 28 | 5 | 33 | 15.2 | 6.6 |
| 5 | Cottonwood Basin | 2,300 | 0[3] | 0 | 0 | 0 | 0 |
| 6 | Cottonwood Creek | 5,660 | 49 | 9 | 58 | 15.5 | 8.3 |
| 7 | Cold Springs | 21,540 | 181 | 27 | 208 | 12.6 | 8.8 |
| 8 | Atturbury | 4,080 | 15 | 3 | 18 | 16.6 | 18.0 |
| 9 | Stockade | 26,866 | 49 | 5 | 54 | 9.3 | 10.8 |
| 10 | Morger Allotment | 26,172 | 128 | 19 | 147 | 12.9 | 8.2 |
| 11 | Sheepheads/Barren Valley | 639,770 | 952 | 176 | 1,128 | 15.6 | 6.9 |
| 12 | Jackies Butte | 78,094 | 186 | 36 | 222 | 16.2 | 8.8 |
| 13 | Three Fingers | 70,868 | 379 | 65 | 444 | 14.6 | 8.7 |
| | Total | 907,600 | 2,061 | 355 | 2,416 | 14.7 | 7.6 |

[1] Numbers refer to locations in Fig. 48.

[2] 1 acre equals 0.405 hectare.

[3] 67 horses claimed but ungathered.

Horses have been regularly counted on the district, but with varying accuracy, since 1968 (Table 16). Two herds, Jackies Butte and Three Fingers, which had been reduced in numbers, increased from 94 to 150 and from 66 to 225, respectively, in the 3-year period 1972-74 (Table 17). Although inaccurate counting and addition of adults to the herds cannot be ruled out in either area, the major increase reflects natural reproduction. The data for Jackies Butte are believed accurate and they suggest a reproductive rate of 60 percent in 3 years or 20 percent per year. Wild horse herds throughout the Western States are known to have high rates of reproduction until feed becomes extremely scarce. Few deaths result from predators and diseases, and confined herds soon increase to and beyond the grazing capacity of their habitats.

Table 17.  Counted numbers of wild horses, Vale District, Bureau of Land Management

| Horse management area | 1968 | Spring 1969 | Fall 1970 | Winter 1972 | Winter 1973 | Spring 1974 | Fall 1974 |
|---|---|---|---|---|---|---|---|
| Hog Creek | - | - | - | 18 [1] | 35 [1] | 17 [1] | 56 |
| Lake Ridge | - | - | - | 11 | 4 [1] | 5 [1] | 5 [1] |
| Pot Holes | - | - | - | 17 | 21 | 4 [1] | 19 |
| Basque | - | - | - | 6 | 6 | 6 | 28 |
| Cottonwood Basin | - | - | - | 2 | 0 | - | 1 |
| Cottonwood Creek | - | - | - | 19 | 34 | 31 [1] | 50 |
| Cold Springs | - | - | - | 52 [1] | 105 | 136 | 164 |
| Atturbury | - | - | - | 6 | 6 | 0 | 0 |
| Stockade | - | - | - | 10 | 13 | 42 | 47 |
| Morger Allotment | - | - | - | 80 | 85 | 132 | 154 |
| Sheepheads/Barren Valley | - | - | - | 539 | 660 | 1,217 | - |
| Jackies Butte | - | 225 | 263 | 94 [2] | 113 | 140 | 150 |
| Three Fingers | 364 | 64 [3] | - | 66 | 120 | 234 | 225 |

[1] Inaccurate.

[2] 181 head of horses removed in November 1970.

[3] 300 head of horses removed in fall of 1968.

In 1975, Cold Springs, Sheepheads/Barren Valley, and Jackies Butte had too many horses. The early signs of damage by horses, enlarged dusting areas and numerous trails, indicated deterioration where horses congregate in the Cold Springs area. Sheepheads/Barren Valley had deteriorating conditions within both winter and summer ranges, and Jackies Butte had denuded winter range area due to wild horses.

We believe that too many free-roaming horses existed in the Vale District in 1975. They grazed to the extent of 28,000 AUM's on 900,000 acres (360 000 ha) designated for horses. Even distribution of grazing remains impossible to attain with wild horses; therefore, some areas become overgrazed and others not grazed at all.

This situation is happening on the three areas mentioned above where numbers of horses should be reduced and maintained at lower levels. A reasonable balance between maintenance of the range and the horses should be attained with 2,000 horses, provided the three management areas receive most of the decrease.

Management of the horses has not been attained. They are creatures of habit and reuse the same trails and dusting areas many times; they paw, especially at springs and other water sources (Fig. 49). Most will not go through a fence unless they are driven to it; however, many learn to crawl under or get through fences. The survey in 1975 found 181 head outside the management area boundaries.

Conflicts between needs of wild horses and those of other users potentially exist. Perhaps 8 percent of the grazing capacity is reserved for wild horses, and we doubt that any local person wants to eliminate them. However, they damage or cross over fences on snow during the winter. The BLM has scheduled gate-openings, removal of existing fences, and changed patterns of livestock grazing to favor the wild horses - not without concern and extra effort by the permittees. Wild horses, in isolated instances, have kept cattle away from water for short periods, but antelope have been observed at water with them. They pay little attention to coyotes.

An unknown and possible conflict may exist because of overlapping diets with the ruminants. Wild horses consume mostly grass but they do feed on forbs and browse, especially in severe winters and when the grass is gone. They tend to "chase" after the early growth of annual grasses from low to high elevations as the growing season develops, thereby grazing too early and trampling wet soil. Cattle, not permitted on high ranges till summer, perhaps do not overlap with the wild horses on more than 20 to 25 percent of the range. Behavior conflicts between cattle and wild horses appear minor. Competition between the horses and bighorn sheep, antelope, and other wildlife is unmeasured and a matter for speculation only. A major effect is most likely to occur through grazing by horses which changes the available feed and cover for other species.

Recreationists make little onsite use of the wild horses. In one year, two persons separately and one party made pack trips to see the wild horses. Of course, many persons have some satisfaction in knowing that wild horses still exist on the Vale District. In actual fact, they are so well adapted to the terrain that their removal would be most difficult. The major problems are to keep them within the designated wild horse management areas and to prevent them from overgrazing their own habitats. Both problems are current and in danger of intensifying.

## Wildlife and Fisheries

This section borrows heavily from an analysis of the wildlife situation in the Vale District by R. R. Kindschy (1971). Kindschy's paper summarizes available data to 1971. We have leaned heavily on Mr. Kindschy's personal observations in the Vale District since 1958, several years before the program started. He estimated in 1971 that 57,000 big game animals plus numerous upland game birds and nongame wildlife resided in the Vale Program area. The number of species is about 300. His analysis used data collected by the Oregon State Game Commission to determine the impact of the Vale Program on selected wildlife species.

Changes in vegetation because of overgrazing, which resulted in extensive and thick stands of brush with little grass, probably favored mule deer and blacktailed jackrabbit; but populations of both tend to be cyclic. Pronghorn antelope, sage-grouse, and bighorn sheep suffered from the increased brush. Bighorn sheep disappeared from the area about 1914 due to changes in vegetation, hunting, and scabies contracted from domestic sheep. Animal population numbers in 1962 reflected

100 years of many kinds of use and abuse. Animal responses to the Vale District
Program give us an entirely new set of population numbers, which are analyzed in
this section without implied desirability. Each may still be far different from
those in the time before domestic livestock.

Fig. 49.  Wild horses (top) damage the soil by trailing and
pawing dust-bath areas (bottom) (Bureau of Land
Management photos).

Mule deer. Unusually high populations of mule deer occurred in the Vale District
in the 1950's, as they did in other western rangeland. Fluctuations in numbers on
the district have paralleled those of other districts, except for indications that
reduction in numbers since 1973 has not been as severe as elsewhere (Fig. 50).

Fig. 50. Mule deer fawn (photo, courtesy R. Kindschy,
Bureau of Land Management, Vale, Oregon).

The ratios of bucks to does appear to be decreasing more rapidly, from 36 to 19
bucks per 100 does on the Vale District, than on other areas in Oregon. That,
however, is a drop of about 50 percent, just the same in the district as elsewhere
in Oregon (Table 18). The ratio continues to be higher in the district than in
the remainder of Oregon. The number of fawns per 100 does remained relatively
stable with a slightly higher ratio in the district than in other parts of Oregon
until 1971, when the Vale District herd was highly successful. Fawns per 100 does
were lowest in 1962. Low numbers of hunter days and relatively poor hunter
success suggest two periods of low deer populations, 1966-68 and 1973-75 (Table 19).
The first followed a severe winter kill in 1964-65, great reductions in permits for
anterless deer, and reductions in hunting pressure. The reasons for the latest
decline are unknown in the Vale District as they are elsewhere.

Many management decisions in the Vale District have successfully increased palatable
browse. These include seedings of browse, no brush control at all on 11 projects,
boundary lines changed to exclude browse from other brush controls, and minimized
late summer and autumn livestock grazing on deer winter range. Kindschy (1971)
found a 25-percent increase in available browse on 22 transects between 1963 and
1971. Mule deer often find grasses attractive during the winters and springs after
fall growth. Crested wheatgrass, cheatgrass, and Sandberg bluegrass often produce
sufficient green leaves in mild autumns to furnish feed for deer and other species

later. In one example, deer have changed their migrations from the Three-Forks area (4,600 feet or 1 400 meters in elevation) to the Rome seedings (3,500 feet or 1 060 meters in elevation) to take advantage of the new feed. Uncontrolled brush and much browse still grow in the canyons, along the streambanks, and on steep slopes which surround and intermingle with the brush controls and seedings. The combinations of seedings, rejuvenating shrubs on them, and the uncontrolled brushland appear to be attractive habitats for mule deer winter range (Fig. 51). In a comparison of deer use before and after spraying of their summer range, Reeher (1969) found in the one example studied that spraying reduced deer use on a summer range. Seedings apparently received light use by deer except when heavy winter snows forced them to lower elevations.

Table 18. Mule deer bucks and fawns on the Vale District and on other Oregon areas

| Year | Bucks per 100 does | | Fawns per 100 does | |
|------|-------------------------|----------------------|-------------------------|----------------------|
|      | Vale District[1] | Other Oregon[2] | Vale District[1] | Other Oregon[2] |
| 1960 | 36 | 24 | 75 | 73 |
| 1961 | 38 | 20 | 94 | 73 |
| 1969 | 20 | 13 | 76 | 69 |
| 1970 | 19 | 12 | 74 | 68 |
| 1971 | - | - | 79 | 40 |

[1] Bureau of Land Management.

[2] Oregon State Game Commission annual reports.

In the period 1963-71, mule deer were estimated to have decreased from 57,000 to 44,000. These numbers are the broadest kind of estimates as no systematic efforts were made to count mule deer populations. Total herd numbers were determined by a formula which used hunting pressure, harvest data, and percentage of herd removal. After 1971, the general deer decline appears to be slightly less in the district than in other western mule deer herds. In general, mule deer exhibited the decline in population typical of the Intermountain west during the establishment of the Vale District rehabilitation program. They declined no more than in most other places. A conservative view is that the Vale Program had no great impact on mule deer populations.

Pronghorn antelope. The dramatic increase in pronghorns during the course of the Vale Program and under increasing hunting pressure has been a most impressive wildlife phenomenon (Fig. 52). The population increased 2.6-fold and the hunters by three times without diminishing the hunter success from 1961 to 1975 (Table 20). The largest population was reached in 1968. Pronghorn antelope were seldom seen in the early 1900's.

Table 19. Hunting pressure and hunter success for mule deer
on Oregon State Game Management units which
include the Vale District, Bureau of Land Management, 1961-75[1]/

| Year | 100 hunter days | Hunter days per deer | Hunter success |
|------|------|------|------|
| | | | Percent |
| 1961[2]/ | 57.3 | – | 70.8 |
| 1962 | 57.4 | 8.2 | 60.0 |
| 1963 | 31.5 | 5.3 | 59.0 |
| 1964 | 35.9 | 4.5 | 62.0 |
| 1965 | 27.3 | 6.1 | 48.3 |
| 1966 | 21.8 | 4.8 | 61.3 |
| 1967 | 19.5 | 4.9 | 47.3 |
| 1968 | 24.3 | 4.4 | 61.8 |
| 1969 | 33.2 | 5.9 | 47.8 |
| 1970 | 35.7 | 6.3 | 53.0 |
| 1971 | 54.1 | 10.8 | 43.8 |
| 1972 | 37.9 | 15.5 | 40.8 |
| 1973 | 37.3 | 14.0 | 28.3 |
| 1974 | 29.1 | 16.5 | 27.0 |
| 1975 | 17.7 | 16.0 | 26.0 |

[1]/ Oregon State Game Commission annual reports.

[2]/ Variable length of hunting season and variable limitations in legal bag among years
reduces precision of data.

In 1970, the Vale District had 143 percent more antelope than in 1962, but other
eastern Oregon antelope populations had increased only 50 percent. A census
showed that numbers had increased from 0.9 to 2.0 antelope per mile (1.6 km) of
transect on the Vale District but the level of their occurrence was constant in
the remainder of Oregon. The actual hunter harvest increased from 123 to 249
(1961-71) on the district but only from 295 to 387 in the other parts of eastern
Oregon during the same period. Each hunter averaged 2.4 days of hunting.

Observations indicate that antelope prefer places where brush has been removed and
crested wheatgrass seeded. Young, tender growth of grasses and forbs attracts
them. They are frequently seen in areas closely used by cattle.

Table 20.   Numbers of antelope and hunter success in the
            Vale District, Bureau of Land Management,
            1961-1976

| Year | Number of antelope | Number of permits | Hunter days | Hunter success |
|------|--------------------|-------------------|-------------|----------------|
|      |                    |                   |             | Percent        |
| 1961 | 947                | –                 | 532         | 56             |
| 1962 | 1,445              | 175               | 386         | 63             |
| 1963 | 1,800              | 175               | 374         | 60             |
| 1964 | 2,039              | 200               | 389         | 64             |
| 1965 | 2,321              | 200               | 448         | 65             |
| 1966 | 2,615              | 250               | 502         | 73             |
| 1967 | 2,823              | 250               | 494         | 56             |
| 1968 | 3,315              | 250               | 500         | 66             |
| 1969 | 2,840              | 300               | 623         | 70             |
| 1970 | 2,957              | 500               | 924         | 60             |
| 1971 | 2,840              | 525               | 1,017       | 62             |
| 1972 | 2,831              | 525               | 991         | 61             |
| 1973 | 2,956              | 625               | 1,166       | 59             |
| 1974 | 2,504              | 625               | 1,164       | 58             |
| 1975 | 1,523[1/]          | 625               | 1,104       | 52             |
| 1976 | 2,979              | 625               | –           | –              |

Source: Oregon State Game Commission.

[1/] Inaccurate census due to weather conditions in 1975.


Nomad alfalfa has been seeded with crested wheatgrass on 56,340 acres (22 818 ha)
on 36 separate areas in the Vale District, and it is highly preferred by antelope
and other animals (Vale District Manager 1974).  The common seeding procedure was
to plow sagebrush in the spring, plant crested wheatgrass in the autumn, and
aerially spread inoculated alfalfa seed at 1 lb/acre (1.1 kg/ha) the following
spring.  A survey of 20 of the seedings in 1973 and 1974 revealed that nomad
alfalfa composed 10.7 percent of the vegetation present on 12 of the seedings
where it was encountered, but it had completely failed or was minor in 8 of the
projects.  Apparently once established, the alfalfa can persist unless blacktailed
jackrabbits dig out the crowns, but its actual persistence is unknown.  Our
observations suggest less alfalfa present in 1975 than was reported in 1973-74
but the differences may have been due to season or method of sampling.  A particularly important characteristic of alfalfa is that it stays green and highly
nutritious all summer.

Plowing of sagebrush and seeding to crested wheatgrass attracts antelope for a few
years after the operation, probably because of high forb content in the vegetation.
Antelope abound on the rehabilitated Cow Creek and Soldier Creek units and on the

Antelope Flat and Deer Flat units which are native sagebrush-grass range in excellent condition (Reeher 1969).  These animals avoid tall stands of big sagebrush, preferring low stands and the short species of sagebrush.  Some ranges do not attract antelope in either the native brush or seeded stands.  For example, the Starvation spray-and-seed project, which lies between winter and summer range, received little use by antelope before and after treatment.  Antelope moved from the Chicken Creek plow-and-seed project to adjacent areas in the year of treatment, but returned the following year and remained in large numbers (Reeher 1969).  It appears that plowing and seeding makes better antelope range than either spraying or spraying and seeding.

Antelope frequently drink at livestock watering points.  Undoubtedly, provision of dry-season water has permitted antelope to use areas in the summer which were not formerly available to them.  Additional water provided in the Vale Program may have benefited the antelope as much as any other practice.  Fences appear not to restrict antelope movements.

Bighorn sheep.  Seventeen California bighorn sheep were reintroduced in November 1965 into the Mahagony unit at Leslie Gulch along the east side of Owyhee Reservoir.  The actual count was 53 (11 rams, 25 ewes, 17 lambs) in 1971, increasing from 6 rams, 8 ewes, and 3 lambs in the original group which came from the Hart Mountain Refuge.  Over 100 sheep were estimated in the herd in 1974, but cursory search revealed only 20 in 1975 (Fig. 53).  They are elusive animals, and many could have been missed in the rugged topography.  Some were believed to have migrated to new ranges.

Fig. 51.  A mixture of bitterbrush, big sagebrush, and bluebunch wheatgrass on winter deer range.

Fig. 52.   Antelope buck (Bureau of Land Management photo).

Bighorn sheep have not extended their range into the brush controls and seedings
but are on native ranges which have improved during the program.   Range management
practices, including controls of livestock numbers and seasons of grazing,
apparently have fostered return of near-climax sagebrush-grass and permitted
bighorn sheep to do well.   Hunters were allowed to draw for two permits (rams
with three-quarters curl or better) in 1973-74 and four permits in 1975.

Rocky mountain elk.   Migratory herds, estimated at 100 head, enter the district
during the winter but numbers vary with severity of winter.   Little potential elk
habitat, especially summer range, exists on the Vale District and there need be
little concern for elk in this area.

Blacktailed jackrabbits.   The last peak in jackrabbit populations in the Vale
District occurred in 1957-58 when large numbers invaded farmlands, causing
thousands of dollars in losses to the farmers and overuse to rangelands.   Neigh-
boring areas in both Oregon and Idaho have experienced subsequent but less severe
increases in populations of jackrabbits.

Fig. 53.  Bighorn sheep (Bureau of Land Management photo).

Reasons for the failure of cycling on the Vale District and lack of synchronism
with cycles in other districts are unclear.  Present jackrabbit populations appear
to be low and stable.  They are known to prefer brush-covered lands with little
grass (Fig. 54).  The change in range condition from poor to good or excellent for
livestock may have greatly reduced favorable jackrabbit habitat in the Vale
District.  Reeher (1969), after comparing four rehabilitation projects with nearby
untouched brushland for 6 years, concluded that the projects did not affect
cottontail and jackrabbit populations or their use of an area.  Sagebrush cover
provided greater winter protection for them than the grasslands.

Chukar partridge.  Chukars were introduced into the Vale District in the 1950's
and have since found their way to many if not all suitable habitats.  Data from
the annual reports of the Oregon State Game Commission (1962 and 1970), as
compiled by Kindschy (1972), show that the numbers of chukars in the Vale District
were higher than in other eastern Oregon areas and that they increased twofold
during the Vale District Program but only by one-fifth outside the district
(Table 21).  In 1969, an estimated 48,000 birds were taken by hunters in the Vale
District.

Chukars feed on insects and seeds.  Cheatgrass and crested wheatgrass seeds commonly
occur in their diets, but grass and weed seeds abound everywhere.  It is doubtful
if the rehabilitation project markedly affected their population numbers (Fig. 55).
Chukars prefer rocky slopes, talus, and steep escarpments - during winter those
facing south.  These topographic types were omitted from the rehabilitation
projects.  The mobility of the birds permits them to feed in the seedings and
return to their favorite habitats.

Table 21. Average numbers of chukar partridge, sagegrouse,
and valley quail counted per 10-mile (16-km)
transect of the Vale District Program, 1961-62
and 1968-70[1]/

| Item | 1961 | 1962 | 1968 | 1969 | 1970 |
|------|------|------|------|------|------|
| Chukar partridge: | | | | | |
| Vale District | 42 | 51 | 170 | 126 | 127 |
| Other eastern Oregon | 24 | 15 | 28 | 22 | 21 |
| Sagegrouse: | | | | | |
| Vale Distrct | 69 | 33 | 132 | 92 | 95 |
| Other eastern Oregon | 23 | 37 | 15 | 7 | 14 |
| Valley quail: | | | | | |
| Vale District | 14 | 8 | 40 | 22 | 29 |
| Other eastern Oregon | 40 | 18 | 28 | 8 | 20 |

[1]/ From Kindschy 1972.

Fig. 54.   Jackrabbit (Bureau of Land Management photo).

Kindschy (1971) believes that development of water for livestock was the practice
giving greatest benefits to chukars.  Reeher (1969) found that spraying of sagebrush did not reduce chukar use of an area and may have increased it.  Variable
use from year to year prevented more definite conclusions from Reeher's study.

Sagegrouse.  The population dynamics, ideal habitat conditions, and impacts of
rangeland rehabilitation on sagegrouse are little understood in the Vale District.
Many thousands of birds inhabited the area in the 1920's and 1930's.  They nearly

disappeared in the 1940's and 1950's but have been increasing since.  The increase
was estimated to be over 100 percent from 1961 to 1970, but similar kinds of census
data suggested a 60-percent decrease in the remainder of eastern Oregon (Table 21).
In 1971 the Vale District was the only area in eastern Oregon that had an open
hunting season for sagegrouse.  The Oregon State Game Commission reported 1,090
sagegrouse taken in the Vale District during the 1969 season.

Fig. 55.   Top, chukar partridge; bottom, sagegrouse (Bureau
           of Land Management photo).

Sagegrouse use big sagebrush for food and cover, especially for nesting and in the
winter, but apparently large areas of continuous big sagebrush are marginal sagegrouse habitat and reduction of wide expanses of brush causes little loss of their
habitats (Fig. 55). They need meadows, seeps, and open areas along the valley
bottoms as well as the big sagebrush. Many are found along the edges and in hay
and grain fields. Concentrations of livestock, which damaged the meadows, may
have caused more loss of sagegrouse habitat than overgrazing in wide expanses of
brushlands. Reeher (1969) found that spraying and spray-seed operations reduced
use by sagegrouse, but it increased following the plow-seed operations. Overall
sagegrouse populations are greater than they were before the program began in 1962,
a situation not matched in other parts of eastern Oregon.

Quail. Both the valley or California quail and the mountain quail occur in the
Vale District. Both species fluctuate widely in population numbers. The valley
quail increased during the course of the rehabilitation program (Table 21). Lack
of data and even of opinions prevents comment on the uncommon mountain quail.

All the rehabilitation projects stated that streambank and other shrub vegetation
along the valley bottoms must be retained. Therefore, the principal native cover
of the valley quail was preserved. Rotational grazing has fostered more vegetation
in sites where cattle normally concentrated along the streams. Improved habitat
for valley quail has resulted, but we doubt that the rehabilitation projects
reached into the mountain quail habitats.

Waterfowl. Mallard and teal have benefited from at least 624 of the reservoirs on
the district, many of which are 1 to 4 surface acres in size. A few have been
fenced to exclude livestock use from the pond edges where increased vegetational
cover provides nesting sites for waterfowl. Rotational grazing and no spring to
early summer grazing often gives the same protection as fencing to the nesting
birds but on an irregular basis. Most of the reservoirs should have been equipped
with a pipeline and trough for livestock watering and fenced at the time of
construction.

The Rock Creek Reservoir, a large, shallow pond near Jordan Valley, and over 200
acres (81 ha) of fenced land around it provide protection for a small population
of Canada geese. Construction included 18 islands for nesting sites which are
regularly used (Fig. 56). In 1971 over 50 goslings were observed at the sites.

Ground squirrels. Several species, but principally *Spermophilus townsendii*, occur
ubiquitously and in large numbers within the Vale District. They prefer the sandy
loam soils and lacustrine sediments. Although these rodents usually cycle, high
numbers have been sustained since 1968 on several crested wheatgrass seedings near
Vale. Forage for livestock may have been reduced but permanent effects on the
grass stands appear to be minor. These rodent populations furnish recreational
shooting for local residents and their continued abundance has permitted an increase
in predators, especially raptorial birds.

Raptorial birds. No census data are available on raptor populations, and none are
being collected. Local wildlife people generally agree that populations are
higher than at any time they can remember. Numerous golden eagles; rough-legged,
redtailed, and marsh hawks; prairie falcon; and several species of owls can be
found with little effort. Sustained ground squirrel populations supply their food,
and national publicity for preservation has increased their chances for survival.

Other predators. A recent high in the observed, but not counted, coyote population
may be diminishing, as few young animals appeared in 1975. Abundance of ground
squirrels and reduced predator controls contributed to the high population; but
reasons for a decline, if one exists, are unclear. Bobcat populations peaked about
1960, dipped to a low in 1968-69, and now are believed to be recovering (Fig. 57).

A timber wolf (identified at the Smithsonian Institution) was shot in 1973.
Mountain lions occur rarely. Badgers and long-tailed weasels associate with rodents,
their principal food supplies. Skunks and raccoons depend more on cultivated areas
than on native rangelands.

Fig. 56. Canada geese (top) and nesting sites constructed
for them (bottom) (photos, courtesy R. Kindschy,
Bureau of Land Management, Vale, Oregon).

Fig. 57.  Bobcats (photo, courtesy R. Kindschy, Bureau of
Land Management, Vale, Oregon).

We estimate that effects of the rehabilitation program upon predator populations
have been minor.  Increases in some species at a few locations might be due to
increased rodent populations which in turn resulted from less brush and more grass
than in the early 1960's or before.  The chain of events cannot be proved because
other factors have contributed to the changes.  A negative conclusion seems more
reasonable - apparently the rehabilitation program has not reduced the populations
of predators.

Fisheries.  The Oregon State Game Commission takes responsibility for fisheries
work within the district, and the BLM actively cooperates with technical assistance
and limited project construction.  Treatment of both the Malheur and Owyhee Rivers
removed nongame or rough fish; and restocking included rainbow trout, smallmouth
bass, and channel catfish, with little involvement in the rangeland rehabilitation
program.

The Alvord cutthroat trout, a threatened subspecies, occurs naturally in three
streams in the Oregon Canyon Range near the southwestern corner of the district.

Fencing of critical portions of the riparian habitat has been accomplished through special funding and the fish has been successfully released in other suitable habitats.  Trash catchers in some of the streams result in resting pools for improved pool/riffle ratios.

The Vale District contains approximately 6,500 surface acres (2 630 ha) of natural lakes and reservoirs, many 2 to 5 acres (0.8–2.0 ha) in size.  Some have been fenced and planted with rainbow trout.  The BLM constructed Squaw Creek Reservoir specifically for a fishery, and it has been a successful recreational project.

Since livestock naturally congregate along the streams and damaged these locations in the past, only intensive rangeland practices can successfully repair many riparian sites.  On the Vale District, rotational systems of grazing and abundant forage on thousands of acres have reduced grazing pressure and permitted vegetation to return on streamside sites, the water to carry fewer sediments, and streambed scouring to decrease.  More places have flowing water throughout the summer. Fencing of some areas is still needed to allow full growth of riparian vegetation. Sport fishing as provided, protected, and improved by the Vale District Program has become a popular activity in the region (Fig. 58).  Many drive miles over poor roads to fish in a relatively small pond.

Fig. 58.  A constructed reservoir which has been protected
          to provide wildlife and fish habitats (photo,
          courtesy R. Kindschy, Bureau of Land Management,
          Vale, Oregon).

An overall view. Wildlife data available to support the analyses and conclusions
in this section leave much to be desired. Few numbers were available for the
periods before 1962 and after 1971. Many projects started after 1971, and the
effects of all extended beyond that time. Our statements use those data, views
expressed by wildlife biologists, and our own assessments. We believe that antelope and sagegrouse have benefited by the project treatments, although their numbers
and their movements may have been temporarily interrupted or even changed. Mule
deer numbers may not have changed greatly, although we suspect favorable responses
before 1971 and less decline in the herd on the Vale District than in other places
after 1971. Many mule deer in the district depend in part on hay meadows, grain
fields, and other irrigated crops, which were only indirectly influenced by the
rehabilitation projects. Widespread native range improvement but not rehabilitation projects per se contributed to the successful release of bighorn sheep.
Sagegrouse have increased, although their numbers are still small. Valley quail
expanded in both range and numbers during the program. Water and steamside site
management practices have improved the fisheries and quail habitat. We find every
animal species on which data or opinions existed to have increased or to be
unchanged because of the Vale District Program. The collared lizard may be an
exception as it prefers bare ground, much less of which exists since the program
ended. Perhaps the large areas of grass discourage jackrabbits. Our concern is
the continued lack of pertinent data on the wildlife responses to particular
factors which cause change.

The importance of the management of public lands for wildlife has gradually
increased in the Vale District Program during the last 20 years, largely because
of three factors: (1) A professional wildlife manager has been a part of the
team throughout the program. (2) Increased knowledge of wildlife requirements has
accumulated. (3) The public has demanded that attention be given to wildlife.
The continuing inability of professional people to predict effects of rehabilitation practices on wildlife populations in the district contributes more than any
other factor to controversy between wildlife enthusiasts and other land users.

Another problem is the lack of a conceptual framework which allows consideration
of all vertebrates in the planning process and the retention of an emphasis on
management of a single or a few species. Still another problem is the lack of a
definition of "ideal habitat" for each species. If ideal habitat were known, it
could be attained through land management (Thomas et al. 1976). These problems
define specific needs and work is beginning on this subject by a team in the
district. Continued generalized criticism by one user group of another will not
help attain these needs whether they are wildlife vs. livestock or some other
multiple use controversy.

The full integration of wildlife planning into the management of rangeland on the
Vale District should recognize several realities: (1) Livestock grazing is, and
likely will remain, the principal land use of the district; (2) wildlife management is the management of habitats, mainly vegetation, because public land
administrators and private landowners cannot by law control wildlife numbers;
(3) livestock grazing management constitutes a powerful tool in the favorable
management of habitats for wildlife; (4) viable populations of wildlife and
reasonable livestock production will result from coordinated effort. The managers
of rangeland need to be able to predict impacts and outcomes of each of their
actions before doing or not doing a job.

*Threatened and Endangered Species*

Species of vertebrate mammals in southeastern Oregon which have been listed as
threatened and endangered are Merriam shrew, white-tailed jackrabbit, Richardson

ground squirrel, little pocket mouse, northern grasshopper mouse, and the sagebrush vole (Dyrness *et al.* 1975). All but the white-tailed jackrabbit appear to be in low numbers due to natural causes. That publication also includes a list of references that describe the species and where they might be found. A study is underway to determine if the long-billed curlew should be added to the threatened list. The bird nests in grass stands on alkaline soils along the Malheur River west of Vale. Data on either good or bad influences on these species resulting from the Vale District Program, or any management program, do not exist.

A list of vascular plants of special interest includes 17 species (Table 22), 10 of which occur on the national list of threatened and endangered species prepared in 1974 (Smithsonian Institution 1974). A majority of those plants were originally collected on bluffs and in the canyon of the Owyhee River, which provides maximum protection from grazing, fire, and other land management practices. The canyon wall effectively prevents livestock use, and man himself can reach much of the area only with great difficulty. It is and will remain an effective wilderness or research natural area, even without official designation. The Jordan Craters were set aside in 1975 as a Research Natural Area.

Table 22. Vascular plants that may be threatened and
endangered in the Vale District

| Species | Distribution |
|---|---|
| *Astragalus iodanthus* var. *vipereus* | Bluffs, eastern Malheur County |
| *Astragalus mulfordae*[1] | Dry sandy ground, lower Owyhee River, eastern Malheur County |
| *Astragalus nudisiliquus* | Gravelly bluffs, northeastern Malheur County |
| *Astragalus purshii* var. *ophiogenes*[1] | Sagebrush desert, Owyhee River, Malheur County |
| *Astragalus solitarius*[1] | Usually in sagebrush, Owyhee River, Malheur County |
| *Astragalus sterilis*[1] | Clay hills, Succor Creek, Malheur County |
| *Cryptantha propria* | Dry hillsides, northern Malheur County |
| *Cymopterus corrugatus*[1] | Dry hills, southern Malheur County |
| *Eriogonum novonudum*[1] | Stony clay hills, eastern Malheur County |
| *Eriogonum ochrocephalus* spp. *calcareum* | In loose, white volcanic ash, Malheur County |
| *Hackelia cronquistii*[1] | Unknown |
| *Hackelia ophiobia*[1] | Cliffs, Three forks of Owyhee River, Malheur County |
| *Hackelia patens* | Between Vale and Harper, Malheur County |
| *Mentzelia mollis*[1] | Clay slopes, eastern Malheur County |
| *Mirabilis bigelovii* | Canyon of Owhyee River, Malheur County |
| *Silene scaposa* var. *lobata*[1] | Unknown |
| *Trifolium owyheense* | Dry slopes, Succor Creek, Malheur County |

Source: Dyrness *et al.* (1975).

[1] Species list of threatened and endangered plants (Smithsonian Institution 1974).

Gathering of field data on threatened and endangered species of all kinds in the
Vale District constitutes a continuing study which should be funded separately and
justified on its own values.  Very likely, more species would be found in such a
study than are presently on the lists.


*Recreational Uses*

The proposal for the Vale District Program stated that 55 tracts would be developed
for recreational purposes (Fig. 59) - 42 were essentially water- and canyon-based
sites to be developed for family camping, picnicking, hunter camping, and scenic
qualities.  Plans called for facilities such as parking, tables, sanitation, and
potable water.  The other 13 sites included a historic monument, wilderness areas,
and natural preserves.  Certainly, most of the planned roads, cattle guards, and
many of the small reservoirs could have been listed for their values to recreationists.  Recreational use in 1961 amounted to 60,000 visitor days.

Recreationists generally congregate around large bodies of water, such as the
Owyhee, Antelope, and Bully Creek Reservoirs, for three main purposes - camping,
boating, and fishing (Table 23, Fig. 60).  Hunting brings large numbers of persons
to the public lands, many from outside the county.  River rafting on the Owyhee
has recently increased.  Rock hounds from all over the United States are increasing
their searches for geodes, petrified wood, agates, jasper picture rocks, and other
minerals.  Traffic counters now record roughly 250,000 visitor days per year in the
Vale District, four times the number in 1961.

Fig. 59.  Chukar Park illustrates a well-developed and
          posted recreation site (Bureau of Land Management
          photo).

Table 23.  Major recreational areas in Malheur County dependent on lakes

| Name of facility | Nearest town | Surface acres [1] | Improvements | Species | Access |
|---|---|---|---|---|---|
| Antelope Reservoir | Jordan Valley | 3,000 | Park, Bureau of Land Management | Trout | Dirt roads |
| Bully Creek Reservoir | Vale | 1,000 | Boat ramp and park | Trout | Oiled road |
| Beulah Reservoir | Juntura | 1,900 | Boat ramp | Trout | Gravel road |
| Batch Lake | Jordan Valley | 50 | None | | |
| Coyote Hole Reservoir | McDermit | | | | |
| Cow Lakes | Jordan Valley | 975 | Boat ramp | Trout | Gravel road |
| | | | Picnic facilities | Bass | Dirt road |
| Chapman Reservoir | Riverside | 18 | | Trout | Gravel road |
| Dunaway Pond | Adrian | 5 | | Bass | Dirt road |
| Granite Creek Reservoir | Riverside | 15 | | Bass-bluegill | Dirt road |
| Littlefield Reservoir | Harper | 34 | | Bass | |
| Malheur Reservoir | Brogan | 1,400 | Roads, pit toilets | Trout | Gravel road |
| Murphy Reservoir | Beulah-Juntura | 15 | | Trout | Dirt road |
| North Indian Creek Reservoir | Westfall | 40 | | Trout | Dirt road |
| Odom Reservoir | Jordan Valley | 40 | | Trout | |
| Owyhee Reservoir | Nyssa | 12,700 | | Bass-crappie | |
| Leslie Gulch | Adrian | | | Bass-crappie | Gravel |
| Dry Creek Arm | Vale | | | Bass-crappie | Dirt |
| Resort and State park | Nyssa | | Boat ramps Picnic and overnight Airstrip | | |
| Deadman's Gulch | Vale | | | Bass-crappie | Paved |
| | | | | Bass-crappie | Road not passable |
| Pole Creek Reservoir | Brogan | 60 | Pit toilets | Trout | Dirt road |
| Rattlesnake | McDermit | 10 | | Trout | Dirt road |
| South Cottonwood Reservoir | Harper | | | Trout | Dirt road |
| Squaw Creek Reservoir | Harper | | | Trout | |
| Vaughn, South Indian Creek | Westfall | 50 | | | Dirt road |
| Warm Springs | Juntura-Riverside | 4,400 | Boat ramp and over-night, etc., in Harney County | Trout-perch Bass | Dirt and gravel road |

1/ 1 acre equals 0.405 hectare.

During the 15 years since the original recreational survey and planning, many
changes have become necessary. Perhaps no more than half of the original sites
were completed as recreational facilities. For those that were, construction of
water and sanitation facilities presented more difficult problems than were expected. BLM pays costs of vandalism, maintenance, and garbage collections. The
recreational public's user fees do not help defray those costs. Construction and
maintenance of camping facilities have been changed to meet the needs of users as
they were demanded, rather than in planned development in the hope of attracting
users. For example, an accurate inventory of all the recreational facilities does
not exist and we found no plans for short-range developments. Table 23 is
incomplete.

Several conflicts between recreationists and other users resulted in major land use
decisions for recreational benefits. The tendency for transients to leave gates
open has resulted in construction of cattle guards. Stockmen rightly continue to
complain about open gates. Cattle need to be eliminated from grazing and travelling through campgrounds, which requires fencing and cattle guards. The road
system was expanded during the course of the program, giving recreationists greater
access to hunting areas and other facilities; it also gives motorized cattle
rustlers greater access. Increasing recreational use results in more wildfires
which cost ranchers the forage and BLM the firefighting efforts. We find these
problems to be relatively minor and that modifications in fencing and in pattern
of grazing cause few difficulties. Stockmen, however, find vandalism on water,
fences, and livestock to be a problem, but their complaint is against people, not
necessarily recreationists.

Overall, the Vale District Program has benefited recreational users directly
through increased roads and reservoirs, and indirectly through better wildlife
habitats. Grazing use by livestock places few restrictions on recreationists.
On the other hand, recreationists need to be more responsible than they now are.


*National Heritage*

Numerous items, located on public and private land in the Vale District and
characterizing national history, should receive increased attention. Historical
sites, such as the Oregon Trail from the mouth of the Boise River into Snake River
through Vale to Farewell Bend of Snake River; Meek's Cutoff following the Malheur
River west from Vale; the Boise-Jordan Valley-Winnemucca stage route; and the Oregon
Central Military Road westward from Jordan Valley to the Rome Crossing and Camp
Smith attracted people during 1976 but not many in other years. Old houses, stage
stations, graves, and the like along these routes warrant an inventory and preservation. These trails should have signs for all to see and remember.

The archeological heritage in the Vale District has never been surveyed. Examinations in 1976 along the lower Owyhee River disclosed many unknown sites of former
Indian occupations. Excavations in the Dirty Shame Rock Shelter southwest of the
three forks of the Owyhee River uncovered artifacts of very early civilizations a
in the Western United States. The Vale District is a rich and promising area for
further archeological exploration.

The range rehabilitation projects before 1969 did little to protect archeological
values and may have inadvertently destroyed or damaged a few sites. Springs
attracted early American man, as they do his counterpart today. Livestock, trails,
and roads followed the routes from one water project to the next. Therefore,
spring developments and reservoirs may have covered, destroyed, or damaged important sites. Onsite archeological examinations before treatments began about 1969.
Archeological values must continue to be considered in locating range improvements.
The Vale Program was finished before these national heritage values became great

public issues; so now an intensive and immediate survey is needed to prevent
further losses.

## Occupancy

Much less pressure exists in the Vale District than in other regions to allow
building of houses, hotels, restaurants, and other structures for use by recreationists and by those who want a summer or retirement home.  Coincident with
increased recreational usage, more and more permits will be requested to build
accommodating structures for them.  This appears to be an issue related to the
rangeland rehabilitation program only to the minor extent that it has increased
recreational use.

## Mining

Mineral resources on the Vale district do not contribute significantly to the local
economy nor greatly influence other users.  Historically, gold has been mined in
Malheur County near Jordan Valley and the historic town of Malheur City, silver
mining occurred in adjacent counties, and mercury deposits have been sporadically
exploited.  Small operations mine sand, gravel, and building stone.  Geothermal
power leases now suggest a potential resource.  Currently, diatomite is mined near
the town of Westfall with a significant impact on nearby vegetation.  The existing
mining laws permit removal of a large hill of diatomite located in the Bully Creek
seeding.  Mine spoil materials cover many acres, making the adjacent seeding only
half usable (Fig. 61).  Rehabilitation of this site will be difficult.

Fig. 61.  Strip mining for diatomite will eliminate the hill
in the background.  The spoil covers a seeding of
crested wheatgrass in the foreground.

*Watershed*

Lack of water of good quality limits agricultural and industrial development in the Vale District. Earlier sections of this report described the climate and effects of water on livestock distribution. The livestock industry and agriculture in Malheur County use water, amounting to about one-half million acre feet (617 million m$^3$) annually for irrigating pastures, haylands, and crops.

Precipitation limits average annual runoff from the Vale District to an estimated 114,425 acre feet (133 million m$^3$) (Bureau of Land Management 1974). Yearly amounts flowing down Bully Creek, 1,000-40,000 acre feet (1.2-4.9 million m$^3$), illustrate the high variability of the runoff. About 75 percent of the irrigation water used in the district comes from the Snake River. Not all irrigable lands in the district have sufficient water and no additional land appears to be susceptible to economic development. Municipal and industrial water is adequate.

Fewer than 250 parts per million (p/m) of dissolved solids occur in the upper Malheur River water. Near Willow Creek east of Vale, and in some of the poorest range in the district, the sediment concentrations vary from 1,000 to 5,000 p/m. Highly alkaline soils occur, contributing to an apparent erosion problem. Jordan Creek has increased sediments during the season of high runoff.

Erosion and its control formed a major thrust of the Vale Program. Although baseline sediments in streams and erosion due to natural processes are unknown, erosion was a problem before the program started.

Soil surface conditions provide the first line of defense against excessive runoff and erosion. Live vegetation and litter retard runoff and increase infiltration. Less of the water that enters the soil is lost by evaporation and more used by plants, appears in springs, or filters to the groundwater when the soil is covered. The extent to which the Vale District Program reduced erosion and changed the pattern of water discharge through increased soil cover should be evident in altered flows of the Malheur and Owyhee Rivers, in less sedimentation of streambeds, healing of gullies, and less sheet erosion. The only flow data available, to our knowledge, comes from regular water measurements in the Malheur and Owyhee Rivers. The highly variable nature of the flows masks any changes in flow that might be due to the rehabilitation program.

Only local areas, for example, Sand Hollow with unstable soil and a naturally high erosion rate, still have active gully formation. Nearly all the district shows evidence of past erosion. Gullies healing with sagebrush and perennial grass in the bottoms are common (Fig. 62). No documentary evidence of decreased sediment input into the Snake and Owyhee Rivers could be found, but such a reduction certainly exists because of the healing gullies.

The Jordan Valley plot referred to previously, where nearly all grazing has been excluded for 40 years, serves as a benchmark for the evaluation of the interaction of grazing and sheet erosion. No significant erosion occurs either inside or outside the fence, the plants tend to be pedestalled in the exclosure, but this is due to the natural accumulation of organic matter within the plant bases and not to erosion.

The district soils appeared well stabilized in 1975. Halting of excessive erosion, as a first priority in the Vale District Program, has been accomplished over a vast majority of the district lands. This benefit to the life of the reservoirs, to the aquatic life, to the quality of water, and to all downstream users of water, although unmeasurable in dollars, has great value. Recreational vehicles may cause as much soil damage and erosion as any other use (Fig. 63).

Fig. 62.  Gullies due to excessive runoff being healed with
          big sagebrush and grasses.  Note that the road in
          lower photo shows little evidence of erosion.

Fig. 63.  Damage to soil and vegetation caused by recreational vehicles.


COSTS AND BENEFITS OF THE VALE DISTRICT PROGRAM

The Vale Program presents a remarkably complex set of problems in economic
analysis which, with the exception of strictly forest uses, encompass most situations encountered in evaluating the multiple uses of natural resources.  Grazing
by livestock dominates the economic and multiple use nature of the program.

The question "Was the Vale Program a cost effective investment of Federal funds?"
does not yield to simple analysis.  Two Ph.D. dissertations have considered
livestock production and use of forage for a few years and on only a portion of
the district (Nielsen 1965; Godfrey 1971).  Other publications (Nielsen *et al*.
1966; Stevens and Godfrey 1972, 1976) also discuss the economics of rangeland
rehabilitation on the Vale District for livestock production.

Stevens and Godfrey (1976) in their analysis of the economics of the Vale Program
included only 20 of the 147 allotments for the period 1960-69.  Data from individual projects were readily available for that timespan and those areas.  They
found rehabilitation costs per acre to be $4.57 ($11.29/ha) for spraying, $7.59
($18.75/ha) for spraying and seeding, and $12.96 ($32/ha) for plowing and seeding.
Improvements on native range cost $0.32/acre ($0.79/ha) (Table 24).  Per acre
(0.405 ha) costs varied for several reasons.  The period 1960-69 covered nationwide
fluctuations in price levels.  Costs were functions of project size, and travel or
other difficulties resulted in a few projects having extremely high costs.  The
incomplete data available for the entire program and for most specific projects
suggest that Stevens and Godfrey selected the most accurate data obtainable.

Table 24.  Average costs of range improvements per acre[1] on
20 Vale District, Bureau of Land Management,
allotments between 1960 and 1969[2]

| Improvement | Spraying | Spraying and seeding | Plowing and seeding | Native range |
|---|---|---|---|---|
| | | Dollars | | |
| Rehabilitation | 2.23 | 4.69 | 8.56 | – |
| Fencing and cattle guards | .95 | 1.20 | 2.03 | 0.16 |
| Water development | .57 | 1.16 | 1.76 | .14 |
| Other | .82 | .53 | .61 | .01 |
| Total | 4.57 | 7.58 | 12.96 | .33 |

[1] 1 acre equals 0.405 hectare.

[2] From Stevens and Godfrey (1976).

Many economic analyses remain undone.  We will not attempt a detailed cost/benefit
analysis of specific practices and benefits within the Vale Program.  That has
been started by others, and it deserves separate funding and more attention than
we can give it.  We take an overview by attempting to evaluate the importance of
several economic factors by drawing attention to areas needing further study and
by advancing results which are pertinent to the question above on cost effectiveness of the whole district program.  Benefit/cost analyses of the separate projects
and of the separate management practices should be done to facilitate further study
into interactions, trade-offs, and decisionmaking.

Three inherent rangeland conditions and the assumptions based on them alter the
analysis of benefits and costs.  First, the benefits accruing from a project do
not depend on independent production functions; for example, forage removal by
livestock affects subsequent forage productivity.  Forage production increased on
untreated pastures because of the additional use made of the treated areas.  The
native pastures also improved in response to enlightened management of livestock
without the introduction of treated areas or without capital investments in
rehabilitation practices.  Since only 10 percent of the Federal rangeland in the
district received any kind of land treatment, an increase in potential productivity
of the whole district appears slight.  The main result of the Vale Program could
have been to speed the rate of recovery, not the extent of it.  Stevens and
Godfrey (1976) attempted to deal with this problem in their simple model to explain
the interdependency of pasture treatments.

A second assumption or condition is that the Vale Program was conceived, justified,
and established as a coordinated set of practices for increasing forage production
over the entire district.  For example, a proposed project in the north may not
have been on as favorable a site as one in the south; yet the northern site was
selected to spread the benefits throughout the district.  Thus, cost/benefit
analysis of an individual project may not truly indicate its worth within the whole
program.  This point is especially important because livestock may be shifted from
one part of the district to another.

Third, the results from the whole district program form the basis of analysis - just

as a whole ranch operation must be used to determine ranch profits.  A benefit/cost
analysis of a range practice on Federal land may be used in a study of both a ranch
business and the district program.  The conclusion reached in the two situations
may be completely different because the benefits occur in two different systems;
for example, the benefits of water development on the Federal land have different
values in the contexts of ranch and district.  One does not measure the other.

Our estimate of the effectiveness of the Vale Program as an investment of public
funds used a simple economic analysis - we estimated and compared cost effectiveness under alternative management plans (Fig. 64).

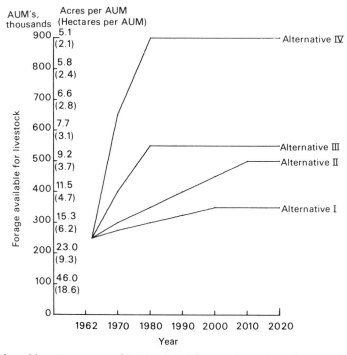

Fig. 64.  Forage available for livestock under alternative
          management programs.

Estimation of forage production (AUM's) on the Vale District has been and will
continue to be a largely subjective exercise.  Before each project commenced, an
estimate of grazing capacity was made by experienced field personnel.  BLM annually
estimates forage production (Table 12) by adding estimated AUM's for individual
allotments.  Each allotment capacity, in 1975 for example, was the actual use
(AUM's) adjusted upward or downward by the number of AUM's that would attain proper
use.  Management objectives and annual variability in production influence the
objectives.  Figure 65 gives estimated grazing capacity in acres per AUM for
various treatments, untreated areas, and the Vale District as a whole.  These data
form the basis for the estimates of potential grazing capacity under the four
alternative management plans (Fig. 64).

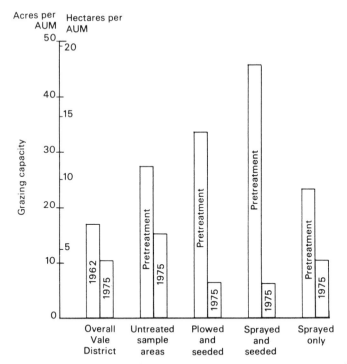

Fig. 65.  Estimated grazing capacity before and after various
          land treatments.

Alternative I defines recommendations by BLM as objected to by lessees before the
Vale Program started.  This alternative provided the incentive for the Vale Program.
Proper range use was to be attained solely by limitations on grazing permits.
Presumably the range would slowly improve.  AUM's would remain low for many years.
Alternative II was initially the same as Alternative I, with the important addition
of water developments and fencing to attain better animal distribution.  Alternative
III is our estimate of the effects of the Vale Program.  Alternative IV estimated
the results of the Vale Program as first proposed if it had been completed in its
original form.  Alternative IV probably was overly optimistic even if full funding
had been available.  Table 25 gives estimated costs and benefits of all four
alternative levels of management.  All values are discounted at a 5-percent rate
to a 1962 constant year.

During the course of the Vale Program, many different amounts have been given for
the cost.  The amount budgeted was to have been $12,392,280 for land treatment,
$2,019,080 for administration, and a third amount for miscellaneous expenses,
resulting in a total of $16,230,460 (Bureau of Land Management [n.d.]).  Yet the
text of the proposal states $12,392,280 as the total cost of the rehabilitation
program but $7,775,000 was added to that for roads and recreational development.
This is the probable source of the statements that the Vale Program cost $20
million.  Fulcher (1975) correctly called the Vale Program a proposed $16.5
million project.  The value of $16,230,000 spent over 7 years discounted to 1962
at 5 percent is $13.0 million (Table 25).

Table 25.  Forage values, improvement and maintenance costs, and benefit/cost ratios for 4 alternative management levels

| Item | Alternative I | Alternative II | Alternative III | Alternative IV |
|---|---|---|---|---|
| | Million dollars | | | |
| Forage value discounted to 1962: | | | | |
| $3.00/AUM | 17.6 | 20.5 | 26.2 | 39.4 |
| $1.51/AUM | 8.8 | 10.25 | 13.1 | 19.7 |
| Improvement costs discounted to 1962 | 0 | 1.4 | 7.0 | 13.0 |
| Maintenance costs discounted to 1962 | 0 | 2.2 | 2.2 | 2.2 |
| Total cost discounted to 1962 | 0 | 3.6 | 9.2 | 15.2 |
| Dollar value of forage increase: | | | | |
| $3.00/AUM | 0 | 2.9 | 8.6 | 21.8 |
| $1.51/AUM | 0 | 1.45 | 4.3 | 10.9 |
| Benefit/cost: | | | | |
| $3.00/AUM | – | .8 | .9 | 1.4 |
| $1.51/AUM | – | .4 | .5 | .7 |

The money actually spent is not known because a separate accounting for the Vale Program was never made.  Then new money was added onto the regular operating budget for the district giving a total of $11.6 million for range conservation for 1962-73 (Table 10).  BLM personnel did not separately account for time spent on either normal or Vale Program activity.  Thus, only a rough estimate of the Vale Program expenditures can be made.  Improvement practices themselves were funded elsewhere, as noted in Table 10, and all BLM districts received about $200,000 per year for 1963-73.  Therefore, a base program budget has been deducted from the total Vale appropriations for a better estimate on new money.  Administrative and maintenance costs are more elusive, and some persons question whether or not the Vale Program contributed significantly to administrative costs.  The original proposal contained an item of $288,000 per year for administration and supervision.  Discounted expenditures were $7 million without administrative and maintenance costs, or $9.2 million including maintenance and administration (Table 25).

Costs to the Government were not covered by grazing fees of $0.30/AUM in 1963, which increased to $1.51 in 1976 (Table 26).  An AUM, the amount of forage needed to maintain one mature cow with calf or its equivalent for 1 month, was worth more than the fee charged by BLM.  The real worth depends on the efficiency of the individual operator, costs of alternative sources of forage, livestock prices, seasonal forage availability, and forage quality.  An underevaluation of forage on Federal lands is reflected by existence of a capitalized value when the grazing permit is attached to private property.  Such properties sell for a higher price than comparable land without Federal permits.  Land assessors in the Vale area estimated the capitalized value of a permit at $25/AUM in 1975.  A study by

BLM (Rumpel 1974) showed that an AUM on private land was worth $5. Stevens and Godfrey (1976) estimated leased forage to cost about $3/AUM during the period 1960-69. A standard appraisal technique prices a Federal AUM at 60 percent of a private AUM because of increased uncertainty and costs of grazing of public lands. This study uses $3 as the market value for a Federal AUM on the Vale District (Table 25).

Table 26.  Fees for grazing on the Vale District, Bureau of Land Management, 1960-76

| Grazing year | Dollars per animal unit month | Grazing year | Dollars per animal unit month |
|---|---|---|---|
| 1960 | 0.22 | 1969 | 0.44 |
| 1961 | .19 | 1970 | .44 |
| 1962 | .19 | 1971 | .64 |
| 1963 | .30 | 1972 | .66 |
| 1964 | .30 | 1973 | .78 |
| 1965 | .30 | 1974 | 1.00 |
| 1966 | .33 | 1975 | 1.00 |
| 1967 | .33 | 1976 | 1.51 |
| 1968 | .33 | | |

At $3/AUM the Vale Program, although it was not designed to be a cost-effective investment, appears to have been a sound investment of Federal funds with a benefit/cost ratio close to unity even including administrative costs (alternative III, Table 25).

All three alternative levels of improvement would have given benefit/cost ratios greater than 1 at $3/AUM except for the high cost of maintenance. Most maintenance costs are incurred in monitoring and maintaining water developments. Since the three levels of improvement, II, III, and IV, include the same amount of water development, a continued yearly cost of $200,000 was assumed for each or discounted to 1962 prices at $2.2 million.

Alternatives I and II, the lower levels of management, were politically unacceptable and ecologically questionable because of the long predicted time for vegetational changes. Alternative IV, we believe, would have been cost effective. At $1.51/AUM, the present grazing fee, no level of management returns the money that BLM spent on rehabilitation (Table 25).

Thus far, this discussion of benefits and costs is based on forage values for livestock. Other users also benefited from the vegetational rehabilitation in the Vale Program. If one considers the AUM price at $3, the other benefits cost only about $600,000. If the $1.51 price is used, the other benefits cost $5 million (Table 25, alternative III), which seems to us to be a low price for the highly vigorous condition of animals and plants, and a countryside with little serious erosion compared with greatly deteriorated conditions 15 years ago. We find that the wise use of public funds in the Vale Program produced exceptional results that are

sound both biologically and economically. It is a truly remarkable result for a
first attempt on so large an area and great expenditure. Under the existing
systems of management, the range continues to improve (Fig. 66). The flexibility
and alternatives in management continue to widen.

Fig. 66.    Top, crested wheatgrass and a dead big sagebrush
            plant (Bureau of Land Management photo).  Bottom,
            bluebunch wheatgrass plant and big sagebrush
            illustrate range conditions on most of the Vale
            District.

## PUBLIC OPINION

Public opinion supported the Vale Program in its beginning, as shown early in this report, but not without some dissent. Little doubt ever existed the the proposed program would help the community. Skeptics argued against the mixtures of project treatments and doubted the ability of BLM to finish the job without massive errors. After all, a program of such a large scale had never been attempted. Crested wheatgrass was a relative newcomer to the district; and cheatgrass, despite all its problems of variable production and poor palatability, at least was a familiar forage resource. The business community generally supported the proposal, but the ranching group was doubtful.

The Ontario Democratic Club, reflecting the ranching community in Malheur County, drafted a letter to the congressional sponsors of the appropriation expressing concern that many acres (hectares) of crested wheatgrass were to be planted to the exclusion of the proven forage producer, cheatgrass. The letter urged that the major thrust of the Vale Program should be to provide additional water developments. The criticisms led the local congressional leaders to insist that land treatment start immediately. Continued funding of the Vale Program may well have hinged on early demonstrations of successful conversion of big sagebrush to grassland.

Public reaction to Federal regulation of use on the free range evolved from resentment, through legal attempts to reduce the authority of BLM, to resigned acceptance, and recently, to a spirit of cooperation. The majority of livestock producers in the Vale District no longer consider BLM an adversary. Abundance of grass aids this relationship. However well accepted the overall rehabilitation program, everyone finds fault with some aspect of Federal regulation.

We sampled public opinions on the current program and asked specifically about future concerns. Our sample is impressionistic and not quantitative because most of the information came from casual conversations with people and from newspaper accounts, letters, and BLM records. Eight formal interviews were held with people having a wide variety of interests. Individual reaction cannot be given so our comments aim for interpretation of general public reactions.

The BLM did an excellent job in selling the Vale Program. Tours with the Advisory Board, user groups, and range management professionals contributed to knowledge of the BLM efforts and to a feeling of participation by the community. Dissemination of information continues, and the program is still regarded as a success. Critical opinion exists, however, in certain areas.

Dissent centers around lack of forage to satisfy obligated demand in the northern resource area, especially around Vale and Ontario. Cheatgrass still persists over thousands of acres and some reseedings of crested wheatgrass have failed. Abundant forage in the southern area brings forth suggestions from the north for reallocation of use permits. Regions with land treatment failures are reservoirs of adverse opinion.

A second area of concern lies in increasing demands from recreationists and wildlife advocates for less grazing by domestic animals and more attention to their own interests. When BLM accedes to these pressures, relationships with the livestock interests become strained. Stockmen claim that attitudes toward wild horses go beyond biological reasonableness and that current court decisions on environmental impact statements restrict rangeland rehabilitation and food production more than they should. Livestock people recognize that poor practices were largely to blame for 75 to 100 years of range deterioration but they point with pride and take part of the credit for much range improvement in recent years, which they claim that other user groups refuse to recognize. Pressures by those groups for land formerly believed not useful for anything but livestock grazing will continue and were recognized by all. The livestock interests have become skeptical of continued

BLM support; yet they know that interests other than for livestock will play an increasing role in the land use of the Vale District. BLM has recognized this fact in the Advisory Board which now has members representing several user interests. Balance among these groups will become increasingly difficult to attain. We note that environmentalists' and protectionists' views about the Vale District from outside are more intense than those from within the district.


ACKNOWLEDGEMENTS

This study was principally funded by the United States Department of the Interior, Bureau of Land Management. The objectives of the study were developed jointly by the Bureau of Land Management, USDA Forest Service, Pacific Northwest Forest and Range Experiment Station, and the authors.

The authors wish to express their appreciation to personnel of both the Vale, Oregon, District and others in the Bureau of Land Management and to the Pacific Northwest Forest and Range Experiment Station. Many persons in both organizations enthusiastically contributed to this study. This report will be used as a case study in the United Nations Environment Program on Desertification.


REFERENCES

Bureau of Land Management. 1974. Malheur County economic profile. Vale Dist. 28 p.

Bureau of Land Management. [n.d.] The Vale Project: A 7 year program for sustained yield natural resource management. Oreg. State Office. 43 p. (Mimeogr.)

Cline, G. G. 1974. Peter Skene Ogden and the Hudson's Bay Company. 279 p. Univ. Okla. Press, Norman.

Daubenmire, R. 1970. Steppe vegetation of Washington. Wash. Agric. Exp. Stn. Tech. Bull. 62, 131 p.

Davies, K. G., A. M. Johnson, and D. O. Johnson. 1961. Peter Skene Ogden's snake country journal, 1826-27. 255 p. Hudson's Bay Rec. Soc., London.

Dyrness, C. T., Jerry F. Franklin, Cris Maser, and others. 1975. Research natural area needs in the Pacific Northwest. USDA For. Serv. Gen. Tech. Rep. PNW-38, 231 p. Pac. Northwest For. and Range Exp. Stn., Portland, Oreg.

Foss, P. O. 1960. Politics and grass: The administration of grazing on the public domain. 236 p. Univ. Wash. Press, Seattle.

Franklin, Jerry F., and C. T. Dyrness. 1969. Vegetation of Oregon and Washington. USDA For. Serv. Res. Pap. PNW-80, 216 p. Pac. Northwest For. and Range Exp. Stn., Portland, Oreg.

Franklin, Jerry F., and C. T. Dyrness. 1973. Natural vegetation of Oregon and Washington. USDA For. Serv. Gen. Tech. Rep. PNW-8, 417 p. Pac. Northwest For. and Range Exp. Stn., Portland, Oreg.

Fulcher, G. D. 1964. Vale evaluation report. Unpubl. rep. 15 p.

Fulcher, G. D. 1975. Resource development on a grazing district. *In* Forest resource management. W. A. Duerr, D. E. Teeguarden, S. Guttenberg, and N. B. Christiansen (eds.). Chapter 48, p. 1-8.

Godfrey, E. B.  1971.  An economic evaluation of range improvements administered
by the Bureau of Land Management in the Vale District of Oregon.  147 p.
Ph. D. Diss., Oreg. State Univ., Corvallis.

Griffiths, David.  1902.  Forage conditions of the northern border of the Great
Basin.  Bur. Plant Ind. Bull. 15, 60 p.

Hanley, M., and E. Lucia.  1974.  Owyhee trails: the West's forgotten corner.
314 p.  Caxton Printers, Ltd., Caldwell, Idaho.

Harris, G. A.  1967.  Some competitive relationships between *Agropyron spicatum*
and *Bromus tectorum*.  Ecol. Monogr.  37:89-111.

Hitchcock, C. L., and A. Cronquist.  1973.  Flora of the Pacific Northwest.
730 p.  Univ. Wash. Press, Seattle.

Hyder, D. N., and F. A. Sneva.  1955.  Effect of form and rate of active
ingredient, spraying season, solution volume, and type of solvent on mortality
of big sagebrush, *Artemisia tridentata*.  Oreg. Agric. Exp. Stn. Tech. Bull. 35.,
16 p.

Irons, K. E.  1964.  Final report - Lodge and Top aerial brush spray project.
Contract No. 14-11-000-1-2562.  Letter dated Dec. 22, 1964, 5 p.

Jackman, E. R., and R. A. Long.  1964.  The Oregon desert.  407 p.  Caxton Printers,
Caldwell, Idaho.

Kindschy, R. R.  1971.  The Vale project and wildlife ecology.  Bur. Land Manage.
Rep.  27 p.  (Mimeogr.)

Kindschy, R. R.  1972.  Untitled summary of wildlife population sizes in the Vale
District.  Bur. Land Manage.  4 p.  (Mimeogr.)

Kittleman, L. R.  1973.  Guide to the geology of the Owyhee region of Oregon.
Mus. Nat. Hist.  Univ. Oreg. Bull. No. 21, 61 p.

Lovell, B. B., M. G. Norgren, D. W. Anderson, and G. H. Simonson.  1969.  Owyhee
drainage basin general soil map report with irrigable areas.  72 p.  Oreg. State
Agric. Exp. Stn. and State Water Resour. Board.

Nielsen, D. B.  1965.  Economics of Federal range use and improvement.  165 p.
Ph. D. Diss., Oreg. State Univ., Corvallis.

Nielsen, D. B., W. G. Brown, D. H. Gates, and T. R. Bunch.  1966.  Economics of
Federal range use and improvement for livestock production.  Oreg. Agric. Exp.
Stn. Bull. 92, 40 p.

Oliphant, J. O.  1968.  On the cattle ranges of the Oregon Country.  372 p.
Univ. Wash. Press, Seattle.

Oregon State Game Commission.  1963-74.  Annual reports.

Piemeisel, R. L.  1938.  Changes in weedy plant cover on cleared sagebrush land
and their probable causes.  U.S. Dep. Agric. Tech. Bull. 654.

Piemeisel, R. L.  1951.  Causes affecting change and rate of change in a vegetation
of annuals in Idaho.  Ecology 32:53-72.

Preston, R. N. 1970. Historical maps of Oregon. 34 p. Treasure Chest Maps, Corvallis, Oreg.

Reeher, J. A. 1969. The effect of large scale livestock range rehabilitation on game species. Oreg. State Game Comm. Rep. 46 p. (Mimeogr.)

Rumpel, P. R. 1974. Master appraisal for commercial forage value. Unpubl. manuscr. 13 p.

Smithsonian Institution. 1974. Report on endangered and threatened plant species of the United States. 200 p. Smithson. Inst., Washington, D. C.

Stevens, J. B., and E. B. Godfrey. 1972. Use rates, resource flows, and efficiency of public investment in range improvements. Am. J. Agric. Econ. (Nov.) p. 611-621.

Stevens, J. B., and E. B. Godfrey. 1976. An economic analysis of public range investments on the Vale project, 1960-1969. Agric. Exp. Stn., Oreg. State Univ. Circ. Inf. 653, 18 p.

Stewart, G., and A. C. Hull. 1949. Cheatgrass (*Bromus tectorum* L.) - an ecologic intruder in southern Idaho. Ecology 30:58-74.

Thomas, J. W., R. J. Miller, H. Black, J. E. Rodiek, and C. Maser. 1976. Guidelines for maintaining and enhancing wildlife habitat in forest management in the Blue Mountains of Oregon and Washington. 41st North Am. Wildl. and Nat. Resour. Conf., Washington, D.C. 45 p. (Mimeogr.)

Uresk, D. W., J. F. Cline, and W. H. Rickard. 1976. Impact of wildlife on three perennial grasses of south-central Washington. J. Range Manage. 29:309-310.

Utah State Fish and Game Commission. 1948. Twenty-eighth biennial report. 80 p. State Utah.

U.S. Department of Agriculture, Forest Service. 1914. Notes on National Forest range plants; Part 1. Grasses. 224 p. Off. Grazing Stud.

Vale District Manager. 1974. Preliminary report on nomad alfalfa seedings, Vale District. 17 p. (Mimeogr.)

Vale, Thomas R. 1975. Presettlement vegetation in the sagebrush-grass area of the Intermountain West. J. Range Manage. 28:32-36.

Williams, G., D. E. Miller, and D. H. Miller. 1971. Peter Skene Ogden's snake country journals. 1827-28 and 1828-29. 201 p. Hudson's Bay Rec. Soc., London.

This paper has been reproduced with the permission of the authors; the Department of the Interior, Bureau of Land Management; and the Department of Agriculture, USDA Forest Service, Pacific Northwest Forest and Range Experiment Station.

PLANT NAMES

Nomenclature for common and scientific plant names used in the text follows
Hitchcock and Cronquist (1973).

| Common name | Scientific name |
|---|---|
| Alfalfa, Nomad | *Medicago sativa* |
| Bitterbrush, antelope | *Purshia tridentata* |
| Bluegrass, Sandberg | *Poa secunda* |
| Cheatgrass | *Bromus tectorum* |
| Cherry, wild | *Prunus* spp. |
| Clover, strawberry | *Trifolium fragiferum* |
| Clover | *Trifolium* spp. |
| Cottonwood, black | *Populus trichocarpa* |
| Fescue, Idaho | *Festuca idahoensis* |
| Greasewood, black | *Sarcobatus vermiculatus* |
| Halogeton | *Halogeton glomeratus* |
| Hawthorn | *Crataegus* spp. |
| Hopsage, spiny | *Grayia spinosa* |
| Indian ricegrass | *Oryzopsis hymenoides* |
| Junegrass, prairie | *Koeleria cristata* |
| Juniper, western | *Juniperus occidentalis* |
| Larkspur | *Delphinium* spp. |
| Mountain-mahogany | *Cercocarpus ledifolius* |
| Mustard | *Brassica* spp. and *Sisymbrium* spp. |
| Needlegrass | *Stipa* spp. |
| Needlegrass, Thurber | *Stipa thurberiana* |
| Needle-and-grass | *Stipa comata* |
| Pine, ponderosa | *Pinus ponderosa* |
| Rabbitbrush | *Chrysothamnus* spp. |
| Sweetclover, yellow | *Melilotus officinalis* |
| Sage, bud | *Artemisia spinescens* |
| Sagebrush, big | *Artemisia tridentata* |
| Sagebrush, low | *Artemisia arbuscula* |
| Shadscale | *Artiplex confertifolia* |
| Squirreltail | *Sitanion hystrix* |
| Thistle, Russian | *Salsola kali* |
| Wheatgrass, bluebunch | *Agropyron spicatum* |
| Wheatgrass, crested | *Agropyron cristatum* and *Agropyron desertorum* |
| Wheatgrass, fairway crested | *Agropyron cristatum* |
| Wheatgrass, pubescent | *Agropyron trichophorum* |
| Wheatgrass, standard crested | *Agropyron desertorum* |
| Wheatgrass, tall | *Agropyron elongatum* |
| Wheatgrass, western | *Agropyron smithii* |
| Wildrye, giant | *Elymus cinereus* |
| Willow | *Salix* spp. |

# The U.S.S.R.

# U.S.S.R. GOLODNAYA (HUNGRY) STEPPE:
## A Case Study of Desertification

*U.S.S.R. Ministry for Reclamation and Water Management*


INTRODUCTION

Abundance of solar heating, prolonged cloudless periods, high temperatures, and high soil fertility, especially of loess-like loams, render vast areas in the arid and semi-arid zones of the U.S.S.R. economically attractive. Under rain-fed conditions these areas are not very productive - 30 to 120 roubles a year and often lower on account of inadequate agricultural management and the impossibility of intensifying agriculture at low cost. Such a situation often results in a transition of semi-deserts into deserts. Irrigation becomes the major instrument allowing these lands to be intensively used.

In the Aral Sea basin in Central Asia and South Kazakhstan, 6.2 million hectares of irrigated lands currently account for some 92 per cent of agricultural output and provide employment opportunities for 95 per cent of the overall agricultural population in this region. It is mainly desert land, and the irrigation potential here amounts to 52 million hectares.

In order to drastically increase the output of such valuable products as cotton, rice, fruits and grapes, in the Aral Sea basin, it is planned to accelerate irrigation development. This will mean that the growth of agricultural production will keep up with the extension of the raw material base for industry, as well as contributing to higher efficiency of the local labour resources management, their annual growth rate being 3.6 to 4.2 per cent. The five-year plan (1976-1980) proposes to add 180,000 to 200,000 hectares of irrigated lands annually. By 1990 the total area will reach 9 million hectares. This will result in almost complete utilization of the available water resources - Syrdarya, Amudarya, Zarafshan, Talas, Assy and other rivers. Further development of irrigation is planned based on the use of the Siberian rivers flow (Ob and Irtysh Rivers). Ambitious plans for their flow transfer to the south is formulated for 1990-1995.

The prevailing features of the majority of areas planned for irrigation in Central Asia are their desertification, poor state in terms of reclamation (soils are susceptible to salinity or they are found at high elevations), inadequate population, and lack of a production base for the areas to be developed.

The Golodnaya Steppe is a typical example in this respect. For almost 100 years this region has witnessed the undertaking of many scientific researches and the introduction of advanced methods in the development of desert and deteriorated lands. More-over, in the past two decades an integrated approach to land irrigation has been developed and inculcated here. It has proved to be highly effective and is currently in use, not only in the U.S.S.R., but in other countries as well.

Following this approach, the land which has been irrigated and developed over the last 20 years has increased four-fold, and also produces higher yields.

These grand-scale construction and development efforts in the Golodnaya Steppe were accompanied by the elaboration of new technology, and engineering methods, which included environmental protection and improvement under irrigation conditions. The specific feature with the Golodnaya Steppe is that here the development was planned to attain certain social and economic targets, increase national income and to attract people into the new regions of development.

Having regard to the above, the Golodnaya Steppe promotes interest as a project which has dramatized the methods of desertification control developed in our country.

### GENERAL DESCRIPTION OF A TERRITORY

*Basic Demographic and Social Features of the Region*

In the "pre-irrigation period" the Golodnaya Steppe was a typical waterless desert where, in a vast area, the only water sources were isolated wells with semi-salt water, which were used by nomads and caravans crossing the Steppe. An accurate description of the Steppe at that time was given by one of its first investigators, N. F. Ulyanov, in 1876:

> "In summer time the Golodnaya (Hungry) Steppe looks like a burnt-out yellow-greyish plain which, being completely lifeless under the scorching sun, quite vindicates its name ... Already in May grass becomes yellow and withered, birds fly away, tortoises look for hiding places and the Steppe again turns into a lifeless torrid area, and in the horizon distant snow peaks are barely discernable through an overheated air. The bones of camels and horses scattered here and there and parts of the stalks of the umbellate, resembling bones, dispersed by the wind, add more to the oppressing impression of the Golodnaya Steppe".

In fact to find means of survival in the Steppe from the end of May to the beginning of October was quite impossible. This is why in the period "before irrigation" this territory was almost unpopulated.

The local population (uzbeks, kirgizes, tadjiks) was confined mainly to piedmont and mountainous areas, rimming the Golodnaya Steppe. The people lived in rural settlements (kishlaks and auls), their main occupation being cattle-raising on distant pastures, sowing small plots to grain crops, and growing fruit trees and vines on the banks of mountain rivers and streams, almost all of which dried up by July. Small communities of uzbeks and tajiks were found along the Syrdarya River. The prevailing occupation of kazakhs was cattle grazing. In the area of over one million hectares there was a single settlement of semi-urban type - Dzhizak. With a population of 8 million, it was located on the periphery of the Steppe. According to the estimates of the economist S. Ponyatovsky, who studied this region in 1878, the whole Steppe supported only 2,000 people.

*Natural Conditions of the Golodnaya Steppe*

Studying the natural conditions of the Golodnaya Steppe is indispensable to the history of its irrigation, known here for over 100 years.

Being one of the most budding regions in terms of irrigation in our country the Golodnaya Steppe has always been a great attraction for reclamation engineers; (N. A. Dimo, M. M. Bushuev, G. K. Rizenkampf, V. A. Obruchev, M. M. Reshetkina, F. N. Morgunov, N. Ya. Makridin, L. P. Rozov, V. A. Kovda, V. V. Yegorov, V. V. Poslavsky, B. V. Fedorov, M. A. Pankov, V. M. Legostajev, L. N. Dounin-Barkovsky, S. F. Averjanov, D. M. Kats, N. A. Kenesarin, A. A. Rachinsky, G. A. Mavlyanov, R. A. Alimov, N. M. Reshetkina, and others).

Extending our knowledge about natural conditions and their role in the irrigation process, the basics of modern reclamation were developed.

The Golodnaya Steppe is located on the left bank of the Syrdarya River (Fig. 1). It begins from the Farkhad gorge where the river valley narrows, squeezed by the spurs of the Turkestan Range on the one side and by the Mogoltau Mountains on the other. The north-east boundary of the Golodnaya Steppe is the Syrdarya River. On the south it borders on the spurs of the Turkestan Range, namely, its northern ridge (Malguzar) merging into the Nuratin Range at Drhizak. Thus the Golodnaya Steppe resembles a triangle with the top at the Chardara Reservoir. The Arnasai lowland and the Tuzkane Lake form the western boundary of the Golodnaya Steppe. On the south-west the Pistalitau and Balyklytau Mountains, the most ancient paleocane formations, are found.

The distance from west to east of the Golodnaya Steppe is about 120 kilometres, and from south to north 70 to 90 kilometres. The total area of arable land exceeds one million hectares, of which 600,000 hectares are found within the Golodnaya Steppe proper, including the Tajik part, 190,000 hectares in the Drhizak Steppe and 200,000 hectares in the Farish Steppe.

Climate. The Golodnaya Steppe has a continental climate, the mean annual temperature being + 12.5°C. The mean temperature for July ranges from +27°C to +30°C, and for January from -2°C to -7°C. Maximum recorded temperature is as high as +48°C (in the shade) and the lowest -36°C.

The growing period of cotton, vines and fruit trees is 210-220 days (from +10°C in spring to +10°C in autumn). The sum of the daily temperatures for the growing period exceeds 4500° and the number of sunny days 150.

The climate of the region is influenced considerably by winds. The so-called "ursatievskia feny" are the strongest, their speed sometimes reaching 40 metres a day, lasting about 3-4 days and recurring 52 days per year. These winds prevail in winter; in summer they are replaced by less strong westerly winds. These winds contribute to the high evaporation in the South Golodnaya Steppe, which amounts to 1,500 millimetres a year (Table 1).

Air humidity in the Golodnaya Steppe is very low, especially in summer. In July-August the relative air humidity ranges in the daytime from 20 per cent in rain-fed areas to 30 per cent in irrigated areas. The annual precipitation increases from 250 to 300 millimetres and reaches 360 millimetres in the piedmont plains (Table 2).

According to the classification of climatic conditions for saline lands (V. A. Kovda, 1966) the Golodnaya Steppe is within the zone of semi-deserts.

Light cloudiness and abundance of sun favour the cultivation of heat-loving crops such as cotton, melon crops, vines, etc. However, a sizeable moisture deficit (600-1000 millimetres), which may be traced to particularly high evaporation in the windy zone, makes irrigation necessary.

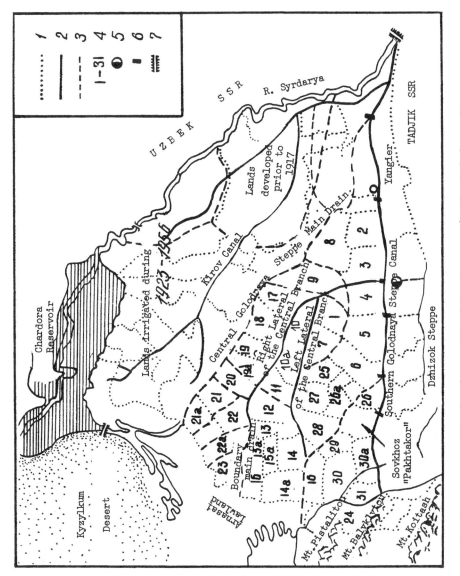

Fig. 1.  Scheme of irrigation and land development in the Golodnaya Steppe
1 – Farm boundary; 2 – Main canals; 3 – Interfarm main drains;
4 – Numerical index of sovkhozes; 5 p Pumping station;
6 – Structures; 7 – Dam

Table 1.  Evaporation from the Ground Surface, mm

| Meteo-stations | Months | | | | | | | | | | | | Total |
|---|---|---|---|---|---|---|---|---|---|---|---|---|---|
| | 1 | 2 | 3 | 4 | 5 | 6 | 7 | 8 | 9 | 10 | 11 | 12 | |
| Ursatievskaya | 18 | 24 | 51 | 98 | 168 | 256 | 272 | 240 | 208 | 120 | 66 | 26 | 1547 |
| Mizarchul | 18 | 19 | 43 | 76 | 136 | 205 | 222 | 200 | 148 | 84 | 42 | 24 | 1217 |
| Dzhizak | 12 | 26 | 45 | 80 | 149 | 221 | 257 | 238 | 178 | 107 | 50 | 27 | 1390 |
| Sovkhozho.[5] | 2 | 5 | 8 | 30 | 74 | 124 | 162 | 155 | 71 | 36 | 11 | 6 | 684 |

Table 2.  Precipitations in the Golodnaya Steppe, mm

| Meteo-stations | Months | | | | | | | | | | | | Total |
|---|---|---|---|---|---|---|---|---|---|---|---|---|---|
| | 1 | 2 | 3 | 4 | 5 | 6 | 7 | 8 | 9 | 10 | 11 | 12 | |
| Ursatievskaya | 36 | 38 | 57 | 46 | 24 | 8 | 2 | 2 | 3 | 17 | 32 | 40 | 305 |
| Mizarchul | 27 | 35 | 60 | 50 | 27 | 7 | 0.4 | 1 | 0.4 | 14 | 38 | 32 | 282 |
| Dzhizak | 45 | 48 | 69 | 56 | 28 | 8 | 1 | 1 | 2 | 21 | 41 | 46 | 366 |

Topography.  The Golodnaya Steppe is a vast valley inclined from the foothills of the Turkestan Range in the south to the Syrdarya River in the north.  Slight inclination is recorded to the west where the Arnasai lowland is found.

The South Golodnaya Steppe occupies the piedmont plain of the Turkestan Range, having absolute elevations of 310-500 metres above sea level.  The piedmont plain has formed as a result of merging of the debris cones of rivers running down the Turkestan Range. It has been subjected to gradual flattening, thus transforming into a plateau having elevations ranging from 260 to 310 metres above sea level and encompassing the greater part of the Golodnaya Steppe.  Running along the Syrdarya River, the plateau passes into a third terrace, breaking steeply to the river.  Within the plateau, the Shuruzyak, Sardoba and Dzhetysai ancient lowlands are found.

Parent rocks in the Golodnaya Steppe are confined to a depth of 200 to 500 metres and are represented by Cretaceous and Tertiary deposits overlaid by more recent layers. The southern part of the Steppe, the zone of the most intensive proluvial activity, is composed of banding layers of pebbles, sands and coarse loams.  The Central Golodnaya Steppe is characterized by a homogeneous structure, the origin of which can

be attributed to the mixed proluvial and eolian processes.  In the central part of
the Golodnaya Steppe the alluvial deposits of the Syrdarya River, which at that time
ran much higher than its present watercourse, have contributed much to the formation
of the upper horizon here.  As time passed the Syrdarya River bed became joined to
the outcrops of parent rocks at Chardara.

Loess-like soils in the south-eastern parts of the Golodnaya Steppe are of a
proluvial origin, and in other areas some are of alluvial origin with partial involvement of deluvial and proluvial processes.

Hydrogeology.  The Golodnaya Steppe depression emerges as a huge hydrogeological
basin, the formation of which was influenced by ground and surface flow from the
Turkestan Range, and also the Syrdarya flow.

Before irrigation commenced ground water was found at a considerable depth (10-20
metres and more).  A higher ground water table was recorded only in the depressions
of Dzhetysai, Sardoba (3-5 metres) and on the slopes of the Shuruzyak lowland (5-10
metres).  The estimations of various investigators for the size of inflow from the
Turkestan Range to the Golodnaya Steppe differ.  V. A. Kovda estimates it at 3.5 -
4 cumecs, D. M. Kats and G. D. Antonov at 2.1 - 3 cumecs, N. N. Khodzhibajev, and
N. A. Kenesarin at 8 cumecs, and H. T. Tulyaganov at 5.8 cumecs.  Regarding the
pressurized inflow to ground water, four zones may be distinguished within the territory under study (Fig. 2):

(a)   zone of ground water sinking located in the piedmont area and underlain by
      pebbles presents the upper part of debris cones (artesian nature does not
      show itself without irrigation);
(b)   zone of artesian water relief is confined to the areas of ground water dis-
      charge at the points where submerged debris cones (often their centres) are
      closest to the ground surface (a piezometric level here is higher than the
      ground water table and quite often self-flowing is observed);
(c)   zone of coincidence of a ground water table with the artesian aquifer or the
      transit zone in a stratum of homogeneous alluvial deposits (a ground water
      depth is 10-20 metres from the ground surface);
(d)   zone where the ground water table is above the piezometric level (deeply occur-
      ring ground water).

In the zone (b) ground water is characterized by the availability of sulphates,
chlorides and sodium in amounts from 3 to 40 grammes/litre and by relatively slow
discharge.  Ground water in the zones (c) and (d) contains chlorides, sulphates and
sodium from 15 to 50 grammes/litre.

It should be mentioned that irrigation has a pronounced effect on ground water.  Poor
natural drainage conditions, low values of the storage coefficient and some other
peculiarities contribute to the change of a ground water table, inducing a sharp rise
under irrigation conditions.  Here the effect of a ground water balance distortion
is felt, caused by infiltration and reduced evaporation from deeper horizons.

Soils.  Over the years our knowledge about the soils of the Golodnaya Steppe has been
increasing.  The soils of the Golodnaya Steppe are mainly light sierozems of various
degrees of alkalinity.  Sometimes meadow soils and solonchaks are encountered.

The first soil survey was undertaken by Professor N. A. Dimo in 1908-1910.  Later, he
supervised the studies of a soil salinization mechanism under irrigation conditions
in 1912-1915 and 1923-1925.  However, the early conclusions of N. A. Dimo were faulty
as he did not trace the dependence of soil salinization on a rise in ground water.

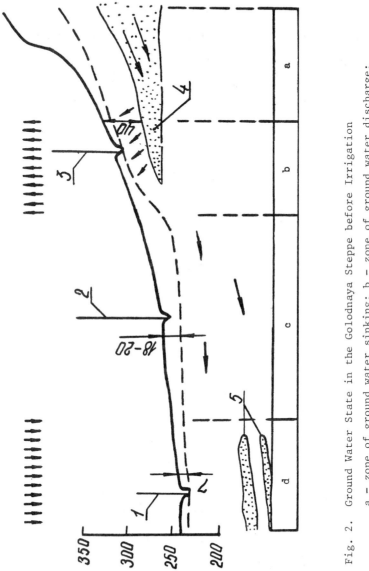

Fig. 2.   Ground Water State in the Golodnaya Steppe before Irrigation

a – zone of ground water sinking; b – zone of ground water discharge;
c – transit zone; d – drainage zone; 1 – Central Golodnaya Steppe Main Drain;
2 – Left Lateral of the Central Branch; 3 – Southern Golodnaya Steppe Canal;
4 – debris cone; 5 – sand lenses in alluvial deposits of the Syrdarya River

The subsequent works of V. A. Kovda (1939), L. P. Rozov (1940), E. G. Petrov (1935) and M. M. Krylov (1957) helped to identify ground water as the major cause of salt build-up and redistribution in soils. They have also deduced that the principal method of controlling soil salinity is by maintaining a ground water table below the critical level. It has been established that the salt composition in an active soil layer is closely related to hydrogeological and geomorphological conditions present in the Golodnaya Steppe. In 1964 N. M. Reshetkina and Z. P. Pushkareva collected all the available data on this subject and divided the area of new irrigation in the Golodnaya Steppe into regions, based on the principles of soil salinity (Table 3, Fig. 3).

Table 3  Regioning of the Golodnaya Steppe acc. to Salt
Composition in the Active Soil Layer

(N. M. Reshetkina, Z. P. Pushkareva)

| Zones | Ground water salinity, | Reference ground water depth, | Salt content in a 3-metres layer, | Salt content in a 20-metres layer, | Drainage conditions | Hydraulic conductivity, | Salinity type |
|---|---|---|---|---|---|---|---|
| | g/l | m | t/ha | t/ha | | m/day | |
| Ia | 40-60 | 2-3 | 920-1000 | 5200-6000 | Poor | 0.1 | Chloride |
| Ib | 7-10 | 6-8 | 700-760 | 1500-1800 | Good | 0.5-2 | Chloride-sulphate |
| II | 18-36 | 8-14 | 135-350 | 1100-2200 | Impeded | 0.3-0.1 | Chloride-sulphate |
| III | 25 | 15-20 | 200-550 | 1600-2500 | Poor | 0.1-0.5 | Chloride-sulphate |

Zone Ia, having highly saline soils to a depth of 20 metres, extends along the Southern Golodnaya Steppe Canal, thus passing the territories of sovkhozes No. 6, 26, 3 and "Pakhtakor". It corresponds to the zone (b) in the hydrogeological regioning. The soils here are mainly represented by solonchaks and meadow-sierozemic with a high gypsum content (from 15 to 25 per cent).

Intensive evaporation from the peripheral parts of a debris cone and largely impeded natural drainage are believed to be the principal factors contributing to the exceptionally high salinity of this zone. The development of these lands requires complicated reclamation measures aimed at salt removal over a prolonged period.

Zone Ib is characterized by heavy salinity of the upper layer, the deeper layers being desalinized. The soils of this zone are meadow and meadow-sierozemic, light sandy loams and light loams. Salt content in the deep layers amounts to 0.3-0.4 per cent of the dry soil weight. This zone corresponds to zone (b) of the hydrogeological regioning. However, in view of better drainage conditions than Zone Ia, intensive salt build-up in ground water aquifers does not occur. Salt accumulation above the aquifer is induced by steady evaporation over a long period. These soils

also need wide reclamation efforts although somewhat less than in zone Ia since here
salts should be removed only from the upper saline layer. Gypsum is found in the
upper layer (to a depth of 2 metres) in the form of a powder. A complicated meso-
relief is quite characteristic of this zone.

Zone II covers the northern parts of the new irrigation area and corresponds to the
zone (d) in the hydrogeological regioning. The prevailing soils here are light
sierozems which were not, or only slightly, saline before irrigation. Quite typical
is the existence of a desalinized upper layer, the thickness of which varies from
one to three metres. Salts have been removed from this layer as a result of the
dissolving and leaching effect of atmospheric precipitations. But below this desalinized layer the salt build-up, accompanied by widespread gypsum, is progressing.
The Syrdarya River largely determines the conditions of this territory. With the
upper location of the river bed intensive soil salinization occurred. As the base
level of erosion was lowered and the natural drainage flow towards a new deeper
river bed was formed, progressive salt accumulation through the soil series was
arrested and desalinization of the upper layer began.

Zone III corresponds to zone (c) in the hydrogeological regioning. The prevailing
soils here are light sierozems underlain by homogeneous loams having an insignificant percentage of sandy loams and high salt content in deeper layers (up to 1.5 per
cent by a dry residue). Ground water is found at a great depth and is highly saline.
The process of salt build-up is similar to that in zone II.

Zone IV extends along the Tokursai and Kly Rivers in the south-western part of the
territory. Here the soil layers at a depth of 6-8 metres appear to be extremely
saline, salt content being 2.5 per cent by a dry residue. Ground water depth is
2-5 metres. The predominant types of soil here are meadow-sierozemic and sierozem-
meadow; their origin is the same as for the soils in zone Ia.

Among other engineering-geological characteristics, the filtration and subsidence
properties of soils in the Golodnaya Steppe need to be emphasized.

The scheme presented in Fig. 4 shows the regioning of the Golodnaya Steppe soils
according to hydraulic conductivity, determined by the inflow to drainage facilities
using the method of inverse problem on the basis of field observations. Hydraulic
conductivity is very low here.

## BRIEF HISTORY OF THE GOLODNAYA STEPPE WITH SPECIAL EMPHASIS ON POLITICAL, ECONOMIC AND SOCIAL ASPECTS

Despite the proximity to ancient oases of Central Asia - the Tashkent, Ferghana and
Zarafshan Valleys being densely populated and having large areas of fertile land and
adequate water resources (the Syrdarya River) - this territory, located at the
intersection of caravan roads during the reign of the khans and emirates and during
the existence of the Soghda, Baktree and other ancient states, was never irrigated
and presented a vast waterless desert.

Using the flow of the Sanzar River, from which branched Murzarabat Canal, irrigation
water supply was provided only for the small areas in the South - West Golodnaya
Steppe. In view of the inadequate flow of this River in the fifteenth century, an
attempt was made to replenish it by constructing the Iskityuyatartar Canal from the
Zarafshan River. These two sources were capable of supplying irrigation to an area
of just over 8,000 hectares near the present city of Dzhizak.

The beginning of irrigation development in the Central Golodnaya Steppe was associated with the joining of Turkestan to Russia in the 1970's and was one of the pioneer
irrigation projects in Russia.

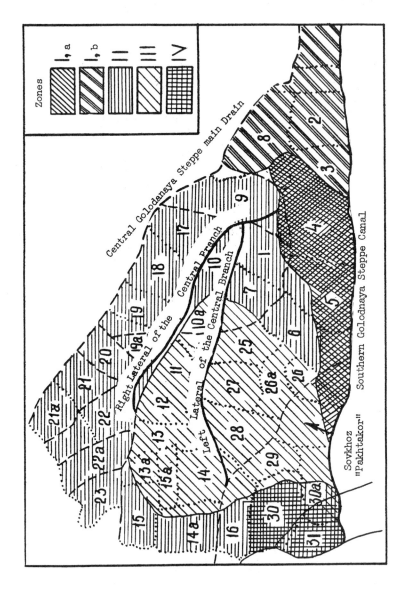

Fig. 3.  Distribution Scheme of Primary Salt Build-up in the New Zone of the
Golodnaya Steppe.

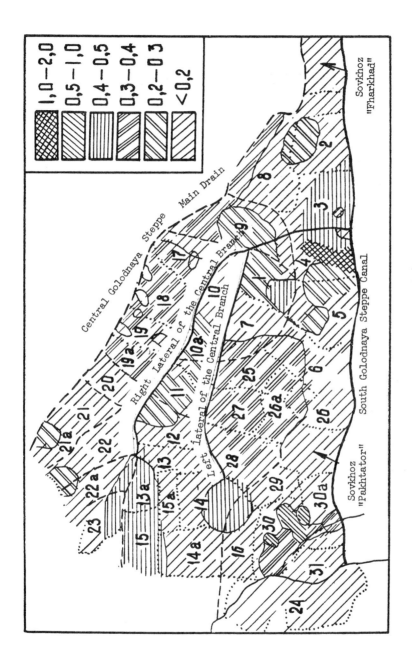

Fig. 4. Regioning of the Golodnaya Steppe by the hydraulic conductivity of the active soil layer, m/day.

Concurrently with the set-up of military settlements, and especially after the building of the Turkestan Railroad was finished in the Uzbekistan, efforts were made to
provide a water supply to settlements situated along the Railroad and the "post road"
Chinaz-Dzhizak.

Irrigation development in the Golodnaya Steppe was undertaken by the tsarist government in 1872, terminated in 1879 and recommenced in 1885.  The first small amount
of water was diverted to the Steppe in 1902, and later the irrigation network was
gradually extended and reconstructed.  In 1913 engineering head structures and a
main supply system were put into operation.

The Government financed only the construction of main canals, distribution networks
and some small escape canals.  The construction of small field ditches was the
tenant's responsibility.

The tsarist government considered that the new irrigation regions should be inhabited
by people of Russian nationality (re-settlers) and a property qualification of 1,000
roubles was induced.  In an unknown situation with new agricultural practices,
and facing the need to cultivate a new crop - cotton - Russian re-resettlers found
themselves in a difficult position and their ineffectiveness was often detrimental.
The "accommodation period" usually took 2 to 3 years.  Apart from this, even the
native population, which had subsisted here for a long time, did not obtain the
right to rent irrigated lands.  Thus, the consequence of the first period in the
Golodnaya Steppe development was the provision of irrigation facilities to an area
of 56,000 hectares, of which 23,000 hectares were actually irrigated.  The implementation of this required over 20 years.

Since the tsarist government did not provide the resources for the installation of
all the necessary structures, the efficacy of land development was very low.w.
Private ownership of land aggravated the situation.  Many landholders were ruined
but this did not affect big capitalists who owned many hundreds, and even thousands,
of hectares of land and ruthlessly exploited local peasants.  The activities of the
tsarist government resulted in a complete degradation of newly-developed lands.

After the victory of the Great October Socialist Revolution the young Soviet State
showed much concern over the condition of irrigated farming in Central Asia.  The
well-known decree "On allocation of 50 million roubles for irrigation developments
in Turkestan", signed by V. I. Lenin on 17 May 1918, carried provisions for supplying irrigation to 500,000 desyatins of lands in the Golodnaya Steppe and setting
up special administration for irrigation development in Turkestan.  However, until
1921 it was impossible to attain an adequate build-up of rehabilitation efforts in
the field of irrigation.  This was because the Soviet State had to concentrate all
its strength on fighting the enemies of the Revolution.

In 1921 the Administration for Irrigation Development in the Golodnaya Steppe was
set up.  During the next four years the irrigation system was restored to use, and
abandoned canals and facilities were reclaimed.  The same period was marked by
land organization and assignment of holdings to land users.  The adjustment of the
whole system operation was concomitant with the improvement of the main canal.  Land
became State property and the size of holdings assigned to land users was regulated
by law.

During the years of Soviet power three main stages could be discerned in the progress
of water economy and agriculture.

The first stage may be called the period of co-operatives and reclamation associations.  It lasted from 1922 to 1930 and corresponded with the transition to the
socialist system in the Soviet Union.

To carry out agricultural jobs, land users formed co-operatives which later merged into Kolkhozes (collective farms). And water users, both individual and collective (co-operatives), formed "reclamation associations" whose members collectively operated, constructed and maintained irrigation systems, obtaining subsidies from the government. At the same time the government established sovkhozes (state farms), functioning on a self-subsistence basis and on government subsidies. The first undertaking of that kind was sovkhoz "Pakhtaaral", organized in the Golodnaya Steppe in 1924.

By 1929 there were already over 30 co-operatives and reclamation associations engaged in extensive rehabilitation efforts and construction of irrigation systems. But most important were the large state farms such as "Pakhtaaral".

Thus, with effect from 1930, the development of large state farms commanding the irrigated area of 5,000 to 10,000 hectares and the extension of land areas assigned to each kolkhoz up to 1,000 hectares was under way. Water resources development was, from that time, the responsibility of water authorities, and reclamation associations were eliminated. During the second period (up to 1956) the method of separate irrigation development and land development was brought into use.

This divided method appeared at a time when development involved only favourable lands in terms of their reclaimability in the regions abundant in labour resources (northern and southern parts of the Ferghana Valley, Zarafshan Valley, the system of Tashkent canals, etc.). A little progress was achieved with existing farms, but it was very slow, and so efforts were mainly confined to undertaking irrigation of plots and, in some cases, to adjusting cropping patterns, and to expanding cultivated areas, etc. Irrigation development was carried out by the state water authorities, and land development was the responsibility of the actual farms.

The pace of land development depended to a great extent on the availability and stability of labour resources. The peculiar variant of this method, which was firstly realized in Uzbekistan and Kazakhstan in 1937-1938, was the formation of "people's construction projects". It was quite understandable that such a method predominated, given the situation of that time - inadequate supplies of machinery coupled with tremendous creative drive of the people. Within a short time, by the efforts of tens of thousands of people, canals were constructed, dozens of kolkhozes were established, and machinery - and tractor stations were built. During those three to four years some 20,000 people were re-settled here and an additional 40,000 hectares were irrigated.

However, this method contributed only to a partial solution of major challenges in land development. The farm authorities had to cope with such problems as labour force stabilization, adequate living conditions for the workers, and they had to find the best technical solutions to the multifarious land development problems, having proper regard for the interaction of man and desert. Such a situation often resulted in low efficiency of land development. By 1959 the area benefitting from irrigation had increased by 200,000 hectares compared to the area in 1917, of which 50,000 hectares became uncultivatable due to salinity and waterlogging problems, managerial ineffectiveness, inadequacy of an irrigation network, or labour shortages. Although, average yields here were three to four times more than in 1917, they were far below their potential and could not compete with advanced state farms.

This period demonstrated all the advantages of large mechanized farms. For the irrigated farming of Central Asia, oriented primarily to cotton growing, wider application of machinery which ensured high land use efficiency became essential. By 1950, machines were used at all stages of cotton growing except for the picking operations. Crop rotation and fertilizers were progressively brought into use. Experience revealed that only large agricultural enterprises - state farms commanding an irrigated area of 5,000-8,000 hectares and collective farms of 2,000 hectares -

could show the highest level of profitability.  In such enterprises cotton production successfully co-survived with other agricultural specializations, e.g. animal husbandry (cattle raising), horticulture, viticulture, sericulture, and others.

Appraising the headway made for the period from 1930 to 1956, it should be emphasized that during those years an irrigation region was established where an area off 250,000 hectares provided over 200,000 tons of cotton.  The annual rate of agricultural development of irrigated lands increased from 5,000-6,000 hectares to 8,000 hectares, which was several times more than that in pre-revolutionary Russia.  Many agricultural enterprises of the region were among the best in the country, measured by yield and the level of profitability.  Apart from irrigation development much was done here to improve the management system and the design of irrigation networks and facilities, irrigation practices, and land levelling.  The construction of collectors and some drainage canals was speeded up.  However, the development in this region was biased towards agricultural orientation.  Such a situation ensued from the system of planning and land development under which all the jobs on the installation of an irrigation network and facilities were the responsibility of water authorities, and agricultural construction and land development were covered by the activities of the agricultural enterprises proper which could use the services of various specialized departments.

The disadvantages mentioned, as well as the increased scientific and technological know-how, reliable material basis and the pressure for accelerated irrigation development in this important region have contributed to the elaboration of an integrated approach to the irrigation and development of desert lands.  The concept of this approach may be represented as follows.  All work on the implementation of irrigation and land development is carried out following a unified plan for a single contractor by a single organization which is completely responsible for the progress of work from project formulation to full territory development.

## ENVIRONMENTAL IMPACTS OF ARID LANDS IRRIGATION

In the irrigation of arid regions, after overcoming the natural water scarcity, the objective is to convert the deserts into highly productive regions.

However, the intrusion of irrigation into the natural environment, disrupting its natural balance, can often produce unpredictable effects, for example, secondary desertification.

This process is intensified under certain conditions:

(i)  irrigating lands with poor natural drainage conditions, when soil salinization progresses;

(ii)  irrigating steep slopes of piedmont valleys, favouring the intensification of erosion.

The Golodnaya Steppe conforms to the first type of condition, causing soil salinization.

Global experience can provide many examples of such phenomenon -- formerly irrigated but now barren desert in the interfluve of the Tigris and Euphrates Rivers, vast areas of saline lands in Pakistan, etc.

Irrigation water supply under inadequate drainage conditions results in the disruption of the established ground water balance and consequently leads to ground water rise.  Evaporation from saline ground water induces the development of a positive salt balance in the aeration zone.  This causes soil salinization and a gradual loss of soil fertility.

As was mentioned above, only a small area of the Golodnaya Steppe has adequate natural drainage conditions and ground water of low salinity. But the bulk of the territory (> 80 per cent) consists of virtually saline lands or lands which became saline after irrigation.

Estimations by G. K. Rizenkampf have indicated that before irrigation was commenced here the area of saline lands amounted to 181,000 hectares, of which solonchaks made up 41,600 hectares. Although irrigation was initially practised on salt-free lands, based on the assumption that many years would pass before ground water salinity reached a hazardous level, the indications of soil salinization have appeared much earlier.

As early as 1907 in some areas, despite the low land use coefficient (< 0.27 per cent) the recorded ground water depth was 1.2-1.6 metres, and that was only after 6 years of irrigation practice. A land strip 100 metres wide and running along the main canal K-3 became completely saline and waterlogged. The careful soil and hydrogeological surveys undertaken in 1908-1910 (N. A. Dimo) have shown that irrigation implications observed in the north-eastern part of the Golodnaya Steppe may be expressed by the following: 6 per cent of all land is irretrievably lost due to salinity; for 38 per cent of land the salinity problem is very severe. G. K. Rizenkampf stated that the area of land becoming saline due to irrigation would amount to 61.8 per cent by 1922.

One of the investigators of the Golodnaya Steppe, M. M. Bushujev, gave a very vividl description of the salinity post-effects in his survey in 1914:

> "The uncontrollable natural phenomena have already done a lot to impair the Golodnaya Steppe for dozens of verstas and turned it into an abomination of desolation due to the lack of wastes and proper irrigation. Life becomes a real nightmare because of malaria, typhus and other diseases prevalent here".

Scientists and engineers, working at the test plot in the Golodnaya Steppe and later at the experimental station from 1902 to 1914, not only traced the causes of soil salinity in this region but also developed a complex of reclamation practices to combat it. Drainage emerges as a major instrument to this end. The tsarist government, however, had no intention of installing drainage; it made provisions for the diversion of drainage water only in the large basin development schemes, but even these plans were not realized. The construction of drainage schemes was initiated only in 1920-1926 after the Great October Revolution.

The provision of main drains in the irrigated area was mainly completed in the 1950's. By 1958, in the old zone of the Golodnaya Steppe, about 12 metres of open main drains and field drains were supplied per each hectare. Although this did not fully eliminate the problem of salinity, it contributed to the reduced areas of solonchaks within irrigated zones, from 35.3 per cent to 9.1 per cent and the area of heavy saline soils decreased from 22.5 to 18.8 per cent.

The investigations carried out by N. M. Reshetkina and H. I. Yakubov in 1964 helped to reveal that, for the majority of lands being irrigated up to 1956 effective soil desalinization could be achieved only in association with vertical drainage through leaching regimes. For the decade, it was only due to the construction of over 250 vertical drainage wells scattered over the whole territory, increasing the average values of a drainage modulus to 0.12-0.15 l/sec/ha/year, that the area of solonchaks within the irrigation zone was reduced to 1,000 hectares and heavy saline soils were almost totally eliminated. This enabled the average cotton yield for the whole territory to reach 32 quint/ha against 17 quint/ha in 1963.

The general dynamics of soil salinization in the old zone of the Golodnaya Steppe is presented in Table 5.

Table 5

| Years | Soil categories | | | | |
|-------|------------------|------------------|-----------------|----------------|------------|
|       | non-saline | slightly saline | medium saline | heavy saline | solonchaks |
| 1908-1911 | 55.9 | 18.8 | 16.2 | 2.2 | 7 |
| 1923-1925 | 29.2 | 21.1 | 26.4 | 12.4 | 10.9 |
| 1934-1935 | 13.4 | 29.9 | 13.3 | 19.6 | 23.8 |
| 1953-1954 | 8.4 | 19.3 | 14.5 | 22.5 | 35.3 |
| 1958-1959 | 12.3 | 42.5 | 16.3 | 18.8 | 9.1 |
| 1970-1971 | 13.5 | 63.5 | 17.2 | 4.6 | 1.2 |

Available data show that, in the Golodnaya Steppe with the initially considerable ground water depth, high crop yields may sometimes be obtained but progressive "secondary desertification" may result in total loss of land fertility if proper measures to abate this process are not taken. Figure 5 gives the dynamics of cotton yields in one region of the Golodnaya Steppe (sovkhoz named after Titov). Here the yields were high in the first two to three years with the initial depth of the saline ground water at 14 metres. However, as a consequence of the salinity process, intensive fertility degradation occurs until drainage construction helps to restore the situation. If deep subsurface drainage (approximately 65-80 metres per hectare) is not provided the land may become unsuitable for further agricultural use, as may be seen from the forecast curve.

So far we have mentioned only principal variations in natural conditions peculiar to this region. In general there may be wider environmental changes due to the irrigation of arid lands. Attempts to categorize them and forecast which of them are especially important for irrigation development are practicable.

Table 6 classifies environmental changes due to irrigation, and their trends. Here, stable and unstable, controllable and uncontrollable changes are distinguished. Stable changes are those which always accompany irrigation, and unstable changes are those which may or may not occur, depending on the combination of other natural factors. Controllable changes cover those whose magnitude or trend can be regulated by man through engineering or other measures, and uncontrollable changes may be defined as those which do not come within the sphere of man's influence.

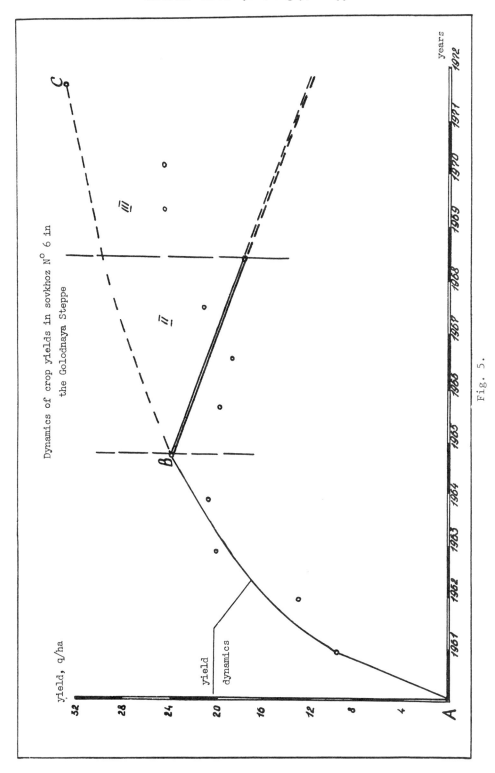

Dynamics of crop yields in sovkhoz N$^o$ 6 in the Golodnaya Steppe

Fig. 5.

Table 6  Types of Environmental Changes of Irrigation

| Types of environmental changes | | Description of environmental changes | Impact | |
|---|---|---|---|---|
| | | | positive | negative |
| stable | uncontrollable | 1. Climate softening | + | |
| | | 2. Changes of flora | + | |
| | | 3. Variations in micro-environment | + | |
| | | 4. Changes of wildlife | + | − |
| | | 5. Less wind force | + | |
| | | 6. Variations in microclimate | + | |
| | | 7. Changes of river flow | + | − |
| | | 8. Changes of cultivated vegetation | + | |
| unstable | controllable | 9. Reduction of non-productive evaporation | + | |
| | | 10. Variations in ground water table | + | − |
| | | 11. Variations in the moisture content of the zone of aeration | + | − |
| | | 12. Variations in ground water salinity | + | − |
| | | 13. Variations in river water salinity | + | − |
| | | 14. Changes of water-physical properties of soils | + | − |
| | | 15. Variations in a salt build-up in the zone of aeration | + | − |
| | | 16. Slope erosion | | − |

More detailed descriptions are given below.

Stable uncontrollable changes produce mainly positive impacts on a natural environment. The most important of them are climatic, for example, higher air humidity on an annual basis, especially in summer time; lowering of the temperature, also on an annual basis and during some seasons.

Using the data on the "Pakhtaaral" state farm in the Golodnaya Steppe, M. I. Budyko has shown that under irrigation conditions the radiation balance, as well as the amount of heat necessary for evaporation, sharply increases. The maximum values of the radiation balance during day time differ between the oasis and desert by 20-25% (R=0.95 and 0.68 cal/cm/min, respectively). As heat in the desert mainly heats the ground surface and very little of it is used for evaporation, the ground is much warmer here. On the basis of theoretical calculations, M. I. Budyko has obtained the possible difference of 10-20°C between the temperatures of ground and air. This causes large streams of heat from the ground to the air.

Under irrigation, evaporation and heat use increases drastically.  This results in
a significant drop in the ground surface temperature.  Under constant moistening
the soil temperature becomes lower than the air temperature.

Figure 6 shows values plotted on the basis of M. I. Budyko's data.  The values show
the differences in temperature and humidity for oases (small – under 3 km, and
large – over 3 km) at a latitude of 42° and at an absolute elevation of 100 m, which
is at the same level as the meteorological station.  In the zone of vegetation this
difference will be even greater.

On the basis of the analysis of the meteorological data, N. G. Gorbunova *et al.* have
calculated the changes in air temperature and humidity (Fig. 7) inside the vegetation cover under irrigation for the whole of Central Asia and Kazakhstan.

Similar data have been obtained by a candidate of physical and mathematical sciences,
B. E. Milkis, by analyzing the changes of climate in Uzbekistan under the influence
of irrigation.

Climatic changes in an area of irrigation reduce the evaporation deficit and the
total evaporation capacity.  Although man is so far unable to enhance this process,
it must be taken into consideration when determining the dynamics of water consumption during the transitional period.

With few exceptions, the changes in items 2, 3 and 4 (see Table 6) are also
favourable.

Meagre vegetation of the Golodnaya Steppe before irrigation in the period under
consideration was represented by giantfennel *(Ferula foctida)*, ephemers *(Poabulbosa,
Carex pachystilis)*, *Halocharis hispida*, and *Salsola scleranta*.  With the development of irrigation these species are vanishing and cultivated crops are being grown
on irrigated lands.  On non-irrigated lands along the conveyance part of the
Southern Golodnaya Steppe Canal and Central Golodnaya Steppe Main Drain and in other
places, reeds, cane, and halophytes such as camel's thorn, etc., have started to
grow.  This is due to the groundwater rise and soil moistening by seepage from the
canal.

Formerly, desert trees were represented only by saxaul.  Now, strips of forest,
orchards, vineyards and windbreaks along roads and irrigation canals are being
established.  In the Golodnaya Steppe the following decorative trees become well
acclimatized: false acacia, smooth-leaved elm, mulberry tree, oriental arborvitae,
Bolle's poplar, and, to a lesser extent, oak, elm, walnut, etc.  Among fruit trees
the following become well acclimatized: apple, peach, cherry, apricot, pomegranate,
plum, quince, and many others.

Before irrigation in the Golodnaya Steppe, 41 species of mites had been identified
as well as 12 species of mosquitoes, some of which were carriers of leishmaniosis
and malaria.  There were also termites, which destroyed timber in buildings and
other structures.  Under the effect of irrigation some of these microfauna are
disappearing and others should be controllable.

Stable controllable changes are also beneficial, in the main, although under certain
conditions a variation in river flow may have adverse effects.

A related phenomenon is the reduction of wind force.  This affects, to a great
extent, evaporative capacity and evaporation, and its beneficial effects can be
seen in the reduction of water consumption, uprise of salts, etc., and in a
reduction of adverse effect of wind on the growth of some crops.  However, this
phenomenon is controllable by the extension of tree plantations, particularly forest
strips around virgin soil fields.

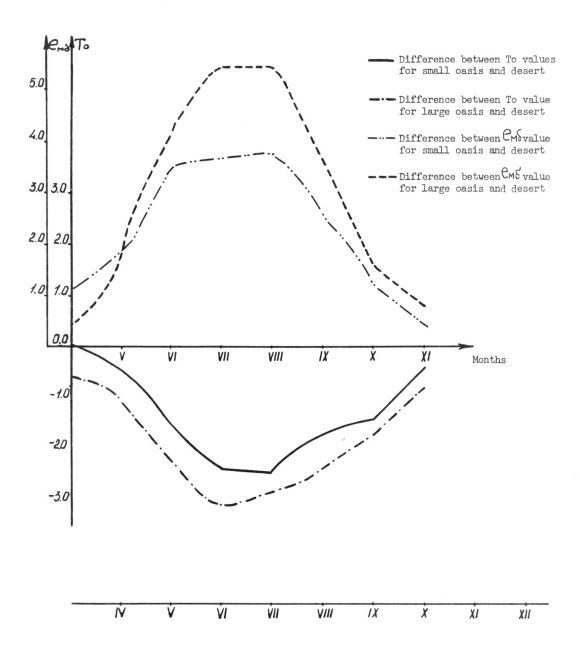

Fig. 6.    Irrigation effect on the meteorological regime

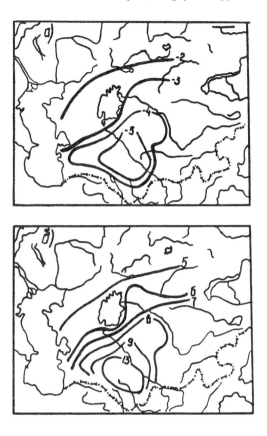

Fig. 7.   Change of air temperature (a) and humidity
(b) inside vegetation cover under irrigation

The design of forest strips for steppe and desert zones elaborated by specialists
(N. G. Petrov, A. I. Molchanova *et al.*) involved in forest improvement permit the
reduction of wind speed within the limits of the irrigated field (300-400 m) to 20%
or more.   The height of the strips should be 10 m, and the wind should blow freely
through them.   The experience of the "Pakhtaaral" state farm and, later, the wind-
break forest strips in the south-eastern part of the Golodnaya Steppe (the "Farkhad"
state farm, the city of Yanguier, etc.) has shown that fast-growing trees should be
selected for this purpose, e.g. Bolle's poplars, with other rows consisting of more
resistant trees, such as black ash, elaeagnus, or false acacia.   In a zone of strips
of 30 to 40 fold height the wind force may drop to 25-30%.

A change in cultivated vegetation (item 8 of Table 6) is evident and self-explana-
tory.   All other changes, with the exception of item 16 (slope erosion), are
closely connected in the process of irrigation development by interaction of soil,
hydrological, hydrogeological, physical and chemical processes which occur in
irrigated areas.

To understand the complex interaction of natural factors, we will describe the
relationship of processes in water, soil, subsoil and salts within the irrigation
area and the irrigation source connected with it (Fig. 8).   Before irrigation there
was evaporation from the soil and transpiration by wild-growing vegetation and dry

crops. Under these conditions transpiration and evaporation account for 150-1300 mm
a year and depend on the types of plant and on the groundwater level. Table 7 shows
evaporation values in non-irrigated areas based on different studies.

Evaporation by aquatic vegetation of surface meadow soils and first terraces, inun-
dated flood-plains, etc. (up to 800-1000 mm a year) reaches its maximum value.
L. V. Dunin-Barkoviskiy studied this phenomenon as far back as 1948. As this
evaporation is, in most cases, unproductive, the development of irrigation reduces
the effect. Under the conditions of water deficiency in the majority of arid areas
the development of flood-plain and delta lands is very effective as only a small
amount of additional irrigation water is needed. For example, transpiration and
evaporation of some crops is 200-300 mm higher than the unproductive evaporation
of wild-grown vegetation.

Unstable controllable effects. Under conditions of irrigation the applied
irrigation water

   - is used for transpiration and evaporation of irrigated crops $(U+T_p)-O_c$;
   - changes water reserve in the soil from $W_o$ to $W_\eta$;
   - creates (if necessary) leaching flows in the field (M);
   - recharges ground-water level caused by the reduction of unproductive
evaporation and seepage from the field and irrigation network, and changes the
ground-water level from $H_o$ to $H$, the ground water salinity being changed from $C_{o2}$ to
$C_2$;
   - is used for evaporation from water surface;
   - enters the drainage network.

If the drainage conditions are favourable, the rise of ground-water level and head
may not occur. If the inflow increases either beyond the boundaries of an
irrigation field or in the field at insufficient outflow, the ground-water head
may rise $(\bar{\pi} - \bar{O}) - (\bar{\pi}_o - \bar{O}_o)$ and the ground-water level also rises.

In order to prevent possible adverse effects of these two phenomena, it is necessary
to enhance the natural drainage conditions by artificial means to such a degree that,
in spite of the increase of inflow to ground-water, the outflow would be sufficient:

$$D - (\bar{\pi} - \bar{O}) \geqslant (1 - \eta c') O_p + (1 - \eta_{T\eta}) O_p + M-(\bar{\pi} - \bar{O}_o)$$

Then, in spite of possible natural deterioration of reclamation conditions, with the
help of drainage it will be possible to ensure beneficial influence on hydrogeological conditions.

The change of moisture content in the aeration zone is very closely related to the
variation of the ground-water level. If, before irrigation, ground-waters are deep,
the moisture content in the aeration zone is usually low and approaches the wilting
moisture content. The variation of moisture content in the aeration zone before
irrigation is observed only in the upper layer (0-3.0 m), due to precipitation and
its infiltration. It is also sometimes observed in piedmont valleys as a result
of mudflow and other flood waters. In the lower layer the moisture content changes
only in the zone of capillary fringe as the ground-water table moves under the
influence of seasonal and other fluctuations. As an example, Fig. 9 shows the
results of our observations on the variations of the ground-water table and moisture
content of the aeration zone in the virgin-land part of the Golodnaya Steppe.

Under the influence of irrigation the increase of moisture content in the aeration
zone is observed in two directions, i.e., upwards, when the capillary fringe rises
together with the rise in the ground-water table, and downwards, when the contour of
suspended infiltrating moisture grows until it joins with the capillary fringe on
the underside. If ground-waters do not rise, the moisture content still increases,
but the nature of its variation is somewhat different.

After Irrigation

б)

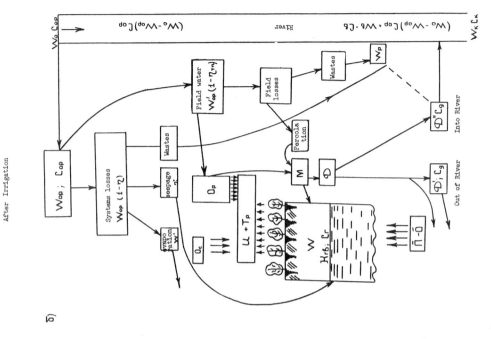

Before Irrigation

а)

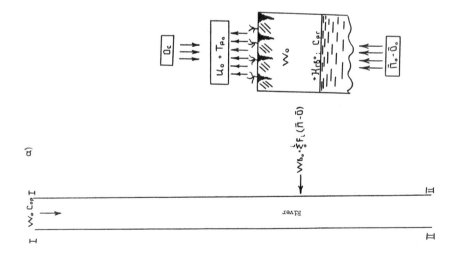

Fig. 8.

Table 7   Value of Total Transpiration and Evaporation from
Non-irrigated Lands

| Item No. | Type of surface | Denomination | Ground water level m | Annual transpiration and evaporation mm | Studied by |
|---|---|---|---|---|---|
| 1. | Solonchaks in delta | – | – | 500 | Egorov, V. V. |
| 2. | Swamps | cane | | 1300 | - do - |
| 3. | Takyr-like soils | – | deep | 200 | - do - |
| 4. | Mean saline soils | – | 0.5 | 350 | Dunin-Barkovskiy, L. V. |
| 5. | - do - | – | 1.0 | 133 | - do - |
| 6. | Slightly saline soils | grass | 1.0 | 1294 | - do - |

V. G. Gussak and Ya. M. Nasyrov have made observations on the variation of the
moisture regime in typical sierozem with deep ground-water table occurrence.  If,
under the influence of precipitation, virgin soil gets wet to a depth of two metres,
from the second metre to the capillary fringe there is a horizon of constant wither-
ing with a moisture content of 5-8%, corresponding to 1.5-fold maximum hydroscopic-
ity.

Under irrigation, the horizon of suspended moisture develops at a depth of 4-10 m
with a moisture content of 18-22% during the whole year, dropping to 17%.  A layer
up to 4 m thick is subject to seasonal fluctuations; here the moisture content
changes under the influence of water application.

Similar data have been obtained by V. M. Maslennikov at the experimental station
near Tashkent.  It is worth mentioning that, according to the author's observations,
the change of moisture content at a depth of 2-3 m depends on the irrigation method.
Under furrow irrigation the moisture content is constant within the limits of 16-18%;
under sprinkling, due to insufficient amount of irrigation water, the moisture content is reduced from 18 to 14% by the end of the vegetation period, thus acting as
a source of moisture recharge.

The opposite may occur, for example, under hydromorphic conditions.  Owing to the
drainage conditions of lands not formerly irrigated the ground-water table and,
consequently, the moisture content in the aeration zone, drop.  It follows from this
that the variation of moisture content in the aeration zone depends on the natural
hydrogeological conditions, irrigation methods and engineering developments to
enhance drainage conditions.

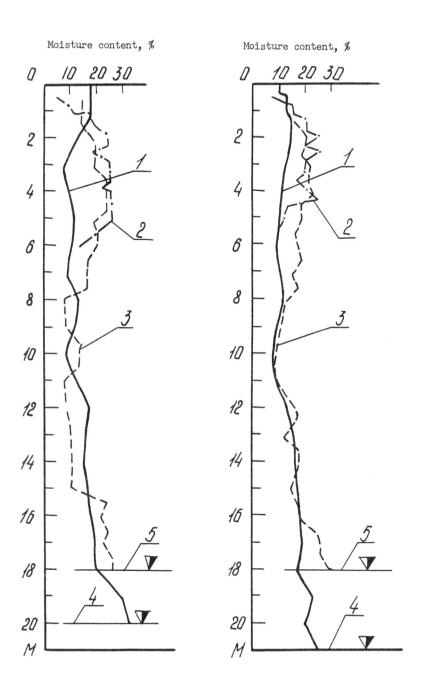

Fig. 9.

Irrigation usually has beneficial effect on the reduction of ground-water salinity because the salinity of infiltrating waters as a result of irrigation, leaching, and losses from canals is usually lower than the salinity of natural ground waters. At the same time there is evidence of an increase in ground-water salinity. It is observed in stagnant zones of impeded exchange and ground-water movement, as well as in places where the rate of water application is insufficient to cover the moisture deficiency.

Favourable drainage conditions and leaching regimes of irrigation are necessary to achieve a decrease in ground-water salinity. This value is determined from the equation of water balance with regard to the salinity of ground water, irrigation and drainage waters:

$$D \cdot C_g \geqslant (\bar{\pi} - \bar{0})\, C_2 + U_{2\beta} \cdot C_2 - [M + O_p(1 - \phi c')] \cdot C_{op}\, \alpha$$

where

> $\alpha$ = factor accounting for the spread of infiltrating waters and its partial use to change the aeration zone;
>
> $C_g$; $C_2$; $C_{\pi p}$ = salinity of drainage water, ground water and irrigation water, respectively.

As seen from the above, the value of the required drainage flow will depend on hydrogeological conditions represented as inflow-outflow, initial ground-water salinity and evaporation from ground water, as a function of ground-water table from the surface.

The variation of the ground-water salinity and its table is closely connected with the variation of salt content in the aeration zone. Under natural conditions, irrigation results in the intensification of salt accumulation under unfavourable natural drainage conditions in the presence of saline irrigation water and when saline ground water rises. In the absence of drainage the type of ground-water salinity greatly affects the nature of salt accumulation.

The irrigation of lands with primary salinization and natural drainage conditions results in their desalinization due to irrigation water supply. The same effect can be achieved through artificial drainage of the required intensity when it is necessary to desalt soils with primary salinization under unfavourable drainage conditions.

Thus, to direct the processes of salt accumulation in the necessary direction, leading to the reduction of salt content in the aeration zone, it is necessary, through drainage and irrigation water supply of definite quantity, to ensure the following condition on the basis of the salt balance of the aeration zone:

$$\Delta S = O_p \cdot C_{op} + O_c \cdot O_{oc} \mp 9\, C_{2p} - D \cdot C_{yp} - Q_{c\delta} - S_{c\delta} - S_{yp} < 0$$

where

> $C_{oc}$; $C_{o\delta}$ = salinity of precipitation and drainage water;
>
> $\mp 9$ = inflow (outflow) of moisture from ground waters to soil;
>
> $S_{yp}$ = removal of salts with biomass of crops.

In the process of irrigation, water and physical properties of soils and subsoils are subject to changes both in connection with the dynamics of salt-accumulation processes in them and without this connection, the character of these changes being rather varied. The main changes are as follows:

(a)   increase of earth compressibility under the effect of natural conditions,
      intensification resulting from moistening (subsidence of I-st type);
(b)   increase of earth compressibility as a result of gradual release of cementing
      links of earth particles under the effect of moistening (subsidence of III-rd
      type);
(c)   reduction of porosity, seepage factors and increase of volume weight under the
      influence of phenomena (a) and (b);
(d)   increase of porosity, seepage factors under the influence of chemical and
      mechanical suffusion of particles, particularly in soils with low sand
      content and in silty soils, with possible formation of cavities, mostly in
      gypsiferous soils;
(e)   reduction of water permeability and loss of aggregate structure of soils and
      subsoils, initiation of compactness under the effect of long-term water supply
      in loams;
(f)   reduction of permeability and degree of structure under the influence of soil
      salinization with salts of sodium, boron, etc.;
(g)   sealing of sandy soils under irrigation.

It is impossible to prevent most of these phenomena, but their direction and development can be regulated. They should be taken into consideration during engineering
design and project construction.

It is very important that sealing of sandy soils (g) should be taken into account
during irrigation. Irrigation water, particularly in the arid zone, carries a
considerable suspended load, the amount of which depends on the season and rivers;
the regulation of river flow also greatly affects it. In all cases the turbidity
remains rather high.

Increased turbidity in rivers contributes to the formation of silt deposits. This
results in a sharp decrease of seepage losses from canals, particularly those in
sandy soils. In this connection such canals may be operated with a year-round
operation regime. Examples of these include the Amubukhara Canal, the Ulyanovskiy
Canal in the Karshi Steppe, the Karakum Canal (in the area of Kelif Lakes), with
discharges ranging from 60 to 400 $m^3$/sec. The stability of their seepage control
is achieved through constantly maintaining the silt deposits and sealant in a wet
state.

Another important practical value of this phenomenon consists in the improvement of
structure and fertility of sandy loams and soils, particularly in the development
of sandy deserts. Along with stabilization, intensive aggregation of these soils
during irrigation, mention should be made of the fact that the solid phase of
irrigation water has many nutrient elements contributing to fast amelioration of
such lands. According to the data of V. A. Kovda, in the Amudarya delta the annual
accumulation of nitrogen, potassium and calcium reaches 20, 1000 and 4500 kg/ha,
respectively.

At the same time, increased turbidity should be taken into account when selecting
the parameters of irrigation canals (slopes and velocities). This is necessary
to minimize silting and to maximize silt removal to the fields.

As seen from the above, most of the controllable changes of natural conditions,
which can be either beneficial or adverse (10, 11, 12, 13, 15), are connected, to a
great extent, with definite hydrogeological and soil conditions. In order to benefit from them it is necessary to provide for artificial drainage conditions (when
the natural drainage is inadequate) and a definite amelioration or soil formation
process.

All the other controllable changes (5, 6, 8, 14, 16) should be taken into account by
definite measures and decision-making in designing and construction.

PRESENT TRENDS IN DEVELOPING DESERT LANDS. INTEGRATED METHOD
FOR IRRIGATION AND LAND DEVELOPMENT IN THE ARID ZONE.

To be successfully and efficiently accomplished, land irrigation in desert areas
demands provision of huge production and non-production assets, and fulfilment of a
great number of various construction, operation, development and other undertakings
which should be closely co-ordinated with the forecasted changes of natural and
economic conditions and the necessity for environmental protection.

In view of this, an integrated method for irrigation construction and development
of newly irrigated lands has been evolved in this country on the basis of experience
in the new zone of the Golodnaya Steppe.

The principles of integrated irrigation construction and large-scale development of
newly irrigated lands in the arid zone of this country are based on the necessity for:

    - integrated utilization of available and imported (water) resources, complying
with the optimal development of the region, aimed at obtaining the highest results
for the national economy, with the consumption of water, the principal resource,
being minimal;
    - planned and well-proportioned development of various economic branches of
the region, proceeding from the required rates of agricultural production established
on the basis of expanding irrigation, its leading branch, and prevention of unproductive use (or idleness) of all the involved or created resources and funds;
    - provision of conditions for the constantly surpassing growth of the national
income in the newly developed areas for the purpose of both ensuring a high
efficiency of irrigation and attracting the required people to the new areas;
    - preventing the deterioration of natural resources in the course of develop-
ment and achieving the maximum gain in their potential productivity.

These principles can be implemented provided that the development of a newly
irrigated land area is treated as the formation of a single complex integrating
natural and production resources, considered to be the optimal combination of controlled natural resources and a special economic production base, intended for the
development of highly productive irrigation farming and all related branches.

A natural-production complex is to be looked upon as a combination of natural
conditions and economic formations, special emphasis being given to the active role
of the natural resources.

The distinctive features of the complex are:

    - common territory and a single water supply system;
    - desert or semi-desert conditions in the regions to be developed;
    - common technological relations conditioned by the objective of speeding up to
the maximum extent the development of intensive irrigation farming;
    - integrated utilization of natural resources, maximum water-use efficiency,
and the manipulation of natural conditions towards improving their potential
productivity;
    - high capital intensity together with high labour efficiency;
    - unity of planning, construction and the major part of financing; establish-
ment of unitary operational bodies.

The main resource of the complex under discussion is water. Apart from its
influence on the entire economy and governing of the principal changes in it, water
has a great effect on other natural resources, dynamically changing their characteristics and being changed itself in the interaction. The success or failure in the
development of the whole complex will depend on the orientation of changes in the
natural environment.

Taking into account the great importance of natural conditions, it is suggested that an irrigation complex should not be classified as a territorial-production project in which the territory and natural environment are a steady background and boundary conditions. It should be regarded as a natural-production complex in which natural factors, primarily water, have an active part.

Hence the structure of the complex (Fig. 10) is formed by the initial natural resources, (water, non-irrigated land, climatic conditions), state resources (finances, materials, fertilizers, mechanisms, etc.), and human resources involved in the complex, mainly as outside help. The resulting natural-production complex consists of the natural and production parts. The former, however, implies not the initial conditions but those changed under the influence of structures, developments and water.

Resulting from the management of complex natural processes, lands are irrigated, climatic, hydrogeological and other conditions are changed in one way or another, return (drainage) water is formed, and the volume and quality of river flow are changed. Irrigated lands imply those transformed by using structures and facilities (canals, drains, water-application means) as well as by reclamation developments (land levelling, amelioration, leaching, etc.). On lands which have not been irrigated before, where fertility has been created (or enhanced), water delivery is ensured in the amounts necessary for growing agricultural crops and meeting the reclamation needs; drainage water is diverted and salts are removed. Although remaining the same territory, the land is now very different in quality. On the other hand, within the complex, certain production activities take shape, and production units are set up with economic relationships established between them. The main sphere (1) is irrigation-based agricultural production ensuring the growing of cotton, rice, grain crops, vegetables, fruit, melons and other crops, as well as highly productive animal husbandry based on the introduction of crop rotation and the growing of fodder. This part of the complex has found its organizational form in sovkhozes and specialized enterprises for fattening of young stock, poultry raising, etc. Normal functioning of the principal agricultural part of the complex requires the setting up of a number of auxiliary services (2): operation and maintenance, supply, and transportation enterprises, for the organization of repair and maintenance of farm machines, supply of agricultural chemicals, fertilizers and spare parts; supply bases providing materials, oil products, fuel, etc. Processing enterprises (3) should be set up to treat agricultural produce: cotton plants and cotton purveying centres producing secondary raw materials - cotton fibre and seeds; butter factories for processing the produce of animal husbandry; canneries and cold stores for processing and storing fruit and vegetables. Normal agricultural activities under conditions of irrigation are possible only where there is an efficiently organized service for the operation of water projects (4), including provision of water resources formation, water distribution, maintenance of interfarm and on-farm structures, maintenance of soil conditions, etc. To achieve this, the complex should include appropriate water-management operational bodies. Likewise, it is necessary to create united operational bodies for power engineering and communications (5), and transport and roads (6). Accommodation of the personnel required for a normal production process, and of their families, and provision of cultural and personal services, demand the establishment of large habitat centres (7) in communities and towns. Alongside this, operation of all the intricate municipal services (heating, water-supply, sewage and gas) requires special operational bodies (8). Finally, a special branch should be created to build and put into use the projects of all these sectors. This branch should be responsible for construction and supply of building materials (9), implying not only construction organizations and their bases, but also enterprises for construction materials (quarries, factories, integrated housing plants). Two functional components of the production process in the complex stand somewhat apart from the others. These are the training of personnel of all skills (engineers, technicians and

workers) for all branches of agriculture, as well as municipal services and construction (10), and managerial authorities including the complex administration, legal
agencies and Soviets (11).

When large areas are irrigated in the arid zone, the necessity for and expediency
of developing desert and semi-desert lands covering an area of F are determined on
the basis on tentative design studies and selection of land most promising from the
viewpoint of irrigation efficiency. The availability of the required water resources
(B), and investments (K) should be guaranteed. Development of large land areas
allows for a more productive use of labour resources in a given region ($\pi_1$) and
drawing labour from the adjacent overpopulated regions ($\pi_2$) where its employment is
difficult. These are the initial elements of the complex. In the course of
development, the initial elements provide the formation of irrigated lands with an
area of $F_i$ and having new productivity $\pi_k > \pi_o$ (where $\pi_o$ = the initial productivity
of the land under irrigation, $\pi_k$ = the final productivity of the land improved by
reclamation developments.

Depending on the speed of putting irrigated lands to use, development time and the
period until optimal formation of the natural-production irrigation complex, the
initial elements have constant vertical and horizontal relationships regulating the
functioning of the system and its components in the period of formation and
development. This is accompanied by the qualitative growth of land productivity,
reduction of (specific) water consumption, etc. (Fig. 11).

The law of planned, well-proportioned development of the socialist economy dictates
both the planned progression of economic branches and the balanced development of
territorial complexes based on the specialized agro-industrial production. This
manifests itself primarily in the fact that all the production and economic components of the complex have distinct organizational and economic relations governing
their mutual co-ordination. Taking into account the area of irrigated lands being
the principal transformed natural factor of irrigation farming it can be used to
determine (Fig. 12) the volume of agricultural production, $V_{i1}=f(F_i)$ and the volume
of operating water projects, $V_{iy}=f(F_i)$.

The production volumes of auxiliary agricultural branches and the processing industry are a function of the volume of agricultural production on irrigated lands,
$V_{2i}=f(F_i)$; $V_{3i}=f(F_i)$.

The amount of required electric power and the volume of transportation are determined as $V_{5i}$; $V_{6i}=f(V_{ni}; V_{4i})$. There exist also more complex relations; the scope
of all branches influences the required volume of construction which, in its turn
determines the scope of the construction base, and these factors dictate the
required amount of electric power, volume of transportation and requisite housing.

The amount of required housing is a function of overall production volume and labour
productivity:

$$V_{\phi i} = f \; \Sigma \; \frac{V_{ni}}{ni} \; ;$$

where $\pi_{ni}$ = annual labour productivity of the (n-th ) branch.

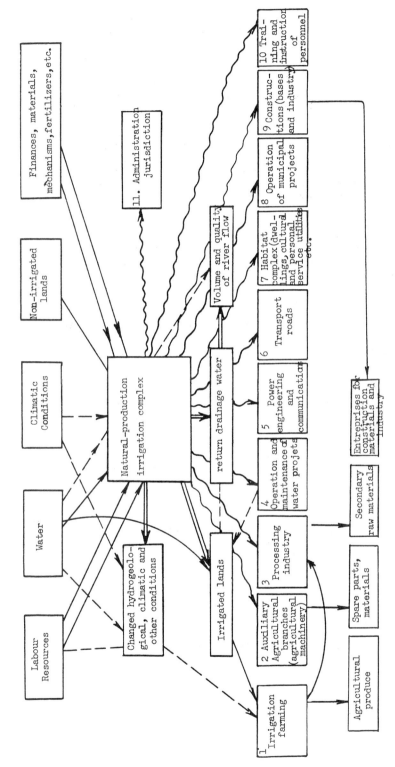

Fig. 10.  Scheme of the natural-production irrigation complex

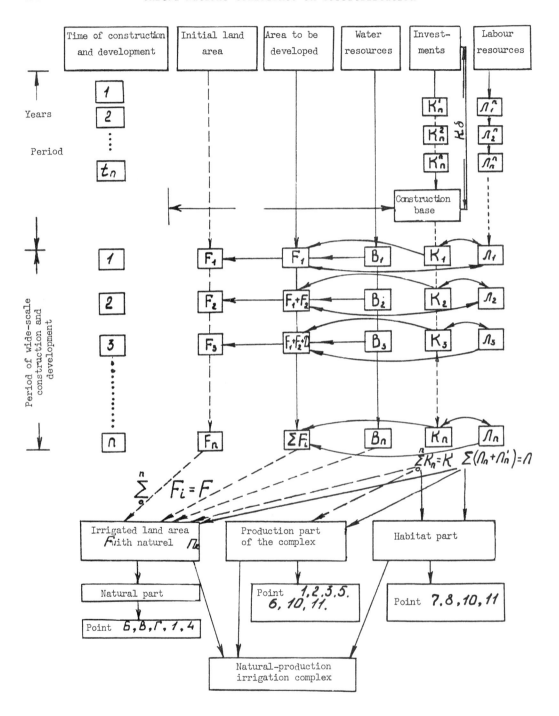

Fig. 11.

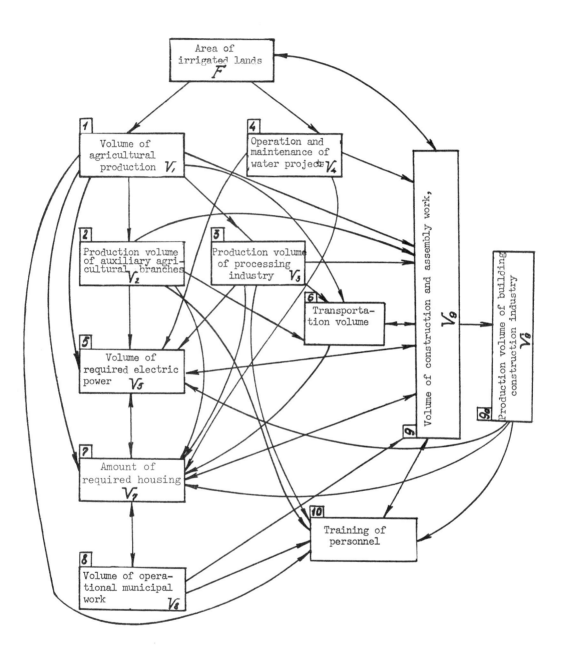

Fig. 12.   Interaction of the elements of the production
           component of the natural-production irrigation
           complex and the related residential component

Proceeding from the planned rates of putting irrigated lands to use and a certain corresponding volume of agricultural production, it is possible to determine precisely the required rates of capacity growth in related (or combined) branches and production enterprises, which will ensure balanced development to proceed as planned.  The capacities of irrigated lands grow by certain individual volumes (team-serviced areas, groups of fields), more or less approximating to the inclined plan curve, while the growth of capacities in related production branches has rather a stepped pattern depending on the individual capacities of the enterprises (ginneries - 40 thousand tons of processed raw cotton each, bases for mineral ferti- lizers - 1 thousand tons, purveying centres - 10-16 thousand tons, etc.).

The volume of construction per year is inferred from the fixed assets required by the beginning of a certain year and the time of the project's construction.

Several periods are to be distinguished in the formation of the complex:

- a preparatory period, in the course of which provision is made for the main construction bases, communications, construction-industry enterprises, builders' settlements, etc., as well as for the main water supply projects;

- the period of wide-scale integrated construction, when sovkhozes are built rapidly and agriculture begins to develop.  Construction is the leading branch at this time, land development having only just started and the technical decisions made for the territory are being tested.  Although growing, the economic effect does not yet cover the investments made in the complex in the current year.  In this period, construction shifts to creating uniform projects at a predetermined rate, since all related branches should develop in proportion to the rate of putting new irrigated lands to use.  This permits organizing flow-line construction of all projects through the use of specialized flows with specified rhythms of work;

- the period of wide-scale development, when agricultural production on the newly-developed lands gains predominance and repays expenditure by the achieved economic effect.  A precise rhythm of construction and land development is established, and the principal objective implies raising the efficiency of agricultural production and all auxiliary branches.  In the preceding period, progress involved only leading crop production, such as cotton and rice growing, in a direction which gave the best results, while the present period sees the necessity for diversified agricultural development of the complex both from the standpoint of the farms' potentialities (the beginning of fruiting in young orchards, rise in the specific portion of grass in crop rotation to create fodder) and in relation to the need for more completely meeting the demands of the region's population for local food products;

- the period of completing the formation of the complex, when the construction of all auxiliary, processing and other related elements envisaged in the general scheme is brought to an end.  Any design alterations made in establishing the complex, and any design drawbacks, are revealed and eliminated, and provisions are made for further progress of production in the complex.  With regard to the new zone in the Golodnaya Steppe (Fig. 13), the preparatory period lasted from 1956 to 1961; the period of wide-scale integrated construction covered the years of 1961-1969; and the period of wide-scale land development started in 1969 and is still going on.  The period for the completion of the complex formation has not yet arrived.  Such a classification shows that in the preparatory period investments are kept idle to a maximum extent and the national economic effect is minimum. Later on, as the irrigated area is increased, the effect grows and finally stabilizes. Analysis of the improved efficiency of the complex components enables the direc- tions of the optimal departmental and structural subordination in different periods of the complex formation to be determined.

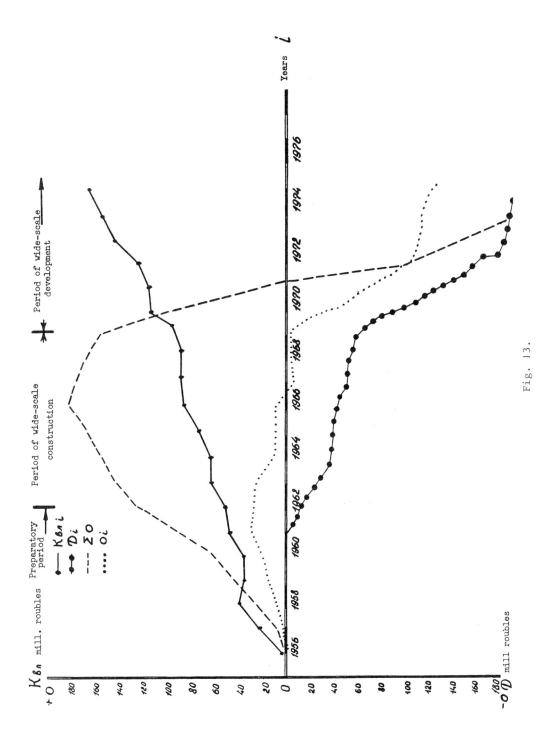

Fig. 13.

The dynamics of the whole complex should be taken into account when considering the role of its natural and geographic components and their changes.

As the area prepared for irrigation is being expanded, water is delivered either for irrigation purposes alone or for initial land development according to the original conditions.

When the initial soil conditions are favourable and the land is potentially fertile, as it is usually with loess automorphic soils, the phenomena to be eliminated in the process of development should include only those which can lead to any deterioration of land productivity in the course of subsequent long-term irrigation. These can be subsidence phenomena, associated with high porosity and compressibility of soil or with chemical processes such as the loosening of cementing bonds in soil. Insufficient natural drainage, not only of the developed lands but also of areas adjoining them or influenced by them, is another failing which is not evident in dry land conditions but can cause undesirable consequences under irrigation. It should be eliminated by using a drainage system. Finally, liability to soil erosion on steep country slopes can be hazardous on lands under irrigation. If such is the case, technological decisions implying special water-application techniques (sprinkling, drip and other types of irrigation), terracing, or stabilization of furrows, are made to rule out the possibility of the degradation of natural soil conditions.

In the case of saline, sandy and stony soils, or other areas of low productivity, such as the ancient takyrs, measures should also be taken to ensure the future high fertility of these lands. Current engineering, soil-improvement and field-management practices can be developed and implemented, turning areas of the worst productivity into highly fertile lands. It is only a matter of time, initial investment and subsequent expenditure.

Emphasis should be laid on the importance of proper forecasting of soil, hydrogeological, geotechnical and other possible changes. This should be done before the work is commenced. The forecasting is intended to determine measures to be taken during the process of construction and development in order to prevent the deterioration of the fertility of the irrigated area under long-term cultivation. This can also be applied to the interrelation of soil and hydrogeological conditions with irrigation water, the former not only being changed by the water's action but also exerting certain influence on its quality in the process of water infiltration and movement across the area to the water-receiving body. It is very important to trace the whole path of this water and, having determined its possible changes, to make assessments as to where and how the return water can be used. It is necessary to find out whether it is reasonable to return it to the river or other water-receiving bodies of the basin, and if any impacts on the water are liable to occur by doing so.

Thus, irrigation development should be accompanied by applying scientific and engineering forecasts to determine the associated changes which will take place in the natural conditions of the region. Engineering, soil-, field-management and other decisions and measures should be used to direct these changes to preserve the natural conditions and to ensure permanent favourable influence on the natural components of the complex.

The reliability of the progressive influence of irrigation on the natural and economic situations depends, in many respects, not only on proper orientation of both components of the complex, but also on their co-ordination. This manifests itself in the timely fulfilment of all the undertakings required to influence the natural and economic conditions, and in the constant control over recording and analyses of the changes in the natural conditions taking place in the region under development.

PROGRESS AND RESULTS OF LAND DEVELOPMENT
IN THE NEW ZONE OF THE GOLODNAYA STEPPE

Land development in the new zone of the Golodnaya Steppe was launched in November 1956. This area is situated in the southern part of the Golodnaya Steppe Lowland. Water is supplied from upstream of the Farkhad headworks by the Southern Golodnaya Steppe Canal, 117 km long, with a head discharge of 300 $m^3$/sec (Fig. 14).

Eight check structures have been built on the canal to maintain the design regime. Water from the canal is supplied to its main branches by gravity, with the exception of the Farkhad branch which is supplied by a pumping station. The main branches of the canal are:

- the Central Branch, with a head discharge of 164 $m^3$/sec., functioning at the same time as an emergency escape 50 $m^3$/sec. in capacity, is designed to irrigate 146 thousand hectares. It is divided into Right and Left Laterals, 55 and 60) $m^3$/sec. in capacity, respectively;

- the Kurgantepa Branch, irrigating 16 thousand hectares, is 20.3 $m^3$/sec. in capacity;

- the Southern Distributor (JP-18), 33.6 $m^3$/sec. in capacity, is designed to irrigate 28 thousand hectares. It also functions as an escape structure to discharge 22 $m^3$/sec. of water. The Southern Canal joins the Tokursai River at 118 km.

In parallel with the construction of the main supply system, provision was made for dense irrigation and drainage networks. The reconstructed Central Golodnaya Steppe Main Drain, 57 km long, 90 $m^3$/sec. in capacity at its tail, is the main collector. Other main collectors are: the Akbulak Collector (49 km long, having a design discharge capacity of 20 $m^3$/sec.), Ts K-6, Ts K-1, Ts K-7, Ts K-6, Ts K-8, Ts K-9, and others, their total length exceeding 470 kilometres.

For interfarm services and communications, the region supplied by the Southern Golodnaya Steppe Canal is divided into three areas:

- the South-Eastern area (sovkhozes No. 1, 2, 3, 4, 5, 6, 7, 8 and "Yangiyer") supplied by the first-stage Southern Golodnaya Steppe Canal and its Kurgantepa Branch;

- the South-Western area (sovkhozes No. 25, 26, 27, 28, 29, 30, 31 and "Pakhtakor") supplied by the second-stage Southern Golodnaya Steppe Canal and its innerfarm distributors, i.e. J P-18, J P-24, J P-25;

- the Central area (sovkhozes No. 9, 10, 11, 12, 13, 14, 15, 16, 17, 18, 19, 20, 21, 22, 23) is supplied by the Left and Right Laterals. In view of the comparative isolation of the "Farkhad" and "Michurin" sovkhozes, they are fed from the Bayaut pumping station, taking water from the Southern Golodnaya Steppe Canal.

The characteristics of these three areas are given in Table 8.

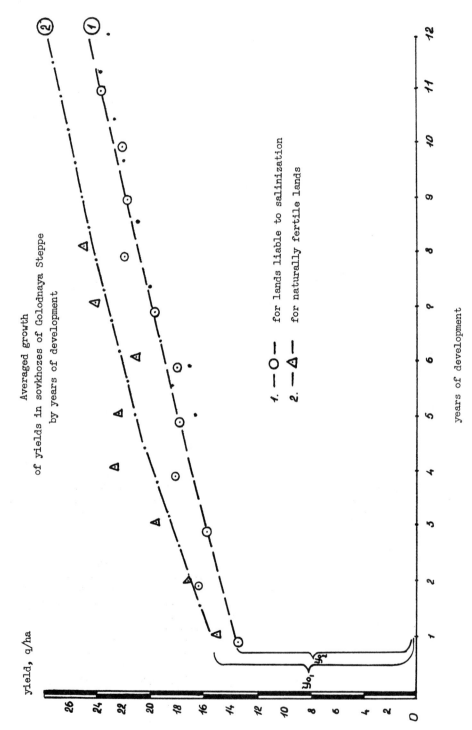

Averaged growth
of yields in sovkhozes of Golodnaya Steppe
by years of development

1. —O—  for lands liable to salinization
2. —△—  for naturally fertile lands

years of development

Fig. 14.

Table 8   Characteristics of areas of the Golodnaya Steppe
          New Zone

| Area | Area, thous. ha | | | Number of sovkhozes | Areas to be leached |
|------|-------|-------|------|------------|---------|
|      | total | gross | net  |            |         |
| South-Eastern | 114.3 | 102.6 | 91.5 | 13 | 67.6 |
| South-Western sovkhoz No. 24 incl. | 90.4 | 82.1 | 75.0 | 12 | 13.0 |
| Central | 165.8 | 154.8 | 139.2 | 25 | 18.5 |
| Farkhad | 14.2 | 12.1 | 10.6 | 2 | 4.6 |
| Total | 384.7 | 351.6 | 316.3 | 52 | 103.7 |

During the preparatory period, from 1956 to 1961, a base for the construction industries was first created.

It was necessary to supply construction materials that would promote new technology in construction and would permit maximum mechanization of construction processes. The primary task was to convert a construction site into an erection site where all (or almost all) processes were aimed at assembling prefabricated articles, the labour required being minimum. This problem was solved by the provision of the industrial bases in the Golodnaya Steppe and at numerous construction sites.

Large-scale developments required that plants be located near raw material sources, taking into account the transportation of the finished products. The towns of Dzhizak, Bekabad, Yangier and Nau became the principal bases for manufacturing construction materials.

During the development period in the Golodnaya Steppe large enterprises of construction and construction materials industry were built, namely: five plants for manufacturing prefabricated reinforced concrete components, two gravel-sorting mills for non-ore materials, a plant for manufacturing tile drainage pipes, a brick-producing plant, two plants for manufacturing silicate-concrete components for houses, etc.

With a view to organizing a repair service, four mechanical-repair workshops were built which, in addition to repairing the construction and earth-moving machinery, also make the required non-standard equipment, metal structures, and technological equipment for the construction materials industry.

The total annual capacity of the above plants, as at the beginning of 1976, was made up as follows:

Prefabricated reinforced concrete ..................... 490 thousand km$^3$

Bricks and wall panels .............................. 42 thousand pcs

Tile drains ......................................... 1800 km

Expanded clay ....................................... 70 thousand m$^3$

Gravel-sand materials ............................... 1.8 million m$^3$

Repair of machinery and metal structures ............. 8 million roubles

During this same period vital services and communications were provided, such as:
the Syrdarya-Dzhizak railroad, 93 km in length; highways, 1746 km long; power
transmission lines, 1805 km; water supply conduits, 187 km; communication lines,
510 km; gas mains, 324 km.  Five communities were also built, with all amenities
to certain construction organizations, their bases, and construction industry plants.
The total living space in these communities exceeds one million square metres,
permitting accommodation for more than 40 thousand builders and industrial workers.

The period of large-scale construction in the Golodnaya Steppe was started in 1961
after completing the first stage of development which envisaged the provision of
the main supply system and the commissioning of the Southern Golodnaya Steppe Canal
in December 1960.

The second stage of development (involving the construction of the Central Branch
of the second stage of the Southern Canal running as far as the 1177-th km St., the
K-7 and Akbulak collectors, as well as the canal Right branch up to the 64-th km
St.) was completed in 1962.

During 1962-1966 third stage developments to provide the main water supply were
carried out, i.e. the construction of the Right Lateral as far as the 246th km
St., the Left Lateral up to the 214th km St., the second stage of the Central Main
Drain designed for a discharge of 90 m$^3$/sec.

As the Canal is extended into the Steppe, main construction jobs are commenced,
i.e. irrigation and drainage of lands, construction of communities and industrial
projects.

It takes 4-5 years to establish sovkhozes, including all the components such as
irrigation and drainage networks, land levelling, construction of industrial and
civil engineering projects.  Tentative assignment of work volumes for each year of
development of a cotton-growing state farm is given in Table 9.

Rates of putting irrigated lands under cultivation have averaged 17-20 thousand
hectares per year in the Golodnaya Steppe.  This has necessitated building 3-5 new
sovkhozes annually, provided with the required irrigation and drainage structures
and industrial projects.

On average each farm has built 150-200 kilometres of canals, either concrete-lined
or divided into flumes and pipelines; 500-600 km of subsurface horizontal drainage,
50-100 km of collectors; 40-50 km of farm roads.  Large volumes of land levelling
and leaching of saline lands were also carried out as well.  During the 15 years
since the beginning of the large-scale development undertaken in the Golodnaya
Steppe, provision has been made for the following:

Dwelling houses, with floor space
    totalling million m ......................................... 2.2

Schools, thousand pupils ...................................... 22.0

Pre-school children's establishments, thousand
    children ...................................................... 10.6

Production and municipal facilities,
    quantity ......................................................   74

Field camps, etc .............................................. 1146

Mechanical-repair workshops,thousand
    conditional repairs ......................................... 2480

Buildings for cattle, head .................................... 6240

Newly irrigated lands put under cultivation,
    thousand ha. .................................................  276

Concrete-lined canals, km .....................................  568

Flumes, km .................................................... 3840

Subsurface pipelines, km ......................................  512

Subsurface horizontal drainage, km ............................ 14980

Open collectors, km ........................................... 2960

Subsurface collectors, km .....................................  560

Vertical drainage wells, km ...................................  368

## *Development of new irrigated lands*

Compared to all other kinds of work taken together, development is responsible to
a greater extent for the efficiency of land irrigation since the justification
period of the project will depend on the rates and skill manifested by new farms
in putting land under cultivation and in organizing on-farm operation and
maintenance services.

The principle of transferring the completed farm sections (group of fields, crop-
rotation area) to the development, as practised in the Golodnaya Steppe, enables
development to occur gradually. This appreciably simplifies the tasks of the
sovkhoz authorities and of the operation and maintenance organizations, which are
thus able to extend their activities.

Re-settlement, training and stabilization of personnel. The yearly rate of putting
irrigated lands under cultivation of 15-20 thousand ha in the new zone of the
Golodnaya Steppe requires considerable manpower for their subsequent development.
In the sovkhozes under "Golodnostepstroi" one worker tills, on average, 6 irrigated
hectares. This implies that 2.5 to 3 thousand workers should be attracted annually
to new sovkhozes, but taking into consideration the sphere of personal services and
family members (a special factor of 3.1 was adopted for the conditions of the
Golodnaya Steppe) the figure amounts to between 6 and 10 thousand people.

One of the important tasks of the construction administration is to provide workers
with sufficient living space. As many as 60-90 thousand square metres of useful
area are to be commissioned annually in the sovkhozes (Table 10).

Table 9  Assignment of work volumes for each year of development of cotton-growing state farm

(Percent of total cost of developments)

| Kind of work | Years of construction and development | | | | | Total | Carried out after commissioning |
| | 1st | 2nd | 3rd | 4th | 5th | | |
| --- | --- | --- | --- | --- | --- | --- | --- |
| Water resources development | 4 | 50 | 46 | – | – | 100 | – |
| Construction of industrial projects | 22 | 25 | 30 | 5 | – | 82 | 18 |
| Construction of community | 9 | 30 | 30 | 16 | – | 85 | 15 |
| Development | – | – | 55 | 45 | – | 100 | – |
| Construction and assembly | 9.0 | 36.8 | 38.5 | 7.8 | – | 92.1 | 7.9 |
| Commissioning of living area | – | 30 | 40 | 15 | – | 85 | 15 |
| Putting lands under cultivation | – | 50 | 50 | – | – | 100 | – |
| Sowing of crops | – | – | 30 | 60 | 85 | 85 | 100 |

It is important to determine the sources for extending the personnel.

These sources are as follows:

(1)    organized re-settlement of people from densely populated regions and districts in accordance with Government decisions;

(2)    assignment of specialists graduated from specialized training schools of machine operators;

(3)    individual employment.

The first source is the most important.  The Golodnaya Steppe absorbs manpower from the Fergana and Zarafshan Valleys, from the mountain regions of the Syrdarya and other districts known for abundant labour resources and low output per worker. Also important is the third source, i.e. employment on a voluntary basis.  In this case the increase in personnel depends entirely on how the new conditions compare with those in their own areas.

Table 10  Formation of Workers' Staff in Golodnaya Steppe
          Sovkhozes

| Year | Number of workers engaged in development by the beginning of the year, persons | Organized recruitment, persons | | Commissioning of living space in sovkhozes, thous. m$^2$ |
|------|------|------|------|------|
| | | re-settlement | assigned from schools of machine operators | |
| 1961 | 2600  | –    | –    | 46.1 |
| 1962 | 5070  | –    | –    | 52.4 |
| 1963 | 6530  | 843  | 43   | 53.9 |
| 1964 | 7700  | 963  | 188  | 44.4 |
| 1965 | 8228  | 977  | 245  | 64.0 |
| 1966 | 10141 | 727  | 47   | 65.5 |
| 1967 | 12024 | 1368 | 22   | 63.0 |
| 1968 | 14141 | 37   | 28   | 52.7 |
| 1969 | 17700 | 3785 | 98   | 55.3 |
| 1970 | 21600 | 2638 | 312  | 82.8 |
| 1971 | 25200 | 3445 | –    | 97.8 |
| 1972 | 28680 | 2894 | 248  | 89.5 |
| 1973 | 32312 | 3240 | 320  | 98.5 |
| 1974 | 36486 | 3390 | 386  | 104.2 |

Social and economic aspects emerge as decisive factors when stabilizing the
personnel.  These involve the provision, on the virgin lands, of housing with all
the modern conveniences.  In this respect the conditions created for the sovkhoz
workers in the Golodnaya Steppe, i.e. houses with 0.08 ha land plots and all
necessary engineering services and communications, are the best in the Republic.

Owing to the high level of mechanization on the newly developed lands, the average
individual output of raw cotton is as high as 19 tons a year in the advanced farms.
Earnings amount to between 2.5 and 3 thousand roubles a year (sovkhozes No.
25, 28, etc.) which is double the average earnings of the Uzbek S.S.R.  This is
enhanced by introducing (for the development period) bonuses estimated at 15 per
cent of the wage.  Other privileges promoted by the Government (increased travelling expenses for re-settlement, credit-financing private house construction) also
help to attract people to the areas to be developed.  Compared to other regions,
the virgin lands are provided with more scarce commodities (cars, motor-cycles,
etc.) which are sold to the best machine operators and workers.  This is decided
by appropriate organizations and authorities of the region.

Sovkhoz workers arriving in the development area are either insufficiently experienced in agricultural jobs or their knowledge can only be partly employed in modern
farms.  In the newly established sovkhozes irrigation, drainage as well as construction of industrial projects are accomplished with the recent advances in science

and technology borne in mind.  To operate and maintain state farm engineering
structures efficiently the new personnel should master new skills and become
familiar with all the details of the structures.

Specialized training of state farm personnel is organized as follows:

     - training at machine operators' schools under "Golodnostepstroi", providing
1500 agricultural machine operators;

     - training courses for improving skills, established in sovkhozes;

     - training at full-time and correspondence technical schools under "Glavsre-
dasirsovkhozstroi", providing 500 specialists annually;

     - training in sovkhoz teams;

     - familiarization of state farm specialists with the advanced experience of
other sovkhozes.

Establishment of farms.  As soon as a certain amount of irrigation and drainage work
is completed and the areas can be put under development, a sovkhoz is established.

Sovkhozes in the Golodnaya Steppe are mainly specialized in cotton growing, their
area under irrigation amounting to 6-7 thousand hectares.  The experience gained
in land development proves that such a size is preferable as it ensures optimum
running of the farm.  A sovkhoz includes a central village where all housing, cultural and personal service facilities and the main production base are concentrated.
The whole territory of the sovkhozes is divided into agroproduction divisions, each
covering 1.5 - 1.8 thousand irrigated hectares.  The division has a production-
utilities centre with premises for storing and maintaining machinery and for
storing implements. Workers are brought by cars from the central village to the
site.  The basic production unit is a team responsible for serving an area of
100-150 ha.  A field camp provided with shower-rooms where workers can rest, and
a shed for small quantities of fertilizers is built for each team.

Organization of agricultural activity of sovkhozes.  Sovkhozes are intended to meet
the following requirements:

     - to make the best use of land prepared for sowing crops envisaged by the
plan, aiming at the maximum effect from agriculture;

     - to combine the high level of agricultural mechanization advanced field
management practices and application of modern methods of crop cultivation.

The experience gained in the Golodnaya Steppe proves that integrated land development complies with the above requirements.

As is known, the basic task of irrigation development is the establishment of a new
cotton-growing region in Central Asia.  Owing to the work of those developing and
constructing the Golodnaya Steppe, this task is being successfully implemented.
The sovkhozes under "Golodnostepstroi" delivered to the State 196 thousand t. of
raw cotton in 1970, 234 thousand t. in 1971 and 338 thousand t. in 1975, or 2.5
million t. since the beginning of the development (during the 15 years).

The integrated method of irrigating the new zone enables as many as 17.5 thousand
ha of new lands, on average to be put to use annually; this is four times the rate
of land increment in the old zone of the Golodnaya Steppe.  The share of cotton
production and the land use factor have appreciably increased.  Table 11 shows
variations in indices of using irrigated lands in the Golodnaya Steppe (new zone).

Table 11   Variations in Indices of using Irrigated Lands
in the New Zone of the Golodnaya Steppe

(in thousand ha)

| Year | Areas irrigated by the beginning of the sowing period | Design plough-land | Actual plough-land | Irrigated land use factor |
|------|------|------|------|------|
| 1 | 2 | 3 | 4 | 5 |
| 1963 | 52.9 | 49.1 | 43.4 | 0.866 |
| 1964 | 69.9 | 65.3 | 57.3 | 0.890 |
| 1965 | 86.5 | 80.5 | 67.2 | 0.840 |
| 1966 | 106.8 | 99.4 | 87.7 | 0.880 |
| 1967 | 125.6 | 116.9 | 98.0 | 0.845 |
| 1968 | 139.4 | 129.8 | 111.6 | 0.860 |
| 1969 | 157.8 | 146.9 | 126.2 | 0.865 |
| 1970 | 172.0 | 161.3 | 143.4 | 0.885 |
| 1971 | 180.8 | 169.7 | 156.8 | 0.925 |
| 1972 | 193.8 | 180.6 | 170.8 | 0.942 |
| 1973 | 219.6 | 202.6 | 190.4 | 0.941 |
| 1974 | 236.1 | 218.5 | 207.1 | 0.942 |
| 1975 | 262.2 | 240.7 | 219.2 | 0.950 |

Advantages of the integrated method of irrigation development of desert lands manifest themselves in the high level of mechanization in farms under establishment. Labour productivity in sovkhozes under "Golodnosterpstroi" is much higher compared to that on farms subordinate to the Uzbek S.S.R. Ministry of Agriculture and to the average level in the Republic.

This has become possible due to the use of recent advances in field management practices, and extensive introduction of modern machines in sovkhozes. It is only natural that the Golodnaya Steppe has become the laboratory of wide-scale promotion of advanced methods of labour in agriculture. Beginning in 1968 they started to introduce wide-row sowing of cotton with rows spaced at 90 cm to apply the method of precise sowing of bare cotton seeds to apply herbicides at the time of cotton sowing to employ wide-range machines while tilling and picking cotton and to widely promote mechanized cotton harvesting.

The efficiency of the high level of mechanization when developing desert lands is evident from the data presented in Table 12.

Table 12  Analysis of Cotton Production and Individual Cotton
Output in "Golodnostepstroi" is much higher compared
1961-1975

| Year | Gross harvest of raw cotton, | Sown area, | Permanent workers, persons | Labour required in cotton production, thous. persons: | Cotton output per one worker, | Sown area served by one worker, |
|------|------|------|------|------|------|------|
|      | t | ha | | | t | ha |
| 1961 | 13965 | 12959 | 1890 | 539 | 7.4 | 6.8 |
| 1962 | 31388 | 31085 | 4020 | 1146 | 7.8 | 7.7 |
| 1963 | 54631 | 38278 | 4776 | 1361 | 11.4 | 8.0 |
| 1964 | 73364 | 46411 | 5512 | 1570 | 13.3 | 8.4 |
| 1965 | 80054 | 53483 | 6786 | 1934 | 11.8 | 7.9 |
| 1966 | 102106 | 64346 | 7473 | 2130 | 13.6 | 8.6 |
| 1967 | 121205 | 75438 | 8609 | 2453 | 14.1 | 8.8 |
| 1968 | 113518 | 77419 | 8009 | 2281 | 14.1 | 9.7 |
| 1969 | 145287 | 91920 | 10439 | 2975 | 13.9 | 8.8 |
| 1970 | 196400 | 109362 | 11080 | 3158 | 17.8 | 9.9 |
| 1971 | 234310 | 128290 | 12849 | 4043 | 18.1 | 10.1 |

*Bringing fertility to newly developed lands and improvement of their potential
productivity*

The construction and land development carried out during the 15 years since 1961
allowed (owing to the provision of drainage, leachings and the leaching regime of
irrigation) soil conditions to be radically improved, probable salinization to be
prevented and soil fertility to be improved.  This is proved both by the 1 m soil
layer salinity dynamics suggested in Table 13 and by the water and salt balances of
the irrigated area presented in Tables 14 and 15.

Another important index is the growth of the yield of the basic crop, cotton.  The
average growth of the cotton yields during the years of development for the
sovkhozes in the Golodnaya Steppe is presented in Fig. 14.

With the exception of construction work (land levelling, drainage, etc.) a series
of reclamation developments carried out in the Golodnaya Steppe, allowing attain-
ment of the above results, includes:

| | For non-saline lands | For non-saline but liable to salinity lands |
|---|---|---|
| Heavy-rate leachings, 10-35 thousand $m^3$/ha | + | - |
| Re-levelling | + | - |
| Sowing crops helping in development | + | - |
| Application of chemical improvers | + | - |
| Application of manure and mineral fertilizers | + | + |
| Preventive leachings, 2-3 thousand $m^3$/ha per year | + | - |
| Leaching regime of irrigation | + | + |

Table 13  Variations in salinity of 1 m soil layer
(thous. ha)

| Degree of salinity | Years | | | | | |
|---|---|---|---|---|---|---|
| | 1961 | 1964 | 1969 | 1970 | 1972 | 1975 |
| Non-saline and slightly saline | 184.8 | 168.7 | 185.0 | 190.5 | 203.5 | 216.2 |
| Moderately saline | 21.2 | 32.1* | 25.1 | 22.2 | 17.3 | 11.6 |
| Highly saline | 36.4 | 41.6* | 32.3 | 29.3 | 21.6 | 13.6 |
| | 242.4 | 242.4 | 242.4 | 242.4 | 242.4 | 242.4 |

EXPENDITURE AND PROFIT

In conformity with the existing method approved by the appropriate Government authorities, the efficiency of capital investments in water resources development is determined by the reimbursement principle

$$T = \frac{K_O}{\Delta} = \frac{K_O}{4\Delta + HO} \qquad \leqslant [T]$$

---

*Some increase in the area of saline land during 1961-1964 was due to drainage construction lagging behind in the initial stage; this failing was later eliminated.

where, T = actual reimbursement period;
   [T] = ditto
   KO = reimbursable capital investments;
   $\Delta$ = national income;
   $4\Delta$ = net income;
   HO = turnover tax share.

This method can be applied to determine reimbursement after commissioning a project, but when establishing a natural-production-irrigation complex such a method is not strictly accurate.

Table 14   Tentative balance of the irrigated area
(thousand $m^3$, net, per 1 ha)

| Item | Years | | | | | | | |
|---|---|---|---|---|---|---|---|---|
| | 1966 | 1967 | 1968 | 1969 | 1970 | 1971 | 1972 | 1973 |
| Input | | | | | | | | |
| Precipitation | 2.22 | 2.57 | 3.24 | 5.71 | 2.86 | 2.92 | 2.46 | 3.12 |
| Irrigation water | 8.64 | 9.54 | 7.5 | 6.28 | 8.2 | 10.60 | 8.95 | 9.03 |
| Inflow from outside | 0.12 | 0.12 | 0.12 | 0.12 | 0.12 | 0.12 | 0.12 | 0.12 |
| Total | 10.98 | 12.23 | 10.86 | 12.11 | 11.48 | 13.64 | 11.43 | 12.27 |
| Output | | | | | | | | |
| Drainage flow | 0.5 | 0.82 | 0.94 | 1.32 | 1.18 | 2.22 | 1.85 | 2.31 |
| Canal wastes during non-vegetation period | 0.41 | 0.33 | 0.48 | 0.40 | 0.38 | 0.51 | 0.28 | 0.36 |
| Transpiration and evaporation | 7.62 | 8.10 | 8.20 | 8.55 | 8.9 | 9.02 | 8.50 | 8.86 |
| Increase of moisture reserve in soil layer | 1.0 | 1.40 | 0.83 | 0.98 | 0.61 | 0.82 | 0.60 | 0.84 |
| Ground water replenishment | 1.08 | 1.14 | 0.35 | 0.89 | 0.36 | 0.66 | 0.53 | 0.77 |
| Total | 10.61 | 11.79 | 10.80 | 12.14 | 11.43 | 11.53 | 11.66 | 12.72 |
| Error | +0.37 | +0.44 | +0.06 | +0.03 | +0.05 | +0.41 | −0.23 | −0.45 |
| In per cent | +3.35 | +3.6 | +0.5 | +0.26 | +0.46 | +3.96 | −2.0 | −3.71 |

Table 15   Salt balance of the Golodnaya Steppe New Zone
(thousand tons)

| Item | Years | | | | | | | |
|---|---|---|---|---|---|---|---|---|
| | 1966 | 1967 | 1968 | 1969 | 1970 | 1971 | 1972 | 1973 |
| **Input** | | | | | | | | |
| Irrigation water | 757 | 1546 | 1354 | 700 | 1171 | 1620 | 1490 | 1916 |
| Precipitation | 31 | 42 | 59 | 113 | 60 | 58 | 54 | 72 |
| Evaporation from ground water | 93 | 117 | 165 | 207 | 123 | 180 | 198 | 221 |
| Underground water inflow from outside | 216 | 252 | 275 | 306 | 324 | 347 | 367 | 387 |
| Total | 1097 | 1957 | 1853 | 1326 | 1688 | 2205 | 2109 | 2596 |
| **Output** | | | | | | | | |
| Drainage flow | 720 | 1201 | 1542 | 2818 | 2021 | 2731 | 3053 | 3109 |
| Wastes | 287 | 231 | 496 | 576 | 377 | 492 | 313 | 406 |
| Total | 1007 | 1432 | 2038 | 3394 | 2398 | 3223 | 3366 | 3515 |
| Accumulated total and decrease of salt content | +90 | +525 | – | – | – | | | |
| | – | – | 185 | 2068 | 710 | 1018 | 1257 | 919 |
| $D_o$, per 1 irrigated ha | +0.6 | +3.6 | −1.0 | 11.5 | −4.0 | −5.4 | −6.0 | −4.6 |
| $D_p$, per 1 ha of lands where ground water table is above drainage level | +2.8 | +10.4 | −3.2 | −29.6 | −12.6 | −15.6 | −17.1 | −13.7 |

While determining the efficiency of the integrated hydraulic construction, the consideration of the time factor is very important.  Provision is made primarily for building preparatory facilities such as:  units of own construction base, industrial projects, and outside services and communications, each of them helping to enhance agricultural efficiency.

Consideration of the time factor enables the efficiency of the entire complex to be properly evaluated and its optimization to be planned.  To this end, having studied all expenditure on integrated construction and development, it is necessary to single out those which can be reimbursed and then to analyse, from the beginning of construction, the distribution of capital investment and the accumulation of profit in different branches of the complex. It seems reasonable to determine the efficiency by the remaining expenses being the difference between annual capital investment and profit in this or that branch.  In this case, every year we shall have:

$$B_i = K_i - \varepsilon_1$$

where,   $B_i$ = remaining expenditures in the branch per "i" year;
         $K_i$ = capital investments in the branch per "i" year;
         $\varepsilon_i$ = efficiency (income in the branch per "i" year).

For a series of years with the participation of "n" branches we shall obtain:

$$B_n^T = \sum_{i=1}^{T} \sum_{0}^{n} (K_i - \varepsilon_i)\, K_g$$

where,   $B_n^T$ = remaining expenditure for a number of years, "T", in "n" branches
              of integrated construction and development;
         $K_g$ = discount rate (coefficient of time consideration).

Time for the capital invested in integrated construction and development to be
reimbursed is, probably, at B=0.

The peculiarity of determining the efficiency in integrated construction is in the
fact that a number of branches involved in this construction are according to the
existing system, non-reimbursable. This refers not only to the construction of
settlements, which is logical and understandable and should be accounted for
neither in the expenditure on capital construction nor on operation. Formally,
non-reimbursable investments are those made in production assets supported by the
budget, i.e. interfarm roads, irrigation and drainage canals and structures, main
water supply conduits, etc.

Capital investments in inter-farm roads with fare-free transport are as socially
useful as those assigned for settlements, and in much the same way as the latter
they are probably non-reimbursable investments though indirectly they aid in
improving the financial figures of construction and the agricultural aspect of
development. Expenditures involved in inter-farm irrigation and drainage projects
are designated only for the production of agricultural produce and, similarly,
operational expenditure including depreciation costs should be accounted for in
total capital investments. They are partially covered by agricultural products,
for example, cotton, rice, etc.

In this case the expression showing the remaining expenditure is converted as
follows:

$$B_n^T = \sum_{i=1}^{T} \sum_{0}^{n} = (K_n - \varepsilon_n + U_i)\, K_g - O\delta$$

where,   $U_i$ = costs involved in the operation of interfarm irrigation structures;
         $\Sigma O\delta$ = the remainder of the circulating capital in all branches.

As is evident from Table 16, by 1974 the capital invested in developing the new
zone totalled 1,459 mill.roubles, including 1.052 mill.roubles (reimbursable
expenses) in industrial projects. By this same period the total income exceeded
the above expenditure by 207 mill.roubles. With effect from 1970, the annual total
income exceeded not only the reimbursable expenses, but the total expenses as well.
Thus, by 1974 the total income of the branches made up 194.6 million roubles,
yearly capital investments making up 143 million roubles (including the reimbursable
investments amounting to 101 million roubles).

These data indicate convincingly that the capital invested in the development of
the Golodnaya Steppe was repaid in 1971 irrespective of the time factor, and had
been repaid by 1974, taking the time factor into account.

Table 16   Calculation of remaining expenditure to assess efficiency of integrated construction and development of lands in the new zone of the Golodnaya Steppe (mill.roubles)

| Year | Total capital investments | Incl. Industrial construction | Incl. Industrial construction (bases and plants) | Agriculture | Incl. agriculture and irrigation | Cotton ginning industry | Roads | Power engineering | Other | Operational costs involved in interfarm network | Income Industry | Income Construction | Income Other branches |
|---|---|---|---|---|---|---|---|---|---|---|---|---|---|
| 1956 | 2.54 | 2.0 | 0.2 | 1.5 | 1.5 | – | 0.3 | – | – | – | – | – | – |
| 1957 | 23.3 | 15.8 | 3.1 | 10.3 | 6.1 | – | 1.8 | – | 4.2 | – | – | 0.1 | – |
| 1958 | 42.6 | 29.9 | 5.5 | 22.4 | 12.8 | – | 2.0 | – | 9.6 | – | – | 0.1 | – |
| 1959 | 33.0 | 22.3 | 6.4 | 13.5 | 13.5 | – | 1.8 | 0.5 | – | – | – | 0.2 | – |
| 1960 | 32.5 | 24.3 | 6.4 | 15.5 | 15.4 | – | 2.1 | 0.4 | – | – | – | 0.0 | – |
| 1961 | 47.5 | 36.6 | 8.7 | 24.6 | 24.6 | – | 2.6 | 0.7 | – | 2.4 | -0.1 | -4.1 | -0.2 |
| 1962 | 50.3 | 38.7 | 3.7 | 31.7 | 30.2 | 0.3 | 2.4 | 0.7 | 1.5 | 2.1 | -0.2 | -4.1 | -0.4 |
| 1963 | 66.4 | 52.4 | 3.9 | 46.0 | 43.9 | 1.0 | 1.0 | 0.4 | 2.1 | 2.3 | -0.1 | -1.3 | -0.8 |
| 1964 | 63.3 | 49.4 | 4.7 | 42.2 | 40.2 | 1.0 | 1.0 | 0.5 | 2.0 | 2.4 | 0.5 | -0.7 | -0.8 |
| 1965 | 74.6 | 54.1 | 5.8 | 45.8 | 43.7 | 1.3 | 1.0 | 0.2 | 2.1 | 2.6 | 1.2 | +2.2 | 0.5 |
| 1966 | 83.8 | 60.8 | 5.6 | 53.0 | 50.1 | 2.6 | 1.0 | 0.4 | 2.9 | 2.8 | 1.9 | +0.7 | 0.7 |
| 1967 | 79.1 | 55.8 | 4.6 | 47.0 | 43.2 | 2.7 | 1.0 | 0.1 | 3.8 | 2.8 | 2.9 | 2.0 | 0.9 |
| 1968 | 79.6 | 55.5 | 3.0 | 48.4 | 46.1 | 2.3 | 1.0 | 0.5 | 2.3 | 3.0 | 4.4 | +1.4 | 1.5 |
| 1969 | 85.5 | 59.5 | 3.1 | 51.8 | 50.3 | 2.7 | 1.0 | 0.4 | 1.5 | 3.4 | 4.7 | +4.3 | 1.4 |
| | 764.1 | 556.8 | 65.3 | 453.6 | 421.6 | 13.9 | 20.0 | 4.8 | 32.0 | | | | |
| 1970 | 115.5 | 79.6 | 2.0 | 72.2 | 69.1 | 2.0 | 1.5 | 1.1 | 3.1 | 3.8 | 6.0 | 10.7 | 2.0 |
| 1971 | 113.1 | 80.7 | 1.3 | 73.6 | 62.2 | 3.2 | 1.6 | – | 11.4 | 3.8 | 3.5 | 10.8 | 0.8 |
| 1972 | 126.5 | 87.5 | 1.6 | 79.2 | 68.0 | 3.4 | 1.7 | – | 11.2 | 4.0 | 6.3 | 17.1 | 2.3 |
| 1973 | 143.0 | 101.0 | 1.0 | 93.0 | 93.0 | 3.6 | 1.8 | 1.6 | 10.0 | 4.2 | 5.5 | 16.4 | 2.1 |
| Total | 1458.9 | 1052 | 88.1 | 897.7 | 851.6 | 29.7 | 31.8 | 6.7 | 76.1 | 42 | | | |

*Capital investments, as of prior to and through 1969, were recalculated in connection with the introduction of new prices for construction.

| Income | | | Remaining expenditures | | | | Remain of circulating capital of branches | Total remaining expenses, accounting for circulating capital | |
|---|---|---|---|---|---|---|---|---|---|
| Agriculture | Cotton ginning, th.t | Turnover tax | Construction and industry | Reduced to 1973 | Agriculture | Reduced to 1973 | | Time factor excluded | Reduced to 1975 |
| – | – | – | 0.2 | 0.9 | 1.5 | 5.5 | 1.4 | 0.3 | 5.0 |
| – | – | – | 3.0 | 15.2 | 6.1 | 21.3 | 2.7 | 8.7 | 40.2 |
| – | – | – | 5.4 | 21.3 | 12.8 | 42.6 | 4.9 | 24.7 | 102.1 |
| – | – | – | 6.2 | 24.0 | 13.5 | 42.2 | 8.6 | 40.7 | 164.6 |
| – | – | – | 6.4 | 22.0 | 15.4 | 45.2 | 9.5 | 61.6 | 230.9 |
| -1.4 | 13.9 | 5.8 | 13.1 | 42.0 | 22.3 | 61.5 | 12.4 | 94.1 | 331.5 |
| -4.0 | 31.4 | 13.2 | 8.4 | 25.2 | 23.1 | 59.4 | 17.8 | 120.2 | 410.7 |
| +3.8 | 54.6 | 23.0 | 6.1 | 16.6 | 19.4 | 46.8 | 19.6 | 143.8 | 472.3 |
| +3.4 | 73.6 | 31.0 | 5.7 | 14.4 | 8.2 | 18.5 | 24.1 | 153.3 | 500.7 |
| +2.2 | 80.1 | 33.4 | 2.1 | 4.9 | 10.7 | 22.5 | 25.9 | 164.3 | 526.3 |
| -3.9 | 102.1 | 43.0 | 2.3 | 5.0 | 13.7 | 26.8 | 27.6 | 178.6 | 556.4 |
| +0.3 | 121.2 | 50.8 | -1.2 | -2.4 | -5.0 | -9.0 | 31.3 | 169.7 | 541.3 |
| -2.4 | 113.5 | 47.6 | -4.3 | -8.1 | 3.9 | 6.5 | 36.2 | 163.4 | 534.8 |
| -11.2 | 145.3 | 61.1 | -7.3 | -12.2 | 3.7 | 4.1 | 41.5 | 154.5 | 521.3 |
| 20.0 | 196.4 | 82.5 | -16.7 | -24.8 | -29.6 | -41.0 | 50.2 | 99.5 | 446.8 |
| 27.8 | 234.3 | 100 | -15.8 | -20.8 | -61.8 | -77.2 | 53.0 | 18.9 | 346.0 |
| 36.5 | 296.3 | 124.3 | -24.1 | -27.8 | -88.8 | -99.5 | 56.0 | -96.8 | 215.7 |
| 40.6 | 309 | 130.0 | -23.0 | -23.0 | -83.4 | -83.4 | 61.0 | -207.2 | 104.3 |
| | | | -33 | 72.5 | -114.2 | 92.8 | | | |

However, it would be wrong to confine the efficiency of the integrated construction and land development to this factor only.  It should be pointed out that in this case some socio-economic facts are not considered, namely, the increase in the income of those who were moved from densely populated areas to the areas to be developed.  Also the methods do not take into consideration the fact that the reclamation efforts undertaken have a long-term effect and that land productivity has increased from the initial $\pi_0$ to the higher value, $\pi_k$.  Consideration of all these factors enables the remaining expenditure involved in a water resources complex during the development period to be generally expressed as:

$$B = \sum_{\phantom{0}}^{T} \sum_{\phantom{0}}^{\pi} (K_{ni} + U_{mxi} - \Delta_{ni})\, K_g \stackrel{-}{+} \sum_{0}^{k} F_k(\pi_k - \pi_0) + \stackrel{0}{\underset{i}{=}} \stackrel{0}{1}$$

$$+ \sum_{0}^{T} (H\,\Delta_k - H\Delta_0)\, l_i$$

where   $K_g$ = discount rate which accounts for the time factor and, calculated using the compound interest method, is equal to:

$$K_g = (1 + \frac{7}{15}\, E_n)^T + \frac{8}{15}\, E_n^T$$

   where   $E_n$ = coefficient of normative efficiency;
            $T$  = period of construction and development;
            $n$  = number of branches;

   $\Delta_{ni}$ = national income of each branch allowing for the turnover tax per "i" year;
   $K_{ni}$ = reimbursable capital investments in "n" branch per "i" year;
   $U_{mxi}$ = inter-farm non-reimbursable costs per "i" year;
   $F_k$ = area of "K" plots with land fertility increased (or decreased) from $\pi_0$ (initial) to $\pi_k$ (final);
$H\Delta_k - H\Delta_0$ = national income for one worker engaged in land development, of the total "l" number of workers moved from densely populated regions prior to and after land development, respectively.

The above supplementary components for the Golodnaya Steppe provided, as of 1973, the following:

$$\sum_{0}^{K} F_K\ (\pi_T - \pi_0) = 29.6 \text{ million roubles.}$$

$$\sum_{0}^{T} (H\Delta_K - H\Delta_0)\, l_i = 94.5 \text{ million roubles.}$$

Thus, considerations of these two factors favours earlier repayment of the capital investments involved in the Golodnaya Steppe irrigation and development, as of 1972.

The capital invested in irrigation and development of the Golodnaya Steppe is evidently paid back in the course of development by the 11th year since the beginning of the large-scale construction. Subsequently, the Golodnaya Steppe provides the State with an income of 60-100 million roubles a year which is continuously increasing despite the growing investments.

At the same time, the national income for one worker engaged in the development averaged 2947 roubles for the development period, as against 1987 roubles in the Republic.

RECOMMENDATIONS

1.  Irrigation is the most efficient means of increasing the productivity of desert lands, allowing other favourable natural conditions, such as abundance of heat, solar radiation, and natural soil fertility, to be markedly intensified. Therefore comprehensive development of irrigation will aid in increasing the agricultural production, extending the raw materials base, improving labour resources employment and intensifying famine control in the developing countries.

2.  Concerning desert lands of the arid zone, the most reasonable approach is an integrated method of irrigation and development implying that all the required measures are to be fulfilled in compliance with a single design and plan, primarily to one order through the services of one organization which is entirely responsible for all stages of work, i.e. from the design to the completed development of the area.

3.  Transformation of natural conditions can be controlled in most cases when irrigating desert lands in the arid zone. To ensure durable improvement of irrigated land fertility and preservation of the environment provision should be made for the appropriate structures and field management practices.

4.  Reliable drainage, land levelling, soil leaching and land amelioration are responsible for the successful development of desert lands in the arid zone.

5.  Establishment of natural-production- irrigation complexes using systems analysis, comprehensive planning and stage-by-stage accomplishment of work make the development of such areas extremely economically attractive permitting, at the same time, the solution of a number of socio-economic problems.

6.  Intensive land development is practicable when, alongside technical efforts, political measures are undertaken, such as: collective use of land and water, elimination of petty farming and provision of high-level mechanization of all operations.

# Integrated Desert Development and Desertification Control in the Turkmenian SSR

A. G. Babaev, A. Batyrov, Z. G. Freikin,
Y. S. Khodzhakuliev, V. T. Lavrinenko,
O. S. Lavronenko, N. T. Nechaeva,
V. N. Nikolaev, N. S. Orlovsky, M. P. Petrov
and M. M. Sarkisov

## INTRODUCTION

The choice of the Turkmenian SSR (Turkmenistan) as the case study to illustrate desertification control in the USSR is quite adequate. Turkmenistan is a typical region in the arid zone of the Soviet Union including Soviet Middle Asia and Kazakhstan where vast territories of deserts are used in combination with comparatively small oases. Therefore, the study of all aspects of economy and the suggested measures of desertification control are relevant for the entire arid zone.

Turkmenistan is a land of deserts. The sandy desert of Kara-Kum and a number of other desert territories cover 90.8%, mountains 5.1% and oases approximately 4.1% of the Republic's territory.

The peculiarities of natural conditions related to the domination of deserts predetermine the orientation of economy in Turkmenistan. Natural conditions were important in the development of the country and in the destinies of the Turkmenian people: the struggle for water and exploration of ways of adaptation to the stern conditions of desert life are salient throughout the history of Turkmenistan and all the Republics of Soviet Middle Asia and Kazakhstan. In the course of this struggle men found many ways in surmounting the unfavourable elements of deserts, specifically when utilizing desert pastures. Thus, the better adapted species of livestock have been selected; ways have been found for using rainfall for drinking and watering; techniques have been worked out for pasturing livestock in spring and winter without watering by making use of the plant moisture; and a method of rational, portional use of pastures which ensures a moderate load and prevents impoverishing of pastures and their disappearance and the forming of barkhanes on pastures, as well as a system of livestock movement to remote seasonal pastures, have been developed.

The application of the rainfall run-off into small saucer-shaped depressions helped work out methods of the so-called "oitach" small-patch farming. Melon crops are being grown without irrigation on sands and takyr-fringe areas. However, the small-scale farms, owing to dismemberment, lack of adequate knowledge and machinery, were not always victorious in the struggle with the desert elements and in many cases lost their livestock, had to excessively exploit the better situated and watered pastures, leaving unexploited the pastures which were remote or did not have enough water. Without other types of fuel the population was intensively cutting shrubs. All this resulted in the impoverishment of the plant cover, the development of barkhanes and desertification.

The primitive modes of using water for irrigation without a system of drainage, the imperfection of the irrigation network have not infrequently led to salination and waterlogging of land in oases which is also regarded as a process of desertification.

With the establishment of Soviet power and the joining of Turkmenistan into the Union of Soviet Socialist Republics the principles of economy were changed. Resting on the achievements of science and technology the economy is growing on an industrial foundation and is steadily becoming more intensive.

The case study illustrates an instance of rapid development of diversified economy where natural conditions and available natural resources have been taken into consideration.

At the entry of the Turkmenian SSR into the Union, and in connection with the rapid improvement of the cultural standard of the Turkmenian people, agriculture and industry were improved on the basis of modern scientific achievements. Agriculture is making progress since more water became available through the utilization of the Amu-Darya discharge thanks to the V.I. Lenin Kara-Kum Canal. Considerable attention is also given to the development of pasture livestock breeding which is based on the utilization of cheap desert forage resources.

The mining industry, which is exploiting tremendous desert resources of raw materials, also plays an important part. All this requires more and more power, improvement of transportation, the development of light and other industries which is being implemented in the Turkmenian SSR.

An objective indicator of the successful development of economy are the following figures: the share of the Turkmenian SSR in the national output of oil comprises 4%, that of sodium sulphate 40%, window pane production, approximately 5%, mineral fertilizers, approximately 3%, table salt 2%. Considerable volumes of iodine and bromine are being mined. Turkmenistan yields 14% of raw cotton, 20% of karakul, 10% of raw silk and 3% of the national output of wool. The mining of combustible gas is growing rapidly.

The development of cottage industry, the construction of canals, roads, communities, the development of desert territories for irrigated farming directly in the desert, alongside with considerable economic advantages leads, in some cases, to desertification.

Man's economic activity is a strong factor which creates irrigated and industrial landscapes in the desert. Great scope of construction of canals, roads, pipelines, communities and other objects, the use of modern mechanisms, transport and earth-moving machines facilitates the development of a technogenous landscape with its intrinsic negative features. Vast territories which were desertified owing to the irrational use of natural resources in the prerevolutionary time have been inherited by the Turkmenian SSR. Even at present, desertification processes may be observed in certain places owing to the fact that the deserts of Turkmenistan have a high economic potential. With its rapid and intensive tapping there is the danger of disrupting natural ecosystems. Belated protective measures intensify some of the undesirable phenomena like deflation and sand accumulation, soil erosion, pasture degradation, soil salinization which lead to the withdrawal of sown areas from economy and to desertification.

Therefore, research is conducted on a nationwide scope to work out and implement plan measures to conserve and reinstate natural ecosystems and to control desertification. It is not accidental that the problem of deserts is one of the major research programmes of the Turkmen Academy of Sciences.

The Institute of Deserts - the sole Soviet arid research centre - is situated in Ashkhabad, the capital of the Turkmen SSR, it conducts research into integrated development of desert territories of the Soviet Union and coordinates the relevant research in this field on the scope of Soviet Middle Asia and Kazakhstan. Functioning with the Institute is a permanent Scientific Council on Deserts ("Integrated Study and Development of the Deserts of Soviet Middle Asia and Kazakhstan"), which affiliates desert students and conducts research on a nationwide scope. The publication which illustrates the results of science and practice in desert development is the *Problemy Osvoyeniya Pustyn* journal.

The idea of conducting this case study is to illustrate the peculiarities of conducting diversified economy in one of the Soviet Republics in an arid zone, the peculiarities which are predetermined by a vast desert territory.

The necessity of ensuring normal economy predetermines the need in preventing desertification and, in case of appearance of desertification foci, their earliest liquidation.

The scientific principles of desert development and the techniques of desertification control in the Turkmenian SSR which are elaborated by Turkmian scientists are of nationwide and international importance.

The study of man-environment interaction in all its diversity comprises the substance of the international programme "Man and the Biosphere" (MAB) in which the Soviet Union is participating. The growth of population requires the improvement of economy to increase the productivity of farm land and prevent desertification. It is imperative for man to learn to conserve the environment, to use it meaningfully and moderately so that the ecosystems of the arid zone should also guarantee the existence of generations of people in future.


NATURAL CONDITIONS

The Turkmenian SSR is situated in the south-west of Middle Asia in the desert zone of the temperate belt. The area is 488,000 km$^2$, or 2.2% of the USSR territory. The bulk of Turkmenistan is covered by deserts which noticeably influence the environment and the economy in the Republic. The small mountainous areas (the altitude of individual summits reaches 3137 m) is in the south and the south-east outskirts.

The *climate* is sharply continental and exceptionally dry. The continentality manifests itself in sharp changes of meteorological elements and in the daily and annual variation, while the aridity - in very small rainfall, considerable air dryness, slight cloudiness and a high evaporation rate. The northward exposure allows cold air masses to reach the Kara-Kum desert territory and induce sharp cooling, specifically in winter. At the same time the south-east mountain ridges retard the influx of moisture from the Indian Ocean.

The weather is extremely unstable in the cold season of the year but it is relatively stable, warm and dry in summer. This is due to a sharp distinction in the synoptic processes; cyclonic activity is pronounced in the cold season, transformation of air masses over the strongly warmed sands in summer.

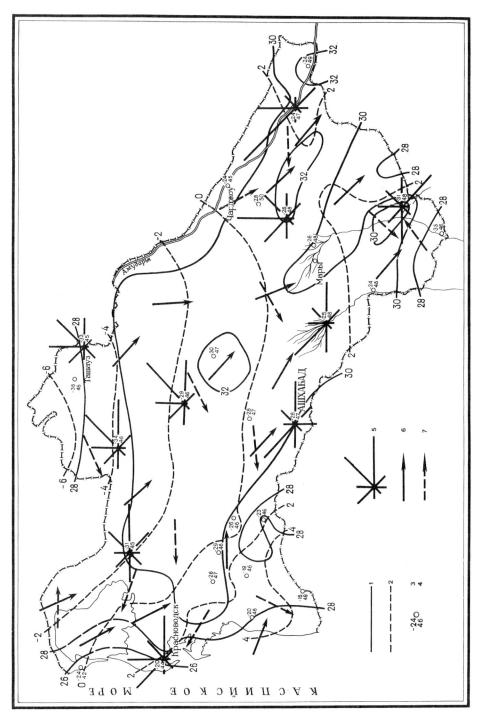

Fig. 1.  Climatic map of the Turkmenian SSR.  Air temperature (C$^o$): 1 - July isotherms; 2 - January isotherms; 3 - absolute minimum; 4 - absolute maximum; 5 - mean annual rose of winds, % = prevailing direction of the wind; 6 - in July; 7 - in January.

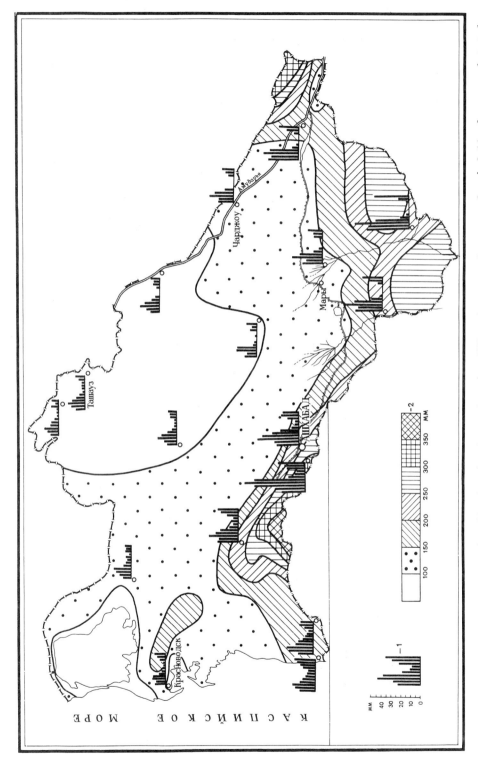

Fig. 2.  Scheme of rainfall distribution in the Turkmenian SSR.  1 - annual curve of rainfall; 2 - annual total of rainfall, mm.

The mean annual temperature in the territory is positive and varies from $11^{0}$ in the north to $18^{0}$ in the south-east over the lowland part of the Republic. Winters are soft and have little snow. The coldest month is January with a mean temperature of $-6^{0}$ in the north-east and $+5^{0}$ in the south-west of the Republic. There are winters of particular severity, persistence of the snow blanket, frosts reaching $-36^{0}$ in the southern districts and $-19^{0}$ in the south-west.

Summer on the lowland part is very warm and dry. Practically the entire incident radiation goes to warm the soil and air. Air temperature, therefore, is high everywhere while the heat reserve suffices to grow cultural thermophylic plants. Mean earth temperature in July reaches $+32^{0}$ while the absolute maximum is $+50^{0}$. Sand surface too in summer is up to $+80^{0}$.

Spring is short with frequent recurrences of cold, frosts are not infrequent. The frost-free period averages 200-250 days and 280-310 days in the south-east in some years.

A characteristic of the climate is the clear sky duration: 100-150 hours in January and 320-400 hours in July or 80-93% of the possible duration.

Turkmenistan belongs to the zone of insufficient humidity. A specific feature of precipitation is not only the exceptionally small volume but the uneven distribution during the year. The average annual rainfall is 80-360 mm. Less than 100 mm is in Northern Turkmenistan, Zaunguz Karakum and in the Kar-Bogaz-Gol Bay district; the Lowland Kara-Kum get up to 150 mm of rainfall; sub-montane zone in the south and south-east up to 250 mm, the rainfall is more than 250 mm in the mountainous districts. Approximately 70% of the annual rainfall comes in the winter-spring season, there is practically no rainfall in summer. Atmospheric precipitation is insufficient for the cultivation of farm crops while the rainfall deficit is replenished by irrigation. Concentration of rainfall, however, in the winter-spring period facilitates the development of a moisture reserve in the soil and the development of pasture vegetation. Annual rainfall totals vary from year to year: at Repetek in 1917 it was 24 mm while in 1920 it was 313 mm.

The highest relative humidity is registered in January - 70-78%. The dryest season, from June to September, when the average monthly relative humidity drops in the desert zone to 22-25% and down to 35-48% in the oases. The low air humidity facilitates intensive water surface evaporation: the annual evaporation varies from 1000 to 2300 mm surmounting atmospheric precipitation (in Central Kara-Kum) 15-20-fold.

North-eastern winds prevail in North Turkmenistan, eastern in the Central and along the Kopetdag submontane plain and northern in the South-east Kara-Kumy. Weak and moderate winds make up 75-85% of all air movement. When wind becomes slightly stronger dust storms arise owing to the character of the surface and they are possible round the year with the greatest recurrence in spring and summer. Winds facilitate the forming of eolian topography. Poorly fixed sands and barkhanes are easily shifted and are liable to cover engineering structure or lay bare pipelines.

*Water Resources*

Most of Turkmenistan has no permanent surface water. Rivers only flow in southern and eastern peripheral districts. All of them are of snow-rainfall origin and spring in the mountains of Iran and Afghanistan. Of greatest economic importance is the full-flowing Amu Darya and smaller rivers - Murgab, Tedjen, Kushka and Atrek. There are many rivers and springs with insignificant discharge of local importance in mountains.

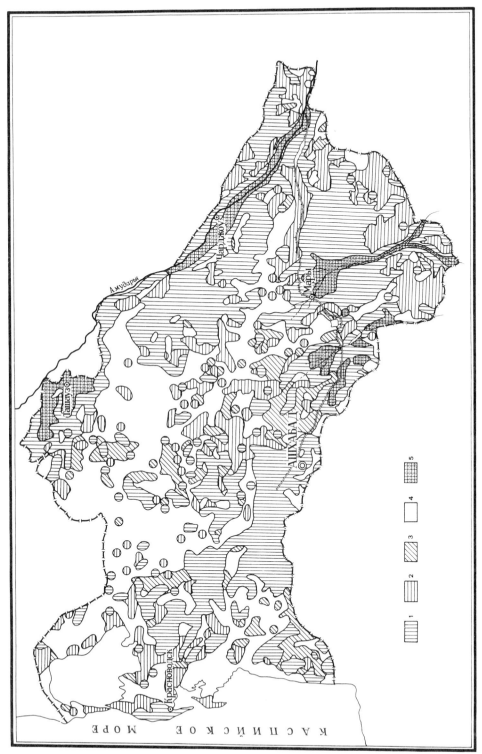

Fig. 3.  Schematic map of the water capacity of pastures in the Turkmenian SSR.  Pastures: 1 – watered in all seasons; 2 – in autumn and winter; 3 – in spring; 4 – unwatered; 5 – cultivated-irrigated and long-fallow lands.

Oases are situated along river valleys and at places where ground waters come to the surface. The largest are the Amu Darya, Khorezm, Charjou, Murgab, Tedjen and Ashkhabad. River waters are fully used for irrigation needs.

Subterranean waters (salinized and sweet) are of great importance in desert districts and the same goes for the winter-spring surface run-off. These waters are used by the local population mainly to water sheep and camels.

*The soil cover* is represented by grey-brown soils in the western part (Ustyurt and Krasnovodskoye plateaus), grey soils in the submontane districts and brown soils in mountains. The developed and formed soils are absent in the sandy desert. Prevailing here are fixed sands and sand dunes. Considerable areas are covered by takyrs and takyr-like surfaces. Meadow type soils predominate in river valleys.

*Vegetation*

Several types of deserts are spread in Turkmenistan: sandy with tall-shrub-grassy vegetation (21 million hectares), gypsum (5 million hectares) and clay (4 million hectares) with semi-shrub-herbage vegetation and the loess submontane (3 million hectares) with herbage vegetation. This plant cover is used both for sheep and camel pasturing and for fuel.

Arboreous vegetation which forms forests and sparse woods is found in river valleys, mountains and in sandy deserts on small sections where ground waters come close to the surface.

The vegetation cover of Middle Asian deserts is represented by 300 species. Particularly widespread are the following families: Chenopodiaceae, Gramineae, Leguminosae, Cruciferae, Compositae, Boraginaceae.

In Kara-Kum it includes different bioforms: trees - 5 species, shrubs - 32 species, semishrub and dwarf-shrub - 39 species, perennial grasses - 60 species, biannual - 2 species, annual - 139 species. Grasses predominate by the number of species but only 30% of them are of a dominant role whereas 73% of shrubs and 66% of semishrub plants are the main components of the plant cover.

There are many useful species among plants used as industrial and medicinal raw material, for decorative, food and other application.

*The fauna* is varied. The foxes and small antelopes are of commercial importance.

Many animals (culan-onager, cheetah, leopard, wild sheep and others) are entered in the "Red Book" and protected by the law.

The flora and fauna and whole natural landscapes are protected by rational utilization and in a number of reserves (Repetek, Badkhyz, Gasan-kuli) and preserves. Before the revolution of 1917 there was only the Repetek reserve which was founded in 1912. All other reserves and preserves were established later. At present, reserve management is developing and the methods of protecting natural ecosystems are being improved; active explanatory work is conducted by publishing posters, pamphlets and reading lectures.

The natural-geographic conditions and consequently the specific features of agriculture divide the territory of the Republic into a zone of irrigated farming and a zone of pasture livestock breeding. The greater part (90.8%) is under deserts; mountains comprise 5.1% and oases 4.1% of the territory.

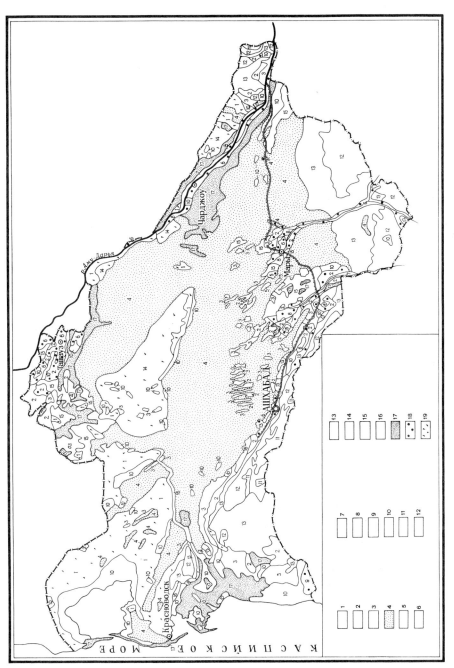

Fig. 4.   Soil map of the Turkmenian SSR.  Soils: 1 – grey-brown; 2 – takyr-like; 3 – takyrs; 4 – sandy deserts; 5 – meadow-residual; 6 – meadow; 7 – meadow-floodland; 8 – meadow-takyr-like; 9 – meadow-bog; 10 – solonchaks; 11 – brown mountain; 12 – dark grey and typical; 13 – dry light; 14 – complex of sandy deserts and takyr-like soils with takyrs; 16 – complex of takyr-like soils, takyrs and solonchaks; 17 – weakly fixed and unfixed sand; 18 – irrigated soils; 19 – rocky soils.

## SOCIAL CONDITIONS AND POPULATION

Prior to the revolution of 1917 this territory, which was populated mainly by Turkmen, was called the Transcaspian Region. Beginning with 1898 it became part of the Turkestanian General Governorship. In the time of Soviet government the Turkestan autonomous Soviet Socialist Republic was formed and within it the Turkmen Autonomous Region.

The Turkmen Soviet Socialist Republic (the Turkmen SSR) was formed in October 1924 following the national alienation, and in February 1925 it joined the Union of Soviet Socialist Republics as an equal constituent republic.

The former Transcaspian Region was a backward colonial province in the Russian Empire. In the Turkmen population, not more than 0.7% could read and write; women were totally illiterate.

Up to 40% of sown areas and 60% of livestock belonged to rich feudals. The main implement was a wooden plough and the hoe. There were only sixty-four metal ploughs throughout the Transcaspian Region. Prevailing sown cultures were grain crops. As for raw cotton the annual harvest reached 70,000 tons; yields of 8-10 centners from a hectare were regarded as adequate. The manufacturers of textiles loaned seed to peasants and later bought up the harvest for negligible sums of money. Breeding farms for work cattle and riding horses of the Akhaltekin breed were situated in the oases. Fat-rumped sheep of low productive capacity but with good stamina as well as the dromedary of the Arvana breed well adapted to desert conditions were raised in Kara-Kum. The karakul sheep were only bred in a few districts of Eastern Kara-Kum.

Nomands, livestock breeders who lived in difficult natural environment, accumulated through centuries the knowledge of desert conditions and evolved the modes of conducting their economy which to a certain extent are still valid.

There was practically no industry. Table salt was extracted from the Kuuli Lake, oil at Cheleken where it was drawn by buckets from wells. In 1913, 129,000 tons of oil was drawn in this way; due to the First Imperialist War of 1914 and the civil wars following the revolution of 1917, oil extraction was completely suspended.

Various crafts like the manufacture of fabrics, carpets, weaponry, etc., were developed among the population. There were repair shops to service the transport facilities in the few towns like Ashkhabad, Krasnovodsk, Kizil-Arvat and Charjou.

Soviet government began the rehabilitation of oil wells on Cheleken, mining of sulphur in Kara-Kum, of sodium sulphate at Kara-Bogaz-Gol, of ozokerite on Cheleken, of bentonite in Western Turkmenistan, of oil in Nebit-Dag and of natural gas in Kara-Kum. Modern industry, light, food, metal working, energetics, engineering, chemical, building materials, etc., were established in towns, and ensured the operation of all branches of economy.

Concurrently, construction and reconstruction of canals and reservoirs in oases and of water wells in the desert was undertaken. Sown areas continued to grow and the very pattern of sowings was altered. Cotton cultivation took the pride of place.

Pasture livestock raising specialized in karakul sheep (70% of the total). The herd of camels was great since they were the sole mode of transportation in the desert and in servicing livestock breeding farms. At present, camel breeding has been curtailed thanks to the mechanization of agriculture and the progress of many other modes of transport.

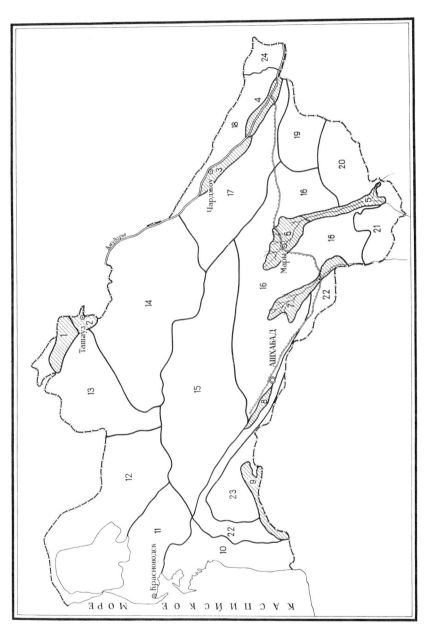

Fig. 5.  Scheme of natural-economic regionalization of Turkmenian SSR.  Regions of the zone of irrigated farming:
1 – Lower Amu-Darya Northern; 2 – Lower Amu-Darya Southern; 3 – Middle Amu-Darya Northern; 4 – Middle Amu-Darya Southern; 5 – Murgab; 6 – Murgab Floodland; 7 – Tedjen Valley-Delta District; 8 – Sub-montane district; 9 – South-western.  Districts of pasture livestock breeding: 10 – Maritime; 11 – Krasnovodsk; 12 – Predustyurt; 13 – Old Delta; 14 – Zaunguz; 15 – Central Kara-Kumy; 16 – Southern Kara-Kumy; 17 – Eastern Kara-Kumy; 18 – Sunduklin; 19 – Obruchevsky; 20 – Karabilsky; 21 – Badkhyz; 22 – Prikopetdag; 23 – Kopetdag; 24 – Kuchitan.

The main providers of farm produce became collective and state farms.  Desert
development turned into a component of the economic policy of the Soviet state and
of its 5-year programmes.

Owing to the radical reorganization of the Republic's economy, relationships
between the oases and the desert took a new shape.  The mining industry as well as
pasture livestock breeding developed in Kara-Kum.  As formerly, cotton-growing,
fruit-growing, vegetable-growing, melon-growing, silk-worm production and livestock
breeding are concentrated at permanent water sources, and directly in the desert
within the zone of large-scale trunk canals (primarily the Kara-Kum Canal).
Industry, processing farm produce and the enterprises servicing the economy (metal-
working and engineering and the production of building materials as well as
several other industries)  are concentrated in the towns of oases.

The form and conditions of labour changed not only at industrial enterprises and
in irrigated farming but in the oldest sector of economy - pasture animal husbandry.
Only the shepherds, their wives and children of preschool age stay at the pastures
with the livestock.  People of older age groups who are not engaged in livestock
breeding and school-age children stay at collective farm communities where there
are schools, hospitals, clubs, cinema houses and other services.

Deep water wells at pastures are fitted out with mechanical water hoisting, camels
are used to draw water from shallow water wells.  Manual water hoisting is
nonexistent.  Latest scientific methods and modern technology are applied for the
development of the Kara-Kum desert; airplanes and helicopters, aerial photography
and sputnik-collected information, as well as motor transport of increased capacity,
water well digging, and other machinery to lay the water mains, oil and gas mains,
etc.

The universal elementary and now the universal secondary education yielded fruit.
There are 1800 general schools and six higher schools in the Republic.  In 1951
the Turkmen Academy of Sciences was opened and it includes fourteen research
centres.  Sixty scientific research institutes function at ministries.  All this
facilitates the growth of intelligentsia, research and engineering personnel,
specifically from among the local population; it also facilitates culture and the
surmounting of the left-overs of feudalism.

The Turkmen SSR consists of five administrative regions and thirty-four districts.
Their boundaries are delimited in a way that every district incorporates a part of
an oasis with urban communities and pasture territory.  This is a precondition
which obliges organs of local government to plan measures for the development and
protection of the desert and to facilitate the development of economy in it.

The population of the Republic is 2,506,000 people (1975), the share of the urban
population is 49% and that of the rural 51%.  The average annual increment is 2.7%
(1974).  Out of 15 towns and 72 urban-type communities 4 towns and 32 communities
are directly in the desert (the towns are Krasnovodsk, Nebit-Dag, Kazandjik and
Cheleken).

The population consists of many nationalities but Turkmen prevail - 65.6%; the
urban population includes Russians, Ukrainians, Caucasian nationalities, etc.

Thanks to the development of industry and urbanization, the growth of population
and the agglomeration of livestock breeding forms, the development of irrigated
farming in oasis, changes have taken place in the distribution of the population in
the Kara-Kum desert, in the types of settlements as well as planning and in
population density.

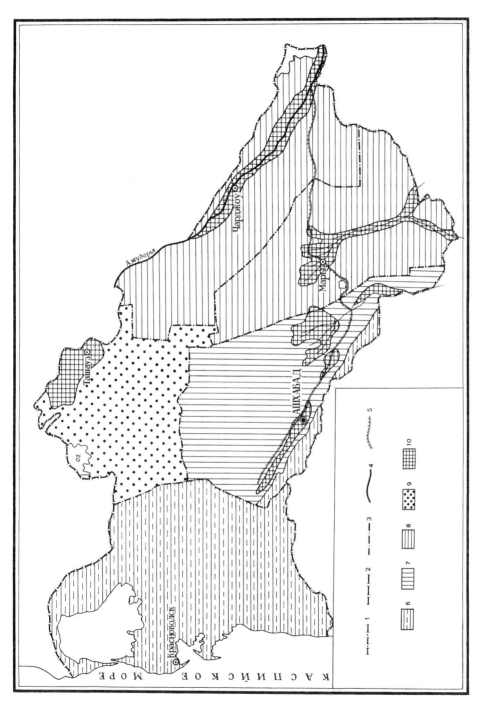

Fig. 6.   Population density of the Turkmenian SSR by regions boundaries.   1 – State; 2 – Union Republics; 3 – regional; 4 – rivers; 5 – canals.  Number of residents per 1 km$^2$: 6 – 1–2; 7 – 0.7–1; 8 – 0.5–1; 9 – more than 0.5; 10 – oases (100–150 per 1 km$^2$).

Urban-type settlements have sprung up at sites of mineral deposits, urban-type and rural communities emerged along railways and trunk canals: district centres, central communities of collective and state farms, communities with transporting, storing, dispatching and other functions with populations ranging from 500 to 4000 people.  The linear pattern of the distribution of communities along the boundary of the Kara-Kum desert facilitates the links between the desert and oases, specifically with regional centres.  Farms with populations ranging from 50 to 100 people and temporary shepherd centres with populations from 10 to 20 people which move to seasonal grazing grounds are located far in the desert.

Livestock breeding communities (central villages of collective and state farms) are situated by water sources or receive their water through water mains which are close to railroads, or by motor transport.  The number of large livestock-breeding communities with populations up to 3000 has increased noticeably.  Within these communities, just as in industrial ones, there are welfare and cultural establishments, schools, kindergartens, hospitals, cinemas, etc.

The industrial communities are characteristic of the mechanical and natural growth of the population, differing national composition and migration.  The characteristic feature of livestock-breeding communities is the natural growth of the population, stability and uniformity of the national composition.

The developed power system made it possible to supply electricity to the remotest parts of deserts where it is not infrequent for the population to use electrical utensils, radio and television sets, etc.  The improvement of the overall cultural standard of the Turkmen people, the progress of Soviet health protection has made it possible to eradicate completely such formerly widespread diseases as trachoma and malaria.


### MINING INDUSTRY

The bulk of oil deposits are in the west of Turkmenistan where oil-fields are successfully exploited.  Prior to the advent of Soviet government exploitation of oil deposits was of extremely low standard and primitive methods were used.  Since Soviet power came the extracting industry has been developing and is based on an industrial foundation.

The extraction of natural gas increased considerably in recent decades.  Gas deposits are so great that they meet own requirements and those of the Centre of the European part of the USSR and several countries which belong to the Council of Mutual Economic Assistance (CMEA).  At present, large gas-bearing deposits and approximately thirty medium-size and small ones which have been switched on to the Middle Asia - Centre gas mains have been prospected.  Up to 90% of the total extraction of natural gas and 59% of oil are exported from the Republic.  The remainder is used as fuel and raw material for oil processing and for the production of chemical goods.  By the end of 1975 the Turkmen SSR accounted for 18% of the nation-wide extraction of natural gas, 3.1% of oil and more than 40% of sulphate.

The construction of the Krasnovodsk oil refinery gave the start to the petrochemical industry of Turkmenistan.  The construction of a refinery in Eastern Kara-Kum is being completed.

High-quality native sulphur plays the leading part among non-metallic minerals. Besides meeting the national needs sulphur is exported.

As for the prospected deposits of iodine and bromine Turkmenistan holds the first place in the USSR with three exploited deposits. The processing of these minerals is conducted at plants in Cheleken and Nebit-Dag.

The Oglanlinskoye deposit of bentonite clays is one of the largest in the USSR. Clay is being used in many branches of economy as an absorbent; in recent years another important sphere of application was found - in the ferrous metallurgy.

The situation of Turkmenistan in the desert zone predetermined the abundance of mineral salts. Of greatest commercial importance is the deposit of Kara-Bogaz-Gol which is unique by its origin and size and here, besides Glauber's salt, mining has been started of epsomite and bischofite. It is planned in the near future to extract bromine and other components.

The deposits of potassium salts in the Guardak-Kugitang district are quite considerable. As for the developed technology, besides the production of potassium fertilizer, plans are made to manufacture bromine, technical and table salt.

The prospected deposits of salt cover the need in raw materials for the operation of a large chlorine-producing combine; and when the prospected deposits of high-quality limestone are put into operation - of soda ash. A number of lake deposits fully meet the requirements of Turkmenistan in table salt.

The available resources of building materials are sufficient for establishing enterprises of the building industry to satisfy the needs of industrial and civil construction. The Republic has its own building stone, materials for the manufacture of cement and light fillers - keramsite.

Survey and prospecting activities on a vast scale resulted in finding one of the largest deposits of sweet water - the Yaskhan deposit which supplies water to industrial towns and communities of Western Turkmenistan and the Kopet-Dag sub-montane plain.

Deposits of thermal mineral waters which are used by the Archman resort place have been prospected in Kopet-Dag.

Survey and exploitation of mineral resources in desert conditions is associated with certain difficulties. The lack of drinking and even of technical water calls for additional investment in the transportation of considerable volumes of water, in sand-fixing operations to protect industrial objects. In places of arduous labour conditions increased pay-rates are applied.

Large-scale application of seismic prospecting with demolition operations which sometimes damages desert landscapes and the cultural land in oases is quite widely used in oil and gas prospecting. To reduce the harmful influence upon the environment local scientists are developing techniques of non-demolition sources of seismic influences.

When prospecting, conducting a survey or sinking commercial drill holes in the construction of gas mains, shrubs and the herbacious cover is destroyed. As a result there are patches and strips of bare sand. A number of measures are taken to reduce or to do away with the harmful after-effects of earth-digging machinery.

The development of mineral deposits not infrequently requires expenditure of water which is then discharged into depressions of the topography. This results in waterlogging the area and salinizing the soil. This may be eliminated by rationalizing water consumption.

The mining industry of the Turkmenian SSR provides 23% of the gross industrial output of the USSR. The few towns of the Turkmen SSR situated in the desert (Krasnovodsk, Nebit-Dag, Kazandjik, Kizyl-Arvat) have well-developed industry which accounts for 35.7% of the fixed industrial assets of the Republic.

Industrial construction in the desert in recent years has been mainly associated with gas extraction. The large Achaksk-Naipsk gas mining district of nation-wide importance has emerged in the Zaunguz Kara-Kum. The largest gas field in southern Kara-Kum is the Shuttlyk deposit.

### TRANSPORT

In connection with the vastness and remoteness of the Turkmenistan's territory from the capital of the Soviet Union and from large towns and resort centres, different modes of transport are developed in this Republic. The local transport is represented by a complex network comprising 2150 km of railways, 8700 km of highways, 1300 km of navigable river ways, a number of marine ports on the Caspian sea coast and 33,000 km of airlines. Turkmenistan is characterized by the predominance of land surface modes of transport.

Characteristic of Turkmenistan's desert districts is the large-scale use of the pipeline method of transportation with a total length of 2000 km which is associated with the development of the gas and oil industry. The pipeline method is represented by the trunk gas mains like Middle Asia - Centre with branches leading across the Kara-Kum desert.

All oil wells of Western Turkmenistan are linked by oil mains which go to the Krasnovodsk refinery and to Cheleken for further sea transport dispatching.

Changes in transport have been particularly great in the desert.

The caravan trails which used to cross the Kara-Kum desert have by now turned into motor roads. Practically all communities in the desert have regular motor or aircraft services. The importance of motor roads which link the oil wells of western Turkmenistan with an outlet on the Caspian Sea is particularly important. As a result of this, the distances which, given the caravan mode of transport were covered in many weeks only, are now covered in several hours. This is of great importance for the development of desert districts, for organizing improved pastures, for afforestation on sands and for sand-fixing measures.

The new waterway across the south-eastern Kara-Kum (450 km) became the V.I. Lenin Kara-Kum Canal which is used for motor boat navigation up to the Khauskhan Reservoir.

The development of transport is the achievement of the Soviet period.

### ENERGETICS

The fuel and power resources of deserts comprise a tremendous and valuable economic potential, which was absolutely latent in the period before Soviet government. Making use of these resources in Turkmenistan is the Krasnovodsk thermal electric power station, the Nebitdag state district electric power station and high-voltage electric transmission lines were built and put into operation as far back as the 1950s.

Thanks to the availability of the tremendous gas deposits in the desert, the construction of the largest state district electric power station in the Soviet Middle Asia (the Maryisk station), with the capacity of the first section being 1,260,000 kW, began in 1959. The first three power units of this electric station have been put into operation.

Another important branch of the power economy is the desalinization of sea water for the needs of desert districts. Commercial desalinization of sea water first began at the Krasnovodsk thermal electric power station in 1946 and was further developed at large desalting plants in Shevchenko and Krasnovodsk.

Alongside the build-up of the power capacities of the existing electric stations, considerable attention is given to the construction of electric transmission lines to unite all electric stations in the oases or in the inland parts of the desert. An inter-republican electric transmission line which went into operation in 1966 has been built across the Kyzyl-Kumy and Kara-Kumy. At present, the pooling of the power grids of Turkmenistan with the single Soviet Middle Asian system has been completed.

The developed network of electric transmission lines across the desert territories (more than 23,000 km) makes possible large-scale application of electric energy, not only for industrial but for domestic needs in remote parts and deserts of Turkmenistan.

## THE V.I. LENIN KARA-KUM CANAL AND ITS PART IN DESERTIFICATION CONTROL

Turkmenistan is the part of Soviet Middle Asia least supplied with water. Its own water resources are negligible and amount to not more than 1.3 $km^3$ and, taking into account the stocks of subterranean waters and the discharge of rivers of the adjacent countries (Afghanistan and Iran) which comes to Turkmenistan, it is 4.3 $km^3$. Even 100% application of this water stock could not resolve desertification control and the needs of developing at least a small part of the deserts in the Republic. At the same time the biggest river of Soviet Middle Asia - the Amu Darya River with a discharge exceeding 62.4 km - flows along the north-eastern boundary of Turkmenistan. A great part of that water used to flow into the Aral Sea and become lost, eventually, in evaporation. For years the people of Turkmenistan dreamed of making use of that water for the development of a part of the deserts for irrigated agriculture and to control desertification. However, this called for shifting tens of cubic kilometres of water to populated desert places remote from Amu Darya where the available land was particularly suitable for development.

The implementation of this magnificent task, despite a number of suggestions made in the early twentieth century, became tangible only following the Great October Socialist Revolution and by the establishment of the Turkmen Soviet Socialist Republic. For the first time anywhere in the world, on a scope of such proportion, the shifting of tremendous volumes of water was carried out across the desert. This has made it possible not only to stop the desertification of the territory but to transform hundreds of thousands of hectares of previously barren desert into blossoming oases.

By the scope of operations, the length, the difficulties of construction and the speed of building - the Kara-Kum Canal has no equal in the world. For instance, it took 11 years to build the Suez Canal which is 166 km long. It took 34 years to build the 82-km-long Panama Canal and only 4 years to build the first section of the Kara-Kum Canal from the Amu-Darya River to the Murgab River, a span of 400 km which cuts across the most forbidding part of the sandy desert.

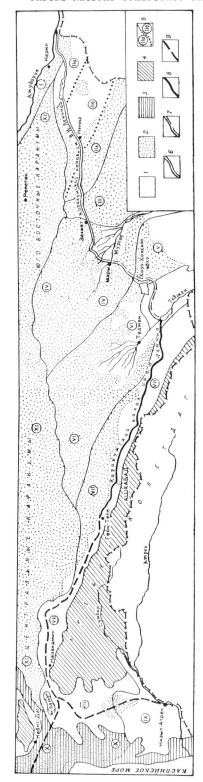

Fig. 7.  Scheme of the V.I. Lenin Kara-Kumy Canal.  1 – Loamy plains; 2 – eoline sandy plains; 3 – moraine sandy plains; 4 – mountain territories; 5 – boundaries of lithological-geographical distracts: I – Amu Darya valley; IIa – solonchak Balkh delta; IIb – sandy-clay Obruchev steppe; IIc – sandy Balkh delta with ridgy eoline topography; III – sandy ridges of Karabil hilly area; IV – loamy Murgab delta; V – Babkhyz elevation; VI – Tedjen delta; VII – proluvial submontane plain of Kopet-Dag; VIII – submontane plain of Western Kopet-Dag; IX – Atrek delta; X – moraine plains; XI – Kara-Kum sand.  Canal construction sections: 6 – first; 7 – second; 8 – third; 9 – fourth and last (project).

The construction of the Kara-Kum Canal is a model not only of active control of desertification but of an integrated settlement of a number of most pressing problems of social and economic character which are peculiar to the arid zone. The shifting of the Amu Darya River water into the desert has resolved the following questions on a vast area of the Kara-Kum Canal zone which surpasses 256,000 km$^2$ and has a population close to 74% of the Republic:

1. Water was supplied to meet the needs of the developing industry and the population in towns and communities.

2. Considerable tracts of virgin desert land became well developed and stable irrigation was ensured on 506,000 hectares where fine fibre cotton is grown together with kenaf, grapes, fruit, vegetables and other valuable farm crops.

3. A vast territory of the Kara-Kum desert pastures was watered.

4. Living conditions were improved, incomes were increased and vast recreation zones were established.

5. A water transport way was established which passes across roadless desert districts.

Fifty-five state farms were set up in the Kara-Kum Canal zone. These include 9 cotton-growing, 21 sheepbreeding, 6 poultry farms, 9 fruit- and grape-growing, 1 for melon crops, 1 beef and dairy, 1 swine-breeding and 1 camel-breeding. In 1975 these farms produced the following volumes of farm products: raw cotton - 455,600 tons; melon crops - 60,200 tons; fruit and grapes - 59,400 tons and wool - 4400 tons; karakul pelts - 593,000; eggs - 783 million; meat (live weight) - 33,100 tons and milk - 55,300 tons. The gross income of only collective farms comprised 339 million roubles, the net income - 128 million roubles.

The construction of the Kara-Kum Canal - the largest irrigation-melioration hydrotechnical project in the deserts of the world - put into existence an artificial river, its length exceeding 900 km, its water discharge in the upper part reaching 400 m$^3$/sec. The annual intake in 1975 exceeded 9 km$^3$. The canal's regimen is completely controlled and adapted to serve the needs of economy. Accordingly, the canal is equipped with a number of large hydrotechnical structures, the discharge of the canal in winter is accumulated in reservoirs, their total capacity exceeding 1 km$^3$.

The specific features of the Amu-Darya regimen, the fact that the canal runs over districts with differing topography (fixed and shifting sands, alluvial and submontane plains), the absence of experience in the construction of such canals in desert conditions and the priority sequence of land development predetermined the arrangement of survey, planning and the construction of the canal in three stages.

The length of the first section (Amu-Darya-Murgab) was 400 km, of which 300 km passes over sandy desert, the annual discharge being 3.5 km$^3$. The construction was completed from 1954 to 1959. The "Pioneer canal" method was used in which the water follows the builders as they progress, ensuring water supply and transport links. It also accelerated the wetting of the canal and stabilized subsequent seepage losses. The "Pioneer canal" was built, in the main, using bulldozers and excavators and its widening was carried out by suction dredges.

Construction of the second span was started in 1960; by November of the same year Amy Darya water reached the Tedjen oasis. The canal became 535 km long, of which 138 km were new and 69 km passed across sandy desert. The canal discharge reached 4.7 km$^3$. Regulation of the canal discharge was started on this stage of

construction.  To do this the Khauskhan reservoir was constructed.  Its initial
capacity reaching 460 million m$^3$.

Then the construction of the third span was started and in 1962 water flowing along
the "Pioneer canal" reached Ashkhabad.  Subsequently, the "Pioneer canal" was made
wider, the capacity of the Khauskhan reservoir increased to 875 million m$^3$, the
Kurtlinskoye reservoir was built to hold 48 million m$^3$ and the Kopet-Dag reservoir
- the last on this stretch - with a capacity of 190 million m$^3$.  The canal's
discharge increased to 8.3 km$^3$.

Further development of the Kara-Kumy Canal is planned.  It will reach western
industrial districts and a new cotton-growing area with an irrigated territory
exceeding 100,000 hectares will be established in the south-western zone. The total
length of the canal will exceed 1500 km; it will irrigate 1 million hectares.  The
upper section will have a reservoir for partial seasonal regulation of the
discharge.  Its capacity will be 3.5 km$^3$.  This is where a considerable part of
the silt from Amu-Darya will be held up.  It is intended to build two more
reservoirs at the canal's ending sections - in the western and south-western
branches - their total capacity exceeding 1 km$^3$.  The water intake of the Kara-Kum
Canal is expected to comprise 17.1 km$^3$; the total storage capacity for the
regulation of the discharge being more than 2.4 km$^3$.

Besides settling its fundamental objectives the Kara-Kum Canal proved to be a
natural laboratory of a kind where the validity of estimates and plan decisions
are tested on a huge scale.  The stage-by-stage construction made it possible to
introduce the necessary adjustments, specifically concerning seepage losses, the
determination of the canal's bed stable dimensions in the easily washed-out rock,
the water losses control at oases, the construction of different types of drainage
systems and an array of other questions.

The experience of canal planning and construction is extremely valuable since it
can be widely applied for desertification control in other regions of the arid
zone by shifting large volumes of water discharge.

The Kara-Kum Canal is a striking instance of desertification control in a socialist
state.  On the whole it positively influenced the ecological situation.  Natural
complexes with lavish vegetation unusual for the territory were developed along
the canal.  The biological productivity increased considerably, new types of
forage appeared, changes took place in the fauna, microclimate and in the soil
cover.  The planting of trees, shrubs and flowers in towns and other communities
increased dozens of times in a considerable part of the canal zone; humidity
increase ranged 1.5-2-fold, the air-dust content decreased, the conditions of life
of the population improved, recreation areas with sport complexes which are unusual
for the desert were established; a number of comfortable communities with all
amenities were built in the canal zone.

However, the ecological situation in this territory is highly liable to change: it
demands and shall continue to demand regular adjustment.  For instance, in some
places of the Kara-Kum Canal zone intra-oasis areas of ground water exhaustion and
salt outcrops occur.  These phenomena are not of a widespread character and are
localized during the development of the territory.  They are easily controlled by
reconstructing the irrigation and drainage systems, by combining discharge and
drainage waters in storage reservoirs for further economic application, for
watering of pastures, and in remote prospective - for the development of spawning
grounds in the Caspian Sea basin.

The control of the overgrowing of the Kara-Kum Canal which took place following
the construction of the first section is an instance of successful liquidation of
unfavourable ecological factors which set in when the discharge was shifted to the

desert. By deepening the canal and breeding plant-eating fishes (*Ctenopharungodon idella, Hypophtalmichthus molitrix*) it became possible not only to arrest the overgrowing of the canal but to considerably increase the biological productivity both of the canal and of reservoirs.

The construction of the Kara-Kum Canal resulted in a gradual formation in the desert territory of anthropogenous landscapes with industrial-agrarian complexes and a developed net of communications.

The experience of the Kara-Kum Canal construction and its operation shows the possibility not only for effective control of desertification but of influencing the scope and rate of environmental changes.

## AGRICULTURE OF THE IRRIGATED ZONE

Agriculture plays a considerable role in the economy of the Turkmenian Soviet Socialist Republic. It accounts for practically 33% of the Republic's national income. On a nation-wide scale Turkmenistan produces 14% of raw cotton, 8% of silk-worm cocoons and more than 20% of karakul pelts.

Gross farming produce in Turkmenistan in the years of Soviet government went up almost 7-fold compared to what it was in 1913 and comprises more than 800 million roubles. Irrigation water is the source of the bulk of output.

Total irrigated area of farm crops in Turkmenistan is close to 745,000 hectares. In the years of Soviet power and compared against the period prior to the revolution of 1917 the irrigated area has grown more than 3.5-fold.

Prior to the revolution the land was irrigated by means of a network of primitive canals. Self-flow irrigation prevailed in the Murgab and Kopet-Dag districts; primitive appliances locally known as "chigir" were used to supply water to the fields for the Amu Darya districts. Fields were irrigated by flooding.

During the Soviet period, not only was the Kara-Kum Canal built but the old irrigation network was reconstructed. The length of trunk canals now exceeds 500 km, the length of canals faced with concrete - 470 km, the storage-drainage network - 12,500 km. There are 65 head locks, 497 water wells with a total yield approximating 8000 litres per second.

To regulate the discharge twelve large storage reservoirs were built with a capacity exceeding 1600 million m$^3$. Hundreds of large-scale hydro-engineering structures, pumping stations and bridges formed an integrated irrigation network combining into a system the rivers of Amu-Darya, Murgab, Tedjen and eliminating water scarcity in the Murgab and Tedjen rivers.

The state of agriculture in the irrigated zone is directly related to investment into melioration and the construction of the storage and drainage network. The highest specific length of the storage-drainage network (exceeding 30.5 running metres per hectare of irrigated area while the average for the Turkmenian SSR is 18.4 running metres) is in the Tashauz oasis. By 1975 the total sown area reached 750,000 hectares including 410,000 hectares sown to cotton, the share of fine fibre cotton being 127,500 hectares.

Table 1.  Phytomass (Surface + Underground) and Forage Yield of Pastures with
Differing Plant Bioforms

Average values for many years (tons per hectare)

(After K. Antonova, S. Karshenas, N. Nechayeva and S. Prikhodko)

| Type of pasture | Surface | | | Under-ground | Total phyto-mass | Harvest changes by years |
|---|---|---|---|---|---|---|
| | Maximum annual harvest (shoots) | Peren-nial part | Total | | | |
| **1. Tall shrub, sandy desert** | | | | | | |
| Saxaul (*Halox-ylon persicum–Carex physodes*) | 0.47 | 3.28 | 3.75 | 4.32 | 8.07 | 0.3-0.8 |
| Kandym (*Calli-gonum rubens–Carex physodes*) | 0.51 | 2.09 | 2.60 | 4.31 | 7.41 | 0.3-0.9 |
| **2. Semi-shrub, clay desert** | | | | | | |
| Sagebrush–Salsola (*Sal-sola gemmascens + Artimisia kemrudica*) | 0.45 | 2.80 | 3.25 | 1.87 | 5.12 | 0.2-1.1 |
| **3. Grassy, loess foothill desert** | | | | | | |
| Blue grass–sedges (*Carex physodes + Poa bulbosa*) | 0.50 | - | 0.50 | 2.47 | 2.97 | 0.13-1.23 |

The main watering source in the desert is underground waters, primarily those
which are strongly or moderately mineralized at a depth of 20-30 m.  Underground
water in the south-eastern parts lies at 150-300 m, their mineralization is slight
- within 2-5 g/l.  The surface run-off from takyrs which is collected in storage
reservoirs plays a considerable part in watering the pastures.  The regular
discharge of rivers is also used to water pastures but in a small measure.

The quality of water determines the season of pasture utilization: areas with fresh
or slightly salinized water wells are used on any season; those with salinized
water wells - in winter only; pastures with reservoirs for collecting the rainfall
run-off are used in spring and early summer.

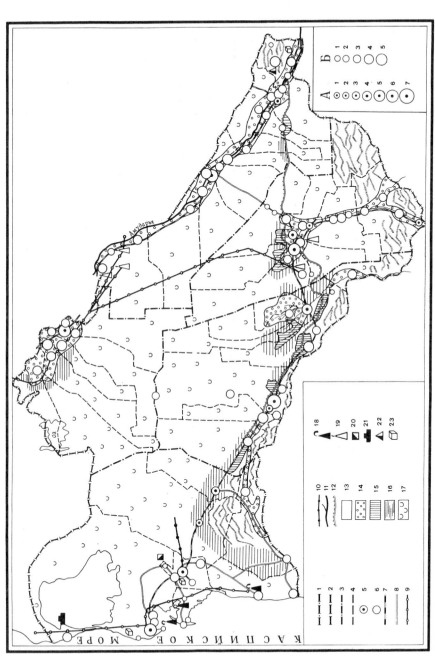

Fig. 8.   Schematic map of desert development in the Turkmenian SSR. Boundaries: 1 – state; 2 – Union Republics; 3 – regional; 4 – administratives districts. Populated points: 5 – towns; 6 – urban type communities (UTC); 7 – railroads; 8 – highways; 9 – gas-mains; 10 – water-mains; 11 – rivers; 12 – canals and storage reservoirs; 13 – lakes. Lands: 14 – old-irrigated; 15 – newly irrigated; 16 – planned for irrigation; 17 – pastures. Mining: 18 – oil and combustible gas; 19 – combustible gas; 20 – bentonite; 21 – Glauber's salt; 22 – sulphur; 23 – table salt. Number of residents (thousands people): A – Towns: 1 – 5–10; 2 – 11–15; 3 – 16–25; 4 – 26–50; 5 – 51–100; 6 – 100–200; 7 – over 200. B – Urban-type settlements: 1 – less than 2; 2 – 2–3; 3 – 3–5; 4 – 5–10; 5 – over 10.

Agriculture of the irrigated zone is clearly cotton-production oriented. More than 75% of commodity production of collective and state farms is made up of raw cotton. Specialization, however, varies from district to district and depends upon water availability. Twenty-four of the thirty-four districts are cotton oriented, five sheep-breeding, two cotton and sheep-breeding, two are specializing in vegetable and grape-growing and sheep-breeding and one district is specializing in sheep- and cattle-breeding. The western districts of Turkmenistan (Kyzyl-Arvatsky, Kyzyl-Atreksky, Kazandjiksky and Gasan-Kuliisky) with the completion of the third and fourth sections of the V.I. Lenin Kara-Kum Canal will be cotton-growing areas.

Cotton production in Turkmenistan in recent years has grown 3-fold (from 384,000 tons in 1958 to 1.078 million tons in 1975), that of vegetables 6-fold and melon crops 3-fold. Increases have been registered in the output and procurement of milk, eggs and other livestock products. The most profitable branch is cotton-growing, its profitability rate reaching 34%. Farm produce yields on irrigated land, in some years, exceed the yields of plough-land for the country as a whole by 4.5-fold.

The forage base of livestock breeding is growing with the progress of irrigated farming. Large-horned cattle was poorly productive, had low live weight (250-270 kg) and low milk yields (300-400 kg per cow). By 1950 total herd of large-horned cattle was 265,300 and it reached 490,000 heads by 1975. Milk yields reached 1592 kg while in some of the foremost collective farms like the "Sovet Turkmenistany" Ashkhabad district, "Leninism" and "Kalinin" of the Kyzyl-Arvatsky district and some other farms - more than 3000 kg per cow.

Poultry as a branch of economy took its start only following the establishment of collective and state farms. By 1929 there were 510,000 poultry heads. At present there are commercial poultry establishments like the Ashkhabad and Nebit-Dag poultry factories, poultry-oriented collective and state farms.

Horse-breeding is centred on riding horses of the Akhaltekin breed which are in high demand on the home and international market. Dozens of pedigree and racing horses of this breed are sold annually at the Moscow international fair for export.

The maintenance of the productivity growth rate at the 1966-1975 level will make it possible to increase the gross farming output in the 1971-1990 period 2.1-fold and the average rate of labour productivity by 7-8%. Thanks to further improvements in specialization and concentration of production gross annual output will be more than trebled.

The increase in water resources poises the danger of a rise in the ground water table in the oases and in the adjacent desert zone, an increase in soil salting and waterlogging which should be viewed as desertification. This requires a closer link of theory and practice, the transition of agriculture to a modern industrial foundation, sparing and effective utilization of the resources of land and water and of machinery.

### PASTURE LIVESTOCK BREEDING

*Pasture Description*

The desert pastures of Turkmenistan divide into three main types subject to the bioforms of plants which comprise them.

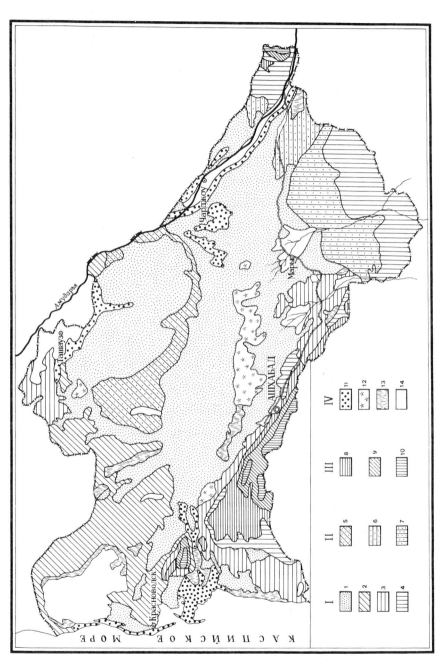

Fig. 9.   The main classes of pastures in the Turkmenian SSR.   I – Pastures of lowland: 1 – sandy desert;
2 – gypsum desert; 3 – clay desert; 4 – loess desert.   II – Desert pasture on the combinations:
5 – sandy and gypsum; 6 – sandy and clay; 7 – sandy and loess.   III – Mountain pastures: 8 – lower
mountain belt (foothills, 400–800 m above sea level); 9 – middle belt of mountains (800–1200 m above
sea level); 10 – upper mountain belt (1200–2800 m above sea level).   IV – Unfit land: 11 – barkhan
land; 12 – takyrs; 13 – solonchaks; 14 – oases.

1.  Tall shrub pastures which include tall and medium shrubs, semi-shrubs and
    grasses, primarily sandy sedge grass and annual plants.  They are applicable
    on any season of the year and are viewed as round-the-year pastures for
    small-horned cattle and camels.  They are widespread in sandy deserts with
    ridge-hilly topography.

2.  Semi-shrub pastures including semi-shrubs, a small number of perennial
    grasses, sedge grasses primarily and annual plants.  Pastures where sedges
    predominate are regarded as "satisfactory" for the spring and summer season
    and as "good" for autumn and winter; they are applicable for small-horned
    cattle and camels.  Areas where the Salsola plants prevail are used in the
    autumn-winter period only; they are "good" for camels and in a smaller
    degree for sheep.  They are confined to clay plains and low gradient
    elevations.

3.  Pastures of herbage communities consist of perennial and annual grasses.
    Submontane pastures consist of blue-grass, sedge brush and forbs and are
    "excellent" in spring and summer for sheep, and "poor" in autumn and winter.
    They are unfit for camels.  Grass-covered pastures on takyr-like clay plains
    are "good" pastures for sheep and camels in autumn and winter.

The harvest of pasture forage and its stability in years is determined greatly by
the total biological output of the phyto-mass (surface and underground).  The
greater the number of perennial parts and roots the higher and more stable is the
forage yield (Table 1).

The main part of the pasture ration are grasses (87% in spring, 75% in summer, 67%
in autumn and 52% in winter, by weight), shrubs are also important, in winter
specifically since they are not covered by snow.  The presence of shrubs when
livestock is kept on pastures round the year is most desirable since they are a
source of fuel for shepherds.

Yield of forage on pastures varies considerably by seasons: in spring and summer
it is 0.3-0.5 ton/hectare, by winter it drops to one-fourth of that while the
nutritive value of forage drops to one-fifth of what it was.  In fact when
seasonal grazing is practiced, not all available forage is utilized (gross stock),
but only the consumable stock (Table 2).

Forest harvest is subject to considerable changes in different years owing to the
influence of meteorological factors (Fig. 1).  In the past 15 years good harvests
in Kara-Kum totalled 46%, medium in 28% and poor in 26%.  In the past 17 years
high harvests in the foothills were observed in 36%, medium in 24% and poor in 40%
of all harvests.

Sharp changes in the yields and in the nutritive content of pasture forage by
seasons and years influence the availability of forage for sheep so that the
animals have to be given additional coarse or concentrated feeds, specifically so
in years of failure of harvest.

*Availability of Water at Pastures*

Effective utilization of desert pastures for livestock is related to the
establishment of structures for cattle watering.  The Turkmenian SSR is classed
with the districts which are poorly supplied with fresh ground water.
Notwithstanding the considerable effort for the construction of water sources in
recent years, the territory of pastures which are not supplied with water is still
considerable.

Table 2. Seasonal Forage Stock (Gross and Consumable)
on Different Pasture Types

Average values for many years, tons per hectare

| Type of pasture | Maxi- mum annual harvest | Spring | | Summer | | Autumn | | Winter | |
|---|---|---|---|---|---|---|---|---|---|
| | | gross | con- sumed | gross | con- sumed | gross | con- sumed | gross | con- sumed |
| Tall shrub, sandy desert | 0.47 | 0.33 | 0.26 | 0.30 | 0.14 | 0.22 | 0.16 | 0.15 | 0.08 |
| Semi-shrub, clay desert | 0.45 | 0.20 | 0.02 | 0.43 | 0.03 | 0.40 | 0.22 | 0.28 | 0.17 |
| Grassy, foot- hill loess desert | 0.45 | 0.45 | 0.40 | 0.40 | 0.31 | 0.30 | 0.15 | 0.20 | 0.11 |

At present 5200 water wells, 54 drill holes, 336 springs and more than 600 surface structures for the collection of rainfall are used as water sources. Watering of pastures is being improved lately by building group trunk water mains to those areas specifically which lack underground waters or where those waters are strongly mineralized. The watered area of pastures is about two-thirds of total territory. The watering of the remaining area will be carried out by building new water mains, making denser the existing network and by repairing the water wells which went out of commission; it will also be conducted by building demineralization plants. It is planned to water 5 million hectares of pastures in the tenth 5-year period.

*Use of Pastures Before the Revolution*

In the pre-revolutionary period pastures were utilized by the nomadic technique. The local population bred karakul and fat-tail sheep, a local coarse-wool breed of goats and dromedaries. Karakul sheep grazed on sandy pastures in south-eastern parts while the local fat-tail sheep and coarse-wool goats prevailed in Turkmenistan's western part. The population engaged in camel-breeding in Central Kara-Kum and in Turkenistan's north-west.

Private cattle-breeding farms of those days conducted a nomadic mode of life with seasonal migrations. The cattle were maintained throughout the year on grazing fodder only and this resulted in wholesale felling of livestock due to lack of fodder in severe winters and in years of crop failures.

At the time there was no strict distribution of pastures among farms and planned management of pastures was therefore impossible. The object of property were not pastures but water wells and rainfall storage reservoirs, the construction of which could be afforded only by a few rich cattle breeders. Even they, however, employed self-made masters and sunk wells using a primitive method in which the shaft was reinforced by timber from local shrubs. In the main, they used the pastures where ground water came close to the surface. The poor availability of water at pastures prevented their full utilization for cattle grazing and was the main development obstacle and at the same time the cause of desertification. There were three farming districts in Turkmenistan before the revolution of 1917.

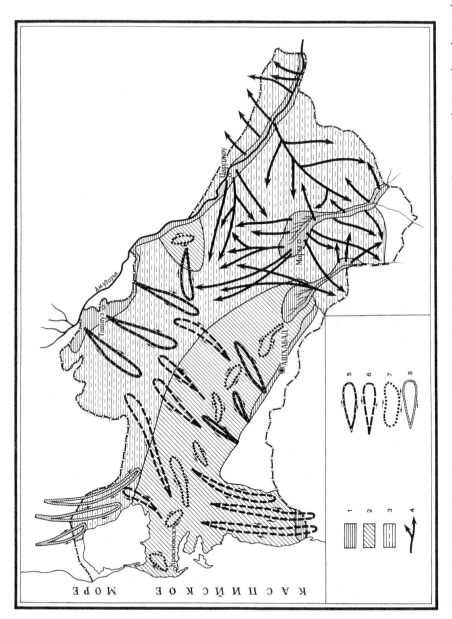

Fig. 10.  Chart of utilization of pastures of Turkmenistan in the pre-revolutionary period.  Districts with permanent population: 1 - farming; 2 - livestock breeding; 3 - unpopulated pasture territories for cattle grazing by driving cattle from farming districts and partially from cattle-breeding districts. Places of grazing for small-horned cattle: 4 - round the year; 5 - for the autumn, winter and spring season; 6 - for the autumn-winter season; 7 - seasonal movement of cattle to pastures around water wells; 8 - movement of cattle from Kazakhstan.

1.  The district of land cultivation (4% of the area) with a permanent population.

2.  The district of livestock breeding (30% of the area) with permanent small-size communities close to the water wells.

3.  The unpopulated pasture territory (66% of the area), only partially used for grazing of cattle which were driven there from the first two districts.

*Pastures Used at Present*

At present the principles and the character of pasture management have been changed. Small nomadic privately owned farms have been amalgamated into large collective and state-farming enterprises.  Following a large-scale geobotanical survey of pastures they were distributed among collective and state farms.

At present, there are twenty-two sheep-breeding, two camel-breeding state farms and 316 sheep-breeding collective farms in the Turkmenian SSR.  The average size of those enterprises in terms of pasture area ranges in different natural districts from 27,000 hectares to 670,000 hectares, while the total area of pastures distributed and fixed among farming enterprises exceeds 30 million hectares.

The establishment of large-scale sheep-breeding and camel-breeding farms made possible planned utilization of pastures on a fixed territory.  This improved the state of watering and care of grazing grounds, ensured more rational pasture use and the construction of cattle sheds and living premises which also prevented the impoverishment of pastures and mitigated the development of desertification.

On the whole, all this facilitated sheep-breeding – the total number of sheep in the Soviet period increased 2.5-fold in Turkmenistan.

A system of rational utilization of pastures has been worked out and put into practice for sheep-breeding farms.  The system is founded on a number of planned organizational and economic measures which preclude the harmful influence of excessive grazing upon pasture vegetation and soil.  This system is conducted on the basis of intrafarm management with long-term programmes of pasture utilization which provide for pasture rotation, the development of a fodder balance for every season of the year and identification of the protein deficit as well as sources of replenishing it, a programme of seasonal siting of cattle by pastures, progressive techniques of grazing and improvement of grazing grounds.

Many measures of pasture management are conducted at state expense.  Specialized building organizations are carrying out a large programme of watering operations. Water mains with a large network of branches and an even coverage of pasture territory are being laid on the remaining unwatered pastures.

Commercial and welfare construction is conducted on a large scope on desert pastures.  In keeping with the programme of integrated pasture development the following main measures have been worked out and are being put into practice: full and even watering of the entire pasture territory and the reconstruction of the existing watering network; further consolidation of the forage base for sheep-breeding by establishing specialized fodder farms on irrigated lands and by improving the existing pastures; amalgamation of sheep-breeding farms to increase specialization and concentration of production; construction of new culture centres at base water wells; radical improvement of the power-generating industry, fire-control measures at grassy pastures in the foothills.

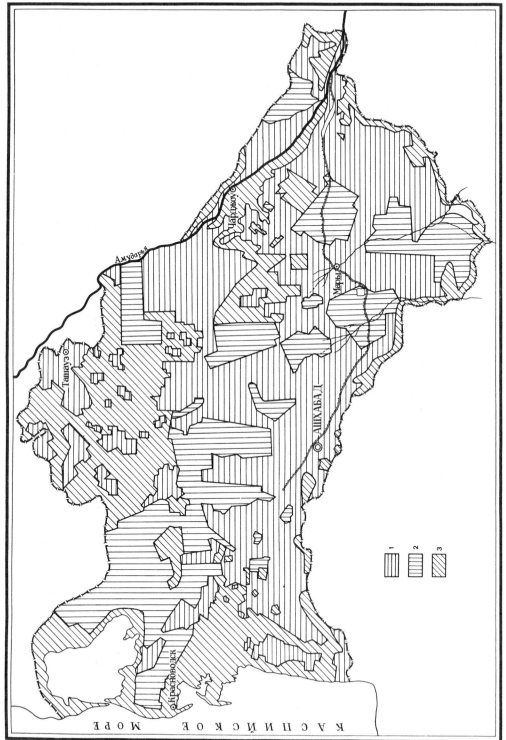

Fig. 11.   Scheme of modern distribution of pastures in the Turkmenian SSR among collective and state farms.
Territory: 1 – collective farms; 2 – state farms; 3 – state land farms.

*Cattle Protection Measures*

A sharp drop in the nutritive value of pasture forage in autumn and specifically
in winter used to lead to quick exhaustion of animals since they had only the
grazing fodder. With the idea of protecting livestock and to maintain its
weight, concentrated feeds are added to winter rations. On years of crop failures
additional subfeeding is conducted with volume feeds.

Accordingly, all sheep-breeding enterprises prepare such feeds directly at
pastures or deliver them from oases. Concentrated feeds (cotton-cake, oil-seed
meal, mixed feeds, barley) are either procured by the farms or produced by them.
On the average, subfeeding in the Turkmenian SSR comprises approximately ninety
fodder units per sheep or 20% of the annual feed requirement.


*Pasture-protection Measures*

Subject to its intensity, grazing can affect the pastures positively or negatively.
It is necessary to distinguish the consequences of grazing from those of cutting
shrubs and semi-shrubs. The impoverishment of the species composition and the
number of shrubs on pastures close to water wells and oases - an indication of
the beginning of desertification - is mainly a result of cutting and to a smaller
extent of grazing. Grazing, in the main, has a negative influence on grasses.

Subject to the season of utilization the grass harvest at shrub pastures ranges
from 0.15 to 0.34 tons/ha. These changes practically coincide with those of the
pasture yield under the influence of meteorological conditions.

The knowledge of seasonal changes in the grassy cover makes possible the pasture
rotation planning, i.e. the alternation of seasons of the utlization of
pastures by years with a moderate grazing load. More favourable are the following
patterns: alternation of grazing consistently in all seasons; alternation of
spring or summer grazing with the autumn or winter grazing seasons. The change
of the season may be annual, bi-annual, every 3 or 4 years. The grazing season
is changed more frequently on sandy pastures and the change is not so frequent
on grazing grounds with more compact soil. The application of pasture rotation
precludes the necessity of resting and ensures good state of pastures.

Given a high load of grazing with an annual withdrawal of more than 70% of the
harvest, pastures degrade in 6-10 years. Resting helps reinstate vegetation on
sandy pastures with low hilly topography and on semi-shrub pastures of clay and
gypsum deserts in 6 years while it takes 15 to 20 years to reinstate vegetation
on pastures with high-ridgy sands.

Also expedient is the application of moderate grazing when 65% of forage fit for
consumption is utilized. In this case subject to the season from 73 to 88% of
grasses and from 9 to 22% of shrubs are used. The estimate of a pasture load
should take into consideration mainly the state and harvest of grasses. It takes
3.5-6 ha of pastures annually to ensure a moderate load per sheep. This estimate
is taken as the basis of calculation when pastures are earmarked for sheep-breeding
collective or state farms.


*The System of Pasture Grazing*

The system is based on earmarking territories proportionally to the number of heads
of cattle in keeping with an estimate ensuring the normal load and uniform grazing.
At present, wherever suitable sources of water are available and the network of
watering places is adequate, the distance of grazing grounds from the water cell is

5-7 km. The pasture territory is divided into grazing sections confined to
individual water wells and the size of the sections is determined by the distance
of the place of grazing from the water well. The pattern of utilization of
pastures conforms to the sections which are used by seasons with pasture rotation.
Small-scale rotational grazing is the basis of utilization of a water-well grazing
section. The grazing strip is set aside for a single period of time between two
waterings, i.e. 1-3 days - a technique that was worked out through the centuries
by Turkmen cattle breeders.

*Pasture Improvement*

Areas with substandard yields (20 to 50% below norm) cover approximately 20% of the
desert territory.

Barkhan sands which are practically devoid of vegetation comprise close to 5%
(1.5 million ha). Large areas approximating 3 million ha in the foothills are
covered by secondary types of herbage communities either without shrubs or semi-
shrubs or when the latter are confined to very limited areas.

All these pastures are distinguished by low yields. However, vegetation is not
taking full advantage of the natural resources. Those lands are fit for the
growing of communities which are much more varied by composition of bioforms and
species which can form pastures with high yields of forage suitable at all seasons.

One of the achievements of Soviet science is the improvement of desert pastures
without irrigation. There is large-scale experimentation into pasture improvement
based on the knowledge of desert ecology and vegetation. Accordingly, methods
have been developed for a radical reorganization of the vegetation cover and for
improving its harvest yield.

Cardinal improvement of pastures is either through soil cultivation or by adding
valuable forage plants to the poor grass stand available on sands. In both cases
new biogenocenoses (phytocenoses) are created by introducing bioforms of plants
of high medium-forming capacity. Surface and underground parts in communities of
shrubs, semi-shrubs and grasses are situated at different levels which ensures 3
to 6 times fuller utilization of pasture forage than on areas which have not been
improved.

Local shrubs, semi-shrubs and perennial grasses in culture develop quickly, yield
lavish fruit and much more production of pasture forage ensuring thereby adequate
round-the-year feeding of sheep and are fit for utilization on the second and
third year. They continue to be operative for not less than 12-30 years. The
investments for pasture cultivation are compensated within 2-4 years.

Pasture-improvement techniques vary in different natural districts. In foothill
deserts where rainfall ranges from 160 to 280 mm the autumn-winter shrubs and
semi-shrubs are planted in keeping with the strip (row) ploughing system. The
width of rows is 10-15 m, the intervals 10-50 m. Pastures on barkhan sands close
to water wells are improved by sowing a mixture of shrubs and semi-shrubs. In
this way good pastures are created in proximity of watering bases and the
improvement of approximately 20% of pasture territory of every farm in the foothill
zone will meet the demands of autumn-winter grazing. Special techniques of
restoring vegetation on close to the water well sands by additional sowing of
shrubs have been recommended for the Kara-Kum desert where rainfall ranges from
120 to 140 mm. Methods of pasture improvement of low-ridge sands of row ploughing
and on takyr-like plains by planting shrubs and semi-shrubs, building moisture
accumulating bands have been worked out. The improved pastures are fit for any
season but are most valuable in winter.

Pasture improvement in the arid zone is a potential to increase the herd and productivity of livestock.

## Economics of Pasture Livestock Breeding

Livestock breeding accounts for 27.2% of gross farming produce of Turkmenistan. The importance of different branches of livestock breeding in the economy are not the same: sheep-breeding in the desert yields large incomes, cattle-breeding and the breeding of other types of livestock is thus far profitless in oases. The explanation is that keeping sheep in the desert throughout the year on pasture fodder is uncostly while the returns from kara-kul pelts and wool are high. For instance, production cost of wool in the Turkmenian SSR is one-quarter or half of that in other republics of the Soviet Union.

The total herd of small-horned cattle in Turkmenistan is 4,465,000 heads including 4,256,000 sheep among which 70% are of the karakul breed (1974). The annual output of karakul sheep-breeding exceeds 1 million pelts and 15,000 tons of wool.

In the past years of the Turkmenian SSR noticeable changes for the better have taken place in pasture livestock breeding. Nomadic mode of economy with its remote seasonal pastures has been replaced by using vacant grazing grounds on the territory which is permanently fixed in the use of a definite farm. This enables farm management to arrange a rational system of grazing with standardized load and pasture location and is binding for every farm to take care of the cattle sheds, watering places and grazing grounds, and to regularly improve pastures preventing their desertification.

In view of the sharp changes in pasture harvest yields from season to season and year to year, emergency stocks of fodder are established on pastures and sheep are given additional feeds so as to ensure a high standard of karakul and be economically advantageous. This has minimized the slaying of animals owing to lack of fodder and ensured the possibility of keeping such a herd of sheep which corresponds to the capacity of developed pastures.

The reserve of further growth of sheep and camel herd and of increasing the yield of livestock products from desert pastures is their complete watering, increase in camel herd in Turkmenistan's western part where there are semi-shrub and Salsola grazing grounds, wider application of combined use of pastures by sheep and camels, pasture improvement with a considerable increase in yields, additional feeding of sheep in winter, the establishment of emergency forage stocks for years of crop failures and further improvement of the pasture management system.

The transition to a regular planned utilization of pastures without driving cattle over long distances has made it possible to improve considerably the living conditions and welfare services for the population engaged in desert livestock breeding.

### HUNTING ECONOMY

Hunting economy in the Turkmenian SSR is based on controlled shooting of definite species of wild game—foxes, the jackal, wild cat and wolf which yield valuable furs. The main commercial object is the fox which provides 93% of the total fur yield. Annual procurement approximates 26,000 fox pelts, nearly 4000 pelts of jackals and approximately 2000 pelts of the wild cat.

Wild ungulates, as a rule, inhabit the same forage areas as the domestic cattle—sheep and camels. Given sufficient number the antelopes are of importance for the development of remote and less watered pastures and yield meat of high quality. Saiga, a small-size antelope, reached such numbers that it is used for commercial meat procurement in Kazakhstan, a Soviet Republic which is adjacent on the Turkmenian SSR.

Rodents (gerbils and ground squirrels) on years of mass breeding rival sheep on pastures. Rodents may be a cause of a number of diseases and are therefore controlled in proximity of human communities.

## FOREST MANAGEMENT, AFFORESTATION AND FIXING OF SHIFTING SANDS

The afforestation and shifting-sand fixing in Turkmenistan prior to the revolution of 1917 was conducted on a very limited scope and only along the Middle Asian Railway. Control of sand drifts in oases was sporadic, based on the initiative of individual peasants and even then conducted on small areas without adequate effect.

The agro-forest melioration works in Turkmenian deserts are three directional:

(a) restoration of *Haloxylon* desert woodlands and of other desert shrubs destroyed by cuttings;

(b) afforestation, fixing and development of intraoases sands with the idea of preventing irrigated land against sand drifts;

(c) control of sand drifts on transport routes, on fringes of communities and industrial enterprises in the desert zone.

### *Forest Management and Agro-forest Melioration*

The tree-shrub vegetation in river deltas and in the sandy desert performs water-conserving, sand-protecting functions and is a source of fuel timber. The stock of timber fuel in *Haloxylon* thickets reaches 40 tons per hectare. For many years desert timber fuel was of great importance, even now it is important in a number of districts.

Rational application of the tree-shrub vegetation in arid regions is most pressing for pasture and woodland conservation, for preventing the formation of shifting sands. Trees and shrubs are widely used for the development of pasture protecting wind-breaks in animal husbandry, for the improvement of pastures and for restoration of forests.

In connection with this the development of effective techniques of exploitation of *Haloxylon* woodlands and of methods of their restoration is highly important.

Scientific principles forest management and prospects of afforestation in the arid zone are intensively studied in connection with the development of desert forest resources. Cutting regulations have been formulated for desert forests and practical recommendations for the nearest future have been issued. The restoration of vegetation on areas where desert forests were cut, subject to their exploitation, have been studied and some of the problems related to mechanization of forest cultivation in the sandy desert have been resolved.

Research continues into rationalization of forest management in *Haloxylon* forests and shrub thickets with the idea of increasing their productivity. In this connection study is made of the productivity of desert woodlands in different soil and climatic conditions of the arid zone, natural and man-made phytocoenoses with the highest productivity of timber, forage and seed are being identified.

Earmarking seed-producing sections to supply planting stock for the growing forest cultivation operations is acquiring particular importance.

## Development of Intraoases Sands

A medium-scale map of the close-to-oases sands of Turkmenistan has been compiled to work out rational methods of developing these sands; besides this, trends of commercial use and the priority list of their application has been determined.

Particular attention is given to agricultural development; promising species and sorts of forage crops and grapes are selected and methods of their cultivation are worked out with account for the hydro-physical and chemical features of eoline sands. Modern sprinkling machines and other latest equipment are being used.

It has been experimentally proved that the near-to-oases eoline sands can be developed for the cultivation of forage crops if sprinkling irrigation is used. The introduction of conventional rates of organic and mineral fertilizers on the irrigated grey-meadow soils and the irrigation rate of 5500-6500 $m^3$/ha on sands may yield from 500 to 1000 centners of green mass of corn and sorgo per hectare.

Concurrently, recommendations are compiled for planting greenery zones around towns and other communities as well as to surround cattle farms and industrial enterprises in different parts of deserts. Integrated research continues into maritime shell-sands on the Caspian and the Aral sea coasts to plant parks on those sands; the possibility of their development for farming, for melon-crop fields and fruit cultures is also being studied.

Research into salinized sands of western Turkmenistan has been completed and recommendations have been compiled for their fixing and afforesting. A detailed investigation of salt resistance of psammophyte shrubs made it possible to select a promising range of plants for the afforestation of salinized sands.

Highly productive machines are designed to mechanize labour-consuming operations in forest melioration in the conditions of sand-hill topography (preparation of protective stock, creation of sand dykes, application of liquid binders on protected surfaces, sowing and planting).

## Fixing and Afforesting Shifting Sands

Soviet agroforest meliorators have developed and are using different techniques of controlling sand drifts outside of oases.

Sand deflation creates considerable problems in developing new territories causing sand drifts and weathering of rock from under the foundations of engineering structures.

To work out scientific principles of deflation control the lowland territory of Turkmenistan has been regionalized in terms of wind erosion extent, a wind erosion map has been compiled with a breakdown for the duration of eoline working of the sand surface, the average intensity and direction of sand shift, thickness of the blown-out layer.

Wind erosion state of the territory of most important economic parts of the desert has been studied and the results have been used as the basis for phytomelioration and engineering methods of fixing shifting sands along the routes of gas-mains, electric transmission lines, motor roads, industrial and farming objects, and communities.

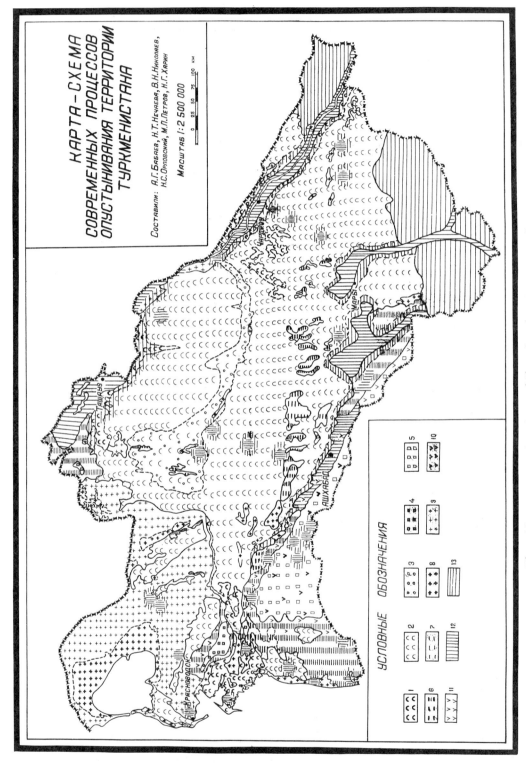

Fig. 12.   Present-day desertification in the Turkmenian SSR.

Fig. 12 note

I.  *Arid Zone. Aridity index $\frac{P}{ETP}$ within 0.06-0.20*

II. *Desertification Danger*

A.  Natural landscape vulnerability

Desertification (soil, topography, vegetation)

Degree of desertification vulnerability (climatic conditions)

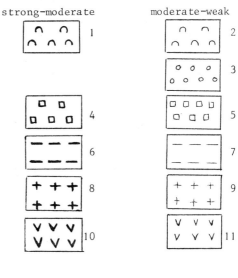

1.  Ridgy, ridgy-hilly, hilly sands, grown in different extent

2.  Accumulations of stones or desert shield caused by wind erosion

3.  Accumulation of rocky outcrops, outcrops of parent rocks

4.  Packed clar surface, takyrs, in some places without vegetation

5.  Salinized grey-brown soils, solon-chaks without vegetation in some places

6.  Territories, subject to water erosion

B.  Anthopogenous influence

1.  Territories with relatively high density of the population (exceeding 7 people per 1 km$^2$)

2.  Territories with relatively high density of cattle per pasture (less than 5 ha per 1 sheep)

C.  Desertification control

1.  Territory where desertification control is effective

D.  Danger of desertification

1.  High: territories ranging from strong to moderate vulnerability to desert-ification plus high density of the population or a high load on the pastures

2.  Moderate: territories with moderate and weak vulnerabilities to desert-ification plus high density of the population or a high load on the pastures

3.  Weak: territories ranging from mod-erate to weak vulnerability to desertification

Recommendations for the selection of the best possible variants of siting economic projects and for their protection against sand and wind erosion are widely applied.

Research continues into eoline sands, physical principles of wind erosion and exploration of more effective methods of protecting economic objects against sand and wind erosion by applying different binding substances.

Proceeding from these studies, agro-forest meliorators of Turkmenistan covered by forest cultivation operations vast territories in recent decades. Specifically, sand-fixing operations have been conducted on an area of 140,000 ha from 1951 to 1968, approximately 300,000 ha were covered by this work from 1971 to 1975. The plan for 1976 to 1980 covers an area of 330,000 ha.

### DESERTIFICATION

Desert territories have been used for pastures since long ago while the shrub thickets are used for the procurement of timber fuel. Certain animals are of commercial importance. As a result of uneven grazing and of shrub cutting, specifically close to watering places and communities, and also owing to uncontrolled shooting of birds and wild ungulates under the influence of protracted economic utilization of the ecosystems of Turkmenistan's deserts considerable changes have taken place there. At present, as a consequence of the non-uniform utilization of the territory before 1917, anthropogenous variants of ecosystems which are characterized by decreasing number, and even complete disappearance, of certain species and bioforms of plants and animals have become widespread on considerable territories, specifically close to the cultivated zone. Particularly intensive cutting concerned the shrubs which were the main type of fuel both for the live-stock breeding population of deserts and for towns and other communities. This resulted in the appearance of anthropogenous types of vegetation. This is the psammophylous vegetation without *Haloxylon* of the southern boundary of the Kara-Kumy desert and the blue-grass sedge herbage communities of the foothills. Concurrently, with the tree-shrub vegetation the antelopes, onagers and many species of birds had also disappeared.

As for the western part of Turkmenistan, besides the pasture economy, oil, ozokerite and other minerals were mined there since long ago. This type of activity in the conditions of soil salinization led to the formation of large foci of shifting sands.

In recent decades economic activity in deserts increased. It was associated with the construction of canals, geological survey and exploitation of oil and gas deposits with the application of earth-moving machinery involving rapid deformation of desert ecosystems, dislocation of their natural integrity and the origination of new anthropogenous variants - technogenous landscapes. Instances are numerous - appearing daily motor tracks which disrupt the surface of land and takyrs, total uprooting of shrubs, unwise shooting of wild animals, etc. The disruption of the surface cover takes place during pipe laying. This gives the beginning to deflation and weakens takyrs' part as rainfall water-collecting areas. All this is predetermined by lack of consideration for the fact that the desert ecosystems function in extremal conditions and therefore are most vulnerable and subject to irreversible changes.

The speed and intensity of the transformation of the structure of biogeocenoses influenced by different commercial uses outstrip by its speed and intensity natural autorestoration processes. In some instances the results are irreversible and catastrophic.

Deflation is particularly vigorous in the western part of Turkmenistan which is known for its unfavourable wind regimen. Stripped of its cover sand turns into shifting sand and sand drifts become a scourge. Cases are infrequent when various premises, roads are overrun by sand, pillars of electric transmission lines collapse because wind has blown the sand out from under their foundation. Sand fixing in these circumstances requires costly and complex measures.

In the years of Soviet government and in recent 20-30 years, specifically, large-scale rational utilization of vegetation in pasture and forest management has become widespread. Owing to the gasification of inhabited communities the rate of cuttings of shrubs for fuel has been reduced considerably. The distribution and fixing of pastures among farms ensured their more sparing utilization. The law on nature conservation entailed the rehabilitation of the desert fauna. The construction of the Kara-Kum Canal did disrupt desert ecosystems along the canal course but did produce absolutely new ecosystems of high productivity - either hydro or shore-line ones.

Planned socialist economy gave the possibility of applying powerful technical facilities specifically for the construction of deep water wells, living and cattle premises in the desert, for hay mowing on large areas, pasture improving, sand fixation and in many other instances. All this opened up considerable prospects for tapping the desert zone potential and also for the elaboration of methods of desertification control since that process is mainly a consequence of irrational utilization of deserts in the past.

In the cultivated-irrigated zone desertification manifests itself, to a certain extent, in the form of salinized and waterlogging sections. Such traces, however, are short-lived and as soon as they are identified they are put into economic use either by means of reclamation or flushing.

To combat desertification in Turkmenistan recommendations in the form of long-term projections or specific annual programmes of assimilating achievements of theory and practice are widely used. These programmes are backed by appropriate allocations both from the state budget and from the budgets of collective and state farms.

It should be considered that not all practical measures that are necessary in deserts are backed by adequate theory. These extensive and urgent tasks of research and practice put to the fore the need in integrated monitoring of desert ecosystems using the following pattern: reserve - anthropogenous variants - cultivated biogeocenoses under different regimens. This will make it possible to supply the most rational practical recommendations at the earliest time.

## RECOMMENDATIONS FOR THE PLAN OF ACTION TO COMBAT DESERTIFICATION

The existing techniques of nature utilization in Turkmenistan's deserts are distinguished by rather high effectiveness. From the point of view of present-day requirements and achievements of science and engineering, however, they can be and should be improved. The steadily growing rate and scope of development of the natural resources in deserts and semideserts require the introduction of new technology for agriculture and industry.

The following ways and rates of Turkmenistan desert development can be projected.

First place goes to irrigated farming which should supply materials for the industry and food for the growing population. More modern methods of irrigation like underground, droplet, sprinkling and other will be applied. The use of the closed and vertical drainage will stop secondary soil salting. Concurrently vast sandy soil areas will be irrigated by sprinkling; and used for farming.

All this will bring to life large farming oases in the desert.  Their area will
be comparatively small, not more than 10% of the total arid zone.  The rest will
as formerly be used in animal husbandry.  In this connection it becomes important
to study comprehensively secondary and primary ecosystem projectivity as the
theoretical foundation of rational use of pastures and finding reserves to increase
the output of livestock products.

Research of many years and recommendations made in pasture management will form
the basis for the following actions:

- further improvements in pasture utilization by introducing in all karakul
  breeding farms long-term plans of pasture management providing for optimal load
  and pasture rotation.  This increases the capacity of grazing grounds and
  prevents damaging of pastures;

- the watering of the remaining unwatered area (approximately 30%) by building
  new water mains, fuller utilization of takyrs and sections with cement facing
  to collect rainfall in areas where ground water is strongly salinized;

- expansion of works related to improvement of pastures particularly of
  impoverished areas and those covered by ridge sands—a considerable potential
  for raising their yielding capacity;

- wider application of machinery in pasture management by serial production of
  machines for the preparation of hay from sedges and coarse grasses and also
  for the preparation of desert plant seeds.

To maintain large numbers and a high level of productivity of karakul sheep desert
grazing should be combined with supplementary feeding in winter and in years of
crop failures.  It is therefore necessary to establish emergency stocks of fodder
which calls for fuller utilization of native hay lands in the foothills and river
valleys, and also greater sowings of fodder crops outside of cotton-crop rotation
with the application of different potential of land and hydro resources: discharge
waters, including those weakly mineralized, sowing of fodder crops on sands with
sprinkling irrigation, etc.

Further improvement of the standard of livestock products and of karakul pelts,
specifically, requires continuation of selection-pedigree work, both in karakul
sheep-breeding and in camel-breeding.

As regards pasture management further studies should include techniques of better
pasture utilization, the study of grazing influence upon pastures to determine
optimal loads and the rates of grazing, the development of methods improving the
vegetation cover; the selection and growing of seed of new forage plants from
native flora; integrated study of primary and secondary pasture productivity;
comprehensive evaluation of the nutritive value of forage plants and rations for
animals, pasture economics and management.

Alongside with pasture animal husbandry industrial livestock breeding based on
alfalfa from the cotton crop rotation and other forage crops grown on irrigated
areas will be further developed.  An important task for livestock breeding is the
development of techniques for the creation of cultivated pastures on irrigated
areas.

Oil and gas mining will be developed at a rapid pace including their conveyance to
processing plants.

The rationalization of industrial techniques of developing mineral deposits in Turkmenistan and their processing requires attention both from the point of view of their fullest utilization and nature conservation. Oil-processing plants which are based on old technology are particularly dangerous as sources of air and water pollution. The reorganization of their technology should be a matter of immediate attention.

In connection with the growing rate of urbanization research is conducted into the planning of such types of communities for the desert zones which would be associated with their economic functions (livestock state-farms, collective-farms, settlements for the workers engaged in mining of minerals, railroad stations, etc.).

The power facilities will be considerably augmented by building new thermal power plants directly in Turkmenistan and by using the electric energy of large mountainous hydro-electric stations of Soviet Middle Asia: Vakhsh, Naryn, Kapchagai and others since the power system of the Turkmen SSR is incorporated into the power-grid of Soviet Middle Asia. The role of heleo-electric plants should be also increased.

The implementation of these measures will be conducted with due consideration for the necessity of the utmost conservation of nature. This can be guaranteed by rational utilization of natural resources and by recultivating desert ecosystems which were rendered derelict during the development of arid territories. Afforestation and fixing of shifting sands as well as deflation control will be regarded with utmost importance. With this objective, scientific and production organizations of Turkmenistan continue research into appraising the intensity and the character of deflation in connection with the wind regimen and the stability of sand surfaces to deflation; the compilation of wind erosion charts with the use of remote sensing techniques from outer space. New binding materials are being sought out for sand fixing (mechanical, chemical and biological binders).

Improved methods are used for the creation of forest tracts for sand- and wind-protecting purposes using psammophytes and arboreal species from oases by utilizing for sand phytomelioration of local waters - rainfall and subterranean waters including those weakly mineralized and by introducing new sand-fixing plants, pasture plants and those for decorative purposes from different deserts of the world.

With the growth of the population the recreational role of arid regions will be much greater. More tourists will be attracted to the desert by its unique beauty, peculiarity of flora and fauna and the undisturbed quiet. The extent of application of the warm and dry desert climate for medical purposes will be increased and the present health establishments for the treatment of kidney disorders (Bairam-Ali) will be supplemented with many others.

All the mentioned trends in economy of arid regions of Turkmenistan will be developing harmoniously.

The psychological aspect is another important factor of environmental protection. Thus far the understanding of the problem is insufficient not only by the bulk of the population but by many local executives.

While the population of Turkmenistan was comparatively small, the damage inflicted by man to nature was self-restored. Now, when the load on desert ecosystems radically increased the necessary self-restoration no longer takes place. As a result of this we see signs of anthropogenous desertification in many districts. In view of this it is necessary to conduct regular education of the population explaining the importance of environmental protection. This will be conducted by publication of posters and pamphlets, short films, by sponsoring photo exhibits and lectures.

Successful and rational development of deserts necessitates a balancing of exploitation of desert natural resources and their protection and restoration. This is an integrated task and it can only be settled by applying ecosystem monitoring and a range of other actions.

Particularly important at the present time is the development of techniques of forecasting the consequences of man's impact on the environment in the development of natural resources. One of the forms of analysing the changes of the landscapes of arid regions under the influence of man are the forecast analyses of ecosystem changes. They are compiled both in the form of charts and forecast maps. The forecast maps might be made for a particular task or integrated (ecological ones). Types of forecasts may differ. They may be short-term ones for the period of construction or for the time of completion and long-term for the period of exploitation of structures. In other words forecasts should be dynamic and subject to regular adjustment.

Long-term forecasting of physical and geographical development at places of man's vigorous action on nature will become particularly important. This is a difficult matter. It calls for consideration of a large number of factors and developments. Forecasting is possible only by applying integrated physical and geographical studies with the utilization of mathematical and physical methods, including the modelling of natural processes which requires knowledge of a large number of dimensions of various phenomena.

Thus, to ensure balanced development of all branches of economy in Turkmenistan's deserts the following science-based measures are to be implemented:

1.  Modernization of agriculture and industry to ensure the fullest development of natural resources, utmost productivity and nature conservation.

2.  Recultivation of derelicted ecosystems to return them back into economy. In particular, introduction of new machinery in irrigated agriculture to prevent secondary salination and waterlogging of irrigated land, to improve pastures, afforestation, for fixing shifting sands, etc.

3.  Identification of maximum loads on ecosystems of arid regions given different techniques of utilization of natural resources to maintain their utmost productivity.

4.  Development of short- and long-term forecasts of the changes in ecosystems for the conservation of environment during its development.

5.  Large-scale propaganda of nature conservation among all groups of the population to ensure people's awareness of the tasks and to involve the population in measures to combat and prevent desertification.

6.  Education of the population in ecological and economic practices of rational utilization of natural resources of arid territories (land, water and vegetation, animal world, minerals, etc.).

7.  The analyses and appraisals of natural and manpower resources in developed territories with the idea of their rational utilization (optimal variants of projects), and to prevent desertification.

REFERENCES

*Agroclimatic Resources of the Turkmenian SSR.* Gidrometeoizdad Publishers, Leningrad, 1974.

Babaev, A.G., Murzaev, A.M., Orazov, A.O. and Freikin, Z.G. (1969) *Turkmenistan. Mysl* Publishers, Moscow.

Babaev, A.G. (1973) *Oasis' Sands of Turkmenistan and Ways of Development. Ylym* Publishers, Ashkhabad.

*Desert Biocomplexes and Intensification of their Productivity. Ylym* Publishers, Ashkhabad, 1971.

*Land and Water Resources of Deserts. Ylym* Publishers, Ashkhabad, 1971.

Morozova, O.I. (1959) *Pastures in Deserts and in Submontane Semi-deserts, their Utilization and Improvement.* The State Publishing House of Agricultural Literature, Moscow.

Nechaeva, N.T., Mordvinov, N.A. and Mosolov, I.A. (1943) *Pastures of Kara-Kums and their Utilization.* The Publishing House of the Turkmen branch of the Academy of Sciences, Ashkhabad.

Nechaeva, N.T. and Prikhodko, S.Y. (1966) *Planted Pastures in Submontane deserts of Soviet Middle Asia (Experience of Developing Artificial Phytocoenosis). Turkmenistan* Publishers, Ashkhabad.

Nikolaev, V.N. (1972) *Natural Forage Resources of Turkmenistan. Ylym* Publishers, Ashkhabad.

Petrov, M.P. (1964) *Deserts of the USSR and Their Development. Nauka* Publishers, Moscow-Leningrad.

*Natural Conditions, Live-stock Breeding and Desert Forage Base.* The Publishing House of the Academy of Sciences of the Turkmen SSR, Ashkhabad.

*Natural Conditions and the Shifting Sands of Deserts. Ylym* Publishers, Ashkhabad, 1974.

*System of Agriculture in the Turkmenian SSR.* The Publishing House of the Academy of Sciences of the Turkmenian SSR, Ashkhabad, 1961.

*Turkmenistan in 50 years. Turkmenistan* Publishers, Ashkhabad, 1974.

Freikin, Z.G. (1957) *Turkmenian SSR.* Geographical Publishing House, Moscow.

Shansutdinov, S.S. (1975) *Establishment of Long-term Pastures in the Arid Zone of Soviet Middle Asia. FAN* Publishers, Tashkent.